Does God Want to Spoil My Fun?

by Edith Bajema

1 LEADER GUIDE AND 10 DISCUSSION HANDOUTS

Copyright ©1994

A MINISTRY OF CRC PUBLICATIONS

2850 Kalamazoo Ave. SE
Grand Rapids, MI 49560

3475 Mainway
Burlington, ON L7M 1A9

Printed in the U.S.A. on recycled paper. ♻
It is illegal to copy this material without written permission from the publisher.

ISBN 1-56212-080-8

Contents

Introduction to Inspirit 5

Session 1: "Where There's Life, There's Bud" 7
  Leader Guide
  10 Discussion Handouts

Session 2: "The One Who Dies With
  the Most Toys Wins" 35
  Leader Guide
  10 Discussion Handouts

Session 3: "Looking Out For Number One" 63
  Leader Guide
  10 Discussion Handouts

Session 4: "Don't Get Mad, Get Even" 91
  Leader Guide
  10 Discussion Handouts

Session 5: "If It Feels Good, Do It" 119
  Leader Guide
  10 Discussion Handouts

Session 6: "I Did It My Way" 149
  Leader Guide
  10 Discussion Handouts

Does God Want to Spoil My Fun?

Introduction to Inspirit

Whether this is your first time leading a small group or you are a veteran leader, welcome to the exciting world of small-group, evangelistic Bible study. These materials were written as an entry-level Bible study for men and women who may never have studied the Bible before. Whether you are leading a group in your workplace, in your home, or another setting, the following guidelines should assist you in your leadership role:

1. PRAY

Nothing will prepare you for leadership more than prayer. Pray for God's direction in making organizational decisions. Pray for the Holy Spirit's direction in whom to invite and for a positive response from those invited. Pray faithfully for group members, and pray for your eyes to be opened to the truths in God's Word and how those truths can best be communicated to your small group. Remember: "More things are wrought by prayer than this world ever dreamed of."

2. PREPARE

Prepare Yourself. The leadership material for each discussion is thorough and reinforces the discovery method of Bible study. We suggest highlighting key phrases or questions for easy reference as you prepare. Take your leader material with you to the small group and be relaxed and informal about using it while you are leading. The perforated discussion copies, located behind the leader material, are to be removed and given to group members each week. If you freely show you have extra help in preparing for the discussion, your group members may dare to ask their questions more readily. They'll see it's not that you're smart and they're ignorant, or that the discussion is just an unguided free-for-all, but it is planned for and focused. Be sure you focus on the discussion element, rather than become a teacher with the "answer book."

Decide whether you will use the **condensed** or the **expanded** format in your group. Time will determine your decision. The condensed format can be done over lunch in a 30- to 40-minute time period. The expanded format can take up to 90 minutes. The leader material includes additional help for use in the expanded format, and is marked with the symbol at right in the leader's guide copy.

Prepare Your Group. State the ground rules before you begin the group and periodically to clarify or as new members join. This will help group members know how the discussion will proceed and know what will be expected of them. Some basic ground rules are:

We're here to see what the Bible has to say, not argue right or wrong.

No previous experience at studying the Bible is needed.

This discussion will not require homework or outside activities.

Respect the confidentiality of the group. "What we say here must stay here." We respect and affirm each group member.

3. PERSEVERE

It takes time to build relationships with non-Christians. The Holy Spirit will already have been at work in some people and they will respond eagerly. Others will be wary. Still others may be in such pain, they'll come because they are desperate. Accept the people God gives you—unconditionally. Often God's timetable is not the same as ours, but be confident that God will use your efforts. Modeling Christ's love may be the most important thing you do. Relax and watch the Spirit work!

Does God Want to Spoil My Fun?

SESSION 1

Does God Want to Spoil My Fun?—Leader Guide

1: "Where There's Life, There's Bud"

Introductory Notes

This may be the first Bible study that some members of your group have ever attended. If so, be aware that this is in some ways a hard-hitting study. It doesn't mince words; it doesn't skirt around sensitive issues. It talks forthrightly about today's struggles with things like sexuality, addiction, materialism, self-centeredness—and what guidelines God has given for living a healthy life.

This is, of course, the strength of this study. People are bombarded daily with evidences of our society's unhealthiness in these areas. They are aware of the struggles. And they want direct answers. This study presents the Bible's honest answers. It does so in a way that is nonthreatening, supportive, and easy to understand.

How can a study on morality be nonthreatening to an unchurched person? By not requiring personal answers unless a group member is ready to give them. By making it clear that Christians—including yourself—also struggle with these things. By providing a supportive group setting where others can share their own stories and weaknesses and encouragement.

Throughout this study, remember to keep your language "easy to understand." Many members of your group may have had no exposure to the religious words that you feel comfortable with: "grace," "righteousness," "atonement," and so on. Even "sin" may be misunderstood. Avoid religious jargon. Use simple words and phrases that have clear meaning for today's unchurched people. As we've said before, find fresh ways to explain the Bible's teaching.

As you prepare to lead this study, take into account that it is based on a common perception of God as a stern judge or father figure who frowns on all human enjoyment and whose rules are meant to make sure that no one has any fun. The stern phrase "thou shalt not" often comes to mind when people think of God's rules for living—the Ten Commandments.

The aim of this study is to turn people's eyes away from the negative and toward the positive. Is God trying to spoil our fun? Or does he have some deeper purpose for setting boundaries and guidelines? Are those limits meant to chain us or to set us free?

And your group should look deeper. What emptiness are they trying to fill with such things as drugs, sexual relationships, material goods, and living only for self? What deep need or longing are they trying to satisfy? Hopefully through this study they will meet the One who can fill that need and bring wholeness to their lives.

Read 1 Corinthians 2:9–16 daily as part of your preparation. Ask the Holy Spirit to work in the minds and emotions of your group members, helping them to discover and understand God's thoughts in this study. Ask also for clear words as you explain and teach—and an open, nonjudgmental heart as you listen. Then entrust your group members to God's care and to the power of his Spirit.

Beginning the Session

If your group has new members, find a nonthreatening way to introduce group members to each other. You might share middle names as well as first names, or ask each person to remember and describe a room in their childhood home that brings back warm memories, or ask them to share their favorite color or sport or TV program or movie (the possibilities are endless).

If members come from various kinds of backgrounds—and especially religious backgrounds—sure to acknowledge that at the outset. To help members become more sensitive to this diversity, say something like, "I'm sure most of us come from a wide variety of backgrounds and experiences. Some may have attended church or Sunday school only in their childhood, others may never have taken the opportunity to attend a church or to read the Bible, and others may have made Bible study a regular part of their life. Let's listen carefully and get to know each other. In this group we can respect each other, affirm each other, and discover what the Bible has to say about things we struggle with in our lives."

 If you are using the longer format for this session, take some extra time here to get to know each other. Keeping your questions low-key, ask members to share a bit about their upbringing—where they were born, if and when they first attended a church, where they first heard of the Bible, and what their church involvement has been as an adult. Be careful not to imply that you expect an active church membership; simply explain that it's helpful to know a little about each other's background as you discuss the Bible's teachings together.

As members give their names, be sure to write them down so that you don't forget them. As your study progresses, you will be following up on each individual and getting to know him or her better. Start out by giving group members the space they need to feel comfortable, however. Make sure they know you're interested in—but not prying into—their private lives. As they get to know you, they will let down their guard more easily.

Again, pray that the Spirit will guide you in your relationship with each person, giving you insights or the right words to say as you talk with each one. Trust God to

9

do drugs like heroin and cocaine offer people today? Why do you think people take these drugs? Why might the reality of their lives be too hard to face? What is comforting about deception? Talk about the bleakness, loneliness, and despair that characterize many people's lives today. It is perhaps understandable that people without any other hope eventually turn to the false illusion of well-being, power, and escape that drugs offer.

Keep in mind that some in your group may feel the emptiness and loneliness that make the allure of drugs so tempting. Others may think it delivers other benefits—social acceptance, escape from reality, fun, or other "perks." The reason they are in this study may be to find the meaning and sense of belonging that has escaped them so far in this life.

 If you are using the longer format, take time to explore this further. **Are these reasons for using alcohol and other addictive substances limited to a particular race or level of society? How broadly does it reach? How is this reflected in the widespread use of addictive substances today?** Note that there is no level of society untouched by the allure of addiction. Even wealthy people who have all the material goods they need still seem drawn to the destructive habit of drugs. **What might their lives be lacking? What do they hope drugs will provide for them?** Adventure, empowerment, excitement, a deeper level of experience, a numbing of inner pain, a feeling of wellbeing in the midst of a life that's empty of meaning—these things can draw even the wealthiest in our society. **How do addictive substances prove deceptive in the end? What do people find that's different from what they expected to find?**

4. What controls the person's life described in these verses from Proverbs?

This question strikes near the heart of the truth of this session. As we noted earlier, the Bible does not forbid drinking alcohol. What it does forbid is giving it control of your life. **What things in the Proverbs passage tell us that this person has lost control of his or her life? What is controlling the mind? The sight? The physical sensations? The desires?**

Perhaps one of the most telling phrases in this passage is the last: "When will I wake up so I can find another drink?" **What is the driving purpose in this person's life? What does he or she live for? How does that compare with those who live from one "high" to the next? What has become this person's highest value?**

Use these questions to help your group discover the Bible's main concern in the misuse of alcohol: it enslaves human beings, changing them from thinking, productive, independent creatures into those who throw away their self-respect, their minds, their families, and work relationships all for the sake of another drink. The drink (or drug) has taken the place of God.

Once a person has allowed an addictive substance to take control of his or her life, what options are left? What principles have organizations like AA discovered that can help people? This is a wonderful opportunity to introduce the first steps of the twelve-step program:
- We admitted we were powerless over alcohol (or drugs or our emotions or workaholism, etc.)—that our lives had become unmanageable.
- We came to believe that a Power greater than ourselves could restore us to wholeness and sanity.
- We made a decision to turn our will and our lives over to the care of God as we understood him.

Introduce your group to these initial steps, explaining that they are used widely in the most successful alcohol- and drug-related therapy groups in North America today. Explore them briefly in your discussion, noting also that you will be returning to them in later sessions as well. **How might these steps be crucial in helping people return their lives to wholeness?** Let your discussion here lead you into the next question, where you will explore further what it means to turn your life over to God.

5. How does an addiction ruin a person's spirit? What alternative does the Bible offer? What do you think this means?

You may get a variety of answers to this question. Already you've touched on how the human spirit is ruined by the desperate need to escape reality through alcohol or drugs. **What happens to a person's self-respect? The ability to make decisions? The ability to meet others' needs? The ability to function normally?**

But look further than the individual. **How can an addiction poison close family relationships as well?** A loving family man can be transformed into a violent abuser. A mother can severely neglect tiny infants and toddlers while under the influence of alcohol or drugs, going against one of the deepest instincts of the human spirit—the maternal instinct. Teenagers use cocaine or alcohol to ease the pain of growing up, of insecurity, of troubled lives—and alienate themselves from their families as a result. All these are evidences of the human spirit that has been ruined.

 In the longer format, look briefly at how the "spirit" of our society has been unraveling also under the influence of drug addiction. **How much inner-city violence and white-collar crime might be due to a person's desperate need for another fix? What might a shot of heroin or a snort of cocaine cost, for example, in comparison to a day's groceries? How much might it cost to support a daily or weekly cocaine habit? Are hardcore addicts able to hold down a job, as a general rule? Where do they often turn for money? Why have drug-related crimes become the number-one law enforcement problem in North America?**

Hopefully your group will see that not only individuals but also our neighborhoods and communities suffer from a "ruined spirit" when drug addictions are present.

But don't just talk "facts" when you deal with this subject. Bring up also the emptiness that plagues our society as a whole. **Do people feel connected with their neighbors? Do they feel safe? Do they reflect a feeling of fulfillment and satisfaction? Or would the word "emptiness" or "searching" better describe the soul of our society? How is this reflected in our cultural "mirror" of movies, popular music, and novels?** Help your group to see that society's addictions, like those of individuals, come from an inner void and longing for meaning.

But look at the Bible's alternative: "Be filled with the Spirit." You cannot, of course, cover this concept completely in the time you have left. And many of your group members may not be ready to understand or accept that concept just yet.

But you can do two things at this point, both of them important. First, find out what group members think it means to be "filled with the Spirit." What they come up with may surprise you, and it will tell you a lot about their ideas about God.

Second, you can introduce them to the idea that human beings are constantly looking for something to drive or to control their lives—whether it be a desire for wealth or beauty, an addiction to drugs, a love relationship, a thirst for power, or the need for acceptance from others.

The Bible offers an alternative to giving our lives over to these things. That alternative is to yield ourselves to the control of God's Spirit. Being "filled with the Spirit" means to allow God—rather than ourselves—to shape and direct our lives. It means allowing that "higher Power" mentioned in the twelve-step program to care for us, remove our shortcomings, and restore our lives to wholeness. Emphasize that the first step is to admit our powerlessness in overcoming our dependencies.

Briefly explain this, after your group members have offered their own opinions as to what being "filled with the Spirit" might mean. The final question should help tie it all together.

6. What difference do you think it would make for a person to have the Spirit of God in his or her life?

Some of your group members may not actually believe in a God—or if they do, may have only the vaguest idea as to what God is really like. So it's important at this point to explore what they think the Spirit of God is like. **What qualities might God's Spirit bring to a person's life? In what way might a person begin to reflect God's character? What do you think God's character is like? How might God's Spirit enable a person to do things he or she might not otherwise have been able to do?**

Again, listen first before you share what the Bible has to say. Members may talk about God as a stern judge, an absentee landlord, a mystical Life Force, a kindly old grandfather, or a crutch for the emotionally impaired. When they have finished, read the brief list of the fruit of the Spirit from Galatians 5:22–23,

The fruit of the Spirit is love, joy, peace, patience, kindness, goodness, faithfulness, gentleness, and self-control.

What do these qualities tell us about God? About the person who is "filled with the Spirit"? Discuss this as much as your group wishes or as time allows, but do explain that they will be able to come back to this subject in later sessions as well. For now it is enough that they begin to think about the idea of giving one's life over to a God who will give them wholeness and spiritual health.

 In the longer format, you may want to explore the Galatians passage a bit further, as time permits. Look at each of these qualities one by one, and compare them to the life of someone who is addicted to alcohol or drugs. **Are these qualities evident when someone is under the control of a chemical substance? What is it that fills our lives?** Return briefly to Ephesians 5:18. Point out the differences between the Spirit-filled life with that of the drug-filled life.

But also look at the positive side. **Are these qualities something that a person might desire in his or her life? How do they reflect wholeness and spiritual maturity? Might these qualities be the very things that people are searching for—love, joy, peace—when they turn to drugs or alcohol?** Use this discussion to help your group see that this mysterious being called "the Spirit of God" may indeed hold the key to happiness and meaning that our culture is searching for.

The Bottom Line

Many people look to drugs and alcohol to escape the pain of their lives. They need something to fill the emptiness in their heart. Others are simply looking for a perpetual good time, an escape from responsibilities. Still others use substances to attain peer approval, social standing, sophistication, and/or respect. But chemical substances are deceiving; they will take control of a person's will and spirit. The Bible offers an alternative that brings wholeness and healing.

Use this brief paragraph to summarize what you've learned today and to refocus members on the central truth of the session. Listen closely to members' responses to this summary and to the session as a whole. There may be some in your group who struggle with chemical addictions, though they will probably not want to admit it to you or to themselves. Pray that the Spirit will help you to discern their struggle and give you wisdom in reaching out to them.

Others may have friends or family members who suffer from some form of addiction. If members are willing to share this information, you may want to include those people in your closing prayer time.

 In the longer format, you will have had time to get to know each other a little better, even though this may be the first time you are meeting together. Mention that you would like to be able to support each member in prayer throughout the week, and ask if anyone has a need or request that they would like remembered in prayer. Don't push here; allow members to get used to the idea of praying with and for others. Some may never have participated in prayer before. Make this time as simple and user-friendly as possible.

Encourage your group to look for answers to these prayers. You may be surprised with what they share at the next session. (God seems to delight particularly in answering the prayers of people who are seeking him for the first time.)

Optional Prayer Time

Close your time with a short prayer—perhaps the one printed below. You may wish to add a few words of your own to this prayer, thanking God for each of the members present and asking him to help them understand and think about what they learned today. Encourage members to take home the discussion handout and to use the prayer below during the coming week if they wish.

As always, be alert for ways in which you can give support to group members during the week. It may be something that other group members can help with too—although you should be the first to set an example here, especially as most of the group members may not know each other well yet. Don't hesitate to give someone a call midweek to see how they're doing, or to offer a meal or transportation where needed.

Prayer

God, help me to see the places in my life where I am looking to other things to give me meaning and fulfillment. Open my eyes to any kind of addiction in my life. Help me to understand what you are offering to me through your Spirit. Amen.

A Final Word

If a person's thinking is controlled by the Spirit, then there is life and peace. *(The apostle Paul in Romans 8:6, New Century Version)*

Does God Want to Spoil My Fun?

1: "Where There's Life, There's Bud"

Beginnings

Think of some commercial slogans that entice us to believe alcohol is the key to happiness (for example, "Weekends were made for Michelob" or "Go for the gusto," etc.). What other addictive substances are in the news lately? Why do you think people use such substances? What are they trying to gain? Is it okay for people to use these as they see fit? Why or why not?

What's Happening Today

"There must be something more than the daily grind of work. There must be some relief, somewhere, to the inner pain and feeling of powerlessness. There must be some way to escape the vague sense of being trapped, of having missed the happiness in life."

Not everyone feels this way, but many do. That's what draws millions every day into the shadowy world of alcohol, heroin, speed, LSD, marijuana, uppers, downers, and cocaine. Feeling empty, sad, or overwhelmed, they seek to fill that void with something that will make them feel powerful, happy, and energetic. They want to get away from the pain, to find a release from fear or boredom. And they seek it in drugs.

Drugs do offer escape—at least a temporary one. Howard, for example, had always gone easy on drinking, but when his business got entangled in tax problems last fall, he began to drink more at home. First it was a couple of beers after dinner "to relax," then harder drinks like whiskey and gin. When his wife confronted him, he began drinking secretly—at work, in bars, or at home after she'd gone to bed.

The increasing pressures of his business have driven Howard to even more drink. His troubles with finances and arguments with employees seem too big to handle. In his clearer moments, Howard knows that he is only a few months away from bankruptcy. But he turns to drink to get away from the painful reality of his failure. So far he has refused all his friends' offers of help and his wife's pleas that he get treatment.

Sandra, on the other hand, is a recovering drug addict. Born to a low-income family, she had started smoking pot and snorting coke shortly after high school. Marrying an ex-Army private, she had two children and moved frequently from place to place, avoiding rent payments and spending much of the family's money on drugs. Their life rapidly became a downward spiral of drugs, unemployment, and running from the law.

When her husband was caught forging checks five years later, Sandra woke up. She got down on her knees and prayed for help.

She admitted that her life had become unmanageable, and that she didn't have the power any more to change it. Hoping that there was a God, she promised to turn her life *and* her will over to him, if only he would restore her life to sanity.

Sandra took her children with her to a homeless shelter, quit drugs, and went into therapy. After a few months, she enrolled in a community college.

Successful beyond her teachers' expectations, Sandra was urged to enter college, using financial aid. Hesitant, she applied—and was accepted. Sandra now maintains a B+ average with a full course load. For two and a half years she's been drug-free. And, instead of hoping at best to find a job as a nurse's aide, she's dreaming of going for a degree in secondary education.

Two real people, two different responses to the alluring addiction of drugs. Drug addiction is an overwhelming problem in our society today. Does the Bible—a book written over 2,000 years ago—speak to the danger of substance abuse? Yes, it does. Read the following Scripture passages for a vivid picture of addiction—and some advice on overcoming it.

What the Bible Tells Us

Who has woe? Who has sorrow?
  Who has strife? Who has complaints?
  Who has needless bruises? Who has bloodshot eyes?

Those who linger over wine,
  who go to sample bowls of mixed wine.

Do not gaze at wine when it is red,
  when it sparkles in the cup.
  when it goes down smoothly!

In the end it bites like a snake
  and poisons like a viper.

Your eyes will see strange sights
  and your mind imagine confusing things.

When will I wake up
  so I can find another drink? (Proverbs 23:29–35)

Copyright ©1994 Church Development Resources   It is illegal to copy this material without permission.

Do not be drunk with wine. That will ruin you spiritually. But be filled with the Spirit. (Ephesians 5:18)

How the Bible Relates

1. What addictive substance is described here? What other addictive substances used today could this passage be describing?

2. What do "those who linger over wine" suffer, according to the first part of this passage?

3. How does alcohol deceive the one who drinks it? How might the same apply to other addictive substances?

4. What controls the person's life described in these verses from Proverbs?

5. How does an addiction ruin a person's spirit? What alternative does the Bible offer? What do you think this means?

6. What difference do you think it would make for a person to have the Spirit of God in his or her life?

The Bottom Line

Many people look to drugs and alcohol to escape the pain of their lives. They need something to fill the emptiness in their heart. Others are simply looking for a perpetual good time, an escape from responsibilities. Still others use substances to attain peer approval, social standing, sophistication, and/or respect. But chemical substances are deceiving; they will take control of a person's will and spirit. The Bible offers an alternative that brings wholeness and healing.

Prayer

God, help me to see the places in my life where I am looking to other things to give me meaning and fulfillment. Open my eyes to any kind of addiction in my life. Help me to understand what you are offering to me through your Spirit. Amen.

A Final Word

If a person's thinking is controlled by the Spirit, then there is life and peace. *(The apostle Paul in Romans 8:6, New Century Version)*

It's a Killer

The heavy use of alcohol affects nearly every organ and system of the body. Here are some common effects of alcohol abuse:

- **Gastrointestinal diseases.** Chronic gastritis, or inflammation of the lining of the stomach, bleeding from the stomach or esophagus, and inflammation of the pancreas.
- **Liver damage.** Hepatitis, fatty infiltration, or alcoholic cirrhosis that can lead to death.
- **Cardiovascular disease.** High blood pressure which, in turn, can lead to impaired functioning, heart attack, or stroke.
- **Nervous-system damage.** Numbness in arms and legs, pain and prickling sensations, light flashes and decreased vision. Can cause permanent brain damage.
- **Cancers.** Cancers of the mouth, larynx, esophagus, lungs, and liver.
- **Fetal alcohol syndrome.** Physical birth defects and mental retardation in infants.
- **Other effects:** Malnutrition, anemia, decrease in resistance to infections, menstrual irregularities, and impotence.

— *Dr. Joyce DeHaan, medical director at Gateway Villa, an addiction-treatment center in Kalamazoo, Michigan. Adapted from* The Banner, *August 15, 1994. Used by permission.*

Does God Want to Spoil My Fun?

1: "Where There's Life, There's Bud"

Beginnings

Think of some commercial slogans that entice us to believe alcohol is the key to happiness (for example, "Weekends were made for Michelob" or "Go for the gusto," etc.). What other addictive substances are in the news lately? Why do you think people use such substances? What are they trying to gain? Is it okay for people to use these as they see fit? Why or why not?

What's Happening Today

"There must be something more than the daily grind of work. There must be some relief, somewhere, to the inner pain and feeling of powerlessness. There must be some way to escape the vague sense of being trapped, of having missed the happiness in life."

Not everyone feels this way, but many do. That's what draws millions every day into the shadowy world of alcohol, heroin, speed, LSD, marijuana, uppers, downers, and cocaine. Feeling empty, sad, or overwhelmed, they seek to fill that void with something that will make them feel powerful, happy, and energetic. They want to get away from the pain, to find a release from fear or boredom. And they seek it in drugs.

Drugs do offer escape—at least a temporary one. Howard, for example, had always gone easy on drinking, but when his business got entangled in tax problems last fall, he began to drink more at home. First it was a couple of beers after dinner "to relax," then harder drinks like whiskey and gin. When his wife confronted him, he began drinking secretly—at work, in bars, or at home after she'd gone to bed.

The increasing pressures of his business have driven Howard to even more drink. His troubles with finances and arguments with employees seem too big to handle. In his clearer moments, Howard knows that he is only a few months away from bankruptcy. But he turns to drink to get away from the painful reality of his failure. So far he has refused all his friends' offers of help and his wife's pleas that he get treatment.

Sandra, on the other hand, is a recovering drug addict. Born to a low-income family, she had started smoking pot and snorting coke shortly after high school. Marrying an ex-Army private, she had two children and moved frequently from place to place, avoiding rent payments and spending much of the family's money on drugs. Their life rapidly became a downward spiral of drugs, unemployment, and running from the law.

When her husband was caught forging checks five years later, Sandra woke up. She got down on her knees and prayed for help.

She admitted that her life had become unmanageable, and that she didn't have the power any more to change it. Hoping that there was a God, she promised to turn her life *and* her will over to him, if only he would restore her life to sanity.

Sandra took her children with her to a homeless shelter, quit drugs, and went into therapy. After a few months, she enrolled in a community college. Successful beyond her teachers' expectations, Sandra was urged to enter college, using financial aid. Hesitant, she applied—and was accepted. Sandra now maintains a B+ average with a full course load. For two and a half years she's been drug-free. And, instead of hoping at best to find a job as a nurse's aide, she's dreaming of going for a degree in secondary education.

Two real people, two different responses to the alluring addiction of drugs. Drug addiction is an overwhelming problem in our society today. Does the Bible—a book written over 2,000 years ago—speak to the danger of substance abuse? Yes, it does. Read the following Scripture passages for a vivid picture of addiction—and some advice on overcoming it.

What the Bible Tells Us

Who has woe? Who has sorrow?
 Who has strife? Who has complaints?
 Who has needless bruises? Who has bloodshot eyes?

Those who linger over wine,
 who go to sample bowls of mixed wine.

Do not gaze at wine when it is red,
 when it sparkles in the cup,
 when it goes down smoothly!

In the end it bites like a snake
 and poisons like a viper.

Your eyes will see strange sights
 and your mind imagine confusing things.

When will I wake up
 so I can find another drink? (Proverbs 23:29–35)

Copyright ©1994 Church Development Resources   It is illegal to copy this material without permission.

Do not be drunk with wine. That will ruin you spiritually. But be filled with the Spirit. (Ephesians 5:18)

How the Bible Relates

1. What addictive substance is described here? What other addictive substances used today could this passage be describing?
2. What do "those who linger over wine" suffer, according to the first part of this passage?
3. How does alcohol deceive the one who drinks it? How might the same apply to other addictive substances?
4. What controls the person's life described in these verses from Proverbs?
5. How does an addiction ruin a person's spirit? What alternative does the Bible offer? What do you think this means?
6. What difference do you think it would make for a person to have the Spirit of God in his or her life?

The Bottom Line

Many people look to drugs and alcohol to escape the pain of their lives. They need something to fill the emptiness in their heart. Others are simply looking for a perpetual good time, an escape from responsibilities. Still others use substances to attain peer approval, social standing, sophistication, and/or respect. But chemical substances are deceiving; they will take control of a person's will and spirit. The Bible offers an alternative that brings wholeness and healing.

Prayer

God, help me to see the places in my life where I am looking to other things to give me meaning and fulfillment. Open my eyes to any kind of addiction in my life. Help me to understand what you are offering to me through your Spirit. Amen.

A Final Word

If a person's thinking is controlled by the Spirit, then there is life and peace. *(The apostle Paul in Romans 8:6, New Century Version)*

It's a Killer

The heavy use of alcohol affects nearly every organ and system of the body. Here are some common effects of alcohol abuse:

- **Gastrointestinal diseases.** Chronic gastritis, or inflammation of the lining of the stomach, bleeding from the stomach or esophagus, and inflammation of the pancreas.
- **Liver damage.** Hepatitis, fatty infiltration, or alcoholic cirrhosis that can lead to death.
- **Cardiovascular disease.** High blood pressure which, in turn, can lead to impaired functioning, heart attack, or stroke.
- **Nervous-system damage.** Numbness in arms and legs, pain and prickling sensations, light flashes and decreased vision. Can cause permanent brain damage.
- **Cancers.** Cancers of the mouth, larynx, esophagus, lungs, and liver.
- **Fetal alcohol syndrome.** Physical birth defects and mental retardation in infants.
- **Other effects:** Malnutrition, anemia, decrease in resistance to infections, menstrual irregularities, and impotence.

— *Dr. Joyce DeHaan, medical director at Gateway Villa, an addiction-treatment center in Kalamazoo, Michigan. Adapted from* The Banner, *August 15, 1994. Used by permission.*

Does God Want to Spoil My Fun?

1: "Where There's Life, There's Bud"

Beginnings

Think of some commercial slogans that entice us to believe alcohol is the key to happiness (for example, "Weekends were made for Michelob" or "Go for the gusto," etc.). What other addictive substances are in the news lately? Why do you think people use such substances? What are they trying to gain? Is it okay for people to use these as they see fit? Why or why not?

What's Happening Today

"There must be something more than the daily grind of work. There must be some relief, somewhere, to the inner pain and feeling of powerlessness. There must be some way to escape the vague sense of being trapped, of having missed the happiness in life."

Not everyone feels this way, but many do. That's what draws millions every day into the shadowy world of alcohol, heroin, speed, LSD, marijuana, uppers, downers, and cocaine. Feeling empty, sad, or overwhelmed, they seek to fill that void with something that will make them feel powerful, happy, and energetic. They want to get away from the pain, to find a release from fear or boredom. And they seek it in drugs.

Drugs do offer escape—at least a temporary one. Howard, for example, had always gone easy on drinking, but when his business got entangled in tax problems last fall, he began to drink more at home. First it was a couple of beers after dinner "to relax," then harder drinks like whiskey and gin. When his wife confronted him, he began drinking secretly—at work, in bars, or at home after she'd gone to bed.

The increasing pressures of his business have driven Howard to even more drink. His troubles with finances and arguments with employees seem too big to handle. In his clearer moments, Howard knows that he is only a few months away from bankruptcy. But he turns to drink to get away from the painful reality of his failure. So far he has refused all his friends' offers of help and his wife's pleas that he get treatment.

Sandra, on the other hand, is a recovering drug addict. Born to a low-income family, she had started smoking pot and snorting coke shortly after high school. Marrying an ex-Army private, she had two children and moved frequently from place to place, avoiding rent payments and spending much of the family's money on drugs. Their life rapidly became a downward spiral of drugs, unemployment, and running from the law.

When her husband was caught forging checks five years later, Sandra woke up. She got down on her knees and prayed for help.

She admitted that her life had become unmanageable, and that she didn't have the power any more to change it. Hoping that there was a God, she promised to turn her life *and* her will over to him, if only he would restore her life to sanity.

Sandra took her children with her to a homeless shelter, quit drugs, and went into therapy. After a few months, she enrolled in a community college.

Successful beyond her teachers' expectations, Sandra was urged to enter college, using financial aid. Hesitant, she applied—and was accepted. Sandra now maintains a B+ average with a full course load. For two and a half years she's been drug-free. And, instead of hoping at best to find a job as a nurse's aide, she's dreaming of going for a degree in secondary education.

Two real people, two different responses to the alluring addiction of drugs. Drug addiction is an overwhelming problem in our society today. Does the Bible—a book written over 2,000 years ago—speak to the danger of substance abuse? Yes, it does. Read the following Scripture passages for a vivid picture of addiction—and some advice on overcoming it.

What the Bible Tells Us

Who has woe? Who has sorrow?
  Who has strife? Who has complaints?
  Who has needless bruises? Who has bloodshot eyes?

Those who linger over wine,
  who go to sample bowls of mixed wine.

Do not gaze at wine when it is red,
  when it sparkles in the cup,
  when it goes down smoothly!

In the end it bites like a snake
  and poisons like a viper.

Your eyes will see strange sights
  and your mind imagine confusing things.

When will I wake up
  so I can find another drink? (Proverbs 23:29–35)

Copyright ©1994 Church Development Resources   It is illegal to copy this material without permission.

Do not be drunk with wine. That will ruin you spiritually. But be filled with the Spirit. (Ephesians 5:18)

How the Bible Relates

1. What addictive substance is described here? What other addictive substances used today could this passage be describing?
2. What do "those who linger over wine" suffer, according to the first part of this passage?
3. How does alcohol deceive the one who drinks it? How might the same apply to other addictive substances?
4. What controls the person's life described in these verses from Proverbs?
5. How does an addiction ruin a person's spirit? What alternative does the Bible offer? What do you think this means?
6. What difference do you think it would make for a person to have the Spirit of God in his or her life?

The Bottom Line

Many people look to drugs and alcohol to escape the pain of their lives. They need something to fill the emptiness in their heart. Others are simply looking for a perpetual good time, an escape from responsibilities. Still others use substances to attain peer approval, social standing, sophistication, and/or respect. But chemical substances are deceiving; they will take control of a person's will and spirit. The Bible offers an alternative that brings wholeness and healing.

Prayer

God, help me to see the places in my life where I am looking to other things to give me meaning and fulfillment. Open my eyes to any kind of addiction in my life. Help me to understand what you are offering to me through your Spirit. Amen.

A Final Word

If a person's thinking is controlled by the Spirit, then there is life and peace. *(The apostle Paul in Romans 8:6, New Century Version)*

It's a Killer

The heavy use of alcohol affects nearly every organ and system of the body. Here are some common effects of alcohol abuse:

- **Gastrointestinal diseases.** Chronic gastritis, or inflammation of the lining of the stomach, bleeding from the stomach or esophagus, and inflammation of the pancreas.
- **Liver damage.** Hepatitis, fatty infiltration, or alcoholic cirrhosis that can lead to death.
- **Cardiovascular disease.** High blood pressure which, in turn, can lead to impaired functioning, heart attack, or stroke.
- **Nervous-system damage.** Numbness in arms and legs, pain and prickling sensations, light flashes and decreased vision. Can cause permanent brain damage.
- **Cancers.** Cancers of the mouth, larynx, esophagus, lungs, and liver.
- **Fetal alcohol syndrome.** Physical birth defects and mental retardation in infants.
- **Other effects:** Malnutrition, anemia, decrease in resistance to infections, menstrual irregularities, and impotence.

— *Dr. Joyce DeHaan, medical director at Gateway Villa, an addiction-treatment center in Kalamazoo, Michigan. Adapted from* The Banner, *August 15, 1994. Used by permission.*

Does God Want to Spoil My Fun?

1: "Where There's Life, There's Bud"

Beginnings

Think of some commercial slogans that entice us to believe alcohol is the key to happiness (for example, "Weekends were made for Michelob" or "Go for the gusto," etc.). What other addictive substances are in the news lately? Why do you think people use such substances? What are they trying to gain? Is it okay for people to use these as they see fit? Why or why not?

What's Happening Today

"There must be something more than the daily grind of work. There must be some relief, somewhere, to the inner pain and feeling of powerlessness. There must be some way to escape the vague sense of being trapped, of having missed the happiness in life."

Not everyone feels this way, but many do. That's what draws millions every day into the shadowy world of alcohol, heroin, speed, LSD, marijuana, uppers, downers, and cocaine. Feeling empty, sad, or overwhelmed, they seek to fill that void with something that will make them feel powerful, happy, and energetic. They want to get away from the pain, to find a release from fear or boredom. And they seek it in drugs.

Drugs do offer escape—at least a temporary one. Howard, for example, had always gone easy on drinking, but when his business got entangled in tax problems last fall, he began to drink more at home. First it was a couple of beers after dinner "to relax," then harder drinks like whiskey and gin. When his wife confronted him, he began drinking secretly—at work, in bars, or at home after she'd gone to bed.

The increasing pressures of his business have driven Howard to even more drink. His troubles with finances and arguments with employees seem too big to handle. In his clearer moments, Howard knows that he is only a few months away from bankruptcy. But he turns to drink to get away from the painful reality of his failure. So far he has refused all his friends' offers of help and his wife's pleas that he get treatment.

Sandra, on the other hand, is a recovering drug addict. Born to a low-income family, she had started smoking pot and snorting coke shortly after high school. Marrying an ex-Army private, she had two children and moved frequently from place to place, avoiding rent payments and spending much of the family's money on drugs. Their life rapidly became a downward spiral of drugs, unemployment, and running from the law.

When her husband was caught forging checks five years later, Sandra woke up. She got down on her knees and prayed for help.

She admitted that her life had become unmanageable, and that she didn't have the power any more to change it. Hoping that there was a God, she promised to turn her life *and* her will over to him, if only he would restore her life to sanity.

Sandra took her children with her to a homeless shelter, quit drugs, and went into therapy. After a few months, she enrolled in a community college.

Successful beyond her teachers' expectations, Sandra was urged to enter college, using financial aid. Hesitant, she applied—and was accepted. Sandra now maintains a B+ average with a full course load. For two and a half years she's been drug-free. And, instead of hoping at best to find a job as a nurse's aide, she's dreaming of going for a degree in secondary education.

Two real people, two different responses to the alluring addiction of drugs. Drug addiction is an overwhelming problem in our society today. Does the Bible—a book written over 2,000 years ago—speak to the danger of substance abuse? Yes, it does. Read the following Scripture passages for a vivid picture of addiction—and some advice on overcoming it.

What the Bible Tells Us

Who has woe? Who has sorrow?
  Who has strife? Who has complaints?
  Who has needless bruises? Who has bloodshot eyes?

Those who linger over wine,
  who go to sample bowls of mixed wine.

Do not gaze at wine when it is red,
  when it sparkles in the cup.
  when it goes down smoothly!

In the end it bites like a snake
  and poisons like a viper.

Your eyes will see strange sights
  and your mind imagine confusing things.

When will I wake up
  so I can find another drink? (Proverbs 23:29–35)

Copyright ©1994 Church Development Resources   It is illegal to copy this material without permission.

Do not be drunk with wine. That will ruin you spiritually. But be filled with the Spirit. (Ephesians 5:18)

How the Bible Relates

1. What addictive substance is described here? What other addictive substances used today could this passage be describing?

2. What do "those who linger over wine" suffer, according to the first part of this passage?

3. How does alcohol deceive the one who drinks it? How might the same apply to other addictive substances?

4. What controls the person's life described in these verses from Proverbs?

5. How does an addiction ruin a person's spirit? What alternative does the Bible offer? What do you think this means?

6. What difference do you think it would make for a person to have the Spirit of God in his or her life?

The Bottom Line

Many people look to drugs and alcohol to escape the pain of their lives. They need something to fill the emptiness in their heart. Others are simply looking for a perpetual good time, an escape from responsibilities. Still others use substances to attain peer approval, social standing, sophistication, and/or respect. But chemical substances are deceiving; they will take control of a person's will and spirit. The Bible offers an alternative that brings wholeness and healing.

Prayer

God, help me to see the places in my life where I am looking to other things to give me meaning and fulfillment. Open my eyes to any kind of addiction in my life. Help me to understand what you are offering to me through your Spirit. Amen.

A Final Word

If a person's thinking is controlled by the Spirit, then there is life and peace. *(The apostle Paul in Romans 8:6, New Century Version)*

It's a Killer

The heavy use of alcohol affects nearly every organ and system of the body. Here are some common effects of alcohol abuse:

- **Gastrointestinal diseases.** Chronic gastritis, or inflammation of the lining of the stomach, bleeding from the stomach or esophagus, and inflammation of the pancreas.
- **Liver damage.** Hepatitis, fatty infiltration, or alcoholic cirrhosis that can lead to death.
- **Cardiovascular disease.** High blood pressure which, in turn, can lead to impaired functioning, heart attack, or stroke.
- **Nervous-system damage.** Numbness in arms and legs, pain and prickling sensations, light flashes and decreased vision. Can cause permanent brain damage.
- **Cancers.** Cancers of the mouth, larynx, esophagus, lungs, and liver.
- **Fetal alcohol syndrome.** Physical birth defects and mental retardation in infants.
- **Other effects:** Malnutrition, anemia, decrease in resistance to infections, menstrual irregularities, and impotence.

— *Dr. Joyce DeHaan, medical director at Gateway Villa, an addiction-treatment center in Kalamazoo, Michigan. Adapted from* The Banner, *August 15, 1994. Used by permission.*

Does God Want to Spoil My Fun?

1: "Where There's Life, There's Bud"

Beginnings

Think of some commercial slogans that entice us to believe alcohol is the key to happiness (for example, "Weekends were made for Michelob" or "Go for the gusto," etc.). What other addictive substances are in the news lately? Why do you think people use such substances? What are they trying to gain? Is it okay for people to use these as they see fit? Why or why not?

What's Happening Today

"There must be something more than the daily grind of work. There must be some relief, somewhere, to the inner pain and feeling of powerlessness. There must be some way to escape the vague sense of being trapped, of having missed the happiness in life."

Not everyone feels this way, but many do. That's what draws millions every day into the shadowy world of alcohol, heroin, speed, LSD, marijuana, uppers, downers, and cocaine. Feeling empty, sad, or overwhelmed, they seek to fill that void with something that will make them feel powerful, happy, and energetic. They want to get away from the pain, to find a release from fear or boredom. And they seek it in drugs.

Drugs do offer escape—at least a temporary one. Howard, for example, had always gone easy on drinking, but when his business got entangled in tax problems last fall, he began to drink more at home. First it was a couple of beers after dinner "to relax," then harder drinks like whiskey and gin. When his wife confronted him, he began drinking secretly—at work, in bars, or at home after she'd gone to bed.

The increasing pressures of his business have driven Howard to even more drink. His troubles with finances and arguments with employees seem too big to handle. In his clearer moments, Howard knows that he is only a few months away from bankruptcy. But he turns to drink to get away from the painful reality of his failure. So far he has refused all his friends' offers of help and his wife's pleas that he get treatment.

Sandra, on the other hand, is a recovering drug addict. Born to a low-income family, she had started smoking pot and snorting coke shortly after high school. Marrying an ex-Army private, she had two children and moved frequently from place to place, avoiding rent payments and spending much of the family's money on drugs. Their life rapidly became a downward spiral of drugs, unemployment, and running from the law.

When her husband was caught forging checks five years later, Sandra woke up. She got down on her knees and prayed for help.

She admitted that her life had become unmanageable, and that she didn't have the power any more to change it. Hoping that there was a God, she promised to turn her life *and* her will over to him, if only he would restore her life to sanity.

Sandra took her children with her to a homeless shelter, quit drugs, and went into therapy. After a few months, she enrolled in a community college.

Successful beyond her teachers' expectations, Sandra was urged to enter college, using financial aid. Hesitant, she applied—and was accepted. Sandra now maintains a B+ average with a full course load. For two and a half years she's been drug-free. And, instead of hoping at best to find a job as a nurse's aide, she's dreaming of going for a degree in secondary education.

Two real people, two different responses to the alluring addiction of drugs. Drug addiction is an overwhelming problem in our society today. Does the Bible—a book written over 2,000 years ago—speak to the danger of substance abuse? Yes, it does. Read the following Scripture passages for a vivid picture of addiction—and some advice on overcoming it.

What the Bible Tells Us

Who has woe? Who has sorrow?
   Who has strife? Who has complaints?
   Who has needless bruises? Who has bloodshot eyes?

Those who linger over wine,
   who go to sample bowls of mixed wine.

Do not gaze at wine when it is red,
   when it sparkles in the cup,
   when it goes down smoothly!

In the end it bites like a snake
   and poisons like a viper.

Your eyes will see strange sights
   and your mind imagine confusing things.

When will I wake up
   so I can find another drink? (Proverbs 23:29–35)

Copyright ©1994 Church Development Resources   It is illegal to copy this material without permission.

Do not be drunk with wine. That will ruin you spiritually. But be filled with the Spirit. (Ephesians 5:18)

How the Bible Relates

1. What addictive substance is described here? What other addictive substances used today could this passage be describing?

2. What do "those who linger over wine" suffer, according to the first part of this passage?

3. How does alcohol deceive the one who drinks it? How might the same apply to other addictive substances?

4. What controls the person's life described in these verses from Proverbs?

5. How does an addiction ruin a person's spirit? What alternative does the Bible offer? What do you think this means?

6. What difference do you think it would make for a person to have the Spirit of God in his or her life?

The Bottom Line

Many people look to drugs and alcohol to escape the pain of their lives. They need something to fill the emptiness in their heart. Others are simply looking for a perpetual good time, an escape from responsibilities. Still others use substances to attain peer approval, social standing, sophistication, and/or respect. But chemical substances are deceiving; they will take control of a person's will and spirit. The Bible offers an alternative that brings wholeness and healing.

Prayer

God, help me to see the places in my life where I am looking to other things to give me meaning and fulfillment. Open my eyes to any kind of addiction in my life. Help me to understand what you are offering to me through your Spirit. Amen.

A Final Word

If a person's thinking is controlled by the Spirit, then there is life and peace. *(The apostle Paul in Romans 8:6, New Century Version)*

It's a Killer

The heavy use of alcohol affects nearly every organ and system of the body. Here are some common effects of alcohol abuse:

- **Gastrointestinal diseases.** Chronic gastritis, or inflammation of the lining of the stomach, bleeding from the stomach or esophagus, and inflammation of the pancreas.
- **Liver damage.** Hepatitis, fatty infiltration, or alcoholic cirrhosis that can lead to death.
- **Cardiovascular disease.** High blood pressure which, in turn, can lead to impaired functioning, heart attack, or stroke.
- **Nervous-system damage.** Numbness in arms and legs, pain and prickling sensations, light flashes and decreased vision. Can cause permanent brain damage.
- **Cancers.** Cancers of the mouth, larynx, esophagus, lungs, and liver.
- **Fetal alcohol syndrome.** Physical birth defects and mental retardation in infants.
- **Other effects:** Malnutrition, anemia, decrease in resistance to infections, menstrual irregularities, and impotence.

— *Dr. Joyce DeHaan, medical director at Gateway Villa, an addiction-treatment center in Kalamazoo, Michigan. Adapted from* The Banner, *August 15, 1994. Used by permission.*

Does God Want to Spoil My Fun?

1: "Where There's Life, There's Bud"

Beginnings

Think of some commercial slogans that entice us to believe alcohol is the key to happiness (for example, "Weekends were made for Michelob" or "Go for the gusto," etc.). What other addictive substances are in the news lately? Why do you think people use such substances? What are they trying to gain? Is it okay for people to use these as they see fit? Why or why not?

What's Happening Today

"There must be something more than the daily grind of work. There must be some relief, somewhere, to the inner pain and feeling of powerlessness. There must be some way to escape the vague sense of being trapped, of having missed the happiness in life."

Not everyone feels this way, but many do. That's what draws millions every day into the shadowy world of alcohol, heroin, speed, LSD, marijuana, uppers, downers, and cocaine. Feeling empty, sad, or overwhelmed, they seek to fill that void with something that will make them feel powerful, happy, and energetic. They want to get away from the pain, to find a release from fear or boredom. And they seek it in drugs.

Drugs do offer escape—at least a temporary one. Howard, for example, had always gone easy on drinking, but when his business got entangled in tax problems last fall, he began to drink more at home. First it was a couple of beers after dinner "to relax," then harder drinks like whiskey and gin. When his wife confronted him, he began drinking secretly—at work, in bars, or at home after she'd gone to bed.

The increasing pressures of his business have driven Howard to even more drink. His troubles with finances and arguments with employees seem too big to handle. In his clearer moments, Howard knows that he is only a few months away from bankruptcy. But he turns to drink to get away from the painful reality of his failure. So far he has refused all his friends' offers of help and his wife's pleas that he get treatment.

Sandra, on the other hand, is a recovering drug addict. Born to a low-income family, she had started smoking pot and snorting coke shortly after high school. Marrying an ex-Army private, she had two children and moved frequently from place to place, avoiding rent payments and spending much of the family's money on drugs. Their life rapidly became a downward spiral of drugs, unemployment, and running from the law.

When her husband was caught forging checks five years later, Sandra woke up. She got down on her knees and prayed for help.

She admitted that her life had become unmanageable, and that she didn't have the power any more to change it. Hoping that there was a God, she promised to turn her life *and* her will over to him, if only he would restore her life to sanity.

Sandra took her children with her to a homeless shelter, quit drugs, and went into therapy. After a few months, she enrolled in a community college. Successful beyond her teachers' expectations, Sandra was urged to enter college, using financial aid. Hesitant, she applied—and was accepted. Sandra now maintains a B+ average with a full course load. For two and a half years she's been drug-free. And, instead of hoping at best to find a job as a nurse's aide, she's dreaming of going for a degree in secondary education.

Two real people, two different responses to the alluring addiction of drugs. Drug addiction is an overwhelming problem in our society today. Does the Bible—a book written over 2,000 years ago—speak to the danger of substance abuse? Yes, it does. Read the following Scripture passages for a vivid picture of addiction—and some advice on overcoming it.

What the Bible Tells Us

Who has woe? Who has sorrow?
  Who has strife? Who has complaints?
  Who has needless bruises? Who has bloodshot eyes?

Those who linger over wine,
  who go to sample bowls of mixed wine.

Do not gaze at wine when it is red,
  when it sparkles in the cup.
  when it goes down smoothly!

In the end it bites like a snake
  and poisons like a viper.

Your eyes will see strange sights
  and your mind imagine confusing things.

When will I wake up
  so I can find another drink? (Proverbs 23:29–35)

Copyright ©1994 Church Development Resources   It is illegal to copy this material without permission.

Do not be drunk with wine. That will ruin you spiritually. But be filled with the Spirit. (Ephesians 5:18)

How the Bible Relates

1. What addictive substance is described here? What other addictive substances used today could this passage be describing?
2. What do "those who linger over wine" suffer, according to the first part of this passage?
3. How does alcohol deceive the one who drinks it? How might the same apply to other addictive substances?
4. What controls the person's life described in these verses from Proverbs?
5. How does an addiction ruin a person's spirit? What alternative does the Bible offer? What do you think this means?
6. What difference do you think it would make for a person to have the Spirit of God in his or her life?

The Bottom Line

Many people look to drugs and alcohol to escape the pain of their lives. They need something to fill the emptiness in their heart. Others are simply looking for a perpetual good time, an escape from responsibilities. Still others use substances to attain peer approval, social standing, sophistication, and/or respect. But chemical substances are deceiving; they will take control of a person's will and spirit. The Bible offers an alternative that brings wholeness and healing.

Prayer

God, help me to see the places in my life where I am looking to other things to give me meaning and fulfillment. Open my eyes to any kind of addiction in my life. Help me to understand what you are offering to me through your Spirit. Amen.

A Final Word

If a person's thinking is controlled by the Spirit, then there is life and peace. *(The apostle Paul in Romans 8:6, New Century Version)*

It's a Killer

The heavy use of alcohol affects nearly every organ and system of the body. Here are some common effects of alcohol abuse:

- **Gastrointestinal diseases.** Chronic gastritis, or inflammation of the lining of the stomach, bleeding from the stomach or esophagus, and inflammation of the pancreas.
- **Liver damage.** Hepatitis, fatty infiltration, or alcoholic cirrhosis that can lead to death.
- **Cardiovascular disease.** High blood pressure which, in turn, can lead to impaired functioning, heart attack, or stroke.
- **Nervous-system damage.** Numbness in arms and legs, pain and prickling sensations, light flashes and decreased vision. Can cause permanent brain damage.
- **Cancers.** Cancers of the mouth, larynx, esophagus, lungs, and liver.
- **Fetal alcohol syndrome.** Physical birth defects and mental retardation in infants.
- **Other effects:** Malnutrition, anemia, decrease in resistance to infections, menstrual irregularities, and impotence.

— *Dr. Joyce DeHaan, medical director at Gateway Villa, an addiction-treatment center in Kalamazoo, Michigan. Adapted from* The Banner, *August 15, 1994. Used by permission.*

Does God Want to Spoil My Fun?

1: "Where There's Life, There's Bud"

Beginnings

Think of some commercial slogans that entice us to believe alcohol is the key to happiness (for example, "Weekends were made for Michelob" or "Go for the gusto," etc.). What other addictive substances are in the news lately? Why do you think people use such substances? What are they trying to gain? Is it okay for people to use these as they see fit? Why or why not?

What's Happening Today

"There must be something more than the daily grind of work. There must be some relief, somewhere, to the inner pain and feeling of powerlessness. There must be some way to escape the vague sense of being trapped, of having missed the happiness in life."

Not everyone feels this way, but many do. That's what draws millions every day into the shadowy world of alcohol, heroin, speed, LSD, marijuana, uppers, downers, and cocaine. Feeling empty, sad, or overwhelmed, they seek to fill that void with something that will make them feel powerful, happy, and energetic. They want to get away from the pain, to find a release from fear or boredom. And they seek it in drugs.

Drugs do offer escape—at least a temporary one. Howard, for example, had always gone easy on drinking, but when his business got entangled in tax problems last fall, he began to drink more at home. First it was a couple of beers after dinner "to relax," then harder drinks like whiskey and gin. When his wife confronted him, he began drinking secretly—at work, in bars, or at home after she'd gone to bed.

The increasing pressures of his business have driven Howard to even more drink. His troubles with finances and arguments with employees seem too big to handle. In his clearer moments, Howard knows that he is only a few months away from bankruptcy. But he turns to drink to get away from the painful reality of his failure. So far he has refused all his friends' offers of help and his wife's pleas that he get treatment.

Sandra, on the other hand, is a recovering drug addict. Born to a low-income family, she had started smoking pot and snorting coke shortly after high school. Marrying an ex-Army private, she had two children and moved frequently from place to place, avoiding rent payments and spending much of the family's money on drugs. Their life rapidly became a downward spiral of drugs, unemployment, and running from the law.

When her husband was caught forging checks five years later, Sandra woke up. She got down on her knees and prayed for help.

She admitted that her life had become unmanageable, and that she didn't have the power any more to change it. Hoping that there was a God, she promised to turn her life *and* her will over to him, if only he would restore her life to sanity.

Sandra took her children with her to a homeless shelter, quit drugs, and went into therapy. After a few months, she enrolled in a community college.

Successful beyond her teachers' expectations, Sandra was urged to enter college, using financial aid. Hesitant, she applied—and was accepted. Sandra now maintains a B+ average with a full course load. For two and a half years she's been drug-free. And, instead of hoping at best to find a job as a nurse's aide, she's dreaming of going for a degree in secondary education.

Two real people, two different responses to the alluring addiction of drugs. Drug addiction is an overwhelming problem in our society today. Does the Bible—a book written over 2,000 years ago—speak to the danger of substance abuse? Yes, it does. Read the following Scripture passages for a vivid picture of addiction—and some advice on overcoming it.

What the Bible Tells Us

Who has woe? Who has sorrow?
  Who has strife? Who has complaints?
  Who has needless bruises? Who has bloodshot eyes?

Those who linger over wine,
  who go to sample bowls of mixed wine.

Do not gaze at wine when it is red,
  when it sparkles in the cup.
  when it goes down smoothly!

In the end it bites like a snake
  and poisons like a viper.

Your eyes will see strange sights
  and your mind imagine confusing things.

When will I wake up
  so I can find another drink? (Proverbs 23:29–35)

Copyright ©1994 Church Development Resources   It is illegal to copy this material without permission.

Do not be drunk with wine. That will ruin you spiritually. But be filled with the Spirit. (Ephesians 5:18)

How the Bible Relates

1. What addictive substance is described here? What other addictive substances used today could this passage be describing?
2. What do "those who linger over wine" suffer, according to the first part of this passage?
3. How does alcohol deceive the one who drinks it? How might the same apply to other addictive substances?
4. What controls the person's life described in these verses from Proverbs?
5. How does an addiction ruin a person's spirit? What alternative does the Bible offer? What do you think this means?
6. What difference do you think it would make for a person to have the Spirit of God in his or her life?

The Bottom Line

Many people look to drugs and alcohol to escape the pain of their lives. They need something to fill the emptiness in their heart. Others are simply looking for a perpetual good time, an escape from responsibilities. Still others use substances to attain peer approval, social standing, sophistication, and/or respect. But chemical substances are deceiving; they will take control of a person's will and spirit. The Bible offers an alternative that brings wholeness and healing.

Prayer

God, help me to see the places in my life where I am looking to other things to give me meaning and fulfillment. Open my eyes to any kind of addiction in my life. Help me to understand what you are offering to me through your Spirit. Amen.

A Final Word

If a person's thinking is controlled by the Spirit, then there is life and peace. *(The apostle Paul in Romans 8:6, New Century Version)*

It's a Killer

The heavy use of alcohol affects nearly every organ and system of the body. Here are some common effects of alcohol abuse:

- **Gastrointestinal diseases.** Chronic gastritis, or inflammation of the lining of the stomach, bleeding from the stomach or esophagus, and inflammation of the pancreas.
- **Liver damage.** Hepatitis, fatty infiltration, or alcoholic cirrhosis that can lead to death.
- **Cardiovascular disease.** High blood pressure which, in turn, can lead to impaired functioning, heart attack, or stroke.
- **Nervous-system damage.** Numbness in arms and legs, pain and prickling sensations, light flashes and decreased vision. Can cause permanent brain damage.
- **Cancers.** Cancers of the mouth, larynx, esophagus, lungs, and liver.
- **Fetal alcohol syndrome.** Physical birth defects and mental retardation in infants.
- **Other effects:** Malnutrition, anemia, decrease in resistance to infections, menstrual irregularities, and impotence.

— *Dr. Joyce DeHaan, medical director at Gateway Villa, an addiction-treatment center in Kalamazoo, Michigan. Adapted from* The Banner, *August 15, 1994. Used by permission.*

Does God Want to Spoil My Fun?

SESSION 2

Does God Want to Spoil My Fun?—Leader Guide

2: "The One Who Dies With the Most Toys Wins"

Introductory Notes

In this session, your group members will be tackling one of the greatest myths of North American society: wealth brings happiness. This is not a new myth. Jesus warned against love of money more often than against any other error. But it is a myth that is hard to shake.

Even Christians in North America struggle with the temptations of a materialistic lifestyle. Much of our working day, budgeting, and education is geared toward one goal: getting ahead financially.

Working to support one's family is, of course, a good thing. But when more of our time and attention is given to financial goals, home improvements, furniture, clothes, and cars—to name a few—than to prayer, spiritual goals, and ministry opportunities, something has begun to take the place of God's call on our lives. And, Jesus says, that something starts with a capital "M."

This session is not meant to be a guilt trip. No one in your group should be left feeling as though God's (or your) finger is pointing at them for their choice of lifestyle.

Rather, this session is meant to give people a chance to step back and look at their goals—and at the meaning of life. Is life more than simply working to meet the basic needs of food and clothing? Are there things so worthwhile that we should carve out time in our hectic day for them—even if they don't help achieve our financial goals? What is driving us—the need for more money, for a better lifestyle? How can we look beyond physical needs to the spiritual?

There is another dimension to this—the dimension of spiritual emptiness. What emptiness in our soul are we trying to fill when we run faster and faster after material goods? Do we feel that they will give us the security, happiness, and sense of self-worth that everyone seems to be striving for?

People today are ripe for this discussion. They are finding out that a new house, two-car garage, and great landscaping do little for that empty feeling inside. The members of your group may already have discovered this truth, or they may still be striving to reach what North Americans know as "the American dream," unaware of its inability to fill their void.

As you prepare for this session, take a good look at your life as well. Where do you struggle in this area? If you were the rich young ruler, would you be able to follow Jesus' suggestion: "Go, sell all you have and give it to the poor, and come and follow me"? Probably not. There are few Christians today who would do so without hesitation. Our houses, our lifestyle, our financial security mean a lot to us.

But don't burden yourself with guilt—and don't do the opposite, which is to push it away and not think about it. Instead, use this as an opportunity to let God work further in your life, to make you more like himself. Ask God to show you the ways in which this Scripture touches your life, too. Be prepared to share with your group your own personal struggles with materialism, your own new insights gained. That will mean more to them than a brilliant explanation of the Bible passage.

Strive for a balance here, too. Take care not to discriminate *against* wealth. God blesses some people with great prosperity. What he expects of them in return is faithful and responsible use of that material blessing out of a heart filled with love for the God who has given them their wealth.

Finally, pray that your group members may be allowed to see that, as the Westminster Catechism puts it, "the chief end of man" is not to glorify money and enjoy it forever but "to glorify *God* and enjoy *him* forever."

Beginning the Session

Welcome everyone warmly, and very briefly follow up on people's sharing or concerns from last week with a few questions. Don't spend too much time on this. You can come back to it at the end of the session during the prayer time, if you wish. You will want to spend most of your time on the Scripture, not on catch-up conversation.

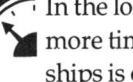 In the longer session, you will want to spend a bit more time here, since building supportive relationships is one of your goals. Remember to keep an open ear for ways in which you can care for each other.

Remind your group of last week's session topic and the theme of this series: "Does God Want to Spoil My Fun?" Review your conclusions from last week: that people who look for escape, fulfillment, or pleasure in drugs and alcohol slowly lose control of their lives and of their personhood. The drug rules them, not the other way around. The Bible tries to warn us about that—not to spoil our fun, but to give us a more healthy, fulfilling life.

But there are other ways in which people try to find meaning and fulfillment in life—ways that can enslave them just as much as alcohol or drugs. Explain that each session in this series will look at these ways and examine what the Bible has to say about each of these.

Beginnings

What "labels" or brand names do people measure success by (in clothing, cars, furniture, titles, positions,

37

etc.)? Do different groups of people have different ways to measure success? Give some examples.**

Your discussion here may resemble a scene out of "Lifestyles of the Rich and Famous": big houses, new cars, vacation homes, private schools—in other words lots of money and expensive possessions. It is what most North Americans consider a sign of success, of "having arrived." It is the rare individual who has not dreamed of winning the lottery, sweeping the Publisher's Clearinghouse sweepstakes, or inheriting a fortune from an unknown relative. No more worries about bills, about working, about budgeting! Sounds great, doesn't it?

But as group members spin their dreams, you may want to follow up with a few brief questions that prepare them for the perspective of the Scriptures that follow: **What kinds of things can money give us? What can't it give us? Do you think sometimes people place an unrealistic expectation on material possessions? Why do you think very wealthy people are sometimes still very unhappy? Is it possible to have no money and still be happy? What might that suggest about the theory that money can buy happiness?**

Don't spend more than a few minutes on this section. When everyone has had the chance to talk, move on to "What's Happening Today."

 In the longer session, explore this topic a bit longer by asking some of the following questions: **How might pursuing such a lifestyle become a taskmaster instead of just a dream? How much time do people pour into their pursuit of things? How does it dominate their family life? Their leisure time? Their physical energy?** Ask these questions to help group members begin to think about the time and energy that much of our culture invests in materialism. This will help prepare them later for Jesus' statement that "you cannot serve both God and Money."

What's Happening Today

Read this section aloud with your group. When you're finished, allow a brief time for comments or questions. Ask them why they think so many women polled say "financial independence is vital." **What are they looking for? What about the turbo-charged executive types? What misperceptions have they bought into? What unhealthy patterns result from the pursuit of things and positions? What impact did the story of the failed financiers have on the group?** After you've dealt with this section, lead into the Scripture reading.

What the Bible Tells Us

Read the Scripture aloud to your group or ask if one of your group members would like to read. This will involve them early on. Be sure to leave time for questions about what you've read. However, if members want to talk about the meaning of the passage at this point, explain that you'll be working with that in more detail once you get to the discussion questions.

How the Bible Relates

1. What two kinds of treasure does Jesus mention?

Jesus contrasts "treasures on earth" with "treasures in heaven." **What would the treasure on earth include? How does that relate to your earlier discussion on the ideal lifestyle? How is that treasure strictly limited to one's existence on earth?** The concept of "treasures on earth" is a relatively easy one; your group should have a lot of ideas here.

However, the idea of "treasures in heaven" may require a little more thought. Explore this thoroughly with your group; make sure that they understand it before you move on to the next question. **What kinds of things could you do on earth to "store up treasures in heaven"? What kind of treasure might there be that doesn't have to do with money or material goods? What might be considered "treasures of the spirit"?**

 In the longer session, you may want to take some time to share some Scriptures that talk about a kind of spiritual wealth:

*Blessed is the man who finds wisdom,
the man who gains understanding,
for she is more profitable than silver
and yields better returns than gold.
She is more precious than rubies;
nothing you desire can compare with her.*
(Proverbs 3:13–15)

Command those who are rich in this present world not to be arrogant nor to put their hope in wealth, which is so uncertain, but to put their hope in God, who richly provides us with everything for our enjoyment. Command them to do good, to be rich in good deeds, and to be generous and willing to share. In this way they will lay up treasure for themselves as a firm foundation for the coming age, so that they may take hold of the life that is truly life. (1 Timothy 6:17–19)

You don't have to read all of these, but you may find a verse or two particularly helpful if your group is unable to think of ways in which we can lay up spiritual treasure. Use the following questions to follow up: **What does it mean to be "rich in good deeds"? What kind of character do these verses talk about? How would you describe or define "wisdom"? How might it "yield better returns than gold"?** Encourage your group to talk about the lasting value of insight and understanding, the value of a life that is filled with good deeds.

2. Which one does he encourage his listeners to store up? Why?

Jesus warns his listeners away from a lifestyle that is absorbed solely in the physical and material world. If necessary, use this question to explore a little more fully what "treasures in heaven" means. It's important especially that this concept be concrete for your group members. If necessary, refer to the additional Scriptures quoted above.

 In the longer format, consider handing out paper and pencils at this point and asking group members to make two simple drawings: one that represents what they see as "treasures on earth," the other representing "treasures in heaven." This may be helpful to people who are more visual than verbal; it will help them think more concretely about these terms. Assure everyone that they don't have to share their pictures with the larger group if they don't wish to—and that they shouldn't feel as if they have to participate if they feel unable to draw even a simple figure. Encourage members to take just a few minutes for this; they should not make the drawings elaborate and complicated.

When they're finished, ask for volunteers to share what they have drawn or thought about. Be sure to share your own as well.

Ask your group to consider these questions also: **Would you rather be a rich person who is an ill-natured fool or a poor person who has gained a deep understanding of life's meaning and whose life is "rich in good deeds"?** Of course, it is possible to be wise, good, and wealthy at the same time. But encourage your group to think about which they would choose, if they had to make a choice.

What can happen to material wealth and possessions? Are they guaranteed and permanent? What threatens them? The truth of Jesus' warning is all too evident in the stories of the ruined financiers ("What's Happening Today"); take a moment to look back on their failures. **What kinds of things eat away at our savings and our financial plans today?** Talk about unexpected illness, car repairs, business failures, family emergencies, and poor budgeting or extravagant spending—just a few of the things that make material wealth precarious and undependable.

How does Jesus contrast this with wealth "laid up in heaven"? What does this imply about the life of a person after death? What is heaven? Here you have the opportunity to share with your group the concept of heaven and to affirm their inner conviction that "there must be something more." But you will want to do more listening than talking. This is an excellent opportunity for you to learn what—if anything—your group members think or believe about these. Don't feel as though you have to give a full and complete explanation here; it is more important initially to get members thinking about the subject and asking questions.

If you do touch on the subject of heaven, keep it very simple, explaining that the Bible portrays heaven as God's home, so to speak—though God is everywhere present. It is a place of rest and joy for those who die with faith in God; it is what will endure when this world is no more. **If we accept the Bible's teaching as true, why would it be important for us to include heaven in our perspectives and priorities? How would it make a difference in our lives and values?**

This discussion touches on questions that lie hidden inside everyone: Is there an afterlife? Is there a God who will hold me accountable? These questions may seem at first glance to have little to do with a lifestyle of materialism and the pursuit of wealth—but in fact they go hand in hand. If there is an afterlife, then there may be something worth living for, worth giving up things for—something of eternal and lasting value. Materialism just looks at the here and now and says, "Grab it while you can, because this is all there is."

 In the longer session, ask group members to think about people close to them who have died—particularly adults, who have had some years to shape their lives. **Did their lives reflect what Jesus is saying here? If not, do you think they had regrets? How might your perspective on money, financial security, and material possessions change when you are facing your own death?** Don't be morbid here, but do encourage the group to entertain these questions and perhaps offer their own ideas and insights.

Finally, look at Jesus' statement that "where your treasure is, there your heart will be also." **What is this "heart" that Jesus mentions? What part of us is he talking about?** Help group members to see that Jesus is referring to our loyalty, emotions, dreams, passions, and values. **Why might it be more beneficial to have these things focused on "heavenly treasure" rather than material possessions?**

3. What does Jesus tell them not to worry about? Why?

Webster defines *worry* as "mental distress or agitation." It explains that the root of the verb *to worry* comes from an old German word meaning "to strangle or constrict." Before you discuss the Bible passage, take a moment to explore this emotional state called "worry." **What kinds of things do we worry most about today?** Your discussion will probably include finances, health and children, job security, and family relationships. Your group may be able to come up with a much longer list.

 In the longer session, ask members to make a "worry list." Give them a minute or two to write, as quickly as they can, all the things, both big and little, that they worry about during the day. Then go over these lists together and see which items are

Inspirit: Does God Want to Spoil My Fun? **LEADER GUIDE** Session 2

most frequently mentioned. (This also is an excellent way to get to know each other better; it reveals the small and not-so-small insecurities that people hide behind their competent and confident exteriors.)

What does worry feel like? What are our emotions? It is true that when we're in the grip of worry, we feel strangled, or constricted—tied up in knots. An inner anxiety drives us, and we are unable to relax.

There are, of course, things that may merit some worry—at least from a human point of view. But Jesus emphasizes that it is pointless to worry about the material part of life—what we eat, drink, and wear—or even about the length of our lives. **What fact of existence does Jesus assume here? Who is looking after us? Who has provided this world with far more materials than we could ever need?** The existence of God is a given in Jesus' teaching here. He teaches not only a God who is powerful and alive, but also a God who cares for what he has made.

As you discuss this, remind your group of the basic premise of the 12-step program that you talked about in your last session: Admitting one's powerlessness and putting oneself in God's hands. **How does that relate to what Jesus is saying?**

What does Jesus say about the important things in life? How does his perspective contrast with that of our culture? Jesus points his listeners beyond the physical needs of this life—food and clothing—to look higher. If we work only to gain material goods, says Jesus, we are missing the point of life. There is much more to life than that.

 In the longer session, if you have already read to your group the additional passage from 1 Timothy, look at how that passage echoes Jesus' words: "In this way they will lay up treasure for themselves as a firm foundation for the coming age, *so that they may take hold of the life that is truly life.*" **What might the "life that is truly life" mean? How might it tie into Jesus' statement that life is "more important than food, and the body more important than clothes"?** Challenge your group to give this some thought; don't offer your own answers, but let them wrestle with it.

4. Who feeds the birds of the air? What relationship does he have to people?

Look especially here at the words Jesus uses for God: "your heavenly Father." **What does that imply about his listeners? What kind of trust was Jesus asking them to put in God? What is a father supposed to supply for his children?** Some in your group may not be ready to allow for the existence of a God, let alone see God as a loving Father who is protective and caring of his human children. Some may have had abusive fathers who forever twisted the meaning of the word "father" for their children. Some may never have known what it is to be loved by any man. Pray that the Holy Spirit will begin to bring healing to that part of their lives. Be sensitive to that need as you lead this discussion.

The trust factor is an important one. Jesus is asking us to trust that God will act toward us like a loving father would. **Why would this kind of trust be necessary before we can take Jesus' advice, "Do not worry"?** Throughout this discussion, listen for comments that will help you understand how your group members see God.

 In the longer session, take some time to explore the picture of God as a heavenly Father. Ask your group to volunteer ideas on all the good things that fathers can do for or give to their children. **What is an ideal father like? What is his attitude toward his children? What does he want to give them?** As they suggest the love and care that a human father can give, they will be gradually painting a picture of the kind of God that Jesus is asking his listeners to trust.

The God Jesus describes is an active, not a passive, God. **What actions does Jesus describe? What is God busy doing?** God feeds the birds of the air, who have nothing to do with planting or harvesting the food they eat. In another place Jesus also mentions that God clothes the lilies of the field, which do not work to spin fabric for their apparel. **What does this suggest as God's role over all creation?** Help your group to see that God intends to look after the creatures he has made—and especially the creatures of highest importance, human beings.

Just for fun, ask your group members to answer the final question in Matthew's passage: "Who of you by worrying can add a single hour to his life?" Help group members to imagine the patience and the humor with which Jesus must have said this. Of course worrying can't lengthen our lifespan. Actually, medical science has proven that worry can *shorten* life by stressing the body and lowering our resistance to disease.

5. What choice of masters does Jesus give his listeners?

This passage is intriguing because it points up the same basic truth that the previous session did: Whatever we use to fill our inner emptiness eventually becomes our master. Both drugs and material possessions will take over our lives, and we will end up serving them rather than finding the fulfillment we seek.

Jesus gives his listeners a choice here. **Why do you think it may not be possible to serve both God and Money? How might there be a constant conflict of interest?** Talk about the difference between a lifestyle that craves material goods and one that puts God first. Help your group to see that serving Money puts self first; serving God requires us, among other things, to live for others as well as for ourselves.

How does this statement of Jesus relate to his teaching about storing up treasures in heaven rather than on earth? How does the one store up treasures on earth,

and the other treasures in heaven? Make sure your group sees that serving Money results only in empty treasure that is unsatisfying and fading. Serving God, on the other hand, will bring meaning and satisfaction that will last beyond this life, according to Jesus. Again, refer to the story of the financiers who spent their lives serving Money, and talk about how their lives may have been different if they had chosen a different Master.

The Bottom Line

God isn't out to deprive us of good, pleasant things. Rather, he wants to free us from being enslaved to them, so that we can see the true meaning of life. Keeping our focus on God will help keep everything else in its right perspective. Only God can fill the emptiness in our souls.

Use this closing part of the session to reaffirm the truths of the Scripture you've just studied. Emphasize that God's wish is not to deprive but to enrich our lives. The myth of happiness through material goods is one that many people spend their lives chasing, only to find emptiness at the end.

 In the longer format, encourage your group to think about this during the coming week and to look at their own lives and the lives of people around them. **How many people can they find who desire material wealth? How many do they know who have been made very happy by their money and possessions?** Encourage members to report back next week on what insights they might have gained from this reflection.

Optional Prayer Time

Close your session with the prayer below. You may wish to add to it, if you want, first mentioning needs of group members and thanking God for everyone who came to today's session. Encourage members, as they leave, to reread the "Final Word" when they get home and to use the prayer in their daily times of reflection.

 In the longer session, take more time to gather prayer requests and follow up on prayer concerns from last week. Assure group members that you've been praying daily for these things; encourage them to look for answers during the coming weeks. Again, listen for ways in which you can be a support to group members with concrete, physical assistance. Then lead the prayer yourself, unless some group members have expressed a desire to participate along with you.

Prayer

God, help me to see whether a desire for material wealth has kept me from seeing the true meaning of life. I would like to begin to trust you for giving me what I need. Amen.

A Final Word

Keep your lives free from the love of money and be content with what you have, because God has said, "Never will I leave you; never will I forsake you." So we say with confidence, "The Lord is my helper; I will not be afraid. What can man do to me?" *(Hebrews 13:5–6)*

devoted to the one and despise the other. You cannot serve both God and Money." (Luke 16:13)

How the Bible Relates

1. What two kinds of treasure does Jesus mention?
2. Which one does he encourage his listeners to store up? Why?
3. What does Jesus tell them not to worry about? Why?
4. Who feeds the birds of the air? What relationship does he have to people?
5. What choice of masters does Jesus give his listeners?

The Bottom Line

God isn't out to deprive you of good, pleasant things. Rather, he wants to free you from being enslaved to them, so that you can see the true meaning of life. Keeping your focus on God will help keep everything else in its right perspective. Only God can fill the emptiness in your soul.

Prayer

God, help me to see whether a desire for material wealth has kept me from seeing the true meaning of life. I would like to begin to trust you for giving me what I need. Amen.

A Final Word

Keep your lives free from the love of money and be content with what you have, because God has said, "Never will I leave you; never will I forsake you." So we say with confidence, "The Lord is my helper; I will not be afraid. What can man do to me?" *(Hebrews 13:5–6)*

Does God Want to Spoil My Fun?

2: "The One Who Dies With the Most Toys Wins"

Beginnings

What "labels" or brand names do people measure success by (in clothing, cars, furniture, titles, positions, etc.)? Do different groups of people have different ways to measure success? Give some examples.

What's Happening Today

Seven Poor Rich Men

In 1928 a group of the world's most successful financiers met at the Edgewater Beach Hotel in Chicago. The following were present:
— the president of the largest steel company
— the greatest wheat speculator
— the president of the New York Stock Exchange
— a member of the President's Cabinet
— the greatest "bear" in Wall Street
— the president of the Bank of International Settlements
— the head of the world's greatest monopoly

Collectively, these tycoons controlled more wealth than there was in the United States Treasury, and for year newspapers and magazines had been printing their success stories and urging the youth of the nation to follow their examples. Twenty-five years later, this is what had happened to these men.

The president of the largest independent steel company, Charles Schwab, lived on borrowed money the last five years of his life and died broke.

The greatest wheat speculator, Arthur Cutten, died abroad, insolvent.

The president of the New York Stock Exchange, Richard Whitney, served a term in Sing Sing Prison.

The member of the President's Cabinet, Albert Fall, was pardoned from prison so he could die at home.

The greatest "bear" in Wall Street, Jesse Livermore, committed suicide.

The president of the Bank of International Settlements, Leon Fraser, committed suicide.

The head of the world's greatest monopoly, Ivar Gruegger, committed suicide.

All of these men had learned how to make money, but not one of them had learned how to live.

Our North American culture is on a continual pursuit to find happiness. In the '80s, it was money; in the '90s, it's personal fulfillment any way you can get it! Earning more and moving up is no longer the only way to go. In the '80s, making a lot of money was viewed as an end in itself. Today it is viewed more as a means to an end—personal fulfillment and happiness. Though nearly 90 percent of American woman say financial independence is vital, fewer than 30 percent think money is key to happiness, according to a poll reported for Avon Products in 1993.

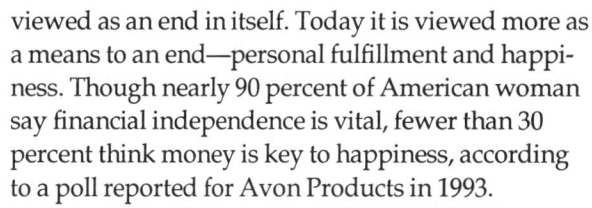

Santa Cruz, California, psychiatrist Alan Sherman counsels many turbo-charged executives from nearby Silicon Valley who come to him "yearning for a life transcending money and career." In a workshop Sherman deals with their concerns. They "reflect on why conventional success seems to taste so bland" and what they can do about it.

Harvard economist Juliet Schor, in her book *The Overworked American*, confirms that thinking: "Affluence is not delivering the kind of meaning and satisfaction it promised." People want more. What is it they are looking for?

What the Bible Tells Us

Do not store up for yourselves treasures on earth, where moth and rust destroy, and where thieves break in and steal. But store up for yourselves treasures in heaven, where moth and rust do not destroy, and where thieves do not break in and steal. For where your treasure is, there your heart will be also . . . .

Therefore I tell you, do not worry about your life, what you will eat or drink; or about your body, what you will wear. Is not life more important than food, and the body more important than clothes? Look at the birds of the air; they do not sow or reap or store away in barns, and yet your heavenly Father feeds them. Are you not much more valuable than they? Who of you by worrying can add a single hour to his life? (Matthew 6:19–21, 25–27)

Jesus said, "No servant can serve two masters. Either he will hate the one and love the other, or he will be

Copyright ©1994 Church Development Resources   It is illegal to copy this material without permission.

devoted to the one and despise the other. You cannot serve both God and Money." (Luke 16:13)

How the Bible Relates

1. What two kinds of treasure does Jesus mention?

2. Which one does he encourage his listeners to store up? Why?

3. What does Jesus tell them not to worry about? Why?

4. Who feeds the birds of the air? What relationship does he have to people?

5. What choice of masters does Jesus give his listeners?

The Bottom Line

God isn't out to deprive you of good, pleasant things. Rather, he wants to free you from being enslaved to them, so that you can see the true meaning of life. Keeping your focus on God will help keep everything else in its right perspective. Only God can fill the emptiness in your soul.

Prayer

God, help me to see whether a desire for material wealth has kept me from seeing the true meaning of life. I would like to begin to trust you for giving me what I need. Amen.

A Final Word

Keep your lives free from the love of money and be content with what you have, because God has said, "Never will I leave you; never will I forsake you." So we say with confidence, "The Lord is my helper; I will not be afraid. What can man do to me?" *(Hebrews 13:5–6)*

Does God Want to Spoil My Fun?

2: "The One Who Dies With the Most Toys Wins"

Beginnings

What "labels" or brand names do people measure success by (in clothing, cars, furniture, titles, positions, etc.)? Do different groups of people have different ways to measure success? Give some examples.

What's Happening Today

Seven Poor Rich Men

In 1928 a group of the world's most successful financiers met at the Edgewater Beach Hotel in Chicago. The following were present:
—the president of the largest steel company
—the greatest wheat speculator
—the president of the New York Stock Exchange
—a member of the President's Cabinet
—the greatest "bear" in Wall Street
—the president of the Bank of International Settlements
— the head of the world's greatest monopoly

Collectively, these tycoons controlled more wealth than there was in the United States Treasury, and for year newspapers and magazines had been printing their success stories and urging the youth of the nation to follow their examples. Twenty-five years later, this is what had happened to these men.

The president of the largest independent steel company, Charles Schwab, lived on borrowed money the last five years of his life and died broke.

The greatest wheat speculator, Arthur Cutten, died abroad, insolvent.

The president of the New York Stock Exchange, Richard Whitney, served a term in Sing Sing Prison.

The member of the President's Cabinet, Albert Fall, was pardoned from prison so he could die at home.

The greatest "bear" in Wall Street, Jesse Livermore, committed suicide.

The president of the Bank of International Settlements, Leon Fraser, committed suicide.

The head of the world's greatest monopoly, Ivar Gruegger, committed suicide.

All of these men had learned how to make money, but not one of them had learned how to live.

Our North American culture is on a continual pursuit to find happiness. In the '80s, it was money; in the '90s, it's personal fulfillment any way you can get it! Earning more and moving up is no longer the only way to go. In the '80s, making a lot of money was viewed as an end in itself. Today it is viewed more as a means to an end—personal fulfillment and happiness. Though nearly 90 percent of American woman say financial independence is vital, fewer than 30 percent think money is key to happiness, according to a poll reported for Avon Products in 1993.

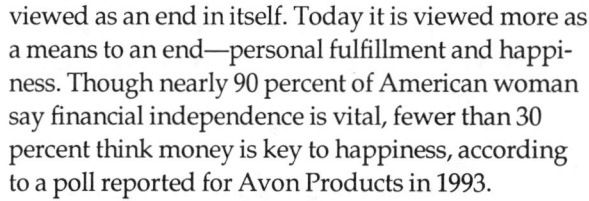

Santa Cruz, California, psychiatrist Alan Sherman counsels many turbo-charged executives from nearby Silicon Valley who come to him "yearning for a life transcending money and career." In a workshop Sherman deals with their concerns. They "reflect on why conventional success seems to taste so bland" and what they can do about it.

Harvard economist Juliet Schor, in her book *The Overworked American*, confirms that thinking: "Affluence is not delivering the kind of meaning and satisfaction it promised." People want more. What is it they are looking for?

What the Bible Tells Us

Do not store up for yourselves treasures on earth, where moth and rust destroy, and where thieves break in and steal. But store up for yourselves treasures in heaven, where moth and rust do not destroy, and where thieves do not break in and steal. For where your treasure is, there your heart will be also . . . .

Therefore I tell you, do not worry about your life, what you will eat or drink; or about your body, what you will wear. Is not life more important than food, and the body more important than clothes? Look at the birds of the air; they do not sow or reap or store away in barns, and yet your heavenly Father feeds them. Are you not much more valuable than they? Who of you by worrying can add a single hour to his life? (Matthew 6:19–21, 25–27)

Jesus said, "No servant can serve two masters. Either he will hate the one and love the other, or he will be

devoted to the one and despise the other. You cannot serve both God and Money." (Luke 16:13)

How the Bible Relates

1. What two kinds of treasure does Jesus mention?

2. Which one does he encourage his listeners to store up? Why?

3. What does Jesus tell them not to worry about? Why?

4. Who feeds the birds of the air? What relationship does he have to people?

5. What choice of masters does Jesus give his listeners?

The Bottom Line

God isn't out to deprive you of good, pleasant things. Rather, he wants to free you from being enslaved to them, so that you can see the true meaning of life. Keeping your focus on God will help keep everything else in its right perspective. Only God can fill the emptiness in your soul.

Prayer

God, help me to see whether a desire for material wealth has kept me from seeing the true meaning of life. I would like to begin to trust you for giving me what I need. Amen.

A Final Word

Keep your lives free from the love of money and be content with what you have, because God has said, "Never will I leave you; never will I forsake you." So we say with confidence, "The Lord is my helper; I will not be afraid. What can man do to me?" *(Hebrews 13:5–6)*

Does God Want to Spoil My Fun?

2: "The One Who Dies With the Most Toys Wins"

Beginnings

What "labels" or brand names do people measure success by (in clothing, cars, furniture, titles, positions, etc.)? Do different groups of people have different ways to measure success? Give some examples.

What's Happening Today

Seven Poor Rich Men

In 1928 a group of the world's most successful financiers met at the Edgewater Beach Hotel in Chicago. The following were present:
—the president of the largest steel company
—the greatest wheat speculator
—the president of the New York Stock Exchange
—a member of the President's Cabinet
—the greatest "bear" in Wall Street
—the president of the Bank of International Settlements
— the head of the world's greatest monopoly

Collectively, these tycoons controlled more wealth than there was in the United States Treasury, and for year newspapers and magazines had been printing their success stories and urging the youth of the nation to follow their examples. Twenty-five years later, this is what had happened to these men.

The president of the largest independent steel company, Charles Schwab, lived on borrowed money the last five years of his life and died broke.

The greatest wheat speculator, Arthur Cutten, died abroad, insolvent.

The president of the New York Stock Exchange, Richard Whitney, served a term in Sing Sing Prison.

The member of the President's Cabinet, Albert Fall, was pardoned from prison so he could die at home.

The greatest "bear" in Wall Street, Jesse Livermore, committed suicide.

The president of the Bank of International Settlements, Leon Fraser, committed suicide.

The head of the world's greatest monopoly, Ivar Gruegger, committed suicide.

All of these men had learned how to make money, but not one of them had learned how to live.

Our North American culture is on a continual pursuit to find happiness. In the '80s, it was money; in the '90s, it's personal fulfillment any way you can get it! Earning more and moving up is no longer the only way to go. In the '80s, making a lot of money was viewed as an end in itself. Today it is viewed more as a means to an end—personal fulfillment and happiness. Though nearly 90 percent of American woman say financial independence is vital, fewer than 30 percent think money is key to happiness, according to a poll reported for Avon Products in 1993.

Santa Cruz, California, psychiatrist Alan Sherman counsels many turbo-charged executives from nearby Silicon Valley who come to him "yearning for a life transcending money and career." In a workshop Sherman deals with their concerns. They "reflect on why conventional success seems to taste so bland" and what they can do about it.

Harvard economist Juliet Schor, in her book *The Overworked American*, confirms that thinking: "Affluence is not delivering the kind of meaning and satisfaction it promised." People want more. What is it they are looking for?

What the Bible Tells Us

Do not store up for yourselves treasures on earth, where moth and rust destroy, and where thieves break in and steal. But store up for yourselves treasures in heaven, where moth and rust do not destroy, and where thieves do not break in and steal. For where your treasure is, there your heart will be also . . . .

Therefore I tell you, do not worry about your life, what you will eat or drink; or about your body, what you will wear. Is not life more important than food, and the body more important than clothes? Look at the birds of the air; they do not sow or reap or store away in barns, and yet your heavenly Father feeds them. Are you not much more valuable than they? Who of you by worrying can add a single hour to his life? (Matthew 6:19–21, 25–27)

Jesus said, "No servant can serve two masters. Either he will hate the one and love the other, or he will be

Copyright ©1994 Church Development Resources   It is illegal to copy this material without permission.

devoted to the one and despise the other. You cannot serve both God and Money." (Luke 16:13)

How the Bible Relates

1. What two kinds of treasure does Jesus mention?

2. Which one does he encourage his listeners to store up? Why?

3. What does Jesus tell them not to worry about? Why?

4. Who feeds the birds of the air? What relationship does he have to people?

5. What choice of masters does Jesus give his listeners?

The Bottom Line

God isn't out to deprive you of good, pleasant things. Rather, he wants to free you from being enslaved to them, so that you can see the true meaning of life. Keeping your focus on God will help keep everything else in its right perspective. Only God can fill the emptiness in your soul.

Prayer

God, help me to see whether a desire for material wealth has kept me from seeing the true meaning of life. I would like to begin to trust you for giving me what I need. Amen.

A Final Word

Keep your lives free from the love of money and be content with what you have, because God has said, "Never will I leave you; never will I forsake you." So we say with confidence, "The Lord is my helper; I will not be afraid. What can man do to me?" *(Hebrews 13:5–6)*

Does God Want to Spoil My Fun?

2: "The One Who Dies With the Most Toys Wins"

Beginnings

What "labels" or brand names do people measure success by (in clothing, cars, furniture, titles, positions, etc.)? Do different groups of people have different ways to measure success? Give some examples.

What's Happening Today

Seven Poor Rich Men

In 1928 a group of the world's most successful financiers met at the Edgewater Beach Hotel in Chicago. The following were present:
— the president of the largest steel company
— the greatest wheat speculator
— the president of the New York Stock Exchange
— a member of the President's Cabinet
— the greatest "bear" in Wall Street
— the president of the Bank of International Settlements
— the head of the world's greatest monopoly

Collectively, these tycoons controlled more wealth than there was in the United States Treasury, and for year newspapers and magazines had been printing their success stories and urging the youth of the nation to follow their examples. Twenty-five years later, this is what had happened to these men.

The president of the largest independent steel company, Charles Schwab, lived on borrowed money the last five years of his life and died broke.

The greatest wheat speculator, Arthur Cutten, died abroad, insolvent.

The president of the New York Stock Exchange, Richard Whitney, served a term in Sing Sing Prison.

The member of the President's Cabinet, Albert Fall, was pardoned from prison so he could die at home.

The greatest "bear" in Wall Street, Jesse Livermore, committed suicide.

The president of the Bank of International Settlements, Leon Fraser, committed suicide.

The head of the world's greatest monopoly, Ivar Gruegger, committed suicide.

All of these men had learned how to make money, but not one of them had learned how to live.

Our North American culture is on a continual pursuit to find happiness. In the '80s, it was money; in the '90s, it's personal fulfillment any way you can get it! Earning more and moving up is no longer the only way to go. In the '80s, making a lot of money was viewed as an end in itself. Today it is viewed more as a means to an end—personal fulfillment and happiness. Though nearly 90 percent of American woman say financial independence is vital, fewer than 30 percent think money is key to happiness, according to a poll reported for Avon Products in 1993.

Santa Cruz, California, psychiatrist Alan Sherman counsels many turbo-charged executives from nearby Silicon Valley who come to him "yearning for a life transcending money and career." In a workshop Sherman deals with their concerns. They "reflect on why conventional success seems to taste so bland" and what they can do about it.

Harvard economist Juliet Schor, in her book *The Overworked American*, confirms that thinking: "Affluence is not delivering the kind of meaning and satisfaction it promised." People want more. What is it they are looking for?

What the Bible Tells Us

Do not store up for yourselves treasures on earth, where moth and rust destroy, and where thieves break in and steal. But store up for yourselves treasures in heaven, where moth and rust do not destroy, and where thieves do not break in and steal. For where your treasure is, there your heart will be also . . . .

Therefore I tell you, do not worry about your life, what you will eat or drink; or about your body, what you will wear. Is not life more important than food, and the body more important than clothes? Look at the birds of the air; they do not sow or reap or store away in barns, and yet your heavenly Father feeds them. Are you not much more valuable than they? Who of you by worrying can add a single hour to his life? (Matthew 6:19–21, 25–27)

Jesus said, "No servant can serve two masters. Either he will hate the one and love the other, or he will be

Copyright ©1994 Church Development Resources   It is illegal to copy this material without permission.

devoted to the one and despise the other. You cannot serve both God and Money." (Luke 16:13)

How the Bible Relates

1. What two kinds of treasure does Jesus mention?

2. Which one does he encourage his listeners to store up? Why?

3. What does Jesus tell them not to worry about? Why?

4. Who feeds the birds of the air? What relationship does he have to people?

5. What choice of masters does Jesus give his listeners?

The Bottom Line

God isn't out to deprive you of good, pleasant things. Rather, he wants to free you from being enslaved to them, so that you can see the true meaning of life. Keeping your focus on God will help keep everything else in its right perspective. Only God can fill the emptiness in your soul.

Prayer

God, help me to see whether a desire for material wealth has kept me from seeing the true meaning of life. I would like to begin to trust you for giving me what I need. Amen.

A Final Word

Keep your lives free from the love of money and be content with what you have, because God has said, "Never will I leave you; never will I forsake you." So we say with confidence, "The Lord is my helper; I will not be afraid. What can man do to me?" *(Hebrews 13:5–6)*

Does God Want to Spoil My Fun?

2: "The One Who Dies With the Most Toys Wins"

Beginnings

What "labels" or brand names do people measure success by (in clothing, cars, furniture, titles, positions, etc.)? Do different groups of people have different ways to measure success? Give some examples.

What's Happening Today

Seven Poor Rich Men

In 1928 a group of the world's most successful financiers met at the Edgewater Beach Hotel in Chicago. The following were present:
—the president of the largest steel company
—the greatest wheat speculator
—the president of the New York Stock Exchange
—a member of the President's Cabinet
—the greatest "bear" in Wall Street
—the president of the Bank of International Settlements
— the head of the world's greatest monopoly

Collectively, these tycoons controlled more wealth than there was in the United States Treasury, and for year newspapers and magazines had been printing their success stories and urging the youth of the nation to follow their examples. Twenty-five years later, this is what had happened to these men.

The president of the largest independent steel company, Charles Schwab, lived on borrowed money the last five years of his life and died broke.

The greatest wheat speculator, Arthur Cutten, died abroad, insolvent.

The president of the New York Stock Exchange, Richard Whitney, served a term in Sing Sing Prison.

The member of the President's Cabinet, Albert Fall, was pardoned from prison so he could die at home.

The greatest "bear" in Wall Street, Jesse Livermore, committed suicide.

The president of the Bank of International Settlements, Leon Fraser, committed suicide.

The head of the world's greatest monopoly, Ivar Gruegger, committed suicide.

All of these men had learned how to make money, but not one of them had learned how to live.

Our North American culture is on a continual pursuit to find happiness. In the '80s, it was money; in the '90s, it's personal fulfillment any way you can get it! Earning more and moving up is no longer the only way to go. In the '80s, making a lot of money was viewed as an end in itself. Today it is viewed more as a means to an end—personal fulfillment and happiness. Though nearly 90 percent of American woman say financial independence is vital, fewer than 30 percent think money is key to happiness, according to a poll reported for Avon Products in 1993.

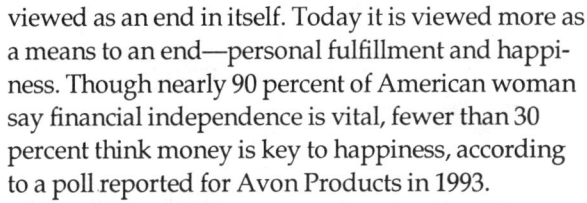

Santa Cruz, California, psychiatrist Alan Sherman counsels many turbo-charged executives from nearby Silicon Valley who come to him "yearning for a life transcending money and career." In a workshop Sherman deals with their concerns. They "reflect on why conventional success seems to taste so bland" and what they can do about it.

Harvard economist Juliet Schor, in her book *The Overworked American*, confirms that thinking: "Affluence is not delivering the kind of meaning and satisfaction it promised." People want more. What is it they are looking for?

What the Bible Tells Us

Do not store up for yourselves treasures on earth, where moth and rust destroy, and where thieves break in and steal. But store up for yourselves treasures in heaven, where moth and rust do not destroy, and where thieves do not break in and steal. For where your treasure is, there your heart will be also . . . .

Therefore I tell you, do not worry about your life, what you will eat or drink; or about your body, what you will wear. Is not life more important than food, and the body more important than clothes? Look at the birds of the air; they do not sow or reap or store away in barns, and yet your heavenly Father feeds them. Are you not much more valuable than they? Who of you by worrying can add a single hour to his life? (Matthew 6:19–21, 25–27)

Jesus said, "No servant can serve two masters. Either he will hate the one and love the other, or he will be

Copyright ©1994 Church Development Resources   It is illegal to copy this material without permission.

devoted to the one and despise the other. You cannot serve both God and Money." (Luke 16:13)

How the Bible Relates

1. What two kinds of treasure does Jesus mention?

2. Which one does he encourage his listeners to store up? Why?

3. What does Jesus tell them not to worry about? Why?

4. Who feeds the birds of the air? What relationship does he have to people?

5. What choice of masters does Jesus give his listeners?

The Bottom Line

God isn't out to deprive you of good, pleasant things. Rather, he wants to free you from being enslaved to them, so that you can see the true meaning of life. Keeping your focus on God will help keep everything else in its right perspective. Only God can fill the emptiness in your soul.

Prayer

God, help me to see whether a desire for material wealth has kept me from seeing the true meaning of life. I would like to begin to trust you for giving me what I need. Amen.

A Final Word

Keep your lives free from the love of money and be content with what you have, because God has said, "Never will I leave you; never will I forsake you." So we say with confidence, "The Lord is my helper; I will not be afraid. What can man do to me?" *(Hebrews 13:5–6)*

Does God Want to Spoil My Fun?

SESSION 3

Does God Want to Spoil My Fun?—Leader Guide

3: "Looking Out for Number One"

Introductory Notes

Today's Scripture teaching may be rather difficult for your group to accept. Our culture has long encouraged people to "look out for Number One," and most people take this for granted as a fact of life.

Your challenge is to begin to move them from their own limited perspective into God's wider, all-embracing one. They won't know it, but they will slowly be changed, as their perspective changes. They will begin to reflect God's qualities and start to become the people God intended them to be.

This, of course, is the work of the Spirit. He's the one who renews our minds, who helps us understand the way God thinks, who begins the process of bringing people into a living relationship with God.

So work hand in hand with the Spirit during this session. Ask him to give you wisdom when some in your group ask tough questions. Pray that you can anticipate group members' reactions and struggles. Ask the Spirit to prepare their minds and hearts for this discussion.

Do some thinking about your own life too. As you well know, no Christian is perfect this side of heaven. Where are you not loving your neighbor as much as you love yourself? Who is your neighbor? (Trick question—remember Jesus' parable of the good Samaritan.) Do you find it easy, or convenient, or natural, to treat others as you would like them to treat you? Do you often think in these terms? How close is your perspective to God's?

As you prepare, remember that this series is meant to show people that God's rules for our lives actually bring health and pleasure, rather than a sense of restriction and imprisonment. It does this by getting at the very areas where we are trapped: our addictions, our ingrained habits, our often-repeated mistakes.

This session may bring to light hurts that have long been festering in members' lives. A parent or guardian may have hurt them so badly that they have never learned the meaning of the word "love." They may have grown up in a competitive, put-down kind of atmosphere. They may have dedicated their entire lives to fulfilling their own dreams, to the exclusion of anyone or anything else.

So you will need the Spirit's help in encouraging your group members to come out of the trap of the "me first" mentality. Pray that they will see it as a way of life where no one really wins—and step into the freedom of a healthy, loving relationship with others.

Beginning the Session

Be sure your welcome is warm and inviting. Greet your group members by name. Be aware of any messages their body language is sending. Your body language is important, too. Your group members may not hear Christ's message, but they will see it in you as you bring Christ's love to them. Also, be sensitive to any group members who may be hurting. Seek opportunities after the session to talk with them individually.

> In the longer session, follow up here on people's thoughts and struggles throughout the past week as they've tried putting the Scriptures from the last session into practice. Be sure to share any of your own experiences that let them see your own struggles with these sessions as well. Don't spend a lot of time on this as you may have opportunity for this discussion at the end of your session.

Beginnings

If someone dropped a $500 bill in a crowd of people and said, "First one to grab this gets it," what do you think would happen? If you were closest to the bill, what would you do? How many times have you been in a scramble for something—a job, a raise, better benefits, or whatever—and someone beat you out? How did you feel? How did it feel when you beat out someone else?

Distribute the discussion handouts and read through the "Beginnings" section aloud, giving group members a brief time to think about and respond to it. A few questions like the following may help them "dig" a little deeper into the subject: **Once you got a hold of that $500 bill, what would you do with it?** Most of the responses here, of course, will reflect financial needs or desired purchases for the group members and their families. And this is not necessarily bad.

But help them to think beyond that for just a minute. **How important is it to try to get the best for yourself and your family? How difficult or easy is it to think of another family's needs? How well do you know your own needs? The needs of others around you?** Don't delve too deeply into this yet. Use these questions to lead into the "What's Happening Today" section.

> If you're using the longer format, take a few more minutes to explore this. Look at your society and the values of your culture. **How does the attitude of "looking out for Number One" show itself in the stock market? In the line at the supermarket?**

In traffic? At a sales table in the department store?

Then take a look at the opposite side of the coin. **When was the last time we can remember that someone treated us courteously in those situations? Why does that often come as a (pleasant) surprise?** Encourage group members to share their own experiences as they begin to relate to the subject of a lifestyle that centers around the needs of one individual or family.

What's Happening Today

Ask group members to follow along as you or someone else in the group reads this section. Encourage more group reading by now. When you've finished, ask if there are any immediate responses to or questions on what has been read.

> If you're using the expanded format, spend a few more minutes here. **When can you remember an incident similar to the three described here? What makes you remember it? What struck you as unusual? How did you feel toward the people involved?** Your group members may have some interesting stories of their own to relate that will help illustrate the ideas you're focusing on today.

What the Bible Tells Us

Ask someone who is comfortable doing so to read the passages aloud. They are short, so don't read through them too quickly. Your group may find it helpful to read through the Scripture aloud twice, just to help get it into their minds.

If there are any questions on what was read, take a few minutes to answer those. Otherwise lead right into the study questions in "How the Bible Relates."

How the Bible Relates

1. What do people owe as a continuing debt to each other?

This Scripture passage is short in length but long on content; don't let any parts go by unnoticed. Look, for example, at the first phrase: "Let no debt remain outstanding."

What kinds of debts do people have today? What are some ways in which we use the word "debt"? There is financial debt, of course—the most common one. Most people carry some financial debt: a house mortgage, car loan, line of credit on a charge card, personal loans, or whatever.

We also speak of a "debt of gratitude," a situation in which we are so grateful for a favor received that we promise to return the favor if we get the chance. There are "debts of honor"—perhaps a gift that someone has given us outright, but we want to pay it back anyway, because we feel we should.

Then look further at this verse: " . . . except the continuing debt to love one another." **How is this kind of debt different from the ones mentioned above? Do we owe only certain people this debt of love? Do the ones we love have to earn it?** Help your group to see that the debt referred to here is something we seem to owe to everyone, whether they've given us anything or not. It doesn't come as a response to someone else's actions; it comes simply out of the principle that we are to love everyone—no matter what.

By nature, we invest most love in those people we are closest to. But this love has a ripple effect outward to others. It does not eliminate our obligation to love others. **Who is the person who can be the recipient of my love?** Anyone whose need I see and whose need I am in a position to meet.

Some in your group may have strong reactions to this statement. "Why should I *owe* love to anyone except my close family or friends?" they might ask. Take a moment to look at this tendency in our human nature to love only those who are close to us. **Who are the people we give the bulk of our love to? How much are we tied in to making sure their needs are met? How aware are we of the needs of our neighbors down the street? Of the people we work with? Of the people we may know in our churches or clubs or sports teams?**

Help your group to see that part of this tendency to love only self or family comes naturally in our society because we often stay isolated from others, even from those living next door. We put up barriers of privacy and choose not to ask questions. That's part of the reason for these limitations on a "debt of love."

Note that these limitations may also come from the idea that love means warm feelings of affection. Ask group members to think about this as they examine the next few verses of the passages, which speak more clearly about what love is.

> In the longer format, take some extra time to explore what group members are thinking of when they use the word "love." You may get some helpful insights into some of the things your group members are struggling with. Be sure that your group understands the meaning of the word "love" as it is used in these verses: not romantic love or selfish love, but an act of the will. **What does it mean to love another person? Can you love someone you don't know? Why or why not? In what ways can you show love? Is it possible to show love to someone you don't know? How?** You will do more listening than talking here, but use these questions to help people begin thinking about love in broader terms than simply having warm feelings for those closest to them.

2. What rule sums up God's entire law regarding other people?

Explain to your group that "the law" and the commandments listed here refer to a set of rules for living that God gave to his people back in the early years of civilization. These rules are known today as the Ten Commandments, and most of the laws of Western civilization are based on these commandments. Explain that many today look at those rules as oppressive, as God's attempt to spoil our fun. Help your group members see them, rather, as necessary for our well-being, even as the laws of nature (such as gravity) are necessary for life and health.

In the longer format, this question will give you an opportunity to go over the Ten Commandments with your group (or at least those commandments that deal with our relationship to others). Since some in your group may not have ever actually heard or read the Ten Commandments, you can read them in full or just the ones that apply to this passage. Following is a condensed version:

1. You shall have no other gods before me.
2. You shall not make for yourself any idols; you shall not bow down to them or worship them.
3. You shall not misuse the name of the Lord your God.
4. Remember the Sabbath day by keeping it holy.
5. Honor your father and your mother.
6. You shall not murder.
7. You shall not commit adultery.
8. You shall not steal.
9. You shall not give false testimony against your neighbor.
10. You shall not covet anything that belongs to your neighbor.

Take some time to look at each commandment specifically. **What kinds of things do these commandments forbid? How would those kinds of things harm another person?** Murder and stealing are rather obvious threats to other people's rights and well-being.

Coveting and adultery might be a little harder for your group to see in the same light, given their everyday occurrence in our society. **What are you wishing when you want someone else's belongings? What kinds of crimes does coveting lead to? What promises does adultery break? How does breaking those promises harm another person?** Point out that adultery, as well as the breaking of any of the commandments, also harms our relationship with God. Following David's adulterous relationship with Bathsheba, he confessed to God, "Against you, you only, have I sinned . . ." These questions may help your group members see that the "I can do it if it doesn't harm anyone else" argument doesn't apply to these commandments either.

What do these commandments do for the rights of others? For the person who reads them? Far from being meant to spoil our fun, these commandments were given to protect others'—and our own—rights. Those who follow these commands will be treating other people as they themselves would expect to be treated. They are loving their neighbors as they love themselves.

Point out also a beautiful little safeguard in the summary of the law: "Love your neighbor *as yourself*." **Why might this be necessary to add? What is the opposite of loving too little? Is it possible to "love too much," or to love in the wrong ways? What does this rule prevent?** These questions address what might be a major concern of some group members: A love for others must be grounded in a healthy love for ourselves. God does not ask that we neglect ourselves or let others run all over us with their demands.

What does a healthy self-love include? What boundaries can we set for ourselves? How might love at times mean saying no to others? Use these questions to explore the meaning of love a little more deeply, especially in the sense of wanting the best for everyone.

In the longer format, encourage group members to add their own examples of "tough love" and of incidents they remember when healthy boundaries were violated in the name of love. Codependence is an unhealthy way to love. It is simply putting someone else's desires, whims, priorities, and choices ahead of your own—and trying to live in a way that pleases or protects another person, regardless of the wrong choices they've made. It is living life through another person rather than living your own life. Codependence damages both parties in the relationship. **How is codependence a form of love that has lost its bearings? How might someone in a codependent relationship have forgotten to love themselves as much as they love others? How do God's rules for living protect us from that?**

3. What is the relationship between God's law and love?

This is a key question for those who have been living according to a "me first" code of behavior. It strikes at a major point in the Bible's teaching: God is looking for a change of heart, not just a change in behavior. "*Love* is the fulfillment of the law."

You can help your group discover this for themselves by using some of the following questions: **What part of ourselves does love involve? Is it just behavior, or does it go deeper than that? What about our will, our heart, our commitment?**

Help your group to see that there is something unique here, different from all other legal codes: It's asking for a change of heart, not of behavior, first of all. **Why is a change of heart more important? Why is it more difficult? Is it better, more effective, more lasting? Why or why not?**

The Bottom Line

God calls us to accept this fact: other people's needs are just as important as our own. We are to treat each other not only with honor, but with affection and kindness. Doing this goes against something deep within our human nature. If we are going to overcome our addiction to "me first," we need God's help.

Prayer

Dear God, help me to see where I can grow in my love for myself and for others. Help me to begin to see other people as you see them. Amen.

A Final Word

Do nothing out of selfish ambition or vain conceit, but in humility consider others better than yourselves. Each of you should look not only to your own interests, but also to the interests of others. *(The apostle Paul in Philippians 2:3–4)*

Does God Want to Spoil My Fun?

3: "Looking Out For Number One"

Beginnings

If someone dropped a $500 bill in a crowd of people and said, "First one to grab this gets it," what do you think would happen? If you were closest to the bill, what would you do? How many times have you been in a scramble for something—a job, a raise, better benefits, or whatever—and someone beat you out? How did you feel? How did it feel when you beat out someone else?

What's Happening Today

Imagine this: A young woman on a TV game show wins a shiny new Oldsmobile. She runs up, screaming with excitement—and decides to give the car to one of the other contestants, whom she has learned is unemployed and without transportation to find a job.

A middle-aged executive on a comfortable salary gets a hefty raise. He comes home with the good news—and he and his wife decide to earmark the extra income for their elderly neighbor, who lives on government assistance.

In another family, the front doorbell rings. When the father goes to answer it, he sees a teenager standing outside the door with a bike. "Here's the bike I stole out of your garage last week," says the boy. "I've been thinking about it, and I had no right to take something that belonged to you. I'm sorry."

Unusual scenes, of course. They are unusual—and surprising—because they run counter to a deeply ingrained habit of human nature. That habit is the one of "me first," the instinct to get the best for ourselves and to hang onto it. In the process, we sometimes treat other people as objects or obstacles.

The interesting thing is, we would all agree—*in principle*—that everyone should be treated as equally as possible. We know that we *shouldn't* demand special treatment and push ourselves to the front of the line. Right?

But in real life things work differently. If there is a bigger slice of the pie, we want it for ourselves. At work, we try to get the promotion over a coworker. If we're bidding on a house against other buyers, we do our best to beat them out. In our area of expertise, we want to shine more brightly than others.

These feelings are fairly commonplace and seemingly harmless. But they have one focus: meeting our own needs, to the exclusion of others'. And pushed to its limits, this basic self-centeredness can lead to darker acts of violence and abuse.

The Bible passages for today challenge us to look at life from a different slant. It questions the "me first" attitude—with some surprising twists. Take a look at things from God's perspective.

What the Bible Tells Us

Let no debt remain outstanding, except the continuing debt to love one another, for he who loves his fellow man has fulfilled the law. The commandment, "Do not commit adultery," "Do not murder," "Do not steal," "Do not covet," and whatever other commandment there may be, are summed up in this one rule: "Love your neighbor as yourself." Love does no harm to its neighbor. Therefore love is the fulfillment of the law. (Romans 13:8–10)

"In everything, do to others what you would have them do to you, for this sums up the Law and the Prophets." (Jesus—Matthew 7:12)

How the Bible Relates

1. What do people owe as a continuing debt to each other?

2. What rule sums up God's entire law regarding other people?

3. What is the relationship between God's law and love?

4. How does Jesus rephrase the summary of the law in Matthew? In what way does the "do" of loving one another fulfill the "do nots" listed in Romans 13:8–10?

5. How would society be different if people actually lived this way? Why do you think they don't?

The Bottom Line

God calls us to accept this fact: other people's needs are just as important as our own. We are to treat each other not only with honor, but with affection and kindness. Doing this goes against something deep within our human nature. If we are going to overcome our addiction to "me first," we need God's help.

Prayer

Dear God, help me to see where I can grow in my love for myself and for others. Help me to begin to see other people as you see them. Amen.

A Final Word

Do nothing out of selfish ambition or vain conceit, but in humility consider others better than yourselves. Each of you should look not only to your own interests, but also to the interests of others. *(The apostle Paul in Philippians 2:3–4)*

Does God Want to Spoil My Fun?

3: "Looking Out For Number One"

Beginnings

If someone dropped a $500 bill in a crowd of people and said, "First one to grab this gets it," what do you think would happen? If you were closest to the bill, what would you do? How many times have you been in a scramble for something—a job, a raise, better benefits, or whatever—and someone beat you out? How did you feel? How did it feel when you beat out someone else?

What's Happening Today

Imagine this: A young woman on a TV game show wins a shiny new Oldsmobile. She runs up, screaming with excitement—and decides to give the car to one of the other contestants, whom she has learned is unemployed and without transportation to find a job.

A middle-aged executive on a comfortable salary gets a hefty raise. He comes home with the good news—and he and his wife decide to earmark the extra income for their elderly neighbor, who lives on government assistance.

In another family, the front doorbell rings. When the father goes to answer it, he sees a teenager standing outside the door with a bike. "Here's the bike I stole out of your garage last week," says the boy. "I've been thinking about it, and I had no right to take something that belonged to you. I'm sorry."

Unusual scenes, of course. They are unusual—and surprising—because they run counter to a deeply ingrained habit of human nature. That habit is the one of "me first," the instinct to get the best for ourselves and to hang onto it. In the process, we sometimes treat other people as objects or obstacles.

The interesting thing is, we would all agree—*in principle*—that everyone should be treated as equally as possible. We know that we *shouldn't* demand special treatment and push ourselves to the front of the line. Right?

But in real life things work differently. If there is a bigger slice of the pie, we want it for ourselves. At work, we try to get the promotion over a coworker. If we're bidding on a house against other buyers, we do our best to beat them out. In our area of expertise, we want to shine more brightly than others.

These feelings are fairly commonplace and seemingly harmless. But they have one focus: meeting our own needs, to the exclusion of others'. And pushed to its limits, this basic self-centeredness can lead to darker acts of violence and abuse.

The Bible passages for today challenge us to look at life from a different slant. It questions the "me first" attitude—with some surprising twists. Take a look at things from God's perspective.

What the Bible Tells Us

Let no debt remain outstanding, except the continuing debt to love one another, for he who loves his fellow man has fulfilled the law. The commandment, "Do not commit adultery," "Do not murder," "Do not steal," "Do not covet," and whatever other commandment there may be, are summed up in this one rule: "Love your neighbor as yourself." Love does no harm to its neighbor. Therefore love is the fulfillment of the law. (Romans 13:8–10)

"In everything, do to others what you would have them do to you, for this sums up the Law and the Prophets." (Jesus—Matthew 7:12)

How the Bible Relates

1. What do people owe as a continuing debt to each other?

2. What rule sums up God's entire law regarding other people?

3. What is the relationship between God's law and love?

4. How does Jesus rephrase the summary of the law in Matthew? In what way does the "do" of loving one another fulfill the "do nots" listed in Romans 13:8–10?

5. How would society be different if people actually lived this way? Why do you think they don't?

Copyright ©1994 Church Development Resources   It is illegal to copy this material without permission.

The Bottom Line

God calls us to accept this fact: other people's needs are just as important as our own. We are to treat each other not only with honor, but with affection and kindness. Doing this goes against something deep within our human nature. If we are going to overcome our addiction to "me first," we need God's help.

Prayer

Dear God, help me to see where I can grow in my love for myself and for others. Help me to begin to see other people as you see them. Amen.

A Final Word

Do nothing out of selfish ambition or vain conceit, but in humility consider others better than yourselves. Each of you should look not only to your own interests, but also to the interests of others. *(The apostle Paul in Philippians 2:3–4)*

Does God Want to Spoil My Fun?

3: "Looking Out For Number One"

Beginnings

If someone dropped a $500 bill in a crowd of people and said, "First one to grab this gets it," what do you think would happen? If you were closest to the bill, what would you do? How many times have you been in a scramble for something—a job, a raise, better benefits, or whatever—and someone beat you out? How did you feel? How did it feel when you beat out someone else?

What's Happening Today

Imagine this: A young woman on a TV game show wins a shiny new Oldsmobile. She runs up, screaming with excitement—and decides to give the car to one of the other contestants, whom she has learned is unemployed and without transportation to find a job.

A middle-aged executive on a comfortable salary gets a hefty raise. He comes home with the good news—and he and his wife decide to earmark the extra income for their elderly neighbor, who lives on government assistance.

In another family, the front doorbell rings. When the father goes to answer it, he sees a teenager standing outside the door with a bike. "Here's the bike I stole out of your garage last week," says the boy. "I've been thinking about it, and I had no right to take something that belonged to you. I'm sorry."

Unusual scenes, of course. They are unusual—and surprising—because they run counter to a deeply ingrained habit of human nature. That habit is the one of "me first," the instinct to get the best for ourselves and to hang onto it. In the process, we sometimes treat other people as objects or obstacles.

The interesting thing is, we would all agree—*in principle*—that everyone should be treated as equally as possible. We know that we *shouldn't* demand special treatment and push ourselves to the front of the line. Right?

But in real life things work differently. If there is a bigger slice of the pie, we want it for ourselves. At work, we try to get the promotion over a coworker. If we're bidding on a house against other buyers, we do our best to beat them out. In our area of expertise, we want to shine more brightly than others.

These feelings are fairly commonplace and seemingly harmless. But they have one focus: meeting our own needs, to the exclusion of others'. And pushed to its limits, this basic self-centeredness can lead to darker acts of violence and abuse.

The Bible passages for today challenge us to look at life from a different slant. It questions the "me first" attitude—with some surprising twists. Take a look at things from God's perspective.

What the Bible Tells Us

Let no debt remain outstanding, except the continuing debt to love one another, for he who loves his fellow man has fulfilled the law. The commandment, "Do not commit adultery," "Do not murder," "Do not steal," "Do not covet," and whatever other commandment there may be, are summed up in this one rule: "Love your neighbor as yourself." Love does no harm to its neighbor. Therefore love is the fulfillment of the law. (Romans 13:8–10)

"In everything, do to others what you would have them do to you, for this sums up the Law and the Prophets." (Jesus—Matthew 7:12)

How the Bible Relates

1. What do people owe as a continuing debt to each other?

2. What rule sums up God's entire law regarding other people?

3. What is the relationship between God's law and love?

4. How does Jesus rephrase the summary of the law in Matthew? In what way does the "do" of loving one another fulfill the "do nots" listed in Romans 13:8–10?

5. How would society be different if people actually lived this way? Why do you think they don't?

Copyright ©1994 Church Development Resources   It is illegal to copy this material without permission.

Does God Want to Spoil My Fun?—Leader Guide

4: "Don't Get Mad, Get Even"

Introductory Notes

This session's topic is less tangible than the previous ones. Addictive substances and a materialistic, self-centered lifestyle are physical realities. But today you will be looking at an attitude of the heart.

The desire for revenge is an attitude that may reveal itself immediately in words and actions; or it may smolder inwardly, unseen and unnoticed for years. It is most certainly an attitude that your group members have experienced more than once in their lifetime. In fact, some of them will be struggling with it now.

"Sweet, sweet revenge"—the satisfaction of seeing someone squirm or pay the price for having wronged you or someone you love. Does God want to spoil even this pleasure by forbidding us to get even? This is a live issue today, with lawsuits spreading like wildfire in legal offices across North America. It also makes for sensational headlines, especially when a world-class football star is accused of murdering his wife and her lover in revenge for their alleged affair.

But this issue also crops up in less sensational ways. For example, we might take revenge for a spouse's insult by giving him or her the cold shoulder for a few days. We get even with a gossiping friend by telling a few choice secrets about her. We pay back a relative who has "done us wrong" by cutting him off from our family get-togethers. Sometimes we try to even the score with people we don't even know. How many of us have laid on the horn to a slower driver or slammed the brakes on a tailgater?

And our children even outdo us, becoming experts in the art of keeping tallies and getting even for the smallest of slights. Taking revenge can be as small as a single word or glance at another person.

The desire for revenge can run deep. Be aware, as you lead this session, that members may have long-standing "roots of bitterness" (see Hebrews 12:15) that may be expressed with strong feelings in your group. Also remember that our culture encourages and cultivates an attitude of getting even—almost to the point of making it one of our "inalienable rights."

So pray with faith beforehand that the Holy Spirit will make inroads into members' entrenched attitudes and emotions. Prepare yourself also to be gentle and patient with others' disagreement, to speak clearly without being dogmatic, and to listen with empathy to feelings of outrage or hurt when members share some of the wrongs they have suffered.

Remember that God is not asking them to stuff feelings back down inside and to pretend that everything is okay. That's like putting a Band-Aid on a traffic accident victim and telling her she'll feel better in a few days.

No, God wants instead to get at the heart of the issue. God wants your group members to see their need to trust in him so completely that they even give him the right to "pay back" their enemies. And God wants them to see that the desire for revenge can make them just as evil as the people who wronged them in the first place.

Do you have any areas in your life where revenge has its hold on you? The best preparation for this session is to bring those to the Lord and ask him to teach you firsthand how to overcome evil with good. Then you can best help others learn how to do the same.

Beginning the Session

Make your welcome of group members as personal as possible. Be warm and natural, using both verbal and nonverbal ways to make them feel welcome. Greet them by name, smile warmly with good eye contact. Use a firm handshake. Laughter is also a good way to make people feel this is a safe place to be.

In the longer session, you may want to briefly review what you discussed last week. Ask the following questions to get them started reflecting on it: **What did you learn as you thought about the last session during your week? Did anything happen during your week that made you remember the things we had talked about? Do you have any new questions or ideas about it?** Use these questions not only to review the last session but also to get to know your group members on a more personal level.

Beginnings

Share a childhood story of a time you "got even" with someone? What does it mean to "even out the score"? What feelings are inside a person who is contemplating revenge?

Use these questions to get group members thinking about the ways in which issues of revenge touch their lives. They may have an experience from the past week or month that is fresh on their minds; or they may recall something as far back as twenty or thirty years ago.

Listen closely to their remarks, especially as they talk about the feelings that creep in when we desire to take revenge. If the feelings are strong and close to the surface, that's a clue that there may be more going on under the surface. You may want to draw this out with more specific questions as the session goes on.

Remember not to push too hard for personal sharing at this point; members are just getting their feet wet on this topic, so to speak. It may take them a bit longer to open up about what's going on inside.

> In the longer format, take the time to ask members to think of some imaginary scenes in which revenge is an issue. **Do they recall any television programs (daytime soaps are a big one here) in which people were trying to get back at each other? What have been some classic stories of revenge in the news? In what situations might people be tempted to take revenge?** Your conversation may run the gamut from tales of murder and intrigue and gang violence to sports events and toddlers fighting. Use these examples to lead into the "What's Happening Today" reading.

What's Happening Today

Have someone read through this section slowly and clearly. Afterwards, leave time for any questions to clarify the meaning of what was read. Some group members may offer comments on how the stories or insights of this section relate to some of their experiences; otherwise, lead right into the Scripture reading.

What the Bible Tells Us

Read this short passage aloud to your group. Since it is fairly simple and straightforward, there should not be any need to go over any words or phrases other than the saying "heap burning coals on his head." If group members ask, explain its meaning (see explanation in question 4) or assure them that it will become clear during the discussion that follows.

How the Bible Relates

1. What repayment plan does the Bible warn against? What does it say to be careful to do?

The repayment plan warned against here is simple. It is best summed up in the ancient rule "An eye for an eye, and a tooth for a tooth" (see Exodus 21:24; Matthew 5:38). **What logic is behind this repayment plan? How easy is it to figure out what to do for revenge?**

(This biblical "eye for eye" rule may seem harsh to some members. Actually, this law was set up early in human civilization by God as a measure of mercy, to prevent people from demanding too great a punishment for an offense. Under this rule, for example, no one could kill another person in revenge for an injured limb or lost tooth. **What legal guidelines do we have that match this today?** The statement "The punishment must fit the crime" is one that some of your members may be familiar with. You may want to mention this information if group members are disturbed by what seems to be a harsh demand for justice here.)

If you have time, look a little more closely at this kind of repayment plan. **What is its main goal?** It should be obvious to your group that justice—repayment for wrongs done—is the concern of revenge. **What other goals might someone have other than paying someone back for what they've done?** Here you might mention, if your group does not, the goals of healing a relationship, restoring friendship, turning an enemy into a friend, and so on. **How might these be just as valid as the goal of revenge? What might make them even more attractive?**

> In the longer session, take a closer look at revenge as a destructive force—even when it's fueled by a desire for justice. One of the most potent examples in the 1990s is the country of Bosnia, where racial hatreds have been simmering for centuries, exploding recently again into unbelievable violence and atrocities.

Three groups of people—Serbs, Muslims, and Croats—have shared this country for centuries, with a long history of civil war and oppression. First one group gets the upper hand, then another.

When any group is in power, it remembers all the wrongs done by the others in the past—rape, murder, burning of homes, economic hardship. It does its best to even the score by oppressing the other two groups and trying to wipe them out. Soldiers involved in these conflicts can tell you stories of awful things done to their ancestors in decades or centuries past—and insist that they are only righting old wrongs.

How might the advice in these verses from Romans have saved centuries of anguish? What will happen if the desire for revenge is left unchecked? Hopefully your group members will begin to see what revenge really accomplishes: further destruction on both sides.

As you look at the second part of the question, ask some of the following to help group members focus their thinking: **Why should a person be careful to "do what is right in the eyes of everybody"? What is the power of a good example? How have people who stood up for what is right changed the course of history? In what sense is it important to go against what everyone is *doing* versus what they know deep inside to be *right*?**

2. How much is it in our power to be at peace with other people? When might it be out of our control?

This is a key question, especially with today's greater awareness of issues of codependency and personal responsibility. **What two "if" statements ("If your enemy is hungry..." and "If he is thirsty...") are really important here? What can we control in a relationship? What can't we control?**

94   Inspirit: Does God Want to Spoil My Fun?   LEADER GUIDE   Session 4

Explore briefly with your group the boundaries of a person's responsibility to maintain peace in his or her relationships. **Can you think of some situations where peace may not be possible, even when one party seeks it wholeheartedly and with a genuine desire to be reconciled? What might be that person's responsibility then?**

Help your group to see that the Scripture is not recommending a "doormat" mentality, where we sacrifice all to maintain peaceful relationships with others. We are not responsible for others' hanging onto grudges, for withholding forgiveness once we've asked for it. Once we have pointed out another person's wrongdoing toward us or acknowledged our own wrongdoing to someone else and asked forgiveness, we have no more control over the situation—except to pray for God to work in that person's life. The other person is responsible for his or her response.

> In the longer session, you may want to ask group members for examples of situations in which one person sought peace but could not get the other person to respond—even after asking forgiveness and communicating in a gentle, nondefensive way. Such stories are sad, but they will effectively point out to your group the destructive force of an unforgiving and vengeful attitude.

Your group may find it helpful to look more closely at the phrase "live at peace." **What does it mean to be "at peace" with someone?** Talk about relationships in which there are no hidden grudges, no unforgiving spirit, but instead a loving honesty. Contrast this with marriage, family, or work relationships that are a constant battleground. **What difference would being "at peace" make in the quality of one's life?**

What does it take to maintain such a relationship? There may be times when "living at peace" means swallowing our pride and taking the first step to mend a broken relationship—even when we think the other person should take the first step.

3. How does God fit into the picture where someone is wronged? What does the Bible say that that person is to allow God to do?

This question gets at something important: God will see that vengeance is carried out. **Does God ask people to give up revenge without any hope of seeing justice done? Who is going to see that justice is carried out?**

Some of your group members may not believe in God. Others may believe that there is a God, but that he's not the kind of God they can trust. The Bible, of course, assumes that God exists; and it addresses people who believe in God.

Look for a moment at the kind of God the Bible asks us to trust. **What kind of interest does this passage suggest that God takes in people's lives? What emotion of God is mentioned here? What do you think causes God's wrath, according to this passage? What does this tell us about God? Why might that be comforting?**

Explore with your group the possibility of a God who is intensely interested in our lives, who is angry when others hurt us maliciously, who asks us to wait for his vengeance.

Why is God better suited than we are to bring judgment and revenge? How capable are people of acting with complete fairness and impartiality? Have you ever acted hastily in a situation and regretted it later? Have you ever made a quick judgment about someone, only to find out that you were mistaken? How much more complete might God's knowledge of the situation be than ours? Use these questions to help your group think through the idea that God is better equipped than us to handle the whole issue of revenge.

When God says in today's passage, "It is mine to avenge; I will repay," what role is he taking on in regard to us? What does he ask of us?

The question of trust is a big one for people. The Bible suggests that God is willing to be their protector. But will God really protect them? Is he interested enough in them to take on their enemies and see that justice is done? What if God doesn't repay right away? What if he doesn't repay at all?

Your group may not be at a point where they can trust God at this level—and that's okay. Don't make them feel guilty for this. Trust comes only as you get to know someone well. If they raise some of the questions above, encourage them to consider trying to get to know God better than they already do. This study and others will give them plenty of opportunity to do so.

4. How are you to treat an enemy in need? Why? What do you think this means?

First of all, take a close look at the situation you are being asked to imagine: You meet up with your enemy when he or she is in need. The Bible says "hungry" and "thirsty," but it could just as easily be some other kind of need. **In what other ways might an opponent be in distressed circumstances?** Perhaps the person who has wronged you is now going through a painful divorce, has lost a job, or is experiencing severe financial difficulty. Maybe someone close to that person has died, or perhaps he or she has been exposed in a scandal. At any rate, whatever the situation, the Scripture asks you to imagine that your enemy is now in a position of weakness and need, and you have the power to help or hurt him or her.

What is your response? Now that the tables are turned, how will you treat this person? Most people's natural response is to dance a little jig of joy: "Great! He (or she) has finally got what's coming to him!" They may gloat, feel smug, and even try to rub it in a little.

According to the Bible, what should be our response? If it is in our power to help, what are we to do? Talk about the concrete ways that a person could help an enemy who has lost a job or who is going through

Inspirit: Does God Want to Spoil My Fun? LEADER GUIDE Session 4

financial difficulty, for example. Try to be as specific as possible.

Of course, treating one's enemy in this way seems preposterous if there's not a good reason behind it. **What reason does the Bible give for doing this? What does it mean to "heap burning coals on his head"?**

To explain this expression, you will have to ask your group members to imagine themselves back in times when fire was the only means for cooking or heating one's home. Even on days when there was no fire blazing, there was a carefully tended pile of hot coals kept on the hearth or in the fire pit.

To heap coals on someone's head could have several meanings back in that ancient culture. The first, and most obvious, is simply a painful punishment for wrongs done. The Bible mentions this as an expression of God's anger on the wicked (see Psalm 11:6 and 140:10). **How might showing kindness to one's enemy be a unique kind of punishment? How might it be an even more bitter pill to swallow than revenge?**

Another way this picture can be interpreted is one of simple kindness and generosity. When wandering desert tribes entertained passing travelers, they would sometimes give the gift of a small pile of burning coals, to be placed in a pan, wrapped carefully, and carried on one's head. **How does this picture fit the kind of nonvengeful attitude that the Bible is talking about?**

The third and perhaps most powerful meaning is connected with the custom in ancient Egypt of walking around with a pan of hot coals on one's head to show sorrow and true repentance for wrongs done. **How might showing kindness to one's enemy bring about a change of heart in even the most stubborn and proud people?**

In the longer session, take time to think of specific examples for some of these meanings. **What stories of this kind of thing have you heard or read about? Can you think of a time when an evil person's life was changed because another person offered to forgive them and showed them kindness?**

5. What does the Bible suggest as the only way to overcome evil?

The first part of this session has focused on holding back on our desire for revenge. The last two questions, however, give your group members something positive to focus on: what they *can* do in a situation when they have been wronged.

If your group members can gain a changed perspective from this session, that will be an evidence of God's Spirit at work. If they can stop thinking in terms of overcoming evil with evil, and instead think of overcoming evil with good, they will have begun to respond to the power of God's Word.

A few questions might help them to turn their thinking around: **What does the Bible suggest might happen to someone who tries to repay evil for evil? What happens to such a person inside? How does he or she become like the person who gave the offense in the first place? How might that person's character eventually be overcome by evil? How is that a loss rather than a victory, even if the score is "evened out"?**

Then look at the positive side of the last sentence in the passage. **What seems to be a stronger force than evil? If you wish to fight back against someone's unfair attack on you, what is your best choice of weapon? What course of action has the power to change your enemy without harming you?** Use these questions to help your group consider in more depth the truth of this passage: the best thing to do when someone hurts you is to respond with good and to place your trust fully in God. Not only will you remain unharmed by the poison of that person's evil, but you will give that person the chance to be changed from evil to good by your example.

In the longer session, take the time to explore this kind of response in greater detail. **What specific situations have you already talked about in this session that have called for revenge? According to the guidelines of this passage, what specific things could someone do in those situations to respond with good instead of evil?** Take the time to imagine these situations and to help group members try to picture the good results that come from doing good rather than evil.

Again, acknowledge that this is a tremendously difficult task. In fact, it is impossible for someone who does not have God's help and who does not trust that there is a higher power who will see that justice is done. Encourage your group to take the opportunity to ask God's help in all this. Emphasize that God does not turn us away or laugh at our weakness; God is always ready and available and wanting us to come to him with our needs and questions.

The Bottom Line

"Sweet, sweet revenge"—Is it so sweet? Or does it poison the person who seeks it? God knows that the desire to get even harms us even more than it does our enemy. He asks us to trust him in seeing that justice is finally done. But God also gives us the secret for healing bitter feelings: overcoming evil with good.

Read through this summary as a way of restating the basic truths of this session—and as an invitation to group members to trust the presence of God in their lives. Also, if there's time, allow for extra questions from group members who may not have been able to find the courage to ask them or to share their experiences until this point.

Prayer

Use the prayer printed on the discussion handout to close your session today. Add to it, if you wish, any personal requests that have come to light as you have discussed today's Scripture. Encourage group members to use this prayer on their own during the week and to come back next time with insights that they've gained as a result.

> In the longer session, take time to review other prayer requests that have come in during past sessions. Follow up on needs that may be ongoing in your group. Be sure to include these in your prayer time; assure members also that you are praying for them daily at home.

Point out the Final Word quote and ask members to read it also throughout the week, asking God to show them how it might apply to their own lives.

> Here is a delightful fable of revenge and forgiveness, written by Lewis Smedes. If you have time toward the end of your session (or if you wish to introduce your session with this story), take time to read it to your group. If you do read it aloud, practice reading it through several times beforehand so that you can read it with ease and expression.

The Magic Eyes— A Little Fable

In the village of Faken in innermost Friesland there lived a long thin baker named Fouke, a righteous man, with a long thin chin and a long thin nose. Fouke was so upright that he seemed to spray righteousness from his thin lips over everyone who came near him; so the people of Faken preferred to stay away.

Fouke's wife, Hilda, was short and round, her arms were round, her bosom was round, her rump was round. Hilda did not keep people at bay with righteousness; her soft roundness seemed to invite them instead to come close to her in order to share the warm cheer of her open heart.

Hilda respected her righteous husband, and loved him too, as much as he allowed her; but her heart ached for something more from him than his worthy righteousness.

And there, in the bed of her need, lay the seed of sadness.

One morning, having worked since dawn to knead his dough for the ovens, Fouke came home and found a stranger in his bedroom lying on Hilda's round bosom.

Hilda's adultery soon became the talk of the tavern and the scandal of the Faken congregation. Everyone assumed that Fouke would cast Hilda out of his house, so righteous was he. But he surprised everyone by keeping Hilda as his wife, saying he forgave her as the Good Book said he should.

In his heart of hearts, however, Fouke could not forgive Hilda for bringing shame to his name. Whenever he thought about her, his feelings toward her were angry and hard; he despised her as if she were a common whore. When it came right down to it, he hated her for betraying him after he had been so good and so faithful a husband to her.

He only pretended to forgive Hilda so that he could punish her with his righteous mercy.

But Fouke's fakery did not sit well in heaven.

So each time that Fouke would feel his secret hate toward Hilda, an angel came to him and dropped a small pebble, hardly the size of a shirt button, into Fouke's heart. Each time a pebble dropped, Fouke would feel a stab of pain like the pain he felt the moment he came on Hilda feeding her hungry heart from a stranger's larder.

Thus he hated her the more; his hate brought him pain and his pain made him hate.

The pebbles multiplied. And Fouke's heart grew very heavy with the weight of them, so heavy that the top half of his body bent forward so far that he had to strain his neck upward in order to see straight ahead. Weary with hurt, Fouke began to wish he were dead.

The angel who dropped the pebbles into his heart came to Fouke one night and told him how he could be healed of his hurt.

There was one remedy, he said, only one, for the hurt of a wounded heart. Fouke would need the miracle of the magic eyes. He would need eyes that could look back to the beginning of his hurt and see his Hilda, not as a wife who betrayed him, but as a weak woman who needed him. Only a new way of looking at things through the magic eyes could heal the hurt flowing from the wounds of yesterday.

Fouke protested. "Nothing can change the past," he said. "Hilda is guilty, a fact that not even an angel can change."

"Yes, poor hurting man, you are right," the angel said. "You cannot change the past, you can only heal the hurt that comes to you from the past. And you can heal it only with the vision of the magic eyes."

"And how can I get your magic eyes?" pouted Fouke.

"Only ask, desiring as you ask, and they will be given you. And each time you see Hilda through your new eyes, one pebble will be lifted from your aching heart."

Fouke could not ask at once, for he had grown to love his hatred. But the pain of his heart finally drove him to want and to ask for the magic eyes that the angel had promised. So he asked. And the angel gave.

Soon Hilda began to change in front of Fouke's eyes, wonderfully and mysteriously. He began to see her as a needy woman who loved him instead of a wicked woman who betrayed him.

The angel kept his promise; he lifted the pebbles from Fouke's heart, one by one, though it took a long time to take them all away. Fouke gradually felt his heart grow lighter; he began to walk straight again, and somehow his nose and his chin seemed less thin and sharp than before. He invited Hilda to come into his heart again, and she came, and together they began again a journey into their second season of humble joy.

Excerpted from Forgive and Forget *by Lewis Smedes. Used by permission of Harper & Row, San Francisco, 1984.*

Does God Want to Spoil My Fun?

4: "Don't Get Mad, Get Even"

Beginnings

Share a childhood story of a time you "got even" with someone? What does it mean to "even out the score"? What feelings are inside a person who is contemplating revenge?

What's Happening Today

A four-year-old grabs a toy from his friend, who promptly hits him. The four-year-old looks surprised, then raises his fist in return. "I'll get you for that!" he yells.

In an office building, a sales rep finds that her coworker has taken over one of her best accounts by lying to their supervisor. The sales rep confronts her supervisor—who chooses to believe the coworker instead. Fuming, the rep walks out and brushes by the coworker, saying, "You'll be sorry you ever did this."

A husband, feeling deeply betrayed by his wife's extramarital affair, sues for divorce and vows to get sole custody of their son and two daughters. "You'll pay for everything you put me through," he tells her.

Revenge. A plan for payback. A way to even the score. Some people are addicted to it. When they are mistreated or when they see a situation that is unfair, they cannot let it go. It comes back constantly in their conversation. They think about it, mull it over, keep the feelings of outrage or hurt or bitterness simmering on the back burner.

We all know that life isn't fair, of course. Our mothers constantly reminded us of that. We see it all around us. But in our heart of hearts, we still wish life were fair. We want to see goodness rewarded, evil punished, and everyone get the same chance in life. Debts should be paid. Hurts should be avenged. Criminals should pay for their crimes.

When we get hurt, our first instinct is to take revenge. We imagine what we might do or say to the person who caused us pain. We think of situations in which we can get the upper hand. When we see that person, our stomach turns over and our breathing comes faster—even if we appear perfectly under control.

Is seeking revenge okay? Is it our right as human beings? What does it do to our enemy? What does it do to us?

The Bible lends a unique perspective on revenge. In fact, it turns our perspective upside down. Read further to find out the secret reality of what revenge can do to you.

What the Bible Tells Us

Do not repay anyone evil for evil. Be careful to do what is right in the eyes of everybody. If it is possible, as far as it depends on you, live at peace with everyone. Do not take revenge, my friends, but leave room for God's wrath, for it is written: "It is mine to avenge; I will repay," says the Lord. On the contrary: "If your enemy is hungry, feed him; if he is thirsty, give him something to drink. In doing this, you will heap burning coals on his head." Do not be overcome by evil, but overcome evil with good. (Romans 12:17–21)

How the Bible Relates

1. What repayment plan does the Bible warn against? What does it say to be careful to do?

2. How much is it in our power to be at peace with other people? When might it be out of our control?

3. How does God fit into the picture when someone is wronged? What does the Bible say that that person is to allow God to do?

4. How are you to treat an enemy in need? Why? What do you think this means?

5. What does the Bible suggest as the only way to overcome evil?

Copyright ©1994 Church Development Resources   It is illegal to copy this material without permission.

The Bottom Line

"Sweet, sweet revenge"—Is it so sweet? Or does it poison the person who seeks it? God knows that the desire to get even harms us even more than it does our enemy. He asks us to trust him in seeing that justice is finally done. But God also gives us the secret for healing bitter feelings: overcoming evil with good.

Prayer

God, teach me how to trust you instead of taking revenge on my own. Help me not to be overcome by the evil that other people do to me. Give me the strength to do good. Amen.

A Final Word

God judges those who do wrong things. And we know that God's judging is right.... On the day God shows his anger, all people will see God's right judgments. God will reward or punish every person for what he has done. *(The apostle Paul in Romans 2:2, 5–6)*

Does God Want to Spoil My Fun?

4: "Don't Get Mad, Get Even"

Beginnings

Share a childhood story of a time you "got even" with someone? What does it mean to "even out the score"? What feelings are inside a person who is contemplating revenge?

What's Happening Today

A four-year-old grabs a toy from his friend, who promptly hits him. The four-year-old looks surprised, then raises his fist in return. "I'll get you for that!" he yells.

In an office building, a sales rep finds that her coworker has taken over one of her best accounts by lying to their supervisor. The sales rep confronts her supervisor—who chooses to believe the coworker instead. Fuming, the rep walks out and brushes by the coworker, saying, "You'll be sorry you ever did this."

A husband, feeling deeply betrayed by his wife's extramarital affair, sues for divorce and vows to get sole custody of their son and two daughters. "You'll pay for everything you put me through," he tells her.

Revenge. A plan for payback. A way to even the score. Some people are addicted to it. When they are mistreated or when they see a situation that is unfair, they cannot let it go. It comes back constantly in their conversation. They think about it, mull it over, keep the feelings of outrage or hurt or bitterness simmering on the back burner.

We all know that life isn't fair, of course. Our mothers constantly reminded us of that. We see it all around us. But in our heart of hearts, we still wish life were fair. We want to see goodness rewarded, evil punished, and everyone get the same chance in life. Debts should be paid. Hurts should be avenged. Criminals should pay for their crimes.

When we get hurt, our first instinct is to take revenge. We imagine what we might do or say to the person who caused us pain. We think of situations in which we can get the upper hand. When we see that person, our stomach turns over and our breathing comes faster—even if we appear perfectly under control.

Is seeking revenge okay? Is it our right as human beings? What does it do to our enemy? What does it do to us?

The Bible lends a unique perspective on revenge. In fact, it turns our perspective upside down. Read further to find out the secret reality of what revenge can do to you.

What the Bible Tells Us

Do not repay anyone evil for evil. Be careful to do what is right in the eyes of everybody. If it is possible, as far as it depends on you, live at peace with everyone. Do not take revenge, my friends, but leave room for God's wrath, for it is written: "It is mine to avenge; I will repay," says the Lord. On the contrary: "If your enemy is hungry, feed him; if he is thirsty, give him something to drink. In doing this, you will heap burning coals on his head." Do not be overcome by evil, but overcome evil with good. (Romans 12:17–21)

How the Bible Relates

1. What repayment plan does the Bible warn against? What does it say to be careful to do?

2. How much is it in our power to be at peace with other people? When might it be out of our control?

3. How does God fit into the picture when someone is wronged? What does the Bible say that that person is to allow God to do?

4. How are you to treat an enemy in need? Why? What do you think this means?

5. What does the Bible suggest as the only way to overcome evil?

Copyright ©1994 Church Development Resources   It is illegal to copy this material without permission.

The Bottom Line

"Sweet, sweet revenge"—Is it so sweet? Or does it poison the person who seeks it? God knows that the desire to get even harms us even more than it does our enemy. He asks us to trust him in seeing that justice is finally done. But God also gives us the secret for healing bitter feelings: overcoming evil with good.

Prayer

God, teach me how to trust you instead of taking revenge on my own. Help me not to be overcome by the evil that other people do to me. Give me the strength to do good. Amen.

A Final Word

God judges those who do wrong things. And we know that God's judging is right.... On the day God shows his anger, all people will see God's right judgments. God will reward or punish every person for what he has done. *(The apostle Paul in Romans 2:2, 5–6)*

Does God Want to Spoil My Fun?

4: "Don't Get Mad, Get Even"

Beginnings

Share a childhood story of a time you "got even" with someone? What does it mean to "even out the score"? What feelings are inside a person who is contemplating revenge?

What's Happening Today

A four-year-old grabs a toy from his friend, who promptly hits him. The four-year-old looks surprised, then raises his fist in return. "I'll get you for that!" he yells.

In an office building, a sales rep finds that her coworker has taken over one of her best accounts by lying to their supervisor. The sales rep confronts her supervisor—who chooses to believe the coworker instead. Fuming, the rep walks out and brushes by the coworker, saying, "You'll be sorry you ever did this."

A husband, feeling deeply betrayed by his wife's extramarital affair, sues for divorce and vows to get sole custody of their son and two daughters. "You'll pay for everything you put me through," he tells her.

Revenge. A plan for payback. A way to even the score. Some people are addicted to it. When they are mistreated or when they see a situation that is unfair, they cannot let it go. It comes back constantly in their conversation. They think about it, mull it over, keep the feelings of outrage or hurt or bitterness simmering on the back burner.

We all know that life isn't fair, of course. Our mothers constantly reminded us of that. We see it all around us. But in our heart of hearts, we still wish life were fair. We want to see goodness rewarded, evil punished, and everyone get the same chance in life. Debts should be paid. Hurts should be avenged. Criminals should pay for their crimes.

When we get hurt, our first instinct is to take revenge. We imagine what we might do or say to the person who caused us pain. We think of situations in which we can get the upper hand. When we see that person, our stomach turns over and our breathing comes faster—even if we appear perfectly under control.

Is seeking revenge okay? Is it our right as human beings? What does it do to our enemy? What does it do to us?

The Bible lends a unique perspective on revenge. In fact, it turns our perspective upside down. Read further to find out the secret reality of what revenge can do to you.

What the Bible Tells Us

Do not repay anyone evil for evil. Be careful to do what is right in the eyes of everybody. If it is possible, as far as it depends on you, live at peace with everyone. Do not take revenge, my friends, but leave room for God's wrath, for it is written: "It is mine to avenge; I will repay," says the Lord. On the contrary: "If your enemy is hungry, feed him; if he is thirsty, give him something to drink. In doing this, you will heap burning coals on his head." Do not be overcome by evil, but overcome evil with good. (Romans 12:17–21)

How the Bible Relates

1. What repayment plan does the Bible warn against? What does it say to be careful to do?

2. How much is it in our power to be at peace with other people? When might it be out of our control?

3. How does God fit into the picture when someone is wronged? What does the Bible say that that person is to allow God to do?

4. How are you to treat an enemy in need? Why? What do you think this means?

5. What does the Bible suggest as the only way to overcome evil?

Copyright ©1994 Church Development Resources   It is illegal to copy this material without permission.

The Bottom Line

"Sweet, sweet revenge"—Is it so sweet? Or does it poison the person who seeks it? God knows that the desire to get even harms us even more than it does our enemy. He asks us to trust him in seeing that justice is finally done. But God also gives us the secret for healing bitter feelings: overcoming evil with good.

Prayer

God, teach me how to trust you instead of taking revenge on my own. Help me not to be overcome by the evil that other people do to me. Give me the strength to do good. Amen.

A Final Word

God judges those who do wrong things. And we know that God's judging is right.... On the day God shows his anger, all people will see God's right judgments. God will reward or punish every person for what he has done. *(The apostle Paul in Romans 2:2, 5–6)*

Does God Want to Spoil My Fun?

4: "Don't Get Mad, Get Even"

Beginnings

Share a childhood story of a time you "got even" with someone? What does it mean to "even out the score"? What feelings are inside a person who is contemplating revenge?

What's Happening Today

A four-year-old grabs a toy from his friend, who promptly hits him. The four-year-old looks surprised, then raises his fist in return. "I'll get you for that!" he yells.

In an office building, a sales rep finds that her coworker has taken over one of her best accounts by lying to their supervisor. The sales rep confronts her supervisor—who chooses to believe the coworker instead. Fuming, the rep walks out and brushes by the coworker, saying, "You'll be sorry you ever did this."

A husband, feeling deeply betrayed by his wife's extramarital affair, sues for divorce and vows to get sole custody of their son and two daughters. "You'll pay for everything you put me through," he tells her.

Revenge. A plan for payback. A way to even the score. Some people are addicted to it. When they are mistreated or when they see a situation that is unfair, they cannot let it go. It comes back constantly in their conversation. They think about it, mull it over, keep the feelings of outrage or hurt or bitterness simmering on the back burner.

We all know that life isn't fair, of course. Our mothers constantly reminded us of that. We see it all around us. But in our heart of hearts, we still wish life were fair. We want to see goodness rewarded, evil punished, and everyone get the same chance in life. Debts should be paid. Hurts should be avenged. Criminals should pay for their crimes.

When we get hurt, our first instinct is to take revenge. We imagine what we might do or say to the person who caused us pain. We think of situations in which we can get the upper hand. When we see that person, our stomach turns over and our breathing comes faster—even if we appear perfectly under control.

Is seeking revenge okay? Is it our right as human beings? What does it do to our enemy? What does it do to us?

The Bible lends a unique perspective on revenge. In fact, it turns our perspective upside down. Read further to find out the secret reality of what revenge can do to you.

What the Bible Tells Us

Do not repay anyone evil for evil. Be careful to do what is right in the eyes of everybody. If it is possible, as far as it depends on you, live at peace with everyone. Do not take revenge, my friends, but leave room for God's wrath, for it is written: "It is mine to avenge; I will repay," says the Lord. On the contrary: "If your enemy is hungry, feed him; if he is thirsty, give him something to drink. In doing this, you will heap burning coals on his head." Do not be overcome by evil, but overcome evil with good. (Romans 12:17–21)

How the Bible Relates

1. What repayment plan does the Bible warn against? What does it say to be careful to do?

2. How much is it in our power to be at peace with other people? When might it be out of our control?

3. How does God fit into the picture when someone is wronged? What does the Bible say that that person is to allow God to do?

4. How are you to treat an enemy in need? Why? What do you think this means?

5. What does the Bible suggest as the only way to overcome evil?

The Bottom Line

"Sweet, sweet revenge"—Is it so sweet? Or does it poison the person who seeks it? God knows that the desire to get even harms us even more than it does our enemy. He asks us to trust him in seeing that justice is finally done. But God also gives us the secret for healing bitter feelings: overcoming evil with good.

Prayer

God, teach me how to trust you instead of taking revenge on my own. Help me not to be overcome by the evil that other people do to me. Give me the strength to do good. Amen.

A Final Word

God judges those who do wrong things. And we know that God's judging is right.... On the day God shows his anger, all people will see God's right judgments. God will reward or punish every person for what he has done. (*The apostle Paul in Romans 2:2, 5–6*)

Does God Want to Spoil My Fun?

4: "Don't Get Mad, Get Even"

Beginnings

Share a childhood story of a time you "got even" with someone? What does it mean to "even out the score"? What feelings are inside a person who is contemplating revenge?

What's Happening Today

A four-year-old grabs a toy from his friend, who promptly hits him. The four-year-old looks surprised, then raises his fist in return. "I'll get you for that!" he yells.

In an office building, a sales rep finds that her coworker has taken over one of her best accounts by lying to their supervisor. The sales rep confronts her supervisor—who chooses to believe the coworker instead. Fuming, the rep walks out and brushes by the coworker, saying, "You'll be sorry you ever did this."

A husband, feeling deeply betrayed by his wife's extramarital affair, sues for divorce and vows to get sole custody of their son and two daughters. "You'll pay for everything you put me through," he tells her.

Revenge. A plan for payback. A way to even the score. Some people are addicted to it. When they are mistreated or when they see a situation that is unfair, they cannot let it go. It comes back constantly in their conversation. They think about it, mull it over, keep the feelings of outrage or hurt or bitterness simmering on the back burner.

We all know that life isn't fair, of course. Our mothers constantly reminded us of that. We see it all around us. But in our heart of hearts, we still wish life were fair. We want to see goodness rewarded, evil punished, and everyone get the same chance in life. Debts should be paid. Hurts should be avenged. Criminals should pay for their crimes.

When we get hurt, our first instinct is to take revenge. We imagine what we might do or say to the person who caused us pain. We think of situations in which we can get the upper hand. When we see that person, our stomach turns over and our breathing comes faster—even if we appear perfectly under control.

Is seeking revenge okay? Is it our right as human beings? What does it do to our enemy? What does it do to us?

The Bible lends a unique perspective on revenge. In fact, it turns our perspective upside down. Read further to find out the secret reality of what revenge can do to you.

What the Bible Tells Us

Do not repay anyone evil for evil. Be careful to do what is right in the eyes of everybody. If it is possible, as far as it depends on you, live at peace with everyone. Do not take revenge, my friends, but leave room for God's wrath, for it is written: "It is mine to avenge; I will repay," says the Lord. On the contrary: "If your enemy is hungry, feed him; if he is thirsty, give him something to drink. In doing this, you will heap burning coals on his head." Do not be overcome by evil, but overcome evil with good. (Romans 12:17–21)

How the Bible Relates

1. What repayment plan does the Bible warn against? What does it say to be careful to do?

2. How much is it in our power to be at peace with other people? When might it be out of our control?

3. How does God fit into the picture when someone is wronged? What does the Bible say that that person is to allow God to do?

4. How are you to treat an enemy in need? Why? What do you think this means?

5. What does the Bible suggest as the only way to overcome evil?

The Bottom Line

"Sweet, sweet revenge"—Is it so sweet? Or does it poison the person who seeks it? God knows that the desire to get even harms us even more than it does our enemy. He asks us to trust him in seeing that justice is finally done. But God also gives us the secret for healing bitter feelings: overcoming evil with good.

Prayer

God, teach me how to trust you instead of taking revenge on my own. Help me not to be overcome by the evil that other people do to me. Give me the strength to do good. Amen.

A Final Word

God judges those who do wrong things. And we know that God's judging is right.... On the day God shows his anger, all people will see God's right judgments. God will reward or punish every person for what he has done. *(The apostle Paul in Romans 2:2, 5–6)*

Does God Want to Spoil My Fun?

4: "Don't Get Mad, Get Even"

Beginnings

Share a childhood story of a time you "got even" with someone? What does it mean to "even out the score"? What feelings are inside a person who is contemplating revenge?

What's Happening Today

A four-year-old grabs a toy from his friend, who promptly hits him. The four-year-old looks surprised, then raises his fist in return. "I'll get you for that!" he yells.

In an office building, a sales rep finds that her coworker has taken over one of her best accounts by lying to their supervisor. The sales rep confronts her supervisor—who chooses to believe the coworker instead. Fuming, the rep walks out and brushes by the coworker, saying, "You'll be sorry you ever did this."

A husband, feeling deeply betrayed by his wife's extramarital affair, sues for divorce and vows to get sole custody of their son and two daughters. "You'll pay for everything you put me through," he tells her.

Revenge. A plan for payback. A way to even the score. Some people are addicted to it. When they are mistreated or when they see a situation that is unfair, they cannot let it go. It comes back constantly in their conversation. They think about it, mull it over, keep the feelings of outrage or hurt or bitterness simmering on the back burner.

We all know that life isn't fair, of course. Our mothers constantly reminded us of that. We see it all around us. But in our heart of hearts, we still wish life were fair. We want to see goodness rewarded, evil punished, and everyone get the same chance in life. Debts should be paid. Hurts should be avenged. Criminals should pay for their crimes.

When we get hurt, our first instinct is to take revenge. We imagine what we might do or say to the person who caused us pain. We think of situations in which we can get the upper hand. When we see that person, our stomach turns over and our breathing comes faster—even if we appear perfectly under control.

Is seeking revenge okay? Is it our right as human beings? What does it do to our enemy? What does it do to us?

The Bible lends a unique perspective on revenge. In fact, it turns our perspective upside down. Read further to find out the secret reality of what revenge can do to you.

What the Bible Tells Us

Do not repay anyone evil for evil. Be careful to do what is right in the eyes of everybody. If it is possible, as far as it depends on you, live at peace with everyone. Do not take revenge, my friends, but leave room for God's wrath, for it is written: "It is mine to avenge; I will repay," says the Lord. On the contrary: "If your enemy is hungry, feed him; if he is thirsty, give him something to drink. In doing this, you will heap burning coals on his head." Do not be overcome by evil, but overcome evil with good. (Romans 12:17–21)

How the Bible Relates

1. What repayment plan does the Bible warn against? What does it say to be careful to do?

2. How much is it in our power to be at peace with other people? When might it be out of our control?

3. How does God fit into the picture when someone is wronged? What does the Bible say that that person is to allow God to do?

4. How are you to treat an enemy in need? Why? What do you think this means?

5. What does the Bible suggest as the only way to overcome evil?

Copyright ©1994 Church Development Resources   It is illegal to copy this material without permission.

3. What did Jesus say to them?

Jesus' reply is full of grace and wisdom. **How did Jesus draw people's attention away from the woman? What was Jesus asking the Pharisees to remember? Whom was he asking them to look at?** Instead of addressing the woman and adding to her shame and discomfort, Jesus turned everyone's eyes and attention to the self-righteous Pharisees. He asked them to look not at her but at themselves. He required them to remember a very simple thing: they were not sinless. **Was anyone present who had not disobeyed God's law in some way during his or her lifetime? Is there anyone alive today who has not at some point disobeyed that law?** Your group should realize the impossibility of anyone's being able to stand up and say, "I am without sin—let me cast the first stone!"

In the longer session, if your group has already discussed some of the ways in which Christians today can act like the Pharisees, take a few minutes to talk about this further. **What might Jesus be saying to the church about passing judgment on others? What are Christians always to remember? How does honesty about one's own failings help to foster a feeling of compassion toward others?** Make sure that your group understands that the "holier than thou" attitude that characterizes some Christians is the very thing that Jesus wanted to get rid of. They need to know that the Jesus who calls to them is full of compassion, not judgment, toward them.

4. What was the Pharisees' and teachers' response?

If there is a scene that brings some delight in this story, this is certainly the scene. **Who are being forced to admit their sin? Whom is the crowd looking at now? What were the Pharisees and teachers of the law saying by their actions at this point?** Jesus has turned the tables, and now it is the Pharisees who are looking down at the ground in embarrassment. We have to give them credit that no one tried to brashly insist that he had never sinned. Perhaps each one was well aware that, if he tried to claim sinlessness, he would be confronted by at least three or four witnesses to the contrary.

Ask your group members to imagine how this scene might have looked if they were in the crowd listening to Jesus. **Did the Pharisees and teachers of the law leave all at once, noisily protesting, or one by one, silently? Why do you think the older ones might have left first?** Don't be afraid to ask group members to put themselves into the story. Sometimes this kind of "imagining" makes the scene come to life for those who have thought the Bible is full of dry, hard-to-understand teachings.

In the longer format, your group might consider what was going on in the Pharisees at this point. **Might some of them already have had stones in their hands? What would have been their first response to Jesus' invitation to stone the woman?** We can imagine a few, especially the younger ones, stepping back and raising their arms to take aim—and waiting for the first stone to be thrown. **What held their arms back? What thoughts and memories may have begun flooding their minds? What things may they have known about themselves and about each other?** Use these questions to help your group see the effect of Jesus' words. **What happens when those who accuse others are forced to take a hard look at their own lives?**

5. What did Jesus say to the woman?

Before you look at Jesus' words to the woman, consider the first part of the story. **Had Jesus spoken to her at all? What kind of attention does this author suggest Jesus gave to her at first? Why might Jesus have done so?** Mercifully, Jesus doesn't seem to have questioned the woman or spoken directly to her. This would have drawn even more attention to her. Fearful, angry, defensive, shamed, she would not have been able to respond.

Perhaps that is why Jesus also bent down and started writing on the ground—simply to give people something else to look at. **What does all this suggest about Jesus? About his sensitivity to hurting people?**

In the longer session, allow group members to put themselves in the woman's place. Imagine a contemporary setting for this story: You have been a prostitute for a number of years. Perhaps from a broken or abusive home, feeling defiant of society, shunned by those who are socially "acceptable," you are alienated from the respect and friendship of any religious people. **What have you come to expect from the "church crowd"? When they catch you soliciting and drag you before one of the city's foremost preachers, what do you expect from the crowd? From the preacher, the "man of God"?** Use these questions to help your group members understand the dynamics of the story and the woman's feelings of apprehension toward Jesus.

Then look at Jesus' conversation with her. **Does he ask her what she has done? Does he demand an explanation? Why not? How might his comments have surprised her?** From all this woman's contact with "religious" people, she would surely expect some of the same from Jesus. But Jesus does not. As your group discusses this, they may well conclude that Jesus, besides wanting to spare the woman any more humiliation, also intentionally distances himself from the self-righteous, condemning people who claimed to be religious.

Instead, he asks her to affirm that none of her accusers are left to throw a stone at her. **What does he want her to realize?** In effect, he may be saying something like, "Look, they're all guilty—it's not just you. Everyone here has done something of which they are ashamed."

This is important also for your group members to know as they come into contact with the sins of the Pharisees in the modern-day church. Even the person with the greatest "holier than thou" attitude and judgmental spirit has done something deserving of God's displeasure. In fact, the only reason such people are able to be part of the church at all is that they have admitted their weakness and mistakes to God and asked for forgiveness. And Jesus, as he did to the Pharisees, may have to remind them from time to time to take a good look at themselves.

But Jesus went further than that. He said, "Then neither do I condemn you." **Why might Jesus, who claimed to be God himself, have been in a position to condemn this woman? What would give him the right?** Here you can share with your group, if they do not already know who Jesus is, that he taught very clearly that he was the Son of God—fully God and fully human at the same time. Though Jesus suffered all the hardships and temptations of being human, the Bible says that he did so without doing anything wrong. Jesus was the only one who would have been able to cast the first stone.

Why do you think Jesus refused to condemn the woman? How did his attitude toward her differ from that of the Pharisees and teachers of the law? Help your group to see that Jesus' gentleness and consideration of this woman arose out of a deep love—God's own love—for her. Do not be afraid at this point to affirm that this is the same attitude with which God looks at each of your group members—no matter what they've done wrong or what mistakes they've made. **What comfort does this give you?**

In the longer session, group members might better grasp what Jesus was offering to the woman if they are able to personalize what Jesus was saying to her. You can suggest that they recall something they've done that they would rather no one know about. Ask them to imagine that they are dragged into God's presence by other people—people who would never do such a thing, who are accusing and pointing the finger. **What will God do to them? What will he say? What has this story taught us about God? About ourselves?**

What did Jesus tell the woman to do? Note that Jesus did not simply ignore what the woman had done. He gently told her that her life needed changing. **How was what she had done against God's will? In what context had God intended human sexuality to flourish and grow?** Recall with your group the earlier discussion on intimacy in a loving, faithful, and caring marriage. This was the ideal that God had in mind, and it was the way also to which Jesus pointed the woman.

6. Who did Jesus say that he is? What do you think this means?

To the woman hopelessly caught in sin, and to everyone else in that dilemma today, Jesus says simply, "I am the light of the world." He doesn't condemn the woman (or anyone else) nor excuse her. In fact, he seems to see both her need and the impossibility of her dealing with that need apart from his help. He doesn't just say, "Leave your life of sin." He says, "I will help you."

What could Jesus have meant by such a statement? Help group members discover Jesus' meaning by looking first at the word "light." **How is light important to us? What does it allow us to do? How would our lives be severely limited if we lived in total darkness?** Use these questions to remind your group of one of light's most important qualities: it enables us to see things clearly. If we have no light, we have nothing to guide us—except a fumbling sense of touch. We are less able to protect ourselves from harm; we are more prone to make mistakes, based on incomplete knowledge of what's around us and where we're going.

How might "living in darkness" describe someone who doesn't have a clue as to life's real meaning? How might it feel to wander without clear directions, to work without any real sense of purpose? This describes the state of many people today—including some who may be in your group. Pray that God's Spirit will help them to admit to themselves that they are unsure of life's meaning, of their direction, and of their ultimate purpose in life—and that they need the One who is the light of the world.

Jesus has said that he is the light of the world. **How might someone like Jesus shed light on life's meaning? Who is Jesus?** This is a key point at which you can learn, if you have not already had a chance to do so, what your group members know about Jesus. Do they think of him as a great teacher or a wise man? Do they have any knowledge about what the Bible says about him? Are their ideas about Jesus accurate? You will want to follow up on what you learn here—both at this point and in the following session, which presents God's offer of forgiveness and grace. Offer to stay later or meet with individuals at another time if your group members seem to be struggling with the question "Who is Jesus?" This is the heart of your purpose. Take the time to answer their questions and to explain, in a few clear and simple words, who Jesus is: the only Son of God, who became human and lived on earth about 2,000 years ago, calling people back into a relationship with God and doing many works of healing. He took on our human nature so that he could suffer the same hardships, temptations, and griefs that we all experience. Having lived completely without sin, he freely gave up his life for us on the cross, taking the punishment for our disobedience so that we could be forgiven and restored to friendship with God. Three days later, God raised his Son from the dead. Jesus, after being seen by his disciples and many eyewitnesses, went back to the Father and now remains in heaven until the last day, when he will come to judge the world and create a new heaven and earth.

⏱ In the longer session, allow more time for this discussion. You will be able to bring in a few more verses that might help group members understand how Jesus is the light of the world. Some helpful passages:

For God so loved the world that he gave his one and only Son, that whoever believes in him shall not perish but have eternal life. For God did not send his Son into the world to condemn the world, but to save the world through him. . . . This is the verdict: Light has come into the world, but men loved darkness instead of light because their deeds were evil. Everyone who does evil hates the light, and will not come into the light for fear that his deeds will be exposed. But whoever lives by the truth comes into the light, so that it may be seen plainly that what he has done has been done through God. (John 3:16–17, 19–21)

In [Jesus] was life, and that life was the light of men. The light shines in the darkness, but the darkness has not understood it. (John 1:4–5)

Use some of the following questions to relate these verses to the story you've just studied: **How did Jesus' words shed light on the situation with the woman caught in adultery? How had the Pharisees tried to bring her sin to light? What were the Pharisees forgetting? What things would they rather have kept hidden in darkness? How did they try to avoid getting exposed to the light?**

Look also at how the woman might have experienced Jesus as the light of the world. **How did Jesus' words shed light on her situation? What did she learn about God? About herself and her lifestyle? About the ones who were accusing her? How might knowing these truths be important for healing in her life?** The woman saw not only her own sin, but also the sins of those accusing her; she was not alone in her shame. But she also saw the surprise of God's astonishing forgiveness for her, through the words and actions of Jesus. Though Jesus let her know that she had been misusing her sexuality, he also offered her understanding and forgiveness. **What is more helpful in helping someone get his or her life back together: critical condemnation or forgiveness and "speaking the truth in love"?**

In the next session you will have the opportunity to present the message of the gospel more clearly and to invite group members to put their trust in Jesus. Pray that your final discussion in this session will stir their thinking and prepare them to respond to Jesus' invitation in the next session. If you sense that any in the group would like to talk more about this, by all means stay afterward to talk with them, or set up a time to meet during the week.

The Bottom Line

God intended our sexuality to be a gift—a delightful part of a nurturing, committed relationship between a man and woman. But when we make mistakes and misuse our sexuality, God does not point the finger in condemnation. Instead, God offers forgiveness and the possibility of a healed and restored life by looking to him.

Use this summary to reaffirm the message of welcome and forgiveness that we find in the story of the woman caught in adultery. Read it aloud to the group and, if there is time, allow for any questions or comments on this summary or on the discussion today as a whole.

⏱ In the longer session, you may have time to relate this "Bottom Line" truth to the story of Janelle ("What's Happening Today"). Ask group members to imagine that Janelle has the opportunity to talk personally with Jesus about her struggles at work and home. **What counsel might Jesus offer to her? What do you think would be his attitude toward Janelle? Would his advice be good? Do you think it would benefit Janelle's life? Why or why not?** Use these questions to help group members relate the story from John to their own struggles today.

Is there an area of your life in which you struggle like Janelle? What might Jesus offer to you? Don't require an answer on these last two questions, but urge group members to think about them seriously.

Then close with the prayer below, allowing a few seconds of silence after the prayer for group members to add their own thoughts to God privately, if they will feel comfortable with that. If you have heard any needs expressed during the session, be sure to mention them in prayer also.

⏱ If you're using the longer format, spend more time asking for prayer needs or following up on requests members have shared in previous weeks. In this particular session, you may want to take out a notepad and pencil and ask for names of people (first names only, to preserve confidentiality) who may be struggling with some of the issues you've talked about in this session. Promise that you'll pray for each of these daily during the coming week, that he or she will receive guidance and help from God.

Draw your group's attention to "A Final Word" and encourage them to think about it during the coming week. Let them know that you're looking forward to seeing them next week for the concluding session of this series.

Prayer

God, please help me to understand the deep places within me—my desires, my weaknesses, my sexuality. Help me also to understand and accept your love for me. Amen.

A Final Word

The temptations that you have are the temptations that all people have. But you can trust God. He will not let you be tempted more than you can stand. But when you are tempted, God will also give you a way to escape that temptation. Then you will be able to stand it. *(The apostle Paul in 1 Corinthians 10:13, New Century Version)*

Does God Want to Spoil My Fun?

5: "If It Feels Good, Do It"

Beginnings

Advertisers know that sex sells. What products can you think of that use sex as a "hook" to get customers? What are the good things and what is the "down" side to our sexuality? Why do you think God made us sexual beings?

What's Happening Today

To observe how morality and sexuality clash in our society today, we need look no further than a woman we'll call Janelle Evans (not her real name). Born in the '60s, Janelle went through her teenage years with a deep desire to find acceptance among her peers. She was on the fringe of a large group of teens who went to movies together, hung out at the mall, and, as they got older, had drinking parties together.

Janelle was confused when boys started making advances to her. She was eager for the popularity part of having a boyfriend, but she didn't know how to handle the physical part of the relationship and felt afraid to say no. "If you really love me, you'll want to do this as much as I do," they said to her. Three boyfriends later, Janelle found herself pregnant. She got an abortion quickly, with the help of her mom. From then on she used birth control pills faithfully.

Janelle went to college and moved in with her current boyfriend, Bill Evans. They got married in the middle of her sophomore year, and the next year she dropped out to work full time while Bill finished his degree. Eight years and two children later, Janelle has a good job as an executive assistant to the owner of a small computer business. She is intelligent, capable, and eager to please, and her boss praises her highly.

That's quite a contrast to what is happening at home, where Bill is now between jobs. He is sullen and moody, and the children are often demanding and fighting. Janelle finds herself emotionally exhausted after a weekend home with the family and eager to get back to the relative peace of the office. She also looks forward to her growing friendship with her boss.

Her boss's attention toward her feels to Janelle like cool water would to a thirsty person. She is confused by her feelings for him but she knows that he is giving her something she badly needs. His glance, his touch, his small signs of physical affection mean more and more to her.

Unsure of herself, Janelle confides in a close friend, Peg, who is single. Peg tells her to go for it. "You deserve more than what you've got with Bill," she says. "What an empty life if you didn't have that kind of intimacy! Just be careful you don't hurt yourself."

Janelle badly wants to take Peg's advice. She knows she is very much attracted to the man she works with every day. But she thinks about herself and her family. Would someone get hurt? What should she do?

Sexual relationships outside of marriage are becoming a socially accepted norm in the United States, with Canada not far behind.

- In an informal 1992 marriage survey by a popular North American magazine, 65 percent of married men interviewed said they had had an extramarital affair. Of the women who responded, 34 percent admitted having slept with a person other than their husband.
- While Europeans commonly accept living together before marriage, Americans lag somewhat behind in social acceptance of this practice. But in a recent survey of 2,000 sexually active adults, 13 percent listed themselves as "never married" and 17 percent were living with an unmarried partner.
- In 1991, unmarried women in the U.S. had a record 1.2 million births—nearly 30 percent of all the births in the U.S., in spite of 1.6 million abortions per year.

What the Bible Tells Us

And God said, "It is not good for the man to be alone. I will make a helper suitable for him. . . . For this reason a man will leave his father and mother and be united to his wife and they will become one flesh." (Genesis 2:18, 24)

Jesus went to the Mount of Olives. At dawn he appeared again in the temple courts, where all the people gathered around him, and he sat down to teach them. The teachers of the law and the Pharisees brought in a woman caught in adultery. They made her stand before the group and said to Jesus, "Teacher, this woman was caught in the act of adultery. In the Law Moses commanded us to stone

Copyright ©1994 Church Development Resources   It is illegal to copy this material without permission.

such women. Now what do you say?" They were using this question as a trap, in order to have a basis for accusing him.

But Jesus bent down and started to write on the ground with his finger. When they kept questioning him, he straightened up and said to them, "If any one of you is without sin, let him be the first to throw a stone at her." Again he stooped down and wrote on the ground.

At this, those who heard began to go away one at a time, the older ones first, until only Jesus was left, with the woman still standing there. Jesus straightened up and asked her, "Woman, where are they? Has no one condemned you?"

"No one, sir," she said.

"Then neither do I condemn you," Jesus declared. "Go now and leave your life of sin."

When Jesus spoke again to the people he said, "I am the light of the world. Whoever follows me will never walk in darkness, but will have the light of life." (John 8:1–12)

Note: The Pharisees were a religious group in Jesus' day. They lived their whole life trying to observe the rules of God's law. However, Jesus often condemned them for their hypocrisy and lack of love.

How the Bible Relates

1. What did God recognize about human nature from the beginning? What might this have to do with our sexuality?

2. Whom had the Pharisees found? What did they think should be done to her? Why did they bring her to Jesus?

3. What did Jesus say to them?

4. What was the Pharisees' and teachers' response?

5. What did Jesus say to the woman?

6. Who did Jesus say that he is? What do you think this means?

The Bottom Line

God intended our sexuality to be a gift—a delightful part of a nurturing, committed relationship between a man and woman. But when we make mistakes and misuse our sexuality, God does not point the finger in condemnation. Instead, God offers forgiveness and the possibility of a healed and restored life by looking to him.

Prayer

God, please help me to understand the deep places within me—my desires, my weaknesses, my sexuality. Help me also to understand and accept your love for me. Amen.

A Final Word

The temptations that you have are the temptations that all people have. But you can trust God. He will not let you be tempted more than you can stand. But when you are tempted, God will also give you a way to escape that temptation. Then you will be able to stand it. *(The apostle Paul in 1 Corinthians 10:13, New Century Version)*

Does God Want to Spoil My Fun?

5: "If It Feels Good, Do It"

Beginnings

Advertisers know that sex sells. What products can you think of that use sex as a "hook" to get customers? What are the good things and what is the "down" side to our sexuality? Why do you think God made us sexual beings?

What's Happening Today

To observe how morality and sexuality clash in our society today, we need look no further than a woman we'll call Janelle Evans (not her real name). Born in the '60s, Janelle went through her teenage years with a deep desire to find acceptance among her peers. She was on the fringe of a large group of teens who went to movies together, hung out at the mall, and, as they got older, had drinking parties together.

Janelle was confused when boys started making advances to her. She was eager for the popularity part of having a boyfriend, but she didn't know how to handle the physical part of the relationship and felt afraid to say no. "If you really love me, you'll want to do this as much as I do," they said to her. Three boyfriends later, Janelle found herself pregnant. She got an abortion quickly, with the help of her mom. From then on she used birth control pills faithfully.

Janelle went to college and moved in with her current boyfriend, Bill Evans. They got married in the middle of her sophomore year, and the next year she dropped out to work full time while Bill finished his degree. Eight years and two children later, Janelle has a good job as an executive assistant to the owner of a small computer business. She is intelligent, capable, and eager to please, and her boss praises her highly.

That's quite a contrast to what is happening at home, where Bill is now between jobs. He is sullen and moody, and the children are often demanding and fighting. Janelle finds herself emotionally exhausted after a weekend home with the family and eager to get back to the relative peace of the office. She also looks forward to her growing friendship with her boss.

Her boss's attention toward her feels to Janelle like cool water would to a thirsty person. She is confused by her feelings for him but she knows that he is giving her something she badly needs. His glance, his touch, his small signs of physical affection mean more and more to her.

Unsure of herself, Janelle confides in a close friend, Peg, who is single. Peg tells her to go for it. "You deserve more than what you've got with Bill," she says. "What an empty life if you didn't have that kind of intimacy! Just be careful you don't hurt yourself."

Janelle badly wants to take Peg's advice. She knows she is very much attracted to the man she works with every day. But she thinks about herself and her family. Would someone get hurt? What should she do?

Sexual relationships outside of marriage are becoming a socially accepted norm in the United States, with Canada not far behind.

- In an informal 1992 marriage survey by a popular North American magazine, 65 percent of married men interviewed said they had had an extramarital affair. Of the women who responded, 34 percent admitted having slept with a person other than their husband.
- While Europeans commonly accept living together before marriage, Americans lag somewhat behind in social acceptance of this practice. But in a recent survey of 2,000 sexually active adults, 13 percent listed themselves as "never married" and 17 percent were living with an unmarried partner.
- In 1991, unmarried women in the U.S. had a record 1.2 million births—nearly 30 percent of all the births in the U.S., in spite of 1.6 million abortions per year.

What the Bible Tells Us

And God said, "It is not good for the man to be alone. I will make a helper suitable for him . . . . For this reason a man will leave his father and mother and be united to his wife and they will become one flesh." (Genesis 2:18, 24)

Jesus went to the Mount of Olives. At dawn he appeared again in the temple courts, where all the people gathered around him, and he sat down to teach them. The teachers of the law and the Pharisees brought in a woman caught in adultery. They made her stand before the group and said to Jesus, "Teacher, this woman was caught in the act of adultery. In the Law Moses commanded us to stone

such women. Now what do you say?" They were using this question as a trap, in order to have a basis for accusing him.

But Jesus bent down and started to write on the ground with his finger. When they kept questioning him, he straightened up and said to them, "If any one of you is without sin, let him be the first to throw a stone at her." Again he stooped down and wrote on the ground.

At this, those who heard began to go away one at a time, the older ones first, until only Jesus was left, with the woman still standing there. Jesus straightened up and asked her, "Woman, where are they? Has no one condemned you?"

"No one, sir," she said.

"Then neither do I condemn you," Jesus declared. "Go now and leave your life of sin."

When Jesus spoke again to the people he said, "I am the light of the world. Whoever follows me will never walk in darkness, but will have the light of life." (John 8:1–12)

Note: The Pharisees were a religious group in Jesus' day. They lived their whole life trying to observe the rules of God's law. However, Jesus often condemned them for their hypocrisy and lack of love.

How the Bible Relates

1. What did God recognize about human nature from the beginning? What might this have to do with our sexuality?

2. Whom had the Pharisees found? What did they think should be done to her? Why did they bring her to Jesus?

3. What did Jesus say to them?

4. What was the Pharisees' and teachers' response?

5. What did Jesus say to the woman?

6. Who did Jesus say that he is? What do you think this means?

The Bottom Line

God intended our sexuality to be a gift—a delightful part of a nurturing, committed relationship between a man and woman. But when we make mistakes and misuse our sexuality, God does not point the finger in condemnation. Instead, God offers forgiveness and the possibility of a healed and restored life by looking to him.

Prayer

God, please help me to understand the deep places within me—my desires, my weaknesses, my sexuality. Help me also to understand and accept your love for me. Amen.

A Final Word

The temptations that you have are the temptations that all people have. But you can trust God. He will not let you be tempted more than you can stand. But when you are tempted, God will also give you a way to escape that temptation. Then you will be able to stand it. *(The apostle Paul in 1 Corinthians 10:13, New Century Version)*

Does God Want to Spoil My Fun?

5: "If It Feels Good, Do It"

Beginnings

Advertisers know that sex sells. What products can you think of that use sex as a "hook" to get customers? What are the good things and what is the "down" side to our sexuality? Why do you think God made us sexual beings?

What's Happening Today

To observe how morality and sexuality clash in our society today, we need look no further than a woman we'll call Janelle Evans (not her real name). Born in the '60s, Janelle went through her teenage years with a deep desire to find acceptance among her peers. She was on the fringe of a large group of teens who went to movies together, hung out at the mall, and, as they got older, had drinking parties together.

Janelle was confused when boys started making advances to her. She was eager for the popularity part of having a boyfriend, but she didn't know how to handle the physical part of the relationship and felt afraid to say no. "If you really love me, you'll want to do this as much as I do," they said to her. Three boyfriends later, Janelle found herself pregnant. She got an abortion quickly, with the help of her mom. From then on she used birth control pills faithfully.

Janelle went to college and moved in with her current boyfriend, Bill Evans. They got married in the middle of her sophomore year, and the next year she dropped out to work full time while Bill finished his degree. Eight years and two children later, Janelle has a good job as an executive assistant to the owner of a small computer business. She is intelligent, capable, and eager to please, and her boss praises her highly.

That's quite a contrast to what is happening at home, where Bill is now between jobs. He is sullen and moody, and the children are often demanding and fighting. Janelle finds herself emotionally exhausted after a weekend home with the family and eager to get back to the relative peace of the office. She also looks forward to her growing friendship with her boss.

Her boss's attention toward her feels to Janelle like cool water would to a thirsty person. She is confused by her feelings for him but she knows that he is giving her something she badly needs. His glance, his touch, his small signs of physical affection mean more and more to her.

Unsure of herself, Janelle confides in a close friend, Peg, who is single. Peg tells her to go for it. "You deserve more than what you've got with Bill," she says. "What an empty life if you didn't have that kind of intimacy! Just be careful you don't hurt yourself."

Janelle badly wants to take Peg's advice. She knows she is very much attracted to the man she works with every day. But she thinks about herself and her family. Would someone get hurt? What should she do?

Sexual relationships outside of marriage are becoming a socially accepted norm in the United States, with Canada not far behind.

- In an informal 1992 marriage survey by a popular North American magazine, 65 percent of married men interviewed said they had had an extramarital affair. Of the women who responded, 34 percent admitted having slept with a person other than their husband.
- While Europeans commonly accept living together before marriage, Americans lag somewhat behind in social acceptance of this practice. But in a recent survey of 2,000 sexually active adults, 13 percent listed themselves as "never married" and 17 percent were living with an unmarried partner.
- In 1991, unmarried women in the U.S. had a record 1.2 million births—nearly 30 percent of all the births in the U.S., in spite of 1.6 million abortions per year.

What the Bible Tells Us

And God said, "It is not good for the man to be alone. I will make a helper suitable for him . . . . For this reason a man will leave his father and mother and be united to his wife and they will become one flesh." (Genesis 2:18, 24)

Jesus went to the Mount of Olives. At dawn he appeared again in the temple courts, where all the people gathered around him, and he sat down to teach them. The teachers of the law and the Pharisees brought in a woman caught in adultery. They made her stand before the group and said to Jesus, "Teacher, this woman was caught in the act of adultery. In the Law Moses commanded us to stone

Copyright ©1994 Church Development Resources   It is illegal to copy this material without permission.

such women. Now what do you say?" They were using this question as a trap, in order to have a basis for accusing him.

But Jesus bent down and started to write on the ground with his finger. When they kept questioning him, he straightened up and said to them, "If any one of you is without sin, let him be the first to throw a stone at her." Again he stooped down and wrote on the ground.

At this, those who heard began to go away one at a time, the older ones first, until only Jesus was left, with the woman still standing there. Jesus straightened up and asked her, "Woman, where are they? Has no one condemned you?"

"No one, sir," she said.

"Then neither do I condemn you," Jesus declared. "Go now and leave your life of sin."

When Jesus spoke again to the people he said, "I am the light of the world. Whoever follows me will never walk in darkness, but will have the light of life." (John 8:1–12)

Note: The Pharisees were a religious group in Jesus' day. They lived their whole life trying to observe the rules of God's law. However, Jesus often condemned them for their hypocrisy and lack of love.

How the Bible Relates

1. What did God recognize about human nature from the beginning? What might this have to do with our sexuality?

2. Whom had the Pharisees found? What did they think should be done to her? Why did they bring her to Jesus?

3. What did Jesus say to them?

4. What was the Pharisees' and teachers' response?

5. What did Jesus say to the woman?

6. Who did Jesus say that he is? What do you think this means?

The Bottom Line

God intended our sexuality to be a gift—a delightful part of a nurturing, committed relationship between a man and woman. But when we make mistakes and misuse our sexuality, God does not point the finger in condemnation. Instead, God offers forgiveness and the possibility of a healed and restored life by looking to him.

Prayer

God, please help me to understand the deep places within me—my desires, my weaknesses, my sexuality. Help me also to understand and accept your love for me. Amen.

A Final Word

The temptations that you have are the temptations that all people have. But you can trust God. He will not let you be tempted more than you can stand. But when you are tempted, God will also give you a way to escape that temptation. Then you will be able to stand it. *(The apostle Paul in 1 Corinthians 10:13, New Century Version)*

Does God Want to Spoil My Fun?

5: "If It Feels Good, Do It"

Beginnings

Advertisers know that sex sells. What products can you think of that use sex as a "hook" to get customers? What are the good things and what is the "down" side to our sexuality? Why do you think God made us sexual beings?

What's Happening Today

To observe how morality and sexuality clash in our society today, we need look no further than a woman we'll call Janelle Evans (not her real name). Born in the '60s, Janelle went through her teenage years with a deep desire to find acceptance among her peers. She was on the fringe of a large group of teens who went to movies together, hung out at the mall, and, as they got older, had drinking parties together.

Janelle was confused when boys started making advances to her. She was eager for the popularity part of having a boyfriend, but she didn't know how to handle the physical part of the relationship and felt afraid to say no. "If you really love me, you'll want to do this as much as I do," they said to her. Three boyfriends later, Janelle found herself pregnant. She got an abortion quickly, with the help of her mom. From then on she used birth control pills faithfully.

Janelle went to college and moved in with her current boyfriend, Bill Evans. They got married in the middle of her sophomore year, and the next year she dropped out to work full time while Bill finished his degree. Eight years and two children later, Janelle has a good job as an executive assistant to the owner of a small computer business. She is intelligent, capable, and eager to please, and her boss praises her highly.

That's quite a contrast to what is happening at home, where Bill is now between jobs. He is sullen and moody, and the children are often demanding and fighting. Janelle finds herself emotionally exhausted after a weekend home with the family and eager to get back to the relative peace of the office. She also looks forward to her growing friendship with her boss.

Her boss's attention toward Janelle feels to Janelle like cool water would to a thirsty person. She is confused by her feelings for him but she knows that he is giving her something she badly needs. His glance, his touch, his small signs of physical affection mean more and more to her.

Unsure of herself, Janelle confides in a close friend, Peg, who is single. Peg tells her to go for it. "You deserve more than what you've got with Bill," she says. "What an empty life if you didn't have that kind of intimacy! Just be careful you don't hurt yourself."

Janelle badly wants to take Peg's advice. She knows she is very much attracted to the man she works with every day. But she thinks about herself and her family. Would someone get hurt? What should she do?

Sexual relationships outside of marriage are becoming a socially accepted norm in the United States, with Canada not far behind.

- In an informal 1992 marriage survey by a popular North American magazine, 65 percent of married men interviewed said they had had an extramarital affair. Of the women who responded, 34 percent admitted having slept with a person other than their husband.
- While Europeans commonly accept living together before marriage, Americans lag somewhat behind in social acceptance of this practice. But in a recent survey of 2,000 sexually active adults, 13 percent listed themselves as "never married" and 17 percent were living with an unmarried partner.
- In 1991, unmarried women in the U.S. had a record 1.2 million births—nearly 30 percent of all the births in the U.S., in spite of 1.6 million abortions per year.

What the Bible Tells Us

And God said, "It is not good for the man to be alone. I will make a helper suitable for him.... For this reason a man will leave his father and mother and be united to his wife and they will become one flesh." (Genesis 2:18, 24)

Jesus went to the Mount of Olives. At dawn he appeared again in the temple courts, where all the people gathered around him, and he sat down to teach them. The teachers of the law and the Pharisees brought in a woman caught in adultery. They made her stand before the group and said to Jesus, "Teacher, this woman was caught in the act of adultery. In the Law Moses commanded us to stone

such women. Now what do you say?" They were using this question as a trap, in order to have a basis for accusing him.

But Jesus bent down and started to write on the ground with his finger. When they kept questioning him, he straightened up and said to them, "If any one of you is without sin, let him be the first to throw a stone at her." Again he stooped down and wrote on the ground.

At this, those who heard began to go away one at a time, the older ones first, until only Jesus was left, with the woman still standing there. Jesus straightened up and asked her, "Woman, where are they? Has no one condemned you?"

"No one, sir," she said.

"Then neither do I condemn you," Jesus declared. "Go now and leave your life of sin."

When Jesus spoke again to the people he said, "I am the light of the world. Whoever follows me will never walk in darkness, but will have the light of life." (John 8:1–12)

Note: The Pharisees were a religious group in Jesus' day. They lived their whole life trying to observe the rules of God's law. However, Jesus often condemned them for their hypocrisy and lack of love.

How the Bible Relates

1. What did God recognize about human nature from the beginning? What might this have to do with our sexuality?

2. Whom had the Pharisees found? What did they think should be done to her? Why did they bring her to Jesus?

3. What did Jesus say to them?

4. What was the Pharisees' and teachers' response?

5. What did Jesus say to the woman?

6. Who did Jesus say that he is? What do you think this means?

The Bottom Line

God intended our sexuality to be a gift—a delightful part of a nurturing, committed relationship between a man and woman. But when we make mistakes and misuse our sexuality, God does not point the finger in condemnation. Instead, God offers forgiveness and the possibility of a healed and restored life by looking to him.

Prayer

God, please help me to understand the deep places within me—my desires, my weaknesses, my sexuality. Help me also to understand and accept your love for me. Amen.

A Final Word

The temptations that you have are the temptations that all people have. But you can trust God. He will not let you be tempted more than you can stand. But when you are tempted, God will also give you a way to escape that temptation. Then you will be able to stand it. *(The apostle Paul in 1 Corinthians 10:13, New Century Version)*

Does God Want to Spoil My Fun?

5: "If It Feels Good, Do It"

Beginnings

Advertisers know that sex sells. What products can you think of that use sex as a "hook" to get customers? What are the good things and what is the "down" side to our sexuality? Why do you think God made us sexual beings?

What's Happening Today

To observe how morality and sexuality clash in our society today, we need look no further than a woman we'll call Janelle Evans (not her real name). Born in the '60s, Janelle went through her teenage years with a deep desire to find acceptance among her peers. She was on the fringe of a large group of teens who went to movies together, hung out at the mall, and, as they got older, had drinking parties together.

Janelle was confused when boys started making advances to her. She was eager for the popularity part of having a boyfriend, but she didn't know how to handle the physical part of the relationship and felt afraid to say no. "If you really love me, you'll want to do this as much as I do," they said to her. Three boyfriends later, Janelle found herself pregnant. She got an abortion quickly, with the help of her mom. From then on she used birth control pills faithfully.

Janelle went to college and moved in with her current boyfriend, Bill Evans. They got married in the middle of her sophomore year, and the next year she dropped out to work full time while Bill finished his degree. Eight years and two children later, Janelle has a good job as an executive assistant to the owner of a small computer business. She is intelligent, capable, and eager to please, and her boss praises her highly.

That's quite a contrast to what is happening at home, where Bill is now between jobs. He is sullen and moody, and the children are often demanding and fighting. Janelle finds herself emotionally exhausted after a weekend home with the family and eager to get back to the relative peace of the office. She also looks forward to her growing friendship with her boss.

Her boss's attention toward her feels to Janelle like cool water would to a thirsty person. She is confused by her feelings for him but she knows that he is giving her something she badly needs. His glance, his touch, his small signs of physical affection mean more and more to her.

Unsure of herself, Janelle confides in a close friend, Peg, who is single. Peg tells her to go for it. "You deserve more than what you've got with Bill," she says. "What an empty life if you didn't have that kind of intimacy! Just be careful you don't hurt yourself."

Janelle badly wants to take Peg's advice. She knows she is very much attracted to the man she works with every day. But she thinks about herself and her family. Would someone get hurt? What should she do?

Sexual relationships outside of marriage are becoming a socially accepted norm in the United States, with Canada not far behind.

- In an informal 1992 marriage survey by a popular North American magazine, 65 percent of married men interviewed said they had had an extramarital affair. Of the women who responded, 34 percent admitted having slept with a person other than their husband.
- While Europeans commonly accept living together before marriage, Americans lag somewhat behind in social acceptance of this practice. But in a recent survey of 2,000 sexually active adults, 13 percent listed themselves as "never married" and 17 percent were living with an unmarried partner.
- In 1991, unmarried women in the U.S. had a record 1.2 million births—nearly 30 percent of all the births in the U.S., in spite of 1.6 million abortions per year.

What the Bible Tells Us

And God said, "It is not good for the man to be alone. I will make a helper suitable for him.... For this reason a man will leave his father and mother and be united to his wife and they will become one flesh." (Genesis 2:18, 24)

Jesus went to the Mount of Olives. At dawn he appeared again in the temple courts, where all the people gathered around him, and he sat down to teach them. The teachers of the law and the Pharisees brought in a woman caught in adultery. They made her stand before the group and said to Jesus, "Teacher, this woman was caught in the act of adultery. In the Law Moses commanded us to stone

Copyright ©1994 Church Development Resources   It is illegal to copy this material without permission.

such women. Now what do you say?" They were using this question as a trap, in order to have a basis for accusing him.

But Jesus bent down and started to write on the ground with his finger. When they kept questioning him, he straightened up and said to them, "If any one of you is without sin, let him be the first to throw a stone at her." Again he stooped down and wrote on the ground.

At this, those who heard began to go away one at a time, the older ones first, until only Jesus was left, with the woman still standing there. Jesus straightened up and asked her, "Woman, where are they? Has no one condemned you?"

"No one, sir," she said.

"Then neither do I condemn you," Jesus declared. "Go now and leave your life of sin."

When Jesus spoke again to the people he said, "I am the light of the world. Whoever follows me will never walk in darkness, but will have the light of life." (John 8:1–12)

Note: The Pharisees were a religious group in Jesus' day. They lived their whole life trying to observe the rules of God's law. However, Jesus often condemned them for their hypocrisy and lack of love.

How the Bible Relates

1. What did God recognize about human nature from the beginning? What might this have to do with our sexuality?

2. Whom had the Pharisees found? What did they think should be done to her? Why did they bring her to Jesus?

3. What did Jesus say to them?

4. What was the Pharisees' and teachers' response?

5. What did Jesus say to the woman?

6. Who did Jesus say that he is? What do you think this means?

The Bottom Line

God intended our sexuality to be a gift—a delightful part of a nurturing, committed relationship between a man and woman. But when we make mistakes and misuse our sexuality, God does not point the finger in condemnation. Instead, God offers forgiveness and the possibility of a healed and restored life by looking to him.

Prayer

God, please help me to understand the deep places within me—my desires, my weaknesses, my sexuality. Help me also to understand and accept your love for me. Amen.

A Final Word

The temptations that you have are the temptations that all people have. But you can trust God. He will not let you be tempted more than you can stand. But when you are tempted, God will also give you a way to escape that temptation. Then you will be able to stand it. (The apostle Paul in 1 Corinthians 10:13, New Century Version)

Does God Want to Spoil My Fun?

5: "If It Feels Good, Do It"

Beginnings

Advertisers know that sex sells. What products can you think of that use sex as a "hook" to get customers? What are the good things and what is the "down" side to our sexuality? Why do you think God made us sexual beings?

What's Happening Today

To observe how morality and sexuality clash in our society today, we need look no further than a woman we'll call Janelle Evans (not her real name). Born in the '60s, Janelle went through her teenage years with a deep desire to find acceptance among her peers. She was on the fringe of a large group of teens who went to movies together, hung out at the mall, and, as they got older, had drinking parties together.

Janelle was confused when boys started making advances to her. She was eager for the popularity part of having a boyfriend, but she didn't know how to handle the physical part of the relationship and felt afraid to say no. "If you really love me, you'll want to do this as much as I do," they said to her. Three boyfriends later, Janelle found herself pregnant. She got an abortion quickly, with the help of her mom. From then on she used birth control pills faithfully.

Janelle went to college and moved in with her current boyfriend, Bill Evans. They got married in the middle of her sophomore year, and the next year she dropped out to work full time while Bill finished his degree. Eight years and two children later, Janelle has a good job as an executive assistant to the owner of a small computer business. She is intelligent, capable, and eager to please, and her boss praises her highly.

That's quite a contrast to what is happening at home, where Bill is now between jobs. He is sullen and moody, and the children are often demanding and fighting. Janelle finds herself emotionally exhausted after a weekend home with the family and eager to get back to the relative peace of the office. She also looks forward to her growing friendship with her boss.

Her boss's attention toward her feels to Janelle like cool water would to a thirsty person. She is confused by her feelings for him but she knows that he is giving her something she badly needs. His glance, his touch, his small signs of physical affection mean more and more to her.

Unsure of herself, Janelle confides in a close friend, Peg, who is single. Peg tells her to go for it. "You deserve more than what you've got with Bill," she says. "What an empty life if you didn't have that kind of intimacy! Just be careful you don't hurt yourself."

Janelle badly wants to take Peg's advice. She knows she is very much attracted to the man she works with every day. But she thinks about herself and her family. Would someone get hurt? What should she do?

Sexual relationships outside of marriage are becoming a socially accepted norm in the United States, with Canada not far behind.

- In an informal 1992 marriage survey by a popular North American magazine, 65 percent of married men interviewed said they had had an extramarital affair. Of the women who responded, 34 percent admitted having slept with a person other than their husband.
- While Europeans commonly accept living together before marriage, Americans lag somewhat behind in social acceptance of this practice. But in a recent survey of 2,000 sexually active adults, 13 percent listed themselves as "never married" and 17 percent were living with an unmarried partner.
- In 1991, unmarried women in the U.S. had a record 1.2 million births—nearly 30 percent of all the births in the U.S., in spite of 1.6 million abortions per year.

What the Bible Tells Us

And God said, "It is not good for the man to be alone. I will make a helper suitable for him . . . . For this reason a man will leave his father and mother and be united to his wife and they will become one flesh." (Genesis 2:18, 24)

Jesus went to the Mount of Olives. At dawn he appeared again in the temple courts, where all the people gathered around him, and he sat down to teach them. The teachers of the law and the Pharisees brought in a woman caught in adultery. They made her stand before the group and said to Jesus, "Teacher, this woman was caught in the act of adultery. In the Law Moses commanded us to stone

such women. Now what do you say?" They were using this question as a trap, in order to have a basis for accusing him.

But Jesus bent down and started to write on the ground with his finger. When they kept questioning him, he straightened up and said to them, "If any one of you is without sin, let him be the first to throw a stone at her." Again he stooped down and wrote on the ground.

At this, those who heard began to go away one at a time, the older ones first, until only Jesus was left, with the woman still standing there. Jesus straightened up and asked her, "Woman, where are they? Has no one condemned you?"

"No one, sir," she said.

"Then neither do I condemn you," Jesus declared. "Go now and leave your life of sin."

When Jesus spoke again to the people he said, "I am the light of the world. Whoever follows me will never walk in darkness, but will have the light of life." (John 8:1–12)

Note: The Pharisees were a religious group in Jesus' day. They lived their whole life trying to observe the rules of God's law. However, Jesus often condemned them for their hypocrisy and lack of love.

How the Bible Relates

1. What did God recognize about human nature from the beginning? What might this have to do with our sexuality?
2. Whom had the Pharisees found? What did they think should be done to her? Why did they bring her to Jesus?
3. What did Jesus say to them?
4. What was the Pharisees' and teachers' response?
5. What did Jesus say to the woman?
6. Who did Jesus say that he is? What do you think this means?

The Bottom Line

God intended our sexuality to be a gift—a delightful part of a nurturing, committed relationship between a man and woman. But when we make mistakes and misuse our sexuality, God does not point the finger in condemnation. Instead, God offers forgiveness and the possibility of a healed and restored life by looking to him.

Prayer

God, please help me to understand the deep places within me—my desires, my weaknesses, my sexuality. Help me also to understand and accept your love for me. Amen.

A Final Word

The temptations that you have are the temptations that all people have. But you can trust God. He will not let you be tempted more than you can stand. But when you are tempted, God will also give you a way to escape that temptation. Then you will be able to stand it. *(The apostle Paul in 1 Corinthians 10:13, New Century Version)*

Does God Want to Spoil My Fun?

5: "If It Feels Good, Do It"

Beginnings

Advertisers know that sex sells. What products can you think of that use sex as a "hook" to get customers? What are the good things and what is the "down" side to our sexuality? Why do you think God made us sexual beings?

What's Happening Today

To observe how morality and sexuality clash in our society today, we need look no further than a woman we'll call Janelle Evans (not her real name). Born in the '60s, Janelle went through her teenage years with a deep desire to find acceptance among her peers. She was on the fringe of a large group of teens who went to movies together, hung out at the mall, and, as they got older, had drinking parties together.

Janelle was confused when boys started making advances to her. She was eager for the popularity part of having a boyfriend, but she didn't know how to handle the physical part of the relationship and felt afraid to say no. "If you really love me, you'll want to do this as much as I do," they said to her. Three boyfriends later, Janelle found herself pregnant. She got an abortion quickly, with the help of her mom. From then on she used birth control pills faithfully.

Janelle went to college and moved in with her current boyfriend, Bill Evans. They got married in the middle of her sophomore year, and the next year she dropped out to work full time while Bill finished his degree. Eight years and two children later, Janelle has a good job as an executive assistant to the owner of a small computer business. She is intelligent, capable, and eager to please, and her boss praises her highly.

That's quite a contrast to what is happening at home, where Bill is now between jobs. He is sullen and moody, and the children are often demanding and fighting. Janelle finds herself emotionally exhausted after a weekend home with the family and eager to get back to the relative peace of the office. She also looks forward to her growing friendship with her boss.

Her boss's attention toward her feels to Janelle like cool water would to a thirsty person. She is confused by her feelings for him but she knows that he is giving her something she badly needs. His glance, his touch, his small signs of physical affection mean more and more to her.

Unsure of herself, Janelle confides in a close friend, Peg, who is single. Peg tells her to go for it. "You deserve more than what you've got with Bill," she says. "What an empty life if you didn't have that kind of intimacy! Just be careful you don't hurt yourself."

Janelle badly wants to take Peg's advice. She knows she is very much attracted to the man she works with every day. But she thinks about herself and her family. Would someone get hurt? What should she do?

Sexual relationships outside of marriage are becoming a socially accepted norm in the United States, with Canada not far behind.

- In an informal 1992 marriage survey by a popular North American magazine, 65 percent of married men interviewed said they had had an extramarital affair. Of the women who responded, 34 percent admitted having slept with a person other than their husband.
- While Europeans commonly accept living together before marriage, Americans lag somewhat behind in social acceptance of this practice. But in a recent survey of 2,000 sexually active adults, 13 percent listed themselves as "never married" and 17 percent were living with an unmarried partner.
- In 1991, unmarried women in the U.S. had a record 1.2 million births—nearly 30 percent of all the births in the U.S., in spite of 1.6 million abortions per year.

What the Bible Tells Us

And God said, "It is not good for the man to be alone. I will make a helper suitable for him . . . . For this reason a man will leave his father and mother and be united to his wife and they will become one flesh." (Genesis 2:18, 24)

Jesus went to the Mount of Olives. At dawn he appeared again in the temple courts, where all the people gathered around him, and he sat down to teach them. The teachers of the law and the Pharisees brought in a woman caught in adultery. They made her stand before the group and said to Jesus, "Teacher, this woman was caught in the act of adultery. In the Law Moses commanded us to stone

Copyright ©1994 Church Development Resources   It is illegal to copy this material without permission.

such women. Now what do you say?" They were using this question as a trap, in order to have a basis for accusing him.

But Jesus bent down and started to write on the ground with his finger. When they kept questioning him, he straightened up and said to them, "If any one of you is without sin, let him be the first to throw a stone at her." Again he stooped down and wrote on the ground.

At this, those who heard began to go away one at a time, the older ones first, until only Jesus was left, with the woman still standing there. Jesus straightened up and asked her, "Woman, where are they? Has no one condemned you?"

"No one, sir," she said.

"Then neither do I condemn you," Jesus declared. "Go now and leave your life of sin."

When Jesus spoke again to the people he said, "I am the light of the world. Whoever follows me will never walk in darkness, but will have the light of life." (John 8:1–12)

Note: The Pharisees were a religious group in Jesus' day. They lived their whole life trying to observe the rules of God's law. However, Jesus often condemned them for their hypocrisy and lack of love.

How the Bible Relates

1. What did God recognize about human nature from the beginning? What might this have to do with our sexuality?

2. Whom had the Pharisees found? What did they think should be done to her? Why did they bring her to Jesus?

3. What did Jesus say to them?

4. What was the Pharisees' and teachers' response?

5. What did Jesus say to the woman?

6. Who did Jesus say that he is? What do you think this means?

The Bottom Line

God intended our sexuality to be a gift—a delightful part of a nurturing, committed relationship between a man and woman. But when we make mistakes and misuse our sexuality, God does not point the finger in condemnation. Instead, God offers forgiveness and the possibility of a healed and restored life by looking to him.

Prayer

God, please help me to understand the deep places within me—my desires, my weaknesses, my sexuality. Help me also to understand and accept your love for me. Amen.

A Final Word

The temptations that you have are the temptations that all people have. But you can trust God. He will not let you be tempted more than you can stand. But when you are tempted, God will also give you a way to escape that temptation. Then you will be able to stand it. (The apostle Paul in 1 Corinthians 10:13, New Century Version)

Does God Want to Spoil My Fun?

5: "If It Feels Good, Do It"

Beginnings

Advertisers know that sex sells. What products can you think of that use sex as a "hook" to get customers? What are the good things and what is the "down" side to our sexuality? Why do you think God made us sexual beings?

What's Happening Today

To observe how morality and sexuality clash in our society today, we need look no further than a woman we'll call Janelle Evans (not her real name). Born in the '60s, Janelle went through her teenage years with a deep desire to find acceptance among her peers. She was on the fringe of a large group of teens who went to movies together, hung out at the mall, and, as they got older, had drinking parties together.

Janelle was confused when boys started making advances to her. She was eager for the popularity part of having a boyfriend, but she didn't know how to handle the physical part of the relationship and felt afraid to say no. "If you really love me, you'll want to do this as much as I do," they said to her. Three boyfriends later, Janelle found herself pregnant. She got an abortion quickly, with the help of her mom. From then on she used birth control pills faithfully.

Janelle went to college and moved in with her current boyfriend, Bill Evans. They got married in the middle of her sophomore year, and the next year she dropped out to work full time while Bill finished his degree. Eight years and two children later, Janelle has a good job as an executive assistant to the owner of a small computer business. She is intelligent, capable, and eager to please, and her boss praises her highly.

That's quite a contrast to what is happening at home, where Bill is now between jobs. He is sullen and moody, and the children are often demanding and fighting. Janelle finds herself emotionally exhausted after a weekend home with the family and eager to get back to the relative peace of the office. She also looks forward to her growing friendship with her boss.

Her boss's attention toward her feels to Janelle like cool water would to a thirsty person. She is confused by her feelings for him but she knows that he is giving her something she badly needs. His glance, his touch, his small signs of physical affection mean more and more to her.

Unsure of herself, Janelle confides in a close friend, Peg, who is single. Peg tells her to go for it. "You deserve more than what you've got with Bill," she says. "What an empty life if you didn't have that kind of intimacy! Just be careful you don't hurt yourself."

Janelle badly wants to take Peg's advice. She knows she is very much attracted to the man she works with every day. But she thinks about herself and her family. Would someone get hurt? What should she do?

Sexual relationships outside of marriage are becoming a socially accepted norm in the United States, with Canada not far behind.

- In an informal 1992 marriage survey by a popular North American magazine, 65 percent of married men interviewed said they had had an extramarital affair. Of the women who responded, 34 percent admitted having slept with a person other than their husband.
- While Europeans commonly accept living together before marriage, Americans lag somewhat behind in social acceptance of this practice. But in a recent survey of 2,000 sexually active adults, 13 percent listed themselves as "never married" and 17 percent were living with an unmarried partner.
- In 1991, unmarried women in the U.S. had a record 1.2 million births—nearly 30 percent of all the births in the U.S., in spite of 1.6 million abortions per year.

What the Bible Tells Us

And God said, "It is not good for the man to be alone. I will make a helper suitable for him . . . . For this reason a man will leave his father and mother and be united to his wife and they will become one flesh." (Genesis 2:18, 24)

Jesus went to the Mount of Olives. At dawn he appeared again in the temple courts, where all the people gathered around him, and he sat down to teach them. The teachers of the law and the Pharisees brought in a woman caught in adultery. They made her stand before the group and said to Jesus, "Teacher, this woman was caught in the act of adultery. In the Law Moses commanded us to stone

Copyright ©1994 Church Development Resources   It is illegal to copy this material without permission.

such women. Now what do you say?" They were using this question as a trap, in order to have a basis for accusing him.

But Jesus bent down and started to write on the ground with his finger. When they kept questioning him, he straightened up and said to them, "If any one of you is without sin, let him be the first to throw a stone at her." Again he stooped down and wrote on the ground.

At this, those who heard began to go away one at a time, the older ones first, until only Jesus was left, with the woman still standing there. Jesus straightened up and asked her, "Woman, where are they? Has no one condemned you?"

"No one, sir," she said.

"Then neither do I condemn you," Jesus declared. "Go now and leave your life of sin."

When Jesus spoke again to the people he said, "I am the light of the world. Whoever follows me will never walk in darkness, but will have the light of life." (John 8:1–12)

Note: The Pharisees were a religious group in Jesus' day. They lived their whole life trying to observe the rules of God's law. However, Jesus often condemned them for their hypocrisy and lack of love.

How the Bible Relates

1. What did God recognize about human nature from the beginning? What might this have to do with our sexuality?

2. Whom had the Pharisees found? What did they think should be done to her? Why did they bring her to Jesus?

3. What did Jesus say to them?

4. What was the Pharisees' and teachers' response?

5. What did Jesus say to the woman?

6. Who did Jesus say that he is? What do you think this means?

The Bottom Line

God intended our sexuality to be a gift—a delightful part of a nurturing, committed relationship between a man and woman. But when we make mistakes and misuse our sexuality, God does not point the finger in condemnation. Instead, God offers forgiveness and the possibility of a healed and restored life by looking to him.

Prayer

God, please help me to understand the deep places within me—my desires, my weaknesses, my sexuality. Help me also to understand and accept your love for me. Amen.

A Final Word

The temptations that you have are the temptations that all people have. But you can trust God. He will not let you be tempted more than you can stand. But when you are tempted, God will also give you a way to escape that temptation. Then you will be able to stand it. *(The apostle Paul in 1 Corinthians 10:13, New Century Version)*

Does God Want to Spoil My Fun?

SESSION 6

Does God Want to Spoil My Fun?—Leader Guide

6: "I Did It My Way"

Introductory Notes

The past five sessions have focused on helping your group to let go of a lot of things and instead to turn their eyes on God. They have been asked to begin trusting God, not material things or chemical substances or sexual relationships or even themselves, for fulfillment and happiness.

This session confronts them with the final letting go—giving up their lives to God, placing their faith in Jesus Christ. They will be faced with the need to give up trying to gain God's favor on their own efforts. Rather, they will be asked to place their complete faith and trust in Jesus Christ as the only way to become right with God.

Your group members may not have been in Bible study very long. Don't be discouraged if they are not yet ready to make this commitment. Some may need more time to ask questions, to think about it, to see if they are really willing to give complete control of their lives and future to God. Claiming Jesus as Savior is one step. Making him Lord requires surrendering and looking at life through his eyes, "cooperating" by living a grateful life.

Be patient and explain things simply and clearly. Remember that often people hear the gospel presentation seven or eight times before they actually respond to God's offer. Others, of course, may be ready to respond immediately.

As you prepare for this session, ask God to allow you to see your group members as he sees them. Meditate on God's deep love for them; reflect on the healing and forgiveness that he wants to pour out on their lives and families.

Also remember as you prepare, however, that the work does not depend on you. Opening your group members' hearts is the work of the Holy Spirit. It is the Spirit who will apply the Word, who will convict consciences, who will woo people's hearts to the love of God. "Flesh gives birth to flesh, but the Spirit gives birth to spirit." You are there only as a kind of midwife, to help the new birth take place. Ask the Spirit to show you how to assist him in this process—and have complete faith that he will show you!

Beginning the Session

As people come in for today's study, greet them warmly and follow up on any needs, concerns, or anticipated events in their lives that they've shared in the past few weeks. Let them know you've been praying for their requests, and assure them that your concern won't end with this session.

Take the time to offer a brief prayer before you begin, thanking God for each person present and for the ways in which God has already answered prayers offered for them or for their family members and friends.

In the longer session, allow time for a few stories of what God has begun to do in group members' lives or how the Bible passages have started to change their perspectives and attitudes. **What specific prayer requests have already been answered? What insights have people gained from the last five weeks? How have situations changed as a result of putting some of these new principles and insights into practice?**

It will be good for your group members to hear these stories, to prepare them for the session today. If they see how God has been already at work in their lives, they will be much more ready to trust him with control in other areas of their lives as well. Pray that group members will be willing to share these experiences and insights.

Beginnings

List phrases and functions that have the word "control" in them (for example, quality control, control panel, etc.). Now list some of the things in your life that you can control. Also list some of the things you can't control. Why do you think control is important to people?

Hand out the discussion sheet and read these beginning questions aloud to your group. It may be helpful at this point also to hand out paper and pencils, because list-making is something that most people feel comfortable with. It also helps them focus on the question without distraction. If you hand out pencils and paper, give members a minute or so to jot down their ideas. Then share them aloud, talking briefly about the ones that are mentioned most often.

Step back from those items for a moment to see the big picture. **In general, what things can't we control?** Obvious things like the weather, catastrophic events, other people's attitudes, and the number of hours in a day should come to mind.

What are the only things we have any control over? This list includes simply the things that we ourselves can do or achieve. But note that even this limited amount of control is not always as great as we would like. **Can we always control our actions, our attitudes, or our thoughts?** Acknowledge that sometimes, no matter how

151

hard we try, we find that our best efforts fall far short of what we want them to be.

What's Happening Today

Read this section aloud to your group. Leave some time for response to what you've read; then move on to the Scripture reading, which should flow from this without needing further explanation.

What the Bible Tells Us

Have a volunteer from your group read aloud these verses from Scripture before going into the discussion questions. Allow time for the meaning to sink in. Some terms may need explanation before you move on: for example, "law," "grace," "sin," and "Jesus Christ." Remember that group members may not have heard these terms before—and if they have, they may have only a vague idea as to their meaning.

If this is the case, explain that "law" refers to the Ten Commandments that God gave people many centuries ago—"You shall not kill, steal, commit adultery," and so on. That law is summed up in the words "Love God with all your heart and soul and mind and strength, and love your neighbor as yourself." (You may have already dealt with this somewhat in previous sessions.)

"Grace" simply means undeserved favor. It means that God loves us and shows us kindness even when we don't deserve it. "Sin" is doing anything to break God's commandments, even the smallest of them. It also involves *not* doing what we should as well as doing what we shouldn't. But sin goes deeper than our actions; it involves our will, emotions, and thoughts.

Explaining who Jesus Christ is may take a bit longer, and you may want to do this as you go along through the study together. You can mention, however, that Jesus is God's Son, whom God sent to live on earth and to teach people about God's love and forgiveness. In God's plan, Jesus died in order to pay the punishment in full for the sins of anyone who would seek God's forgiveness. God raised his Son from death, and now Jesus is alive in heaven; and he will come again, at a time set by God, to bring healing and justice and a new heavens and earth.

Use your judgment as to how much explanation is needed at this point. Don't belabor points, but also be careful not to leave members confused when a simple explanation will help them understand.

How the Bible Relates

1. What is one way to be made right with God?

Your discussion here will be very important in setting the stage for God's offer of salvation later in the session. You see, most non-Christians today believe that this is the only way to be made right with God. (Sadly, some Christians do too.) Gently probe your group's understanding; it's important to know what they think before you can teach them the truth.

Explore that brief first statement in the Bible passage with some questions: **What do you think is "the law" referred to here? According to the Bible, who gave us this law?** If you haven't yet discussed what "the law" refers to, do so here (see explanation above). If necessary, read through it briefly again as it's found in Exodus 20 or Deuteronomy 5.

If we lived this law perfectly, what effect do you think it would have on our lives? On our relationship to God? Again, you have probably dealt with these questions in an earlier session, so you may need only to refresh group members' memories here. Help your group to see that if we were indeed able to follow God's law perfectly, our lives would be whole and our relationship with God would be without friction, guilt, or fear.

In other words, it is true: the law *can* make us right with God—but only if we are able to obey the law perfectly in every way. Keeping most of the commandments most of the time is not enough. If you think it may be helpful to your group, consider reading this passage from James 2:

> *A person might follow all of God's law. But if he fails to obey even one command, he is guilty of breaking all the commands in that law. God said, "You must not be guilty of adultery." The same God also said, "You must not murder anyone." So if you do not take part in adultery, but you murder someone, then you are guilty of breaking all of God's law.*

In the longer session, take a little more time to explore this. **How much does it take to break God's law? Does God intend these laws to apply only to our actions, or also to our thoughts and desires?** You may want to look with your group at Jesus' words in Matthew 5:27–28:

> *You have heard that it was said, "You must not be guilty of adultery." But I tell you that if anyone looks at a woman and wants to sin sexually with her, then he has already done that sin with the woman in his mind.*

What other commands of God are just as easy to break in thought as well as action? What about the sin of coveting? Murder? Lying? Help your group to see that if you look at the law of God in this way, it's almost impossible to claim that you are able to keep it perfectly.

Some group members might object that not everyone has heard of God's law or the Ten Commandments. In a literal sense, that may be true. But that does not mean that they are not aware of God's law. **In what way is this law "built in"—programmed into human beings? What part of our psychological makeup lets us know when we've done something right or wrong?** Talk about the role of conscience and how God has given everyone a built-in

152 Inspirit: Does God Want to Spoil My Fun? **LEADER GUIDE** Session 6

safeguard (even though it might be twisted or dulled after years of misuse).

If this question is an issue for some in your group, you may consider reading an excerpt from Romans 2 that was not included in today's passage:

> Many people . . . do not have the law. But . . . they show in their hearts they know what is right and wrong, just as the law commands. And they also show this by the way they feel about right and wrong. Sometimes their thoughts tell them they did wrong. And sometimes their thoughts tell them they did right. (Romans 2:15)

Finally, look at the element of control here. **How much control does this way of becoming right with God give us over our destiny? Over our relationship with God?** Note that this way of being made right with God gives the control entirely into the hands of the person who's trying to do it. That person is on his own, trying in his own efforts to keep his relationship with God open.

2. What is difficult, if not impossible, about this way?

At first glance, the idea of trying to get right with God by "living right" may seem workable to your group members. But, as you began to touch on in the previous question, it is not as easy as it seems at first. Help your group to see this by asking some of the following questions: **How many times have you done something absolutely perfectly—without mistakes—in your life? Or how many times have you told yourself, "I'm not going to do that"—and then gone ahead and done it anyway? Or said, "I'm *going* to do this"—and then failed to do it?** Their answers should show that our lives and even our best intentions are beset by weakness. It is rare, if it happens at all, that we actually do something absolutely perfectly.

How are all people the same, according to these verses? How do they measure up to God's glory? Why? Make sure that your group realizes that the condition of sin—the inability to follow God's law perfectly—is something that infects absolutely everyone. From drug dealers to terrorists to housewives to business executives, everyone has in common the fact that they have disobeyed God's law.

Do you think that God knows this about us? If so, then why did God give us the law—especially if he knew that we weren't going to be able to keep it perfectly? This question is an important one for your group. They need to hear that God *knows* our weaknesses. He didn't give us the law because he thought we would be able to keep it perfectly. He gave us the law to help us see our weakness and our need for him.

The law teaches us a valuable lesson: We are not God, and we are as much in need of God's forgiveness and undeserved kindness as everyone else. Something very good happens to us when we are able to say, "I'm not God. I can't do this on my own." We begin to let go of our need to control. We begin to face reality—the effects of sin in our daily lives.

In the longer session you may want to address this question: **"Why can't God just overlook our mistakes, if he loves us so much?"** In answer, you may find it helpful to ask group members to imagine that they are sitting in a court of law, waiting for a trial to begin. The defendant, a young man, is accused of driving recklessly under the influence of alcohol and of having killed a young mother and her child as a result.

As the trial progresses, it becomes clear that he did indeed commit this crime. The jury returns the verdict of guilty, and the judge turns to address the young man.

"It looks like you're guilty, son," he says kindly. "But I've taken such a liking to you that I can't really hold you guilty for this. I'm going to let you go free, with just a warning. Try not to do it again, okay?"

What are your responses to this judge's words? Why do you feel that way? What does his approach do to the integrity of the law, of what is right and wrong? Is his approach just? Why or why not? Your group will most likely feel a sense of outrage or at least discomfort with this judge's approach.

Then look at how this story relates to God's position as giver of a good and just law. **How is God's situation similar to that of the judge? How might it be unfair of God to let everyone off the hook, even if he loves them with a deep love?** Let the group wrestle with these questions for a few minutes. Then note that, fortunately, God has left us with another alternative.

3. What other way has God made for people to be made right with him?

It is important for your group members to catch the difference between this new way of being made right with God and the old way—the one they may have thought was the only way. Ask the Spirit to help them change their perspective from one of earning God's favor to one of receiving it as a free gift, with absolutely no strings attached.

Some of the following questions may help group members discover this for themselves: **How does the law figure into this way of being made right with God? Does God still expect us to be perfect? Or even close to perfect? What seems to be the only requirement in this way of being made right with God?**

These verses make it clear that obeying the law has absolutely nothing to do with this new way of being made right with God. No, God does not expect us to be perfect. He doesn't require that we be even half-good before he will accept and forgive us. He requires only one thing: faith in Jesus Christ.

At this point, if you haven't yet explained to your group who Jesus is and what the Bible means by "faith in Christ," do so here, using the explanation given above (see "What the Bible Tells Us") as a basis. Be sure to keep your explanation simple and free from any religious jargon that might be unfamiliar to members.

In the longer session, if you've used the illustration of the judge and the young offender, pursue that a little further here to give your group a clearer idea of what God is offering them in Jesus Christ. Ask them to suppose that the jury has convicted the young man of manslaughter and drunk driving. The judge looks at him sternly and says, "Son, your crime was terrible, and there is no excuse for it. Because of your carelessness, two lives were destroyed. The penalty is 45 years in prison without parole."

The young man begins to weep. He is obviously sorry for what he has done and terror-stricken at the thought of spending most of his life behind bars.

The judge looks at him with compassion and love. Suddenly he stands up, walks down from the judge's stand, and takes off his official robe. "Your sentence will stand," he says. "Justice must be carried out. But there is a provision in the law that if someone willingly takes your place and endures your sentence for you, then you may go free. I will take your place. You are free to go."

How does the judge's offer satisfy the demands of the law? How does it still uphold justice? From a technical point of view, the judge is making a legal offer that the law recognizes as acceptable. **How did Jesus offer to do the same thing for us? In what way has God himself acted like that judge?**

Look even more closely, however, at the "why" of this offer. **What moved the judge to make such an offer? What did he feel toward this young man? Do you think God might feel the same way toward us? Might God love us deeply, in spite of our weakness? If so, how has God proved his love?** Make sure that group members don't see this only as a cold legal transaction. John 3:16 says, "For God *so loved* the world, that he gave his one and only Son, that whoever believes in him shall not perish but have eternal life." Pray that group members will see, perhaps for the first time, that God truly loves them deeply and without any reservations. Ask the Spirit to help them respond to that love as you discuss these things together.

4. What happens when people put their faith in Jesus Christ?

Once people have accepted God's offer of forgiveness through Jesus Christ, something changes dramatically. **What is their relationship with God like, once they have put their faith in Jesus? What are they free from? What has God done with their sin?** This is truly good news that you have to share with your group members. Once they put their faith in Jesus, their relationship with God will be made right. They will be made "free from sin." God will forgive whatever sin they have committed. And the best part is this: It's absolutely free! **What price do people have to pay for being restored to God's favor? Do they have to buy it or earn it in some way? How does the Bible describe God's grace?** Look again at the words "free gift." You cannot emphasize this point enough: There is absolutely no way to earn God's friendship and his forgiveness. All the work has been done for us; it is out from under our control. All we can do now is to receive it, with thankfulness and a glad heart.

Make sure that your group members do not miss the point of Jesus' life, death, and resurrection. He was not merely a good teacher, as some would like to think. God did not send his only Son as a good example. Look at the passage closely. **Why did God give his Son, Jesus, to us? What did the blood of Jesus' death do for us?** This passage makes it clear that God's main desire in sending Jesus was that he would be able to forgive us—by taking our death sentence on himself.

Yet, in spite of this good news, many people today turn down this offer from God. What stands in the way of their accepting it? The next question will help your group members come to grips with what it will mean for them to say yes to God's free gift in Jesus Christ.

5. What would a person have to give up in order to put his or her faith in Jesus? What would that person gain, according to this passage?

There are a number of possible answers to the first question. Some of them will reveal something of what your members are struggling with as they consider the invitation to receive God's forgiveness as a free gift.

Help your group members think this through by asking the following questions: **How easy or difficult is it to admit that we can't achieve a right relationship with God through our own efforts? What do we have to acknowledge about ourselves? Why might that be hard?** Pride, a desire for control, a fear of giving up independence, a reluctance to admit sin, or an enjoyment of sinful behavior and a refusal to see its consequences—all these can stand in the way of our taking advantage of God's incredible offer.

As you deal with this important question, keep in mind that some people are willing to accept the offer of salvation, but fail to act in response to make Jesus Lord of their lives. Lordship, like sanctification, is a process. Sensitively challenge those who may need a push to put wheels on their faith, but be very careful not to threaten or overwhelm the genuinely seeking person who is for the first time seeing the need for Jesus as Savior. Yes, surrendering control means making Jesus *Lord*, but even Christians struggle with that. Don't discourage those new to the faith, but assure them that God honors and responds to his genuinely repentant, obedient children.

> In the longer session, encourage group members to talk honestly—and personally, if they feel safe enough—about their feelings and hesitations. If they sense that you are quick to listen and slow to judge, they may take the risk of opening up their feelings at this point. Acknowledge your own struggles in giving up control to God; talk about the fears that you may have faced in deciding to put your faith in Christ.

Then look at the positive side of this decision: what a person will gain. **What benefits have we discussed so far? What other things come to mind?** Here you might share some of the benefits you have experienced in your own life: peace of heart and mind, a growing Father/child relationship with God, freedom from a guilty conscience, strength to overcome certain problems or habits, a sense of relief at not having to be perfect or to have complete control any more.

> In the longer session, you may have a new Christian in your group who is willing to speak about how his or her life has changed. If so, you might ask that person to share what he or she has experienced as tangible benefits after having placed faith in Jesus and received God's forgiveness.

Affirm that God's offer is good right now, and that anyone who wishes to can simply pray and ask God to accept their faith in Jesus and forgive them completely. Explain that, as a result of this prayer, God will give them a completely new beginning, and God will consider them his children.

If you are using the shorter version of this study, you may not have time for personal prayer with members during the lesson time. Yet you may have some whose hearts are ready—even desperate—for the offer of new life in Christ.

So it's essential to let members know that you are available to talk with them during the coming weeks about what they've studied today. Note those who seem to be on the brink of committing their lives to Christ. Call them during the week. Follow up on their questions and their prayer requests. Find out who is interested in further Bible study—as a group or as individuals. By written notes or telephone, make sure that each group member feels your continuing love and support during the next few weeks.

> In the longer session, offer your group members the time they need to ask questions, talk, and pray

about God's offer through Jesus. You may find the following narrative helpful as you lead them through this discussion and prayer:

Listen now to what God is saying to you.

You may be aware of things in your life that keep you from coming near to God. You may have thought of God as someone who is unsympathetic, angry, and punishing. You may feel like you don't know how to pray to God or how to come near to him.

Listen to what God is saying to you through Jesus. He is an understanding, loving God. He knows first-hand what it's like to live in a sinful, broken world. He knows how hard it is to overcome the constant temptation to sin. He has already taken the punishment for your sin, clearing the way for you to come near to God.

So now come near to God. It's as simple as A–B–C:

*A*dmit that you have sinned, and that you need God's forgiveness.

*B*elieve that God loves you and that Jesus already paid the price for your sins.

*C*ommit your life to God in prayer, asking him to forgive your sins, make you his child, and fill you with his Holy Spirit.

Prayer of Commitment
Here's a prayer to help you draw near to God:

Dear God, I believe that you love me. Please forgive me for all the things in my life that stand between you and me. Thank you for giving your only Son, Jesus, to die for my sins.

Now help me to believe in Jesus with all my heart. Help me to really accept that you came into the world to save me, not to condemn me. I believe that my sins are completely forgiven because of what Jesus did for me. Help me to remember that what I did in the past no longer makes me feel guilty or unworthy of being your child.

Thank you that you are making me completely new, that you will teach me through the Bible how to be your child. Give me your Holy Spirit now, to help me pray and to teach me from your Word.

In Jesus' name, amen.

Do not pressure anyone to respond at this point; remember that they may need time to think, reflect, and pray about God's offer to them. They may need to hear it again from you, in a personal conversation or further Bible study. But let them know that God's offer is real and that they have a real hope for change and renewal in their lives.

When you discuss any questions that group members may have, let them know that you are available after the study or during the coming weeks to talk with them further about God's offer in Christ. Make sure they have your phone number and know what hours they can reach you. Encourage them as warmly as you can to contact you with any questions.

The Bottom Line

The final control—trying to earn our way into God's good graces—is impossible. Because we are unable to live a perfect life, that way is blocked for us. But God has made another way: He offers us his love and forgiveness on the basis of what his Son did for us. The question is, can we give up trying to control our destiny and allow God to do it for us? Can we acknowledge that happiness, success, and fulfillment in life is not found by doing it "my way," but rather by surrendering to him?

Use this summary to restate the heart of this session. If you have time, allow for any questions that remain or any responses that might have been held back until now. Don't prod or push; simply listen and allow God to open hearts to this message of good news.

Close your time with prayer, mentioning specific needs that have been shared during this session and previous ones. If you have not used the prayer and discussion suggested in the longer session, encourage group members to pray silently along with you as you read through the prayer written below. Suggest before you leave that they use this prayer during the week if they are considering God's offer of his free gift of forgiveness.

Prayer

God, help me to understand what you will do if I put my faith in Jesus Christ. Help me to get to know you better so that I can trust you with the control of my life. Amen.

A Final Word

A person is not made right with God by following the law. No! It is trusting in Jesus Christ that makes a person right with God. *(The apostle Paul in Galatians 2:16)*

Does God Want to Spoil My Fun?

6: "I Did It My Way"

Beginnings

List phrases and functions that have the word "control" in them (for example, quality control, control panel, etc.). Now list some of the things in your life that you can control. Also list some of the things you can't control. Why do you think control is important to people?

What's Happening Today

Control. Many people today believe control is the key to a better life. Perhaps that is because so many things seem out of control. Governments try to control out-of-control spending by requiring elaborate paperwork to verify every expenditure. Out-of-control violence has led to gun control laws and crime prevention legislation. In an era of political correctness, we even find that some people want to control what we may or may not think.

Laws are not the only means of controlling people; people try to control people as well. Husbands beat their wives in an attempt to control them. Wives withhold sexual favors from their husbands in an effort to control or manipulate what they want. Parents abuse their children in order to control their behavior. Both men and women play mind games with one another in an attempt to come out on top.

Some of these controls are good and necessary. It is good to control inappropriate behaviors, for example. Abuse is often simply control gone awry.

We try as much as possible to control the direction and destination of our lives. We try to control our reputation, our income, our standard of living. We work hard to set the right course for our career, for our financial security, and for our children's future happiness.

Sometimes control is an illusion, however. Laws cannot stop crime if people do not obey the laws. People cannot control other people if the person being controlled doesn't cooperate. (Have you ever been at the mercy of an uncooperative two-year-old throwing a temper tantrum in the grocery store?)

There is another aspect of our lives that is beyond our ability to control. Can we control what happens to us when we die? Where do we go? Can we, by trying hard enough, claim a right to be on God's good side? What does it take?

Some people believe that God is all about keeping rules. But the Bible lets us in on a secret: forget thinking you can keep the rules. God knows we're not perfect. He knows we're not in control: *he* is. Actually, the way God has things set up, there's not a thing we can do to earn our way into heaven. Read further to see how God has taken things out of our control.

What the Bible Tells Us

The law makes people right with God only if they obey what the law says....

But God has a way to make people right with him without the law.... God makes people right with himself through their faith in Jesus Christ. This is true for all who believe in Christ, because all are the same. All people have sinned and are not good enough for God's glory. People are made right with God by his grace, which is a free gift. They are made right with God by being made free from sin through Jesus Christ. God gave Jesus as a way to forgive sin through faith. And all of this is because of the blood of Jesus' death. (Romans 2:13–15; 3:21–25)

How the Bible Relates

1. What is one way to be made right with God?

2. What is difficult, if not impossible, about this way?

3. What other way has God made for people to be made right with him?

4. What happens when people put their faith in Jesus Christ?

5. What would a person have to give up in order to put his or her faith in Jesus? What would that person gain, according to this passage?

The Bottom Line

The final control—trying to earn our way into God's good graces—is impossible. Because we are unable to live a perfect life, that way is blocked for us. But God has made another way: He offers us his love and forgiveness on the basis of what his Son did for us. The question is, can we give up trying to control our destiny and allow God to do it for us? Can we acknowledge that happiness, success, and fulfillment in life is not found by doing it "my way," but rather by surrendering to him?

Prayer

God, help me to understand what you will do if I put my faith in Jesus Christ. Help me to get to know you better so that I can trust you with the control of my life. Amen.

A Final Word

A person is not made right with God by following the law. No! It is trusting in Jesus Christ that makes a person right with God.
(The apostle Paul in Galatians 2:16)

Does God Want to Spoil My Fun?

6: "I Did It My Way"

Beginnings

List phrases and functions that have the word "control" in them (for example, quality control, control panel, etc.). Now list some of the things in your life that you can control. Also list some of the things you can't control. Why do you think control is important to people?

What's Happening Today

Control. Many people today believe control is the key to a better life. Perhaps that is because so many things seem out of control. Governments try to control out-of-control spending by requiring elaborate paperwork to verify every expenditure. Out-of-control violence has led to gun control laws and crime prevention legislation. In an era of political correctness, we even find that some people want to control what we may or may not think.

Laws are not the only means of controlling people; people try to control people as well. Husbands beat their wives in an attempt to control them. Wives withhold sexual favors from their husbands in an effort to control or manipulate what they want. Parents abuse their children in order to control their behavior. Both men and women play mind games with one another in an attempt to come out on top.

Some of these controls are good and necessary. It is good to control inappropriate behaviors, for example. Abuse is often simply control gone awry.

We try as much as possible to control the direction and destination of our lives. We try to control our reputation, our income, our standard of living. We work hard to set the right course for our career, for our financial security, and for our children's future happiness.

Sometimes control is an illusion, however. Laws cannot stop crime if people do not obey the laws. People cannot control other people if the person being controlled doesn't cooperate. (Have you ever been at the mercy of an uncooperative two-year-old throwing a temper tantrum in the grocery store?)

There is another aspect of our lives that is beyond our ability to control. Can we control what happens to us when we die? Where do we go? Can we, by trying hard enough, claim a right to be on God's good side? What does it take?

Some people believe that God is all about keeping rules. But the Bible lets us in on a secret: forget thinking you can keep the rules. God knows we're not perfect. He knows we're not in control: *he* is. Actually, the way God has things set up, there's not a thing we can do to earn our way into heaven. Read further to see how God has taken things out of our control.

What the Bible Tells Us

The law makes people right with God only if they obey what the law says. . . .

But God has a way to make people right with him without the law. . . . God makes people right with himself through their faith in Jesus Christ. This is true for all who believe in Christ, because all are the same. All people have sinned and are not good enough for God's glory. People are made right with God by his grace, which is a free gift. They are made right with God by being made free from sin through Jesus Christ. God gave Jesus as a way to forgive sin through faith. And all of this is because of the blood of Jesus' death. (Romans 2:13–15; 3:21–25)

How the Bible Relates

1. What is one way to be made right with God?

2. What is difficult, if not impossible, about this way?

3. What other way has God made for people to be made right with him?

4. What happens when people put their faith in Jesus Christ?

5. What would a person have to give up in order to put his or her faith in Jesus? What would that person gain, according to this passage?

The Bottom Line

The final control—trying to earn our way into God's good graces—is impossible. Because we are unable to live a perfect life, that way is blocked for us. But God has made another way: He offers us his love and forgiveness on the basis of what his Son did for us. The question is, can we give up trying to control our destiny and allow God to do it for us? Can we acknowledge that happiness, success, and fulfillment in life is not found by doing it "my way," but rather by surrendering to him?

Prayer

God, help me to understand what you will do if I put my faith in Jesus Christ. Help me to get to know you better so that I can trust you with the control of my life. Amen.

A Final Word

A person is not made right with God by following the law. No! It is trusting in Jesus Christ that makes a person right with God.
(The apostle Paul in Galatians 2:16)

Does God Want to Spoil My Fun?

6: "I Did It My Way"

Beginnings

List phrases and functions that have the word "control" in them (for example, quality control, control panel, etc.). Now list some of the things in your life that you can control. Also list some of the things you can't control. Why do you think control is important to people?

What's Happening Today

Control. Many people today believe control is the key to a better life. Perhaps that is because so many things seem out of control. Governments try to control out-of-control spending by requiring elaborate paperwork to verify every expenditure. Out-of-control violence has led to gun control laws and crime prevention legislation. In an era of political correctness, we even find that some people want to control what we may or may not think.

Laws are not the only means of controlling people; people try to control people as well. Husbands beat their wives in an attempt to control them. Wives withhold sexual favors from their husbands in an effort to control or manipulate what they want. Parents abuse their children in order to control their behavior. Both men and women play mind games with one another in an attempt to come out on top.

Some of these controls are good and necessary. It is good to control inappropriate behaviors, for example. Abuse is often simply control gone awry.

We try as much as possible to control the direction and destination of our lives. We try to control our reputation, our income, our standard of living. We work hard to set the right course for our career, for our financial security, and for our children's future happiness.

Sometimes control is an illusion, however. Laws cannot stop crime if people do not obey the laws. People cannot control other people if the person being controlled doesn't cooperate. (Have you ever been at the mercy of an uncooperative two-year-old throwing a temper tantrum in the grocery store?)

There is another aspect of our lives that is beyond our ability to control. Can we control what happens to us when we die? Where do we go? Can we, by trying hard enough, claim a right to be on God's good side? What does it take?

Some people believe that God is all about keeping rules. But the Bible lets us in on a secret: forget thinking you can keep the rules. God knows we're not perfect. He knows we're not in control: *he* is. Actually, the way God has things set up, there's not a thing we can do to earn our way into heaven. Read further to see how God has taken things out of our control.

What the Bible Tells Us

The law makes people right with God only if they obey what the law says....

But God has a way to make people right with him without the law.... God makes people right with himself through their faith in Jesus Christ. This is true for all who believe in Christ, because all are the same. All people have sinned and are not good enough for God's glory. People are made right with God by his grace, which is a free gift. They are made right with God by being made free from sin through Jesus Christ. God gave Jesus as a way to forgive sin through faith. And all of this is because of the blood of Jesus' death. (Romans 2:13–15; 3:21–25)

How the Bible Relates

1. What is one way to be made right with God?

2. What is difficult, if not impossible, about this way?

3. What other way has God made for people to be made right with him?

4. What happens when people put their faith in Jesus Christ?

5. What would a person have to give up in order to put his or her faith in Jesus? What would that person gain, according to this passage?

Copyright ©1994 Church Development Resources   It is illegal to copy this material without permission.

The Bottom Line

The final control—trying to earn our way into God's good graces—is impossible. Because we are unable to live a perfect life, that way is blocked for us. But God has made another way: He offers us his love and forgiveness on the basis of what his Son did for us. The question is, can we give up trying to control our destiny and allow God to do it for us? Can we acknowledge that happiness, success, and fulfillment in life is not found by doing it "my way," but rather by surrendering to him?

Prayer

God, help me to understand what you will do if I put my faith in Jesus Christ. Help me to get to know you better so that I can trust you with the control of my life. Amen.

A Final Word

A person is not made right with God by following the law. No! It is trusting in Jesus Christ that makes a person right with God. *(The apostle Paul in Galatians 2:16)*

Does God Want to Spoil My Fun?

6: "I Did It My Way"

Beginnings

List phrases and functions that have the word "control" in them (for example, quality control, control panel, etc.). Now list some of the things in your life that you can control. Also list some of the things you can't control. Why do you think control is important to people?

What's Happening Today

Control. Many people today believe control is the key to a better life. Perhaps that is because so many things seem out of control. Governments try to control out-of-control spending by requiring elaborate paperwork to verify every expenditure. Out-of-control violence has led to gun control laws and crime prevention legislation. In an era of political correctness, we even find that some people want to control what we may or may not think.

Laws are not the only means of controlling people; people try to control people as well. Husbands beat their wives in an attempt to control them. Wives withhold sexual favors from their husbands in an effort to control or manipulate what they want. Parents abuse their children in order to control their behavior. Both men and women play mind games with one another in an attempt to come out on top.

Some of these controls are good and necessary. It is good to control inappropriate behaviors, for example. Abuse is often simply control gone awry.

We try as much as possible to control the direction and destination of our lives. We try to control our reputation, our income, our standard of living. We work hard to set the right course for our career, for our financial security, and for our children's future happiness.

Sometimes control is an illusion, however. Laws cannot stop crime if people do not obey the laws. People cannot control other people if the person being controlled doesn't cooperate. (Have you ever been at the mercy of an uncooperative two-year-old throwing a temper tantrum in the grocery store?)

There is another aspect of our lives that is beyond our ability to control. Can we control what happens to us when we die? Where do we go? Can we, by trying hard enough, claim a right to be on God's good side? What does it take?

Some people believe that God is all about keeping rules. But the Bible lets us in on a secret: forget thinking you can keep the rules. God knows we're not perfect. He knows we're not in control: *he* is. Actually, the way God has things set up, there's not a thing we can do to earn our way into heaven. Read further to see how God has taken things out of our control.

What the Bible Tells Us

The law makes people right with God only if they obey what the law says. . . .

But God has a way to make people right with him without the law. . . . God makes people right with himself through their faith in Jesus Christ. This is true for all who believe in Christ, because all are the same. All people have sinned and are not good enough for God's glory. People are made right with God by his grace, which is a free gift. They are made right with God by being made free from sin through Jesus Christ. God gave Jesus as a way to forgive sin through faith. And all of this is because of the blood of Jesus' death. (Romans 2:13–15; 3:21–25)

How the Bible Relates

1. What is one way to be made right with God?

2. What is difficult, if not impossible, about this way?

3. What other way has God made for people to be made right with him?

4. What happens when people put their faith in Jesus Christ?

5. What would a person have to give up in order to put his or her faith in Jesus? What would that person gain, according to this passage?

The Bottom Line

The final control—trying to earn our way into God's good graces—is impossible. Because we are unable to live a perfect life, that way is blocked for us. But God has made another way: He offers us his love and forgiveness on the basis of what his Son did for us. The question is, can we give up trying to control our destiny and allow God to do it for us? Can we acknowledge that happiness, success, and fulfillment in life is not found by doing it "my way," but rather by surrendering to him?

Prayer

God, help me to understand what you will do if I put my faith in Jesus Christ. Help me to get to know you better so that I can trust you with the control of my life. Amen.

A Final Word

A person is not made right with God by following the law. No! It is trusting in Jesus Christ that makes a person right with God. *(The apostle Paul in Galatians 2:16)*

Does God Want to Spoil My Fun?

6: "I Did It My Way"

Beginnings

List phrases and functions that have the word "control" in them (for example, quality control, control panel, etc.). Now list some of the things in your life that you can control. Also list some of the things you can't control. Why do you think control is important to people?

What's Happening Today

Control. Many people today believe control is the key to a better life. Perhaps that is because so many things seem out of control. Governments try to control out-of-control spending by requiring elaborate paperwork to verify every expenditure. Out-of-control violence has led to gun control laws and crime prevention legislation. In an era of political correctness, we even find that some people want to control what we may or may not think.

Laws are not the only means of controlling people; people try to control people as well. Husbands beat their wives in an attempt to control them. Wives withhold sexual favors from their husbands in an effort to control or manipulate what they want. Parents abuse their children in order to control their behavior. Both men and women play mind games with one another in an attempt to come out on top.

Some of these controls are good and necessary. It is good to control inappropriate behaviors, for example. Abuse is often simply control gone awry.

We try as much as possible to control the direction and destination of our lives. We try to control our reputation, our income, our standard of living. We work hard to set the right course for our career, for our financial security, and for our children's future happiness.

Sometimes control is an illusion, however. Laws cannot stop crime if people do not obey the laws. People cannot control other people if the person being controlled doesn't cooperate. (Have you ever been at the mercy of an uncooperative two-year-old throwing a temper tantrum in the grocery store?)

There is another aspect of our lives that is beyond our ability to control. Can we control what happens to us when we die? Where do we go? Can we, by trying hard enough, claim a right to be on God's good side? What does it take?

Some people believe that God is all about keeping rules. But the Bible lets us in on a secret: forget thinking you can keep the rules. God knows we're not perfect. He knows we're not in control: *he* is. Actually, the way God has things set up, there's not a thing we can do to earn our way into heaven. Read further to see how God has taken things out of our control.

What the Bible Tells Us

The law makes people right with God only if they obey what the law says....

But God has a way to make people right with him without the law.... God makes people right with himself through their faith in Jesus Christ. This is true for all who believe in Christ, because all are the same. All people have sinned and are not good enough for God's glory. People are made right with God by his grace, which is a free gift. They are made right with God by being made free from sin through Jesus Christ. God gave Jesus as a way to forgive sin through faith. And all of this is because of the blood of Jesus' death. (Romans 2:13–15; 3:21–25)

How the Bible Relates

1. What is one way to be made right with God?

2. What is difficult, if not impossible, about this way?

3. What other way has God made for people to be made right with him?

4. What happens when people put their faith in Jesus Christ?

5. What would a person have to give up in order to put his or her faith in Jesus? What would that person gain, according to this passage?

Copyright ©1994 Church Development Resources   It is illegal to copy this material without permission.

The Bottom Line

The final control—trying to earn our way into God's good graces—is impossible. Because we are unable to live a perfect life, that way is blocked for us. But God has made another way: He offers us his love and forgiveness on the basis of what his Son did for us. The question is, can we give up trying to control our destiny and allow God to do it for us? Can we acknowledge that happiness, success, and fulfillment in life is not found by doing it "my way," but rather by surrendering to him?

Prayer

God, help me to understand what you will do if I put my faith in Jesus Christ. Help me to get to know you better so that I can trust you with the control of my life. Amen.

A Final Word

A person is not made right with God by following the law. No! It is trusting in Jesus Christ that makes a person right with God.
(The apostle Paul in Galatians 2:16)

Does God Want to Spoil My Fun?

6: "I Did It My Way"

Beginnings

List phrases and functions that have the word "control" in them (for example, quality control, control panel, etc.). Now list some of the things in your life that you can control. Also list some of the things you can't control. Why do you think control is important to people?

What's Happening Today

Control. Many people today believe control is the key to a better life. Perhaps that is because so many things seem out of control. Governments try to control out-of-control spending by requiring elaborate paperwork to verify every expenditure. Out-of-control violence has led to gun control laws and crime prevention legislation. In an era of political correctness, we even find that some people want to control what we may or may not think.

Laws are not the only means of controlling people; people try to control people as well. Husbands beat their wives in an attempt to control them. Wives withhold sexual favors from their husbands in an effort to control or manipulate what they want. Parents abuse their children in order to control their behavior. Both men and women play mind games with one another in an attempt to come out on top.

Some of these controls are good and necessary. It is good to control inappropriate behaviors, for example. Abuse is often simply control gone awry.

We try as much as possible to control the direction and destination of our lives. We try to control our reputation, our income, our standard of living. We work hard to set the right course for our career, for our financial security, and for our children's future happiness.

Sometimes control is an illusion, however. Laws cannot stop crime if people do not obey the laws. People cannot control other people if the person being controlled doesn't cooperate. (Have you ever been at the mercy of an uncooperative two-year-old throwing a temper tantrum in the grocery store?)

There is another aspect of our lives that is beyond our ability to control. Can we control what happens to us when we die? Where do we go? Can we, by trying hard enough, claim a right to be on God's good side? What does it take?

Some people believe that God is all about keeping rules. But the Bible lets us in on a secret: forget thinking you can keep the rules. God knows we're not perfect. He knows we're not in control: *he* is. Actually, the way God has things set up, there's not a thing we can do to earn our way into heaven. Read further to see how God has taken things out of our control.

What the Bible Tells Us

The law makes people right with God only if they obey what the law says....

But God has a way to make people right with him without the law.... God makes people right with himself through their faith in Jesus Christ. This is true for all who believe in Christ, because all are the same. All people have sinned and are not good enough for God's glory. People are made right with God by his grace, which is a free gift. They are made right with God by being made free from sin through Jesus Christ. God gave Jesus as a way to forgive sin through faith. And all of this is because of the blood of Jesus' death. (Romans 2:13–15; 3:21–25)

How the Bible Relates

1. What is one way to be made right with God?

2. What is difficult, if not impossible, about this way?

3. What other way has God made for people to be made right with him?

4. What happens when people put their faith in Jesus Christ?

5. What would a person have to give up in order to put his or her faith in Jesus? What would that person gain, according to this passage?

Copyright ©1994 Church Development Resources   It is illegal to copy this material without permission.

The Bottom Line

The final control—trying to earn our way into God's good graces—is impossible. Because we are unable to live a perfect life, that way is blocked for us. But God has made another way: He offers us his love and forgiveness on the basis of what his Son did for us. The question is, can we give up trying to control our destiny and allow God to do it for us? Can we acknowledge that happiness, success, and fulfillment in life is not found by doing it "my way," but rather by surrendering to him?

Prayer

God, help me to understand what you will do if I put my faith in Jesus Christ. Help me to get to know you better so that I can trust you with the control of my life. Amen.

A Final Word

A person is not made right with God by following the law. No! It is trusting in Jesus Christ that makes a person right with God. *(The apostle Paul in Galatians 2:16)*

Does God Want to Spoil My Fun?

6: "I Did It My Way"

Beginnings

List phrases and functions that have the word "control" in them (for example, quality control, control panel, etc.). Now list some of the things in your life that you can control. Also list some of the things you can't control. Why do you think control is important to people?

What's Happening Today

Control. Many people today believe control is the key to a better life. Perhaps that is because so many things seem out of control. Governments try to control out-of-control spending by requiring elaborate paperwork to verify every expenditure. Out-of-control violence has led to gun control laws and crime prevention legislation. In an era of political correctness, we even find that some people want to control what we may or may not think.

Laws are not the only means of controlling people; people try to control people as well. Husbands beat their wives in an attempt to control them. Wives withhold sexual favors from their husbands in an effort to control or manipulate what they want. Parents abuse their children in order to control their behavior. Both men and women play mind games with one another in an attempt to come out on top.

Some of these controls are good and necessary. It is good to control inappropriate behaviors, for example. Abuse is often simply control gone awry.

We try as much as possible to control the direction and destination of our lives. We try to control our reputation, our income, our standard of living. We work hard to set the right course for our career, for our financial security, and for our children's future happiness.

Sometimes control is an illusion, however. Laws cannot stop crime if people do not obey the laws. People cannot control other people if the person being controlled doesn't cooperate. (Have you ever been at the mercy of an uncooperative two-year-old throwing a temper tantrum in the grocery store?)

There is another aspect of our lives that is beyond our ability to control. Can we control what happens to us when we die? Where do we go? Can we, by trying hard enough, claim a right to be on God's good side? What does it take?

Some people believe that God is all about keeping rules. But the Bible lets us in on a secret: forget thinking you can keep the rules. God knows we're not perfect. He knows we're not in control: *he* is. Actually, the way God has things set up, there's not a thing we can do to earn our way into heaven. Read further to see how God has taken things out of our control.

What the Bible Tells Us

The law makes people right with God only if they obey what the law says. . . .

But God has a way to make people right with him without the law. . . . God makes people right with himself through their faith in Jesus Christ. This is true for all who believe in Christ, because all are the same. All people have sinned and are not good enough for God's glory. People are made right with God by his grace, which is a free gift. They are made right with God by being made free from sin through Jesus Christ. God gave Jesus as a way to forgive sin through faith. And all of this is because of the blood of Jesus' death. (Romans 2:13–15; 3:21–25)

How the Bible Relates

1. What is one way to be made right with God?

2. What is difficult, if not impossible, about this way?

3. What other way has God made for people to be made right with him?

4. What happens when people put their faith in Jesus Christ?

5. What would a person have to give up in order to put his or her faith in Jesus? What would that person gain, according to this passage?

Copyright ©1994 Church Development Resources   It is illegal to copy this material without permission.

The Bottom Line

The final control—trying to earn our way into God's good graces—is impossible. Because we are unable to live a perfect life, that way is blocked for us. But God has made another way: He offers us his love and forgiveness on the basis of what his Son did for us. The question is, can we give up trying to control our destiny and allow God to do it for us? Can we acknowledge that happiness, success, and fulfillment in life is not found by doing it "my way," but rather by surrendering to him?

Prayer

God, help me to understand what you will do if I put my faith in Jesus Christ. Help me to get to know you better so that I can trust you with the control of my life. Amen.

A Final Word

A person is not made right with God by following the law. No! It is trusting in Jesus Christ that makes a person right with God. *(The apostle Paul in Galatians 2:16)*

Does God Want to Spoil My Fun?

6: "I Did It My Way"

Beginnings

List phrases and functions that have the word "control" in them (for example, quality control, control panel, etc.). Now list some of the things in your life that you can control. Also list some of the things you can't control. Why do you think control is important to people?

What's Happening Today

Control. Many people today believe control is the key to a better life. Perhaps that is because so many things seem out of control. Governments try to control out-of-control spending by requiring elaborate paperwork to verify every expenditure. Out-of-control violence has led to gun control laws and crime prevention legislation. In an era of political correctness, we even find that some people want to control what we may or may not think.

Laws are not the only means of controlling people; people try to control people as well. Husbands beat their wives in an attempt to control them. Wives withhold sexual favors from their husbands in an effort to control or manipulate what they want. Parents abuse their children in order to control their behavior. Both men and women play mind games with one another in an attempt to come out on top.

Some of these controls are good and necessary. It is good to control inappropriate behaviors, for example. Abuse is often simply control gone awry.

We try as much as possible to control the direction and destination of our lives. We try to control our reputation, our income, our standard of living. We work hard to set the right course for our career, for our financial security, and for our children's future happiness.

Sometimes control is an illusion, however. Laws cannot stop crime if people do not obey the laws. People cannot control other people if the person being controlled doesn't cooperate. (Have you ever been at the mercy of an uncooperative two-year-old throwing a temper tantrum in the grocery store?)

There is another aspect of our lives that is beyond our ability to control. Can we control what happens to us when we die? Where do we go? Can we, by trying hard enough, claim a right to be on God's good side? What does it take?

Some people believe that God is all about keeping rules. But the Bible lets us in on a secret: forget thinking you can keep the rules. God knows we're not perfect. He knows we're not in control: *he* is. Actually, the way God has things set up, there's not a thing we can do to earn our way into heaven. Read further to see how God has taken things out of our control.

What the Bible Tells Us

The law makes people right with God only if they obey what the law says....

But God has a way to make people right with him without the law.... God makes people right with himself through their faith in Jesus Christ. This is true for all who believe in Christ, because all are the same. All people have sinned and are not good enough for God's glory. People are made right with God by his grace, which is a free gift. They are made right with God by being made free from sin through Jesus Christ. God gave Jesus as a way to forgive sin through faith. And all of this is because of the blood of Jesus' death. (Romans 2:13–15; 3:21–25)

How the Bible Relates

1. What is one way to be made right with God?

2. What is difficult, if not impossible, about this way?

3. What other way has God made for people to be made right with him?

4. What happens when people put their faith in Jesus Christ?

5. What would a person have to give up in order to put his or her faith in Jesus? What would that person gain, according to this passage?

Copyright ©1994 Church Development Resources   It is illegal to copy this material without permission.

The Bottom Line

The final control—trying to earn our way into God's good graces—is impossible. Because we are unable to live a perfect life, that way is blocked for us. But God has made another way: He offers us his love and forgiveness on the basis of what his Son did for us. The question is, can we give up trying to control our destiny and allow God to do it for us? Can we acknowledge that happiness, success, and fulfillment in life is not found by doing it "my way," but rather by surrendering to him?

Prayer

God, help me to understand what you will do if I put my faith in Jesus Christ. Help me to get to know you better so that I can trust you with the control of my life. Amen.

A Final Word

A person is not made right with God by following the law. No! It is trusting in Jesus Christ that makes a person right with God. *(The apostle Paul in Galatians 2:16)*

Does God Want to Spoil My Fun?

6: "I Did It My Way"

Beginnings

List phrases and functions that have the word "control" in them (for example, quality control, control panel, etc.). Now list some of the things in your life that you can control. Also list some of the things you can't control. Why do you think control is important to people?

What's Happening Today

Control. Many people today believe control is the key to a better life. Perhaps that is because so many things seem out of control. Governments try to control out-of-control spending by requiring elaborate paperwork to verify every expenditure. Out-of-control violence has led to gun control laws and crime prevention legislation. In an era of political correctness, we even find that some people want to control what we may or may not think.

Laws are not the only means of controlling people; people try to control people as well. Husbands beat their wives in an attempt to control them. Wives withhold sexual favors from their husbands in an effort to control or manipulate what they want. Parents abuse their children in order to control their behavior. Both men and women play mind games with one another in an attempt to come out on top.

Some of these controls are good and necessary. It is good to control inappropriate behaviors, for example. Abuse is often simply control gone awry.

We try as much as possible to control the direction and destination of our lives. We try to control our reputation, our income, our standard of living. We work hard to set the right course for our career, for our financial security, and for our children's future happiness.

Sometimes control is an illusion, however. Laws cannot stop crime if people do not obey the laws. People cannot control other people if the person being controlled doesn't cooperate. (Have you ever been at the mercy of an uncooperative two-year-old throwing a temper tantrum in the grocery store?)

There is another aspect of our lives that is beyond our ability to control. Can we control what happens to us when we die? Where do we go? Can we, by trying hard enough, claim a right to be on God's good side? What does it take?

Some people believe that God is all about keeping rules. But the Bible lets us in on a secret: forget thinking you can keep the rules. God knows we're not perfect. He knows we're not in control: *he* is. Actually, the way God has things set up, there's not a thing we can do to earn our way into heaven. Read further to see how God has taken things out of our control.

What the Bible Tells Us

The law makes people right with God only if they obey what the law says. . . .

But God has a way to make people right with him without the law. . . . God makes people right with himself through their faith in Jesus Christ. This is true for all who believe in Christ, because all are the same. All people have sinned and are not good enough for God's glory. People are made right with God by his grace, which is a free gift. They are made right with God by being made free from sin through Jesus Christ. God gave Jesus as a way to forgive sin through faith. And all of this is because of the blood of Jesus' death. (Romans 2:13–15; 3:21–25)

How the Bible Relates

1. What is one way to be made right with God?
2. What is difficult, if not impossible, about this way?
3. What other way has God made for people to be made right with him?
4. What happens when people put their faith in Jesus Christ?
5. What would a person have to give up in order to put his or her faith in Jesus? What would that person gain, according to this passage?

Copyright ©1994 Church Development Resources   It is illegal to copy this material without permission.

The Bottom Line

The final control—trying to earn our way into God's good graces—is impossible. Because we are unable to live a perfect life, that way is blocked for us. But God has made another way: He offers us his love and forgiveness on the basis of what his Son did for us. The question is, can we give up trying to control our destiny and allow God to do it for us? Can we acknowledge that happiness, success, and fulfillment in life is not found by doing it "my way," but rather by surrendering to him?

Prayer

God, help me to understand what you will do if I put my faith in Jesus Christ. Help me to get to know you better so that I can trust you with the control of my life. Amen.

A Final Word

A person is not made right with God by following the law. No! It is trusting in Jesus Christ that makes a person right with God. *(The apostle Paul in Galatians 2:16)*

Does God Want to Spoil My Fun?

6: "I Did It My Way"

Beginnings

List phrases and functions that have the word "control" in them (for example, quality control, control panel, etc.). Now list some of the things in your life that you can control. Also list some of the things you can't control. Why do you think control is important to people?

What's Happening Today

Control. Many people today believe control is the key to a better life. Perhaps that is because so many things seem out of control. Governments try to control out-of-control spending by requiring elaborate paperwork to verify every expenditure. Out-of-control violence has led to gun control laws and crime prevention legislation. In an era of political correctness, we even find that some people want to control what we may or may not think.

Laws are not the only means of controlling people; people try to control people as well. Husbands beat their wives in an attempt to control them. Wives withhold sexual favors from their husbands in an effort to control or manipulate what they want. Parents abuse their children in order to control their behavior. Both men and women play mind games with one another in an attempt to come out on top.

Some of these controls are good and necessary. It is good to control inappropriate behaviors, for example. Abuse is often simply control gone awry.

We try as much as possible to control the direction and destination of our lives. We try to control our reputation, our income, our standard of living. We work hard to set the right course for our career, for our financial security, and for our children's future happiness.

Sometimes control is an illusion, however. Laws cannot stop crime if people do not obey the laws. People cannot control other people if the person being controlled doesn't cooperate. (Have you ever been at the mercy of an uncooperative two-year-old throwing a temper tantrum in the grocery store?)

There is another aspect of our lives that is beyond our ability to control. Can we control what happens to us when we die? Where do we go? Can we, by trying hard enough, claim a right to be on God's good side? What does it take?

Some people believe that God is all about keeping rules. But the Bible lets us in on a secret: forget thinking you can keep the rules. God knows we're not perfect. He knows we're not in control: *he* is. Actually, the way God has things set up, there's not a thing we can do to earn our way into heaven. Read further to see how God has taken things out of our control.

What the Bible Tells Us

The law makes people right with God only if they obey what the law says....

But God has a way to make people right with him without the law.... God makes people right with himself through their faith in Jesus Christ. This is true for all who believe in Christ, because all are the same. All people have sinned and are not good enough for God's glory. People are made right with God by his grace, which is a free gift. They are made right with God by being made free from sin through Jesus Christ. God gave Jesus as a way to forgive sin through faith. And all of this is because of the blood of Jesus' death. (Romans 2:13–15; 3:21–25)

How the Bible Relates

1. What is one way to be made right with God?
2. What is difficult, if not impossible, about this way?
3. What other way has God made for people to be made right with him?
4. What happens when people put their faith in Jesus Christ?
5. What would a person have to give up in order to put his or her faith in Jesus? What would that person gain, according to this passage?

Copyright ©1994 Church Development Resources   It is illegal to copy this material without permission.

The Bottom Line

The final control—trying to earn our way into God's good graces—is impossible. Because we are unable to live a perfect life, that way is blocked for us. But God has made another way: He offers us his love and forgiveness on the basis of what his Son did for us. The question is, can we give up trying to control our destiny and allow God to do it for us? Can we acknowledge that happiness, success, and fulfillment in life is not found by doing it "my way," but rather by surrendering to him?

Prayer

God, help me to understand what you will do if I put my faith in Jesus Christ. Help me to get to know you better so that I can trust you with the control of my life. Amen.

A Final Word

A person is not made right with God by following the law. No! It is trusting in Jesus Christ that makes a person right with God.
(The apostle Paul in Galatians 2:16)

Instrument Procedures

JEPPESEN
A BOEING COMPANY

Jeppesen is a registered trademark of Jeppesen Sanderson, Inc. All other trademarks, registered trademarks, product names, and company names or logos mentioned herein are the property of their respective owners.

All rights reserved. No part of this publication may be reproduced, stored in a retrieval system, or transmitted in any form or by any means, electronic, mechanical, photocopying, recording, or otherwise, without the prior permission of the publisher.

The charts, tables, and graphs used in this publication are for illustration purposes only and cannot be used for navigation or to determine actual aircraft performance.

ISBN-13: 978-0-88487-330-3

Jeppesen
55 Inverness Drive East
Englewood, CO 80112-5498
Web Site: www.jeppesen.com
Email: Captain@jeppesen.com
Copyright © Jeppesen
All Rights Reserved. Published 2004, 2011, 2014
Printed in the United States of America

10001933-001

INTRODUCTION

The *Instrument Procedures Guide* is designed primarily as a technical reference for instrument-rated pilots who are pursuing careers as pilots, and for professional pilots using Jeppesen charts who are conducting flights under IFR in the National Airspace System (NAS). Certificated instrument flight instructors, instrument-rated pilots, and instrument students who want to enhance their knowledge of instrument procedures and the IFR environment also will find this guide a valuable training aid.

Chapter 1 provides an overview of IFR operations in the NAS and highlights the latest equipment, facilities, and services that enable safe and efficient IFR operations. Chapters 2 through 5 provide expanded and detailed coverage of Jeppesen instrument charts and of instrument procedures during all phases of flight under IFR including takeoff and departure, enroute, arrival, and approach. Although the emphasis of this guide is airplane operations, Chapter 6 includes guidelines specific to helicopter IFR operations. The *Instrument Procedures Guide* also explores IFR safety topics such as runway incursion, land and hold short operations (LAHSO), and controlled flight into terrain (CFIT).

Appendix A is a useful reference for airborne navigation databases and Appendix B provides valuable information about instrument procedure design to help ensure you stay within protected airspace. Appendix C contains an extensive list of acronyms and a glossary that defines important terms used throughout the guide.

To use the *Instrument Procedures Guide* most effectively, you should also be familiar with the applicable sections of the *Aeronautical Information Manual* (AIM) and of Title 14 of the Code of Regulations (14 CFR), referred to in this guide as the Federal Aviation Regulations (FARs). Occasionally, this guide uses the word "must" or similar language where the desired action is deemed critical. The use of such language is not intended to add to, interpret, or relieve pilots of their responsibility imposed by 14 CFR.

Jeppesen supplies a wide variety of products in both electronic and print formats that you can use in combination with the Instrument Procedures Guide, such as IFR enroute and terminal charts, the FAR/AIM, and reprints of the Instrument Rating and Airline Transport Pilot Practical Test Standards. The Jeppesen *Instrument/Commercial* textbook, available as an e-book or in print, provides clear and concise content essential to obtaining an instrument rating and can be used as a reference for fundamental IFR concepts.

For information about Jeppesen products and services, contact Jeppesen at:
Web Site: www.jeppesen.com
Online Store: jeppdirect.jeppesen.com

You can forward comments regarding the *Instrument Procedures Guide* to:
Jeppesen Aviation Training Solutions
55 Inverness Drive East
Englewood CO 80112-5498
Email: Captain@Jeppesen.com

CONTENTS

Chapter 1 — IFR Operations in the National Airspace System

NAS Safety 1-1
  Controlled Flight Into Terrain Prevention 1-1
  Runway Incursion Avoidance 1-2
    Planning 1-2
    Situational Awareness 1-3
    Written Taxi Instructions 1-3
    Flight Crew Verbal Communication 1-3
    ATC/Pilot Communication 1-3
    Taxi 1-4
    Exterior Aircraft Lighting 1-4
  Approach and Landing Accident Reduction 1-4
NAS Components 1-5
  Users 1-5
    Airlines 1-5
    Air Charter 1-6
    General Aviation 1-6
    Military 1-6
  ATC Facilities 1-6
    Air Traffic Control System Command Center 1-7
    Air Route Traffic Control Center 1-7
    Terminal Radar Approach Control 1-7
    Air Traffic Control Tower 1-8
    Flight Service 1-8
NAS Design 1-9
  FAA Radar Systems 1-9
    Air Route Surveillance Radar 1-9
    Airport Surveillance Radar 1-9
    Precision Runway Monitor 1-10
  Automatic Dependent Surveillance-Broadcast 1-10
    Traffic Information 1-12
    Flight Information Service-Broadcast 1-12
  Performance-Based Navigation 1-12
    RNAV 1-12
      Wide Area Augmentation System 1-12
      Ground-Based Augmentation System 1-14
      RNAV (GPS) Approach Equipment 1-14
    RNP 1-14
    PBN Dashboard 1-16
    Optimized Profile Descent 1-17
    Reduced Vertical Separation Minimums 1-17
NAS Tools 1-17
  Flight Preparation 1-17
    Common Support Services-Weather 1-17
    Flight Plans 1-18
    Electronic Flight Bag 1-18
    Release Times 1-19
    IFR Slots 1-19
  Surface Movement 1-20
    Surface Movement Guidance and Control System 1-20
    Airport Surface Detection Equipment-Model X 1-20
    EFB-Surface Movement 1-21
  Flight Operations 1-21
    Aircraft Communications Addressing and Reporting System ... 1-21

Data Communications	1-22
Advanced Technologies and Oceanic Procedures	1-22
Aviation Environmental Design Tool	1-22
Collision Avoidance Systems	1-22
Vision Systems	1-23
Enhanced and Synthetic Vision Systems	1-23
Combined Vision System	1-23
Enhanced Flight Vision System	1-24
Automated Terminal Proximity Alert	1-24
Flight Management System	1-24
EFB-Enroute and Approach	1-24
Disseminating Aeronautical Information	1-24
Publication Criteria	1-25
Jeppesen Charts and Flight Information	1-26
IFR Enroute Low Altitude Charts	1-26
IFR Enroute High Altitude Charts	1-28
Terminal Charts	1-30
Airport Qualification Charts	1-31
Jeppesen NOTAM Service	1-32

Chapter 2 — Takeoffs And Departures

Surface Movement Safety	2-1
Taxi Diagram and Airport Moving Map	2-1
Airport Charts	2-2
Airport Signs/Markings/Lighting	2-3
SMGCS Low Visibility Taxi Plans	2-4
Runway Hot Spots	2-6
Standard Taxi Routes	2-7
Runway Safety	2-7
Takeoff Minimums	2-8
Operations Specifications	2-8
Takeoff Minimum Considerations	2-9
Ceiling and Visibility Requirements	2-9
Runway Visual Range	2-9
Prevailing Visibility	2-10
Tower Visibility	2-10
Automated Weather Observing Systems and Automated Surface Observing Systems	2-11
Automatic Terminal Information Service and Digital ATIS	2-12
IFR Alternate Minimums	2-12
Part 91 Alternate Requirements	2-12
Part 121 and Part 135 Requirements	2-13
Departure Procedures	2-13
Obstacle Departure Procedures	2-14
Standard Instrument Departures	2-14
Vector SIDs	2-17
Pilot Navigation SIDs	2-18
RNAV SIDs	2-19
Departure Procedure Responsibility	2-20
Procedures Assigned by ATC	2-20
Procedures Not Assigned by ATC	2-21
Departures from Tower-Controlled Airports	2-21
Departures from Airports Without an Operating Control Tower	2-21
Radar Departure	2-22
Noise Abatement Procedures	2-22
Safety Considerations	2-22
Sterile Cockpit	2-24
CFIT Prevention	2-24

Chapter 3 — Enroute Operations

Air Route Traffic Control Centers ... 3-1
IFR Navigation ... 3-2
    VHF Airways/Routes ... 3-2
        Navaid Service Volume ... 3-3
        Navigational Gaps ... 3-3
        Changeover Points ... 3-3
    RNAV Routes ... 3-4
        Waypoints ... 3-4
            User-Defined Waypoints ... 3-4
            Floating Waypoints ... 3-5
            Database Identifiers ... 3-5
            Navigation Reference System ... 3-5
        RNAV Route Planning ... 3-6
            Q-Routes ... 3-6
            Random RNAV Routes ... 3-6
            Non-Restrictive Routing ... 3-7
            T-Routes ... 3-8
    LF Airways/Routes ... 3-8
    Preferred IFR Routes ... 3-8
    Tower Enroute Control ... 3-9
    Route Designators ... 3-10
        Use of Designators in Communications ... 3-10
IFR Enroute Altitudes ... 3-10
    Minimum Enroute Altitude ... 3-11
    Minimum Crossing Altitude ... 3-11
    Minimum Obstruction Clearance Altitude ... 3-12
    Minimum Reception Altitude ... 3-12
    Maximum Authorized Altitude ... 3-12
    Minimum Vectoring Altitude ... 3-13
    Minimum Off-Route Altitude ... 3-13
    IFR Cruising Altitude or Flight Level ... 3-14
    Lowest Usable Flight Level ... 3-14
Reporting Procedures ... 3-15
    Nonradar Position Reports ... 3-16
Communication Failure ... 3-16
Climbing and Descending Enroute ... 3-17
    Climb at Pilot's Discretion ... 3-17
    Expedite Climb ... 3-17
    Descent Clearances ... 3-18
Holding Procedures ... 3-18
    ATC Holding Instructions ... 3-18
    Maximum Holding Speed ... 3-20
    High-Performance Holding ... 3-20
Fuel State Awareness ... 3-20
Required Navigation Performance ... 3-20
Reduced Vertical Separation Minimums ... 3-22
Diversion Procedures ... 3-22

Chapter 4 — Arrivals

Planning the Descent ... 4-1
    Top of Descent ... 4-1
    Time, Fuel, and Distance ... 4-2
Arriving in the Terminal Area ... 4-3
    Airspeed Restrictions ... 4-3
    Altitude Restrictions ... 4-4
    Standard Terminal Arrival Routes ... 4-5

RNAV STARS 4-5
    STAR Procedure Responsibility 4-9
  Radar Vectors to Final Approach Course 4-10
  Tailored Arrivals 4-11
Special Airport Qualification 4-11
CFIT Prevention 4-13

Chapter 5 — Approaches

Approach Procedure Types 5-1
Instrument Approach Procedure Segments 5-1
  Enroute Transition 5-2
  Initial Approach Segment 5-2
  Intermediate Approach Segment 5-2
  Final Approach Segment 5-4
  Missed Approach Segment 5-4
Approach Procedure Considerations 5-4
  Straight-In Landing vs. Circling Approach 5-5
  Straight-In Approaches vs. Course Reversals 5-7
  Altitudes 5-7
    Minimum Safe/Sector Altitude 5-7
    FAF or Glide-Slope/Glide-Path Intercept Altitude 5-8
    Minimum Descent Altitude, Decision Altitude, and Decision Height 5-9
  Landing Minimums and Ops Specs 5-10
  Vertical Descent Angle 5-11
Types of Approaches 5-11
  Visual Approache 5-12
  Contact Approach 5-12
  Charted Visual Flight Procedure 5-13
  RNAV (GPS) Approach 5-14
    RNAV (GPS) Approach Design 5-14
    GPS Approach Equipment 5-15
      Baro-VNAV 5-16
      WAAS-Certified GPS 5-16
    Landing Minimums 5-18
      LNAV 5-18
      LNAV/VNAV and LPV 5-19
      LP 5-21
      Determining Landing Minimums 5-22
    RAIM Failure During an Approach 5-22
  RNAV (RNP) Approach 5-22
  ILS Approach 5-23
    ILS Approach Categories 5-24
      CAT I ILS Approaches 5-24
      CAT II ILS Approaches 5-24
      CAT III ILS Approaches 5-26
  GLS Approach 5-26
  Parallel Approaches 5-28
    Parallel Approaches (Dependent) 5-28
    Simultaneous Parallel Approaches (Independent) 5-28
    Simultaneous Close Parallel PRM Approaches (Independent) 5-29
      Simultaneous Offset Instrument Approaches 5-30
      RNAV PRM and GLS PRM Options 5-32
      PRM Approach Requirements 5-33
  Simultaneous Converging Approaches 5-33
  Localizer Approaches 5-33
    Localizer and Localizer DME 5-34
    Localizer Back Course 5-35

  Localizer-Type Directional Aid 5-35
 VOR Approach.. 5-35
 NDB Approach.. 5-38
 Radar Approaches 5-38
  Airport Surveillance Radar 5-38
  Precision Approach Radar 5-40
Approach Planning 5-40
 Gathering Weather Information 5-40
  Weather Sources 5-40
  Weather Source Considerations 5-41
  In-Flight Weather.. 5-41
  Regulatory Requirements 5-42
   Part 91 Operators 5-42
   Part 135 and Part 121 Operators 5-42
 Performing an Operational Briefing 5-43
  Airport and Runway Information 5-43
  Aircraft Performance and Configuration 5-43
  Approach Speed and Category 5-45
 Setting Up Equipment 5-45
 Performing an Approach Briefing 5-46
Flying the Approach 5-46
 Approach Clearance 5-46
  Vectors to Final Approach Course 5-46
  Nonradar Environment 5-48
 Use of the Autopilot 5-49
 Stabilized Approach 5-49
 Continuous Descent Final Approach 5-50
 Transition to Visual Flight 5-51
 Missed Approach 5-51
CFIT Prevention 5-52

Chapter 6 — Helicopter IFR Operations

Helicopter IFR Certification 6-1
 Flight and Navigation Equipment 6-1
 Miscellaneous Requirements 6-2
 Stabilization and Automatic Flight Control Systems 6-2
 Helicopter Flight Manual Limitations 6-3
 Operations Specifications 6-5
 Minimum Equipment List 6-5
Pilot Proficiency 6-6
Helicopter VFR Minimums 6-7
Helicopter IFR Takeoff Minimums 6-7
Helicopter IFR Alternates 6-7
 Part 91 Operators 6-8
 Part 135 Operators 6-8
Helicopter Instrument Approaches 6-8
 Standard Instrument Approach Procedures to an Airport 6-8
 Copter Only Approaches 6-9
 Copter GPS Approaches to an Airport or Heliport 6-10
 Approach Procedures to a VFR Heliport 6-10
  Approaches to a Specific Landing Site 6-11
  Point-In-Space Approaches 6-11
 Special Approaches 6-13
Inadvertent Flight into IMC 6-13

Appendix A — Airborne Navigation Databases

Evolution of Airborne Navigation Databases A-1
    Database Capabilities A-2
Production and Distribution A-2
    Role of the Database Provider A-2
    Role of the Avionics Manufacturer A-3
    Role of the User A-3
Composition of Airborne Navigation Databases A-4
    The WGS-84 Reference Datum A-4
    ARINC 424 .... A-4
        Records A-4
            Fix Records A-4
            Simple Route Records A-5
            Complex Route Records A-5
            Miscellaneous Records A-5
    Path/Terminator Concept A-6
Operational Limitations of Airborne Navigation Databases A-6
    Reliance on Navigation Automation A-6
    Storage Limitations A-7
    Path/Terminator Limitations A-8
    Inconsistencies Between Charts and Databases A-8
        Naming Conventions A-8
        Magnetic Variation A-8
        Differences in Revision Cycles A-9
    Evolution of RNAV A-10

Appendix B — Staying Within Protected Airspace

What Is Protected Airspace? B-1
Courses and Fixes B-2
Terms B-2
Protected Airspace Factors B-4
Takeoff and Departure B-5
Enroute B-7
    VHF Navigation B-7
        Primary Area B-8
            Non-Mountainous Areas B-8
            Mountainous Areas B-9
        Secondary Area B-9
        Turning Area B-11
    RNAV B-12
Holding B-12
Arrival and Approach B-13
    Initial Approach Segment B-14
    Intermediate Segment B-14
    Final Approach Segment B-15
    Missed Approach Segment B-16

Appendix C — Acronyms and Glossary C-1

Index I-1

x

Chapter 1
IFR Operations in the National Airspace System

The National Airspace System (NAS) combines a vast collection of facilities, equipment, procedures, and airports operated by thousands of people. NAS improvements are ongoing to provide a safer and more efficient flying environment. Because of the dynamic nature of the NAS, you must constantly update your knowledge of the system and maintain proficiency on the latest procedures to operate effectively as a professional pilot. The innovative forces that transform the NAS also drive similar developments on a global scale. You must meet the challenge of complying with international aviation standards and using current technology worldwide and within the NAS. [Figure 1-1]

NextGen is the Federal Aviation Administration's (FAA's) plan to improve the NAS by guiding and tracking aircraft more precisely, developing new technologies, enhancing safety, reducing delays, saving fuel, and decreasing aircraft exhaust emissions. This chapter provides a foundation for exploring the structure and operation of the evolving NAS. Much of this structure is already in place. However, some programs, procedures, and services are still being implemented. New technology is developed every day, so to stay abreast of changes, visit the FAA's website, which describes the NextGen plan and provides frequent updates.

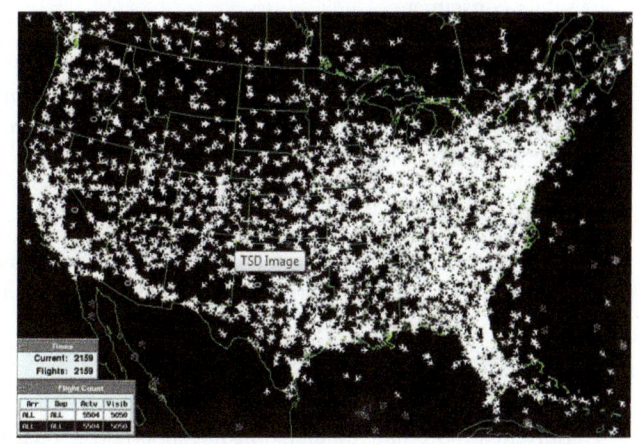

Figure 1-1. Statistics show that 4,000 to 6,000 aircraft operate simultaneously within the NAS during peak traffic periods.

NAS SAFETY
The ultimate goal of the FAA and the aviation industry is to improve safety in the NAS. Three areas of focus are controlled flight into terrain (CFIT) prevention, runway incursion avoidance, and approach and landing accident reduction (ALAR).

CONTROLLED FLIGHT INTO TERRAIN PREVENTION
The term CFIT defines an accident in which a fully qualified and certificated crew flies a properly functioning airplane into the ground, water, or obstacles with no apparent awareness by the pilots. To decrease your risk of a CFIT accident, know CFIT risk factors and take actions in each phase of flight to mitigate these factors. For example, limited ATC services, mountainous terrain, minimal runway lighting, and pilot/controller language barriers increase CFIT risk. Your company's type of operation, the country in which you operate, the weather conditions, your crew configuration, and your fatigue level also play a role in CFIT risk. Risk is reduced when your company culture values safety, you follow standard operating procedures (SOPs), you receive hazard awareness training, and your aircraft is equipped with a terrain awareness warning system (TAWS). All turbine-powered aircraft with six or more passenger seats (not including the pilot and copilot) must be equipped with TAWS. [Figure 1-2]

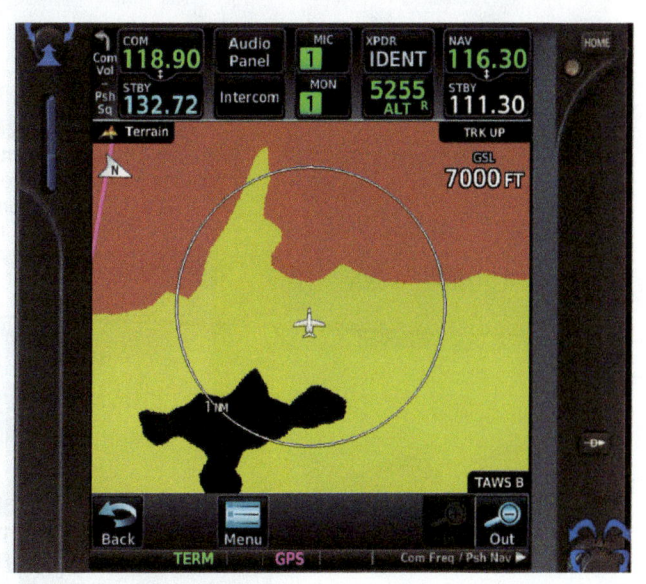

Figure 1-2. Part 135 aircraft with 10 or more seats and Part 121 aircraft must have a Class A TAWS and Part 135 aircraft with six to nine seats are required to have a Class B TAWS as shown here.

1-1

Evaluate your CFIT risk so you can take actions to mitigate it by using the CFIT Checklist prepared by the Flight Safety Foundation. Subsequent chapters describe specific actions you can take during the departure, enroute, arrival, and approach phases of flight to prevent CFIT.

RUNWAY INCURSION AVOIDANCE

A runway incursion is formally defined by the FAA as "any occurrence at an aerodrome involving the incorrect presence of an aircraft, vehicle, or person on the protected area of a surface designated for the landing and takeoff of aircraft." Detailed investigations of runway incursions have identified three major factors contributing to these events: failure to comply with ATC instructions; lack of airport familiarity; and nonconformance with SOPs. There are four categories of runway incursions:

- Category A—a serious incident in which a collision is narrowly avoided.

- Category B—an incident in which separation decreases and there is a significant potential for a collision; this might result in a time critical corrective/evasive response to avoid a collision.

- Category C—an incident with ample time and/or distance to avoid a collision.

- Category D—an incident that meets the definition of runway incursion, such as the incorrect presence of a single vehicle/person/aircraft on the protected area of a surface designated for the landing and takeoff of aircraft but with no immediate safety consequences.

A key to preventing runway incursions is adhering to SOPs for taxiing. Operators must develop SOPs that increase flight crew situational awareness but that do not increase workload during taxi. Effective SOPs cover seven major categories: planning, situational awareness, written taxi instructions, flight crew verbal communication, ATC/pilot communication, taxi, and exterior aircraft lighting.

PLANNING

Plan for the airport surface movement portion of the flight just as you plan for other phases of flight. Planning for taxi operations consists of review items and briefing items. Review items include:

- NOTAMs and automatic terminal information service (ATIS) for runway and taxiway closures, construction activity, and other airport-specific risks.

- Current airport diagram including hot spots and standard taxi routes.

- FAA updates on airport signage, markings, and lighting, including surface movement guidance and control system (SMGCS) lights and runway status lights (RWSL). [Figure 1-3]

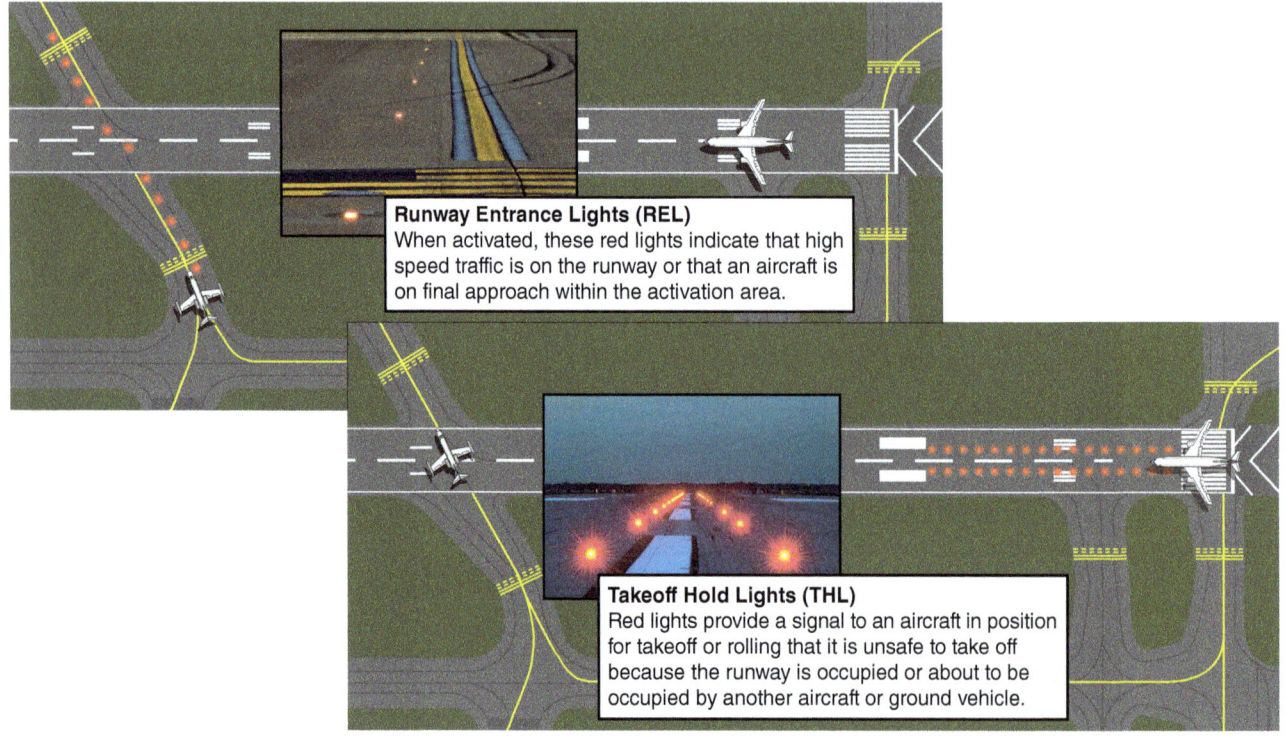

Figure 1-3. Runway status lights are designed to reduce the number and severity of runway incursions.

Just as you would for an approach procedure, you should brief taxi operations before taxi on departure and prior to initial descent on arrival. Brief these items:

- When and where to perform aircraft checklists and company communication.
- The taxi route, including hold-short lines, crossing runways, and hot spots.
- Turning off your cell phones and devices to prevent any distractions.
- Procedures during taxi, such as maintaining a sterile cockpit and displaying the airport diagram or low visibility taxi chart (if applicable).

SITUATIONAL AWARENESS

Use a continuous-loop process to actively monitor and update your progress during taxi. Know the aircraft's present location and mentally calculate the next location on the route that requires increased attention; a turn onto another taxiway, an intersecting runway, or hot spot. To maintain situational awareness:

- Prior to entering or crossing any runway, scan the full length of the runway and final approach. If you see a conflicting aircraft, stop taxiing and query ATC.
- Before performing operational duties and checklists, bring the aircraft to a complete stop or ensure you are in a phase of taxiing that has no risk of a runway incursion.
- Be especially vigilant if another aircraft with a similar call sign is on the same frequency.
- Never stop on a runway to communicate with ATC if you become disoriented.
- When instructed to taxi and line up and wait (LUAW), ensure your traffic alert/advisory system is on so you can monitor aircraft that might be landing on your runway.
- During landing, do not accept last-minute turnoff instructions unless you are certain that you can safely comply.
- Use caution after landing on a runway that intersects another runway, or on a runway where the exit taxiway is in close proximity to another runway's hold short line.
- After landing at a non-towered airport, listen on the CTAF for inbound aircraft information and scan the full length of the runway, including the final approach and departure paths of any runways you intend to cross.

WRITTEN TAXI INSTRUCTIONS

Write down complex taxi instructions as a reference for reading back the instructions to ATC and to confirm the taxi route and any restrictions. You might choose to enter taxi instructions into the flight management system (FMS) scratchpad. [Figure 1-4]

FLIGHT CREW VERBAL COMMUNICATION

Verbally confirm that you understand all ATC instructions to the other flight crewmember so you have a chance to discover and correct any misunderstandings. For example, when ATC issues a clearance for an arrival or a departure, refer to the airport diagram and confirm and verbalize the assigned runway and taxi route, including any instructions to hold short of, or cross, a runway. Contact ATC to resolve any persistent disagreement or uncertainty among crewmembers about any clearance. When it becomes necessary for you to stop monitoring any ATC frequency to prepare for takeoff or landing, tell the other flight crewmember when you stop and when you resume monitoring the ATC frequency.

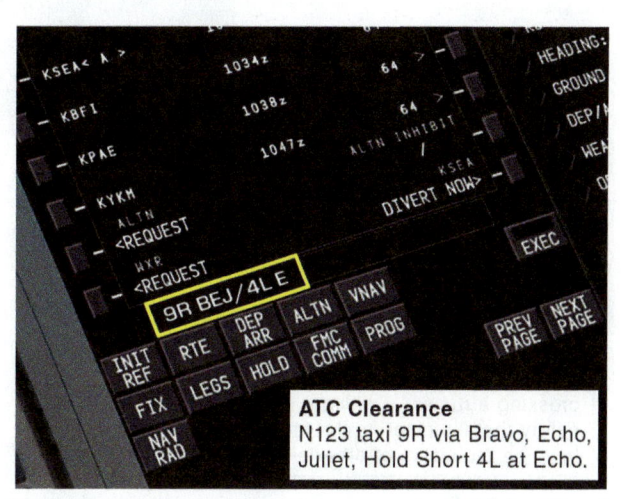

Figure 1-4. The forward slash / represents the hold short line of Runway 4 Left at Echo – the clearance limit.

ATC Clearance: N123 taxi 9R via Bravo, Echo, Juliet, Hold Short 4L at Echo.

ATC/PILOT COMMUNICATION

Use standard phraseology and read back clearances to communicate effectively with ATC. However, simply reading back a clearance is not enough to prevent a runway incursion. Many runway incursions occur even after the pilot reads back the hold short instruction, so develop a technique to remind yourself to hold short. For example, place something on an instrument knob or on the control yoke. At non-towered airports, when you are in position for takeoff or on final approach, monitor the CTAF for potential conflicts involving your runway, or a crossing runway. The risk of miscommunication increases when operating at foreign airports so ensure that you understand accents, terminology, and International Civil Aviation Organization (ICAO) procedures.

TAXI

Prior to taxi, complete all aircraft pre-taxi checklist items and enter all the flight navigation data. As you taxi, use the airport diagram and refer to the aircraft's heading indicator to confirm the correct taxiway or runway alignment. If you are unsure of your location, stop the aircraft—do not stop on a runway—and immediately advise ATC. When you are cleared to take off or to cross a runway, or when you are exiting a runway, do so in a timely manner: inform ATC of any anticipated delay. Never exit the landing runway onto another runway without an ATC clearance.

EXTERIOR AIRCRAFT LIGHTING

Use exterior aircraft lights to make your aircraft more conspicuous when operating on the airport surface. You can use various combinations of exterior lights to convey your location and intent to other pilots, ATC, and ground personnel. Do not illuminate strobe lights if they will adversely affect the vision of other pilots and ensure you comply with your aircraft lighting system's operating limitations. [Figure 1-5]

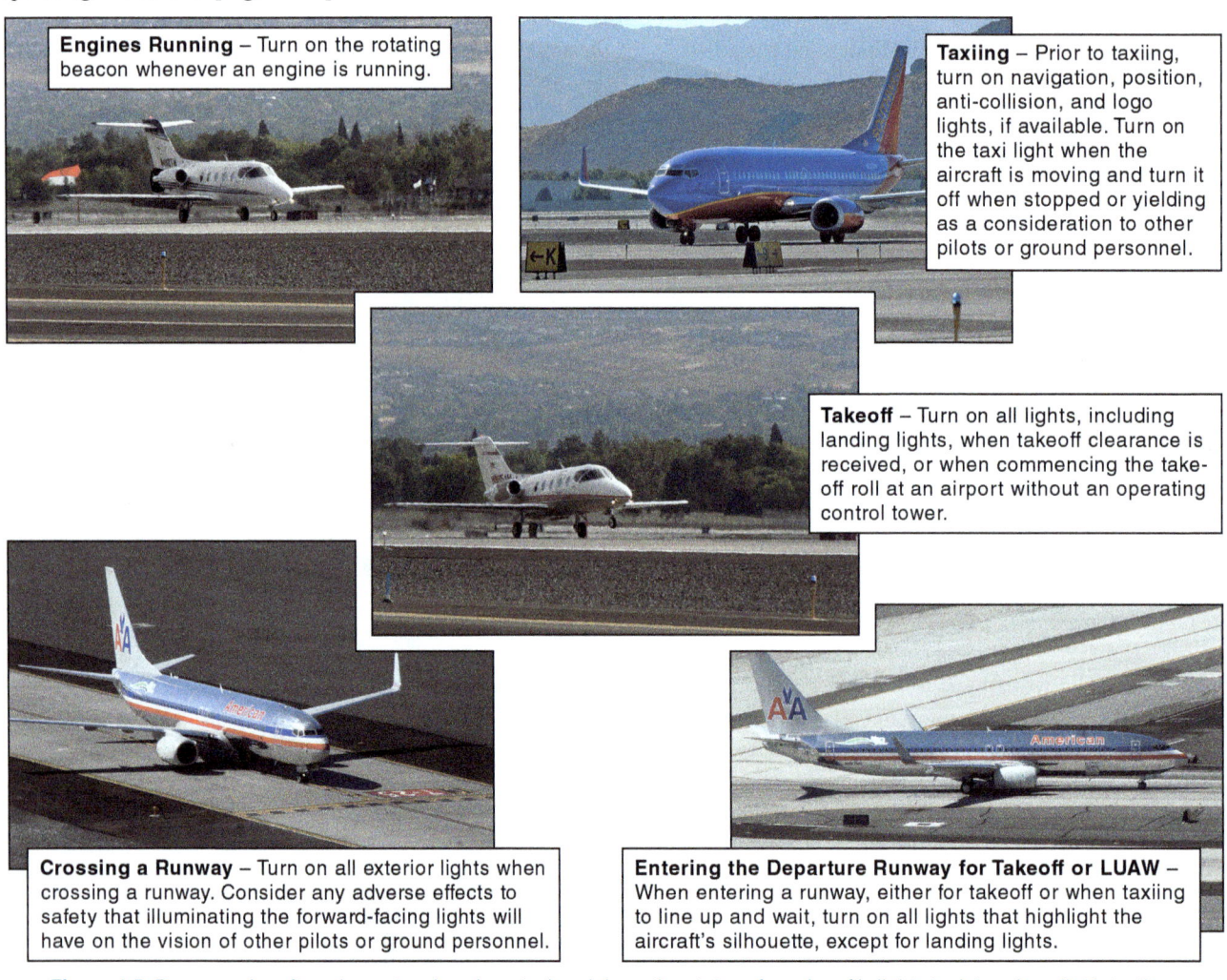

Engines Running – Turn on the rotating beacon whenever an engine is running.

Taxiing – Prior to taxiing, turn on navigation, position, anti-collision, and logo lights, if available. Turn on the taxi light when the aircraft is moving and turn it off when stopped or yielding as a consideration to other pilots or ground personnel.

Takeoff – Turn on all lights, including landing lights, when takeoff clearance is received, or when commencing the take-off roll at an airport without an operating control tower.

Crossing a Runway – Turn on all exterior lights when crossing a runway. Consider any adverse effects to safety that illuminating the forward-facing lights will have on the vision of other pilots or ground personnel.

Entering the Departure Runway for Takeoff or LUAW – When entering a runway, either for takeoff or when taxiing to line up and wait, turn on all lights that highlight the aircraft's silhouette, except for landing lights.

Figure 1-5. Because aircraft equipment varies, do not rely solely on the status of an aircraft's lights to determine pilot intentions.

APPROACH AND LANDING ACCIDENT REDUCTION

Approach and landing accident reduction (ALAR) involves three primary areas: maintaining a stabilized approach, avoiding hazards during landings; and orienting toward a proactive go-around. The Flight Safety Foundation provides an ALAR Tool Kit—a unique set of pilot briefing notes, videos, presentations, risk-awareness checklists and other products designed to prevent approach and landing accidents. ALAR training typically includes basic airmanship, advanced aircraft maneuvering, non-normal aircraft conditions, and approach procedures and briefings. [Figure 1-6]

Basic Airmanship
- Basic stick and rudder skills
- SOPs for transferring aircraft control
- Advanced aircraft/swept-wing and fan jet training

Advanced Aircraft Maneuvering
- Mountain flying and high altitude airports
- Upset and unusual attitude recoveries
- Steep turns and high angle of attack (AOA) maneuvers and awareness

Non-Normal Aircraft Conditions
- Typical aircraft emergencies for the aircraft type
- Line-oriented scenarios
- Resource use during emergencies

Approach Procedures and Briefings
- Approach briefings that include items such as NOTAMs, weather, inoperative equipment, terrain, missed approach procedures, and special airport considerations
- Constant-angle approach profiles
- Explicit go-around gates

Figure 1-6. ALAR training typically encompasses a wide variety of pilot skills.

NAS COMPONENTS

The NAS comprises the common network of U.S. airspace, air navigation facilities, equipment, services, airports, aeronautical charts, rules and regulations, procedures, personnel, and technical information. Included are system components shared jointly with the military. The components of the NAS must work together to meet the demand for air commerce, people's desire to travel for business and pleasure, and to ship cargo by air. As this demand grows, the amount of IFR flight plans filed by airlines and other airspace users to access the system increases.

USERS

Users of the NAS cover a wide spectrum in pilot skill and experience, aircraft types, and air traffic service demands, creating a challenge to the NAS to provide a variety of services that accommodate all types of traffic. NAS users range from professional airline, commuter, and corporate pilots to single-engine piston pilots, as well as owner-operators of personal jets to military jet fighter trainees.

AIRLINES

Major air carriers operate exclusively under IFR at altitudes above 18,000 feet. Airline flights adhere to established schedules and operate in and out of large and well-equipped airports. Commuter/regional airlines also follow established schedules but typically operate smaller and lower performance aircraft in airspace that must often be shared by general aviation aircraft, including VFR traffic. Commuter/regional airlines, which operate both turboprop aircraft and regional jets (RJs) with seating capacities of 100 seats or less, use hub airports along with other commercial carriers and small community airports capable of IFR operation.

AIR CHARTER

Air charter companies, which use a wide variety of aircraft, including turboprops, business jets, airliners, and helicopters, operate at small community airports and major hubs. Air charter flights range from transporting individuals for business or recreation to carrying time-sensitive cargo to conducting air ambulance operations.

GENERAL AVIATION

General aviation (GA) is all civil aviation operations other than scheduled air services and non-scheduled air transport operations for hire. By using larger high-performance airplanes and equipping them with the latest avionics, the business portion of the GA fleet —corporate aircraft and fractionals—has created demands for ATC services that more closely resemble commercial operators. Although one company might own one or more corporate aircraft with unlimited access, fractional jet owners buy a share of the airplane and have guaranteed access (50-400 hours annually, depending on share size) with as little as four hours' notice.

The tendency of GA aircraft owners at the upper end of the spectrum to upgrade the performance and avionics of their aircraft increases the demand for IFR services and for terminal airspace at airports. The majority of air traffic falls into this category, and most airports serve general aviation exclusively. The measures to separate and control both IFR and VFR traffic create more restrictions on airspace use and raise the level of aircraft equipage and pilot qualification necessary for access.

MILITARY

From an operational point of view, military flight activities comprise a subsystem that is fully integrated within the NAS. However, military aviation has unique requirements that often are different from civil aviation users. The military's need for designated training areas and low-level routes located near bases sometimes conflicts with civilian users who must circumnavigate these areas. In coordinating the development of ATC systems and services for the armed forces, the FAA is challenged to achieve a maximum degree of compatibility between civil and military aviation objectives.

ATC FACILITIES

The NAS includes public and private airports, the air traffic control system command center, air route traffic control centers, terminal radar approach control facilities, air traffic control towers, flight service, and air navigation facilities. Several thousand pieces of maintainable equipment including radar, communication systems, ground-based navigation aids, computer displays, and radios are used in NAS operations. FAA employees provide air traffic control, security, field maintenance, certification, system acquisition, and other essential services. [Figure 1-7]

Air Traffic Control System Command Center (ATCSCC)
The ATCSCC oversees all air traffic control and manages air traffic control at centers where there are issues causing delays, such as poor weather, traffic overload, or closed runways.

Air Traffic Control Tower (ATCT)
Control towers manage aircraft surface movement, relay IFR departure clearances, and separate IFR aircraft in the terminal area.

Air Route Traffic Control Center (ARTCC)
ARTCCs provide air traffic control service to aircraft operating on IFR flight plans within controlled airspace, principally during the enroute phase of flight.

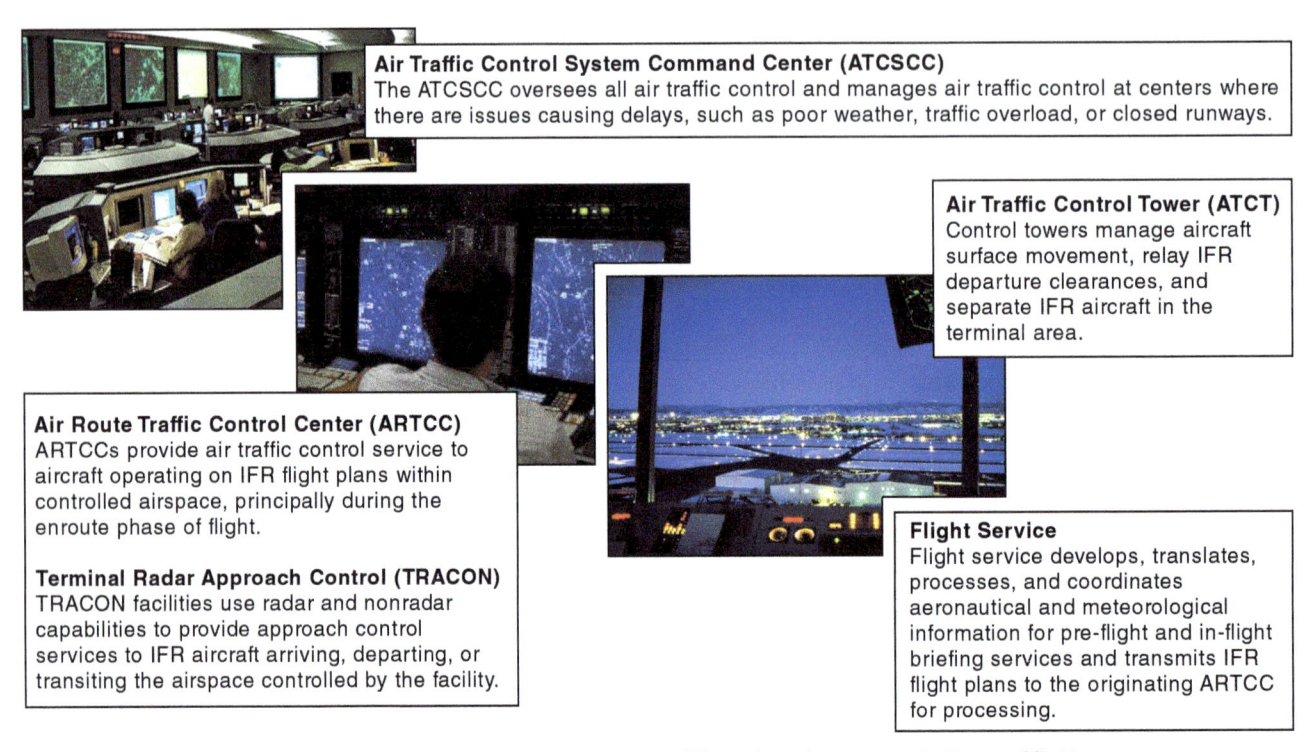

Terminal Radar Approach Control (TRACON)
TRACON facilities use radar and nonradar capabilities to provide approach control services to IFR aircraft arriving, departing, or transiting the airspace controlled by the facility.

Flight Service
Flight service develops, translates, processes, and coordinates aeronautical and meteorological information for pre-flight and in-flight briefing services and transmits IFR flight plans to the originating ARTCC for processing.

Figure 1-7. A network of ATC facilities provides IFR services throughout all phases of flight.

AIR TRAFFIC CONTROL SYSTEM COMMAND CENTER

The task of managing the flow of air traffic within the NAS is assigned to the ATCSCC. Headquartered in Herndon, Virginia, the ATCSCC regulates air traffic at a national level when weather, equipment, runway closures, or other conditions place stress on the NAS. In these instances, traffic management specialists at the ATCSCC work with airline personnel and controllers at the affected facilities to analyze, coordinate, and reroute (if necessary) traffic to maximize efficiency and remain within the capacity of the NAS. [Figure 1-8]

ATCSCC traffic management personnel use the enhanced traffic management system (ETMS) to predict, traffic surges, gaps, and volume on national and local scales based on current and anticipated airborne aircraft. Traffic management personnel evaluate the projected traffic flow into airports and sectors and then provide routes and spacing to ensure that traffic demand does not exceed system capacity. [Figure 1-9]

AIR ROUTE TRAFFIC CONTROL CENTER

An ARTCC's (center's) primary function is to control and separate air traffic within a designated airspace that might cover more than 100,000 square miles, traverse over several states, and extend from the base of the underlying controlled airspace up to flight level (FL) 600. There are 22 centers located throughout the U.S., each of which is divided into sectors. Controllers assigned to these sectors, which range from 50 to over 200 miles wide, guide aircraft toward their intended destination by assigning vectors or a specific airway and routing aircraft around weather and other traffic.

TERMINAL RADAR APPROACH CONTROL

Terminal radar approach control (TRACON) controllers typically monitor an area with a 50-mile radius and up to an altitude of 17,000 feet on radarscopes. This airspace is configured to provide service to a primary airport, but might include other airports that are within 50 miles of the radar service area. In addition to providing IFR separation, TRACON controllers provide vectors to airports, around terrain, and to avoid hazardous weather. Controllers in TRACONs determine the arrival sequence for the control tower's designated airspace.

On the basis of the current and future traffic flow, traffic management coordinators (TMCs) create a plan to deliver aircraft, safely separated, to the TRACON at a rate that does not exceed the capacity of the TRACON and the destination airports. The TMC's plan consists of sequences and scheduled times of arrival (STAs) at meter fixes—published points that lie on the center-TRACON boundary. The center controllers issue clearances to aircraft to cross the meter fixes at the STAs specified in the TMC's plan.

Two tools that can assist TMCs are the Traffic Management Advisor (TMA) and the Final Approach Spacing Tool (FAST). The TMA computes the sequences

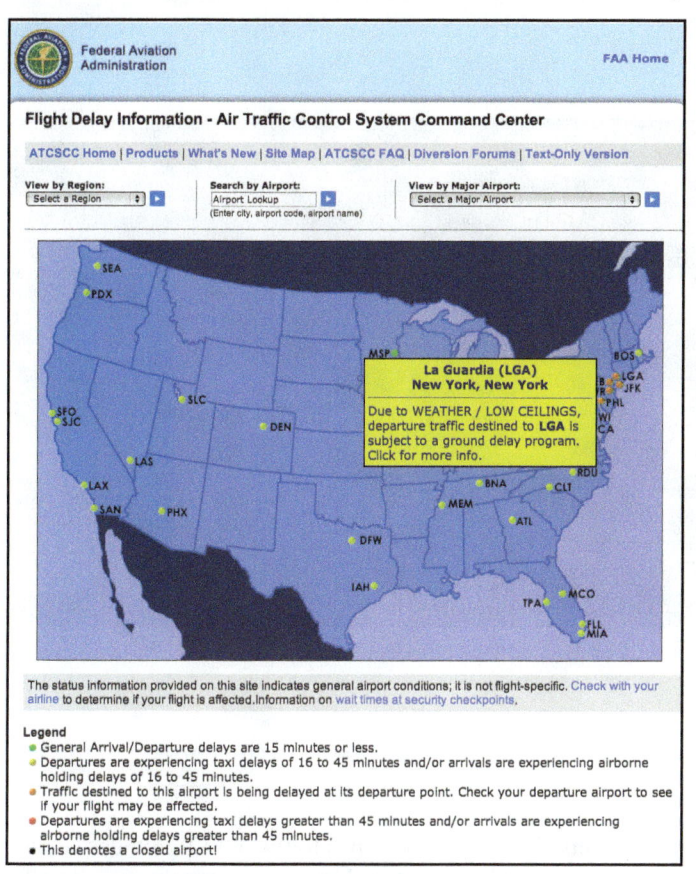

Figure 1-8. Real-time Airport Status pages displayed on the ATCSCC website provide general airport condition status and indicate trouble spots in the NAS.

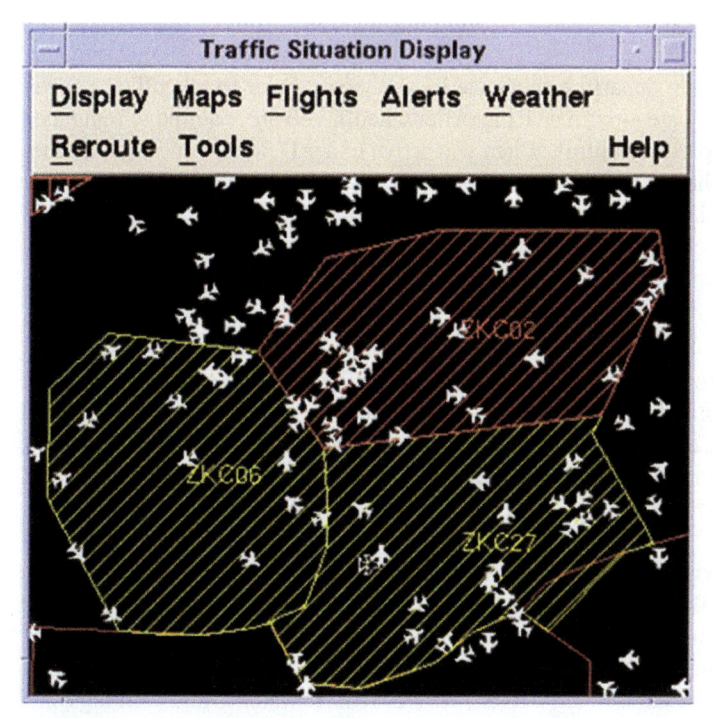

Figure 1-9. Monitor Alert, a part of ETMS, analyzes traffic demand for all airports, sectors, and airborne reporting fixes in the continental U.S. and then automatically displays an alert when demand is predicted to exceed capacity in a particular area.

1-7

and STAs to the outer meter arc, meter fix, final approach fix, and runway threshold for each aircraft to meet the sequencing and scheduling constraints entered by the TMC. The TMA continually updates its results at a speed comparable to the live radar update rate in response to changing events and controller inputs. [Figure 1-10]

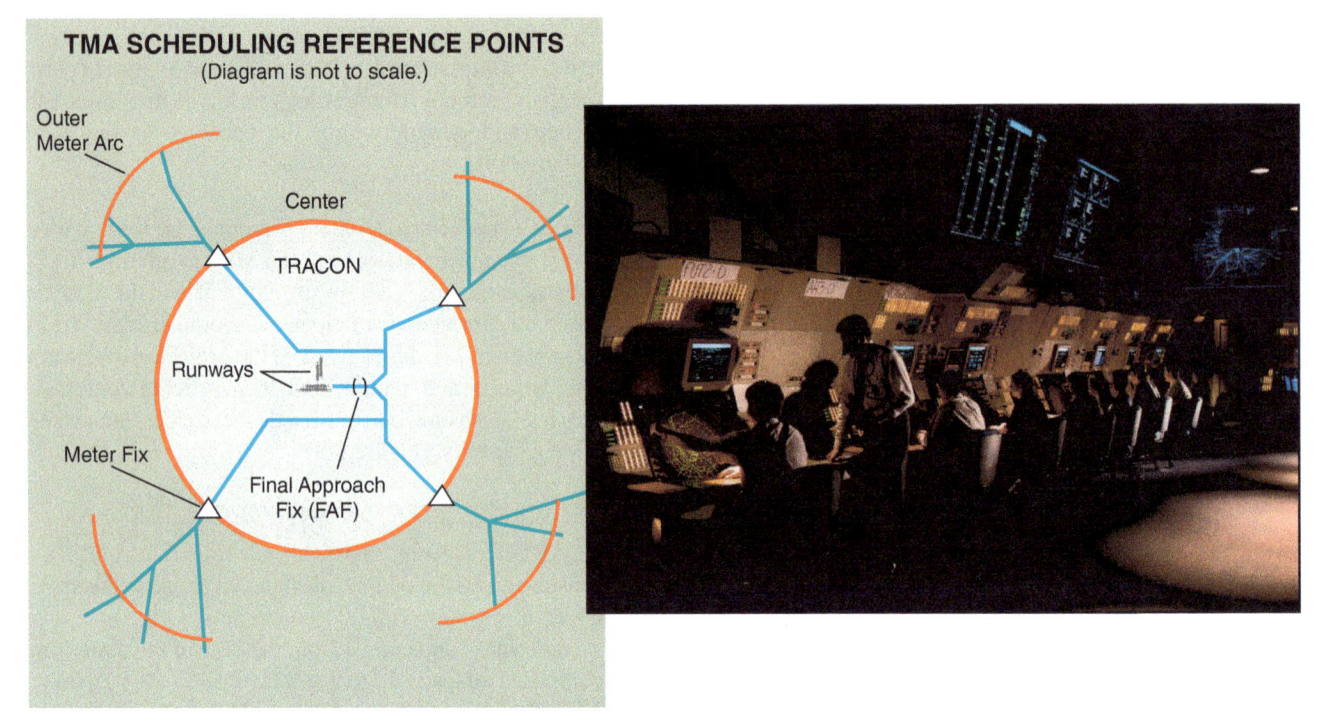

Figure 1-10. The TMA increases controller situational awareness through graphical displays and alerts. It also generates statistics and reports about the traffic flow.

FAST is an automation system for helping terminal area controllers efficiently manage arrival traffic. FAST provides landing sequences and landing runway assignments, as well as speed and heading advisories to achieve an accurately spaced traffic flow on final approach. The FAST system is designed to operate either independently or in direct coordination with the other controller tools.

AIR TRAFFIC CONTROL TOWER
Aircraft that are departing under IFR are integrated into the departure sequence by the tower. Prior to takeoff, the tower controller coordinates with departure control to ensure adequate aircraft spacing. After takeoff, you are required to remain on the tower frequency until you are instructed to contact departure control. When you arrive under IFR at a controlled airport, you are sequenced by approach control for spacing and then advised to contact the tower for landing clearance. The tower controller issues your landing clearance, which might include wind direction, wind velocity, current visibility, and if appropriate, special instructions. After landing, the tower controller automatically closes your IFR flight plan.

FLIGHT SERVICE
Lockheed Martin Flight Service (LMFS) air traffic control specialists are certified as pilot weather briefers by FAA Flight Service Safety and Operations. These briefers are authorized to translate and interpret available National Weather Service (NWS) products and provide standard, abbreviated, and outlook briefings. LMFS also provides a variety of online briefing and flight planning tools. By logging into the Pilot Portal, you can obtain a weather briefing, airport information, and NOTAMs. You can file and save favorite flight plans and aircraft data, as well as link to information such as GPS RAIM data and IFR terminal and enroute charts. [Figure 1-11]

By registering for the free Adverse Conditions Alerting Service (ACAS), you are notified when a new adverse condition arises after you obtain a briefing for a flight or file a flight plan in the Pilot Portal. The alerts are specific to a particular flight plan and are sent to you by text messages, email messages, or short messages that are transmitted via the Iridium satellite constellation directly to special devices in the cockpit. The ACAS generates alerts for TFRs, NOTAMs for closed airports or runways, AIRMETs, SIGMETs, convective SIGMETs, center weather advisories (CWAs), severe weather watches and warnings, and urgent PIREPs or AIREPs. Contact LMFS to obtain complete details for the adverse condition or go to your home page on the Pilot Portal to view and acknowledge ACAS alerts without calling a specialist. [Figure 1-12]

Figure 1-11. You can obtain a wide variety of briefing and flight planning tools online, including a comprehensive weather picture for your route of flight.

NAS DESIGN

Satellite-based and digital technologies provide the foundation for NAS design and for the procedures that guide and track aircraft precisely, enhance safety, reduce delays, and decrease aircraft exhaust emissions. These technologies consist of both ground infrastructure and avionics.

FAA RADAR SYSTEMS

The FAA operates two basic radar systems: air route surveillance radar (ARSR) and airport surveillance radar (ASR). Both of these surveillance systems use primary and secondary radar returns, as well as sophisticated computers and software programs designed to give the controller additional information, such as aircraft speed and altitude.

AIR ROUTE SURVEILLANCE RADAR

Figure 1-12. An adverse condition must intersect or be within a standard 25-NM briefing corridor of the flight plan route in order for an alert to be generated.

The long-range radar equipment used in controlled airspace to manage traffic is the ARSR system. ARSR facilities relay traffic information to radar controllers at ARTCCs to direct and coordinate IFR traffic. Some of these facilities can detect only transponder-equipped aircraft and are referred to as beacon-only sites. Each ARSR site can monitor aircraft flying within a 200-mile radius of the antenna, although some stations can monitor aircraft as far away as 600 miles through the use of remote sites.

AIRPORT SURVEILLANCE RADAR

TRACON facilities use ASR to direct and coordinate IFR traffic within specific terminal areas. ASR provides relatively short-range coverage in the airport vicinity and serves as an expeditious means of managing terminal area traffic. ATC also uses ASR as an instrument approach aid.

ASR facilities use the common automated radar terminal system (CARTS) or the standard terminal automation replacement system (STARS). Each of these systems provides a display of an aircraft's position, altitude, groundspeed, and other pertinent information. This information is updated continuously as the aircraft progresses through the terminal area. CARTS has several different configurations that depend on the computer equipment and software programs used. STARS is designed to provide the software and hardware platform necessary to support future air traffic control enhancements and incorporates tools like minimum distance lines between aircraft and projected track lines that show where aircraft will be in one, two, or three minutes. [Figure 1-13]

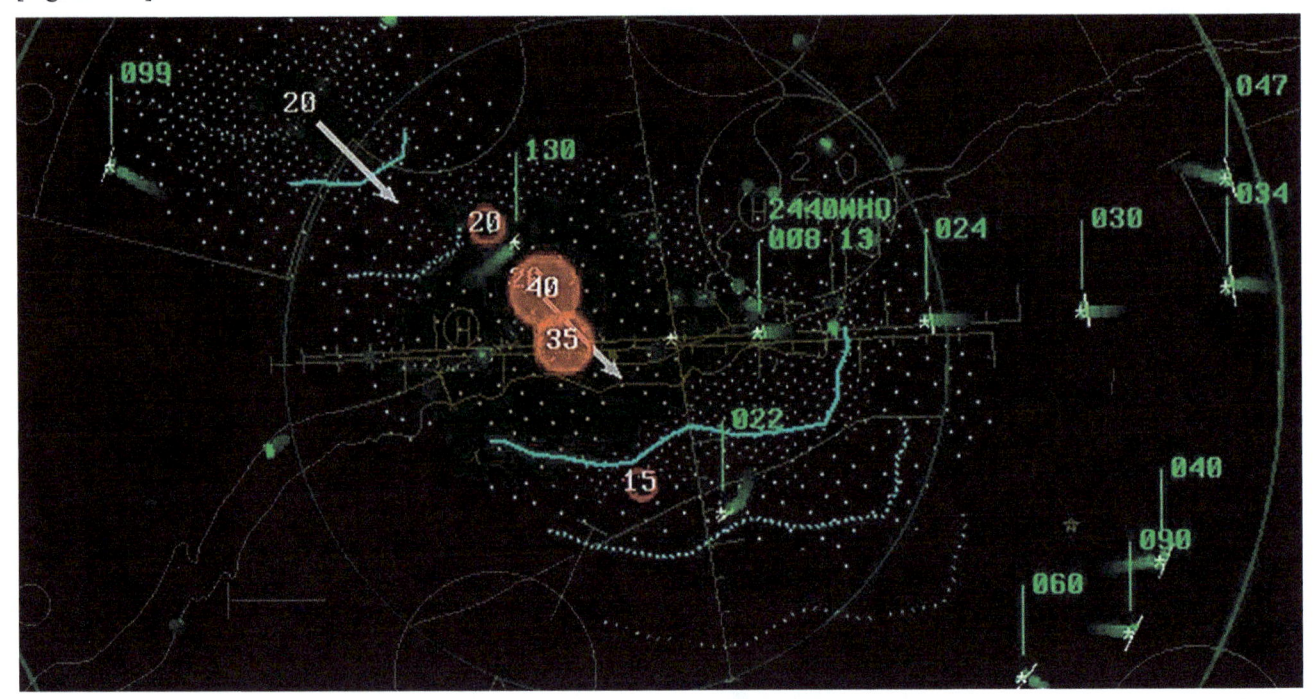

Figure 1-13. STARS presents flight and weather data on high-resolution 20x20 displays. Six levels of weather information identified by different colors simultaneously displayed with air traffic enables controllers to direct aircraft around adverse weather.

PRECISION RUNWAY MONITOR

Precision runway monitor (PRM) is a high-update-rate radar surveillance system used at selected capacity-constrained airports to provide simultaneous close parallel PRM approaches. ATC also uses PRM in conjunction with simultaneous offset instrument approaches (SOIA), which allow simultaneous approaches to two parallel runways spaced at least 750 feet but less than 3,000 feet apart. For example, the SOIA procedure utilizes an ILS PRM approach to one runway and an offset localizer-type directional aid (LDA) PRM approach with glide slope to the adjacent runway. These approach procedures are covered in more detail in Chapter 5 – Approaches.

PRM updates every second to display an accurate picture of the aircraft's location on final approach and to give the controller significantly more time to react to potential aircraft separation problems. The controller also sees target trails that provide very accurate trend information. With PRM, it is immediately apparent when an aircraft starts to drift off the runway centerline and toward the no-transgression zone. PRM also predicts the aircraft track and provides aural and visual alarms when an aircraft is within 10 seconds of penetrating the no-transgression zone. During PRM sessions, a separate controller monitors each final approach course and a coordinator manages the overall situation.

Flying simultaneous close parallel PRM approaches does not require any additional aircraft equipment, but you must have special training and qualifications. If you choose not to participate in PRM operations when arriving at an airport where PRM procedures are underway, expect to be held until ATC can accommodate your aircraft without disrupting the PRM arrival streams.

AUTOMATIC DEPENDENT SURVEILLANCE-BROADCAST

The automatic dependent surveillance broadcast (ADS-B) system incorporates GPS satellites, aircraft transmitters, and aircraft and ground receivers to provide pilots and ground control personnel with specific information about the position and speed of aircraft in the area. Two forms of ADS-B equipment apply to aircraft—ADS-B Out and ADS-B In. ADS-B Out signals travel line-of-sight from transmitting aircraft to ATC ground receivers or aircraft receivers. In order to receive the signal and display traffic information in your aircraft you must also have ADS-B In capability. [Figure 1-14]

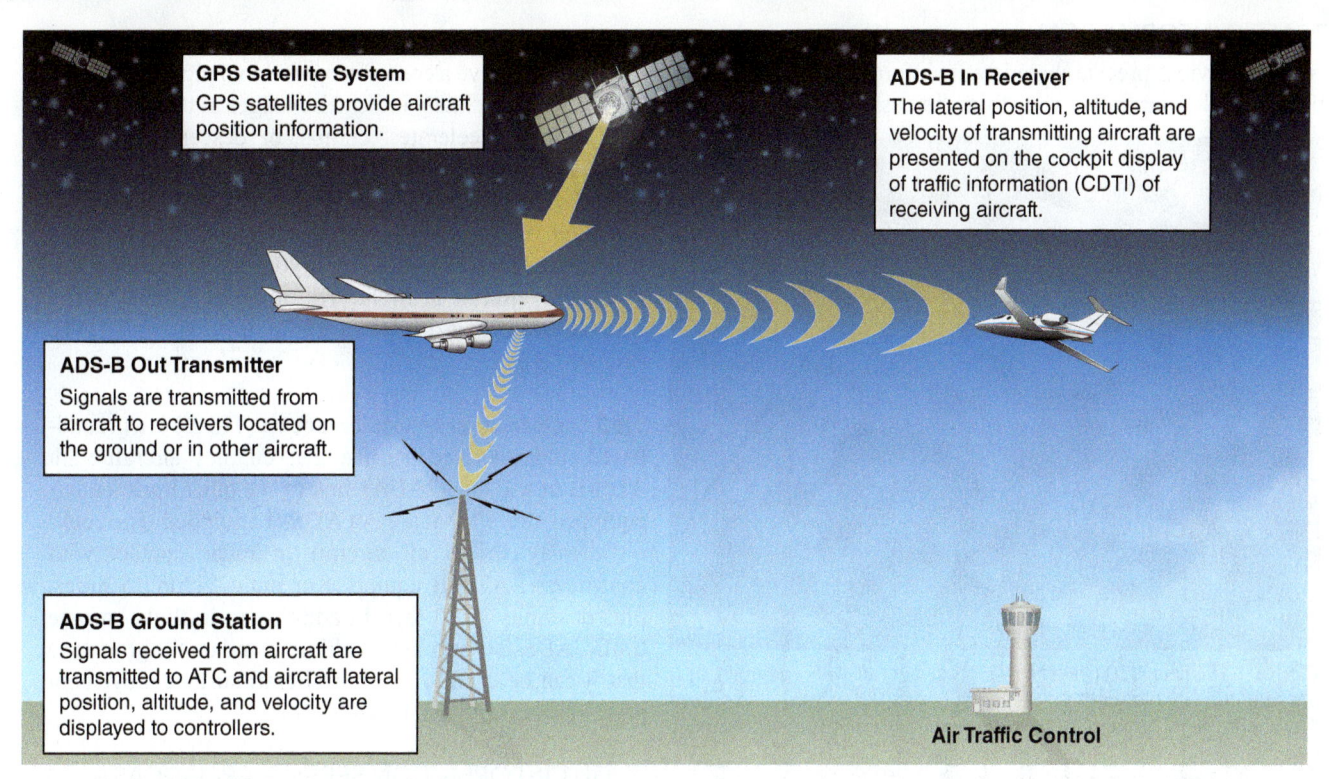

Figure 1-14. ADS-B helps you maintain situational awareness regarding your airplane's position in relation to other aircraft.

ADS-B continuously and automatically broadcasts aircraft speed, altitude, position, and other data once per second. Aircraft transmit and receive ADS-B data on one of two frequencies: the 1090 extended squitter (ES) or the 978 MHz universal access transceiver (UAT). [Figure 1-15]

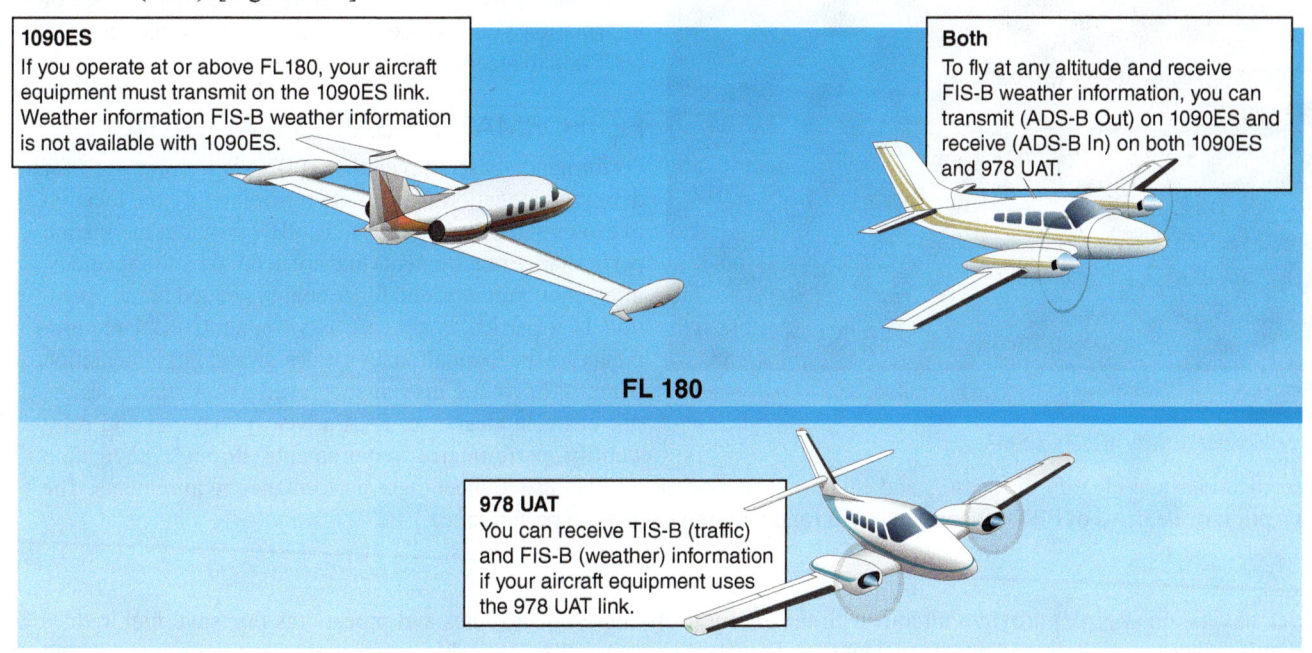

1090ES
If you operate at or above FL180, your aircraft equipment must transmit on the 1090ES link. Weather information FIS-B weather information is not available with 1090ES.

Both
To fly at any altitude and receive FIS-B weather information, you can transmit (ADS-B Out) on 1090ES and receive (ADS-B In) on both 1090ES and 978 UAT.

FL 180

978 UAT
You can receive TIS-B (traffic) and FIS-B (weather) information if your aircraft equipment uses the 978 UAT link.

Figure 1-15. The altitudes at which your aircraft operates determine the ADS-B data link that your aircraft requires.

Two additional ADS applications are ADS-Rebroadcast (ADS-R) and ADS-Contract (ADS-C). If you do not have both 1090ES and UAT equipment, your ADS-B equipment cannot see aircraft on the other frequency. ADS-R compensates for this by taking position information received on the ground from UAT-equipped aircraft and rebroadcasting the data on the 1090 frequency and vice versa. ADS-C functions similarly to ADS-B but is primarily used in sparsely trafficked transcontinental areas or oceanic crossings. ADS-C data is transmitted and acknowledged based on a contract between the ground system and an aircraft.

TRAFFIC INFORMATION

ADS-B provides precise shared traffic information so both pilots and controllers have a common operational picture and real-time data when aircraft deviate from their assigned flight paths. It clearly and immediately indicates changes as the conflicting traffic turns, accelerates, climbs, or descends. With an effective range of 100 nautical miles, the system gives controllers a large margin in which to implement conflict detection and resolution. Traffic situational awareness with alerts (TSAA) warns you if your aircraft is too close to another aircraft in flight. You monitor ADS-B traffic data on the cockpit display of traffic information (CDTI). [Figure 1-16]

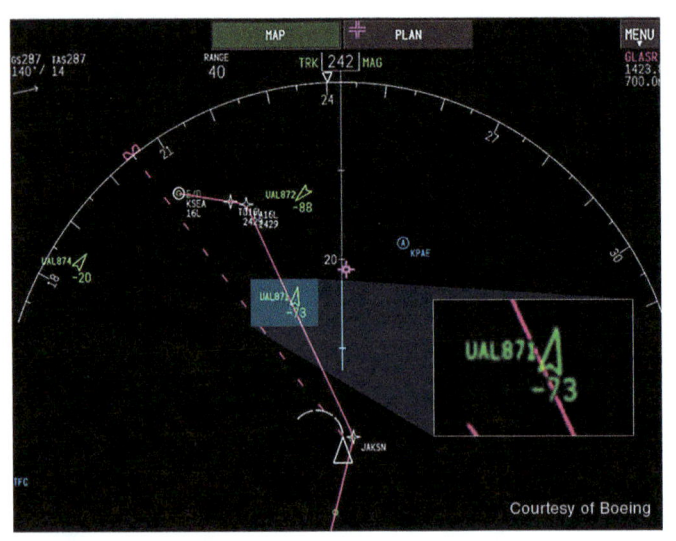

Figure 1-16. This CDTI represents other aircraft with chevrons that are oriented to the aircraft's direction of travel. The display also shows the aircraft flight ID and altitude and vertical trend data to indicate whether the aircraft is climbing or descending.

Traffic information service-broadcast (TIS-B) is a ground-based, radar-derived service that enables aircraft with ADS-B In and the 978 UAT link to see other transponder-equipped aircraft that are not ADS-B equipped. The cockpit display shows all aircraft in radar contact with controllers—ADS-B equipped or not—within 15 miles, plus or minus 3,500 feet. In addition to in-flight enroute traffic, ADS-B works at low altitudes and on the ground so that it can be used to monitor aircraft surface movement and airport operations. [Figure 1-17]

FLIGHT INFORMATION SERVICE-BROADCAST

Flight information service-broadcast (FIS-B) provides graphical and textual weather, as well as aeronautical information to aircraft equipped with the 978 UAT link. METARs, TAFs, NEXRAD precipitation maps, NOTAMs, TFRs, and PIREPS are just some of the many types of information you receive. Your aircraft must use the 978 UAT link to receive FIS-B.

PERFORMANCE-BASED NAVIGATION

Performance-based navigation (PBN) is a framework for defining navigation that is not constrained by the location of ground-based navigation aids. PBN provides navigation performance requirements that are defined by the accuracy, integrity, continuity, and functionality needed for an operation in a particular airspace environment. PBN requirements are the foundation for the design and implementation of air traffic routes, instrument procedures, airspace design, and obstacle clearance. FAA advisory material and rules identify performance requirements through navigation specifications and identify the sensors and equipment that operators may use to meet these performance requirements. The two primary elements of PBN are area navigation and required navigation performance.

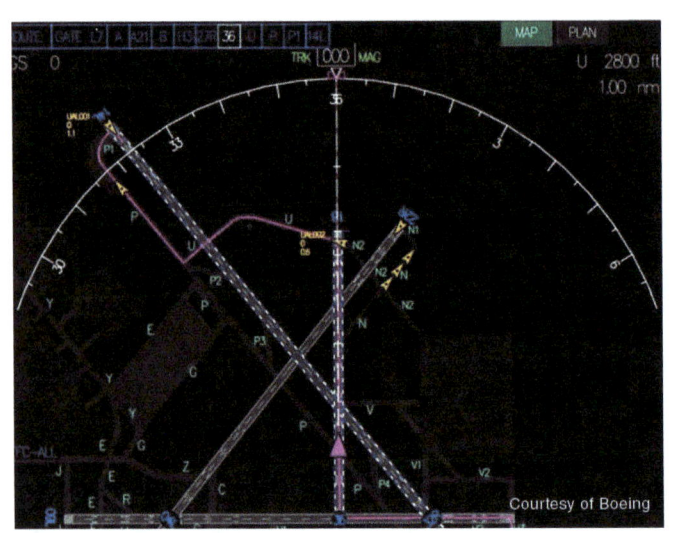

Figure 1-17. ADS-B provides surface movement data to increase your situational awareness while taxiing and reduce the risk of runway incursion, especially in low visibility conditions.

RNAV

Area navigation (RNAV) provides aircraft with the ability to fly more direct routes and procedures that save fuel, reduce aircraft exhaust emissions, and make efficient use of available airspace. RNAV enables controllers to assign routes without overflying navaids, reduce the lateral separation between aircraft tracks, and assign lower altitudes where VOR reception requires higher minimum altitudes. [Figure 1-18]

Wide Area Augmentation System

The accuracy of GPS is enhanced with the use of the wide area augmentation system (WAAS), a series of ground stations that generate a corrective message that is transmitted to the aircraft by a geostationary satellite. This corrective message improves navigational accuracy by accounting for positional drift of the satellites and signal delays caused by the ionosphere and other

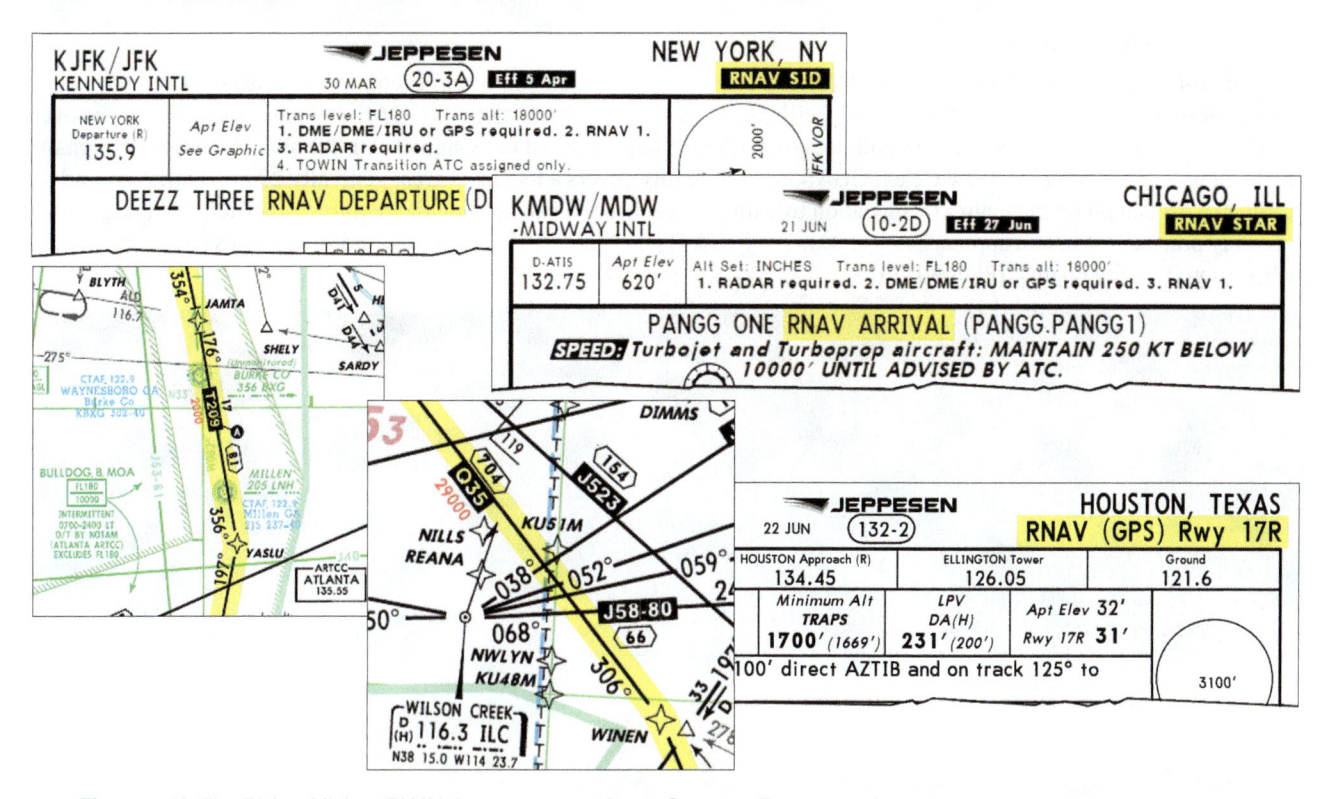

Figure 1-18. The FAA publishes RNAV departure procedures, Q-routes, T-routes, arrival procedures and approach procedures.

atmospheric factors. In addition, WAAS-certified GPS equipment provides vertical glide path information for RNAV (GPS) instrument approach procedures. [Figure 1-19]

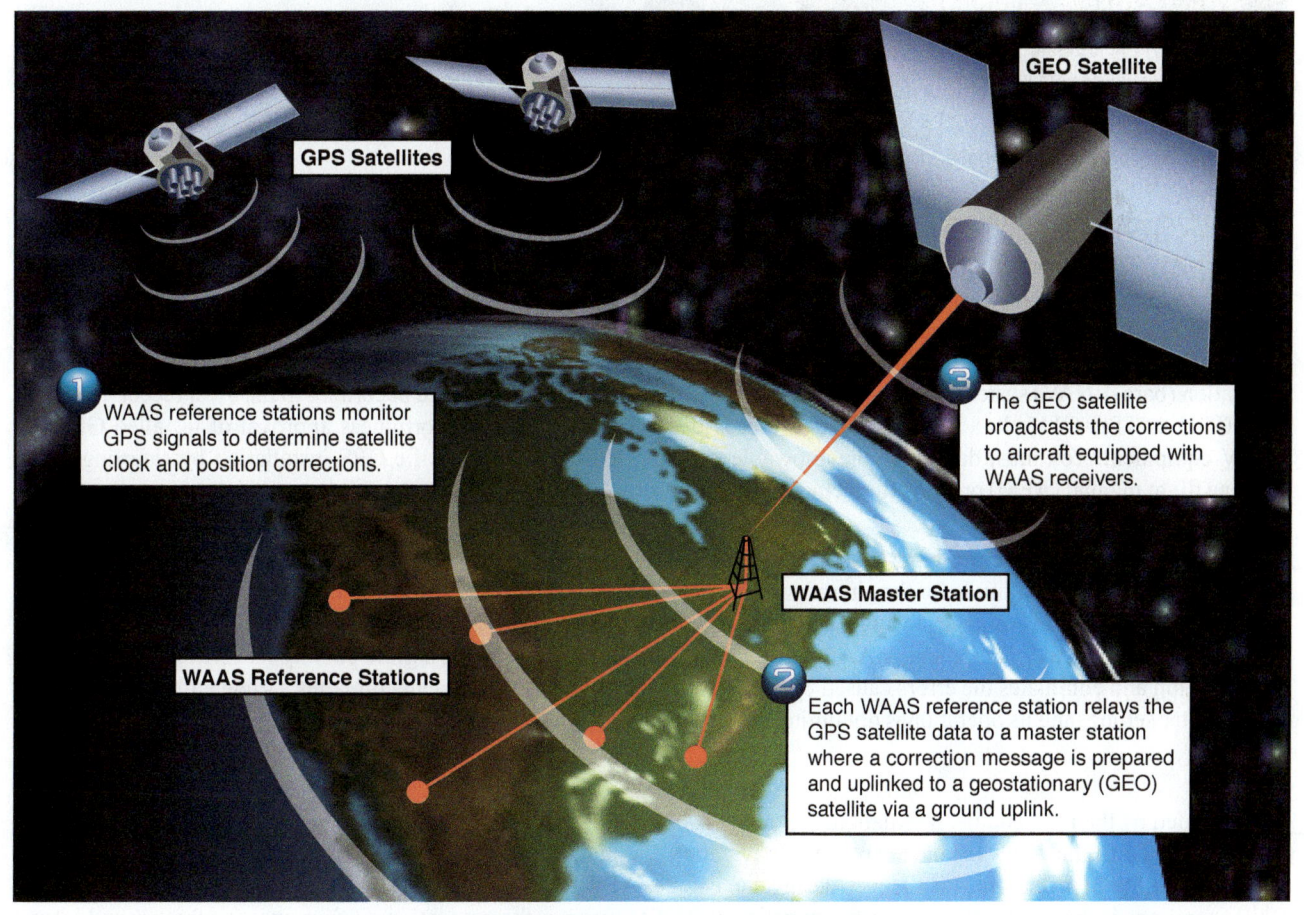

Figure 1-19. WAAS components work with the existing constellation of over 30 GPS satellites.

1-13

Ground-Based Augmentation System

The ground-based augmentation system (GBAS) provides a GPS position correction even more precise than WAAS. Local receivers send corrections to an airport ground facility that transmits the corrections to GBAS-compatible GPS receivers over a VHF radio data link. The aircraft GPS unit uses this information to correct GPS signals. Unlike WAAS correction signals, which are broadcast over a wide area, each GBAS ground facility covers a localized area, generally 20 to 30 miles around an airport. GBAS can pinpoint an aircraft's location to within three feet and can provide the required precision and integrity for extremely precise instrument approaches with Category (CAT) I and CAT II/III minimums and for airport surface operations, such as low-visibility taxiing. [Figure 1-20]

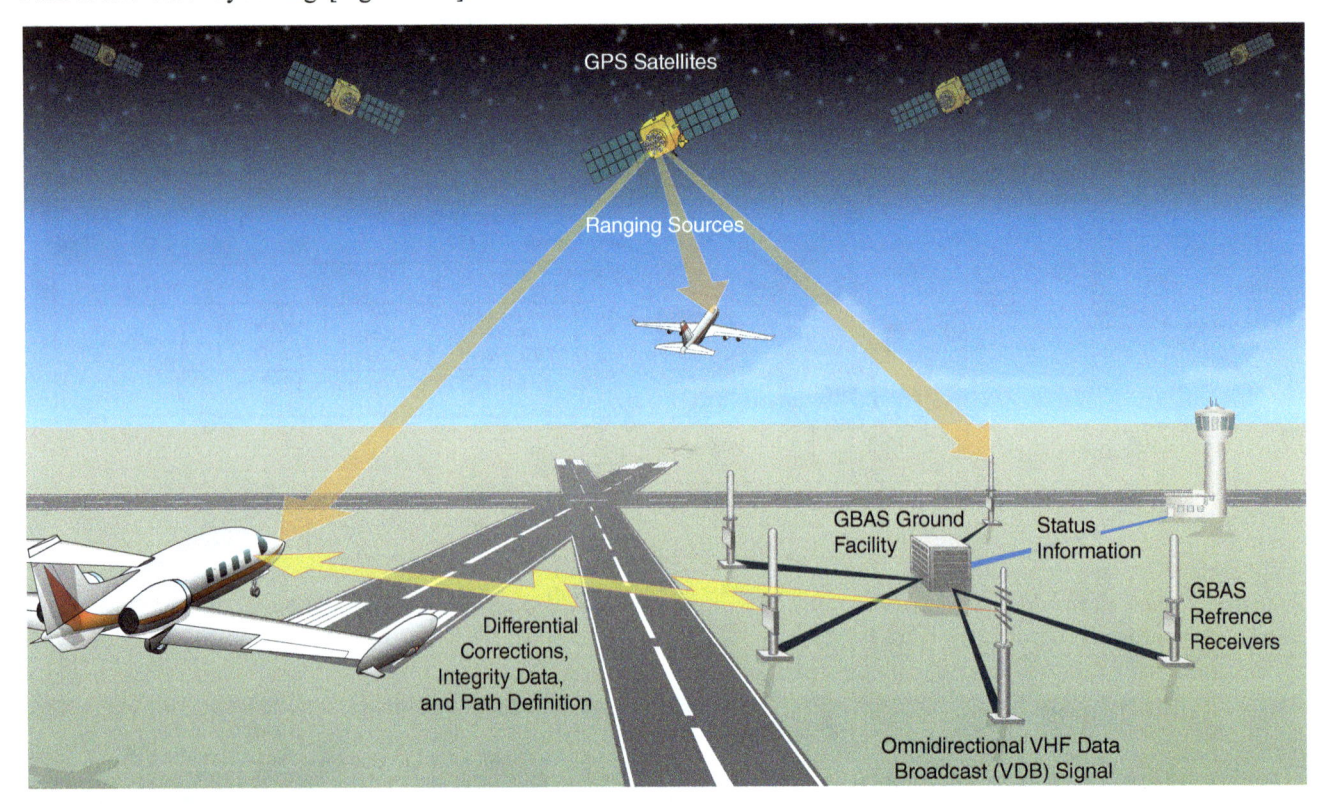

Figure 1-20. GBAS is a ground-based augmentation to GPS that focuses its service on the airport area for precision approaches, departure procedures, and terminal area operations.

RNAV (GPS) Approach Equipment

To fly RNAV (GPS) approach procedures with lateral navigation, GPS equipment must be certified not just for IFR enroute and terminal navigation but must also be approved for IFR approaches according to the current version of technical standard order (TSO) C129. Additional equipment requirements must be met to fly RNAV (GPS) approaches that incorporate vertical navigation. The primary types of equipment used to perform GPS approaches with vertical navigation are barometric vertical navigation (baro-VNAV) systems or WAAS-certified GPS equipment that is approved according to the most recent version of TSO-C145 or TSO-C146. In addition, AC 20-138 provides guidance for the airworthiness approval of installed GPS and RNAV equipment. You must determine the allowable uses for your aircraft's specific GPS installation by referring to the airplane flight manual (AFM) or AFM supplement.

Used primarily in larger aircraft, baro-VNAV equipment builds a glide path by sensing and then comparing the airplane's altitude with a calculated altitude for the aircraft's position on the glide path. You must enter the current local altimeter setting on the GPS equipment to ensure an accurate calculated glide path. In addition, there are high and low temperature limitations for the use of baro-VNAV equipment. WAAS-certified GPS equipment determines a glide path by its vertical and horizontal GPS position and eliminates the errors caused by barometric altimetry. This equipment computes a glide path independent of the altimeter setting, and its operation is not limited by temperature.

RNP

Implemented by the FAA and the International Civil Aviation Organization (ICAO), required navigation performance (RNP) is a set of standards that apply to both airspace and navigation equipment. The use of RNP in conjunction with RNAV provides greater flexibility in procedure and airspace design and enables ATC to offer more direct routing. A defining characteristic of RNP operations is the ability of the aircraft navigation system to monitor the navigation performance it achieves and inform you if the requirement is not met during an operation. This onboard monitoring and alerting capability enhances your situational awareness, reduces obstacle clearance, and enables closer route spacing without ATC intervention.

The RNP value designates the lateral performance requirement associated with a procedure. The required performance is obtained through a combination of aircraft capability and the level of service provided by the corresponding navigation infrastructure. From a broad perspective:

Aircraft Capability + Level of Service = Access

In this context, aircraft capability refers to the airworthiness certification and operational approval elements, such as avionics, maintenance, database, human factors, pilot procedures, and training. The level of service element refers to the NAS infrastructure, including published routes, signal-in-space performance and availability, and air traffic management. When considered collectively, these elements result in providing access. Access provides the desired benefit (airspace, procedures, routes of flight, etc.).

A key feature of RNP is the concept of on-board monitoring and alerting. This means the navigation equipment is accurate enough to keep the aircraft in a specific volume of airspace that moves along with the aircraft. The aircraft is expected to remain within this block of airspace for at least 95 percent of the flight time. Additional airspace outside the 95 percent area is provided for continuity and integrity, so that the combined areas ensure aircraft containment 99.9 percent of the time. RNP levels are actual distances from the centerline of the flight path that must be maintained for aircraft and obstacle separation. The specific performance required on the final approach segment of an instrument approach is an example of this RNP level. [Figure 1-21]

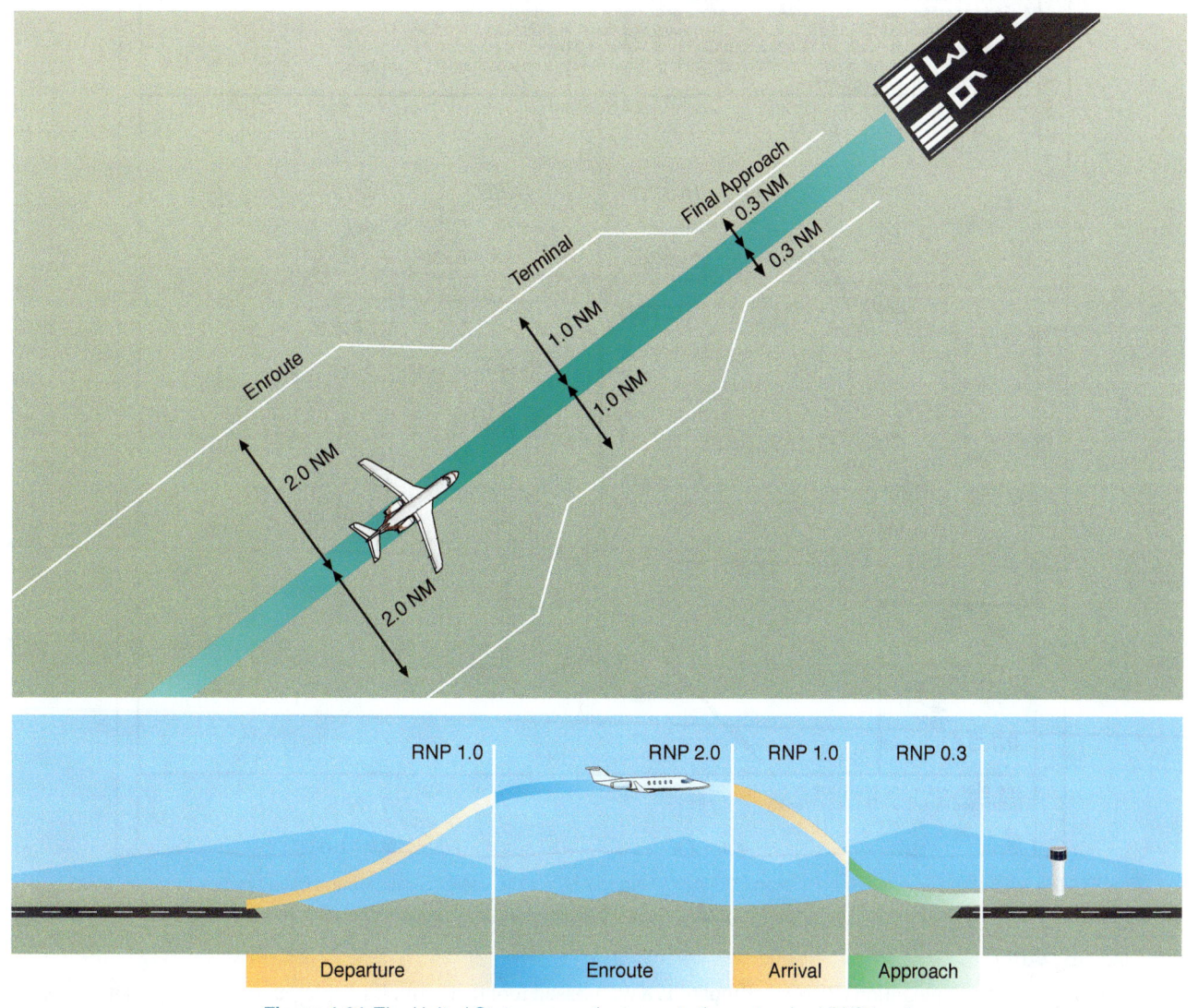

Figure 1-21. The United States currently supports three standard RNP levels.

For international operations, the FAA and ICAO member states have led initiatives to apply RNP concepts to oceanic routes. The ICAO RNP levels supported for international operations are:

- RNP-1 – European precision RNAV (P-RNAV)

- RNP-4 – Projected for oceanic/remote areas where 30 NM horizontal separation is applied

- RNP-5 – European basic RNAV (B-RNAV)

- RNP-10 – Oceanic/remote areas where 50 NM lateral separation is applied

RNAV (RNP) approaches are designed to be flown with any type of equipment that meets the RNP integrity requirements specified for the approach procedure. However, to perform RNAV (RNP) approaches, you and your aircraft must meet authorization required (AR) performance criteria. [Figure 1-22]

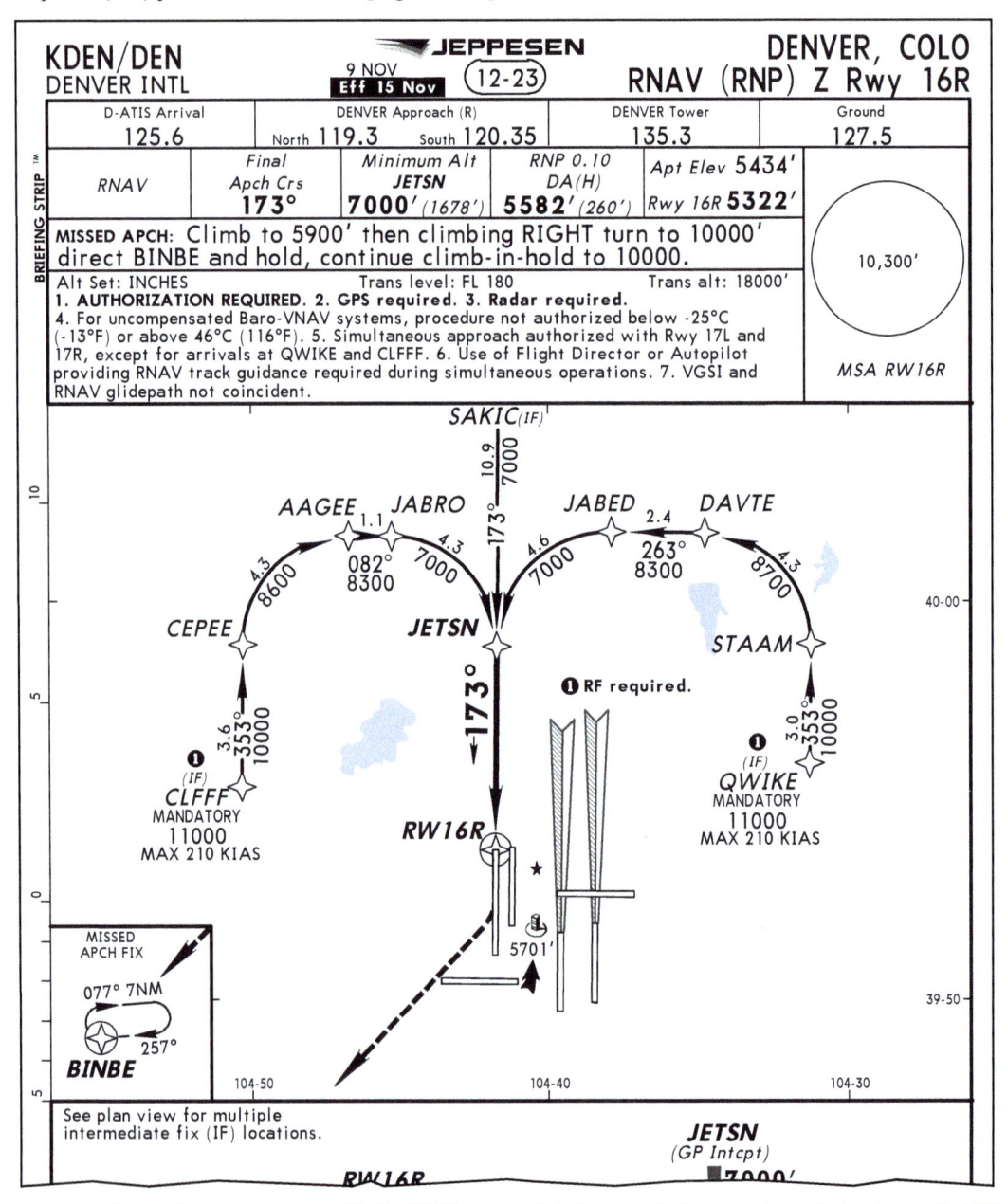

Figure 1-22. One of the unique features of an RNAV (RNP) approach is the use of circular paths called radius to fix (RF) legs.

PBN DASHBOARD

The Performance-Based Navigation (PBN) Dashboard is a web-based tool that provides deployment and usage data on every RNAV and RNP airport procedure in the NAS as well as the operators using the airport. This information supports analysis of current PBN operations and aids in developing new procedures. [Figure 1-23]

DECEMBER 20__ OPERATORS			
Carrier	Full Name	Operations	Percent of Operations
SKW	SKYWEST AIRLINES	1594	32.1%
GA	GENERAL AVIATION	872	17.5%
MIL	MIL	529	10.6%
RPA	REPUBLIC AIRLINES	529	10.6%
AAL	AMERICAN AIRLINES	399	8%
FFT	FRONTIER AIRLINES	228	4.6%
ASQ	EXPRESSJET	209	4.2%
FDX	FEDEX		
DAL	DELTA AIR LINE		
LYM	KEY LIME AIR		

AVAILABLE PBN PROCEDURES CALENDAR YEAR 20__		
Procedure Name	Procedure Type	Usage Data Available
OZZZY1	RNAV STAR	YES
R17LZ	RNP APPROACH	YES
R17RZ	RNP APPROACH	YES
R35LZ	RNP APPROACH	YES
		YES

DECEMBER 20__ RNAV STAR USAGE		
Procedure Name	Average Daily Usage Count	Average Daily Usage Percent Of Arrivals
OZZZY1	9.7	12.2%

Figure 1-23. On the PBN Dashboard, you can select an airport and review data regarding RNAV SIDs and STARs, RNAV (RNP) approaches, and the various operators at the airport.

OPTIMIZED PROFILE DESCENT

Another element of PBN is the optimized profile descent (OPD). An OPD as part of an arrival procedure enables you to perform a continuous descent from the top of descent to touchdown using a vertical descent profile. OPD flight procedures use the capabilities of the aircraft FMS to fly a continuous, descending path without level segments, based on the actual performance of the aircraft under current flight conditions.

REDUCED VERTICAL SEPARATION MINIMUMS

Reduced vertical separation minimums (RVSM) airspace is between FL290 and FL410 where aircraft are separated by 1,000 feet vertically. The operator and aircraft must be approved to operate in RVSM airspace. Exceptions to this rule in U.S. domestic RVSM airspace require FAA approval and include operations such as department of defense flights and air ambulance flights. RVSM is implemented worldwide to increase ATC flexibility, mitigate conflict points, reduce controller workload, and enable crossing traffic. In RVSM airspace, aircraft are able to operate at more fuel-efficient flight levels and have greater options for user-preferred routing.

NAS TOOLS

A wide variety of NAS programs and services provide support in each phase of flight under IFR, from flight planning and surface movement to departure, cruise, approach, and landing. ATC and aircraft tools to facilitate these programs and services range from computer software that compiles and disseminates weather data and IFR flight plans to electronic flight bags and enhanced visual systems in the cockpit.

FLIGHT PREPARATION

Flight preparation in the NAS involves ATC facilities, operators, and pilots using a wide variety of tools to plan and schedule flights. Collaboration between the FAA and flight operations centers (FOCs) is key to effective use of the NAS under IFR. To determine flow assignments, FAA traffic flow automation must incorporate FOC priorities. Frequent updates from airlines on departure schedules and the "earliest off block" time for each flight enables ATC to predict capacity and demand at individual airports and minimize queue lengths.

COMMON SUPPORT SERVICES–WEATHER

Common Support Services–Weather (CSS-Wx) is a single disseminator of weather information implemented by the FAA. A virtual repository of weather data from disparate data contributors and locations provides a common weather picture for all users of the NAS. This enables collaborative and dynamic decision making among controllers, air traffic managers, and pilots to give them the ability to proactively plan and execute operations ahead of weather impacts. CSS-Wx incorporates standardized weather information provided by the NextGen weather processor (NWP), the National Oceanic and Atmospheric Administration's (NOAA's) 4-dimensional weather cube, and other weather sources.

The NWP is a platform that processes information from textual, graphical and digital weather observations, analyses, and forecasts to create standardized, aviation-specific weather information, providing a measurement of the constraint that weather will place on NAS operations. Planners use the translated information to assess weather-related impacts on traffic flows and individual aircraft trajectories.

FLIGHT PLANS

Flight plans provide ARTCC computers with accurate and precise routes required for flight data processing. The computer contains every route (published and unpublished) and navaid, most intersections, and all airports, and only processes a flight plan if the proposed route and fixes connect properly. Center computers also identify preferred routes and recognize that forecast or real-time weather might change arrival routes. Centers and TRACONs have a computer graphic that displays the flight plan information and presents the position of every aircraft on a flight plan in the U.S.

ELECTRONIC FLIGHT BAG

The electronic flight bag (EFB) exists both as a mobile device or as equipment that is installed in the aircraft. You can use EFB features during flight planning and during each phase of flight. EFBs display flight plans, routes, checklists, flight operations manuals, regulations, minimum equipment lists (MELs), moving map and weather displays, approach charts, airport diagrams, logbooks, and operating procedures. You can also use the EFB to calculate aircraft performance and accomplish many tasks traditionally handled by a dispatcher. [Figure 1-24]

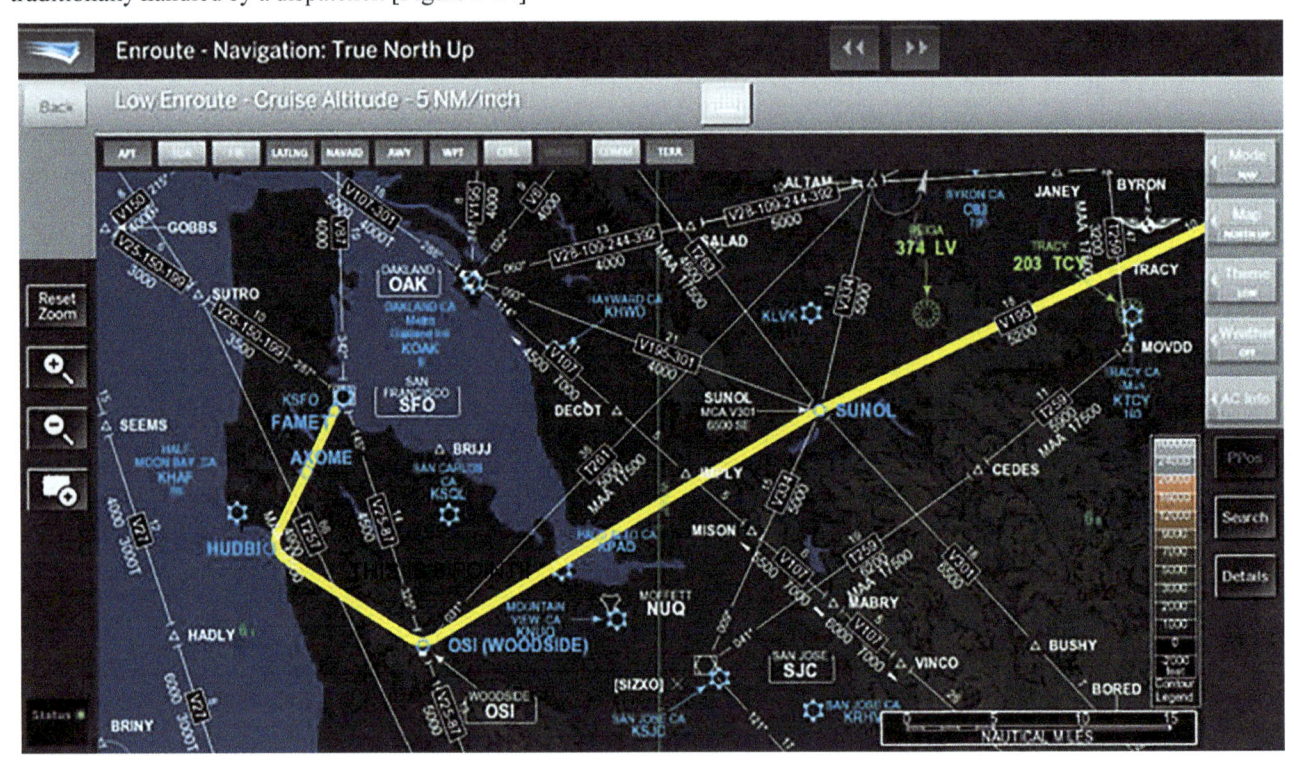

Figure 1-24. You can enter and modify your flight plan on the EFB.

AC 120-76, *Guidelines for the Certification, Airworthiness, and Operational Use of Electronic Flight Bags*, provides information for obtaining certification and approval for EFB use. This AC also describes three types of EFB software applications. Type A applications are primarily intended for use during flight planning, on the ground, or during noncritical phases of flight. Type B applications provide the aeronautical information required to be accessible to you during all phases of flight and Type C applications include communication, navigation, and surveillance functions that require FAA design, production, and installation approval.

AC 120-76 also outlines the capabilities and limitations of each of the three classes of EFBs. Classes are primarily based on whether the EFB is portable and the placement of the equipment in the cockpit.

- Class 1 EFBs are mobile devices that are not mounted to the aircraft. To use a Class 1 EFB for IFR charts and electronic checklists, you must ensure that it is secured and viewable during critical phases of flight and that it does not interfere with flight control movement.

- Class 2 EFBs are typically mounted to the aircraft and may be connected to a data source, a hard-wired power source, and an installed antenna. For a Class 2 EFB to be considered portable, you must be able to remove it from the flight deck without the use of tools.

- Class 3 EFBs are built into the aircraft panel and require a supplemental type certificate (STC) or certification design approval with the aircraft as part of its equipment. Depending on the model, the EFB might connect to the GPS or FMS, and it might combine GPS position with the locations and speed vectors of other aircraft and graphic weather information into a single, detailed moving map display. Its database can also provide obstacle and terrain warnings. It is important to remember that an EFB does not replace any system or equipment required by the regulations. [Figure 1-25]

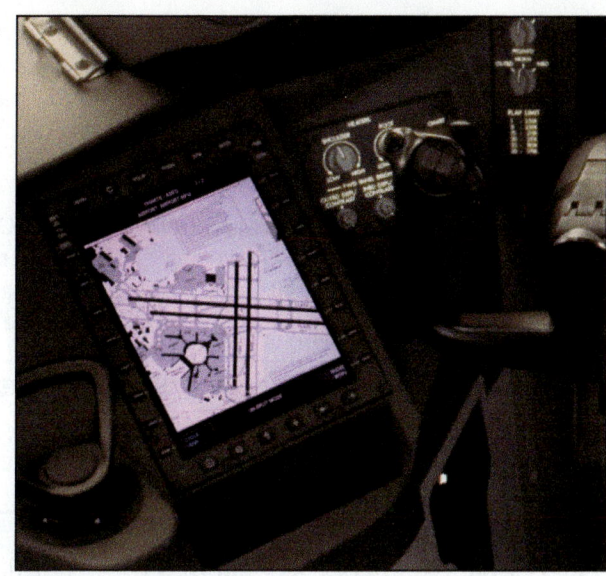

RELEASE TIMES

ATC uses an IFR release time—a departure restriction issued by ATC specifying the earliest and latest time you may depart—in conjunction with traffic management procedures to separate departing aircraft from other traffic. For example, when controlling departures from an airport without a tower, the controller limits the departure release to one aircraft at any given time. After that aircraft is airborne and radar identified, then the following aircraft may be released for departure, provided it meets the approved radar separation (3 miles laterally or 1,000 feet vertically). Controllers must take aircraft performance into account when releasing successive departures. For example, ATC does not release a Boeing 747 immediately after a departing Cessna 172. Besides releasing fast aircraft before slow ones, another technique that ATC uses for successive departures is to have the first aircraft turn 30° to 40° from runway heading after departure, and then have the second aircraft depart on a SID or on runway heading. ATC uses these techniques as common practice to maximize airport traffic capacity.

Figure 1-25. A Class 3 EFB is installed in the cockpit according to applicable airworthiness regulations.

IFR SLOTS

ATC uses IFR slots to promote a smooth flow of traffic at airports in close proximity to special events and specific high-density airports. Slot reservations required for unscheduled aircraft operations restrict the number of IFR takeoffs and landings at each airport during certain hours of the day. Web interfaces simplify the reservation process and provide more reservation flexibility. [Figure 1-26] Departure queue management systems at major airports can also determine efficient IFR departure slot times using automation that exchanges information about airport capacity from surface surveillance systems and specific company ramp operations over a data network.

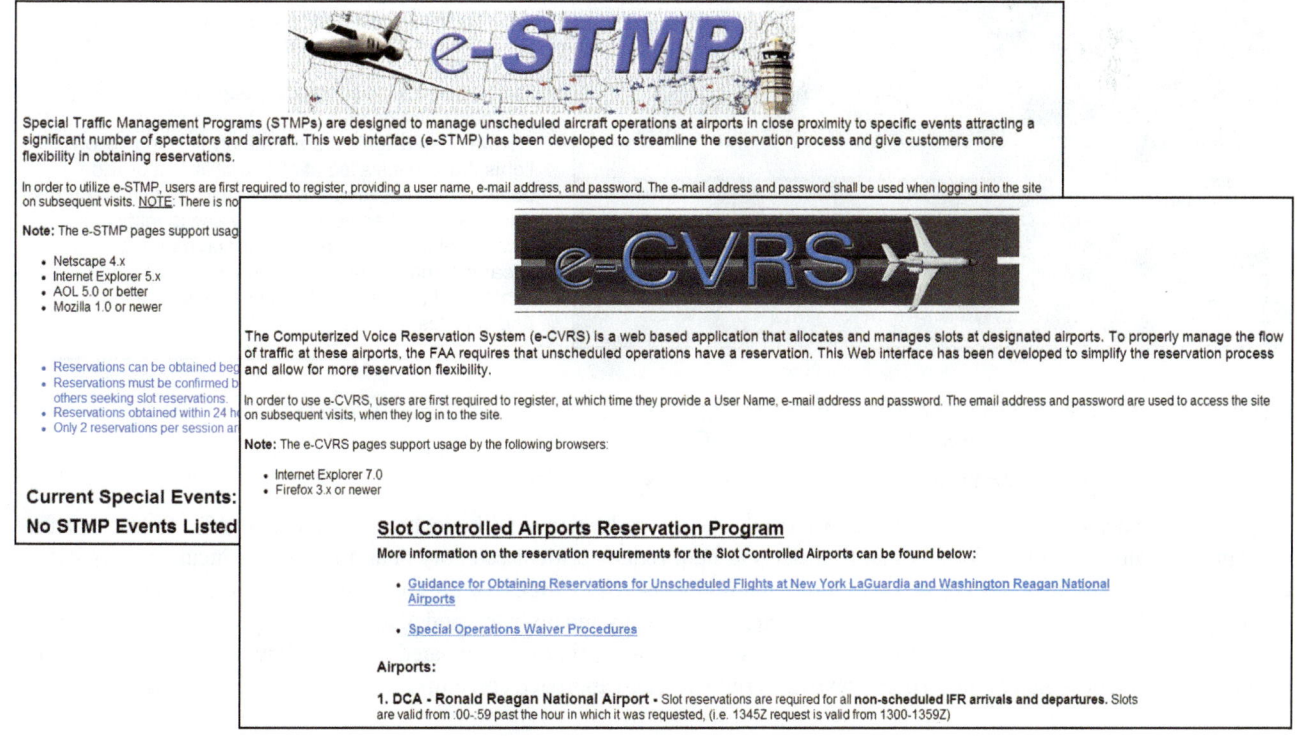

Figure 1-26. Register online to obtain slot reservations beginning 72 hours in advance of the proposed operation.

1-19

SURFACE MOVEMENT

Both controllers and pilots use a wide variety of tools to enhance safety on the airport surface. Taxi, takeoff, and landing operations at busy airports in low visibility conditions increase the risk of runway incursion accidents so airports have installed extensive lighting and radar systems to track surface movement.

SURFACE MOVEMENT GUIDANCE AND CONTROL SYSTEM

The surface movement guidance and control system (SMGCS) facilitates the safe movement of aircraft and vehicles at airports where scheduled air carriers are conducting authorized operations. The SMGCS program provides guidelines for the creation of low visibility taxi plans for all airports with takeoff or landing operations using visibility minimums less than RVR 1200. SMGCS plans apply to both flight crews and airport vehicle operators. [Figure 1-27]

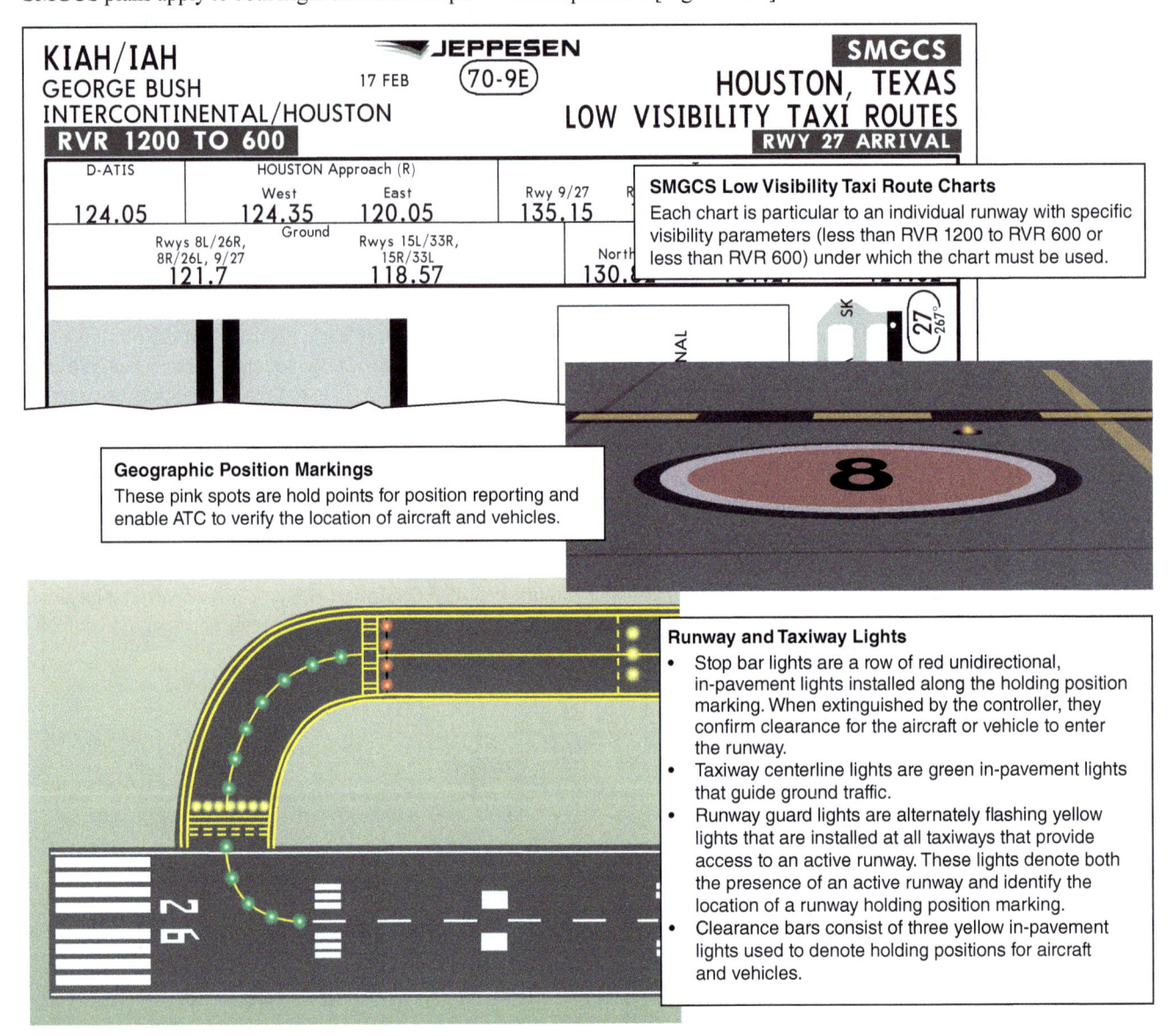

SMGCS Low Visibility Taxi Route Charts
Each chart is particular to an individual runway with specific visibility parameters (less than RVR 1200 to RVR 600 or less than RVR 600) under which the chart must be used.

Geographic Position Markings
These pink spots are hold points for position reporting and enable ATC to verify the location of aircraft and vehicles.

Runway and Taxiway Lights
- Stop bar lights are a row of red unidirectional, in-pavement lights installed along the holding position marking. When extinguished by the controller, they confirm clearance for the aircraft or vehicle to enter the runway.
- Taxiway centerline lights are green in-pavement lights that guide ground traffic.
- Runway guard lights are alternately flashing yellow lights that are installed at all taxiways that provide access to an active runway. These lights denote both the presence of an active runway and identify the location of a runway holding position marking.
- Clearance bars consist of three yellow in-pavement lights used to denote holding positions for aircraft and vehicles.

Figure 1-27. Low-visibility taxi route charts are published for SMGCS airports. Specialized runway and taxiway markings are displayed and specific lighting systems are installed at airports with SMGCS.

AIRPORT SURFACE DETECTION EQUIPMENT–MODEL X

Airport surface detection equipment–model X (ASDE-X) uses radar and satellite technology to enable ATC to track surface movement of aircraft and vehicles at major airports to help reduce critical category A and B runway incursions. ASDE-X collects data from surface surveillance radar, multilateral sensors, ADS-B sensors, the terminal automation system, and aircraft transponders to provide detailed coverage of movement on runways and taxiways and of aircraft flying within five miles of the airport. To spot potential collisions, tower controllers monitor a continuously-updated color display of aircraft and vehicle positions overlaid on a map of the airport's taxiways, runways, and approach corridors.

EFB – SURFACE MOVEMENT

EFBs store airport charts that help you maintain situational awareness during taxi operations, especially in poor visibility at an unfamiliar airport. Using moving map technology, you can see your cleared taxi route and the position of your aircraft. Some EFBs automatically display the airport chart after landing to decrease workload in the cockpit. ADS-B enables you to see the positions of other aircraft on the airport and ADS-B-equipped ground vehicles. [Figure 1-28]

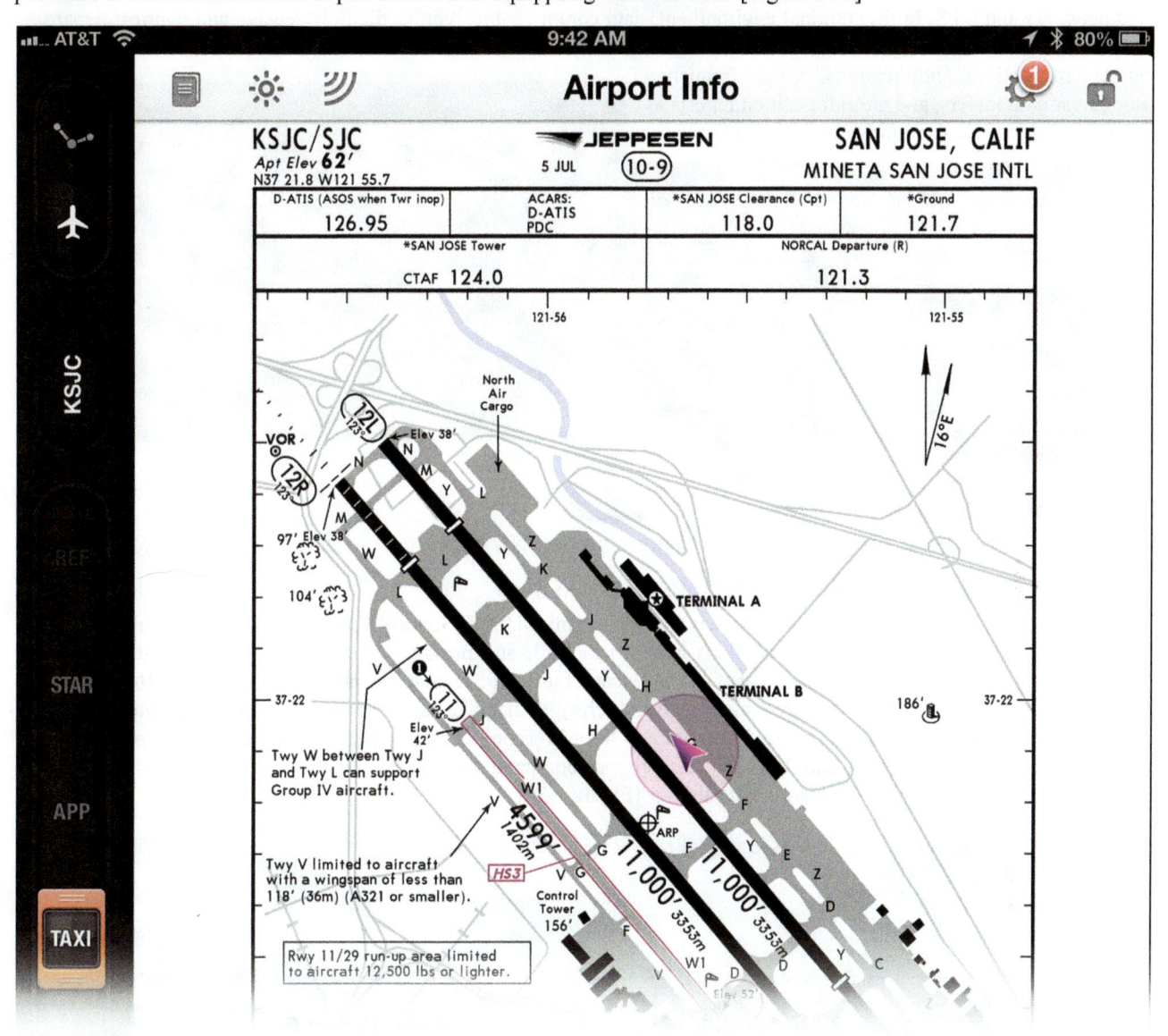

Figure 1-28. On the EFB the aircraft symbol (ownship) shows your position on an airport diagram as you taxi.

FLIGHT OPERATIONS

Tools that you use during flight operations are designed to enhance communications with ATC, avoid traffic conflicts, and increase your situational awareness in low visibility conditions. ATC automation helps decrease controller workload and provide separation for increasing numbers of aircraft in the NAS.

AIRCRAFT COMMUNICATIONS ADDRESSING AND REPORTING SYSTEM

The aircraft communications addressing and reporting system (ACARS) is a digital commercial system that enables you to communicate with company personnel and send email-type messaging to ATC without verbal transmission. Many messages to company personnel are sent and received automatically, such as when the flight leaves the gate (triggered by the release of the parking brake), during takeoff and touchdown (triggered by landing gear switches), and on arrival (triggered when a cabin door is opened). Other information received or transmitted through ACARS can include abnormal flight condition identification, flight plans, enroute and destination weather, crew lists, cargo manifests, ATIS reports, clearances, fuel reports, engine reports, and maintenance plans.

DATA COMMUNICATIONS

The data communications (data comm) program moves some communication off the voice channel using data link technology. This capability provides a verifiable record to reduce communication errors and increases air traffic efficiency by decreasing the time spent on routine tasks, such as communication transfers. Using systems, such as the future air navigation system (FANS), enables flight crews and air traffic controllers to communicate information through data links established on satellite-based networks and GPS. In the terminal environment, data comm enables you to digitally receive and confirm departure clearances and revisions and taxi instructions. During enroute operations, controllers and flight crews send ATC clearances, requests, instructions, notifications, voice frequency communication transfers, and aircraft position reports as a supplement to voice communications. [Figure 1-29]

Figure 1-29. Using data comm, an ATC message is sent to a display and you respond to the message digitally.

ADVANCED TECHNOLOGIES AND OCEANIC PROCEDURES

Advanced technologies and oceanic procedures (ATOP) is an oceanic air traffic control automation system that fully integrates flight and radar data processing, detects conflicts between aircraft, and provides satellite data link communication and surveillance capabilities. As the key component of ATOP, Ocean21 uses GPS-enabled technologies to free air traffic controllers from many routine, manual tasks and enables aircraft altitude changes that take advantage of more favorable winds to provide better fuel economy and smoother conditions. For example, Ocean21's conflict probe determines if there is adequate separation available for a climb or descent. Controllers can clear aircraft equipped with ADS-C to climb or descend to their desired altitude between aircraft flying at an intermediate altitude [Figure 1-30]

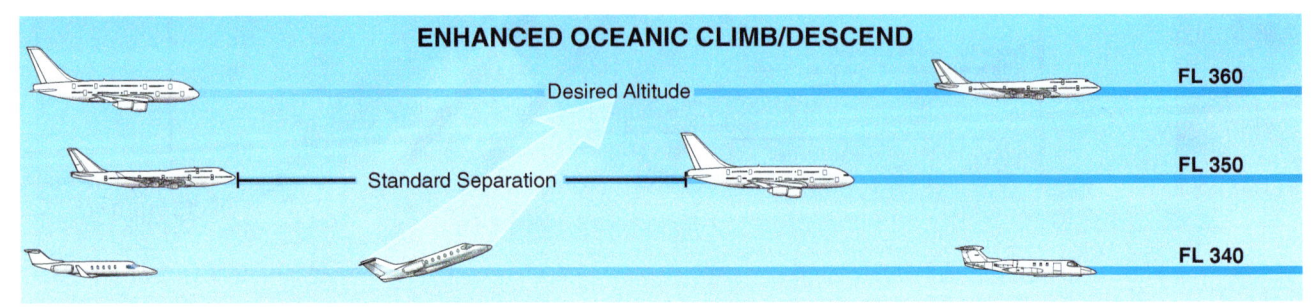

Figure 1-30. To take advantage of the climb/descend procedure (CDP), the aircraft's navigation system verifies the aircraft's position using GPS signals and ADS-C.

AVIATION ENVIRONMENTAL DESIGN TOOL

Aircraft noise, air quality, climate, and energy issues influence the capacity and flexibility of the NAS. The FAA continues to develop strategies to reduce environmental and energy impacts to levels that promote sustainability without constraining growth. The aviation environmental design tool (AEDT) is a software system that models the performance of specific aircraft types to produce fuel burn, emissions, and noise data. The AEDT system provides full flight gate-to-gate analyses for single flights at one airport to multiple aircraft at the regional, national, and global levels. The FAA uses the AEDT to study the interdependencies between fuel burn, emissions, and noise.

COLLISION AVOIDANCE SYSTEMS

The traffic alert and collision avoidance system (TCAS)—internationally known as the airborne collision avoidance system (ACAS)—enables you to maintain awareness of the traffic situation in the vicinity of your aircraft. TCAS uses three separate systems to plot the positions of nearby aircraft. First, directional antennae that receive Mode S transponder signals provide a bearing to neighboring aircraft that is accurate to a few degrees. Next, the system uses Mode C altitude broadcasts to plot the

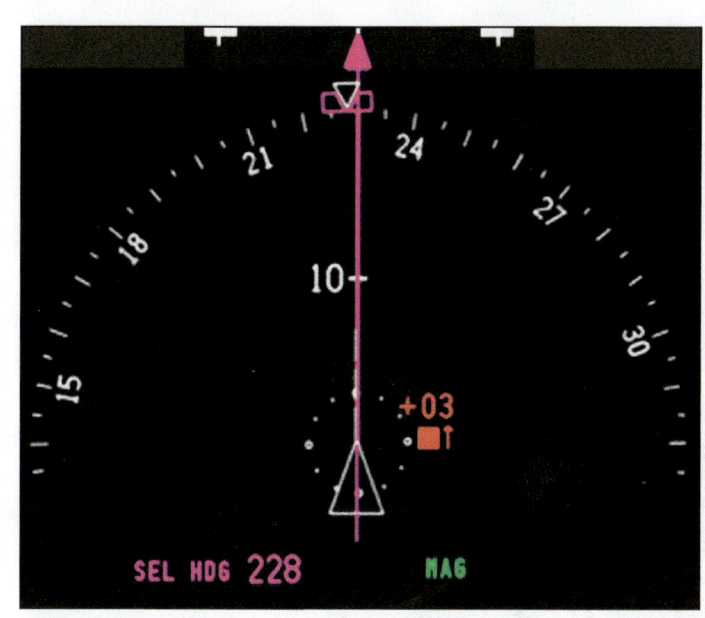

Figure 1-31. TCAS and similar traffic avoidance systems provide safety independent of ATC and supplement and enhance ATC's ability to prevent air-to-air collisions.

altitude of aircraft in the vicinity. Finally, the timing of the Mode S interrogation/response protocol is measured to ascertain the distance of an aircraft from the TCAS aircraft. [Figure 1-31]

TCAS continues to evolve. TCAS I—the first generation of TCAS—displays the relative position and velocity of other transponder-equipped aircraft within a 10 to 20-mile range and provides a warning when an aircraft gets too close. However, TCAS I does not provide instructions on how to maneuver to avoid the aircraft.

TCAS II provides airspace surveillance, intruder tracking, threat detection, and avoidance maneuver generations. TCAS II determines whether each aircraft is climbing, descending, or flying straight and level, and commands an evasive maneuver to either climb or descend to avoid conflicting traffic. If both aircraft in conflict are equipped with TCAS II, then the evasive maneuvers are well coordinated via air-to-air transmissions over the Mode S data link and the commanded maneuvers do not cancel out each other. TCAS II can reduced vertical separation above FL290 and enables aircraft to track multiple targets at long ranges. The next generation of TCAS—ACAS-X—uses ADS-B technology to provide improved traffic surveillance and tracking and advanced collision avoidance logic.

VISION SYSTEMS

Vision systems technology can improve your situational awareness and in some cases, reduce takeoff and landing minimums. Vision systems fall under four categories based on their features and how you use them during flight operations. Enhanced vision systems, synthetic vision systems, and combined vision systems can be displayed on primary flight displays (PFD), navigation displays, or class 3 EFBs. The enhanced flight vision system must be displayed on a conformal head-up display (HUD).

Enhanced and Synthetic Vision Systems

An enhanced vision system (EVS) provides a display of the forward external scene topography through the use of imaging sensors, such as forward looking infrared, millimeter wave radiometry or radar, and low-light-level image intensifying. A synthetic vision system (SVS) is a computer-generated image of the surrounding topography and airport environment created from a database of terrain, obstacles, and cultural features and a navigation source for the aircraft's position, altitude, heading, and track. The image is displayed from the flight crew's perspective or as a plan view moving map. [Figure 1-32]

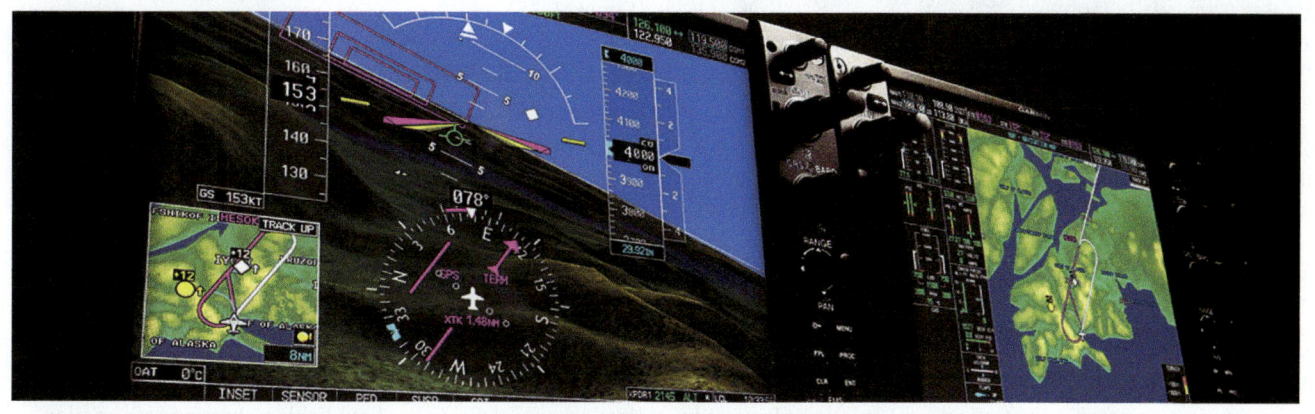

Figure 1-32. SVS real-time, color 3-D imagery of the flight environment enhances situational awareness.

Combined Vision System

A combined vision system (CVS) unites synthetic and enhanced systems. For example a CVS might include database-driven synthetic vision images combined with real-time sensor images superimposed and correlated on the same display. You might use the CVS technology while flying an approach. For example, during most of the approach procedure, you would refer to the SVS picture. As the aircraft nears the runway, the picture gradually and smoothly transitions from synthetic to enhanced vision to display the runway environment.

1-23

Enhanced Flight Vision System

An enhanced flight vision system (EFVS) uses a real-time imaging sensor that provides highly accurate vision performance in low visibility conditions. The EFVS projects an image onto a HUD. Required visual references become visible in the image before they are visible naturally out the window. In addition, depending on atmospheric conditions and the strength of energy emitted and/or reflected from the scene, you can see these visual references on the display in more detail than you can looking through the window without enhanced vision. FAR 91.175(l) allows you to continue an approach below the DA or MDA to 100 feet above the runway using an EFVS provided specific conditions outlined in the regulation are met. [Figure 1-33]

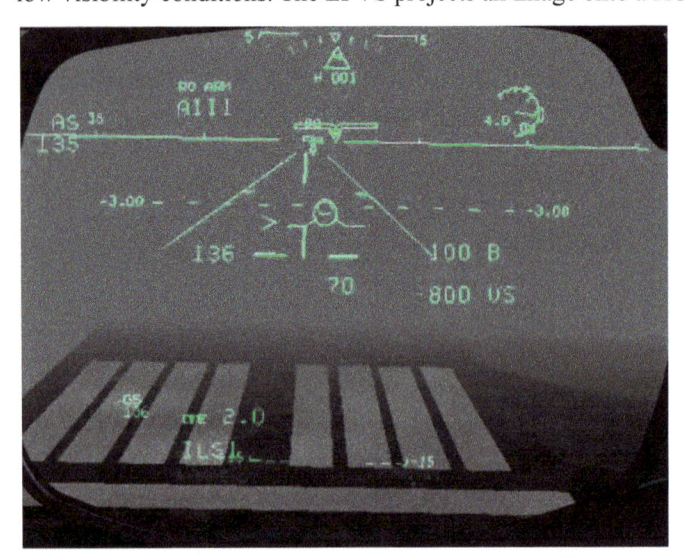

Figure 1-33. A HUD enables you to look outside the flight deck, scanning for traffic or flying an approach, and simultaneously view primary flight instruments.

AUTOMATED TERMINAL PROXIMITY ALERT

The automated terminal proximity alert (ATPA) is a tool that provides decision support information to controllers to make adjustments needed to safely achieve optimal final approach spacing and efficiency. Cones displayed between aircraft on the controller's radar screen show the minimum required separation distance for aircraft flying in-line instrument approaches, which is three to ten miles depending on the aircraft type. An additional line shows a continuous mileage-readout between aircraft, accurate to 100th of a mile. If the ATPA system projects that the trailing aircraft might be too close, the mileage-readout display and the cone changes color to alert the controller. The alert gives the controller time to adjust the aircraft's speed. [Figure 1-34]

FLIGHT MANAGEMENT SYSTEM

A flight management system (FMS) is a flight computer system that uses a large database to allow routes to be pre-programmed and fed into the system by means of a data loader. The FMS is constantly updated with respect to position accuracy by reference to conventional navigation aids, inertial reference system technology, or GPS. The sophisticated program and its associated database ensure that the most appropriate navigation aids or inputs are automatically selected during the information update cycle. [Figure 1-35]

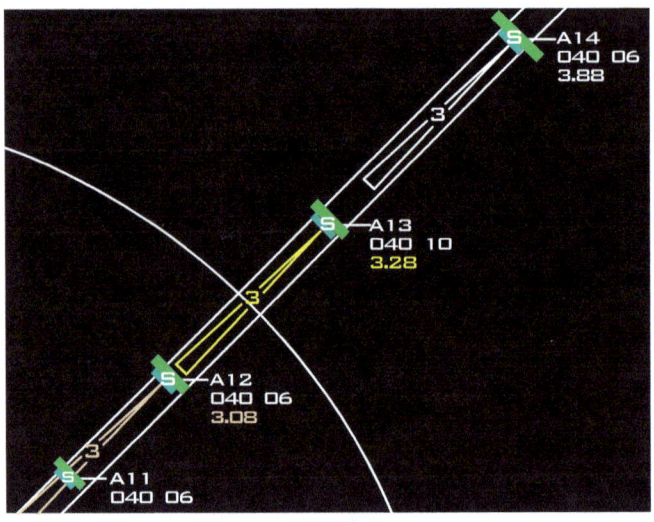

Figure 1-34. The ATPA system provides data that gives the controller time to request an aircraft speed adjustment to ensure adequate spacing rather than vectoring the aircraft off the approach course.

EFB – ENROUTE AND APPROACH

The ability to display enroute and terminal charts and view your aircraft symbol on an EFB moving map increases your situational awareness during flight operations. You can receive in-flight weather and perform real-time calculations based on current weather and runway conditions. The EFB can interface with ground systems to include a dashboard for dispatchers to monitor data. In addition, the EFB can replace paper logbooks with computer-based logs that can be stored and shared . You can report technical status and faults, maintain flight logs, and store maintenance actions, deferrals, release, and servicing records. [Figure 1-36]

DISSEMINATING AERONAUTICAL INFORMATION

The FAA is the official source of aeronautical information. The Aeronautical Navigation Products (AeroNav Products) division supports pilots, air traffic controllers, and aviation planners by collecting, maintaining, and publishing charting information. AeroNav Products develops and maintains the FAA's instrument flight procedures (IFPs) and performance-based navigation procedures. AeroNav Products also compiles and publishes the FAA's IFR and VFR digital and paper aeronautical chart products and produces specialized aeronautical products to support ATC.

Figure 1-35. A typical FMS provides information for continuous automatic navigation, guidance, and aircraft performance management, and includes a control display unit (CDU)

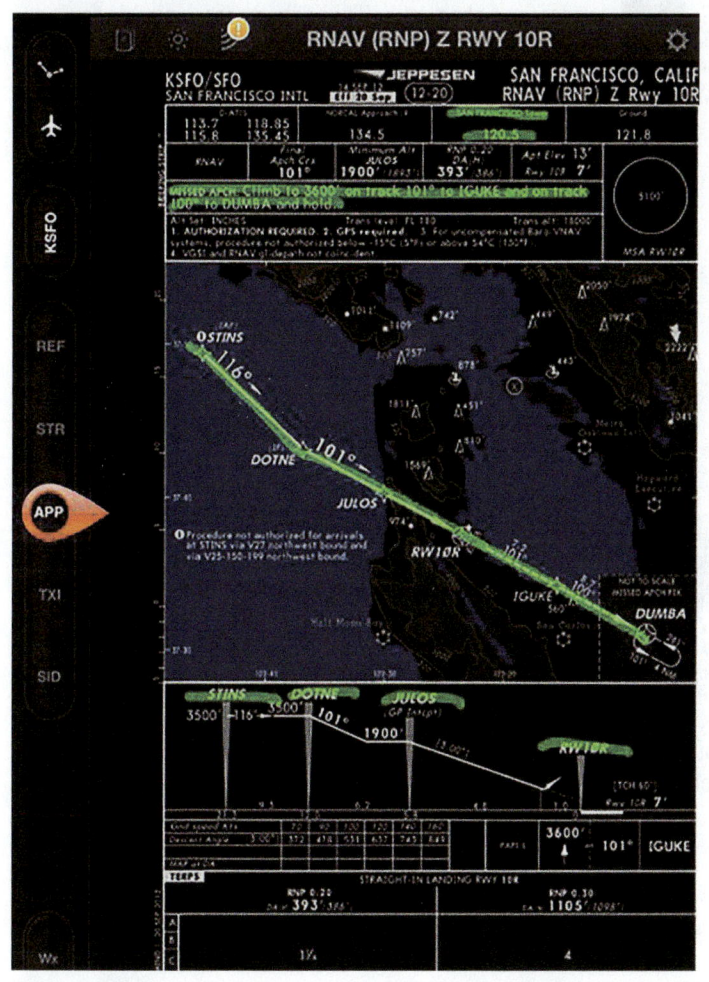

Figure 1-36. EFB technology can include the ability to zoom and highlight information on electronic charts and select a night theme for increased readability.

PUBLICATION CRITERIA

The National Flight Data Center (NFDC) is the primary authority and official repository within the FAA responsible for the collection, validation and quality control of aeronautical information disseminated to support NAS operations. NFDC aeronautical information is used to develop and update instrument approach procedures, digital products, aeronautical charts and related publications. This information is disseminated in accordance with standards established by the International Civil Aviation Organization (ICAO) and in accordance with the aeronautical information regulation and control cycle (AIRAC). The AIRAC cycle produces charting revisions every 56 days (double AIRAC cycle) or every 28 days (single AIRAC cycle). The following conditions or categories of information are forwarded to the NFDC for inclusion in government source material used as the basis for flight information publications and aeronautical charts:

- Navaid commissioning, decommissioning, outages, restrictions, frequency changes, and changes in monitoring status.

- Commissioning, decommissioning, and changes in the hours of operation of FAA ATC facilities.

- Changes in the hours of operations of surface areas and airspace.

- Remote communications outlet (RCO) and remote center air/ground (RCAG) commissioning, decomissioning, and changes in voice control or monitoring facility.

- Weather reporting station commissioning, decommissioning, failure, and unavailability or unreliable operations.

- Public airport commissioning, decommissioning, opening, closing, and abandonment and some airport operating area changes.

- Aircraft rescue and fire fighting capability, including restrictions to air carrier operations.

- Changes to runway identifiers, dimensions, threshold placements, and surface compositions.

- NAS lighting system commissioning, decommissioning, outages, and change in classification or operation.

- IFR area charts.

JEPPESEN CHARTS AND FLIGHT INFORMATION

Jeppesen is the premier commercial provider of aeronautical charts, publications, and additional flight information for pilots in both paper and electronic formats. Jeppesen uses the flight information from the official government source material and, presents the data in a well researched, user-friendly format. Jeppesen flight information is available for virtually every country in the world.

Jeppesen NavData provides navigation databases for GPS equipment used by airlines, general aviation pilots, and corporate flight departments and almost every major avionics manufacturer worldwide. Jeppesen paper and digital chart services include enroute low and high altitude charts; area charts; enroute and terminal chart NOTAMs; terminal approach charts; arrival and departure procedures; and text pages that include critical flight information such as radio aids, meteorology, tables, codes, and chart ends. These charts are available for locations around the world. [Figure 1-37]

Aeronautical charts are available as a one time purchase or, more commonly, as a subscription that is tailored to meet the needs of all instrument pilots, from individuals to commercial airlines. Both paper and electronic formats are available in a variety of service types. Although Jeppesen charts are most commonly referred to as the standard *Jeppesen Airway Manual,* there are numerous other available chart options. In order to provide the most current, up-to-date flight information, as a subscriber, you receive revisions in accordance with the type of service chosen. For most subscriptions, revisions are normally disseminated every 14 days.

Jeppesen also provides several other publications pertinent to flight information. These publications include reprints of the Federal Aviation Regulations and *Aeronautical Information Manual* (FAR/AIM) for pilots, maintenance technicians, and FAA inspectors. Additional products include explanations of FARs, recurrent training programs, chart training programs, and FAA

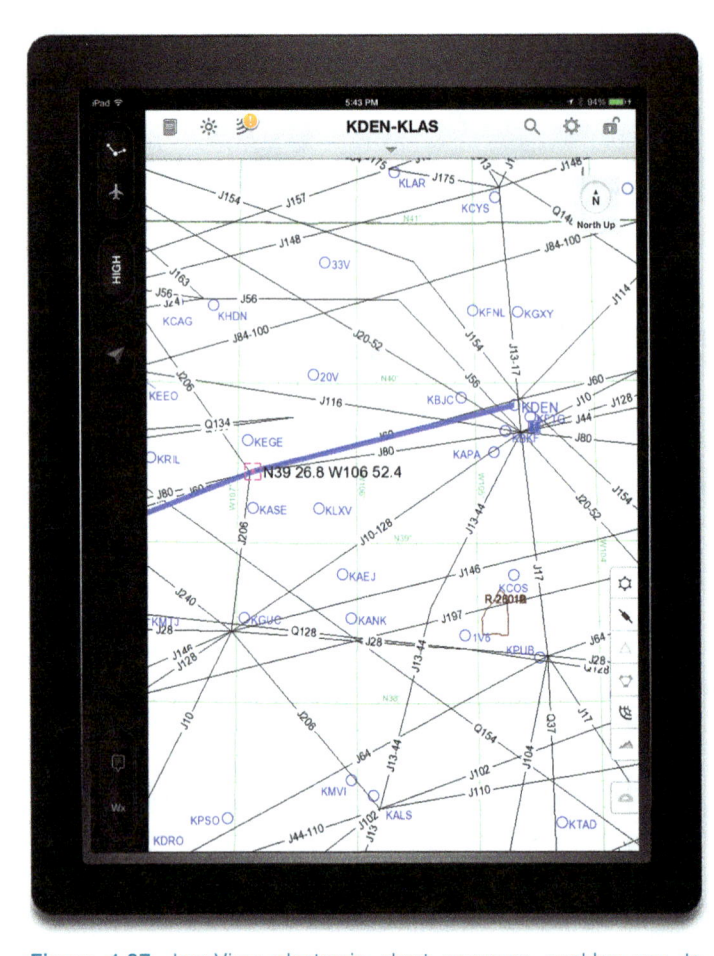

Figure 1-37. JeppView electronic chart coverage enables you to download to Mobile FliteDeck and MobileTC and update charts and NavData anytime via the internet.

VFR charts. Charts, chart services, and additional publications are available for purchase directly from Jeppesen or an authorized Jeppesen dealer. Catalogs that describe each type of chart subscription are also available. For information about Jeppesen products and services, contact Jeppesen at:

Web Site: www.jeppesen.com

Online Store: jeppdirect.jeppesen.com

IFR ENROUTE LOW ALTITUDE CHARTS

IFR enroute low altitude charts provide aeronautical information for navigation under IFR below 18,000 feet MSL. Chart data includes airways; limits of controlled airspace; VHF navaids with frequency, Morse code identifier, and 3-letter identifier; VFR and IFR airports; communication frequencies; minimum enroute and obstruction clearance altitudes; airway distances; reporting points; and special use airspace. Scales vary from chart to chart with the scale for a particular chart noted along the top of the chart. [Figure 1-38]

Figure 1-38. Enroute low altitude chart subscriptions cover the entire U.S. or specific regions. Worldwide coverage is available.

Area charts provide individual enlargements of several high density air traffic areas to improve readability and provide more detail. Area charts do not provide approach or departure information, but can help with the transition from departure to the enroute structure and from enroute to approach by providing information such as arrival and departure routes, reporting points, speed limit points, distance rings, and airspace designations. Selected area charts with terrain in excess of 4,000 feet above the main airport elevation might contain generalized contour information to help you visualize the layout of the terrain in the area. However, this does not ensure clearance around terrain or man-made structures because there might be higher uncharted obstacles in the same vicinity. Comply with all minimum IFR altitudes dictated by the airway and route structure to ensure terrain and obstruction clearance. Area chart locations are shown on the low altitude enroute index and the low altitude flight planning chart. [Figure 1-39]

IFR ENROUTE HIGH ALTITUDE CHARTS

Enroute high altitude charts are designed for navigation at or above 18,000 feet MSL. This four-color chart series includes the jet route structure; VHF navaids with frequencies, identifiers, and geographic coordinates; reporting points; and minimum altitudes. Like low altitude enroute charts, the scales vary from chart to chart. [Figure 1-40]

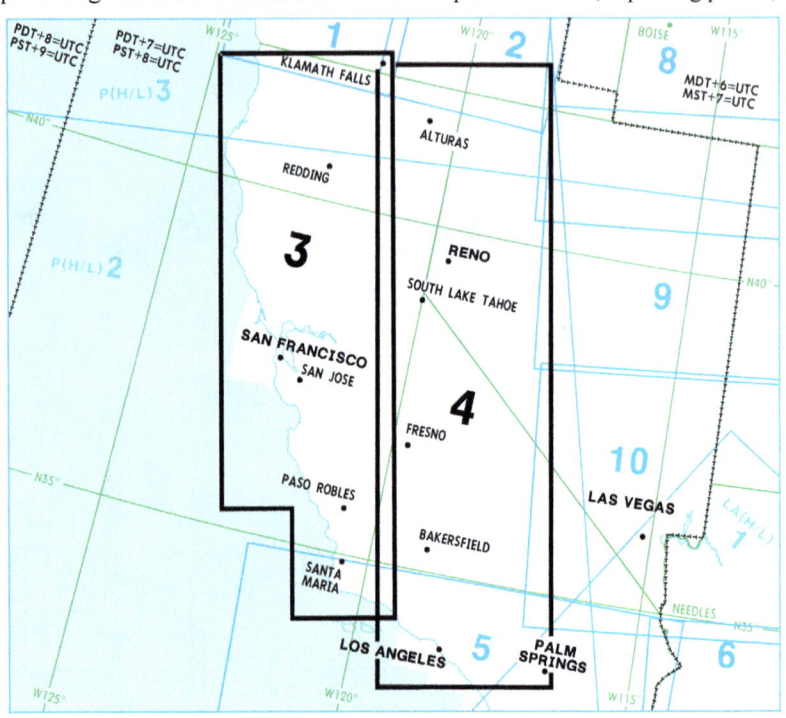

Figure 1-39. The front panel and the face of low altitude enroute charts show area chart coverage. For example, this front panel shows that area charts are published for San Francisco, Reno, Los Angeles, Palm Springs, and Las Vegas.

Figure 1-40. Each IFR high altitude chart covers a larger area than an IFR low altitude chart.

TERMINAL CHARTS

Approach charts depict instrument approach procedures in both a plan and profile view and include altitude, navigation, and communication information. Each procedure is designated for use with a specific type of navigational aid such as an ILS, VOR, NDB, LOC, RNAV (GPS), and RNAV (RNP). There are two types of departure procedures: standard instrument departures (SIDs) and obstacle departure procedures (ODPs). SIDs are depicted in a graphic format and are designed to assist ATC by expediting clearance delivery and to facilitate transition between takeoff and enroute operations. ODPs are established to ensure obstacle clearance and might be depicted textually or graphically, depending on complexity. Standard terminal arrival route (STAR) charts are designed to expedite ATC arrival procedures and to facilitate the transition between enroute and instrument approach operations. Each STAR chart graphically depicts a preplanned IFR ATC arrival procedure and might serve either a single airport or more than one airport in a given geographic area. Airport charts present detailed runway and taxiway information and include takeoff and alternate minimums. [Figure 1-41]

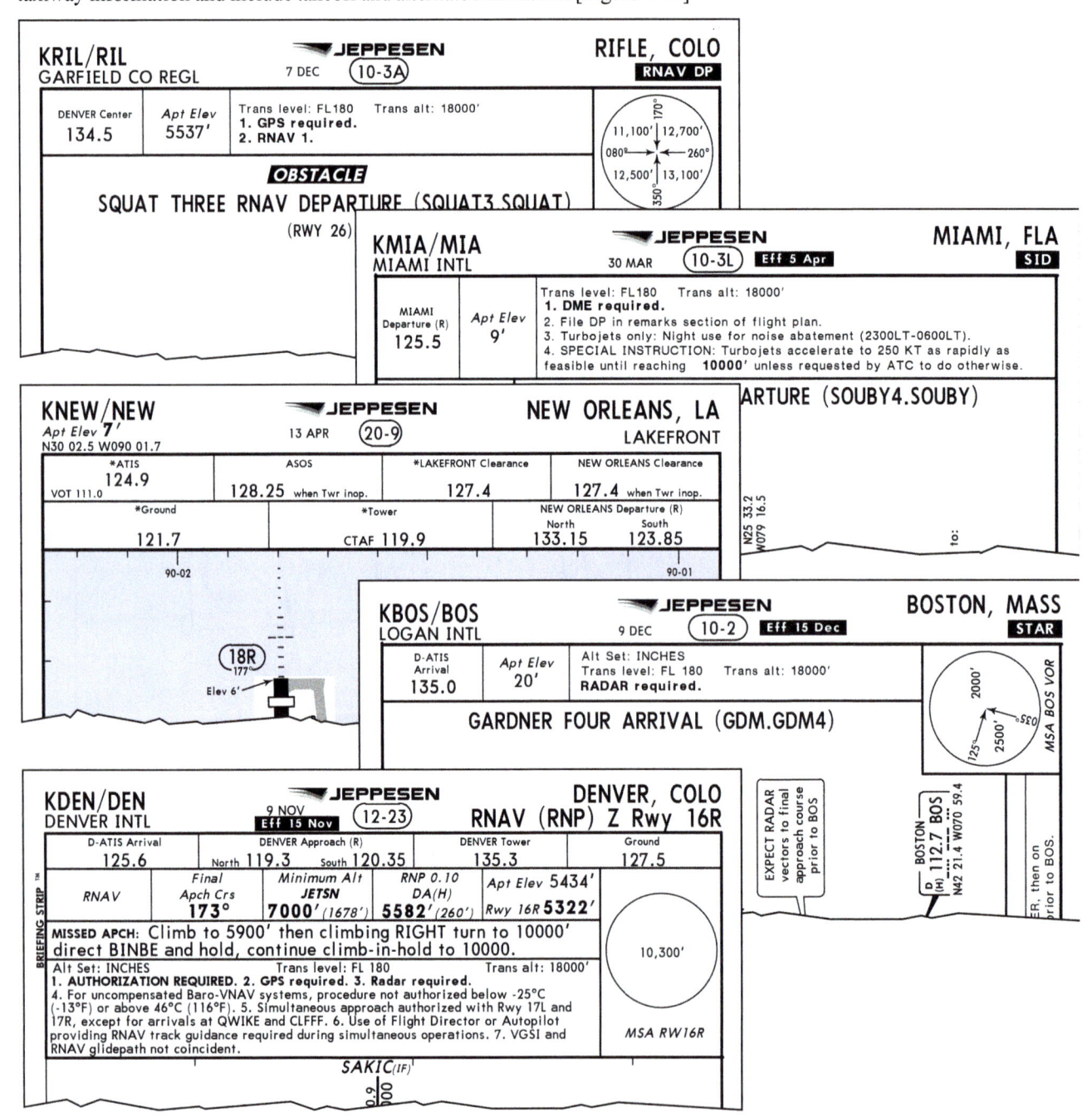

Figure 1-41. There are a variety of terminal charts including ODP, SID, STAR, approach, and airport charts.

AIRPORT QUALIFICATION CHARTS

The operating rules governing domestic and flag air carriers under FAR 121.445 require you to be qualified to fly on certain routes and operate at certain airports. Airport qualification charts help meet this requirement with full-color photographs of selected airports and surrounding areas. The charts include operational procedure information, notes on prevailing weather patterns, and descriptive overviews. [Figure 1-42]

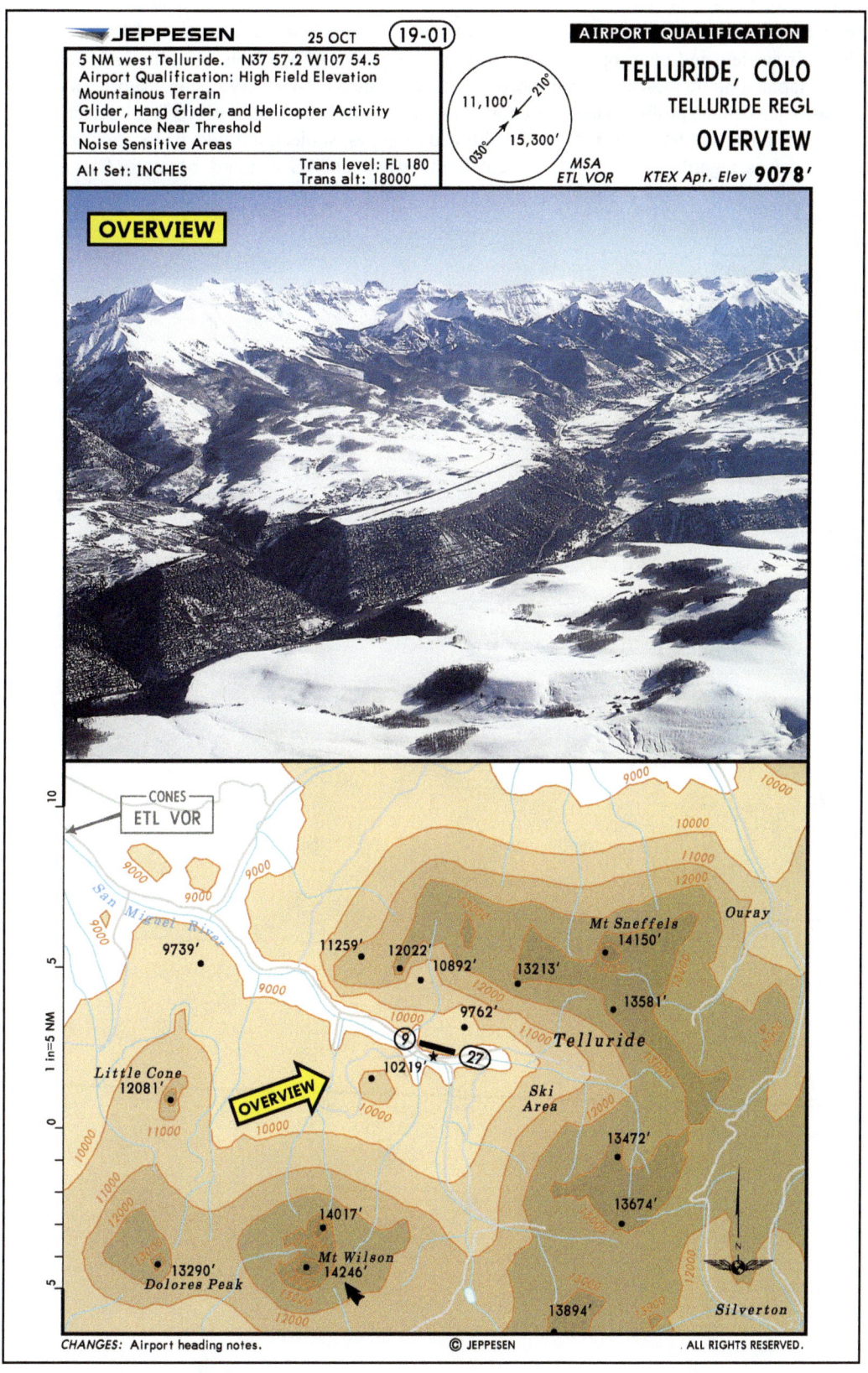

Figure 1-42. Airport qualification charts provide you with detailed, visual information as a means of increasing situational awareness and improving safety at airports located in regions of treacherous terrain or surrounded by numerous obstacles.

JEPPESEN NOTAM SERVICE

Because the NAS is continually evolving, notices to airmen (NOTAMs) provide the most current essential flight operation information available, not known sufficiently in advance to publicize in the most recent aeronautical charts or *Airport/Facility Directory*. NOTAMs provide information on airports and changes that affect the NAS that are time critical and applicable to IFR operations.

More than 150 countries issue NOTAMs. There is not, however, an official repository that stores and disseminates this NOTAM information. Since air carriers and other operators are required to gather all available information, this limitation greatly complicates pre-flight planning. Jeppesen solves this problem by offering NOTAM services on a subscription basis. Jeppesen offers the use of customer-defined profiles that permit maintenance of individual customer NOTAM databases. These profiles can filter out NOTAMs a specific operator does not need based on types, subject, altitude, or location of operations. Every NOTAM Jeppesen receives, regardless of origin or content, is edited to the ICAO standard format for Class 1 NOTAMs.

Chapter 2
Takeoffs and Departures

Thousands of IFR takeoffs and departures occur daily in the NAS. In order to accommodate this volume of traffic, ATC must rely on flight crews to use airport charts, obstacle departure procedures (ODPs), and standard instrument departures (SIDs). Although many charted (and uncharted) departures are based on radar vectors, the bulk of IFR departures in the NAS require you to fly a procedure to navigate from the terminal environment to the enroute phase.

SURFACE MOVEMENT SAFETY

One of the biggest safety concerns in aviation is surface movement accidents. To fully support the improvement of safety in the airport environment, Jeppesen publishes detailed charts of all airports, both VFR and IFR, and provides chart users with frequent updates as information changes. Jeppesen also works with industry leaders in partnership with the FAA to create and implement new procedures as well as to develop educational and awareness programs for flight crews. By working with the aviation community, Jeppesen continues to promote and support the foundations of the company as set forth by its founder, Elrey B. Jeppesen, who in the early years of instrument flying, began charting for reasons of safety and survival.

TAXI DIAGRAM AND AIRPORT MOVING MAP

Jeppesen FliteDeck Pro EFB application includes a taxi diagram on which you can monitor your position on the airport surface by referring to an airport symbol (ownship) on an airport chart. The Jeppesen Airport Moving Map application certified by the FAA for Class 2 and 3 EFBs provides similar information but uses a detailed database to dynamically render maps of an airport's runways, taxiways, and structures. [Figure 2-1]

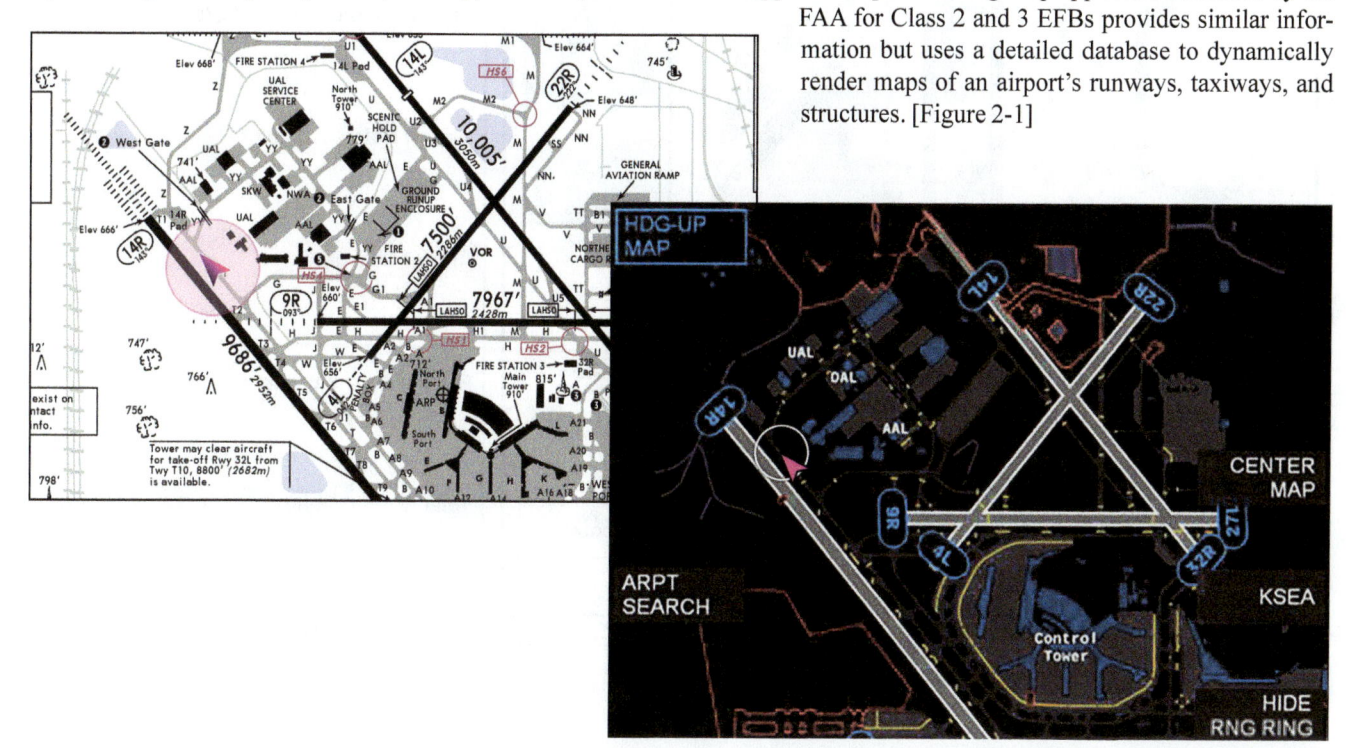

Figure 2-1. Both of these EFB applications help you identify and anticipate the airplane's location on the surface to aid in situational awareness.

AIRPORT CHARTS

Airport charts provide graphical depictions of airport layouts. Jeppesen IFR terminal chart subscriptions include a separate airport chart for every airport with an instrument approach. Each airport chart depicts information such as runway data, taxiway identifiers, airport latitude and longitude, communication frequencies, and building identification. [Figure 2-2] Takeoff minimums and alternate airport minimums might be depicted on the same chart or on a separate chart along with items such as notices, runway incursion hot spot descriptions, and obstacle departure procedures. [Figure 2-3]

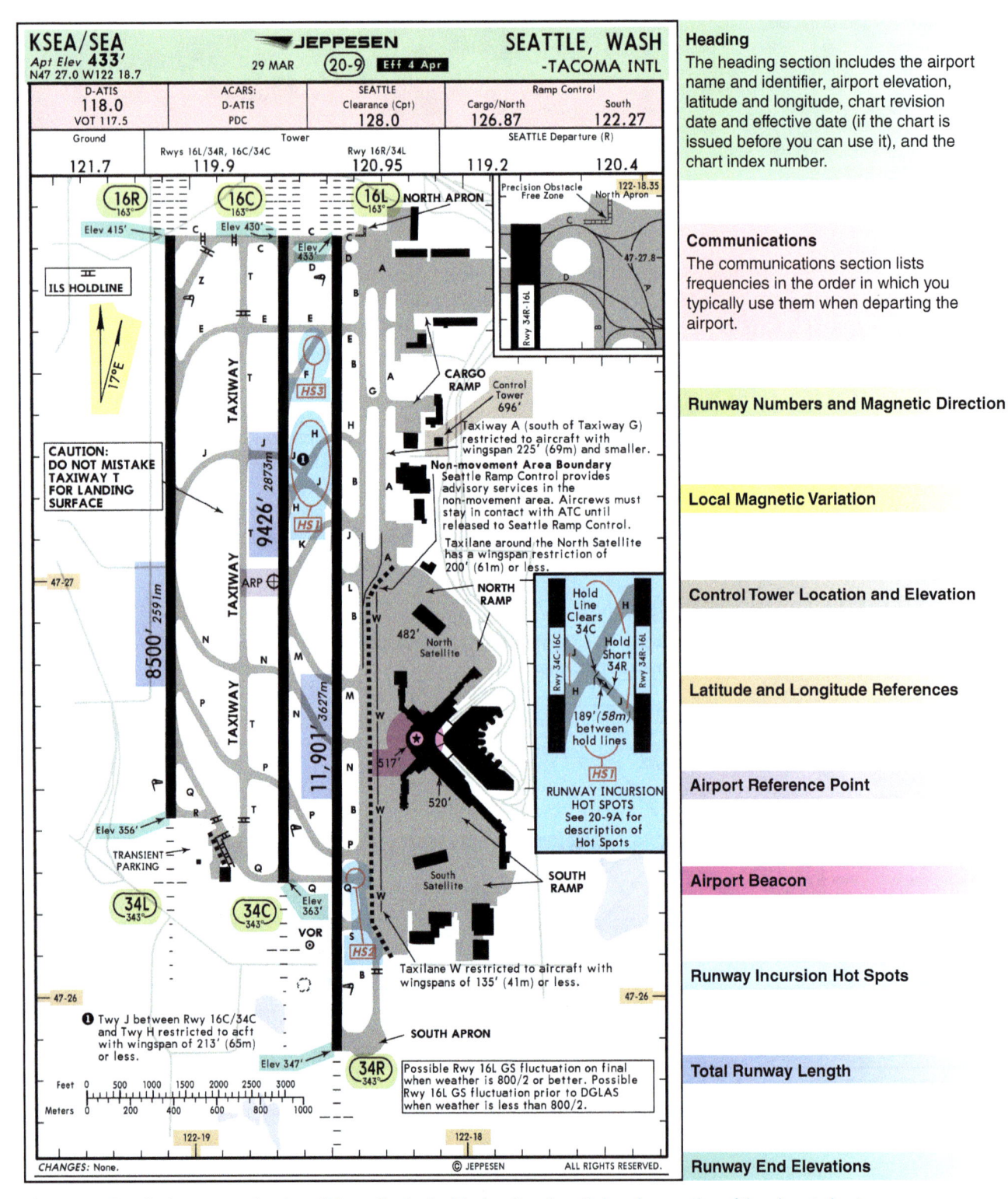

Figure 2-2. Detailed runway and taxiway information is depicted on the airport plan view section of the airport chart.

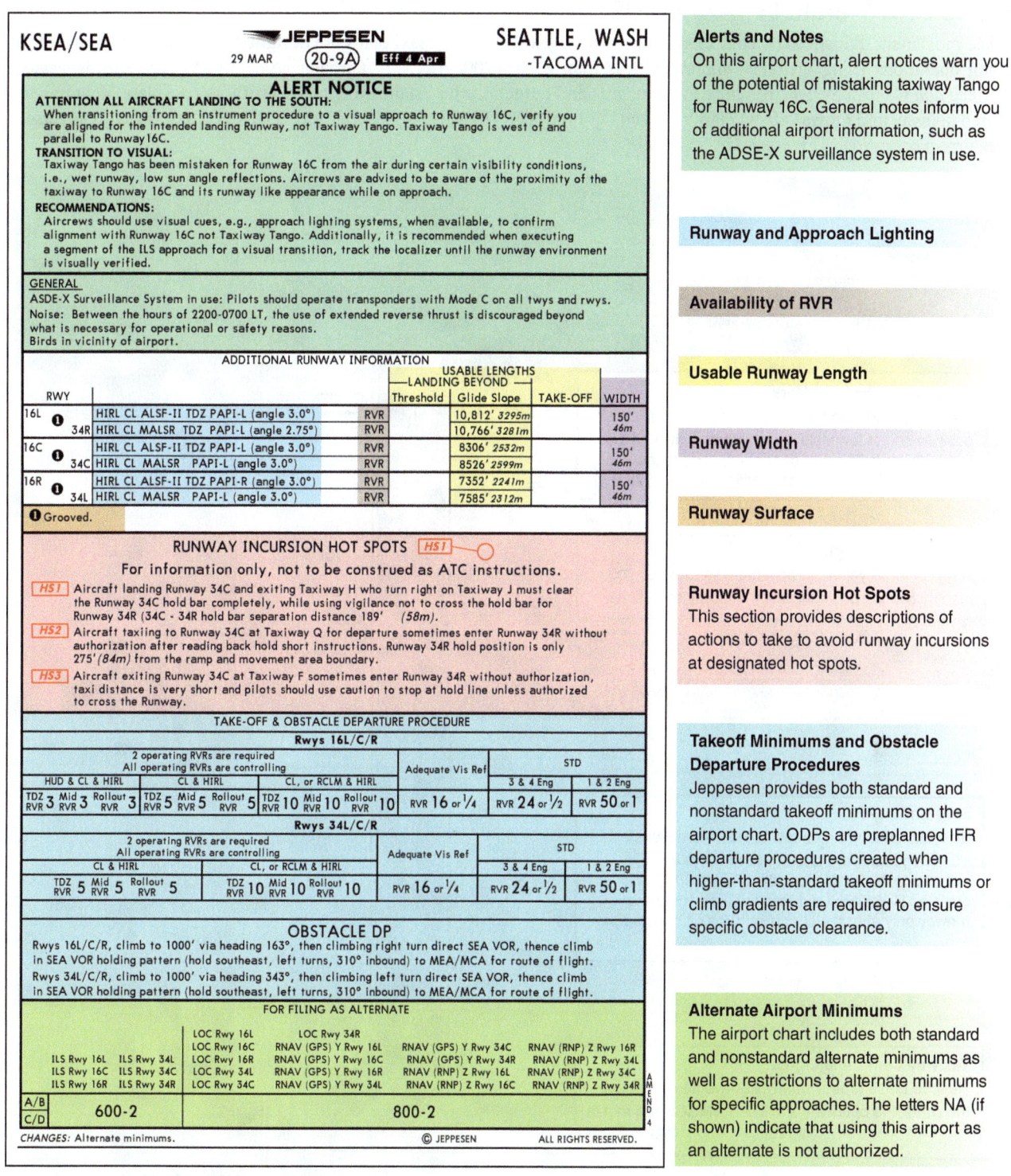

Figure 2-3. Additional airport charts provide more detailed runway information and takeoff and alternate minimums.

AIRPORT SIGNS/MARKINGS/LIGHTING

You use airport signs, markings, and lighting, to help maintain situational awareness when operating on the ground and in the air. These visual aids provide information concerning the aircraft's location on the airport, the taxiway in use, and the runway entrance being used. Often this information is overlooked, which can lead to ground accidents that are preventable. If you encounter unfamiliar signs, markings, or lighting, contact ATC for clarification and, if necessary, request progressive taxi instructions. It is your responsibility to notify the appropriate authorities of erroneous, misleading, or decaying signs or lighting that might contribute to unsafe ground operations.

SMGCS LOW VISIBILITY TAXI PLANS

Surface movement guidance and control system (SMGCS) low visibility taxi plans are designed for airports with takeoff or landing operations using visibility minimums less than RVR 1200. Advisory Circular (AC) 120-57, *Surface Movement Guidance and Control System*, provides the standards and guidelines for establishing a low visibility taxi plan, including the required taxiway and runway signs, markings, and lighting. A NOTAM is issued when any SMGCS outages would adversely affect airport operations. [Figure 2-4]

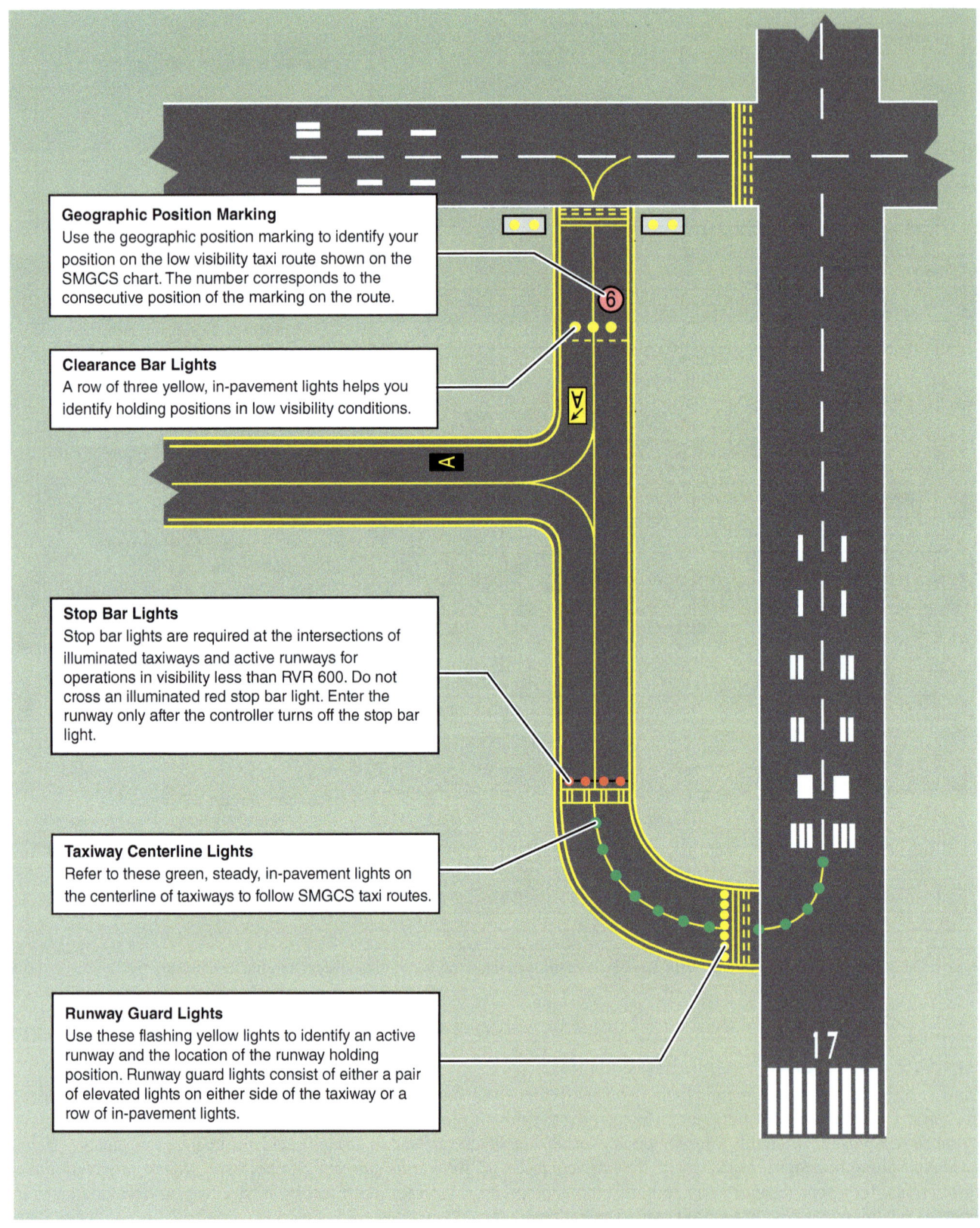

Geographic Position Marking
Use the geographic position marking to identify your position on the low visibility taxi route shown on the SMGCS chart. The number corresponds to the consecutive position of the marking on the route.

Clearance Bar Lights
A row of three yellow, in-pavement lights helps you identify holding positions in low visibility conditions.

Stop Bar Lights
Stop bar lights are required at the intersections of illuminated taxiways and active runways for operations in visibility less than RVR 600. Do not cross an illuminated red stop bar light. Enter the runway only after the controller turns off the stop bar light.

Taxiway Centerline Lights
Refer to these green, steady, in-pavement lights on the centerline of taxiways to follow SMGCS taxi routes.

Runway Guard Lights
Use these flashing yellow lights to identify an active runway and the location of the runway holding position. Runway guard lights consist of either a pair of elevated lights on either side of the taxiway or a row of in-pavement lights.

Figure 2-4. SMGCS taxiway and runway signs, marking, and lighting help guide you during taxi in low visibility conditions.

Both flight and ground crews must comply with SMGCS plans when implemented. All airport tenants are responsible for disseminating information to their employees and for conducting training in low visibility operating procedures. If you are operating in conjunction with a SMGCS plan, you must have a copy of the low visibility taxi route chart for the airport. These charts outline the taxi routes and other detailed information concerning low visibility operations. [Figure 2-5]

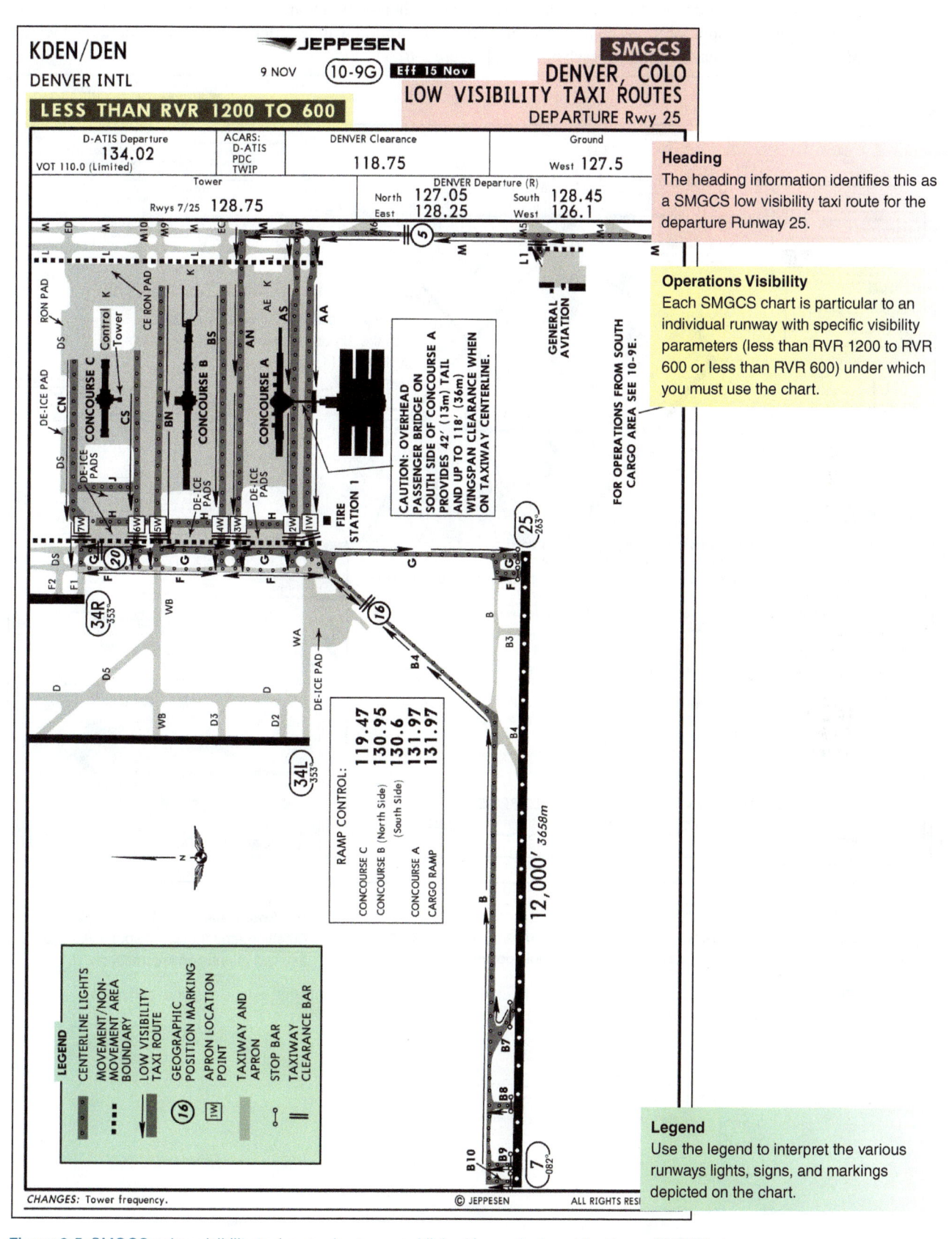

Figure 2-5. SMGCS or low visibility taxi route charts are published for each airport that has a SMGCS plan.

RUNWAY INCURSION HOT SPOTS

Runway incursion hot spots are locations that have been identified by an airport's controlling authority as having a history of collision risk or runway incursion where pilots and airport vehicle drivers must heighten their attention. Typically these hot spots are locations of intersecting runways, or areas that cannot be seen from the tower. You need to be aware that these hazardous intersections exist and you must be increasingly vigilant when approaching or taxiing through these locations. Jeppesen visually depicts hot spot locations on airport charts for those airports with reported hot spots and includes a textual description of the nature of the hazard found at each hot spot. [Figure 2-6]

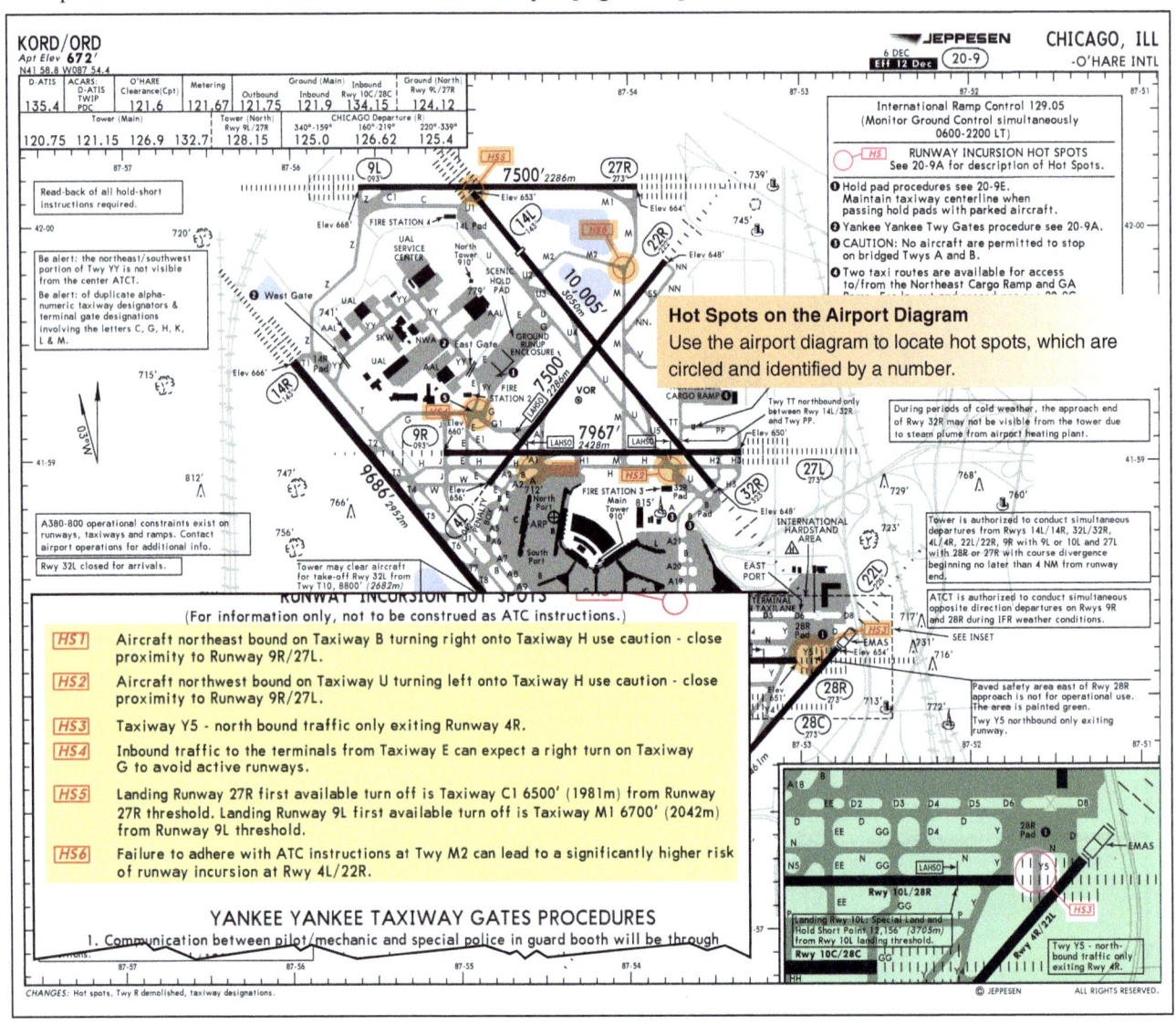

Hot Spots on the Airport Diagram
Use the airport diagram to locate hot spots, which are circled and identified by a number.

Hot Spot Descriptions
Refer to the hot spot descriptions, which are often on an additional airport information chart, for specific cautions and actions to take at the hot spot location.

Hot Spot Details
An enlargement of a hot spot gives you more detailed orientation information.

Figure 2-6. Prior to taxi, use the airport chart to brief the location of the hot spots that exist along your taxi route.

2-6

STANDARD TAXI ROUTES

Standard taxi routes improve ground management at high-density airports with scheduled airline service. At these airports, typical taxiway traffic patterns that are used to move aircraft between the gate and the runway are determined and coded. ATC can reduce radio communication time and eliminate taxi instruction misinterpretation by simply clearing you to taxi via a specifically named route. If you are unable to comply with a standard taxi route, advise ground control on initial contact. It is your responsibility to know if a particular airport has standard taxi routes, to be familiar with them, and to have the taxi descriptions in your possession. [Figure 2-7]

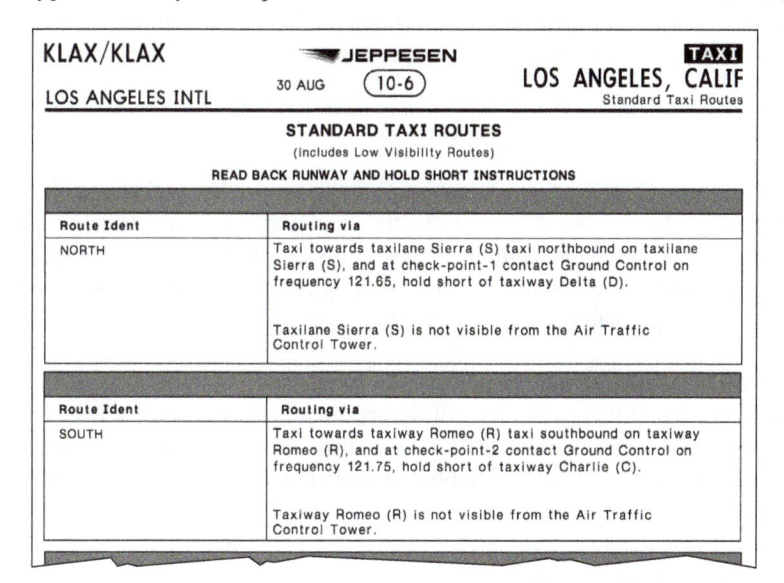

Figure 2-7. Jeppesen publishes standard taxi route descriptions with other terminal charts for the airport.

RUNWAY SAFETY

Runway safety is one of the FAA's top priorities and the Runway Safety web page provides guidance, resources, and information on the latest FAA initiatives to increase runway safety, such as runway status lights (RWSL). The takeoff and departure phases of flight are critical since the majority of this time is spent on the ground with multiple actions occurring. The FAA and the aviation industry want to reduce runway surface events of all types, but this cannot be done simply through policy changes and educational programs—you must take responsibility for ensuring safety during surface operations and continue to educate yourself through government and industry runway safety programs. [Figure 2-8]

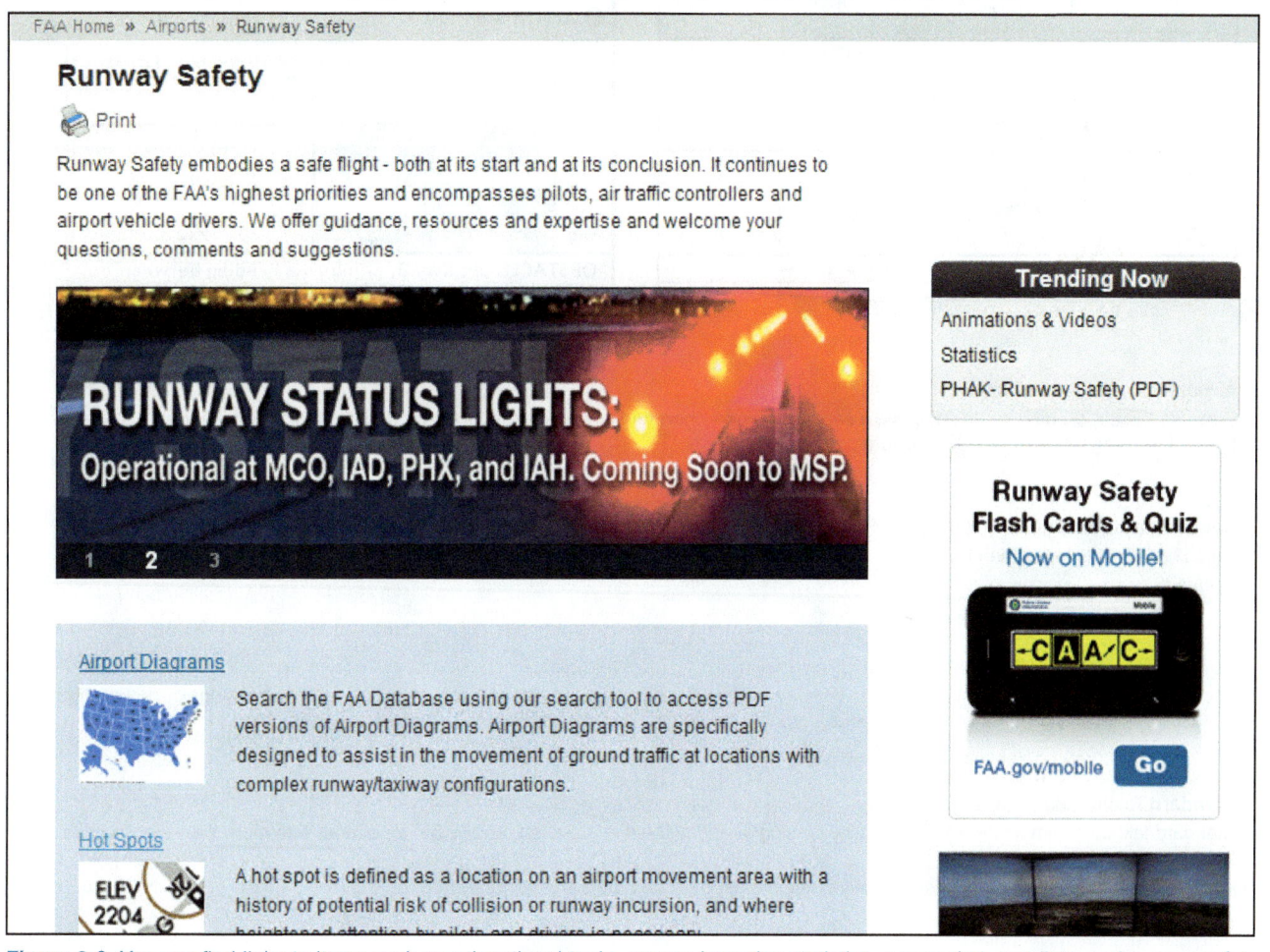

Figure 2-8. You can find links to items such as educational tools, runway incursion statistics, runway hot spot lists, and runway safety news on the FAA Runway Safety web page.

TAKEOFF MINIMUMS

The FAA establishes takeoff minimums for every airport that has published standard instrument procedures. These minimums are used by aircraft operated under Parts 121, 125, 129, or 135. At airports where minimums are not established, these same carriers must use FAA-designated standard minimums, which are specified in the regulations. These standard takeoff minimums are one statute mile visibility for single- and twin-engine aircraft, and one-half statute mile for helicopters and aircraft with more than two engines.

OPERATIONS SPECIFICATIONS

If you are operating under Part 121 or Part 135, your operations specifications (OpsSpecs) may approve lower-than-standard takeoff minimums. OpsSpecs are required by FAR 119.5 to be issued to commercial operators to define appropriate authorizations, limitations, and procedures based on the type of operation, equipment, and pilot qualifications. The OpsSpecs are an extension of the regulations; therefore, they are legal, binding contracts between a properly certificated air transportation organization and the FAA for compliance with the regulations applicable to their operation.

A visibility of RVR 1,600 feet or 1/4 statute mile is below standard and may be approved for specific commercial operators if contained in an OpsSpecs approval. OpsSpecs may indicate that the flight can still depart the airport if visibility is below standard minimums or specific visibility reporting equipment is out of service if you can maintain adequate visual reference. An appropriate visual aid must be available to ensure the takeoff surface can be continuously identified and directional control can be maintained throughout the takeoff run. [Figure 2-9]

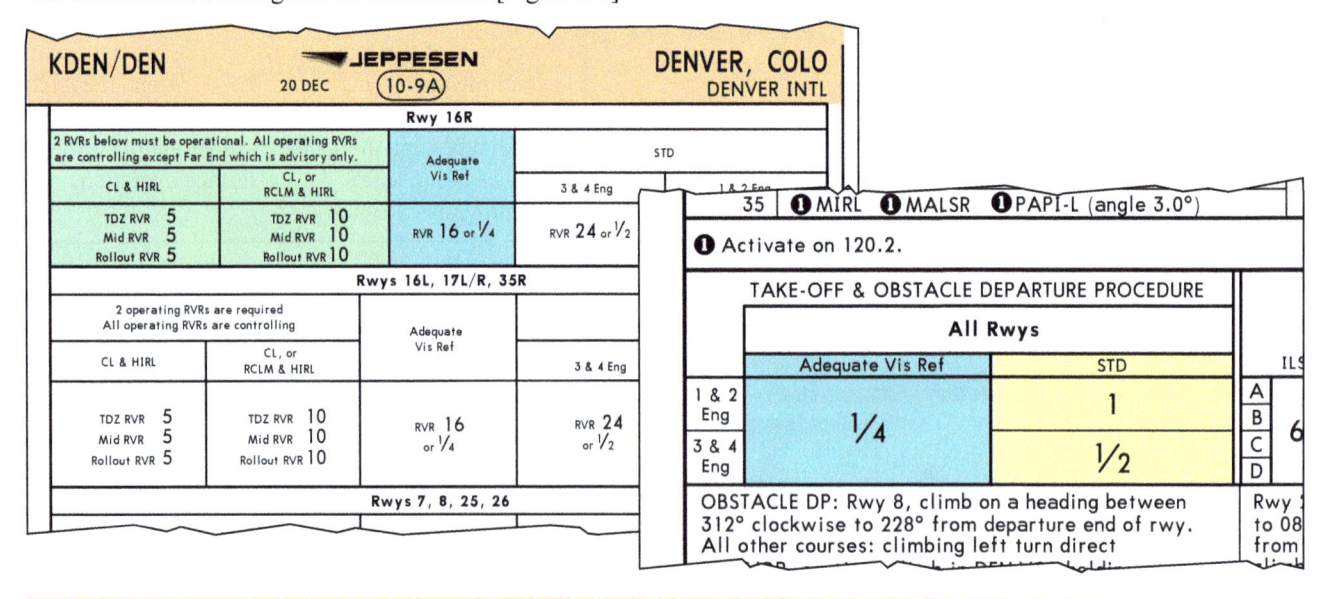

Airport Info and Takeoff Minimums
Because the airport diagram is complex, a separate airport chart for Denver International Airport shows additional airport information, takeoff minimums, and obstacle departure procedures.

Nonstandard Takeoff Minimums — RVR 5 or RVR 10
Takeoff minimums lower than RVR 16 (¼ SM) are based on the runway lighting available and whether RVR-measuring equipment is operating.

Nonstandard Takeoff Minimum
The nonstandard takeoff minimum of ¼ SM visibility applies if you have adequate visual reference—runway markings or runway lighting that provides you with reference to continuously identify the takeoff surface and maintain directional control throughout the takeoff run.

Standard Takeoff Minimums
Standard takeoff minimums are 1 SM visibility for single- and twin-engine aircraft, and ½ SM for aircraft with more than two engines.

Figure 2-9. Jeppesen lists all published takeoff minimums, both standard and nonstandard, on the lower left portion of the airport chart or at larger airports, on a separate page.

Depending on the equipment installed in a specific type of aircraft, the crew training, and the type of equipment installed at a particular airport, a company's OpsSpecs might approve flight crews to take off with as little as RVR 300. Jeppesen's tailored chart services use approved OpsSpecs for lower-than-standard takeoff and landing minimums and customizes charts specific to individual operators at their request. An enhanced flight vision system (EFVS) is an example of equipment that may lower takeoff minimums. [Figure 2-10]

TAKEOFF MINIMUM CONSIDERATIONS

If you are operating under Part 91, you are not required to comply with established takeoff minimums—legally, a zero/zero departure is acceptable but it is never advisable. If commercial airliners must comply with takeoff minimums, then good judgment and common sense would dictate that all instrument-rated pilots follow established minimums as well. Another consideration regarding takeoff minimums is the possibility that you might have to return to the airport in the event of an emergency. Although mechanical failure is potentially hazardous during any phase of flight, a failure during takeoff under IFR weather conditions is extremely critical. You must decide to either return to the departure airport or fly directly to a takeoff alternate. If conditions are below the landing minimums for the departure airport, you are unable to return for landing, leaving few options and little time to reach a takeoff alternate.

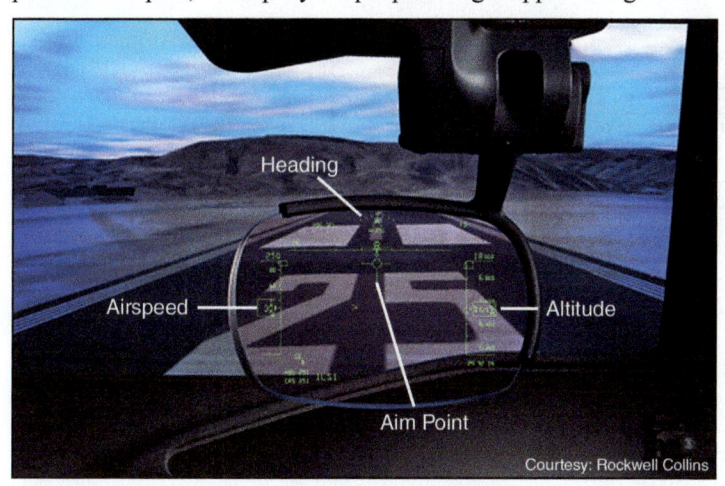

Figure 2-10. The Rockwell Collins Head-up Guidance System (HGS™) is an example of an EFVS with a low visibility takeoff capability of RVR 300.

CEILING AND VISIBILITY REQUIREMENTS

All takeoffs and departures have visibility minimums, and some may have minimum ceiling requirements, incorporated into the procedure. When ceiling and visibility minimums are specified for an IFR departure procedure both are applicable. Never launch an IFR flight without obtaining current visibility information immediately prior to departure. [Figure 2-11]

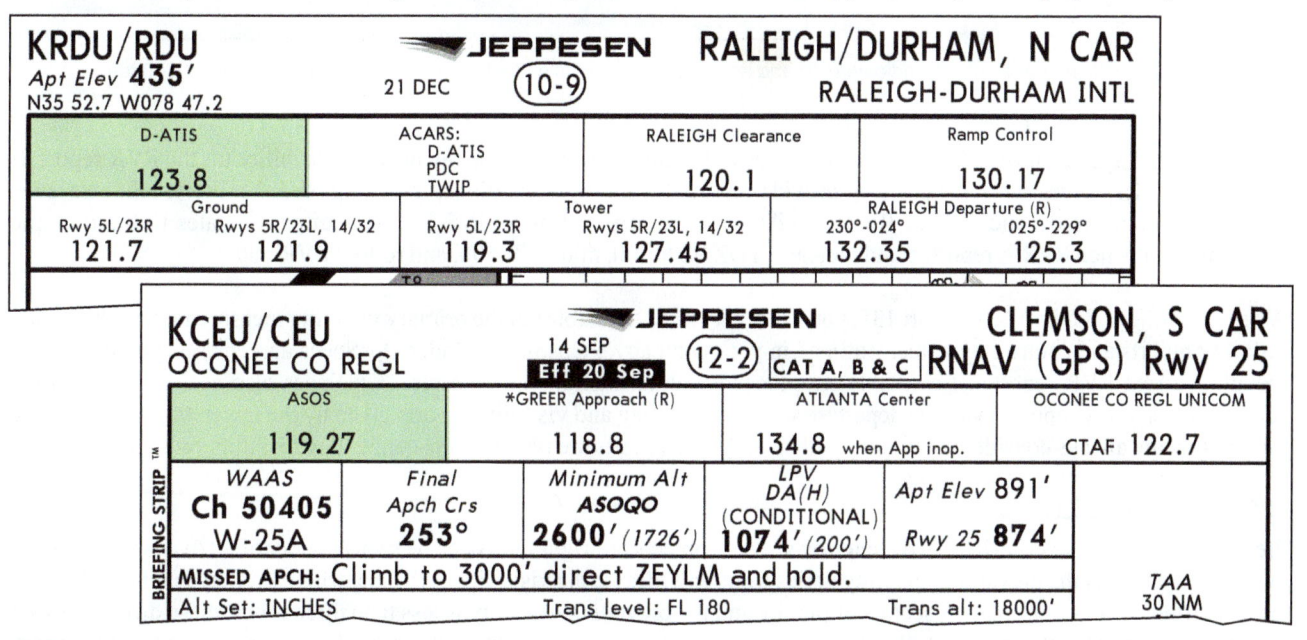

Figure 2-11. Frequencies for weather information—ATIS, digital ATIS (D-ATIS), the automated weather observing system (AWOS), and the automated surface observing system (ASOS)—are published on airport and approach charts.

RUNWAY VISUAL RANGE

Runway visual range (RVR) is an instrumentally derived value, based on standard calibrations, that represents the horizontal distance a pilot can see down the runway. It is based on the sighting of either high intensity runway lights or on the visual contrast of other targets, whichever yields the greater visual range. Unlike prevailing or runway visibility, RVR is based on what a pilot in a moving aircraft should see looking down the runway and is reported in hundreds of feet. You must use the RVR value for takeoff minimums below RVR 1600. However, RVR values of 1,600 feet or greater may be converted to statute miles if RVR is not being reported. [Figure 2-12]

TAKE-OFF							
Rwys 6R, 24L, 36			Rwy 18				Other
Adequate Vis Ref	STD		Adequate Vis Ref	With Mim climb of 290'/NM to 1300'			
	3 & 4 Eng	1 & 2 Eng		STD		
				3 & 4 Eng	1 & 2 Eng		
RVR 16 or ¼	RVR 24 or ½	RVR 50 or 1	RVR 16 or ¼	RVR 24 or ½	RVR 50 or 1	300-1

RVR to Statute Miles
The visibility minimum for takeoff with adequate visual reference is RVR 16 or 1,600 feet. If RVR is not reported, ¼ statute mile visibility applies.

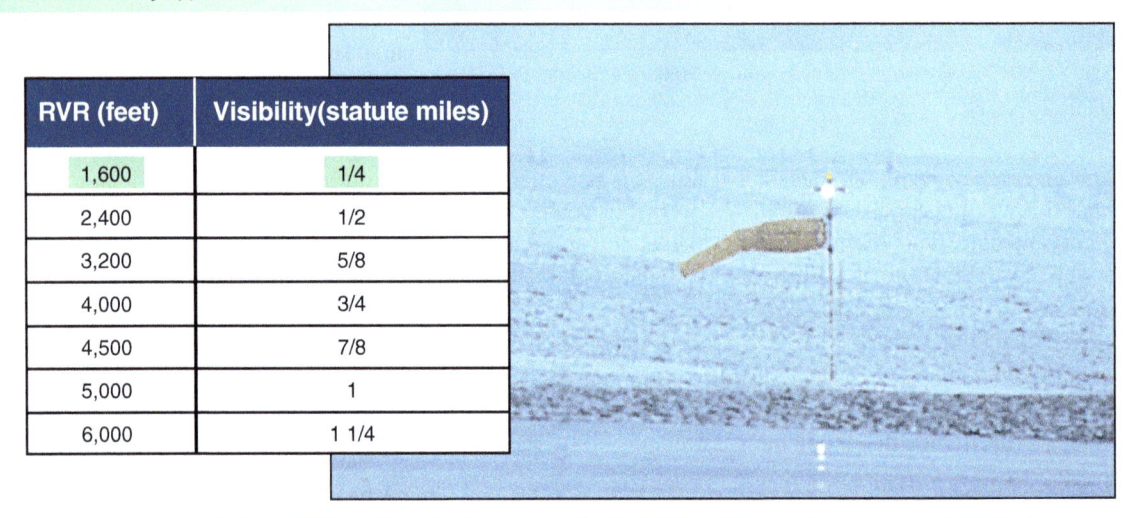

RVR (feet)	Visibility (statute miles)
1,600	1/4
2,400	1/2
3,200	5/8
4,000	3/4
4,500	7/8
5,000	1
6,000	1 1/4

Figure 2-12. Jeppesen charts indicate RVR and its value in statute miles for RVR visibility minimums above 1,600 feet.

Sensor systems, such as forward scatter meters or transmissometers near the runway measure visibility for the RVR report. If multiple sensor systems are installed, they provide reports for multiple locations, including RVR for the touchdown zone (TDZ), mid-point (mid), and rollout. RVR visibility may be reported as RVR 5-5-5. This directly relates to the multiple locations from which RVR is reported and indicates TDZ RVR 500, mid RVR 500, and rollout RVR 500.

When operating under Part 121 or Part 135, you use RVR (when available) as the primary visibility measurement with specific visibility reports and controlling values outlined in your company's OpsSpecs. Under OpsSpecs agreements, you must have specific, current RVR reports (if available) to proceed with an instrument departure. OpsSpecs also outline which is the controlling visibility report in various departure scenarios. Ceiling and visibility reports given by the tower with the departure information are always considered official weather, and RVR reports are typically the controlling visibility reference.

PREVAILING VISIBILITY

Prevailing visibility is the horizontal distance over which objects or bright lights can be seen and identified over at least half of the horizon circle. If the prevailing visibility varies from area to area, the visibility of the majority of the sky is reported. When critical differences exist in various sectors of the sky and the prevailing visibility is less than three miles, these differences are reported at manned stations. Typically, this is referred to as sector visibility in the remarks section of a METAR report. Prevailing visibility is reported in statute miles or fractions of miles.

TOWER VISIBILITY

Tower visibility is the prevailing visibility as determined from the control tower. If visibility is determined from only one point on the airport and it is the tower, then it is considered the usual point of observation. Otherwise, when the visibility is measured from multiple points, the control tower observation is referred to as the tower visibility. It too is measured in statute miles or fractions of miles.

AUTOMATED WEATHER OBSERVING SYSTEMS AND AUTOMATED SURFACE OBSERVING SYSTEMS

Automated weather observing systems (AWOS) and automated surface observing systems (ASOS) are installed at airports and maintained by both government (FAA and NWS) and private entities. AWOS and ASOS offer a wide variety of capabilities and progressively broader weather reports. Automated systems typically transmit weather every one to two minutes so the most up-to-date weather information is constantly broadcast. Basic AWOS includes only altimeter setting, wind speed, wind direction, temperature, and dewpoint information. More advanced systems such as the AWOS-3 provide additional information, such as cloud and ceiling data and precipitation type. Stations providing service levels A or B also report RVR. [Figure 2-13]

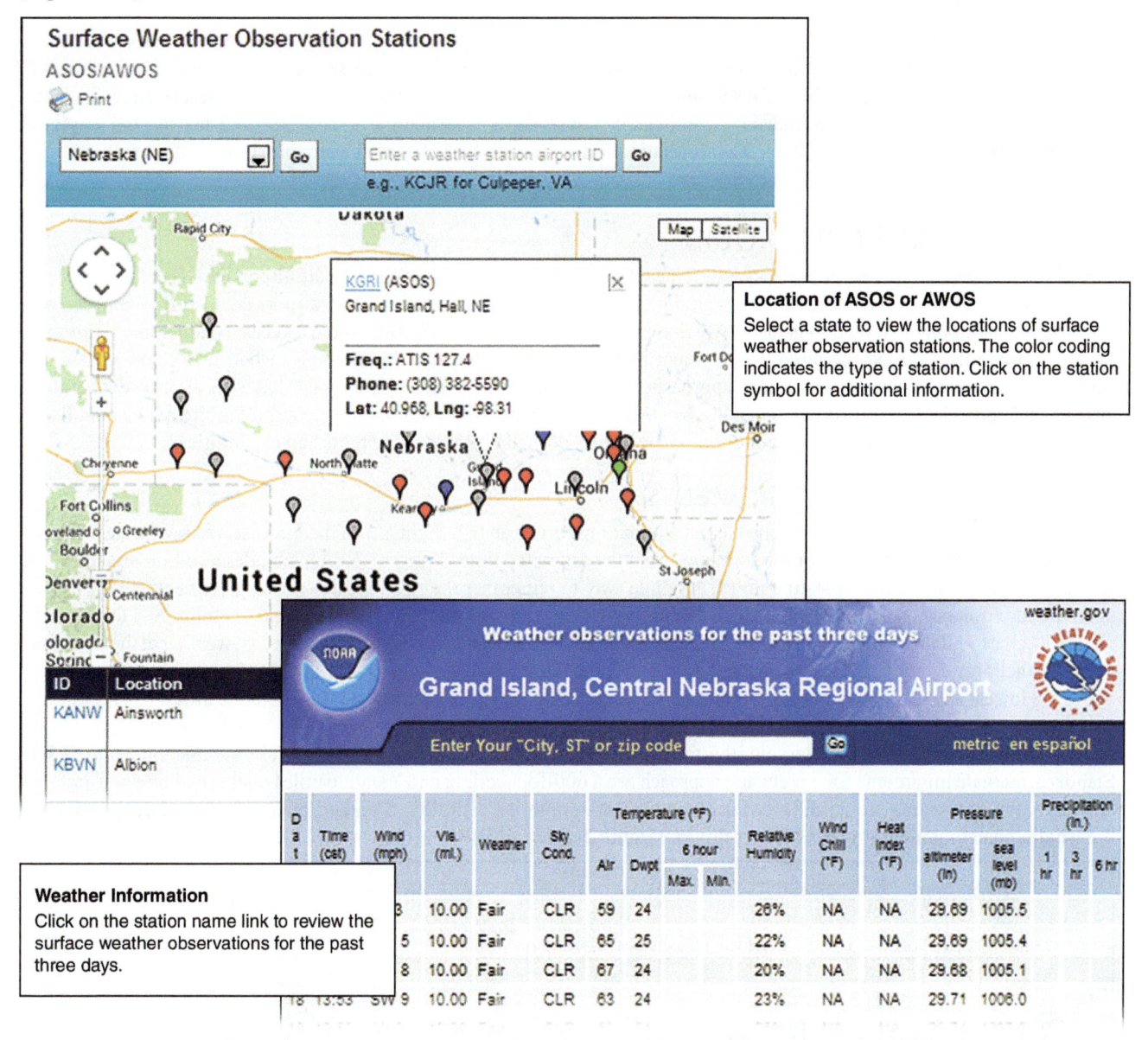

Figure 2-13. You can determine the location and type of AWOS and ASOS stations through various flight information sources, including the Surface Weather Observation Stations page of the FAA web site.

You are typically required by your OpsSpecs to use weather reports that come from a specific approved source such as the National Weather Service (NWS). While every operator's specifications are individually tailored, most operators are required to use ATIS information, RVR reports, and selected reports from automated weather stations. Each type of automated station has different levels of approval as outlined in FAA Order 8400.10 and individual OpsSpecs. All reports coming from an AWOS-3 station are usable for Part 121 and 135 operators.

AUTOMATIC TERMINAL INFORMATION SERVICE AND DIGITAL ATIS

Automatic terminal information service (ATIS) is available at most airports that have an operating control tower. At some airports that operate part-time towers, ASOS information is broadcast over the ATIS frequency when the tower is closed. This service is available only at those airports that have both an ASOS on the field and an ATIS/ASOS interface switch installed in the tower. Each ATIS report includes essential information, such as the runways and instrument approaches in use, specific outages, runup procedures at the airport, and current weather conditions including visibility reported in statute miles. ATIS weather information comes from a variety of NWS-approved sources depending on the equipment installed at the airport. A manual observer, weather instruments located in the tower, or an automated weather station might provide the weather conditions for the ATIS report.

Digital ATIS (D-ATIS) is an alternative method of receiving ATIS reports. A dispatcher receives ATIS information at a central location and then transmits it via datalink to the aircraft. Aircraft equipped with datalink services are capable of receiving ATIS information in the cockpit over the ACARS unit. You can read and print out the ATIS report inside the aircraft, thereby increasing report accuracy and decreasing workload. Because ATIS information is only updated hourly and anytime a significant change in the weather occurs, the information is not the most current report available. Prior to departing, you must obtain the latest weather information from the tower.

IFR ALTERNATE MINIMUMS

Part of your planing prior to departure is to determine whether your flight requires an alternate airport and if so, the airports that meet alternate minimum requirements. The ceiling and visibility requirements to list an airport on an IFR flight plan as an alternate are based on the regulations under which the flight is operating. In addition to the forecast weather, the requirement for an alternate depends on the aircraft equipment and the approach navaid. For example, when using non-WAAS GPS equipment for navigation and instrument approaches, any required alternate airport must have an approved operational instrument approach procedure other than GPS. Not all airports can be used as alternates. An airport might not be qualified for alternate use if the airport navaid is unmonitored or the airport does not have weather reporting capabilities.

PART 91 ALTERNATE REQUIREMENTS

For airplane Part 91 requirements, you must list an alternate airport on an IFR flight plan if the forecast weather at the destination airport, from a time period of plus or minus 1 hour from the estimated time of arrival (ETA), includes a ceiling less than 2,000 feet and/or visibility less than 3 statute miles. A simple way to remember the rules for determining the necessity of filing an alternate for airplanes is the "1, 2, 3 Rule"(plus or minus 1 hour, ceiling less than 2,000 feet, and visibility less than 3 statute miles). For Part 91 helicopter operations, you must list an alternate on an IFR flight plan if the forecast weather at the destination airport or heliport, from the ETA to 1 hour after the ETA, includes ceilings of less than 1,000 feet or ceilings below 400 feet above the lowest applicable approach minimums, whichever is higher, and visibility less than 2 statute miles.

For an airport to be used as an alternate, the forecast weather at that airport must meet certain qualifications at the ETA. Standard alternate minimums for a precision approach are a 600-foot ceiling and 2 statute miles visibility. For a non-precision approach, the minimums are an 800-foot ceiling and 2 statute miles visibility. Standard alternate minimums apply unless higher alternate minimums are listed for an airport. [Figure 2-14]

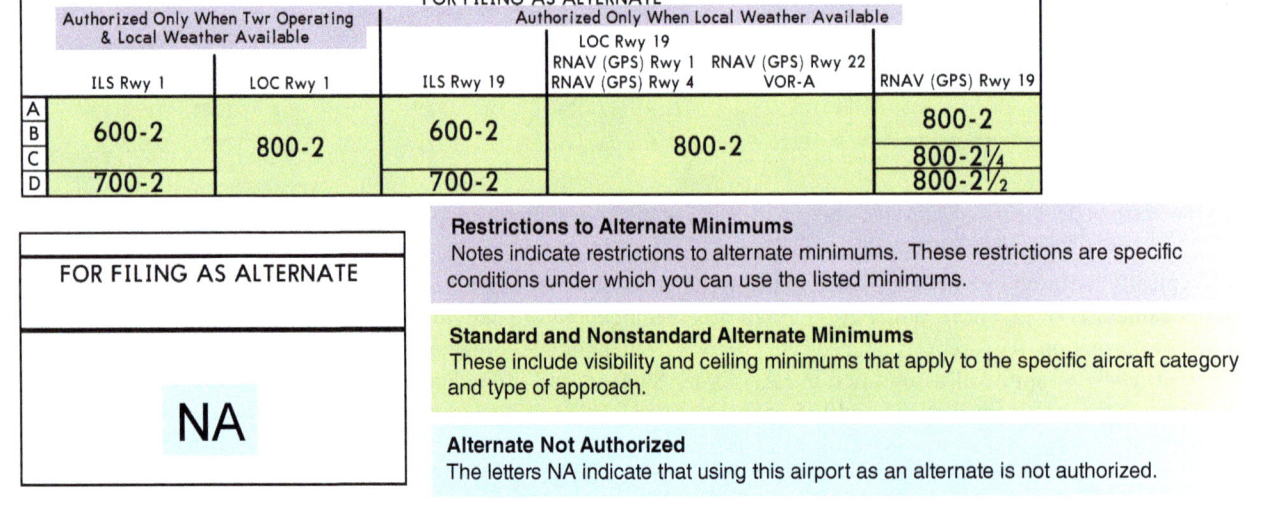

Figure 2-14. Jeppesen charts include both standard and nonstandard alternate minimums.

PART 121 AND PART 135 REQUIREMENTS

The requirements for an alternate depend on the type of aircraft and its installed equipment and the forecast weather. Alternate minimums for Part 121 and 135 are outlined in detail in their OpsSpecs. In addition to meeting the alternate requirements for the airport of intended landing, Part 121 operators are required by their OpsSpecs and by FARs 121.617 and 121.625 to have a takeoff alternate airport if the weather at the departure airport is below the landing minimums for that airport specified in the certificate holder's OpsSpecs. The alternate must be within two hours flying time for an aircraft with three or more engines with an engine out in normal cruise in still air. For two-engine aircraft, the alternate must be within one hour. The airport of intended landing may be used in lieu of an alternate if it meets all the requirements. Part 121 operators must also file for alternate airports when the weather at their destination airport, from one hour before to one hour after their ETA, is forecast to be below a 2,000-foot ceiling and/or less than three statute miles visibility.

An example of Part 121 OpsSpecs requirements for calculating alternate minimums is as follows: for airports with at least one operational navigational facility that provides a straight-in non-precision approach, a straight-in precision approach, or a circling maneuver from an instrument approach procedure, determine the ceiling and visibility minimums by:

- Adding 400 feet to the authorized CAT I HAT/HAA for ceiling.

- Adding one statute mile to the authorized CAT I for visibility.

Part 135 operators are also subject to their own specific rules regarding the selection and use of alternate minimums as outlined in their OpsSpecs and FAR 135.219 through FAR 135.225, and they differ widely from those used by Part 121 operators.

Typically, dispatchers for Part 121 and Part 135 operators are responsible for determining alternate airports by considering aircraft performance, aircraft equipment and its condition, and the route of flight. If changes need to be made to the flight plan enroute due to deteriorating weather, the dispatcher maintains contact with the flight crew and reroutes the flight as necessary. To aid in the planning of alternates, dispatchers have a list of airports that are approved as alternates so they can quickly determine which airports should be used for a particular flight. Dispatchers also use flight-planning software and services provided by Jeppesen and other private sources, that is tailored for individual operators to plan routes, including alternates.

Although you are the final authority for the flight and ultimately have full responsibility, the dispatcher is responsible for creating accurate and law abiding flight plans. Alternate minimum criteria are only used as planning tools to ensure that you and the dispatcher are thinking ahead to the approach phase of flight. In the event the flight would actually need to divert to an alternate, you must use the published approach minimums or lower-than-standard minimums as addressed in OpsSpecs documents.

DEPARTURE PROCEDURES

Departure procedures are preplanned routes that provide transitions from the departure airport to the enroute structure. Primarily, these procedures are designed to provide obstacle protection for departing aircraft. They also enable efficient routing of traffic and reductions in pilot/controller workloads. There are two types of departure procedures: those developed to assist you in obstruction avoidance, obstacle departure procedures and those developed to communicate air traffic control clearances, standard instrument departures. Both types are based on the design criteria outlined in the U.S. Standard for Terminal Instrument Procedures (TERPS).

Departure design, including climb gradients, does not take into consideration the performance of the aircraft; it only considers obstacle protection for all aircraft. TERPS criteria assumes the aircraft is operating with all available engines and systems fully functioning. When a climb gradient is required for a specific departure, you must fully understand the performance of your aircraft and determine if it can comply with the required climb. The standard climb of 200 feet per nautical mile is not an issue for most aircraft. When an increased climb gradient is specified due to obstacle issues, it is important to calculate aircraft performance, particularly when flying out of airports at higher altitudes on warm days. To help you calculate climb rate, Jeppesen includes gradient-to-rate tables on SID charts and with the terminal data in their charting services. [Figure 2-15]

Another factor to consider when you depart in IFR conditions is the possibility of an engine failure. During preflight planning, use the aircraft performance charts to determine if the aircraft can still maintain the required climb performance in the event of an engine failure. Aircraft that are performance limited might be unable to maintain altitude, let alone complete a climb to altitude. Using the performance expectations for the aircraft, construct an emergency plan of action that includes emergency checklists and the actions to take to ensure safety in this situation.

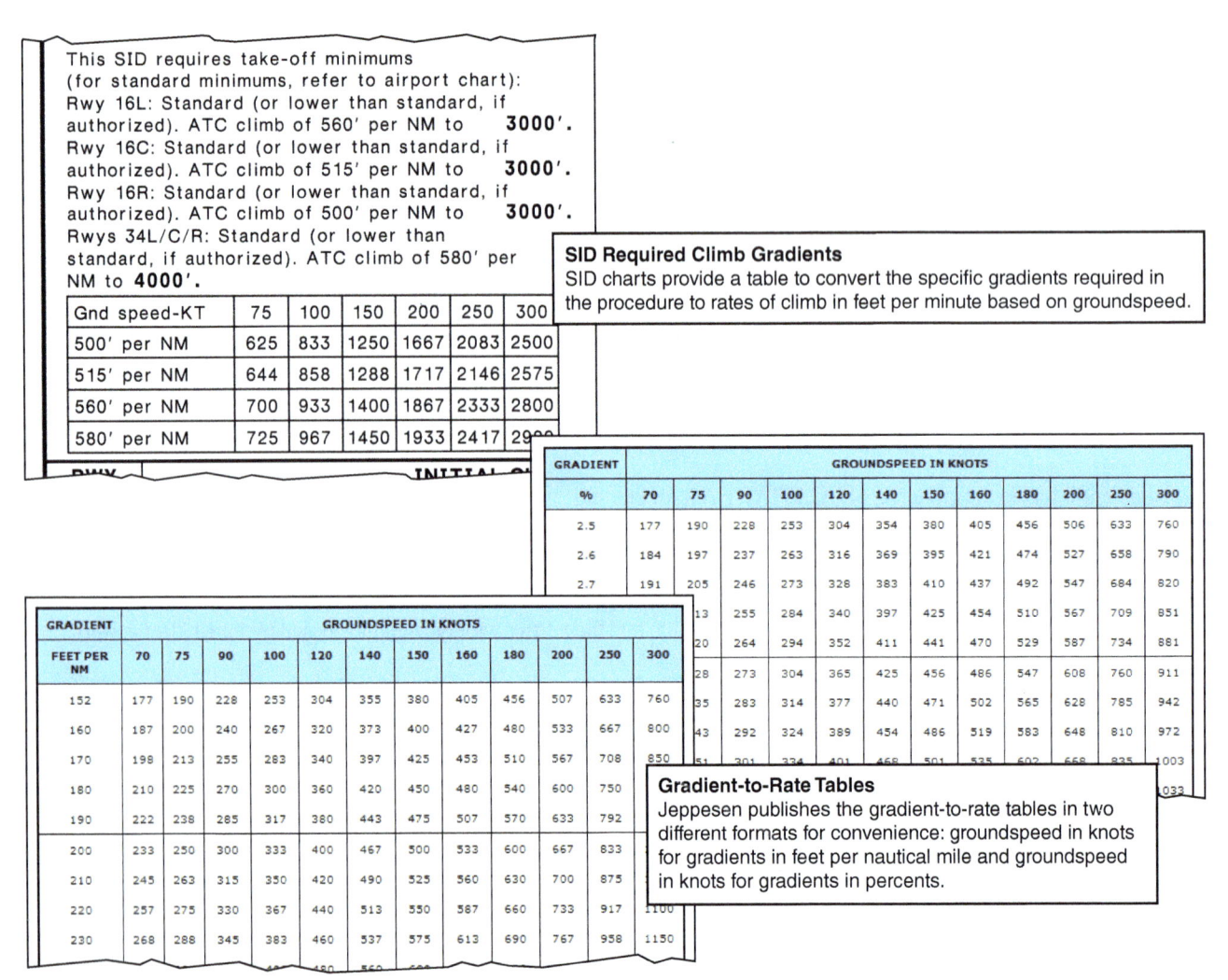

This SID requires take-off minimums (for standard minimums, refer to airport chart):
Rwy 16L: Standard (or lower than standard, if authorized). ATC climb of 560' per NM to **3000'**.
Rwy 16C: Standard (or lower than standard, if authorized). ATC climb of 515' per NM to **3000'**.
Rwy 16R: Standard (or lower than standard, if authorized). ATC climb of 500' per NM to **3000'**.
Rwys 34L/C/R: Standard (or lower than standard, if authorized). ATC climb of 580' per NM to **4000'**.

Gnd speed-KT	75	100	150	200	250	300
500' per NM	625	833	1250	1667	2083	2500
515' per NM	644	858	1288	1717	2146	2575
560' per NM	700	933	1400	1867	2333	2800
580' per NM	725	967	1450	1933	2417	2900

SID Required Climb Gradients
SID charts provide a table to convert the specific gradients required in the procedure to rates of climb in feet per minute based on groundspeed.

GRADIENT %	\multicolumn{11}{c	}{GROUNDSPEED IN KNOTS}
	70	75	90	100	120	140	150	160	180	200	250	300
2.5	177	190	228	253	304	354	380	405	456	506	633	760
2.6	184	197	237	263	316	369	395	421	474	527	658	790
2.7	191	205	246	273	328	383	410	437	492	547	684	820
13	255	284	340	397	425	454	510	567	709	851		
20	264	294	352	411	441	470	529	587	734	881		
28	273	304	365	425	456	486	547	608	760	911		
35	283	314	377	440	471	502	565	628	785	942		
43	292	324	389	454	486	519	583	648	810	972		
51	301	334	401	468	501	535	602	668	835	1003		

GRADIENT FEET PER NM	\multicolumn{11}{c	}{GROUNDSPEED IN KNOTS}
	70	75	90	100	120	140	150	160	180	200	250	300
152	177	190	228	253	304	355	380	405	456	507	633	760
160	187	200	240	267	320	373	400	427	480	533	667	800
170	198	213	255	283	340	397	425	453	510	567	708	850
180	210	225	270	300	360	420	450	480	540	600	750	
190	222	238	285	317	380	443	475	507	570	633	792	
200	233	250	300	333	400	467	500	533	600	667	833	
210	245	263	315	350	420	490	525	560	630	700	875	
220	257	275	330	367	440	513	550	587	660	733	917	
230	268	288	345	383	460	537	575	613	690	767	958	1150

Gradient-to-Rate Tables
Jeppesen publishes the gradient-to-rate tables in two different formats for convenience: groundspeed in knots for gradients in feet per nautical mile and groundspeed in knots for gradients in percents.

Figure 2-15. Gradient-to-rate tables relate specific climb gradients and typical airspeeds.

OBSTACLE DEPARTURE PROCEDURES

The term obstacle departure procedure (ODP) is used to define procedures that simply provide obstacle clearance—they do not include ATC-related climb requirements. The primary emphasis of ODP design is to use the least onerous route of flight to the enroute structure while attempting to accommodate typical departure routes. [Figure 2-16]

A visual climb over airport (VCOA) is a departure method that might be included in an ODP for aircraft unable to meet required climb gradients and for airports at which a conventional instrument departure procedure is impossible to design due to terrain or other obstacle hazards. VCOA procedures are developed when obstacles more than three statue miles from the departure end of the runway require a climb gradient greater than 200 feet per nautical mile. [Figure 2-17]

During planning, you must determine whether the departure airport has an ODP. An ODP might drastically affect the initial part of the flight plan. You might have to depart at a higher than normal climb rate, or depart in a direction opposite the intended heading and maintain that for a period of time, which requires an alteration in the flight plan and initial headings. To plan the departure, consider the forecast weather, the departure runway, the ODP, and the aircraft's climb performance and fuel burn.

Additionally, when close-in obstacles are noted in the Takeoff and Obstacle Departure Procedure section of the airport chart, you might be required to take action to avoid these obstacles. Consider the decreased climb performance from an inoperative engine and the amount of runway required for takeoff. If your aircraft requires most of the available runway for takeoff, it might not have the standard required obstacle clearance when climbing at the normal 200 feet per nautical mile.

STANDARD INSTRUMENT DEPARTURES

Standard instrument departures (SIDs) are designed at the request of ATC to increase the capacity of terminal airspace, effectively control the flow of traffic with minimal communication, and reduce environmental impact through noise abatement procedures. While obstacle protection is always considered in SID routing, the primary goal is to reduce ATC/pilot workload

ODP Title
The word OBSTACLE in the title identifies this as an ODP. You may include a graphic ODP in an instrument flight plan by using the computer code in the procedure title.

Obstacle Description
You must maintain situational awareness regarding the obstacles near the departure end of the runway to ensure safe clearance over those obstacles.

RNAV ODP
RNAV ODPs are always in graphical form and include the word RNAV in the procedure heading and title.

Takeoff Minimums and Climb Gradient

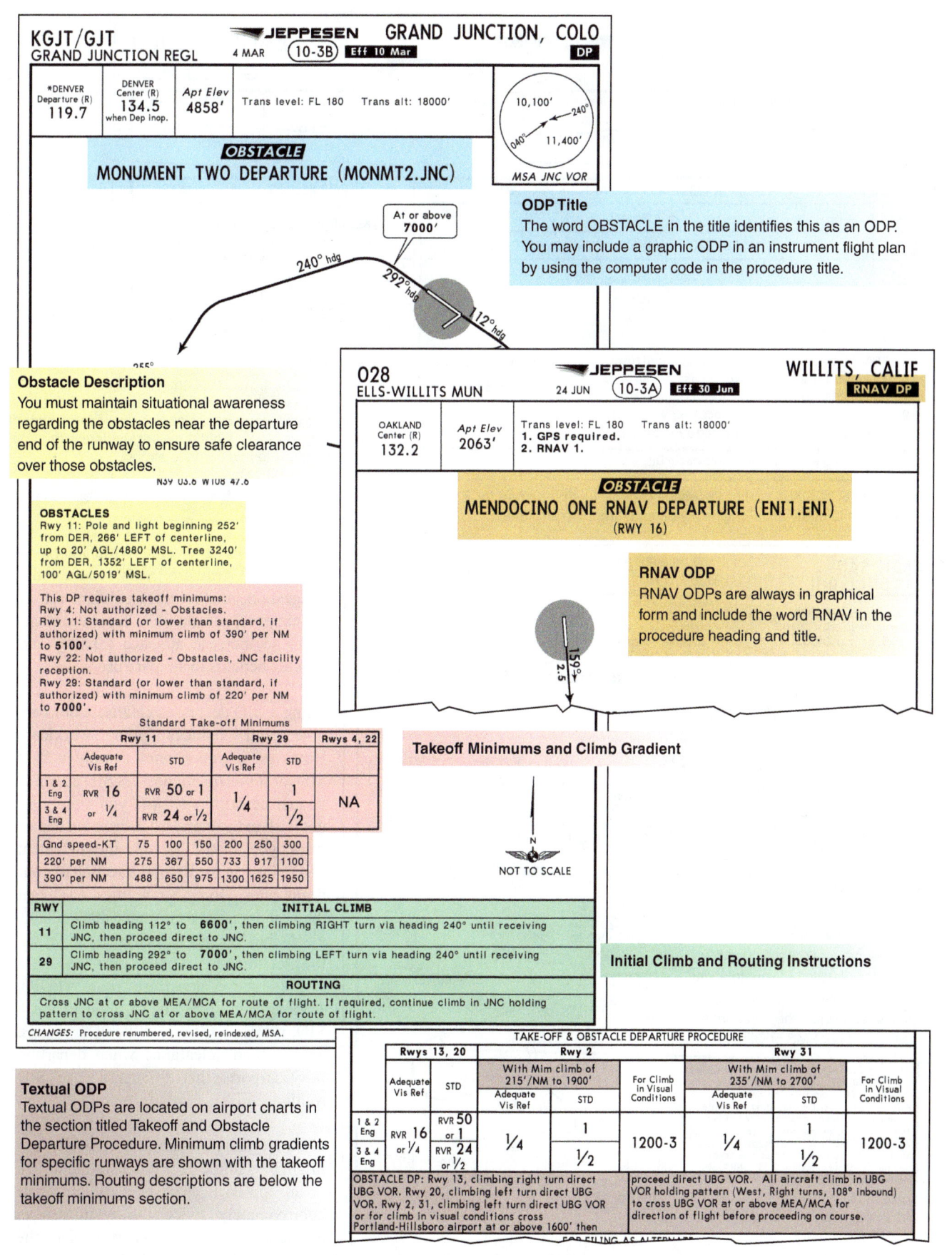

Initial Climb and Routing Instructions

Textual ODP
Textual ODPs are located on airport charts in the section titled Takeoff and Obstacle Departure Procedure. Minimum climb gradients for specific runways are shown with the takeoff minimums. Routing descriptions are below the takeoff minimums section.

Figure 2-16. ODPs are published in textual or graphic form. RNAV ODPs are always in graphical form.

2-15

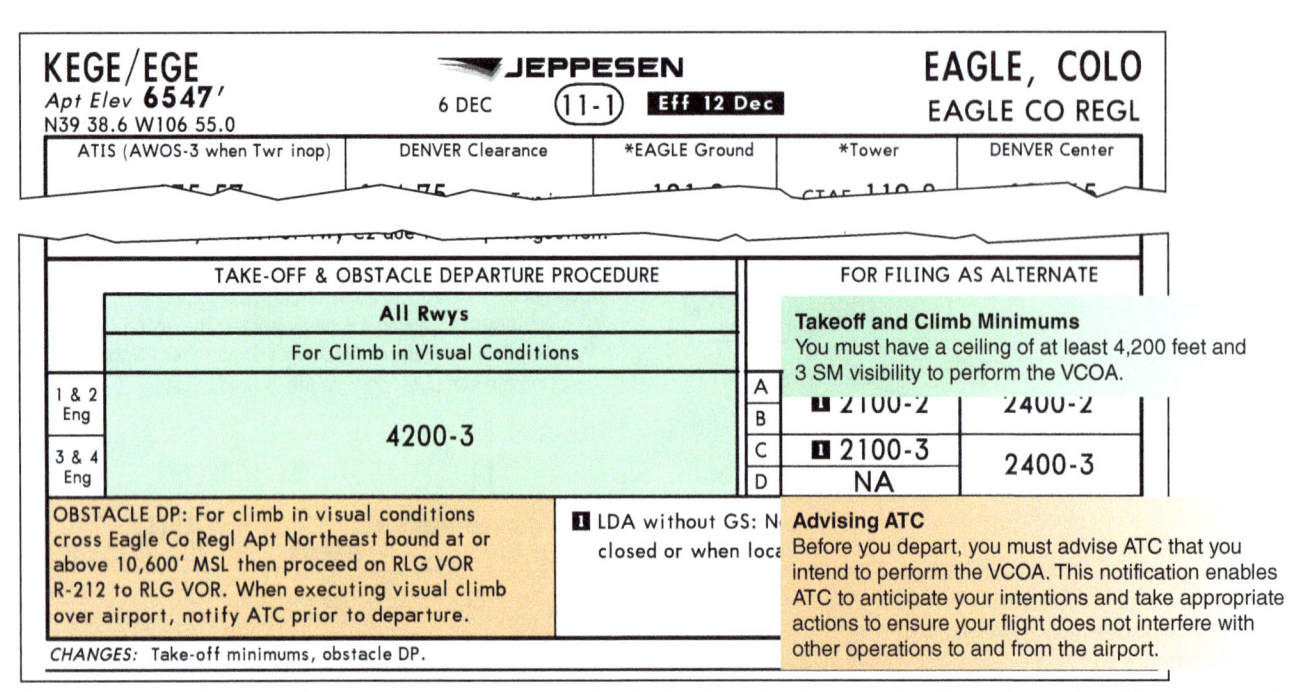

Figure 2-17. A VCOA is part of the obstacle departure procedure for Eagle, Colorado where the climb rate to fly the SID can exceed the performance of many multi-engine piston and turboprop airplanes.

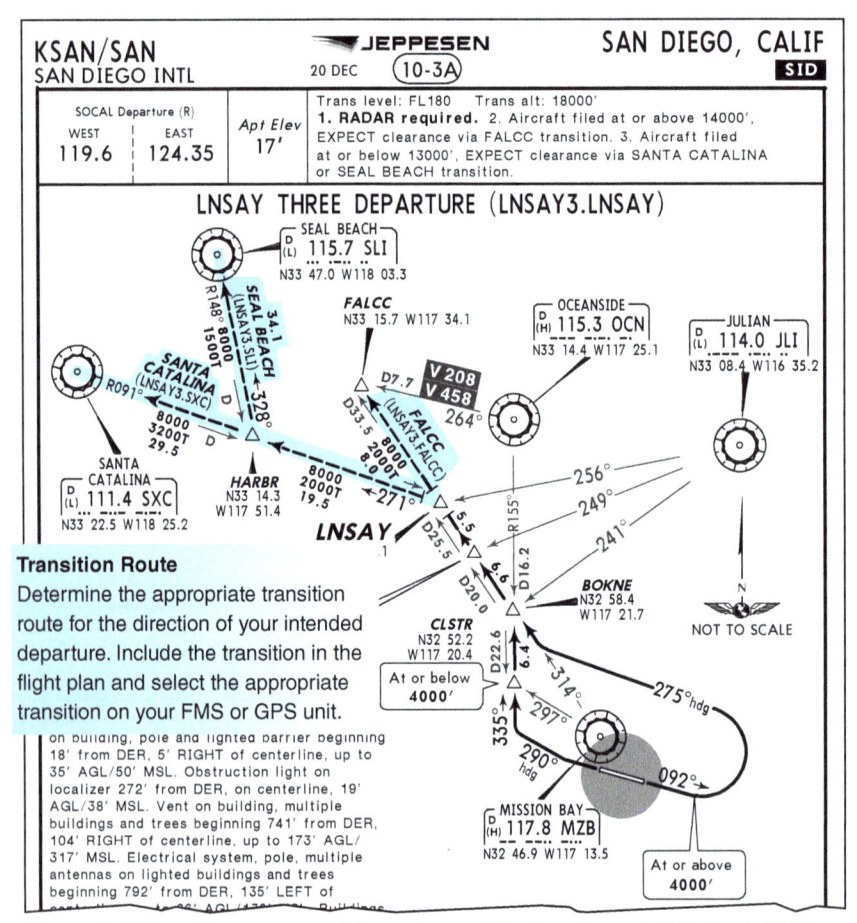

Figure 2-18. Transition routes enable you to transition from the end of the basic SID to a location in the enroute structure.

while providing seamless transitions to the enroute structure. SIDs reduce radio congestion, enable more efficient use of the airspace, and simplify departure clearances to increase airspace capacity and provide benefits to airspace users.

Using a SID decreases clearance delivery time and reduces your workload. However, if you cannot comply with a SID, or if you do not possess SID charts or textual descriptions, or if you simply do not wish to use standard instrument departures, you should include the statement "NO SIDs" in the Remarks section of your flight plan. Doing so notifies ATC that they cannot issue a clearance that contains a SID, but instead will clear the flight via the filed route to the extent possible, or via a preferential departure route (PDR). Although, you are not required to use a SID, it might be more difficult to receive an "as filed" clearance when departing busy airports that frequently use SID routing.

SIDs are always charted graphically and might be a single page chart similar in size to an approach chart or a pullout chart approximately twice the width of an approach chart. Each chart depicts the departure route, navigational fixes, required altitudes, and transition routes (if applicable). [Figure 2-18] The takeoff and departure instructions outline the particular procedure for each runway. SIDs are categorized by the type of navigation used to fly the departure, so they are considered either pilot navigation or vector SIDs.

VECTOR SIDS

Vector SIDs require ATC to provide radar vectors from just after takeoff until reaching the assigned route or a fix depicted on the SID chart. The procedure typically includes an initial heading and altitude and then ATC expects you to comply with radar vectors. Advise the controller if an instruction will cause a compromise of safety due to obstructions or traffic. When you review vector SID charts prior to flight, ensure you understand any nonstandard lost communication procedures. If you were to lose radio contact while being vectored by ATC, you are expected to comply with the lost communication procedure as outlined on the chart. [Figure 2-19]

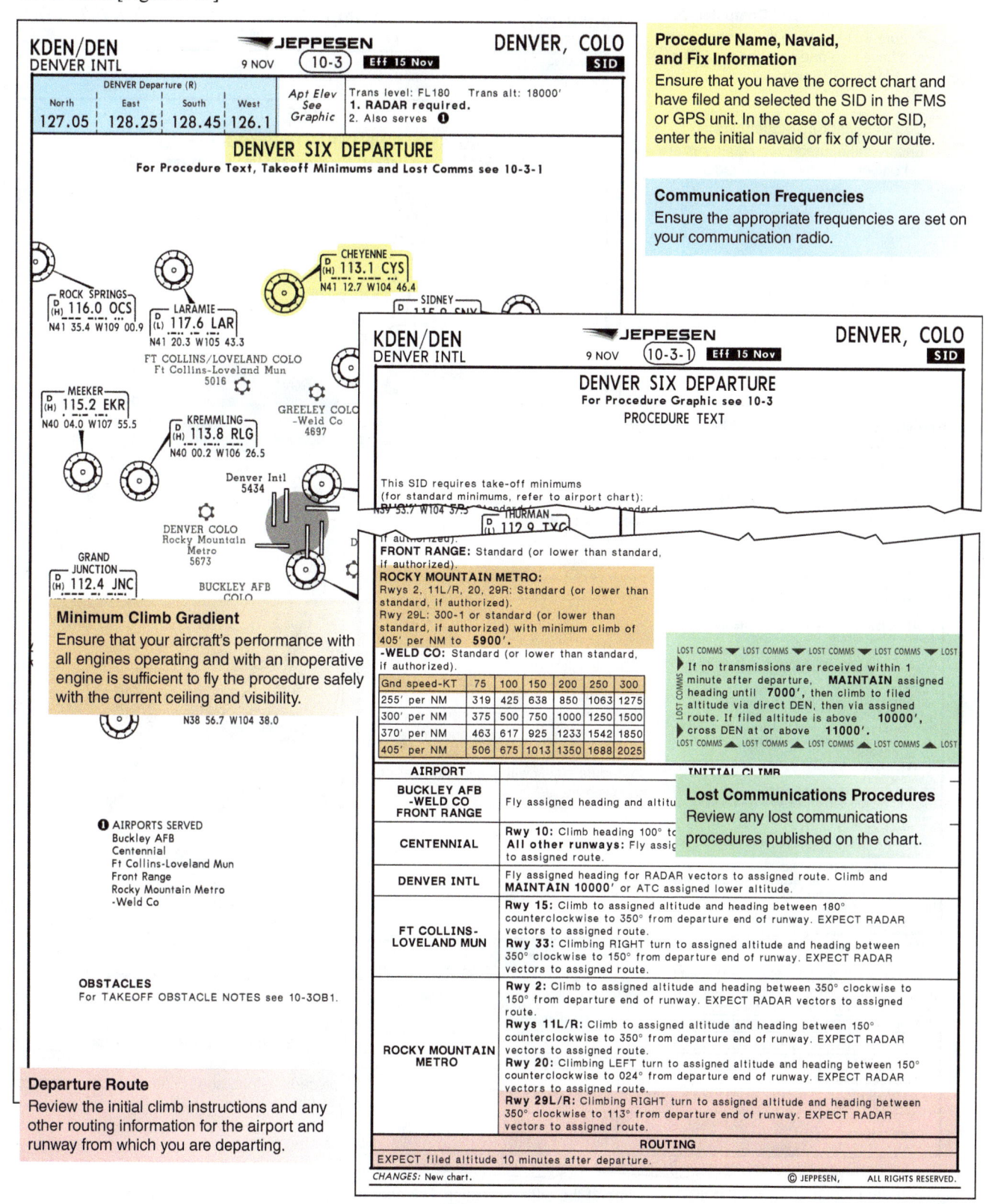

Figure 2-19. Prepare for and brief the key points of the vector SID prior to departure according to your standard operating procedures.

2-17

PILOT NAVIGATION SIDS

Pilot navigation SIDs enable you to provide your own navigation with minimal radio communication. This type of procedure usually contains an initial set of departure instructions followed by one or more transition routes. A pilot navigation SID might include an initial segment requiring radar vectors to help the flight join the procedure, but the majority of the navigation remains your responsibility. These SIDs reduce ATC workload by requiring minimal communication and navigation support. [Figure 2-20]

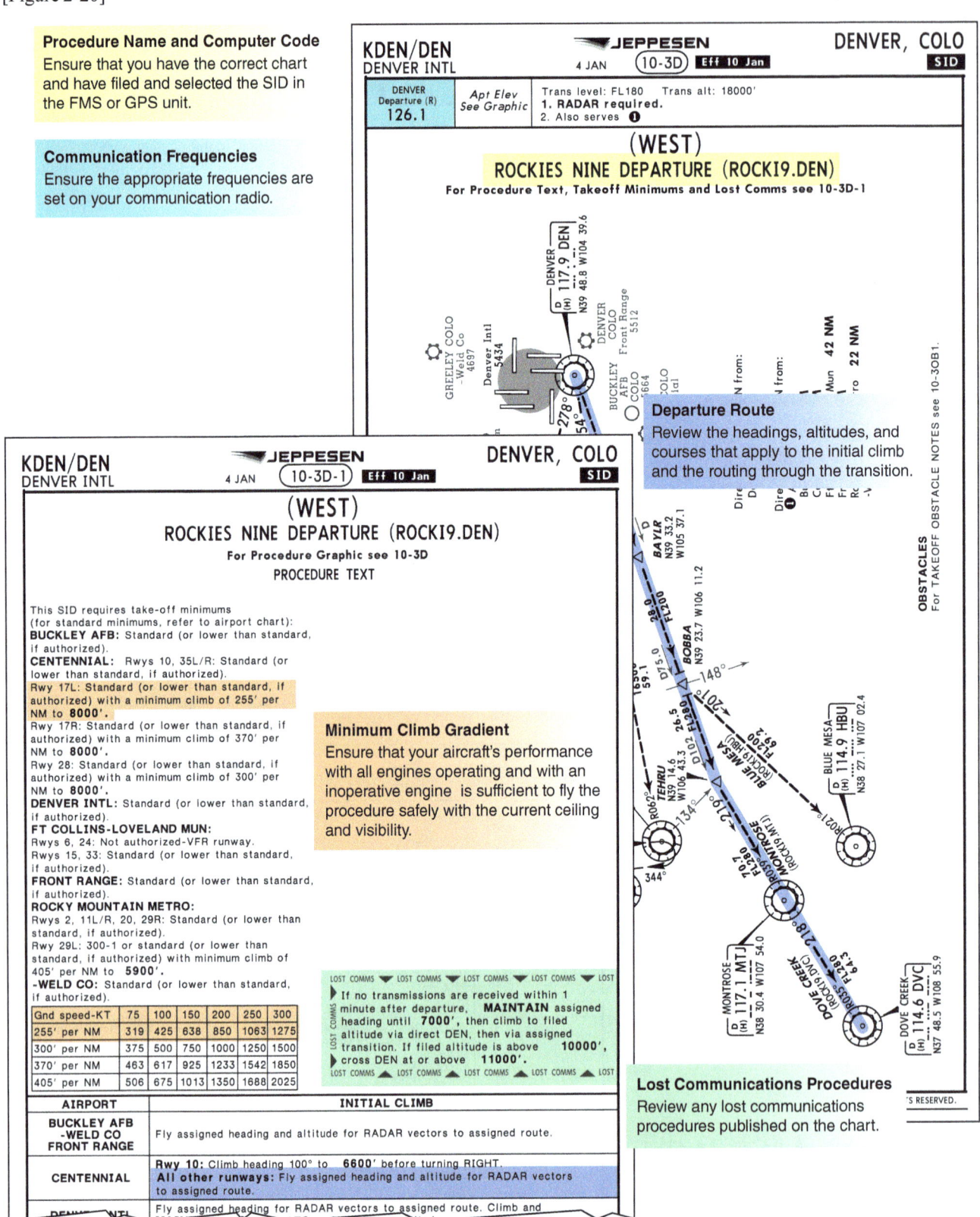

Figure 2-20. Prepare for and brief the key points of the pilot navigation SID prior to departure according to your standard operating procedures.

2-18

RNAV SIDS

An RNAV SID is identifiable as such by the inclusion of the term RNAV in the title. AC 90-100, *U.S. Terminal and Enroute Area Navigation (RNAV) Operations* provides operational and airworthiness guidance for operation on U.S. RNAV routes and IFR departure and arrival procedures. According to AC 90-100, your aircraft must meet specific equipment and performance standards for you to fly RNAV SIDs.

If your aircraft does not have GPS, you must use DME/DME/IRU updating. DME/DME updating uses the DME from two different VORs to determine the aircraft location, DME/DME/IRU adds an inertial reference unit (IRU) that indicates the aircraft position and this unit is updated by means of DME/DME. In addition, your RNAV equipment must meet RNAV 1 standards, which require a total system error of not more than one nautical mile for 95 percent of the total flight time. You must engage RNAV equipment no later than 500 feet above airport elevation and you must use a CDI/flight director and/or autopilot in lateral navigation mode. The type of equipment and performance standards are indicated on the SID chart. An RNAV SID routing might consist solely of pilot navigation or a combination of vectors and pilot navigation. [Figures 2-21 and 2-22]

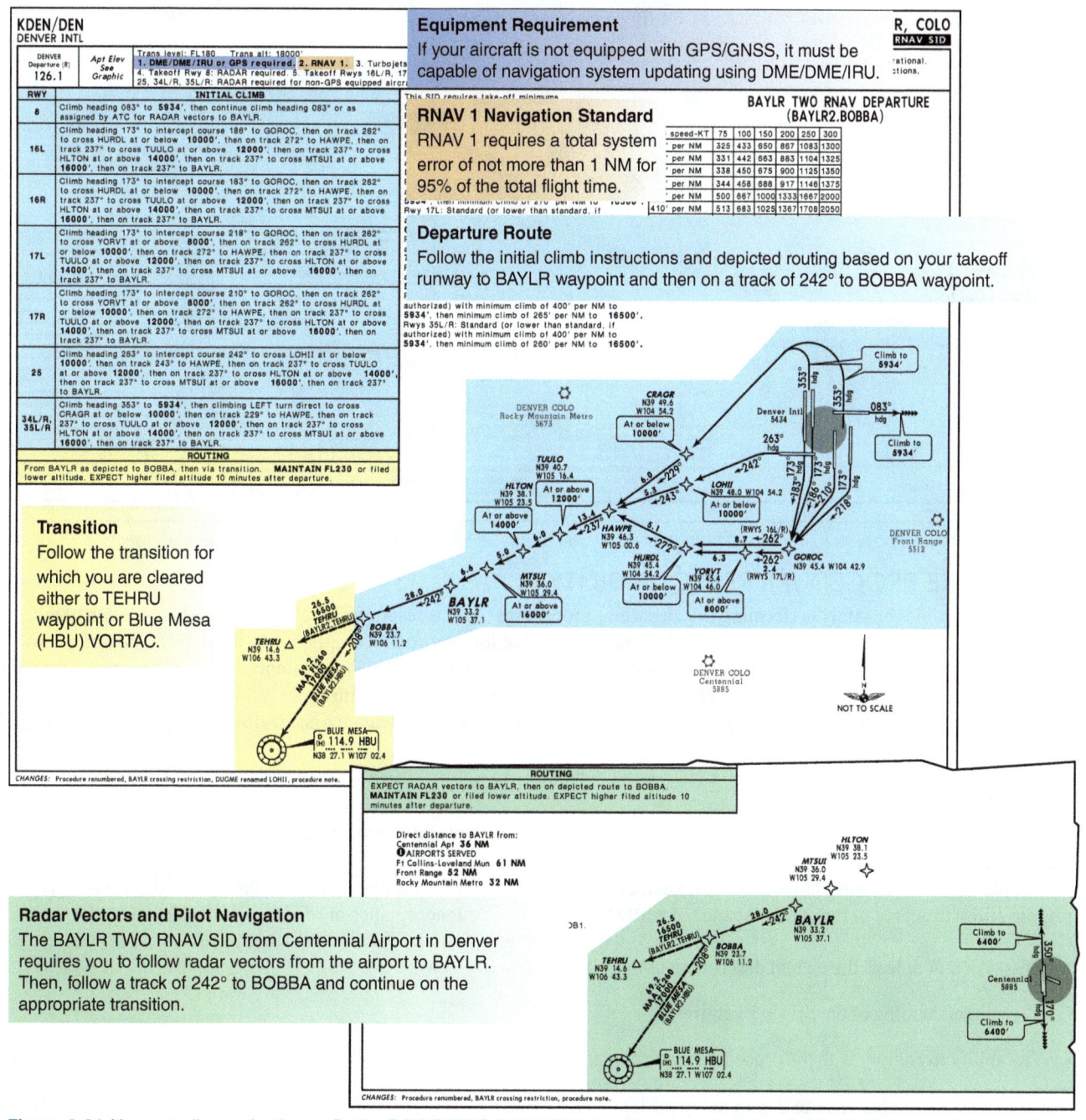

Figure 2-21. You use pilot navigation to fly the BAYLR TWO RNAV SID from Denver International Airport. However, when you depart Centennial Airport using this same departure, you follow radar vectors to the BAYLR waypoint.

2-19

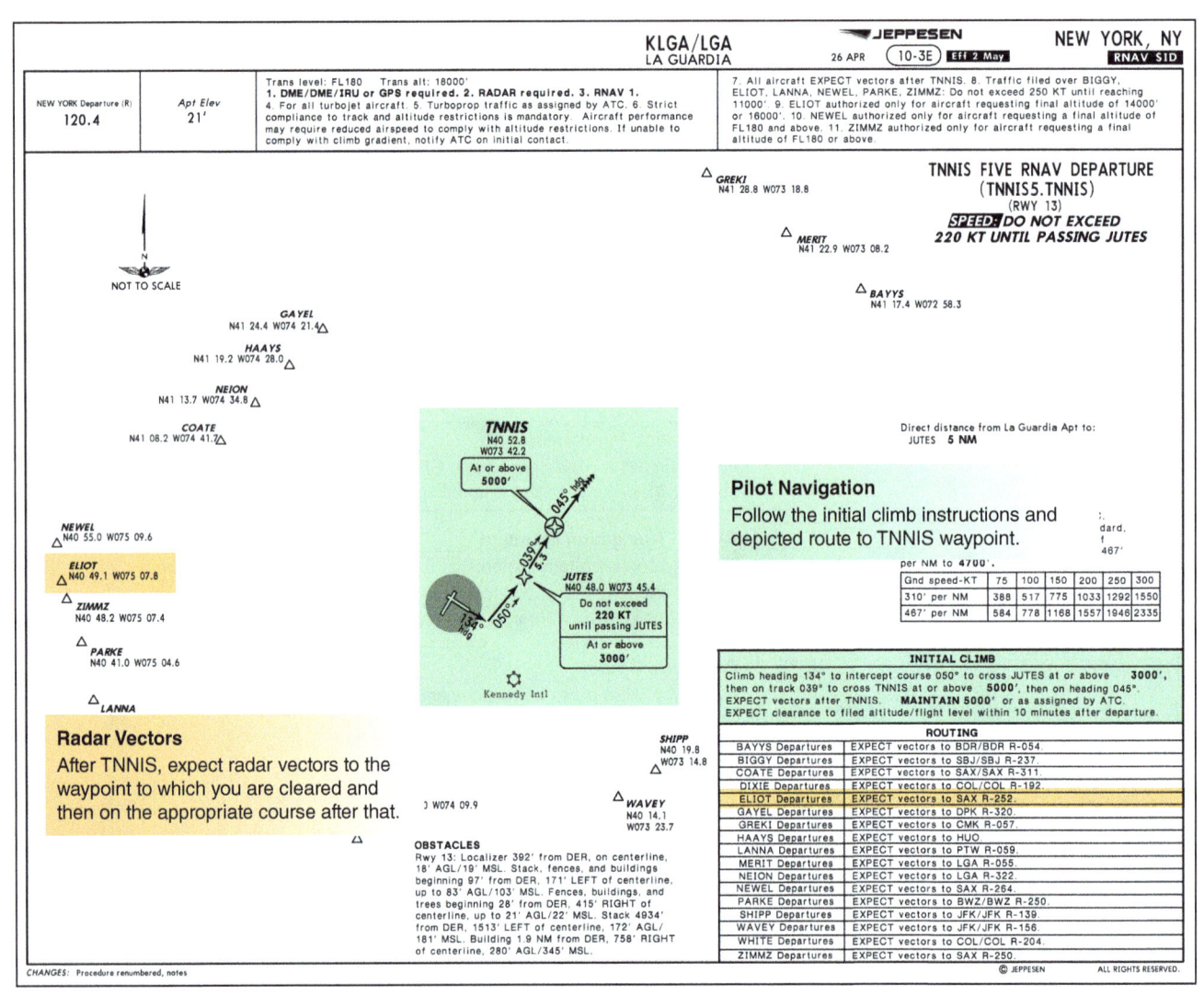

Figure 2-22. To fly the TNNIS FIVE RNAV SID, you use a combination of pilot navigation and radar vectors.

DEPARTURE PROCEDURE RESPONSIBILITY

You are responsible for safely performing IFR departure procedures. ATC is responsible for specifying the direction of takeoff or initial heading when necessary, obtaining pilot concurrence that the procedure complies with local traffic patterns, terrain, and obstruction clearance, and including departure procedures as part of the ATC clearance when pilot compliance for separation is necessary. By simply complying with departure procedures in their entirety as published, obstacle clearance is guaranteed. Depending on the type of departure used, responsibility for terrain clearance and traffic separation might be shared between you and the controller.

PROCEDURES ASSIGNED BY ATC

ATC can assign SIDs or radar vectors as necessary for traffic management and convenience. You can also request a SID in your initial flight plan, or from ATC. To fly a SID, you must receive approval to do so in a clearance. In order to accept a clearance that includes a SID, you must have at least a textual description of the SID in your possession at the time of departure. It is your responsibility to accept or reject the issuance of a SID by ATC. Base your acceptance or rejection of the clearance on:

- Possession of at least the textual description of the SID.

- Your understanding of the SID in its entirety.

- The ability to comply with the procedure requirements. [Figure 2-23]

When you accept a clearance to depart using a SID or radar vectors, ATC is responsible for traffic separation and obstacle clearance. When departing with a SID, ATC expects you to fly the procedure as charted because the procedure design considers obstacle clearance. It is also expected that you will remain vigilant in scanning for traffic when departing in visual conditions. Furthermore, it is your responsibility to notify ATC if the clearance would compromise safety.

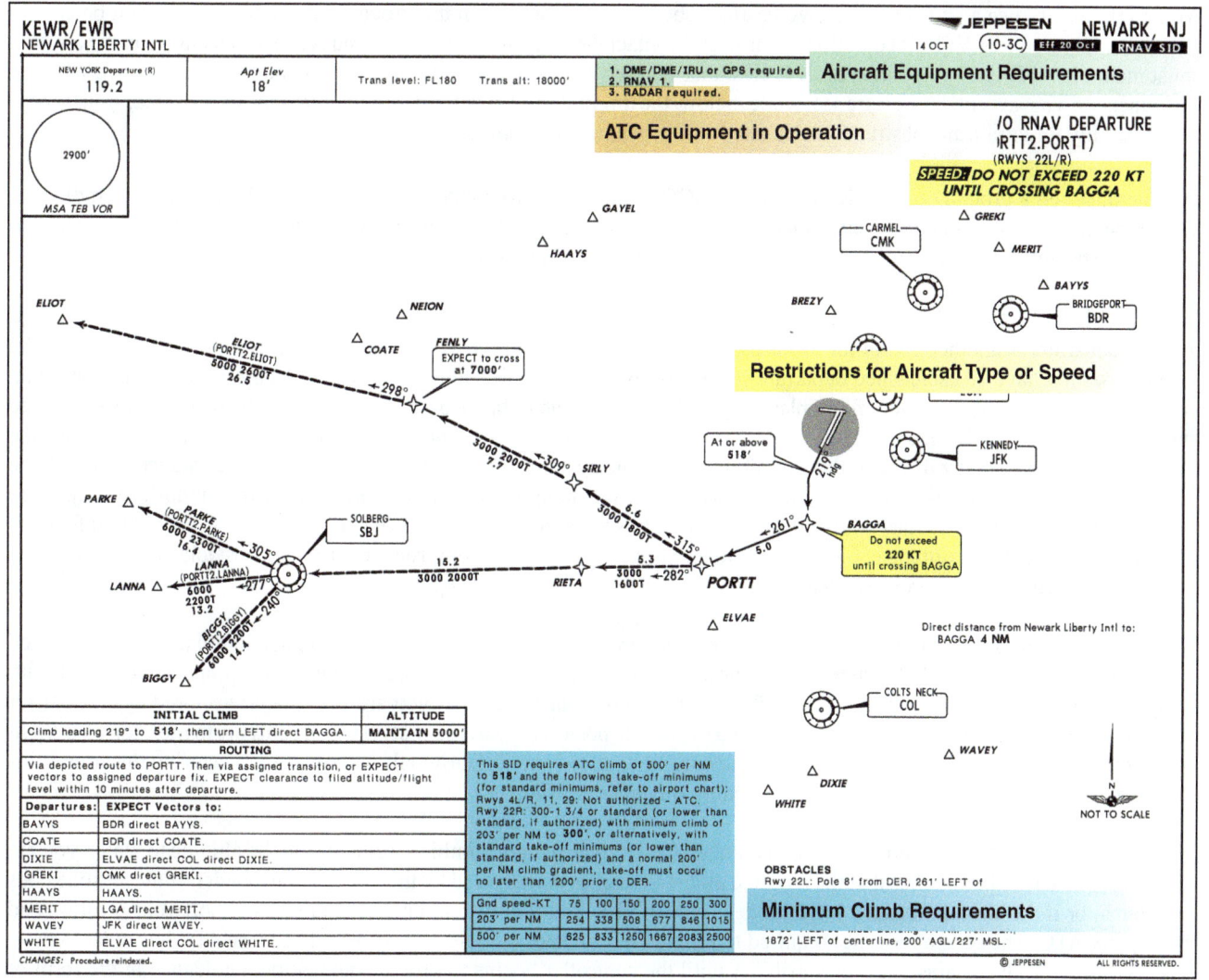

Figure 2-23. Review the departure requirements to determine if you can comply with the procedure.

PROCEDURES NOT ASSIGNED BY ATC

Obstacle departure procedures are not assigned by ATC unless absolutely necessary to achieve aircraft separation. You are responsible for determining if there is an ODP published for that airport. If you are not given a clearance for a SID or radar vectors and an ODP exists, you must use the ODP. Additionally, ATC expects you to comply with the published procedure unless the weather at the departure airport enables you to depart under VFR conditions.

DEPARTURES FROM TOWER-CONTROLLED AIRPORTS

Normally, you request your IFR clearance through ground control or clearance delivery at a tower-controlled airport. Communication frequencies for the various controllers are listed on departure, approach, and airport charts. At some airports, you might have the option of receiving a pre-taxi clearance. This program allows you to contact ground control or clearance delivery no more than ten minutes prior to beginning taxi operations to receive your IFR clearance. A pre-departure clearance (PDC) program is available for Part 121 and 135 operators and enables you to receive a clearance from a dispatcher via a datalink. The clearance is given to the dispatcher who in turn relays it to you, enabling you to bypass communication with clearance delivery, thus reducing frequency congestion. After you have received your clearance, it is your responsibility to comply with the instructions as given and notify ATC if you are unable to comply. If you do not understand the clearance or if you think that you have missed a portion of the clearance, you must contact ATC immediately for clarification.

DEPARTURES FROM AIRPORTS WITHOUT AN OPERATING CONTROL TOWER

During the planning phase, determine the departure airport's method for receiving an instrument clearance. You can contact flight service on the ground by telephone and flight service will request your clearance from ATC. Typically, when a clearance is given in this manner, the clearance includes a void time. You must depart the airport before the clearance void time; if you fail to depart, you must contact ATC by a specified notification time, which is within 30 minutes of the original void time. After the clearance void time, the space reserved for the flight within the IFR system is released for other traffic. Another way to receive a clearance at a non-towered airport is to request your clearance by contacting flight service or ATC on the radio.

You might experience a situation where you cannot obtain your clearance on the ground. In this case, you might be able to depart the airport under VFR, if conditions permit, and contact the controlling authority and request a clearance in the air. You must maintain VFR until you obtain an IFR clearance and have ATC approval to proceed on course in accordance with the clearance. If you accept this clearance while below the minimum IFR altitude for operations in the area, you accept responsibility for terrain and obstruction clearance until reaching that altitude.

A system, called a ground communication outlet (GCO) enables you to contact flight service and ATC by VHF radio to a telephone connection to obtain an instrument clearance or close a VFR/IFR flight plan. Use four key clicks on the radio to contact the nearest ATC facility and use six key clicks to contact flight service.

RADAR DEPARTURE

A radar departure is another option for departing an airport on an IFR flight. You might may receive a radar departure if the airport does not have an established departure procedure, if you are unable to comply with a departure procedure, or if you request "No SIDs" as a part of your flight plan. Expect ATC to issue an initial departure heading if you are being radar vectored immediately after takeoff. Do not expect to be given a purpose for the specific vector heading—the controller knows the proposed flight route and will vector the aircraft into position. By nature of the departure type, once a clearance is issued, the responsibility for coordination of the flight rests with ATC, including the tower controller and, after handoff, the departure controller who remains in contact with you until the aircraft is released to *"resume own navigation."* However, if you feel that any assigned heading or altitude could cause a violation of a regulation or compromise terrain or obstacle clearance, advise ATC immediately to obtain a revised clearance.

For all practical purposes, a radar departure is the easiest type of departure to use. It is also a good alternative to a published departure procedure, particularly when none of the available departure procedures are conducive to a proposed route of flight. However, you should always maintain a detailed awareness of your location as you are being radar vectored by ATC. If for some reason radar contact is lost, you will be asked to provide position reports so that ATC can continue to monitor your flight progress. Also, ATC might release you to *"resume own navigation"* on your original clearance after vectoring the aircraft off course momentarily for a variety of reasons including weather or traffic.

Upon initial contact, state the aircraft or flight number, the altitude you are climbing through, and the altitude to which you are climbing. The controller verifies that the reported altitude matches that emitted by the aircraft transponder. If the altitude does not match, or if the aircraft does not have Mode C capabilities, you will be continually required to report your position and altitude for ATC. The controller is not required to provide terrain and obstacle clearance just because ATC has radar contact with your aircraft. It remains your responsibility until the controller begins to provide navigational guidance in the form of radar vectors. Once radar vectors are given, pilots and flight crews are expected to promptly comply with headings and altitudes as assigned.

ATC may establish a minimum vectoring altitude (MVA) around certain airports. This altitude is based on terrain and obstruction clearance and provides controllers with minimum altitudes to vector aircraft in and around a particular location. However, it may be necessary to vector aircraft below this altitude to assist in the efficient flow of departing traffic. For this reason, an airport may have established a diverse vector area (DVA). DVA design requirements are outlined in TERPS and allow for the vectoring of aircraft immediately off the departure end of the runway below the MVA. [Figure 2-24]

NOISE ABATEMENT PROCEDURES

FAR Part 150 specifies the FAA's responsibilities to investigate the recommendations of the airport operator in a noise compatibility program and approve or disapprove the noise abatement suggestions. This is a crucial step in ensuring that the airport is not unduly inhibited by noise requirements ad that air traffic workload and efficiency are not significantly impacted, all while considering the noise problems addressed by the surrounding community. During a radar departure. ATC might require you to turn away from their intended course or vector you around a particular area. Typically, noise restrictions are incorporated into the main body of SIDs—higher departure altitudes, larger climb gradients, reduced airspeeds, and turns to avoid specific areas. Some SIDs are developed solely to comply with noise abatement requirements. [Figure 2-25]

SAFETY CONSIDERATIONS

Understanding how to interpret charted procedures to safely perform taxiing, takeoff, and departure under IFR is critical to flight safety. You also must consider other actions to mitigate risk during these operations, such as maintaining a sterile cockpit and using procedures to reduce the risk of CFIT.

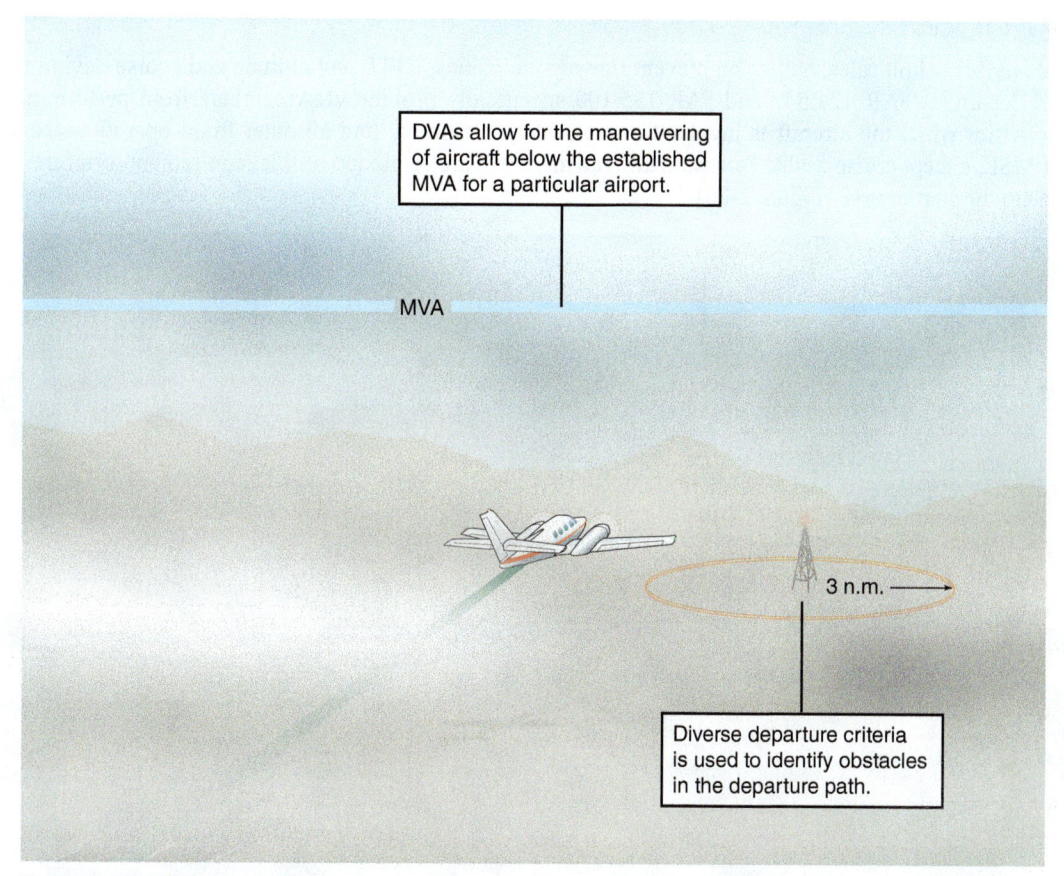

Figure 2-24. A DVA is valid only when aircraft are permitted to climb uninterrupted from the departure runway to the MVA or higher.

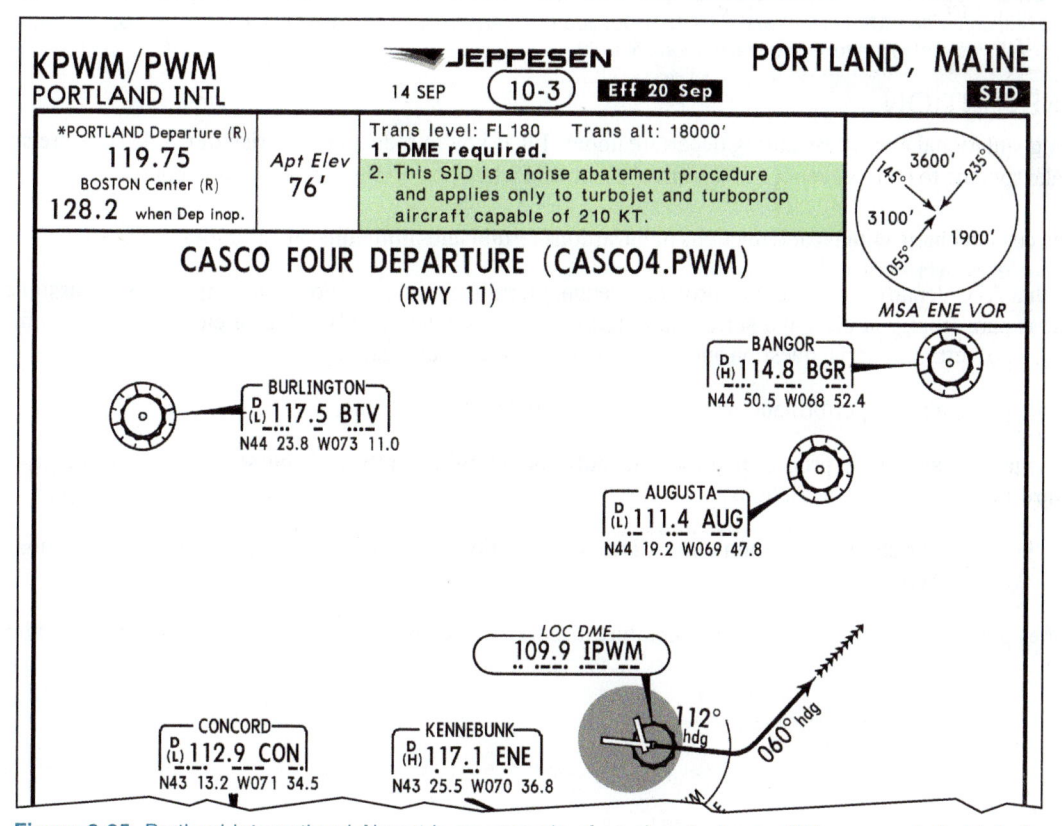

Figure 2-25. Portland International Airport is an example of an airport where a SID was created strictly for noise abatement purposes as noted in parentheses below the title of the departure procedure.

2-23

STERILE COCKPIT

Adhering to sterile cockpit rules, helps you prevent runway incursions, CFIT, and altitude and course deviations during taxi, takeoff, and departure. FAR 121.542 and FAR 135.100 specifically prohibit crewmembers from performing nonessential duties or activities while the aircraft is involved in taxi, takeoff, landing, and all other flight operations conducted below 10,000 feet MSL, except cruise flight. To ensure all crewmembers are reminded of this requirement, brief the sterile cockpit rule prior to engine start or taxi. [Figure 2-26]

During all ground operations involving taxi, takeoff and landing, and all other flight operations conducted below 10,000 feet, except cruise flight:

- Do not perform any duties, such as ordering galley supplies, confirming passenger connections, promoting the air carrier, pointing out sights of interest, and filling out company records during a critical phase of flight except those duties required for the safe operation of the aircraft.

- Do not engage in or permit any activity, such as eating meals, engaging in nonessential conversations and communications, and reading publications not related to the flight during a critical phase of flight that could distract any flight crewmember from the performance of his or her duties or which could interfere in any way with the proper conduct of those duties.

Figure 2-26. According to FAR 121.542 and FAR 135.100, you must ensure that non-essential conversations, activities, and otherwise distracting actions do not occur during critical portions of flight.

CFIT PREVENTION

Maintaining situational awareness during departure under IFR is key to reducing your risk of CFIT. Here are specific actions you can take specific to help prevent CFIT on initial climb and when performing departure procedures:

- Review current charts with clear depictions of hazardous terrain and minimum safe altitudes.

- Verify that ATC departure instructions provide adequate terrain clearance—do not assume that your assigned course and altitude ensures that you clear the surrounding terrain and obstacles. If ATC gives a clearance that conflicts with your assessment of terrain criteria, question and, if necessary, refuse the clearance.

- Ensure that your aircraft performance can meet any required climb gradients.

- Brief the takeoff and climb procedure prior to takeoff, including the outbound course, direction of the first turn, and any departure altitude crossing restrictions.

- During the takeoff briefing, set all communication and navigation frequencies and course selectors to eliminate distractions below 1,000 feet AGL.

- Brief the approach procedure in use at the departure airport to be ready in the event you must return to the airport.

Chapter 3
Enroute Operations

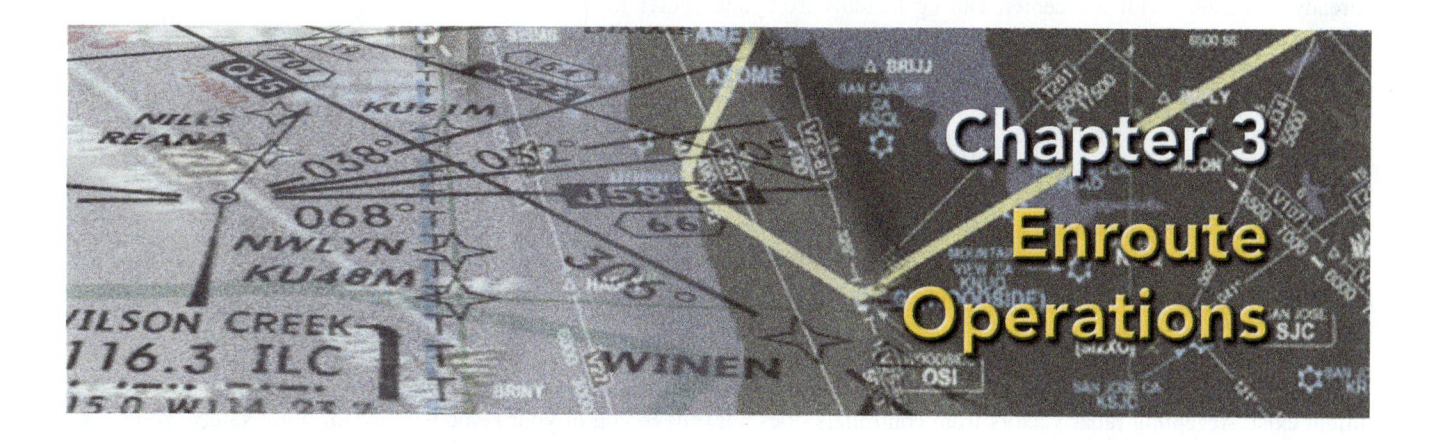

To fly enroute under IFR, you must be skilled in interpreting charts and in operating avionics equipment for precise navigation. You must be able to effectively communicate with ATC, monitor systems, and maintain situational awareness regarding the flight environment and your aircraft. In the event that you lose communications, you must follow the proper lost communications procedures.

AIR ROUTE TRAFFIC CONTROL CENTERS

ARTCCs provide the central authority for issuing IFR clearances and for nationwide monitoring of each IFR flight. These responsibilities apply primarily to the enroute phase of flight and include providing weather information and other in-flight services. Each ARTCC contains between 20 to 80 sectors, with their size, shape, and altitudes determined by traffic flow, airway structure, and workload. [Figure 3-1]

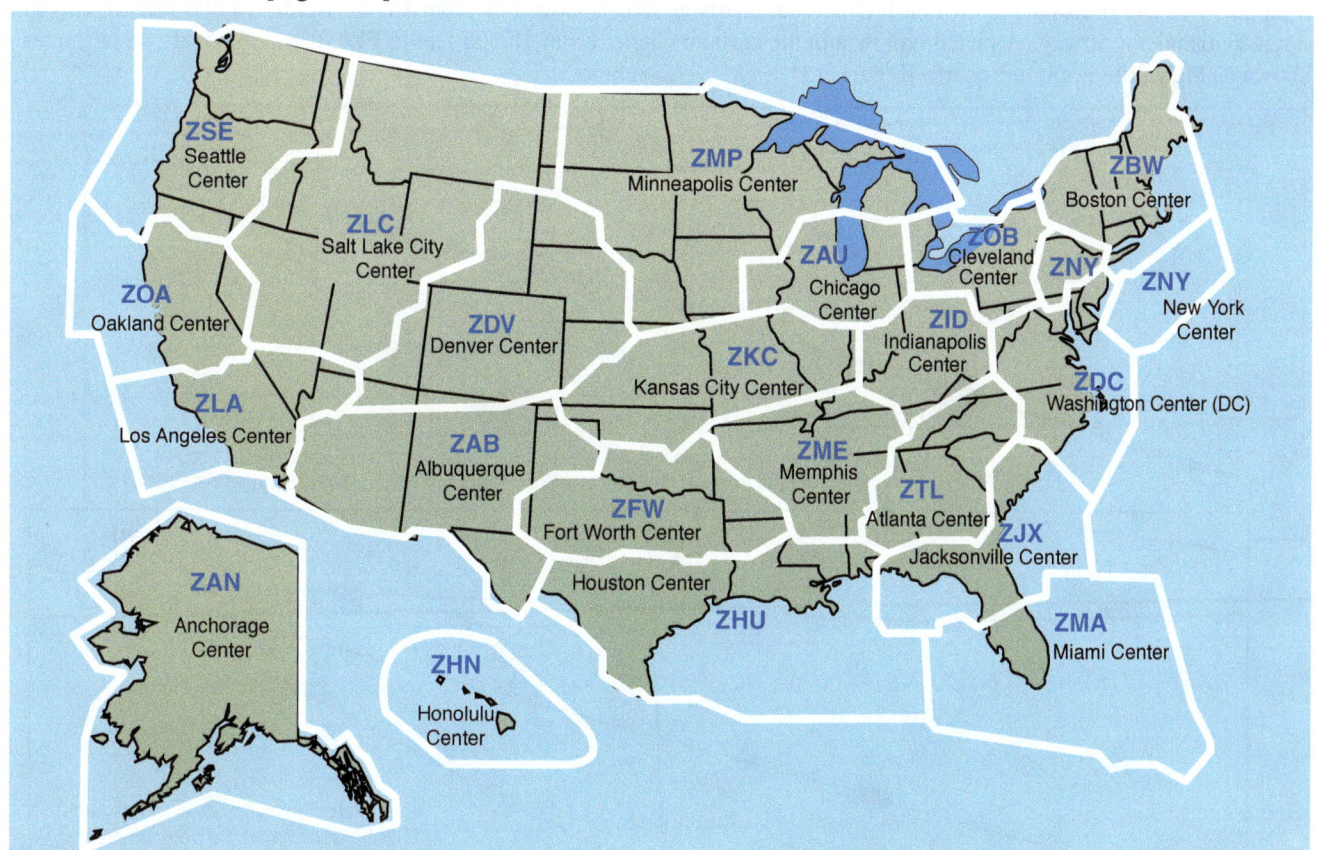

Figure 3-1. Appropriate radar and communication sites are connected to the centers by microwave links and telephone lines.

The regulations require you to continuously monitor an appropriate center or control frequency under IFR in controlled airspace. When climbing after takeoff, you are either in contact with a radar-equipped local departure control or, in some areas, an ARTCC facility. As your flight transitions to the enroute phase, expect a handoff from departure control to a center frequency if not

3-1

already in contact with the center. During handoff from one center to another, the previous controller assigns a new frequency. [Figure 3-2]

During the enroute phase, as your flight transitions from one center facility to the next, a handoff or transfer of control is required as previously described. The handoff procedure is similar to the handoff between other radar facilities, such as departure or approach control. During the handoff, the controller whose airspace is being vacated issues instructions that include the name of the facility to contact, the appropriate frequency, and other pertinent remarks.

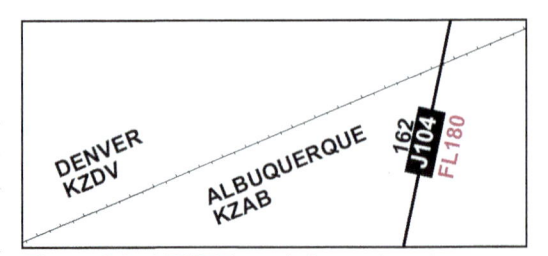

Figure 3-2. ARTCC boundaries and center names are indicated on high altitude and low altitude enroute charts.

While the center is monitoring a flight by radar, it is possible for ATC computers to go down, the power to fail, or radio communication to fail, leaving a flight without ATC guidance. In other cases, gaps in radar coverage along the route of flight might exist. Accepting radar vectors from controllers does not relieve you of your responsibility for flight safety. You must maintain a safe altitude, keep track of your position, and the location of traffic in your vicinity. It is your obligation to question controllers, request an amended clearance, or, in an emergency, deviate from a clearance if you believe flight safety is at risk. TAWS and TCAS equipment can help you detect and correct unsafe altitudes and traffic conflicts.

IFR NAVIGATION

You might be navigating enroute using routes based on VORs or on courses defined by GPS waypoints. The procedures you perform in the enroute phase of flight take place in three flight strata of the NAS. The first, or lower stratum, is an airway structure that extends from the base of controlled airspace up to but not including 18,000 feet mean sea level (MSL). The second stratum is an area containing identifiable jet routes as opposed to designated airways, and extends from 18,000 feet MSL to flight level (FL) 450. The third stratum, FL450 and above, is intended for random, point-to-point navigation.

VHF AIRWAYS/ROUTES

VHF airways and routes are shown on IFR enroute charts as radials extending from VORs. Below 18,000 feet MSL, you navigate on Victor airways depicted on low altitude enroute charts. From 18,000 feet to FL450, you navigate on jet routes shown on high altitude enroute charts. [Figure 3-3]

Distance
Low altitude airways typically have shorter distances between navaids than jet routes For example, V210 extends from PGS to GSN to TBC. However, J64-128 bypasses GCN.

Design
Victor airways and jet routes might be designated between different VORs and do not necessarily overlap. Airspace, terrain, and other factors determine the low and high altitude enroute structure.

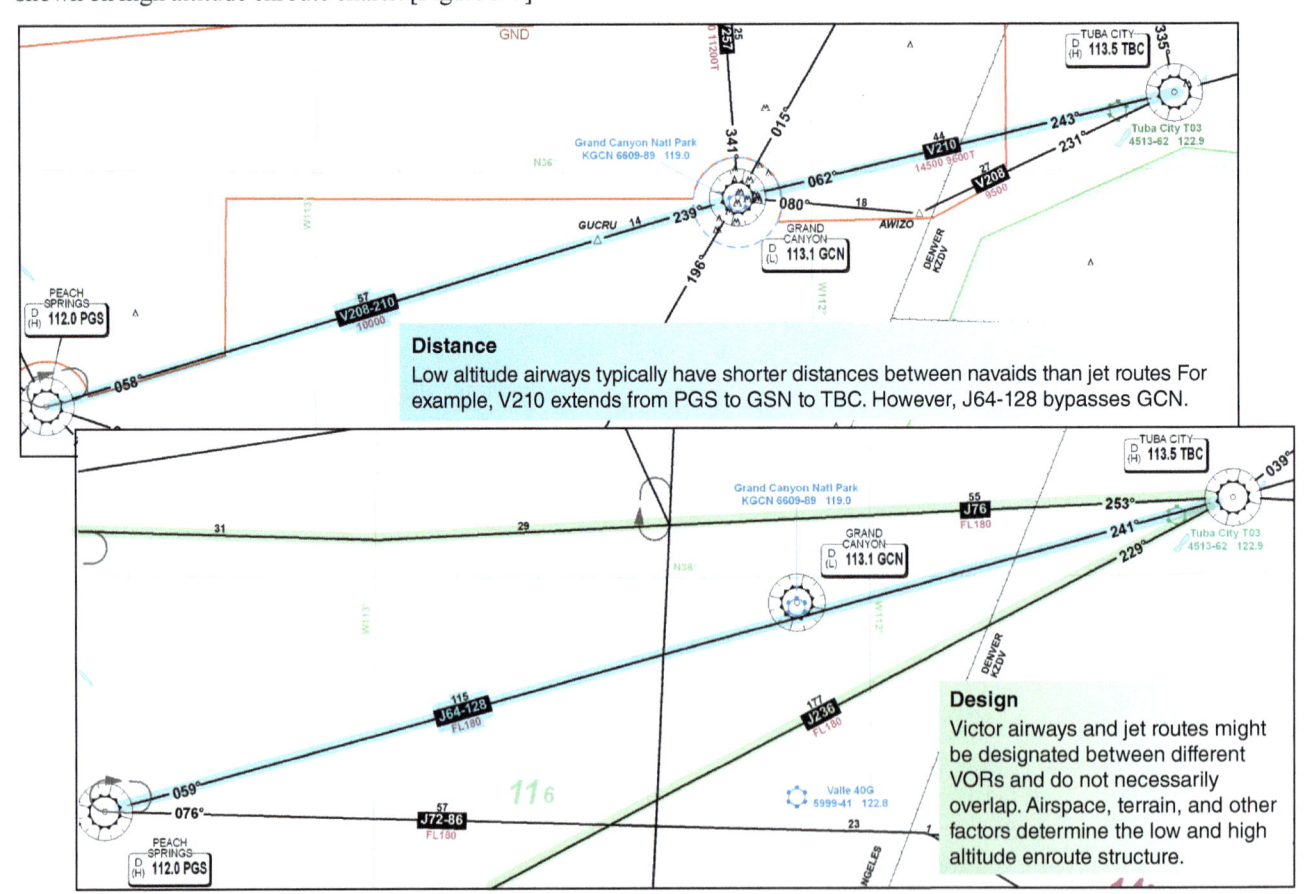

Figure 3-3. Victor airway and jet route depiction is similar, as shown on the EFB. However, the low and high enroute structure varies.

NAVAID SERVICE VOLUME

Each class of VHF navaid has an established operational service volume to ensure adequate signal coverage and frequency protection from other navaids on the same frequency. [Figure 3-4] There might be a time when ATC clears you for a direct route that exceeds the stated distances. When that happens, ATC provides radar monitoring and navigational assistance as necessary.

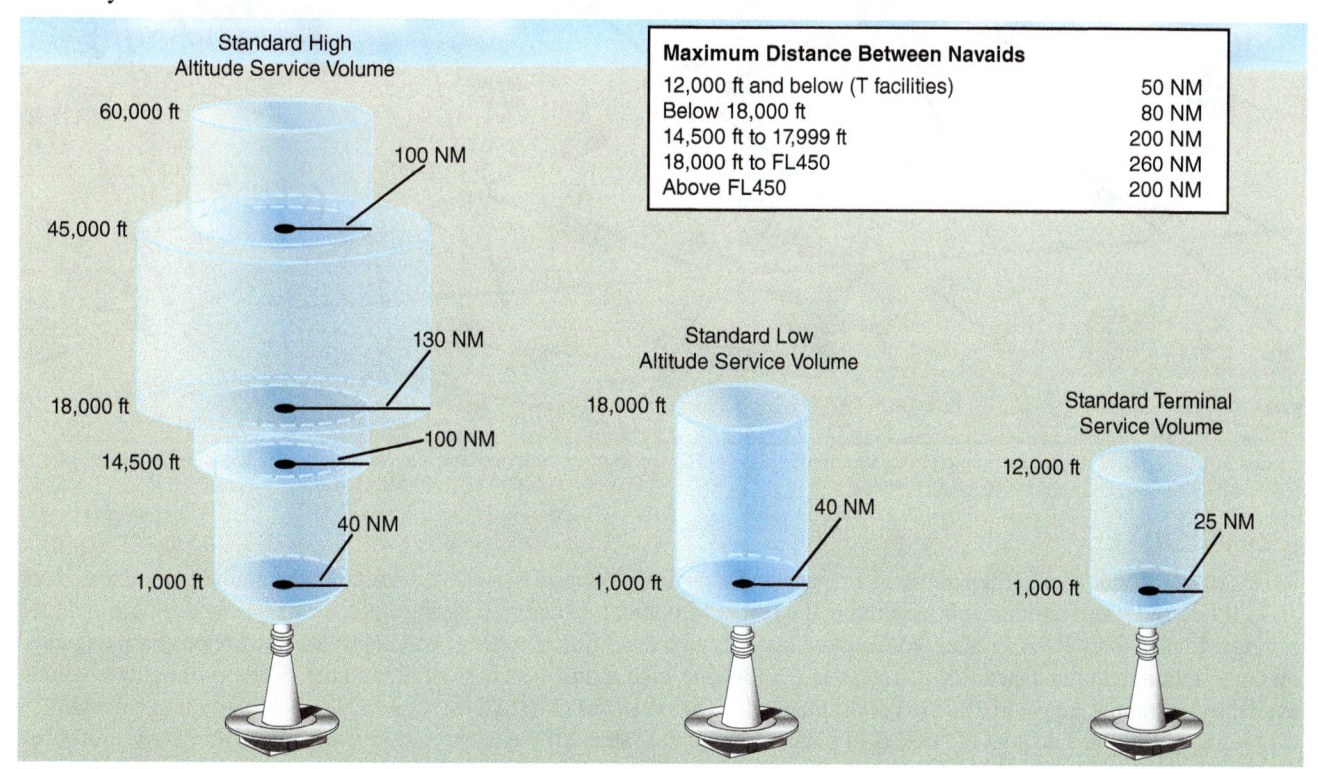

Maximum Distance Between Navaids	
12,000 ft and below (T facilities)	50 NM
Below 18,000 ft	80 NM
14,500 ft to 17,999 ft	200 NM
18,000 ft to FL450	260 NM
Above FL450	200 NM

Figure 3-4. For direct route navigation, be aware of the maximum distances between VORs at which you can receive a signal.

NAVIGATIONAL GAPS

Where a navigational course guidance gap (MEA gap) exists, the airway or route segment may still be approved for navigation. The navigational gap may not exceed a specific distance that varies directly with altitude, from zero nautical miles at sea level to 65 nautical miles at 45,000 feet MSL and not more than one gap may exist in the airspace structure for the airway or route segment. Additionally, a gap usually does not occur at any airway or route turning point. To help ensure the maximum amount of continuous positive course guidance available when flying, route criteria are established for both straight and turning segments. Where large gaps exist that require altitude changes, MEA "steps" may be established at increments of not less than 2,000 feet below 18,000 feet MSL, or not less than 4,000 feet at 18,000 feet MSL and above, provided that a total gap does not exist for the entire segment within the airspace structure. MEA steps are limited to one step between any two facilities to eliminate continuous or repeated changes of altitude in problem areas. [Figure 3-5]

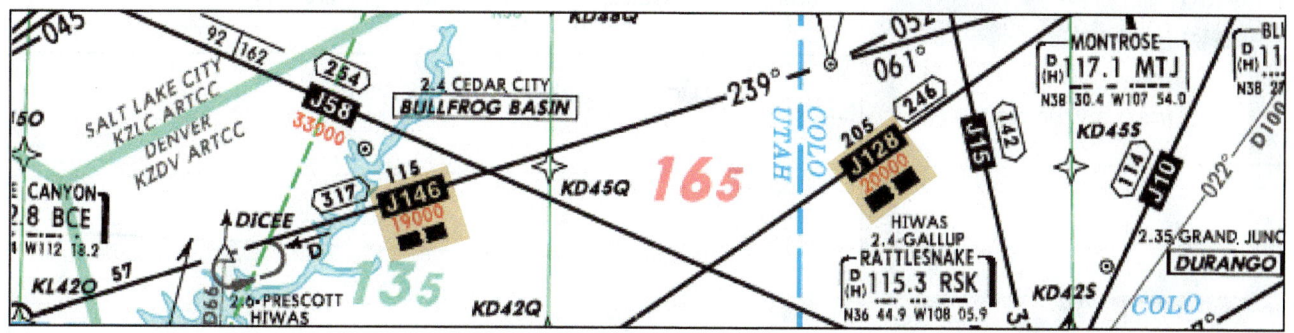

Figure 3-5. MEA gaps are shown by a broken bar symbol.

CHANGEOVER POINTS

When flying airways and jet routes, you normally change frequencies midway between navaids, although there are times when this is not practical. If the navigation signals cannot be received from the second VOR at the midpoint of the route, a changeover point (COP) indicates the distance to each navaid in nautical miles where a frequency change is necessary to receive course guidance from the facility ahead of the aircraft instead of the facility behind. These changeover points ensure continuous reception of navigation signals at the prescribed minimum enroute IFR altitude. They also ensure that other aircraft operating within the same portion of an airway or route segment receive consistent azimuth signals from the same navigation facilities regardless of the direction of flight. [Figure 3-6]

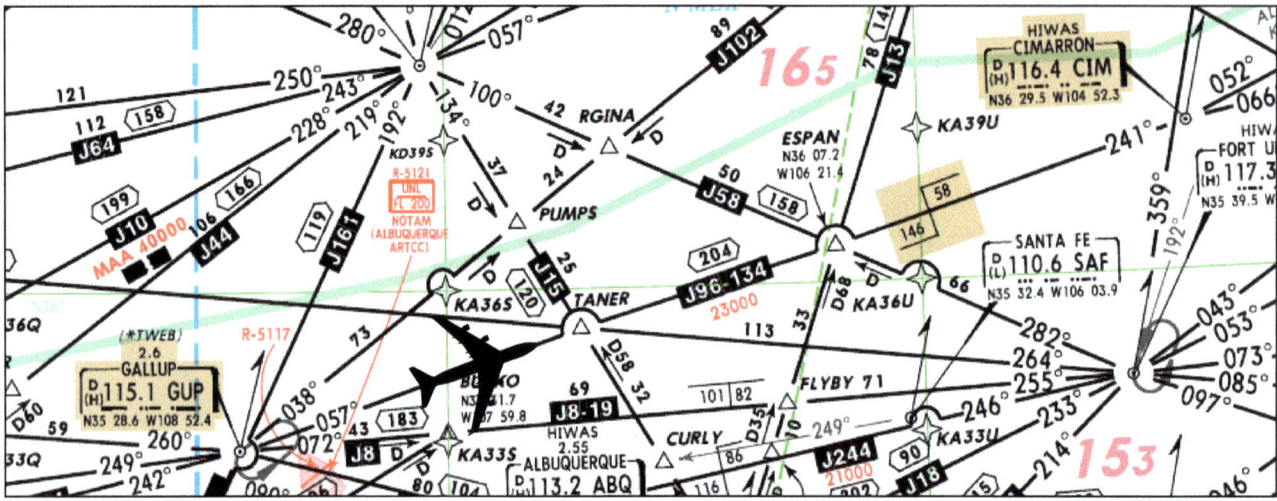

Figure 3-6. To ensure adequate navigational signal reception when flying northeast bound on J96-134, change the VOR frequency from 115.1 to 116.4 when you reach 146 nautical miles.

RNAV ROUTES

RNAV routes enable more efficient use of airspace and reduce ATC transmissions by decreasing the amount of radar vectors and altitude and speed assignments required in the IFR environment. In addition, flying RNAV routes provides time and fuel savings. To plan to fly RNAV routes, you must be familiar with the different types of waypoints and the options for navigating on both random and published RNAV routes in the low and high altitude enroute environments. Some of the route options available at altitudes above FL180 are part of the High Altitude Redesign (HAR) system, which is initially implemented for flights above FL390. The goal of HAR is to obtain maximum system efficiency by introducing advanced RNAV routes for suitably equipped aircraft to use.

WAYPOINTS

Waypoints used to define an RNAV route might be any of the following types: user-defined waypoints, floating waypoints, and navigation reference system waypoints. Published waypoints are defined relative to VOR/DME or VORTAC stations or in terms of latitude/longitude coordinates.

User-Defined Waypoints

You can create user-defined waypoints for use in your own RNAV equipment. User-defined waypoints are unpublished airspace fixes that are designated geographic locations to help provide positive course guidance for navigation and a means of checking progress on a flight. You communicate these waypoints to ATC in terms of bearing and distance, or latitude/longitude. [Figure 3-7]

Figure 3-7. You can determine latitude and longitude coordinates for user-defined waypoints by using a flight planning program or an EFB.

3-4

Another example is an offset phantom waypoint, which is a point in space formed by a bearing and distance from a navaid, such as a VORTAC. When specifying unpublished waypoints in a flight plan, use the frequency/bearing/distance format or latitude and longitude, and these waypoints automatically become compulsory reporting points unless otherwise advised by ATC. All aircraft with latitude/longitude navigation systems flying above FL390 must use latitude and longitude to define turning points.

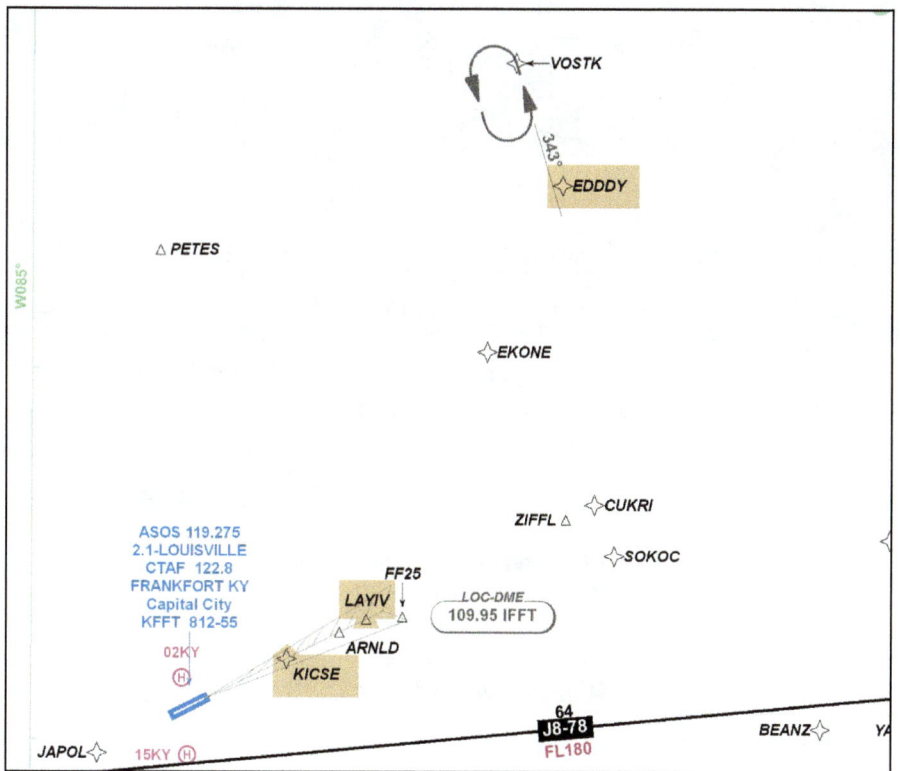

Figure 3-8. Floating waypoints are designated for a wide variety of reasons. For example, EDDDY waypoint is a holding fix and KICSE and LAYIV are associated with approach procedures at Capital City Airport

Floating Waypoints

Floating waypoints represent airspace fixes at a point in space not directly associated with a conventional airway. Floating waypoints might be established for such purposes as ATC metering fixes, holding points, RNAV-direct routing, gateway waypoints, STAR origination points, and SID terminating points. Waypoints are named with five-letter identifiers that are unique and pronounceable but you must be careful of similar waypoint names and verify that you have correctly entered each waypoint into your navigation system. [Figure 3-8]

Database Identifiers

You use database identifiers to maintain orientation with a database navigation system. Do not use these identifiers when filing flight plans or when communicating with ATC. Outside the U.S., these fixes are established by the country as computer navigation fixes (CNFs). [Figure 3-9]

Navigation Reference System

The navigation reference system (NRS) is a grid of waypoints overlying the U.S. that provides flexible flight planning and gives ATC the ability to more efficiently manage tactical route changes for aircraft separation, traffic flow management, and weather avoidance. As part of the HAR, you can file NRS waypoints in your flight plan and use these waypoints when you request route deviations around weather areas. Specifying NRS waypoints helps you and ATC obtain a common understanding of the desired flight path. The NRS includes waypoints every 30 minutes of latitude and every 2° of longitude. [Figure 3-10]

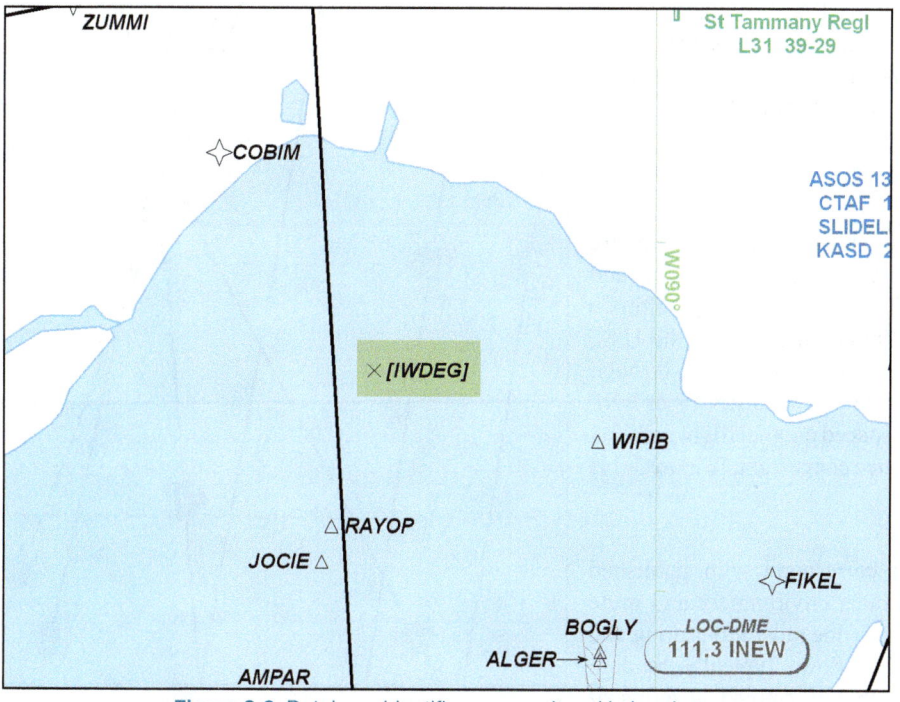

Figure 3-9. Database identifiers are enclosed in brackets.

3-5

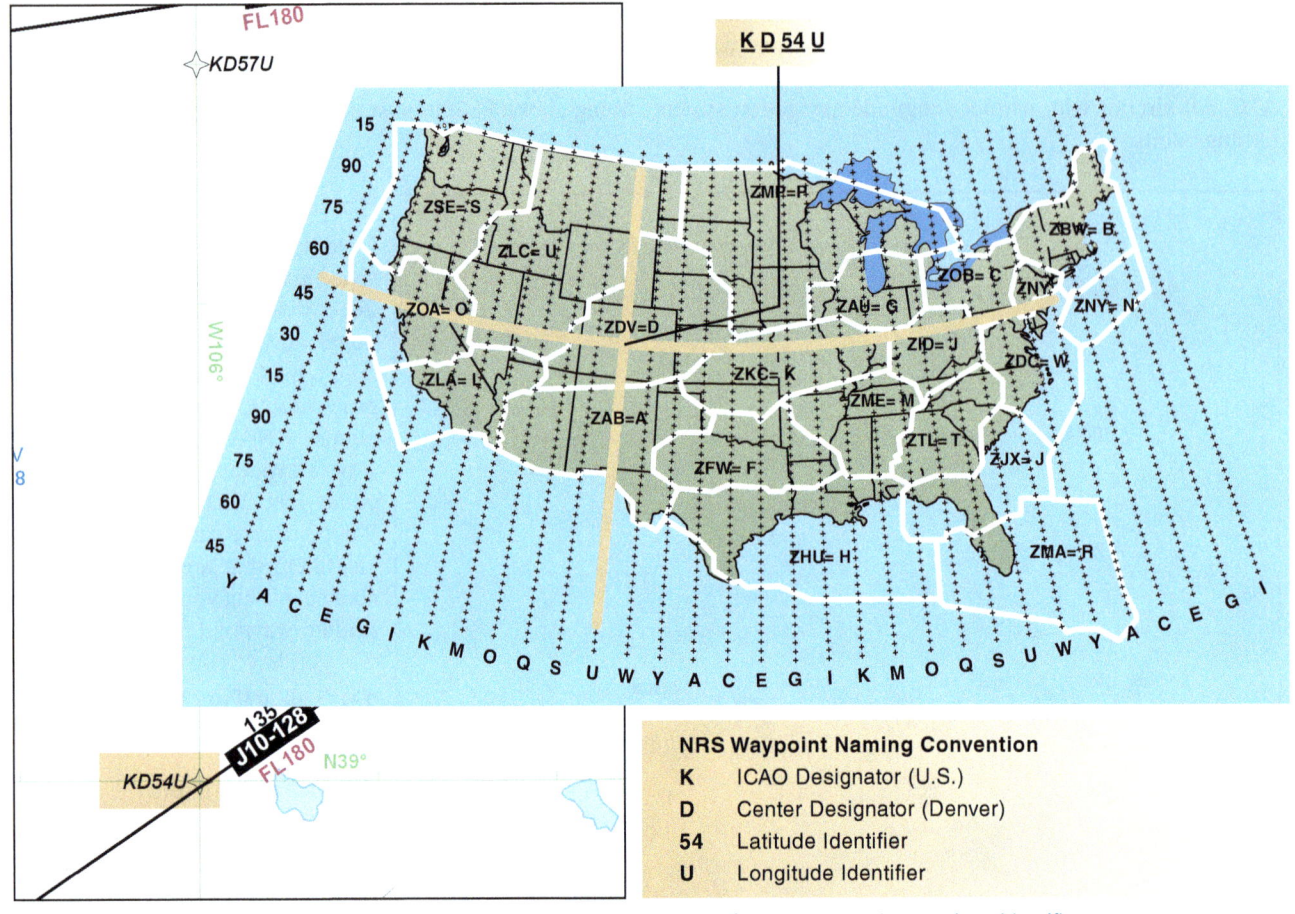

Figure 3-10. Waypoints that are part of the navigation reference system have unique identifiers.

RNAV ROUTE PLANNING

The options for RNAV route planning depend on your aircraft's RNAV equipment, your company's OpsSpecs, and the altitude at which you are operating. You might use RNAV to navigate on airways or jet routes based on conventional navaids or you might used published RNAV routes. The AIM provides guidelines for planning random RNAV routes both at lower altitudes and above FL390 using NRS waypoints.

Q-Routes

The routes between some points are very popular, so these paths are given route designators and published on charts. The U.S. and Canada use "Q" as a designator for RNAV routes on high-altitude enroute charts. Q-routes 1 through 499 are allocated to the U.S., while Canada is allocated Q-routes numbered from 500 through 999. One benefit of this system is that aircraft with RNAV or RNP capability can fly safely along closely spaced parallel flight paths on high-density routes, which eases airspace congestion. [Figure 3-11]

Random RNAV Routes

Random RNAV routes that do not correspond with published courses can only be authorized in a radar environment and route approval depends on ATC's ability to provide radar monitoring and compatibility with traffic volume and flow. Typically random RNAV routes are flown between waypoints defined in terms of latitude and longitude coordinates, degree and distance fixes, or offsets from established airways at a specified distance and

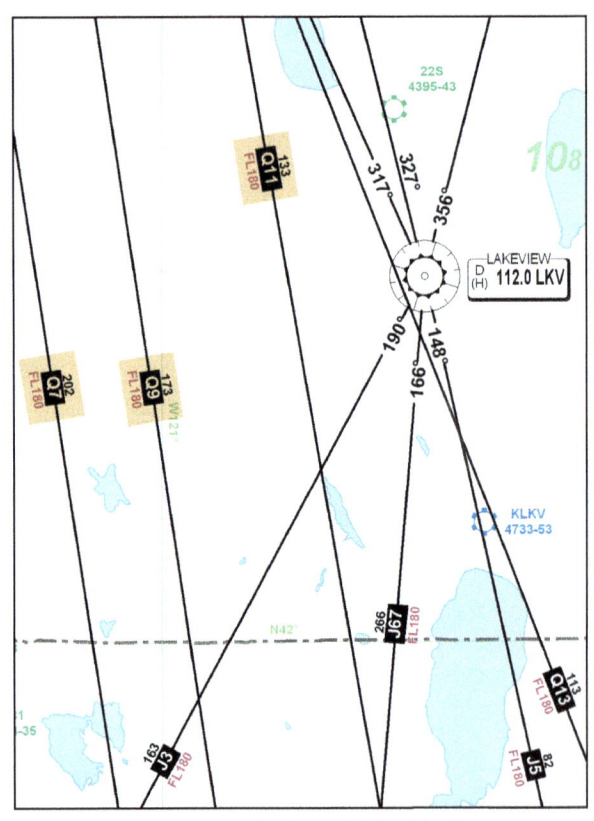

Figure 3-11. Q-routes facilitate high-altitude. long-range direct flights and closely-spaced Q-routes can accommodate increased operations within congested airspace areas, such as the east and west coasts of the U.S.

direction. Although ATC monitors your flight, navigation on a random RNAV route is your responsibility, so create a flight plan with multiple waypoints to enhance situational awareness. When you file a random RNAV route, you must file the appropriate RNAV capability certification suffix in your flight plan. Be aware that ATC might not approve direct routing due to traffic flow and other considerations. When planning your flight comply with the guidelines for using RNAV for IFR flight planning outlined in the AIM. [Figure 3-12]

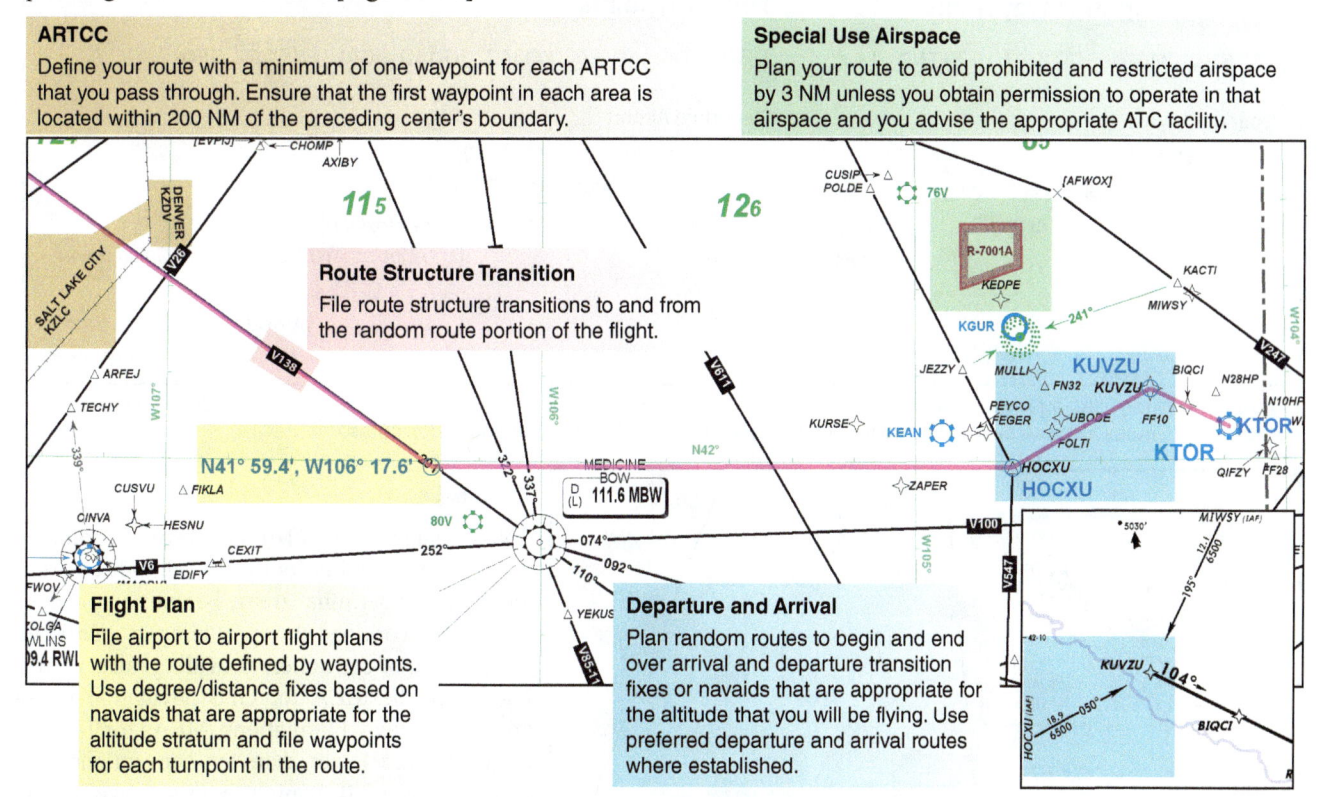

ARTCC
Define your route with a minimum of one waypoint for each ARTCC that you pass through. Ensure that the first waypoint in each area is located within 200 NM of the preceding center's boundary.

Special Use Airspace
Plan your route to avoid prohibited and restricted airspace by 3 NM unless you obtain permission to operate in that airspace and you advise the appropriate ATC facility.

Route Structure Transition
File route structure transitions to and from the random route portion of the flight.

Flight Plan
File airport to airport flight plans with the route defined by waypoints. Use degree/distance fixes based on navaids that are appropriate for the altitude stratum and file waypoints for each turnpoint in the route.

Departure and Arrival
Plan random routes to begin and end over arrival and departure transition fixes or navaids that are appropriate for the altitude that you will be flying. Use preferred departure and arrival routes where established.

Figure 3-12. Plan your route by using all the waypoints required to ensure accurate navigation via the filed route of flight. Navigation on the route is your responsibility unless you request ATC assistance.

Non-Restrictive Routing

If your aircraft is equipped with latitude/longitude coordinate navigation capability, independent of VOR/TACAN references, you may file for random RNAV routes at and above FL390 within the conterminous U.S. This routing is called non-restrictive routing (NRR) and is part of the HAR. You must define the route of flight after the departure fix, including each intermediate fix (turnpoint) and the arrival fix for the destination airport in terms of latitude/longitude coordinates plotted to the nearest minute or in terms of NRS waypoints. You must fly all routes and route segments on Great Circle tracks. Make any in-flight requests for random RNAV clearances or route amendments to an enroute ATC facility. For latitude/longitude filing, the arrival fix must be identified by both the latitude/longitude coordinates and a fix identifier. NRR uses specific pitch and catch points. Pitch points indicate the end of a departure procedure, preferred IFR routing, or other established route where you can begin a segment of the NRR. The catch point indicates where your flight ends a segment of the NRR and joins published arrival procedures, preferred IFR routing, or other established routes. [Figure 3-13]

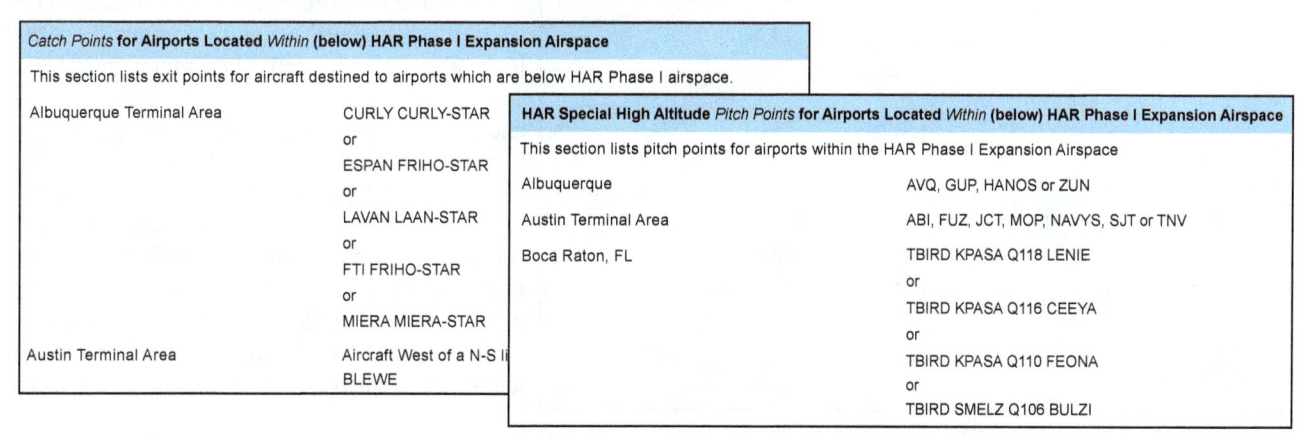

Catch Points for Airports Located *Within* (below) HAR Phase I Expansion Airspace

This section lists exit points for aircraft destined to airports which are below HAR Phase I airspace.

Albuquerque Terminal Area	CURLY CURLY-STAR or
	ESPAN FRIHO-STAR or
	LAVAN LAAN-STAR or
	FTI FRIHO-STAR or
	MIERA MIERA-STAR
Austin Terminal Area	Aircraft West of a N-S li
	BLEWE

HAR Special High Altitude *Pitch Points* for Airports Located *Within* (below) HAR Phase I Expansion Airspace

This section lists pitch points for airports within the HAR Phase I Expansion Airspace

Albuquerque	AVQ, GUP, HANOS or ZUN
Austin Terminal Area	ABI, FUZ, JCT, MOP, NAVYS, SJT or TNV
Boca Raton, FL	TBIRD KPASA Q118 LENIE or
	TBIRD KPASA Q116 CEEYA or
	TBIRD KPASA Q110 FEONA or
	TBIRD SMELZ Q106 BULZI

Figure 3-13. Jeppesen provides a list of HAR routing pitch and catch points with high-altitude charting services.

3-7

There are two ways to designate an NRR route on your flight plan. One method, point-to-point (PTP), uses the traditional fixes in the aircraft equipment database and is shown by placing "PTP" in the first part of the "Remarks" block of the flight plan. For aircraft that have the NRS waypoints in their databases, "HAR" is placed in the first part of the "Remarks" block. The AIM provides guidelines for filing random RNAV routes for flights at and above FL390. [Figure 3-14]

Latitude/Longitude Waypoints

MIA — Departure Airport
SRQ — Departure Fix
3407/10615 — Intermediate Fix (Turning Point)
3407/11546 — Arrival Fix
TNP LAX — Destination Airport

NRS Waypoints

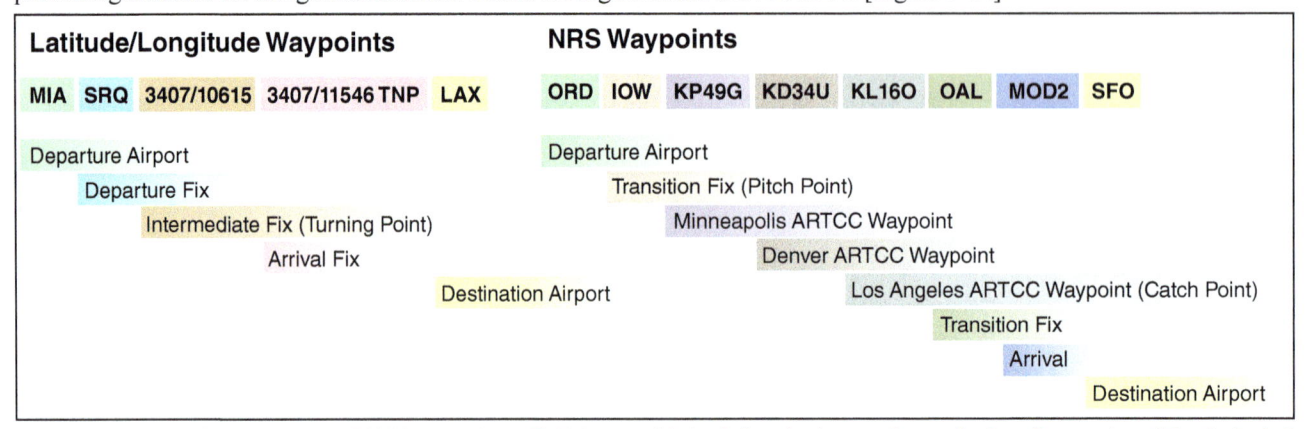

ORD — Departure Airport
IOW — Transition Fix (Pitch Point)
KP49G — Minneapolis ARTCC Waypoint
KD34U — Denver ARTCC Waypoint
KL16O — Los Angeles ARTCC Waypoint (Catch Point)
OAL — Transition Fix
MOD2 — Arrival
SFO — Destination Airport

Figure 3-14. When filing a random RNAV route about FL390, record latitude/longitude coordinates by four figures describing latitude in degrees and minutes followed by a slash and five figures describing longitude in degrees and minutes.

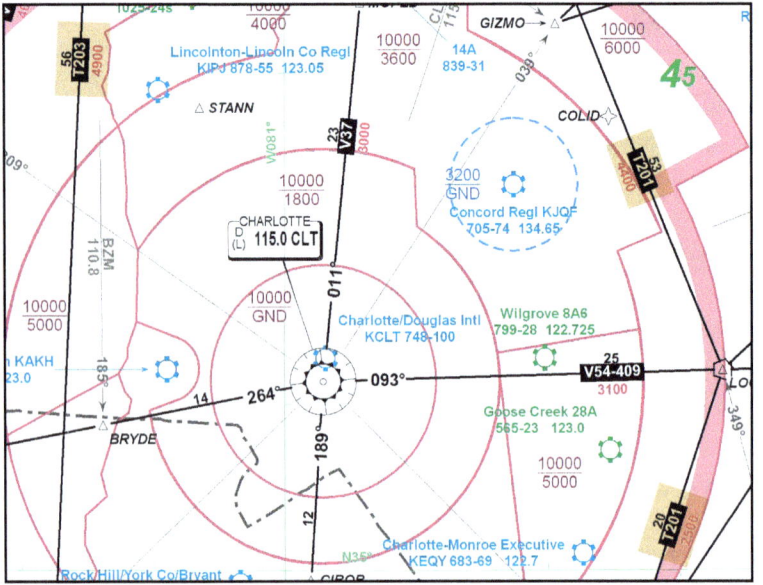

Figure 3-15. Several T-routes enable you to navigate in Charlotte's terminal area.

T-Routes

RNAV Tango routes (T-routes) provide point-to-point route capability for the low altitude environment. In busy terminal areas, T-routes help reduce controller workload by providing a published route in lieu of controllers providing radar vectoring. Since the MEA for GPS navigation is not affected by navaid limitations, MEAs for T-routes frequently are lower than for conventional airways. A lower MEA might help you avoid icing conditions if you can fly below the freezing level. [Figure 3-15]

LF AIRWAYS/ROUTES

Low frequency (LF) airways and routes that are based on NDBs still exist in Alaska and in other countries. These routes are shown on both low and high-altitude enroute charts. [Figure 3-16]

PREFERRED IFR ROUTES

A system of preferred IFR routes helps you and dispatchers plan a flight to minimize route changes and to aid in the efficient, orderly management of air traffic using airways and jet routes. Low and high altitude preferred IFR routes provide a systematic flow of air traffic in the major terminal and enroute flight environments. Filing preferred routes results in fewer air traffic delays and better efficiency for departure, enroute, and arrival ATC service. Jeppesen publishes preferred IFR routes for the low and high altitude stratum. Where more than one route is listed, the routes have equal priority for use. Official location identifiers are used in the route description and intersection names are spelled out. The route is direct where

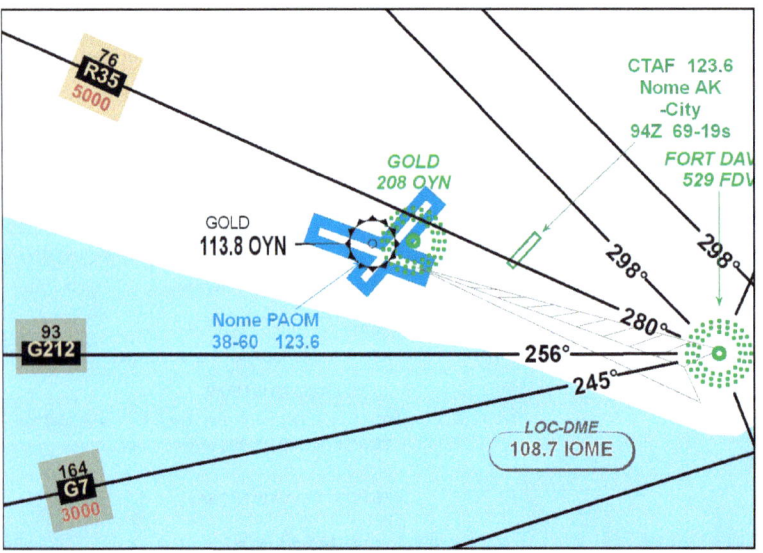

Figure 3-16. LF airways R35, G212, and G7 are LF airways based on the Fort Davis NDB.

two navaids, an intersection and a navaid, a navaid and a navaid radial and distance point, or any navigable combination of these route descriptions follow in succession. [Figure 3-17]

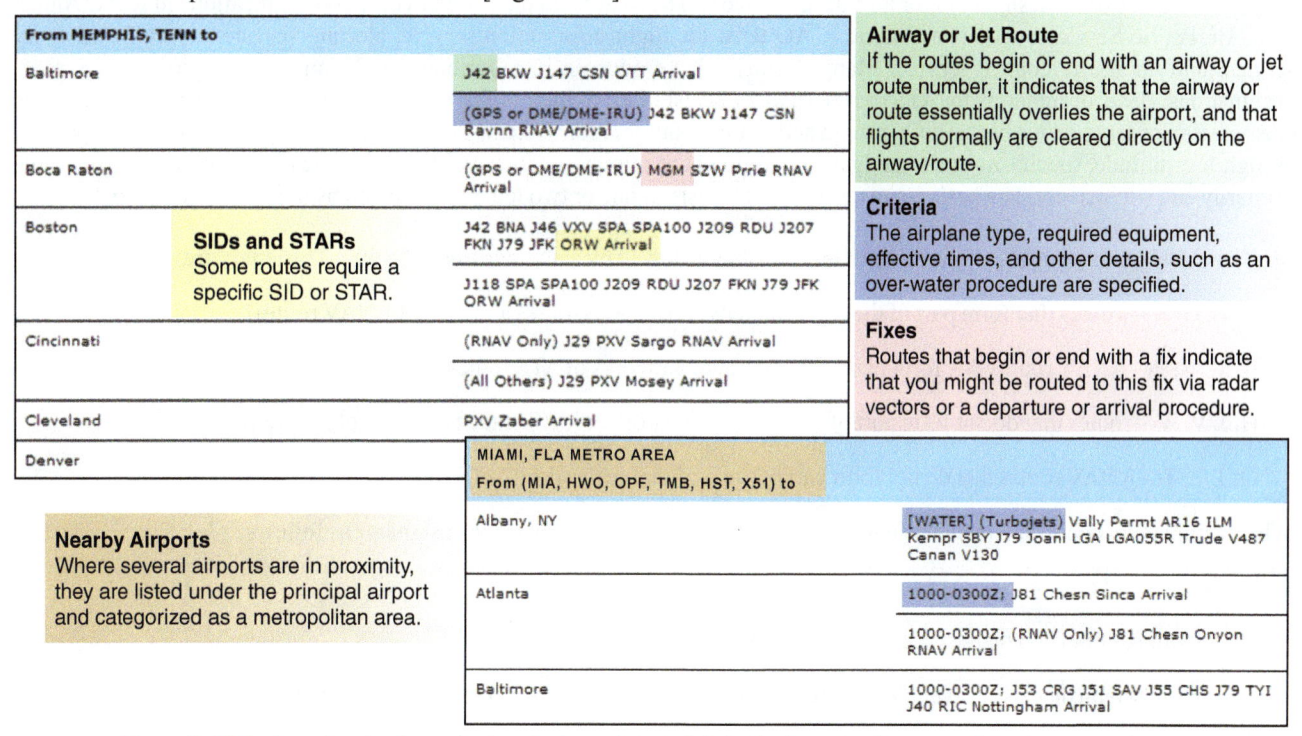

From MEMPHIS, TENN to	
Baltimore	J42 BKW J147 CSN OTT Arrival
	(GPS or DME/DME-IRU) J42 BKW J147 CSN Ravnn RNAV Arrival
Boca Raton	(GPS or DME/DME-IRU) MGM SZW Prrie RNAV Arrival
Boston	J42 BNA J46 VXV SPA SPA100 J209 RDU J207 FKN J79 JFK ORW Arrival
	J118 SPA SPA100 J209 RDU J207 FKN J79 JFK ORW Arrival
Cincinnati	(RNAV Only) J29 PXV Sargo RNAV Arrival
	(All Others) J29 PXV Mosey Arrival
Cleveland	PXV Zaber Arrival
Denver	

SIDs and STARs
Some routes require a specific SID or STAR.

Airway or Jet Route
If the routes begin or end with an airway or jet route number, it indicates that the airway or route essentially overlies the airport, and that flights normally are cleared directly on the airway/route.

Criteria
The airplane type, required equipment, effective times, and other details, such as an over-water procedure are specified.

Fixes
Routes that begin or end with a fix indicate that you might be routed to this fix via radar vectors or a departure or arrival procedure.

MIAMI, FLA METRO AREA From (MIA, HWO, OPF, TMB, HST, X51) to	
Albany, NY	[WATER] (Turbojets) Vally Permt AR16 ILM Kempr SBY J79 Joani LGA LGA055R Trude V487 Canan V130
Atlanta	1000-0300Z; J81 Chesn Sinca Arrival
	1000-0300Z; (RNAV Only) J81 Chesn Onyon RNAV Arrival
Baltimore	1000-0300Z; J53 CRG J51 SAV J55 CHS J79 TYI J40 RIC Nottingham Arrival

Nearby Airports
Where several airports are in proximity, they are listed under the principal airport and categorized as a metropolitan area.

Figure 3-17. Preferred routes for major terminals are listed alphabetically under the name of the departure airport.

TOWER ENROUTE CONTROL

Within the NAS, it is possible to fly an IFR flight without leaving approach control airspace using tower enroute control (TEC) service. This service helps expedite air traffic and reduces ATC and pilot communication requirements. TEC is referred to as "tower enroute," or "tower-to-tower," and allows flight beneath the enroute structure. Tower enroute control reallocates airspace both vertically and geographically to allow flight planning between city pairs while remaining within approach control airspace. You are encouraged to use the TEC route descriptions when filing flight plans. [Figure 3-18]

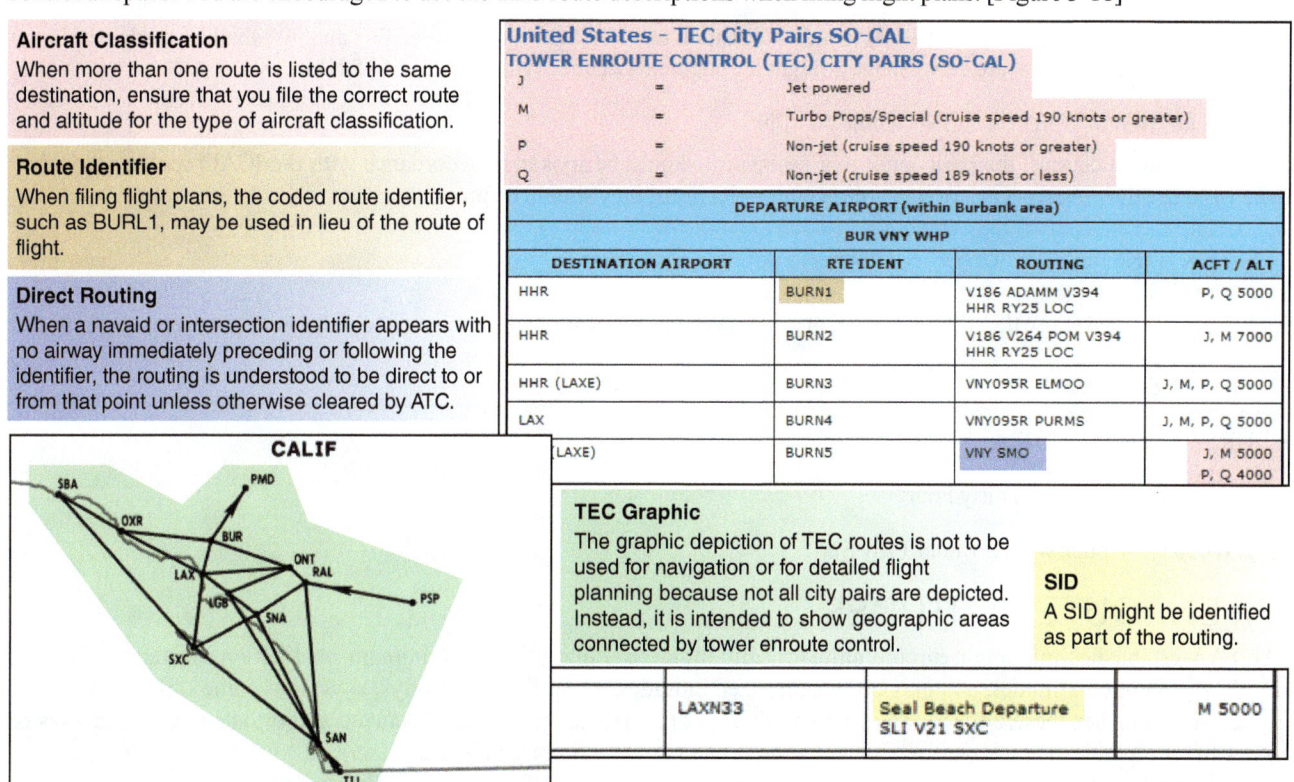

Aircraft Classification
When more than one route is listed to the same destination, ensure that you file the correct route and altitude for the type of aircraft classification.

Route Identifier
When filing flight plans, the coded route identifier, such as BURL1, may be used in lieu of the route of flight.

Direct Routing
When a navaid or intersection identifier appears with no airway immediately preceding or following the identifier, the routing is understood to be direct to or from that point unless otherwise cleared by ATC.

United States - TEC City Pairs SO-CAL
TOWER ENROUTE CONTROL (TEC) CITY PAIRS (SO-CAL)

J	=	Jet powered
M	=	Turbo Props/Special (cruise speed 190 knots or greater)
P	=	Non-jet (cruise speed 190 knots or greater)
Q	=	Non-jet (cruise speed 189 knots or less)

DEPARTURE AIRPORT (within Burbank area)			
BUR VNY WHP			
DESTINATION AIRPORT	RTE IDENT	ROUTING	ACFT / ALT
HHR	BURN1	V186 ADAMM V394 HHR RY25 LOC	P, Q 5000
HHR	BURN2	V186 V264 POM V394 HHR RY25 LOC	J, M 7000
HHR (LAXE)	BURN3	VNY095R ELMOO	J, M, P, Q 5000
LAX	BURN4	VNY095R PURMS	J, M, P, Q 5000
(LAXE)	BURN5	VNY SMO	J, M 5000 P, Q 4000
	LAXN33	Seal Beach Departure SLI V21 SXC	M 5000

TEC Graphic
The graphic depiction of TEC routes is not to be used for navigation or for detailed flight planning because not all city pairs are depicted. Instead, it is intended to show geographic areas connected by tower enroute control.

SID
A SID might be identified as part of the routing.

Figure 3-18. All published TEC routes are designed to avoid enroute airspace and the majority are within radar coverage.

ROUTE DESIGNATORS

ICAO establishes basic designators for air traffic service (ATS) routes and their use in voice communications in ICAO Annex 11 – Air Traffic Services. ATS is a generic ICAO term for flight information service, alerting service, air traffic advisory service, and air traffic control service. Many countries have adopted ICAO recommendations with regard to ATS route designations. Basic designators for ATS routes usually consist of a maximum of five, and in no case exceed six, alpha/numeric characters in order to be usable by both ground and airborne automation systems. The designator indicates the route type such as high/low altitude, specific airborne navigation equipment requirements such as RNAV, and the aircraft type using the route primarily and exclusively. The basic route designator consists of one or two letter(s) followed by a number from 1 to 999.

The basic designator consists of one letter of the alphabet followed by a number from 1 to 999. The letters are:

- A, B, G, R— routes that form part of the regional networks of ATS routes and are not RNAV routes.
- L, M, N, P—RNAV routes that form part of the regional networks of ATS routes.
- H, J, V, W—routes that do not form part of the regional networks of ATS routes and are not RNAV routes.
- Q, T, Y, Z—RNAV routes that do not form part of the regional networks of ATS routes.

Where applicable, one supplementary letter must be added as a prefix to the basic designator as follows:

- K—a low level route established for use primarily by helicopters.
- U—the route or portion thereof is established in the upper airspace.
- S—a route established exclusively for use by supersonic airplanes during acceleration/deceleration and while in supersonic flight.

Where applicable, a supplementary letter may be added after the basic designator of the ATS route as a suffix as follows:

- F—on the route or portion thereof advisory service only is provided.
- G—on the route or portion thereof flight information service only is provided.
- Y—RNP 1 routes at and above FL200 to indicate that all turns on the route between 30° and 90° shall be made within the tolerance of a tangential arc between the straight leg segments defined with a radius of 22.5 NM.
- Z—RNP 1 routes at and below FL190 to indicate that all turns on the route between 30° and 90° shall be made within the tolerance of a tangential arc between the straight leg segments defined with a radius of 15 NM.

USE OF DESIGNATORS IN COMMUNICATIONS

In voice communications, the basic letter of a designator should be spoken in accordance with the ICAO spelling alphabet. When you use the prefixes K, U, or S in voice communications, they should be pronounced as:

K = "Kopter" U = "Upper" S = "Supersonic"

You are not required to use the suffixes F, G, Y, or Z in voice communications. These are examples of designator pronunciations:

- A11—Alfa Eleven
- UR5—Upper Romeo Five
- KB34—Kopter Bravo Thirty Four
- UW456 F—Upper Whiskey Four Fifty Six

IFR ENROUTE ALTITUDES

The FAA establishes minimum enroute altitudes, minimum crossing altitudes, minimum obstruction clearance altitudes, minimum reception altitudes, and maximum authorized altitudes, along federal airways, as well as some off-airway routes. The FAA establishes these altitudes after determining that the navigation aids are adequate and oriented on the airways or routes for acceptable signal coverage and that aircraft can maintain flight within the prescribed route widths. The FAA also determines minimum vectoring altitudes and minimum off-route altitudes for use off of published routes.

According to the regulations, except when necessary for takeoff or landing, you may not operate an aircraft under IFR below applicable minimum altitudes. If no applicable minimum altitude is prescribed, in the case of operations over an area designated as mountainous, you must maintain an altitude of 2,000 feet above the highest obstacle within a horizontal distance of four nautical miles from the course to be flown. In any other case, you must maintain an altitude of 1,000 feet above the highest obstacle within a horizontal distance of four nautical miles from the course to be flown. If both an MEA and a minimum obstruction clearance altitude (MOCA) are prescribed for a particular route or route segment, you may operate an aircraft below the MEA down to, but not below, the MOCA, only when within 22 nautical miles of the VOR. When climbing to a higher minimum IFR altitude, you must begin climbing immediately after passing the point beyond which that minimum altitude applies. However, when ground obstructions intervene, you must cross the point beyond which the higher minimum altitude applies at or above the applicable minimum crossing altitude (MCA) for the VOR.

If on an IFR flight plan, but cleared by ATC to maintain VFR conditions on top, you may not fly below minimum enroute IFR altitudes. The FAA designs minimum altitude rules to ensure safe vertical separation between the aircraft and the terrain. These minimum altitude rules apply to all IFR flights, whether in IFR or VFR weather conditions, and whether assigned a specific altitude or VFR conditions on top. [Figure 3-19]

Minimum Crossing Altitude (MCA)
An MCA is the lowest altitude at certain fixes at which your aircraft must cross when proceeding in the direction of a higher minimum enroute IFR altitude. To reduce clutter around navaids, a reference number corresponds to a nearby box that shows the airway number, altitude, and direction to which the crossing restriction applies.

Grid Minimum Off-Route Altitude (Grid MORA)
A grid MORA is an altitude that provides terrain and man-made structure clearance of 2,000 feet in mountainous areas and 1,000 feet in non-mountainous areas.

Minimum Enroute Altitude (MEA)
The MEA is the lowest published altitude between radio fixes that ensures acceptable navigational signal coverage and meets obstacle clearance requirements between those fixes.

Minimum Reception Altitude (MRA)
The MRA is the minimum altitude at which you can receive the navigation signal for the route and for off-course navaid facilities that determine a fix.

Minimum Obstruction Clearance Altitude (MOCA)
The MOCA is the lowest published altitude in effect between radio fixes on VOR airways, off-airway routes, or route segments that meets obstacle clearance requirements for the entire route segment.

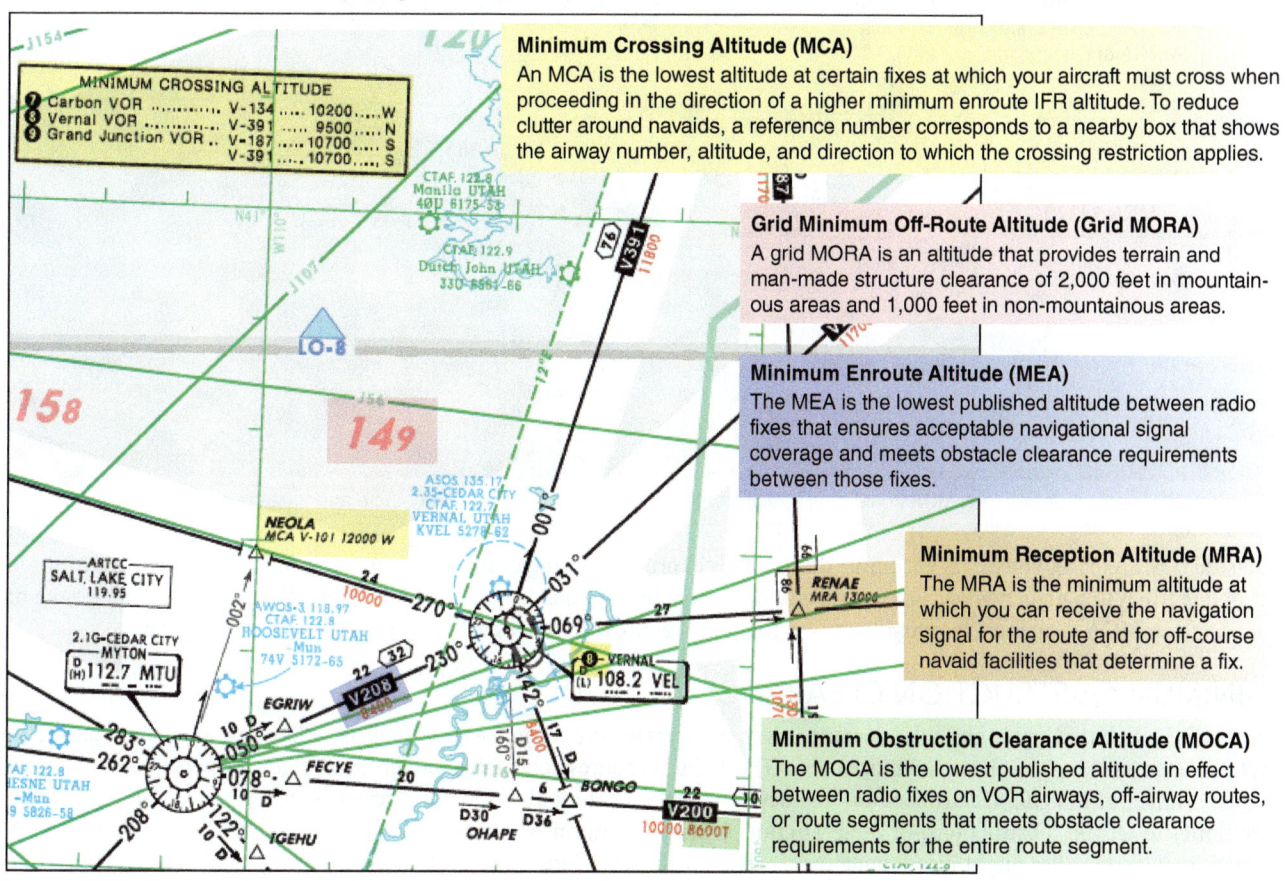

Figure 3-19. You must adhere to the minimum IFR altitudes that are indicated on enroute charts.

MINIMUM ENROUTE ALTITUDE

The MEA prescribed for a federal airway or segment, RNAV low or high route, or other direct route applies to the entire width of the airway, segment, or route between the fixes defining the airway, segment, or route. MEAs for routes wholly contained within controlled airspace normally provide a buffer above the floor of controlled airspace consisting of at least 300 feet within transition areas and 500 feet within control areas. MEAs are based upon obstacle clearance over terrain and man-made objects, adequacy of navigation facility performance, and communications requirements, although adequate communication at the MEA is not guaranteed. MEAs are indicated along the airway or jet route. Some T-routes in Alaska that coincide with Victor airways have a specific MEA for GPS use indicated by the suffix G after the altitude shown along the route.

MINIMUM CROSSING ALTITUDE

When an MEA changes to a higher altitude, you normally begin your climb upon reaching the fix where the change occurs, unless an MCA is established at the fix. MCAs are established in all cases in which obstacles intervene to prevent aircraft from maintaining obstacle clearance during a normal climb to a higher MEA after passing a point beyond which the higher MEA applies. The standard for determining the MCA is based upon the following climb gradients and is computed from the flight altitude:

- Sea level through 5,000 feet MSL — 150 feet per NM
- 5000 feet through 10,000 feet MSL — 120 feet per NM
- 10,000 feet MSL and over — 100 feet per NM

To determine the MCA shown on an enroute chart, the distance from the obstacle to the fix is computed from the point where the centerline of the enroute course in the direction of flight intersects the farthest displacement from the fix. [Figure 3-20] When a change of altitude is involved with a course change, course guidance must be provided if the change of altitude is more than 1,500 feet or if the course change is more than 45°. However, there is an exception to this rule. In some cases, course changes of up to 90° may be approved without course guidance provided that no obstacles penetrate the established MEA requirement of the previous airway or route segment.

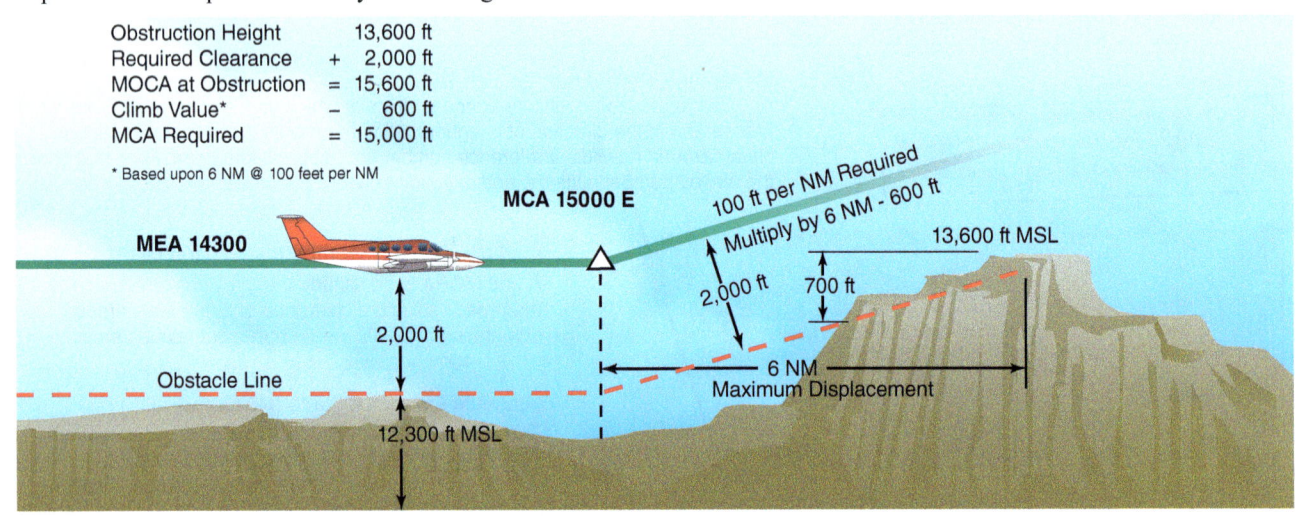

Figure 3-20. The FAA determines MCAs based on specific criteria to ensure aircraft meet obstacle and terrain clearance requirements.

Outside U.S. airspace, you might encounter different flight procedures regarding minimum crossing altitudes and transitioning from one MEA to a higher MEA. For example, when operating in Canada, you must be at the higher MEA crossing each fix, similar to an MCA. You must thoroughly review flight procedure differences when flying outside U.S. airspace.

MINIMUM OBSTRUCTION CLEARANCE ALTITUDE

The MOCA is based upon obstacle clearance over the terrain or over man-made objects, adequacy of navigation facility performance, and communication requirements. The MOCA ensures acceptable navigational signal coverage only within 22 nautical miles of a VOR. Controllers are instructed to issue a safety alert if your aircraft is in a position that is in unsafe proximity to terrain, obstructions, or other aircraft. After you inform ATC of the action that you are taking to resolve the situation, the controller might discontinue the issuance of further alerts. A typical terrain/obstruction alert might sound like this: *"Low altitude alert. Check your altitude immediately. The MOCA in your area is 12,000."*

MINIMUM RECEPTION ALTITUDE

FAA flight inspectors determine MRAs by traversing an entire route of flight to establish the minimum altitude at which the navigation signal can be received for the route and for off-course navaid facilities that determine a fix. When the MRA at the fix is higher than the MEA, an MRA is established for the fix, and is the lowest altitude at which the fix can be determined.

MAXIMUM AUTHORIZED ALTITUDE

A maximum authorized altitude (MAA) is a published altitude representing the maximum usable altitude or flight level for an airspace structure or route segment. An MAA might be established to maintain aircraft below a particular altitude for ATC purposes or the MAA might be the highest altitude on the airway or jet route at which you are ensured adequate reception of navigation signals.

MINIMUM VECTORING ALTITUDE

The FAA established minimum vectoring altitudes (MVAs) for use by ATC in radar areas where ATC provides radar vectors. The MVA provides 1,000 feet of clearance above the highest obstacle in nonmountainous areas and 2,000 feet above the highest obstacle in designated mountainous areas. Because of the ability to isolate specific obstacles, some MVAs may be lower than MEAs, MOCAs, or other minimum altitudes depicted on charts for a given location. While being radar vectored, IFR altitude assignments by ATC are normally at or above the MVA.

Controllers use MVAs only when they are sure they are receiving an adequate radar return from the aircraft. Charts depicting minimum vectoring altitudes are available to controllers and in some cases to pilots as well to help provide increased situational awareness. When climbing, you should not be vectored into a sector with a higher MVA unless at or above the next sector's MVA, except where diverse vector areas have been established. Where lower MVAs are required in designated mountainous areas to achieve compatibility with terminal routes or to permit vectoring to an instrument approach procedure, 1,000 feet of obstacle clearance may be authorized with the use of airport surveillance radar (ASR). The MVA provides at least 300 feet above the floor of controlled airspace. [Figure 3-21]

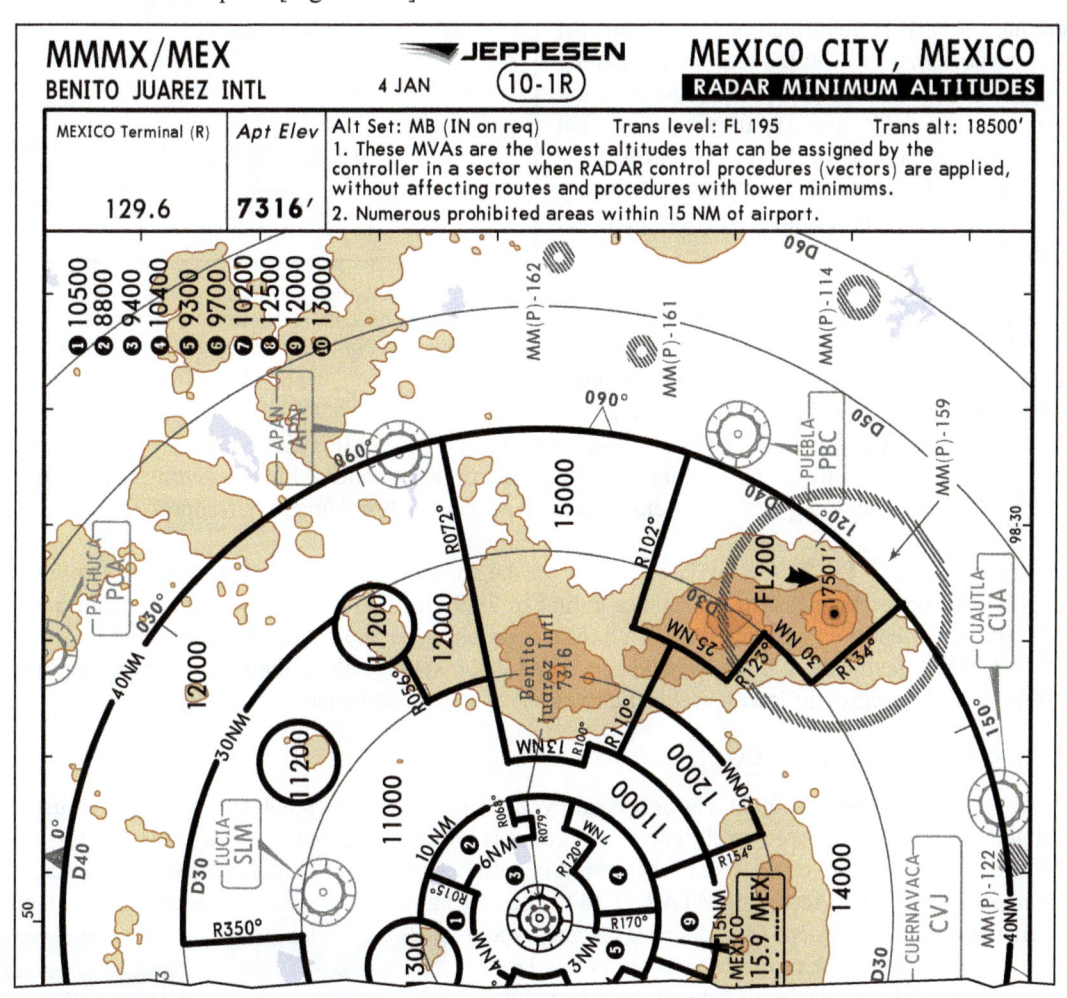

Figure 3-21. This minimum radar altitudes chart for Benito Juarez International Airport helps you maintain situational awareness, especially when you are being vectored during a climb into an area with progressively higher MVA sectors.

MINIMUM OFF-ROUTE ALTITUDE

Grid MORAs are altitudes derived by Jeppesen or provided by state authorities (government civil aviation authority). Grid MORA values determined by Jeppesen clear all terrain and man-made structures by 1,000 feet in areas where the highest elevations are 5,000 feet MSL or lower. MORA values clear all terrain and man-made structures by 2,000 feet in areas where the highest elevations are 5,001 feet MSL or higher. When a Grid MORA is shown as "Unsurveyed" it is due to incomplete or insufficient information. Grid MORA values followed by a +/- denote doubtful accuracy, but are believed to provide sufficient reference point clearance.

Grid MORAs supplied by the state authority provide 2,000 feet clearance in mountainous areas and 1,000 feet in non-mountainous areas. MORAs do not ensure signal reception from ground-based navaids or ensure ATC radar and communication coverage. They are intended primarily as a tool for emergencies and situational awareness. MORAs depicted on enroute charts do not provide acceptable altitudes for terrain and obstruction clearance for off-route, random RNAV direct flights in either controlled or uncontrolled airspace. If you depart an airport under VFR and must obtain an air-filed (popup) IFR clearance, you must be aware of the surrounding terrain and obstructions.

IFR CRUISING ALTITUDE OR FLIGHT LEVEL

In controlled airspace, you must maintain the altitude or flight level assigned by ATC. If you operate an aircraft under IFR in level cruising flight in uncontrolled airspace (except while in a holding pattern of two minutes or less or while turning), you must maintain an appropriate altitude based on your direction of flight. [Figure 3-22]

When operating on an IFR flight plan below 18,000 feet MSL in accordance with a VFR-on-top clearance, you may select any VFR cruising altitude appropriate to the direction of flight between the MEA and 18,000 feet MSL that enables the flight to remain in VFR conditions. You must report any change in altitude to ATC and you must comply with all other IFR reporting procedures. VFR-on-top is not authorized in Class A airspace.

When cruising below 18,000 feet MSL, you must set the altimeter to the current setting, as reported by a station within 100 nautical miles of your aircraft position. In areas where weather reporting stations are more than 100 nautical miles from the route, use the altimeter setting of the closest station. ATC advises IFR flights periodically of the current altimeter setting, but it is your responsibility to update altimeter settings in a timely manner. Altimeter settings and weather information are available from weather reporting facilities operated or approved by the NWS or an FAA-approved source.

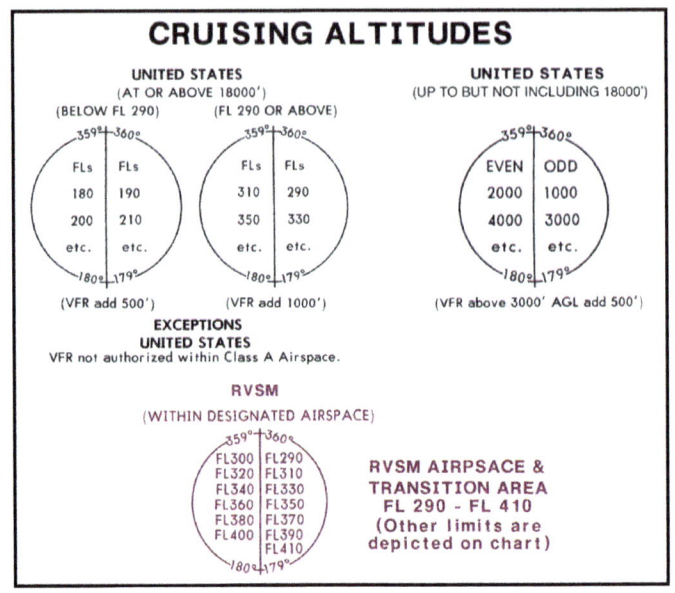

Figure 3-22. Although ATC assigns you an altitude in your IFR clearance, you typically select an altitude for your flight plan based on your direction of flight as shown in this cruising altitude reference, the minimum altitudes along your route of flight, your aircraft's performance, weather conditions, and other factors.

When operating at or above 18,000 feet MSL, you must set the altimeter to 29.92 in. Hg. A flight level (FL) is a level of constant atmospheric pressure related to a reference datum of 29.92 in. Hg. Each flight level is stated in three digits that represents hundreds of feet. For example, FL250 represents an altimeter indication of 25,000 feet. Conflicts with traffic operating below 18,000 feet MSL might arise when actual altimeter settings along the route of flight are lower than 29.92. Therefore, FAR 91.121 specifies the lowest usable flight levels for a given altimeter setting range.

LOWEST USABLE FLIGHT LEVEL

When the barometric pressure is 31.00 in. Hg or less and you are flying below 18,000 feet MSL, you must use the current reported altimeter setting because the true altitude of an aircraft is lower than indicated when sea level pressure is lower than standard. When you are enroute on an IFR flight plan, ATC provides this information at least once while you are in the controller's area of jurisdiction. According to FAR 91.144, when the barometric pressure exceeds 31.00 in. Hg, the following procedures are placed in effect by NOTAM defining the geographic area affected: set 31.00 inches for enroute operations below 18,000 feet MSL and maintain this setting until beyond the affected area. ATC issues actual altimeter settings and advises you to set 31.00 inches in your altimeter, for enroute operations below 18,000 feet MSL in affected areas. If your aircraft has the capability of setting the current altimeter setting and operating into airports with the capability of measuring the current altimeter setting, no additional restrictions apply. At or above 18,000 feet MSL, you must set your altimeter to 29.92 in. Hg (standard setting). As local altimeter settings fall below 29.92, if you are operating in Class A airspace, you must cruise at progressively higher indicated altitudes to ensure separation from aircraft operating in the low altitude structure. [Figure 3-23]

Usable Altitudes	
Current Altimeter Setting	Lowest Usable Flight Level
29.92 (or higher)	180
29.91 — 29.42	185
29.41 — 28.92	190
28.91 — 28.42	195
28.41 — 27.92	200
27.91 — 27.42	205
27.41 — 26.92	210

Figure 3-23. The lowest usable flight level is determined by the atmospheric pressure in the area of operation.

3-14

When the minimum altitude, as prescribed in FARs 91.159 and 91.177, is above 18,000 feet MSL, the lowest usable flight level is the flight level equivalent of the minimum altitude plus the number of feet specified according to the lowest flight level correction factor. [Figure 3-24]

You should be familiar with ICAO terminology for altimeter settings:

- QNE—the standard altimeter setting of 29.92 in. Hg or 1013.2 mb/hPa (used to display pressure altitude)

- QNH—the barometric pressure as reported by a particular station—the local altimeter setting (used to display height above sea level)

- QFE— mean sea level pressure corrected for temperature, adjusted for a specific site or datum like an airfield

Altimeter Setting	Correction Factor
29.92 (or higher)	None
29.91 — 29.42	500 feet
29.41 — 28.92	1,000 feet
28.91 — 28.42	1,500 feet
28.41 — 27.92	2,000 feet
27.91 — 27.42	2,500 feet

Figure 3-24. Apply these correction factors to determine the lowest usable flight level when the minimum IFR altitude is above 18,000 feet MSL.

As you climb and descend to flight levels, your aircraft passes through a transition layer. For example in the U.S. with the altimeter set at QNH below FL180, you are at the transition altitude. The transition level is the lowest flight level available to use above the transition altitude. The transition layer is the airspace between the transition altitude and the transition level. If you are descending through the transition layer, set the altimeter to local station pressure (QNH). When climbing through the transition layer, use the standard altimeter setting of 29.92 in. Hg or 1013 (QNE). When you operate in other countries, these procedures might vary and you must be aware of the specific altimeter setting that you are required to use.

REPORTING PROCEDURES

In addition to acknowledging a handoff to another center enroute controller, there are reports you should make without a specific request from ATC. You should make certain reports at all times regardless of whether your flight is in radar contact with ATC, although others are necessary only if radar contact is lost or terminated. [Figure 3-25]

RADAR/NONRADAR REPORTS

These reports should be made at all times without a specific ATC request.

REPORTS	EXAMPLE
Leaving one assigned flight altitude or flight level for another	"Marathon 564, leaving 8,000, climb to 10,000."
VFR-on-top change in altitude	"Marathon 564, VFR-on-top, climbing to 10,500."
Leaving any assigned holding fix or point	"Marathon 564, leaving FARGO Intersection."
Missed approach	"Marathon 564, missed approach, request clearance to Chicago."
Unable to climb or descend at least 500 feet per minute	"Marathon 564, maximum climb rate 400 feet per minute."
TAS variation from filed speed of 5% or 10 knots, whichever is greater	"Marathon 564, advises TAS decrease to140 knots."
Time and altitude or flight level upon reaching a holding fix or clearance limit	"Marathon 564, FARGO Intersection at 05, 10,000, holding east."
Loss of nav/comm capability (required by FAR 91.187)	"Marathon 564, ILS receiver inoperative."
Unforecast weather conditions or other information relating to the safety of flight (required by FAR 91.183)	"Marathon 564, experiencing moderate turbulence at 10,000."

NONRADAR REPORTS

When not in radar contact, these reports should be made without a specific request from ATC.

REPORTS	EXAMPLE
Leaving FAF or OM inbound on final approach	"Marathon 564, outer marker inbound, leaving 2,000."
Revised ETA of more than three minutes	"Marathon 564, revising SCURRY estimate to 55."
Position reporting at compulsory reporting points (required by FAR 91.183)	See figure 3-26 for position report items.

Figure 3-25. Reporting changes in altitude, aircraft performance, and navigation equipment status, and making position reports in the nonradar environment provides ATC with information to manage traffic and maintaining aircraft separation in the IFR environment.

NONRADAR POSITION REPORTS

If radar contact is lost or radar service terminated, the regulations require you to provide ATC with position reports over designated VORs and fixes along your route of flight. Solid triangles depict these compulsory reporting points on IFR enroute charts. Fixes shown as open triangles indicate noncompulsory reporting points, and position reports are only necessary when requested by ATC. If you are on a direct course that is not on an established airway or jet route, report over the fixes used in your flight plan that define the route since they automatically become compulsory reporting points. Compulsory reporting points also apply when conducting an IFR flight in accordance with a VFR-on-top clearance. Whether on a published airway or route or proceeding direct, position reports are mandatory in a nonradar environment, and they must include specific information. [Figure 3-26]

COMMUNICATION FAILURE

Two-way radio communication failure procedures for IFR operations are outlined in FAR 91.185. Unless otherwise authorized by ATC, you are expected to comply with this regulation when you are operating under IFR. Use the transponder to alert ATC to a radio communication failure by squawking code 7600. [Figure 3-27]

Position Report Items	
Identification	"Marathon 564,
Position	Sidney
Time	15, (minutes after the hour)
Altitude/Flight Level	9,000,
IFR or VFR (in a report to Flight Service only)	IFR,
ETA Over the Next Reporting Fix	Akron 35, (minutes after the hour)
Following Reporting Point	Thurman next."
Pertinent Remarks	(If necessary)

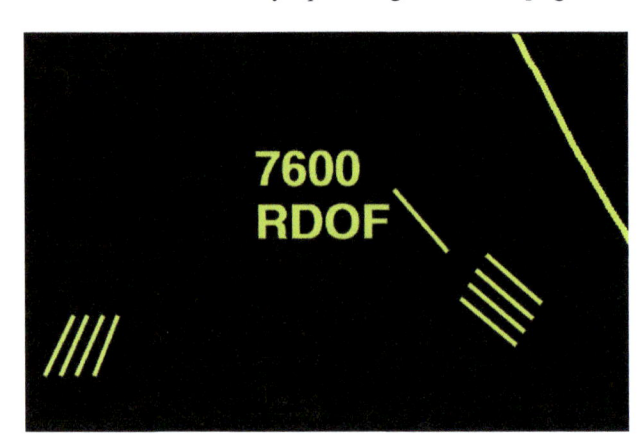

Figure 3-27. When an aircraft squawks code 7600 during a two-way radio communication failure, the information block on the radar screen flashes RDOF (radio failure) to alert the controller.

If only the transmitter is inoperative, you should listen for ATC instructions on any operational receiver, including the navigation receivers. It is possible ATC might try to contact you over a VOR, VORTAC, NDB, or localizer frequency. In addition to monitoring navaid receivers, attempt to reestablish communication by contacting ATC on a previously assigned frequency or by calling flight service or Aeronautical Radio, Incorporated (ARINC).

The primary objective of the regulations governing communication failures is to preclude extended IFR operations within the ATC system because these operations might adversely affect other users of the airspace. If the radio fails while operating on an IFR clearance, but in VFR conditions, or if encountering VFR conditions at any time after the failure, you should continue the flight under VFR conditions, if possible, and land as soon as practicable. The requirement to land as soon as practicable should not be construed to mean as soon as

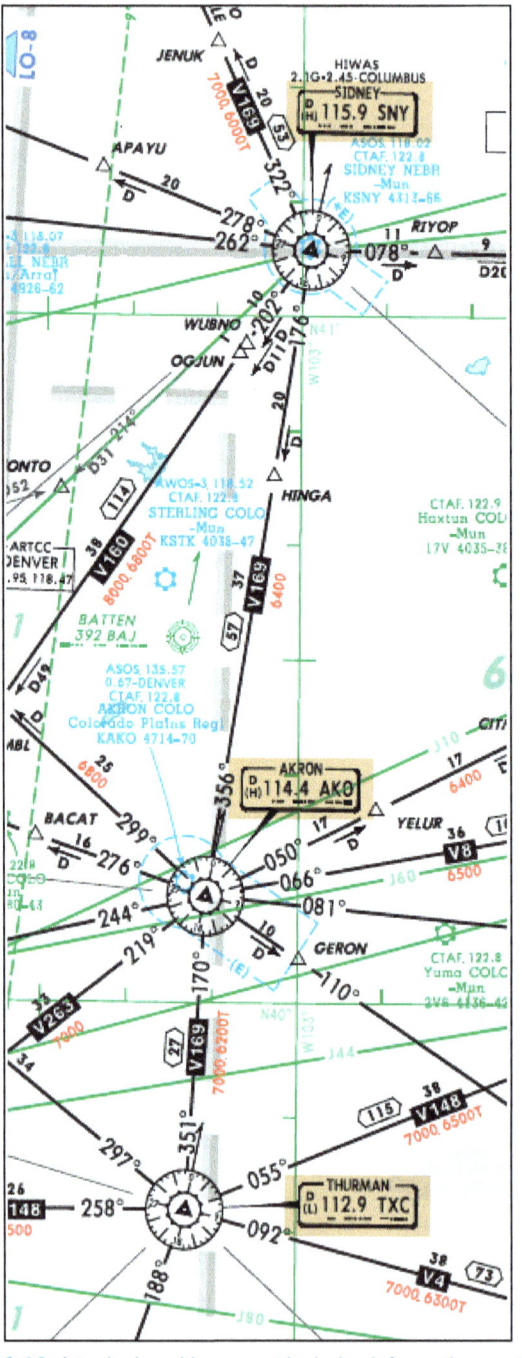

Figure 3-26. A typical position report includes information pertaining to aircraft position, expected route, and estimated time of arrival (ETA). Time may be stated in minutes only when no misunderstanding is likely to occur.

possible. You retain the prerogative of exercising your best judgment and are not required to land at an unauthorized airport, at an airport unsuitable for the type of aircraft flown, or to land only minutes short of your intended destination. However, if IFR conditions prevail, you must comply with regulatory procedures to ensure aircraft separation.

If you must continue your flight under IFR after experiencing two-way radio communication failure, you should fly one of the following routes:

- The route assigned by ATC in the last clearance received.

- If being radar vectored, the direct route from the point of radio failure to the fix, route, or airway specified in the radar vector clearance.

- In the absence of an assigned route, the route ATC has advised you to expect in a further clearance.

- In the absence of an assigned or expected route, the route filed in the flight plan.

You must also fly a specific altitude if you lose two-way radio communication. The altitude to fly after a communication failure can be found in FAR 91.185 and must be the highest of the following altitudes for each route segment flown:

- The altitude or flight level assigned in the last ATC clearance.

- The minimum altitude or flight level for IFR operations.

- The altitude or flight level ATC has advised to expect in a further clearance.

In some cases, the assigned or expected altitude might not be as high as the MEA on the next route segment. In this situation, begin a climb to the higher MEA when you reach the fix where the MEA rises. If the fix also has a published MCA, start the climb so you will be at or above the MCA when reaching the fix. If the next succeeding route segment has a lower MEA, descend to the applicable altitude — either the last assigned altitude or the altitude expected in a further clearance — when reaching the fix where the MEA is lower.

CLIMBING AND DESCENDING ENROUTE

You might request a climb or descent to a different enroute altitude to avoid icing or turbulence or ATC might direct you to climb or descend for aircraft separation purposes or traffic conflicts. When ATC issues a clearance or instruction, you are expected to execute its provisions upon receipt. In some cases, controllers include words that modify their expectation. For example, a controller uses the word *"immediately"* in a clearance or instruction to impress urgency to avoid an imminent situation, and ATC expects you to comply without delay.

CLIMB AT PILOT'S DISCRETION

If you receive the direction to *"climb at pilot's discretion"* in the altitude information of an ATC clearance, it means you are authorized to start a climb when you wish, to climb at any rate, and to temporarily level off at any intermediate altitude, although after you vacate an altitude you may not return to that altitude. When ATC does not use the term *"at pilot's discretion"* or impose any climb restrictions, you should climb promptly on acknowledgment of the clearance. You should climb at an optimum rate consistent with the operating characteristics of the aircraft to 1,000 feet below the assigned altitude, and then attempt to climb at a rate of between 500 and 1,500 feet per minute until reaching the assigned altitude. If at any time you are unable to climb at a rate of at least 500 feet per minute, or if it is necessary to level off at an intermediate altitude during climb, you should advise ATC.

EXPEDITE CLIMB

"Expedite climb" normally indicates that you should use the approximate best rate of climb without an exceptional change in aircraft handling characteristics. Normally controllers inform you of the reason for an instruction to expedite. If flying a turbojet airplane equipped with afterburner engines, such as a military aircraft, you should advise ATC prior to takeoff if you intend to use afterburning during your climb to the enroute altitude. Often, the controller can plan traffic to accommodate a high-performance climb and allow you to climb to the planned altitude without restriction. If you receive an expedite clearance and ATC subsequently changes the altitude or restates the clearance without an expedite instruction, the expedite instruction is canceled.

During enroute climb, as in any other phase of flight, it is essential that you clearly communicate with ATC regarding clearances to avoid readback/hearback errors. For example, *"reaching"* and *"leaving"* are commonly used ATC terms having different usages. They might be used in clearances involving climbs, descents, turns, or speed changes. On the flight deck, the words *"reaching"* and *"leaving"* sound much alike. [Figure 3-28]

```
Departing IFR, clearance was to maintain 5,000 feet, expect 12,000 in ten minutes. After
handoff to center, we understood and read back, "Leaving 5,000 turn left heading 240° for
vector on course." The First Officer turned to the assigned heading climbing through 5,000
feet. At 5,300 feet center advised assigned altitude was 5,000 feet. We immediately
descended to 5,000. Center then informed us we had traffic at 12 o'clock and a mile at
6,000. After passing traffic, a higher altitude was assigned and climb resumed. We now
believe the clearance was probably "reaching" 5,000, etc. Even our readback to the
controller with "leaving" didn't catch the different wording.
```

Figure 3-28. In this Aviation Safety Reporting System (ASRS) account, a flight crew experienced an apparent clearance readback/hearback error that resulted in confusion about the clearance, and ultimately to inadequate separation from another aircraft.

For altitude awareness during climb, call out altitudes on the flight deck according to your SOPs. The pilot monitoring (PM) might call 2,000 and 1,000 feet to the pilot flying (PF) prior to reaching an assigned altitude. The callout might be, *"two to go"* and *"one to go."* Climbing through the transition altitude, both pilots set their altimeters to 29.92 in. Hg and announce *"2992 inches"* (or 'standard,' on some aircraft) and the flight level passing. For example, *"2992 inches" ('standard'), flight level one eight zero."* On international flights, you might need to differentiate between barometric pressure equivalents indicated as in. Hg and those indicated as millibars or hectopascals to eliminate any potential errors, such as setting 996 millibars as 2996.

DESCENT CLEARANCES
ATC issues two basic descent clearances. The controller might ask you to descend to and maintain a specific altitude. Generally, this clearance is for enroute traffic separation purposes and you must respond to it promptly. You should descend at the optimum rate for your aircraft, until 1,000 feet above the assigned altitude. Descend at a rate of 500 to 1,000 feet per minute for the last 1,000 feet of descent. The second type of descent clearance allows you to descend *"...at pilot's discretion."* When ATC issues a clearance at pilot's discretion, you may begin the descent whenever you choose. You are also authorized to level off, temporarily, at any intermediate altitude during the descent, although once you leave an altitude, you may not return to it.

HOLDING PROCEDURES
There are many factors that affect aircraft during holding maneuvers, including navaid ground and airborne tolerance, the effect of wind, flight procedures, ATC instructions, outbound leg length, maximum holding airspeeds, fix to navaid distance, DME slant range effect, holding airspace size, and altitude holding levels.

ATC HOLDING INSTRUCTIONS
When a controller anticipates a delay at a the clearance limit or fix, a holding clearance is usually issued to the flight at least five minutes before the ETA at the clearance limit or fix. If the holding pattern assigned by ATC is depicted on the appropriate aeronautical chart, you are expected to hold as published. In this situation, the controller issues a holding clearance that includes the name of the fix, the instructions to hold as published, and issues an expect further clearance (EFC) time. An example of such a clearance is: *"Marathon five sixty four, hold east of MIKEY Intersection as published, expect further clearance at 1521."*

When ATC issues a clearance that requires a hold at a fix where a holding pattern is not charted, the controller issues complete holding instructions. This information includes the direction from the fix, name of the fix, course, leg length, if appropriate, direction of turns (if left turns are required), and the EFC time. You must maintain your last assigned altitude unless a new altitude is specifically included in the holding clearance, and fly right turns unless ATC assigns left turns. Note that all holding instructions should include an EFC time. If you lose two-way radio communication, the EFC allows you to depart the holding fix at a definite time. You should plan the last circuit of the holding pattern to leave the fix as close as possible to the exact time. [Figure 3-29]

If you are approaching the clearance limit and you have not received holding instructions from ATC, you are expected to follow certain procedures. First, call ATC and request further clearance before reaching the fix. If the controller does not issue a clearance, ATC expects you to enter a hold at the fix in compliance with the published holding pattern. If a holding pattern is not charted at the fix, you are expected to hold on the inbound course using right turns. [Figure 3-30]

Charted Holding Pattern

- Direction to hold from the holding fix
- Holding fix
- Expect further clearance time

"...Hold southeast
Of GOULL intersection
as published"

Uncharted Holding Pattern

- Direction to hold from holding fix
- Holding fix
- The holding course (a specified radial, magnetic bearing, airway or route number)
- The outbound leg length in minutes or nautical miles when DME is used
- Nonstandard pattern, if used
- Expect further clearance time

"...Hold west
of Horst Intersection
on Victor 8
5 mile legs
left turns
expect further clearance at 1430."

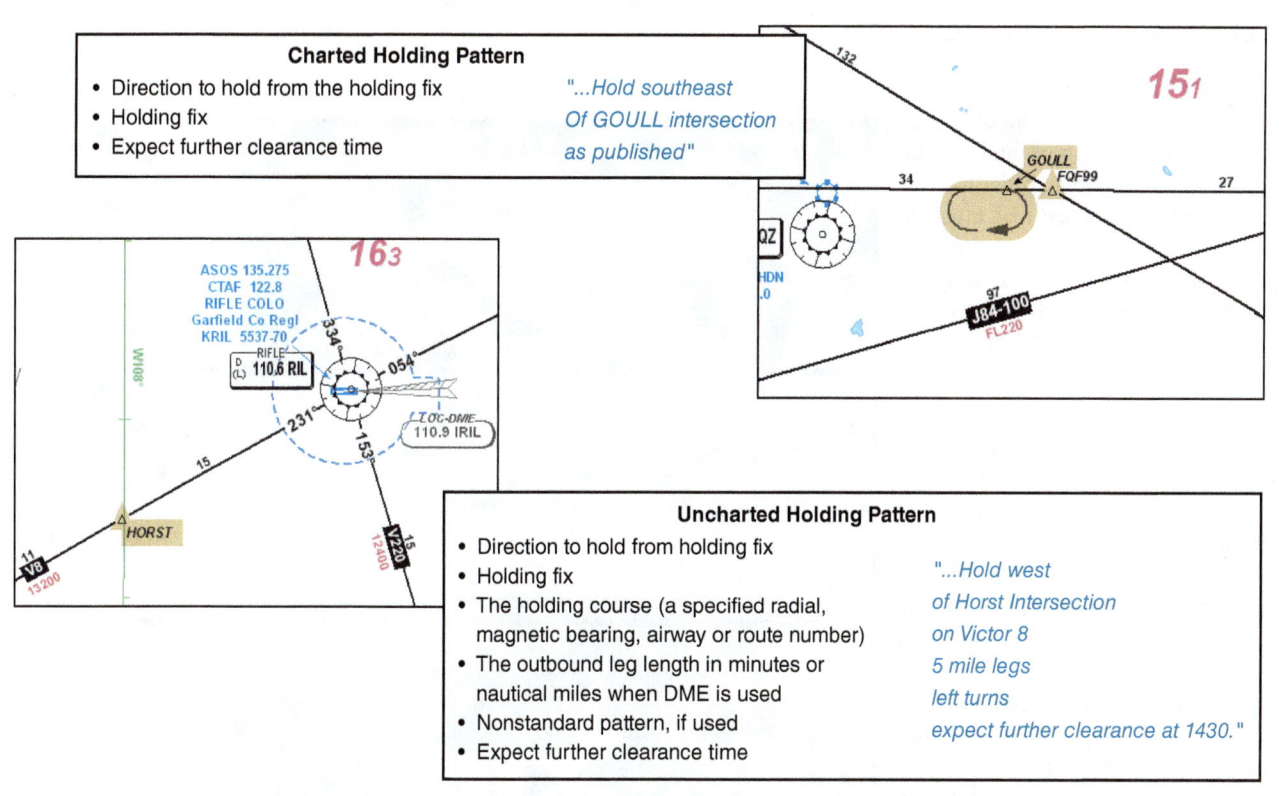

Figure 3-29. Clearances for charted holding patterns and uncharted holding patterns contain specific information.

Clearance Limit — Charted Holding Pattern
You are established on J64-128 and the Peach Springs VORTAC is your clearance limit. If you do not obtain further clearance and do not receive holding instructions, plan to hold northeast on the 076° radial, as charted.

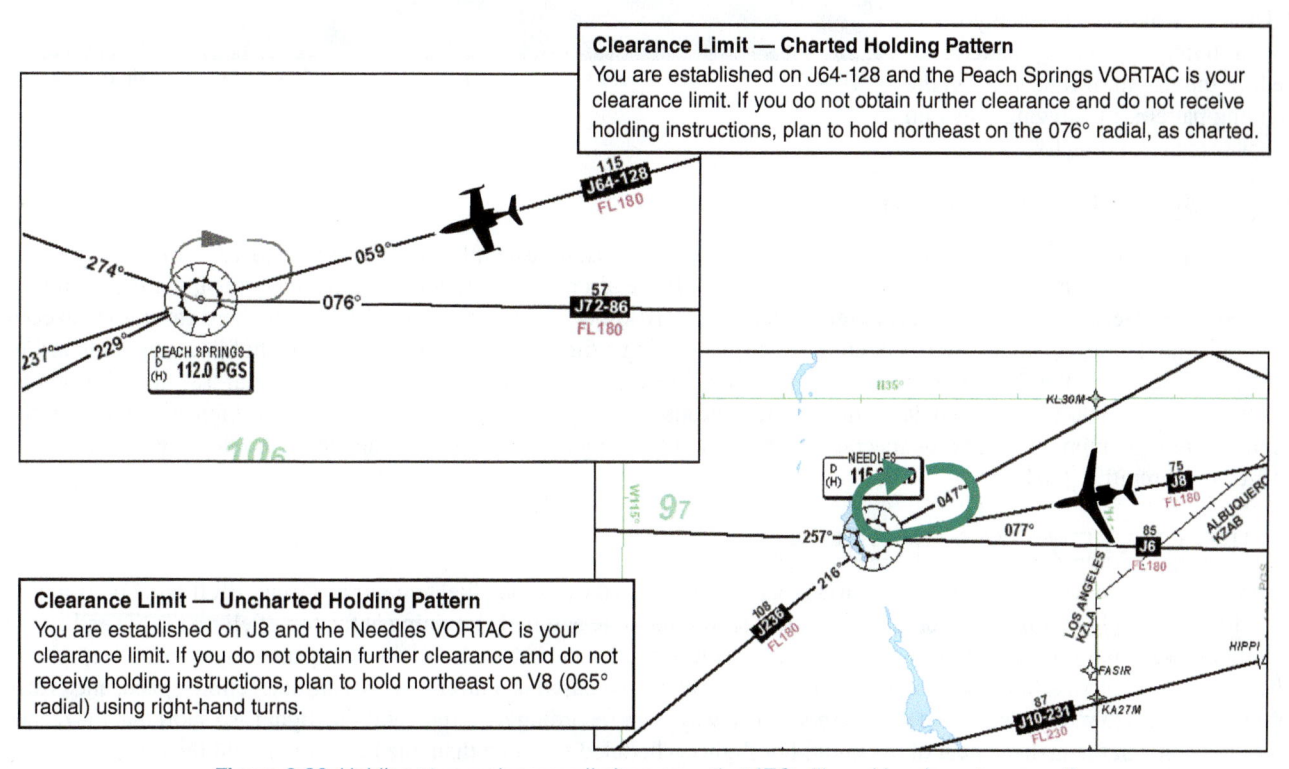

Clearance Limit — Uncharted Holding Pattern
You are established on J8 and the Needles VORTAC is your clearance limit. If you do not obtain further clearance and do not receive holding instructions, plan to hold northeast on V8 (065° radial) using right-hand turns.

Figure 3-30. Holding at your clearance limit ensures that ATC will provide adequate separation.

Where required for aircraft separation, ATC might request that you hold at any designated reporting point in a standard holding pattern at the MEA or the MRA, whichever altitude is higher at locations where a minimum holding altitude has not been established. Unplanned holding at enroute fixes may be expected on airway or route radials, bearings, or courses. If the fix is a facility, unplanned holding could be on any radial or bearing. Holding limitations might be required if standard holding cannot be accomplished at the MEA or MRA.

MAXIMUM HOLDING SPEED

Because the size of the holding pattern is directly proportional to the speed of the airplane, in order to limit the amount of airspace that must be protected by ATC, maximum holding speeds in knots indicated airspeed (KIAS) are designated for specific altitude ranges. [Figure 3-31]

Even so, some holding patterns may have additional speed restrictions to keep faster airplanes from flying out of the protected area. If a holding pattern has a nonstandard speed restriction, it is depicted with the limiting airspeed and its blocked altitude. If the holding speed limit is less than you feel is necessary, advise ATC of your revised holding speed. Also, if the indicated airspeed exceeds the applicable maximum holding speed, ATC expects the flight to slow to the speed limit within three minutes of the ETA at the holding fix. Often you can avoid flying a holding pattern, or reduce the length of time spent in the holding pattern, by slowing down on the way to the holding fix.

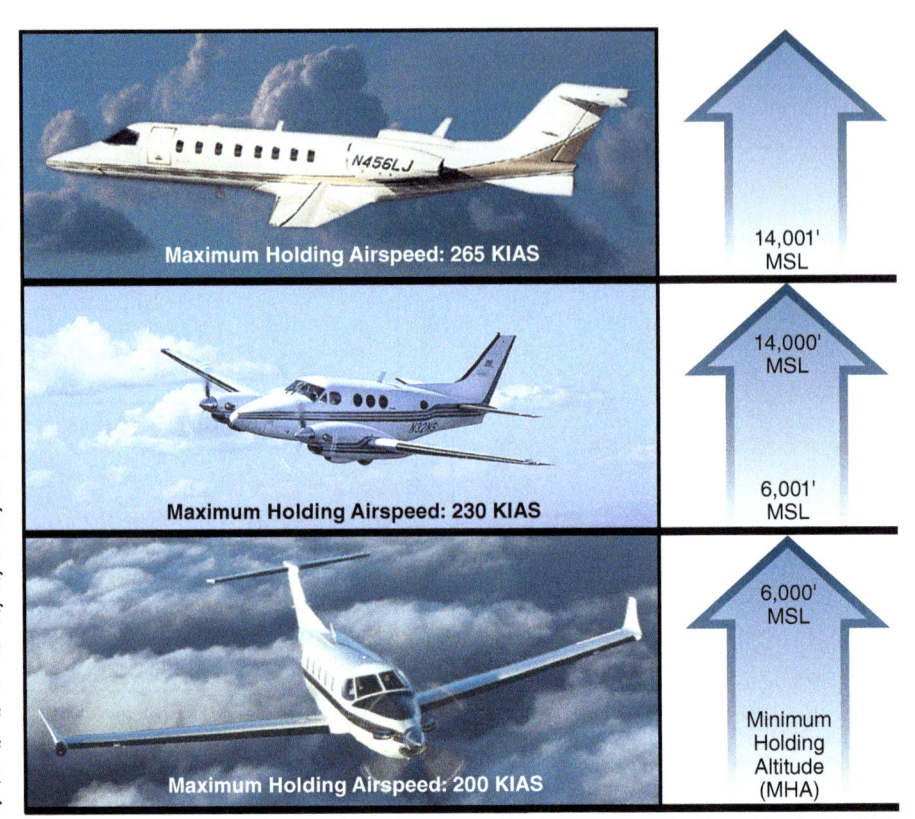

Figure 3-31. You must adhere to the holding speed limitations based on the altitude at which you are operating.

HIGH-PERFORMANCE HOLDING

Certain limitations come into play when you operate at higher speeds; for example, do not make standard rate turns in holding patterns if the your aircraft's bank angle will exceed 30°. If the aircraft is using a flight director system, the bank angle is limited to 25°. Because the speed of an aircraft must be over 210 knots TAS for the bank angle in a standard-rate turn to exceed 30°, this limit applies to relatively fast aircraft. An airplane using a flight director would have to be holding at more than 170 knots TAS to reach the 25° limit. These true airspeeds correspond to indicated airspeeds of about 183 and 156 knots, respectively, at 6,000 feet in a standard atmosphere. Because some military aircraft need to hold at higher speeds than the civilian limits, maximum speeds for specific military aircraft are higher. For example, the maximum holding airspeed for a USAF F-4 aircraft is 280 KIAS.

FUEL STATE AWARENESS

In order to increase fuel state awareness, you are required to record the time and fuel remaining during IFR flight. For example, on a flight scheduled for one hour or less, you might record the time and fuel remaining at the top of climb (TOC) and at one additional waypoint listed in the flight plan. Generally, TOC is used in aircraft with a flight management system, and represents the point at which cruise altitude is first reached. TOC is calculated based on current aircraft altitude, climb speed, and cruise altitude. The captain might elect to delete the additional waypoint recording requirement if the flight is so short that the record does not assist in the management of the flight. For flights scheduled for more than one hour, you might record the time and fuel remaining shortly after the TOC and at selected waypoints listed in the flight plan, conveniently spaced approximately one hour apart. You compare actual fuel burn to planned fuel burn by monitoring each fuel tank to verify proper burnoff and appropriate fuel remaining. On two-pilot aircraft, the PM keeps the flight plan record.

REQUIRED NAVIGATION PERFORMANCE

ICAO defines required navigation performance as a statement of required navigation accuracy in the horizontal plane (lateral and longitudinal position fixing) necessary for operation in a defined airspace. For federal airways that extend four nautical miles either side of the airway centerline, the airway has an equivalent RNP of 2, which refers to a required navigational performance accuracy of two nautical miles of the desired flight path at least 95 percent of the time flying. ICAO has established RNP containment parameters that include lateral and longitudinal total system errors (TSEs). [Figure 3-32]

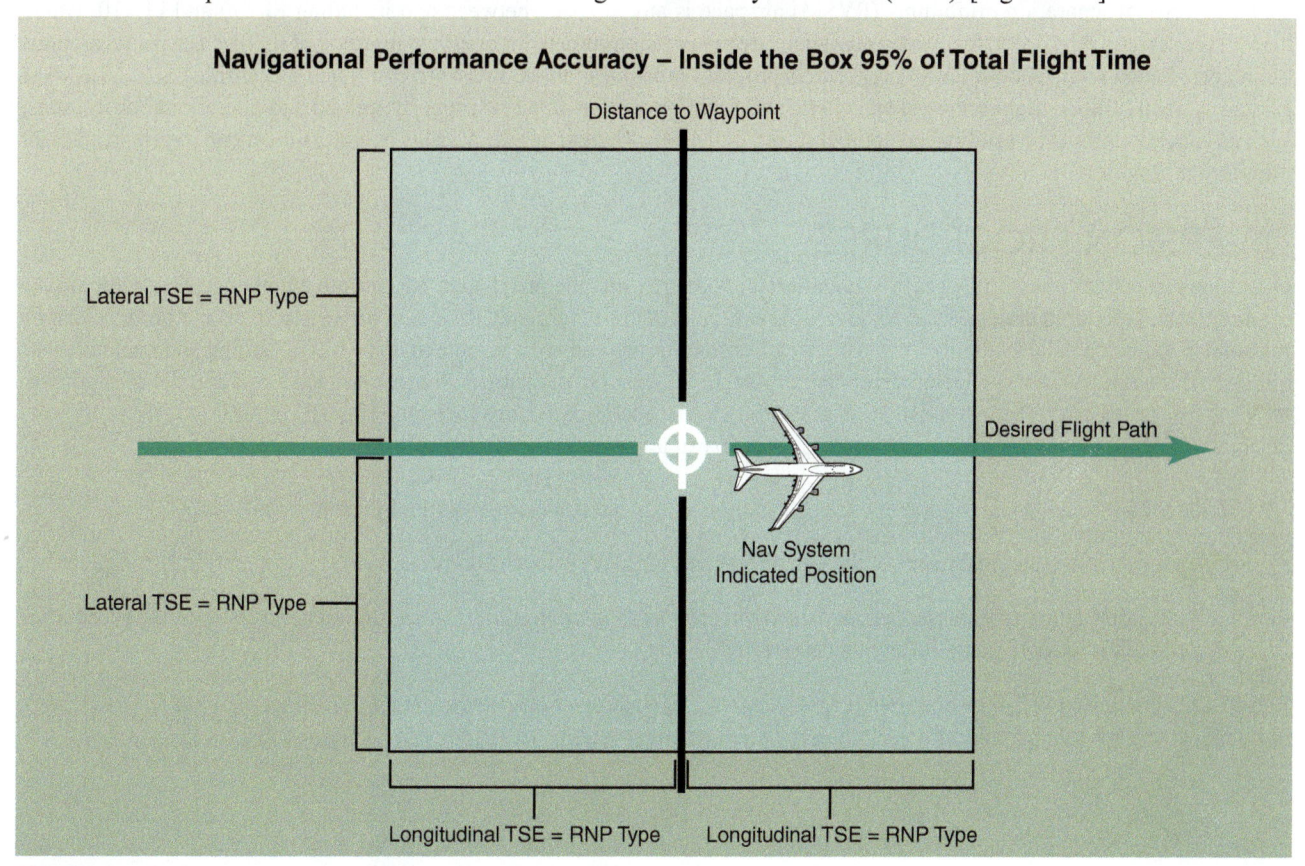

Figure 3-32. ICAO containment parameters indicate that the aircraft must be within a specified distance of the airway at least 95 percent of the time.

An additional lateral containment limit specifies a requirement on navigation system uncertainty beyond the ICAO concept of 95 percent accuracy performance. The lateral (cross-track) dimension of this containment limit is twice the size of the RNP value and centered on the aircraft's defined path. The navigation system must ensure that the aircraft remain within this containment region 99.999 percent of the flight time. [Figure 3-33]

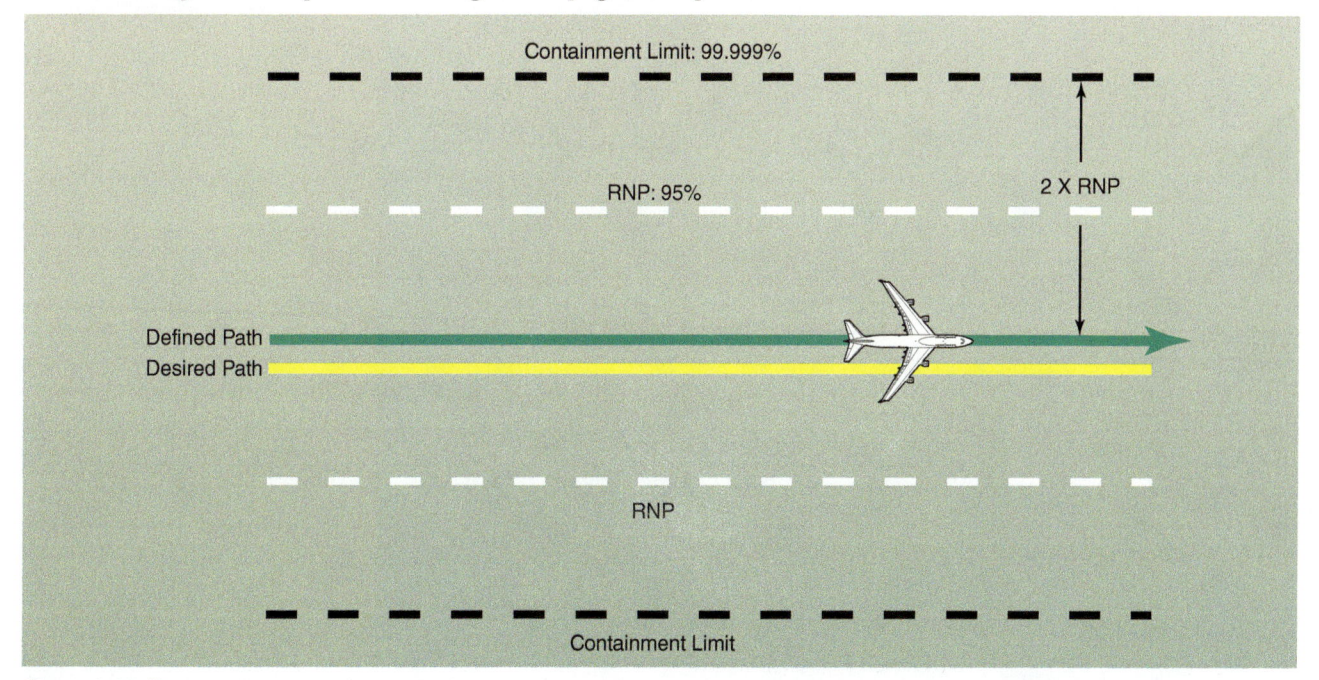

Figure 3-33. The outer linear containment region is used to assess the safe separation of aircraft and obstacle clearance when developing routes, areas, and procedures.

REDUCED VERTICAL SEPARATION MINIMUMS

Reduced vertical separation minimums (RVSM) airspace is any airspace between and including FL290 and FL410, where aircraft are separated by 1,000 feet vertically. There are many requirements for operator approval of RVSM. Each aircraft must be in compliance with specific RVSM criteria. A program must be in place to assure continued airworthiness of all RVSM critical systems. Pilots, flight crews, dispatchers, and flight operations must be properly trained and operational procedures, such as checklists, must be established and published in the Ops Manual and AFM, plus operators must participate in a height monitoring program.

DIVERSION PROCEDURES

Operations specifications (OpsSpecs) for commercial operators include provisions for enroute emergency diversion airport requirements. Operators are expected to develop a sufficient set of emergency diversion airports so that one or more can be reasonably expected to be available in varying weather conditions. You must be able to make a safe landing and maneuver the aircraft off the runway at the selected diversion airport. In the event of a disabled aircraft following landing, the capability to move the disabled aircraft must exist so as not to block the operation of any recovery aircraft. In addition, those airports designated for use must be capable of protecting the safety of all personnel by being able to:

- Offload the passengers and flight crew in a safe manner during possible adverse weather conditions.

- Provide for the physiological needs of the passengers and flight crew for the duration until safe evacuation is completed.

- Be able to safely extract the passengers and the flight crew as soon as possible. Execution and completion of the recovery is expected within 12 to 48 hours following diversion.

Part 91 operators also need to be prepared for a diversion. Designation of an alternate in the IFR flight plan is a good first step; although, changing weather conditions or equipment issues might require you to consider other options.

Chapter 4
Arrivals

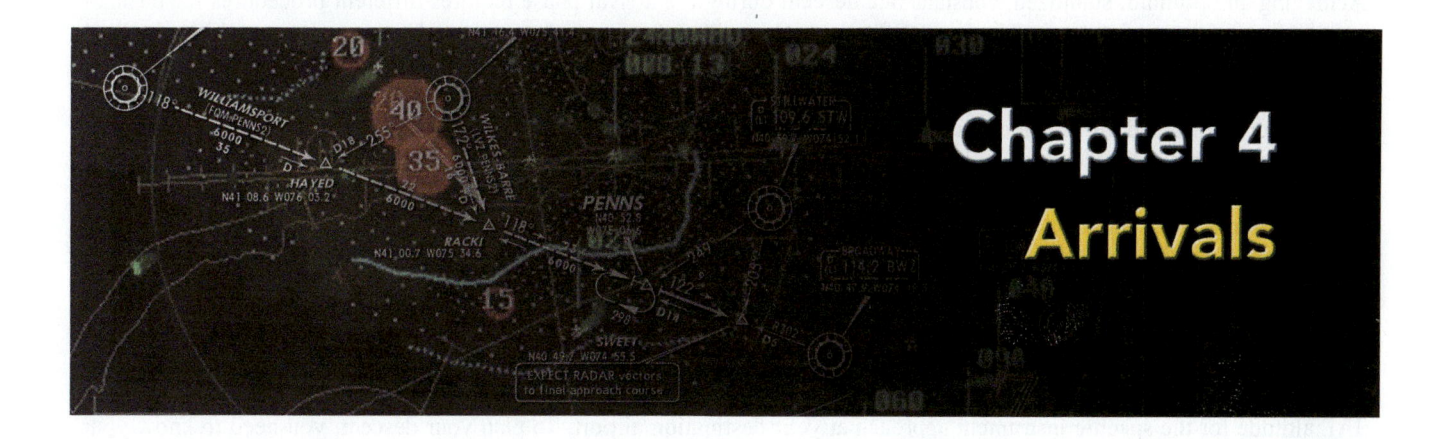

Preparing for the arrival and approach phases of flight begins long before you start a descent from the enroute environment. Planning early, while there are fewer demands on your attention, leaves you free to concentrate on precise aircraft control and better equips you to deal with the increased workload that applies to these phases of flight. During arrival, you might descend from your enroute altitude directly to an initial approach fix (IAF) or approach gate, receive radar vectors from the enroute phase to join an approach procedure, or fly a standard terminal arrival route (STAR) procedure to transition to a visual or instrument approach. ATC issues a descent clearance so that you arrive in approach control airspace at an appropriate minimum altitude.

PLANNING THE DESCENT

Planning the descent from cruise is important because you need to dissipate altitude and airspeed in order to arrive with the aircraft properly configured at the IAF or approach gate—an imaginary point used by ATC to vector aircraft to the final approach course. The approach gate is established at one nautical mile from the final approach fix (FAF) on the side of the final approach course away from the airport and is located no closer than five nautical miles from the landing threshold.

TOP OF DESCENT

Descending early results in more flight at low altitudes with increased fuel consumption, and starting down late results in problems controlling both airspeed and descent rates on the approach. The top of descent (TOD) is the point at which you initiate a descent from cruise altitude. You calculate the TOD manually or through an FMS, based upon the altitude of the approach gate or IAF. To determine a time and distance for the TOD, subtract the altitude of the approach gate or IAF and apply the target rate of descent and groundspeed. [Figure 4-1]

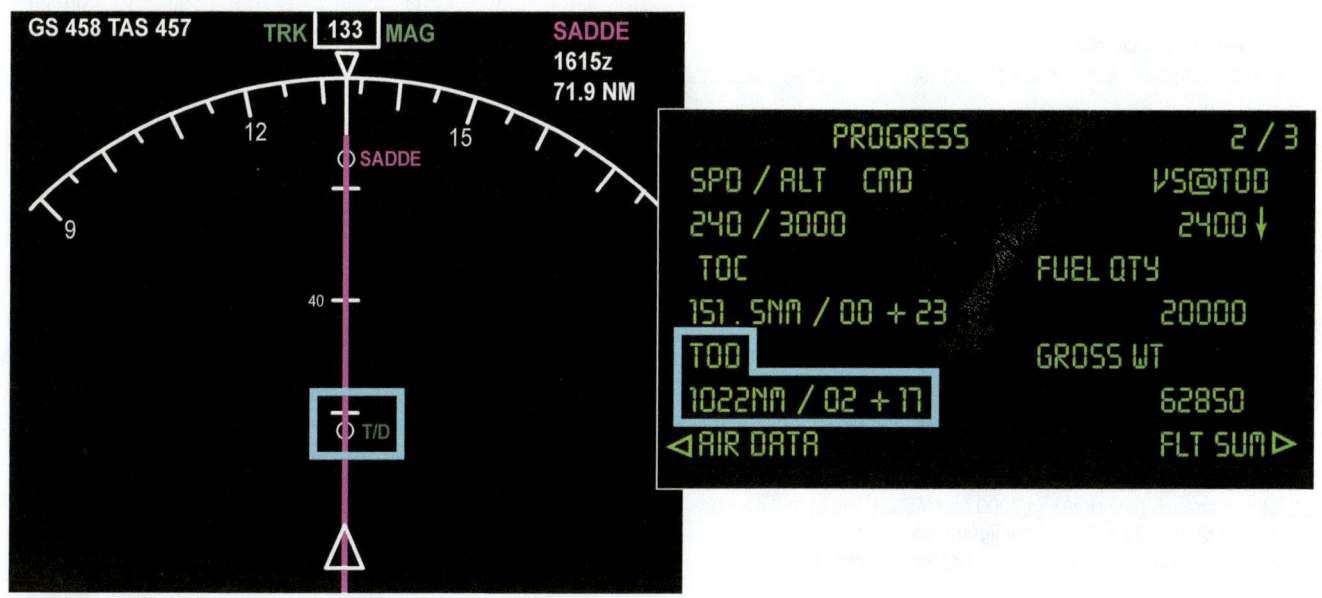

Figure 4-1. The FMS calculates and displays the distance and time at which the aircraft will reach the top of descent. Your navigation display shows the TOD along your flight path as you near the destination.

Achieving an optimum, stabilized, constant-rate descent during the arrival phase requires different procedures for turbine-powered and reciprocating-engine airplanes. Effectively controlling the airspeed and rate of descent creates a stabilized arrival and approach with minimum time and fuel consumption. Reciprocating-engine airplanes require engine performance and temperature management for maximum engine longevity, especially for turbocharged engines. If you fly a turbine-powered airplane, do not exceed the airplane's maximum operating limit speed above 10,000 feet or exceed the 250-knot limit below 10,000 feet. If necessary, use speed brakes.

Controllers anticipate and plan that you might need to level off at 10,000 feet MSL to comply with the indicated airspeed limit of 250 knots. Leveling off at any other time on descent might seriously affect air traffic handling by ATC. You must make every effort to fulfill ATC expected actions on descent to aid in safely handling and expediting air traffic.

TIME, FUEL, AND DISTANCE

Prior to flight, you calculate the time, fuel, and distance required to descend from your cruising altitude to the approach gate or IAF altitude for the specific instrument approach at your destination airport. To plan your descent, you need to know your cruise altitude, approach gate altitude or IAF altitude, descent groundspeed, and descent rate. You should determine time, fuel, and distance to descend before the flight and update this information while in flight for changes in altitude, weather, wind, and specific procedure flown. For example, from a charted STAR procedure, you might plan a descent based on an expected clearance to *"cross 40 DME west of Brown VOR at 6,000"* and then apply rules of thumb for slowing down from 250 knots. These might include planning your airspeed at 25 nautical miles from the runway threshold to be 250 knots, 200 knots at 20 nautical miles and 150 knots at 15 nautical miles until the aircraft reaches gear and flap speeds, never to fall below approach speed.

The need to plan the IFR descent into the airport environment during the preflight planning stage of flight is particularly important for turbojet airplanes. Although, you should always refer to the performance charts for your airplane, a general rule of thumb for initial IFR descent planning in jets is the 3 to 1 formula. This means that it takes 3 nautical miles to descend 1,000 feet. For example, if your airplane is at FL310 and the approach gate or IAF is at 6,000 feet MSL, the initial descent requirement equals 25,000 feet (31,000 - 6,000). Multiplying 25 by 3 equals 75, therefore, begin the descent 75 nautical miles from the approach gate, based on a normal jet airplane, idle thrust, a speed of Mach 0.74 to 0.78, and a descent rate of 1,800 to 2,200 feet per minute. [Figure 4-2]

Conditions
- The chart data is based on an airspeed of Mach .80 until the aircraft reaches 280 knots.
- The 250-knot airspeed limitation below 10,000 feet MSL is not included on the chart, because its effect is minimal.
- The effects of temperature and weight variation are omitted because they are negligible.

Descent to Sea Level
At FL310, it takes 16 minutes, 600 pounds of fuel, and 86 NM to descend to sea level.

Descent to Approach Gate or IAF
If the approach gate or IAF is 7,000 feet MSL, subtract 252 seconds (36 × 7) and 210 pounds of fuel (30 × 7) from the figures determined for descent to sea level for a time of approximately 12 minutes and a fuel burn of 390 pounds.

.80/280

Press Alt - 1000 Ft	Time - Min	Fuel - Lbs	Dist - NAM
39	20	850	124
37	19	800	112
35	18	700	101
33	17	650	92
31	16	600	86
29	15	600	80
27	14	550	74
25	13	550	68
23	12	500	63
21	11	500	58
19	10	450	52
17	10	450	46
15	9	400	41
10	6	300	26
5	3	150	13

Note: Subtract 30 lb of fuel and 36 seconds for each 1,000 feet that the destination airport is above sea level.

Figure 4-2. A typical jet descent planning table enables you to determine time, fuel, and distance to descend.

During the descent planning stage, try to determine the runway in use at the destination airport because distances depend on the active runway and STAR. Due to the increased cockpit workload during arrival, complete as many tasks ahead of time as possible. Some aircraft manufacturers provide a graph for descent planning. [Figure 4-3]

ARRIVING IN THE TERMINAL AREA

The procedure you used to transition from the enroute phase of flight to arriving in the terminal area depends on the published procedures and ATC services available, traffic, and weather conditions. ATC might provide radar vectors, clear you to descend direct to a fix, or assign a STAR or tailored arrival. In addition to issuing your arrival clearance, during your descent ATC might ask you to adjust your airspeed and altitude to achieve proper traffic sequencing and separation and to reduce the amount of radar vectoring required in the terminal area.

AIRSPEED RESTRICTIONS

ATC might ask you to increase or decrease your speed by 10 knots, or multiples thereof. ATC expects you to maintain the specified airspeed within ±10 knots. If your aircraft cannot maintain the assigned airspeed, you must advise the controller. When ATC no longer requires the speed adjustment, the controller advises you to *"...resume normal speed."*

Keep in mind that the maximum speeds specified in FAR 91.117 still apply during speed adjustments. It is your responsibility to advise ATC if an assigned speed adjustment would cause the aircraft to exceed these limits. For operations in Class C or Class D airspace at or below 2,500 feet AGL, within 4 nautical miles of the primary airport, ATC has the authority to request or approve a higher speed than those prescribed in FAR 91.117. If you are operating at or above 10,000 feet MSL on an assigned speed adjustment that is greater than 250 knots, you are expected to comply with FAR 91.117(a) when cleared below 10,000 feet MSL within domestic airspace. You should comply with the 250 knot speed adjustment and the other provisions of FAR 91.117 without notifying the controller. In airspace underlying a Class B airspace area designated for an airport, you are expected to comply with the 200 knot speed limit specified in FAR 91.117(c). Approach clearances cancel any previously assigned speed adjustment. You are expected to make necessary speed adjustments to complete the approach unless the restriction is restated.

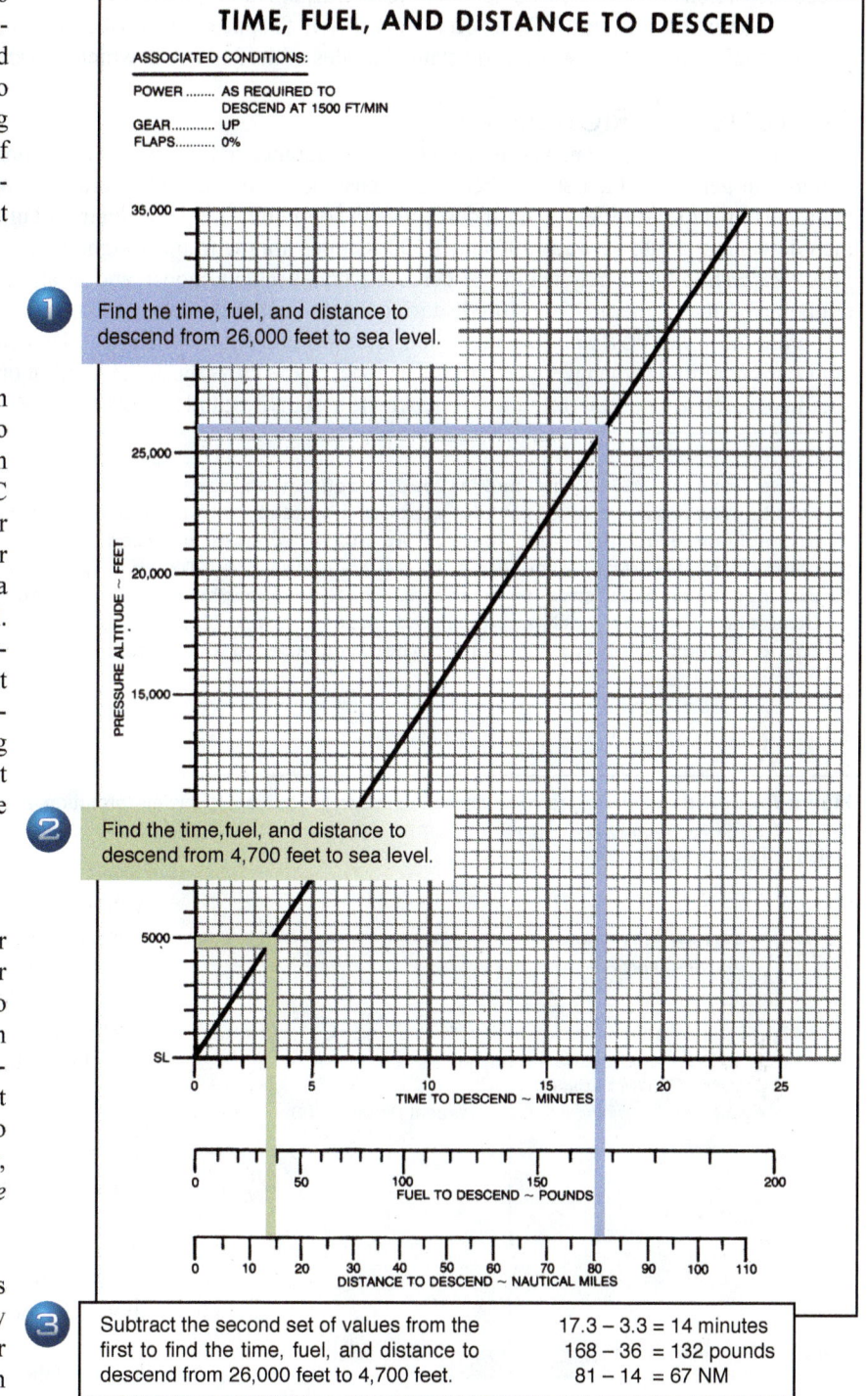

Figure 4-3. Consult the proper performance charts to compute your fuel requirements as well as the time and distance needed for your descent.

TIME, FUEL, AND DISTANCE TO DESCEND

ASSOCIATED CONDITIONS:
POWER........ AS REQUIRED TO DESCEND AT 1500 FT/MIN
GEAR............ UP
FLAPS........... 0%

1. Find the time, fuel, and distance to descend from 26,000 feet to sea level.
2. Find the time, fuel, and distance to descend from 4,700 feet to sea level.
3. Subtract the second set of values from the first to find the time, fuel, and distance to descend from 26,000 feet to 4,700 feet.

17.3 − 3.3 = 14 minutes
168 − 36 = 132 pounds
81 − 14 = 67 NM

Speed restrictions of 250 knots do not apply to aircraft operating beyond 12 nautical miles from the coastline within the U.S. Flight Information Region (FIR) in offshore Class E airspace below 10,000 feet MSL. Also, speed restrictions vary for international flight, so ensure you understand the rules of the country in which you are operating.

ALTITUDE RESTRICTIONS

As you near your destination, ATC issues a descent clearance so that you arrive in approach control's airspace at an appropriate altitude. In general, ATC issues either of two basic kinds of descent clearances. When ATC clears you to descend to and maintain a specific altitude, you must descend at the optimum rate for your aircraft until 1,000 feet above the assigned altitude, then descend at a rate between 500 and 1,500 feet per minute to the assigned altitude. If you are cleared to descend *"... at pilot's discretion"* you may begin the descent whenever you choose and at any rate you choose and you may level off, temporarily, at any intermediate altitude during the descent. A descent clearance may also contain a crossing restriction, such as *"cross the Joliet VOR at or above 12,000, descend and maintain 5,000."* This clearance authorizes you to descend from your current altitude whenever you choose, as long as you cross the Joliet VOR at or above 12,000 feet MSL. After that, you should descend at a normal rate until you reach the assigned altitude of 5,000 feet MSL. [Figure 4-4]

```
...We were at FL310 and had already programmed the "expect-crossing altitude" of 17,000 feet
at the VOR. When the altitude alerter sounded, I advised center that we were leaving FL310.
ATC acknowledged with a "Roger." At FL270, center quizzed us about our descent. I told the
controller we were descending so as to cross the VOR at 17,000 feet. ATC advised us that we
did not have clearance to descend. What we thought was a clearance was in fact an "expect"
clearance. We are both experienced pilots...which just means that experience is no substitute
for a direct question to center when you are in doubt about a clearance.
```

Figure 4-4. Speed and altitude restrictions in clearances are subject to misinterpretation, as evidenced in this ASRS account. A corporate flight crew treats instructions in a published procedure as a clearance and perceives *"Roger"* as an understanding of their transmission instead of simply an acknowledgement.

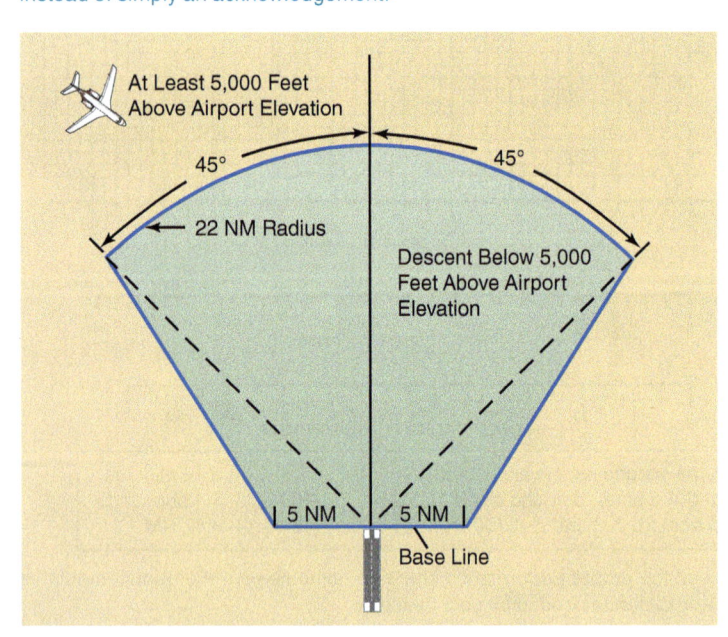

Figure 4-5. Descent areas are established for all straight-in instrument approach procedures at an airport and might be established for runways not served by an instrument approach procedure to accommodate visual and contact approaches. A typical descent area for a straight-in instrument approach is shown here.

Although standardization of altitude procedures for terminal locations is subject to local considerations, specific criteria apply in developing new or revised arrival procedures. Ideally, high-performance airplanes enter the terminal area at or above 10,000 feet above the airport elevation and begin descent between 40 and 30 flight path nautical miles from touchdown on the landing runway. Unless you indicate an operational need for a lower altitude, descent below 5,000 feet above the airport elevation is typically limited to the descent area where you can perform a final descent and intercept the glide slope intercept without exceeding specific obstacle clearance and other related arrival, approach, and landing criteria. [Figure 4-5]

Arrival delays typically are absorbed at a metering fix along an established route prior to entering terminal airspace, at or above 10,000 feet above the airport elevation to facilitate a profile descent, rather than controllers using delaying vectors or a holding pattern at low altitudes. Descent restrictions normally are applied prior to reaching the final approach phase to preclude relatively high descent rates close to the destination airport. At least 10 nautical miles from initial descent from 10,000 feet above the airport elevation, the controller issues an advisory that details when to expect to commence the descent. ATC typically uses the phraseology, *"Expect descent in (number) miles."* If cleared for a visual or contact approach, ATC usually restricts you to at least 5,000 feet above the airport elevation until entering the descent area. Standard ATC phraseology is, *"Maintain (altitude) until (specified point; e.g., abeam landing runway end), cleared for visual approach or expect visual or contact approach clearance in (number of miles, minutes, or specified point)."*

STANDARD TERMINAL ARRIVAL ROUTES

STARs provide a transition from the enroute structure to an approach gate, outer fix, instrument approach fix, or arrival waypoint in the terminal area, and they usually terminate with an instrument or visual approach procedure. The STAR and approach procedure should connect to one another in such a way as to maintain the overall descent and deceleration profiles. The STAR officially begins at the common navaid, intersection, or fix where all the various transitions to the arrival come together. [Figure 4-6]

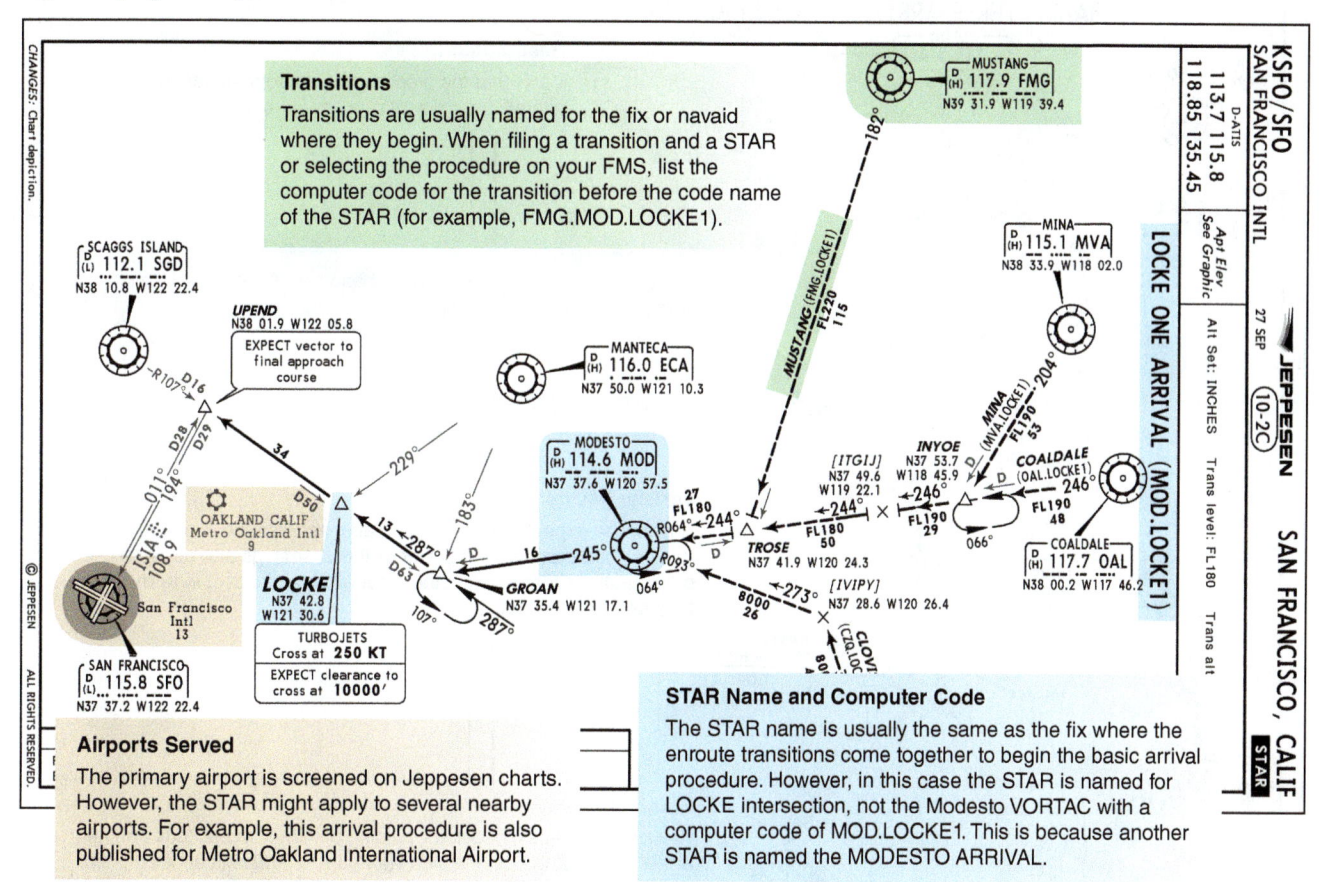

Figure 4-6. Use the transition and STAR computer codes to file the procedure in your flight plan and to select the procedure on your FMS.

For STARs based on conventional navaids, the procedure design and obstacle clearance criteria are essentially the same as that for the enroute environment. At and above 10,000 feet MSL, STAR procedures typically include a standardized descent gradient of 318 feet per nautical mile or 3°. Below 10,000 feet MSL, the maximum descent rate is 330 feet per nautical mile, or approximately 3.1°. In addition to standardized descent gradients, STARs allow for deceleration segments at any waypoint that has a speed restriction. As a general guideline, deceleration considerations typically add 1 nautical mile of distance for each 10 knots of speed reduction required.

If ATC issues a STAR clearance, review and thoroughly brief the procedure. Your workload typically increases throughout the arrival and approach and without advance preparation, it is easy to become overloaded, make mistakes, and lag behind the aircraft, especially if there are numerous airspeed and crossing restrictions. Altitude crossing and airspeed restrictions are included on the chart when they are assigned by ATC a majority of the time. [Figure 4-7]

RNAV STARS

An RNAV STAR is identified as such by the inclusion of the term RNAV in the title. Just as it does for RNAV SIDs, AC 90-100, *U.S. Terminal and Enroute Area Navigation (RNAV) Operations* provides operational and airworthiness guidance for RNAV arrival procedures. Your aircraft must meet specific equipment and performance standards for you to fly RNAV STARs. If your aircraft does not have GPS equipment, you must use DME/DME/IRU updating and your RNAV equipment must meet RNAV 1 standards, which require a total system error of not more than 1 nautical mile for 95 percent of the total flight time. You must use a CDI/flight director and/or autopilot in lateral navigation mode. The type of equipment and performance standards are indicated on the STAR chart.

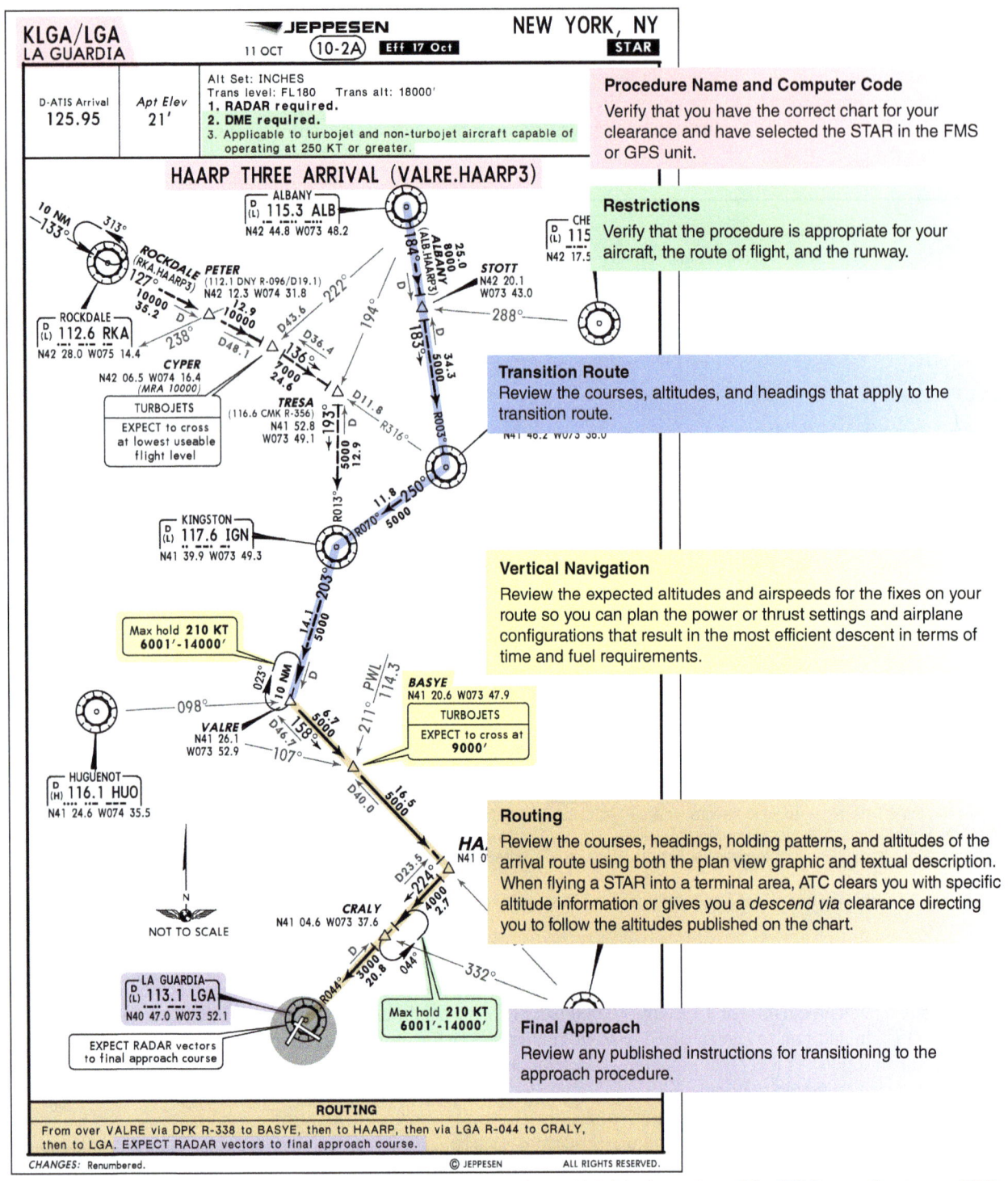

Figure 4-7. Prior to your descent from the enroute structure, prepare for and brief the key points of the STAR according to your SOPs.

RNAV STARs might be designed with vertical profiles optimized to facilitate a continuous descent from the TOD to touchdown. Optimized profile descents (OPDs) are designed to reduce fuel consumption, emissions, and noise by enabling you to set aircraft engines near idle throttle to descend. OPDs use the capabilities of the FMS to fly a continuous, descending path without level segments. [Figure 4-8]

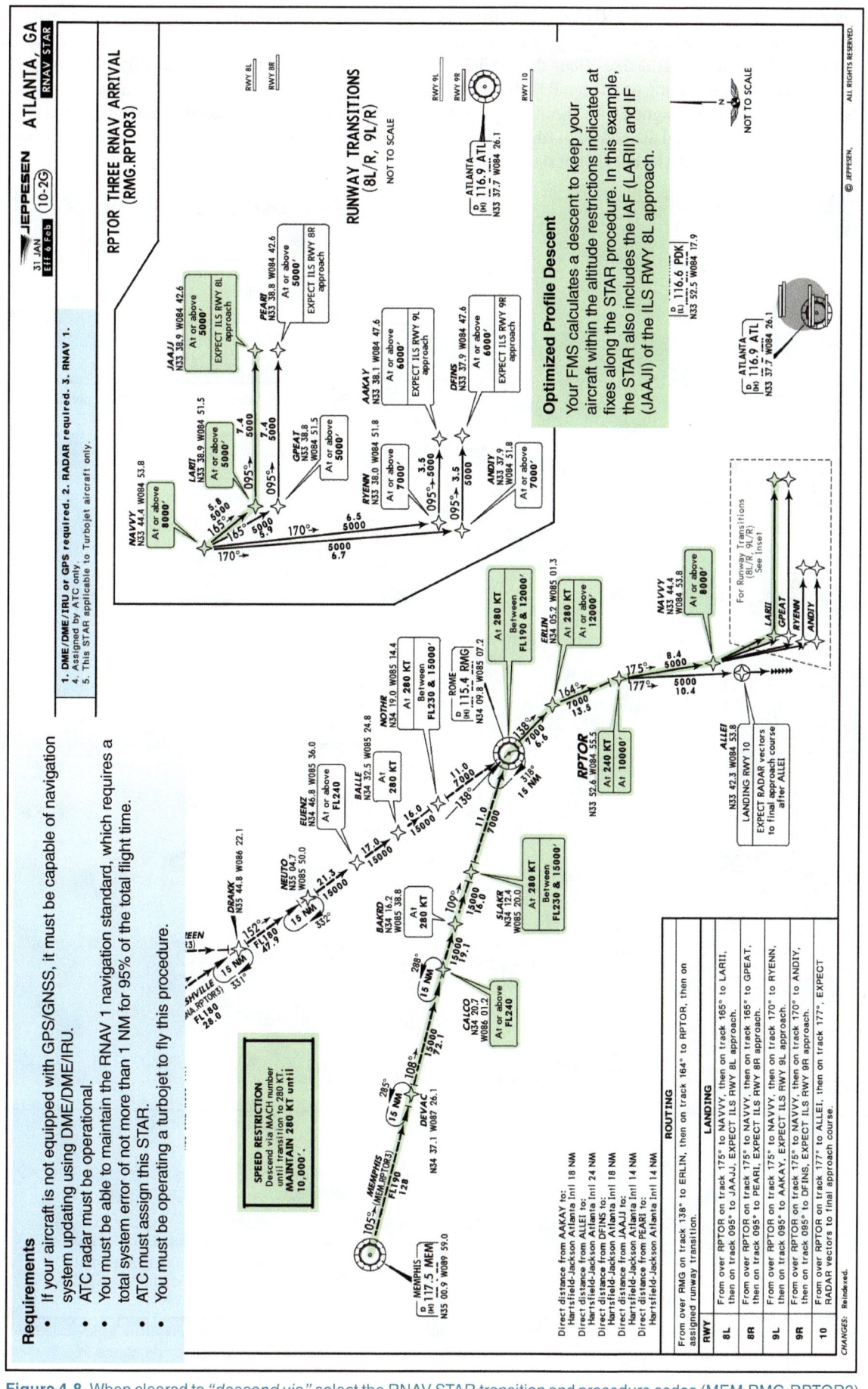

Figure 4-8. When cleared to *"descend via,"* select the RNAV STAR transition and procedure codes (MEM.RMG.RPTOR3) from your onboard navigation database and conform to altitude and speed restrictions on the charted procedure.

4-7

Whenever possible, you must extract RNAV routes from your database in their entirety, rather than loading RNAV route waypoints from the database into the flight plan individually. You may select and insert individual, named fixes from the database, provided you insert all the fixes along the published route to be flown. You must not manually enter waypoints using latitude/longitude or place/bearing or change RNAV STAR database waypoint type from a fly-by to a fly-over or vice versa. RNAV STARs and SIDs are designed with specific leg types, which are identified by a two-letter code that describes the path (heading, course, track, etc.) and the end point (the path ends at an altitude, distance, fix, etc.). These coded leg types are used by the aircraft navigation database, but are not shown on the chart. [Figure 4-9]

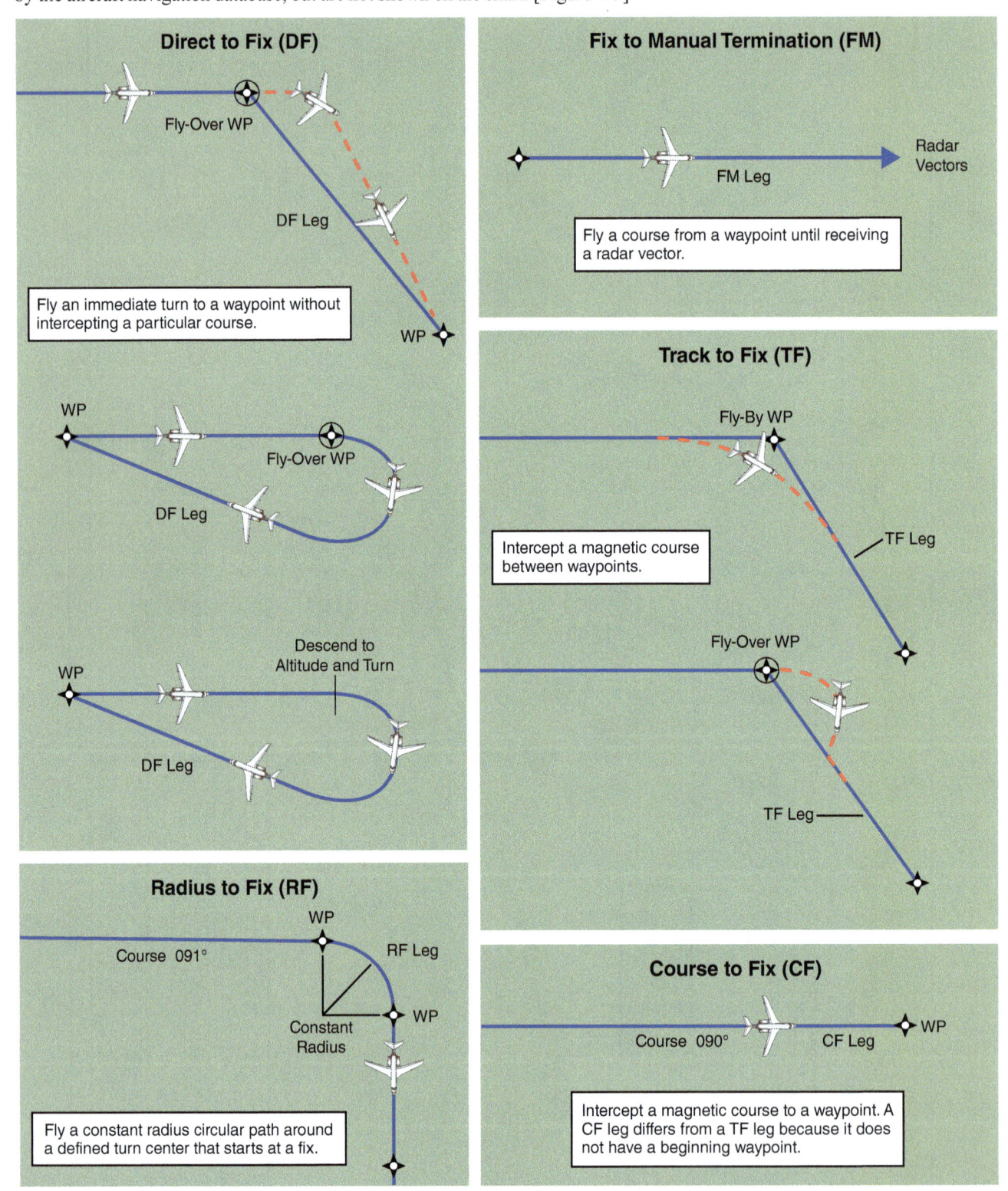

Figure 4-9. These are examples of leg types used in RNAV procedures that are coded into your navigation database. You fly the procedure based on the textual and graphic depiction shown on the chart.

STAR PROCEDURE RESPONSIBILITY

You may accept a STAR within a clearance or you may file a STAR in your flight plan. As you near the destination airport, ATC might add a STAR procedure to your original clearance. You must keep in mind that ATC may assign a STAR even if you have not requested one. If you accept the clearance, you must have at least a textual description of the procedure in your possession. If you do not want to use a STAR, you must specify "No STAR" in the remarks section of your flight plan. It is your responsibility to accept or reject the issuance of a STAR by ATC and notify ATC if the clearance would compromise safety.

Obtain destination airport and weather information as early as practical and prior to flying the STAR. If you are landing at an airport with approach control services that has two or more published instrument approach procedures, ATC or ATIS provides advance notice of which instrument approaches to expect. An instrument approach in use might not be specified when the visibility is three statute miles or better and the ceiling is at or above the highest initial approach altitude established for any instrument approach procedure for the airport. Review the STAR and expected approach thoroughly before you enter the terminal area. Check the aircraft fuel level and verify that a prolonged hold or increased headwinds have not cut into your fuel reserves because there is always a chance you will have to make a missed approach or fly to an alternate.

When you accept a clearance for a STAR, ATC expects you to fly the procedure as charted because the procedure design considers obstacle clearance. Minimum crossing altitudes and airspeed restrictions are expected and are not part of your clearance until ATC includes them verbally. A STAR is simply a published routing; it does not have the force of a clearance until issued specifically by ATC. For example, MEAs printed on STARs are not valid unless stated within an ATC clearance or in cases of lost communication. As you near the terminal area, ATC either clears you to a specific altitude, or the controller gives you a *descend via* clearance that instructs you to follow the altitudes published on the STAR. You are not authorized to leave your last assigned altitude unless specifically cleared to do so. If ATC amends the altitude or route to one that is different from the published procedure, the rest of the charted descent procedure is canceled. ATC assigns you any further route, altitude, or airspeed clearances, as necessary. [Figure 4-10]

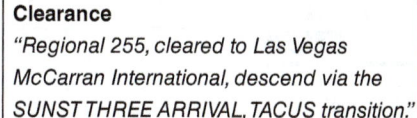

Clearance
"Regional 255, cleared to Las Vegas McCarran International, descend via the SUNST THREE ARRIVAL, TACUS transition."

Lost Communications
If you lose communications, perform the RWY 25 ILS at PRINO. If unable due to weather conditions or other circumstances, maintain 8,000 feet MSL and proceed to the Las Vegas VORTAC (LAS) and then to Boulder City VORTAC (BLD) and hold as depicted.

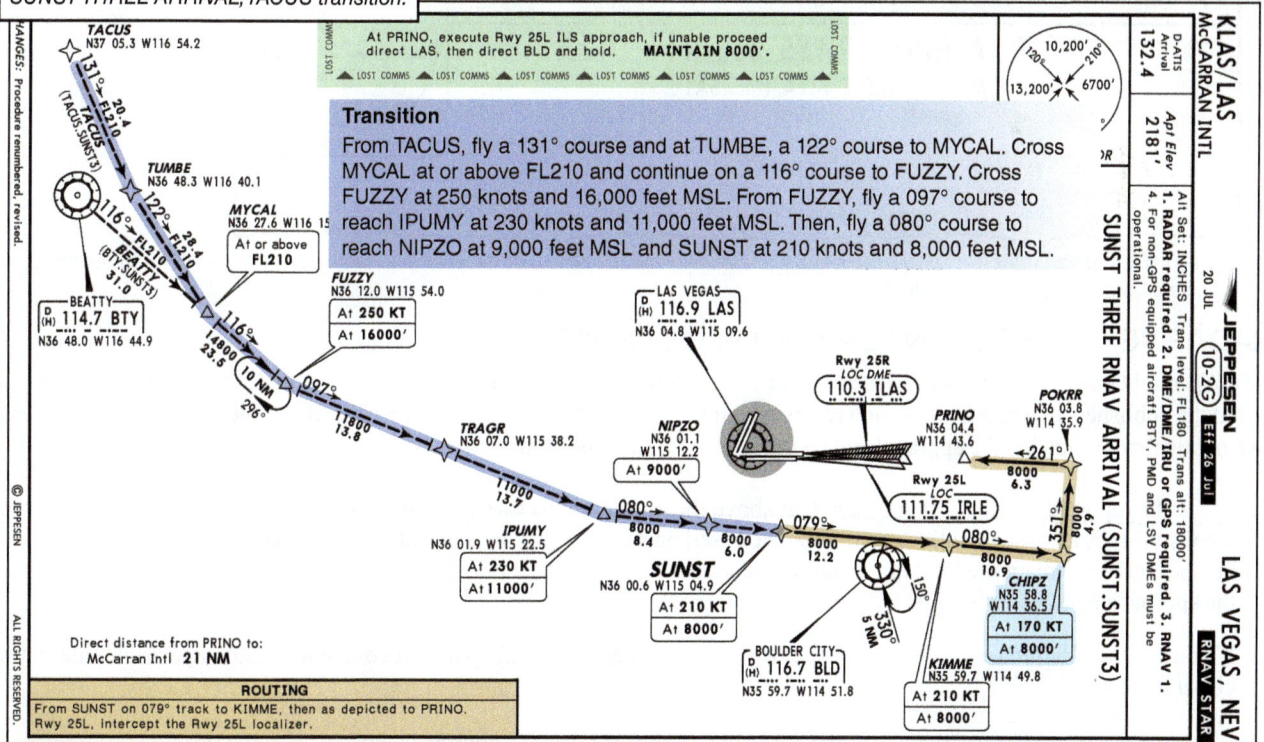

Transition
From TACUS, fly a 131° course and at TUMBE, a 122° course to MYCAL. Cross MYCAL at or above FL210 and continue on a 116° course to FUZZY. Cross FUZZY at 250 knots and 16,000 feet MSL. From FUZZY, fly a 097° course to reach IPUMY at 230 knots and 11,000 feet MSL. Then, fly a 080° course to reach NIPZO at 9,000 feet MSL and SUNST at 210 knots and 8,000 feet MSL.

STAR Procedure
At SUNST, maintain 210 knots and 8,000 feet MSL on a 079° course to KIMME. At KIMME, fly a 080° course and slow down to arrive at CHIPZ at 170 knots and 8,000 feet MSL. Continue on a 351° course to POKKR and a 261° course to PRINO, the IAF for ILS RWY 25L. Then, intercept the localizer at 8,000 feet MSL.

Vertical Navigation Planning
You must plan your descent and airspeed to reach CHIPZ at 8,000 feet MSL and 170 knots.

Figure 4-10. Ensure that you understand the charted procedure and plan your descent to meet any crossing restrictions.

In the United States, Canada, and many other countries, when you descend through FL180, you change the altimeter setting from 29.92 in. Hg (1013.2 hectopascals or millibars) to the local altimeter setting. This transition altitude is indicated on the STAR chart. In some countries, a different transition altitude applies or the STAR chart indicates that the transition level is assigned to you by ATC. [Figure 4-11]

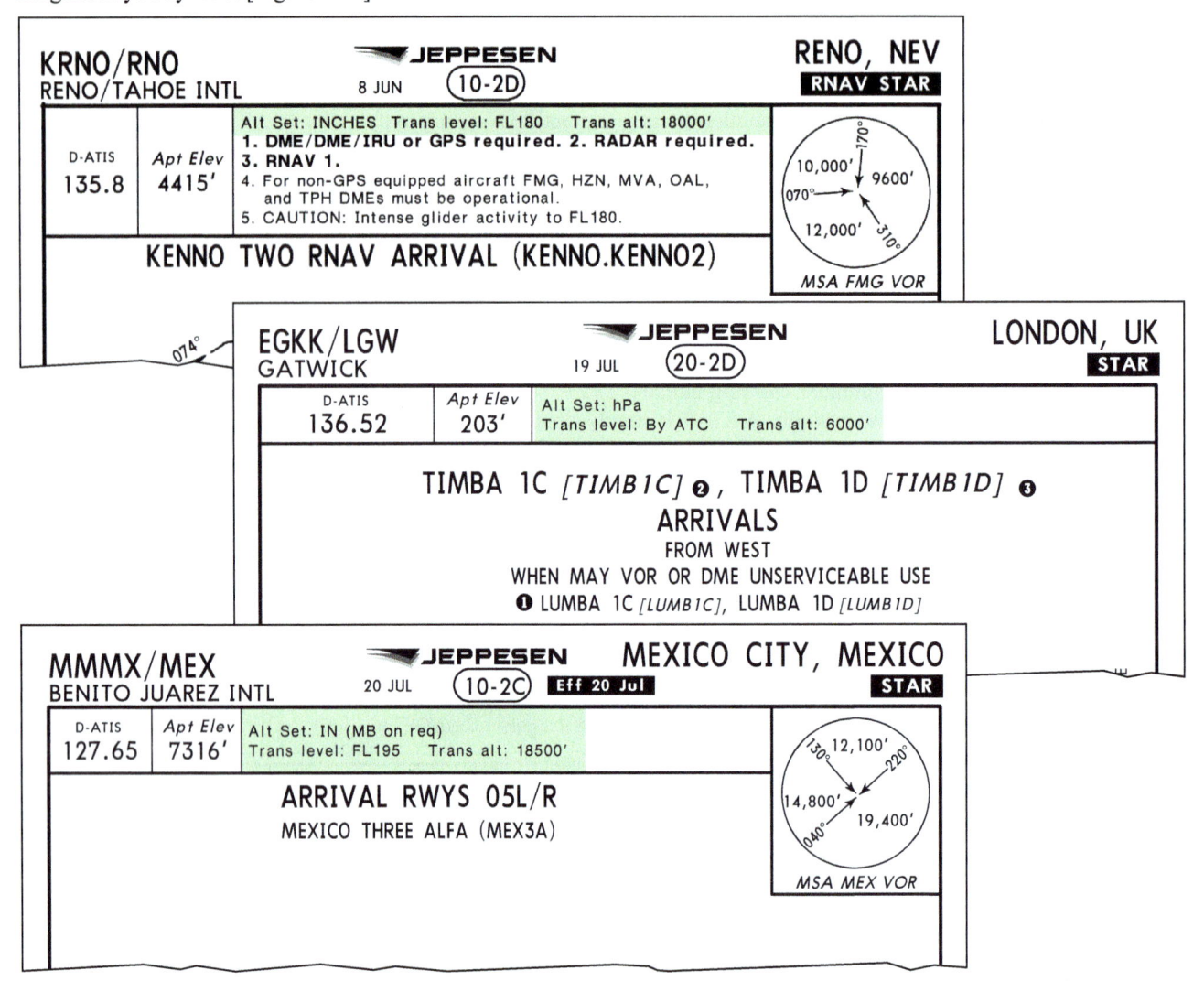

Figure 4-11. In other countries, transition levels and altitudes might vary from 18,000 feet or might be assigned by ATC. Altitudes above the transition altitude are flight levels, not feet.

RADAR VECTORS TO FINAL APPROACH COURSE

A STAR might end in radar vectors to the approach procedure or you might receive a clearance to descend to your destination without a published arrival procedure and receive radar vectors to the final approach course. ATC typically vectors you at least two nautical miles outside the approach gate unless one of these conditions exists:

1. When the reported ceiling is at least 500 feet above the minimum vectoring altitude (MVA) or minimum IFR altitude and the visibility is at least 3 nautical miles (may be based on a pilot report if no weather is reported for the airport), ATC may vector you to intercept the final approach course closer than 2 nautical miles outside the approach gate but no closer than the approach gate.

2. If you specifically request it, ATC may vector you to intercept the final approach course inside the approach gate but no closer than the FAF.

ATC issues these arrival instructions to you before your aircraft reaches the approach gate:

1. Position relative to a fix on the final approach course. If none is portrayed on the controller's radar display or if none is prescribed in the instrument approach procedure, ATC issues position information relative to the airport or relative to the navigation aid that provides final approach guidance.

2. Vector to intercept the final approach course if required.

3. Approach clearance except when conducting a radar approach. ATC typically issues the approach clearance only after you are established on a segment of a published route or instrument approach procedure.

TAILORED ARRIVALS

Tailored arrivals enable you to fly a continuous near-idle descent from the TOD to the runway. The final cruise segment routing and the descent profile are tailored to achieve the waypoint arrival times required for spacing. Ground automation generates custom routes that are reviewed and uplinked by ATC to your FMS well prior to the TOD. A tailored arrival clearance contains vertical, lateral, and speed constraints from the enroute phase of flight to the destination runway, including the approach procedure. Tailored arrivals reduce pilot and controller workload and the risk of error. Arrival "windows' enable controllers to effectively sequence aircraft to avoid traffic conflicts and meet aircraft schedule constraints. Aircraft experience increased predictability and lower fuel burn, which reduces their environmental impact. [Figure 4-12]

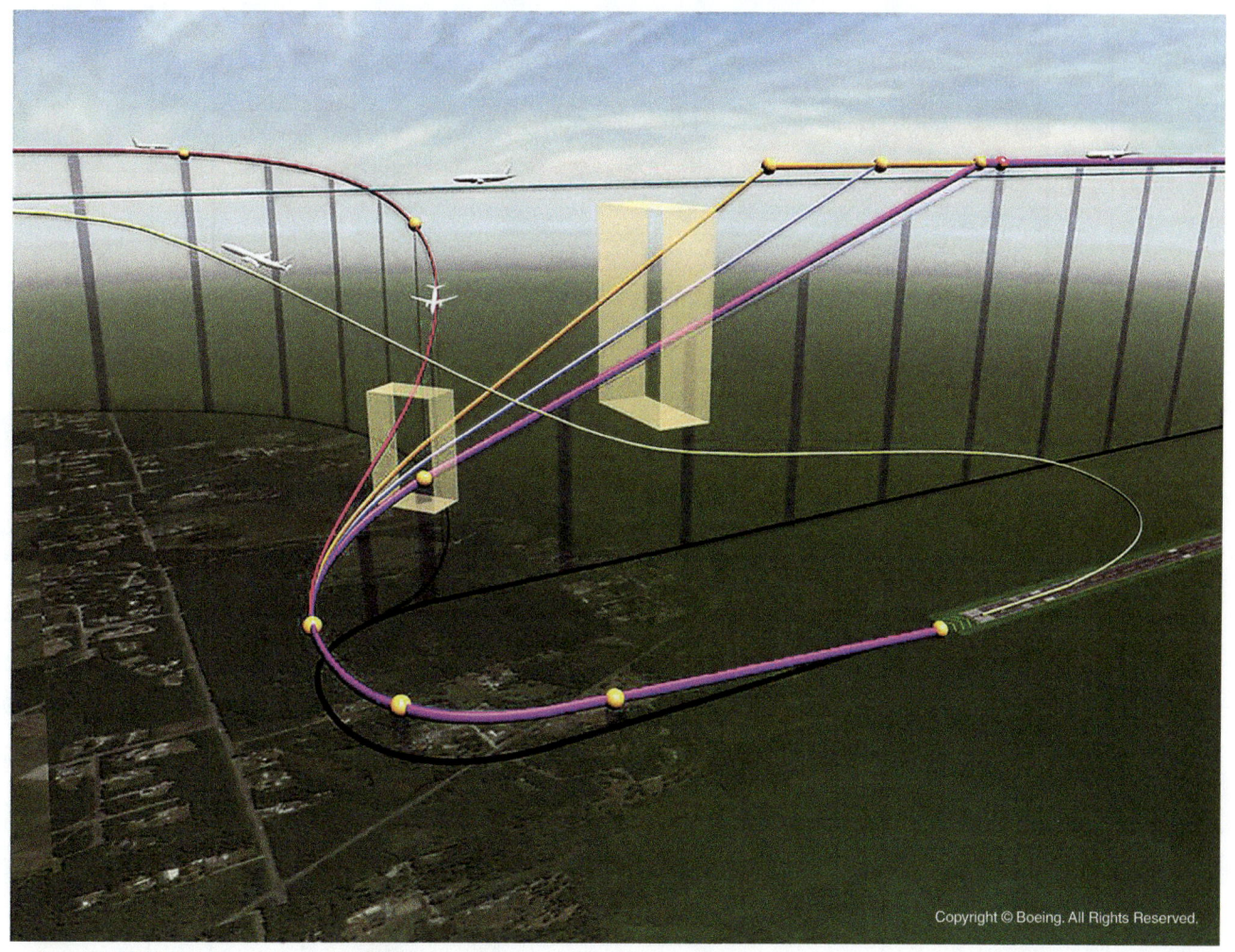

Figure 4-12. Tailored arrivals use "windows" to ensure separation from other traffic streams and to optimize routing for aircraft types.

SPECIAL AIRPORT QUALIFICATION

The operating rules governing domestic and flag air carriers require you, as pilot in command, to be qualified over the routes and into airports where scheduled operations are conducted, including areas, routes, and airports that require special pilot or navigation qualifications. Most of the airports that require special qualification are surrounded by mountainous terrain or have special procedures, such as Aspen, Colorado. Another example is Butte, Montana, which has numerous obstructions and no tower. Airports in other countries, which have limited information available about conditions also require special qualification. For Part 119 certificate holders who conduct operations under FARs 121.443 and 121.445, OpSpecs include provisions under which operators can comply with this regulation. One way to meet these qualifications is for you to have performed a takeoff and landing at the applicable airport as a flight crewmember within the preceding 12 calendar months. Another method is through the use of acceptable pictorial means. [Figure 4-13]

Figure 4-13. To help you meet regulatory requirements and enhance situational awareness during arrival and approach, Jeppesen airport qualification charts include full-color photographs of airports and surrounding areas, operational procedure information, notes on prevailing weather patterns, and descriptive overviews.

CFIT PREVENTION

Inappropriate descent planning and errors made during arrivals have been contributing factors to many fatal aircraft accidents. Maintaining situational awareness during the descent from the enroute phase of flight and while arriving in the terminal area is key to preventing CFIT accidents. The inability of controllers and flight crews to properly communicate has been a factor in many CFIT accidents. Heavy workloads can lead to hurried communication and the use of abbreviated or non-standard phraseology. [Figure 4-14]

```
We were vectored off the JAWWS 2 Arrival to a left downwind to 12R at SJC. We were cleared to
descend to 5500 feet west of the airport over the mountains where the MSA is 5600 feet. I was
watching our position closely on the area chart and saw the highest terrain in our area was
4100 feet. The First Officer had TERR ON ND selected on his side and I had the radar on for
weather in the area. I had voiced concern over the low altitude we were assigned. Right after
that we got a TERRAIN TERRAIN GPWS warning to which I responded immediately by climbing… We
advised ATC and had climbed to 8000 feet. After restoring automation, we resumed being
vectored and descended slowly to get over the valley and gain more terrain separation than the
minimum. Due to rapidly changing weather conditions and a very low altimeter of 29.26 inches,
there may have been an altimeter error that caused the warning since we were at minimum
vectoring altitude.
```

```
While getting vectors after the COMMO Arrival to Runway 11 at OAK, we were given a descent
from 5,000 feet to what we thought was 2,100 feet. That is what I understood and set into the
altitude window, and that is what my First Officer read back to ATC. My First Officer and I
thought that was kind of low for where we were in relation to the airport and discussed it. My
First Officer then asked ATC what the MVA was in this area and he replied 5,000 feet where we
were previously, a small band of 4,000 feet, and then 3,000 feet. We assumed that he was
descending us into an area ahead of that with an even lower MVA. As we passed through about
2,700 feet ATC said the altitude was supposed to be 3,100 feet. I immediately started a climb
to 3,100 feet and then I got a single GPWS caution, "Caution, terrain." I disconnected the
autopilot and continued correcting the flight path of the aircraft. We leveled at 3,100 feet
and continued to the airport without further problems.
```

Figure 4-14. These two ASRS accounts emphasize the importance of maintaining situational awareness and verifying ATC instructions when being vectored during arrival.

The following are excerpts from CFIT accidents related to descending on arrival: "…delayed the initiation of the descent…"; "Aircraft prematurely descended too early…"; "…late getting down…"; "During a descent…incorrectly cleared down…"; "…aircraft prematurely let down…"; "…lost situational awareness…"; "Premature descent clearance…"; "Prematurely descended…"; "Premature descent clearance while on vector…"; "During initial descent…" Take these actions to prevent CFIT on arrival:

- Thoroughly brief the arrival procedure and aircraft operation. Include the minimum safe or sector altitudes and the highest terrain in the area.

- Understand the procedure well enough to know when ATC issues an unsafe clearance or when the pilot flying is not following the published procedure.

- Verify all ATC clearances. Question an ATC clearance that assigns a heading and/or altitude that, based upon your situational awareness, places the aircraft at risk of CFIT.

- Ask for clarification when in doubt about any ATC instruction.

- Follow the sterile cockpit rule and company SOPs for descent and arrival.

- Be aware of the limitations and operation of automation, navigation equipment, and barometric altimeters.

- Do not operate below minimum safe altitudes if uncertain of your position or of the ATC clearance.

- Be especially vigilant when operating outside the United States or in an unfamiliar area.

Chapter 5
Approaches

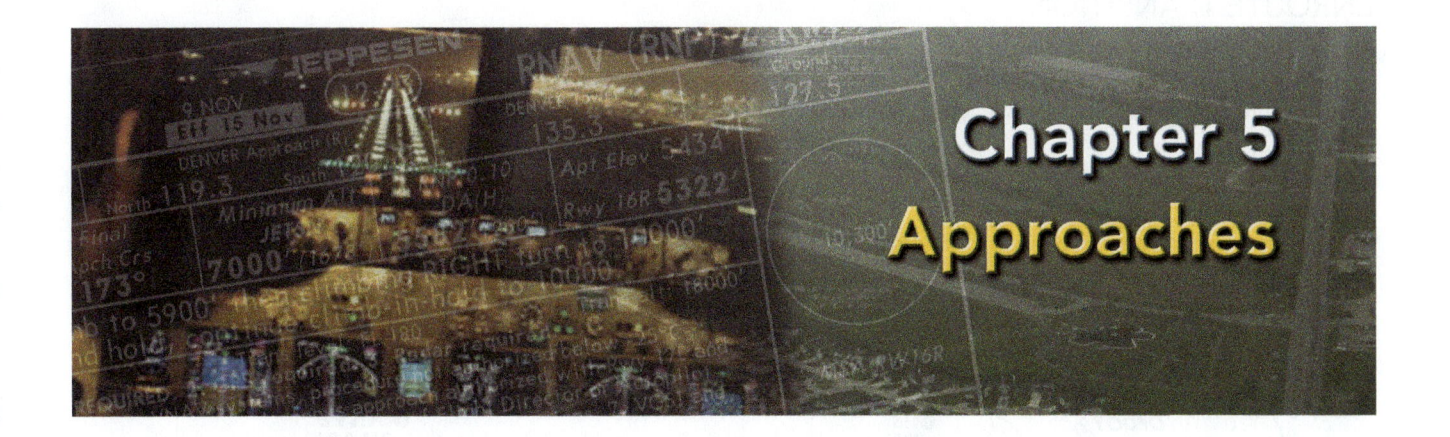

The approach phase of flight is challenging and workload is high during this period. Interpreting instrument approach charts correctly, briefing the approach procedure thoroughly, following SOPs, and maintaining a stabilized approach are key to completing an approach precisely and safely. Your OpsSpecs, SOPs, and any other FAA-approved documents for your specific company are the final authorities for individual authorizations and limitations as they relate to instrument approaches.

APPROACH PROCEDURE TYPES
The three instrument approach procedure (IAP) types are based on the final approach course guidance provided and are further classified according to the primary navigation system:

- Precision approach (PA)—provides lateral guidance and vertical guidance in the form of a glide slope. This approach provides the most accurate guidance and must meet specific standards of precision and integrity limits. The most common precision approach is the ILS.

- Approach with vertical guidance (APV)—provides lateral guidance and vertical guidance in the form of a glide path display. APVs do not meet precision approach criteria to be classified as precision approaches. RNAV (GPS) and RNAV (RNP) approaches that use vertical guidance are APVs.

- Nonprecision approach (NPA)—provides only lateral guidance. Examples of nonprecision approaches include localizer, VOR, and NDB approaches, and RNAV (GPS) approaches without vertical guidance.

INSTRUMENT APPROACH PROCEDURE SEGMENTS
Reviewing the characteristics of IAP segments provides a foundation for interpreting the wide variety of charted approach procedures. An instrument approach may be divided into as many as four approach segments: initial, intermediate, final, and missed approach. In addition, there are several types of enroute transitions—methods that enable you to transition from the enroute structure to the initial approach segment. [Figure 5-1]

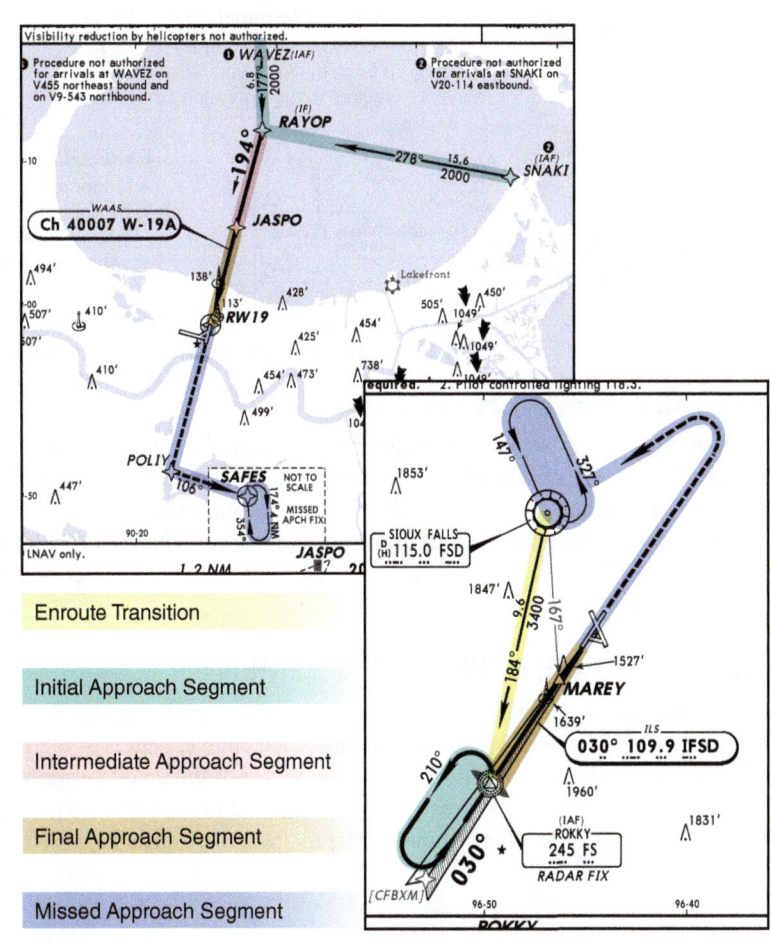

Figure 5-1. Although approach procedures vary widely, the same basic approach segments apply to each IAP. Identifying the segments helps you effectively interpret approach charts.

ENROUTE TRANSITION

Transitions from the enroute structure to the approach structure include STARs, feeder routes, terminal arrival areas (TAAs), and radar vectors. When the IAF is part of the enroute structure, there might be no need to designate additional routes for aircraft to proceed to the IAF. The route you fly depends on your navigation equipment, your position, and your ATC clearance. [Figure 5-2]

Radar Vectors
Radar vectors direct you to an IAF or IF or provide a heading to intercept the approach course on the intermediate segment.

Terminal Arrival Area
For many RNAV (GPS) approaches, the terminal arrival area typically describes a volume of airspace with a 30-NM radius within which you navigate to an IAF.

Standard Terminal Arrival Route
A STAR might end at an IAF or at a fix from which you receive radar vectors to the approach course.

Feeder Route
A feeder route designates a course for you to fly from the enroute structure to the IAF. Although an approach procedure might have several feeder routes, you generally use the one closest to your enroute arrival point.

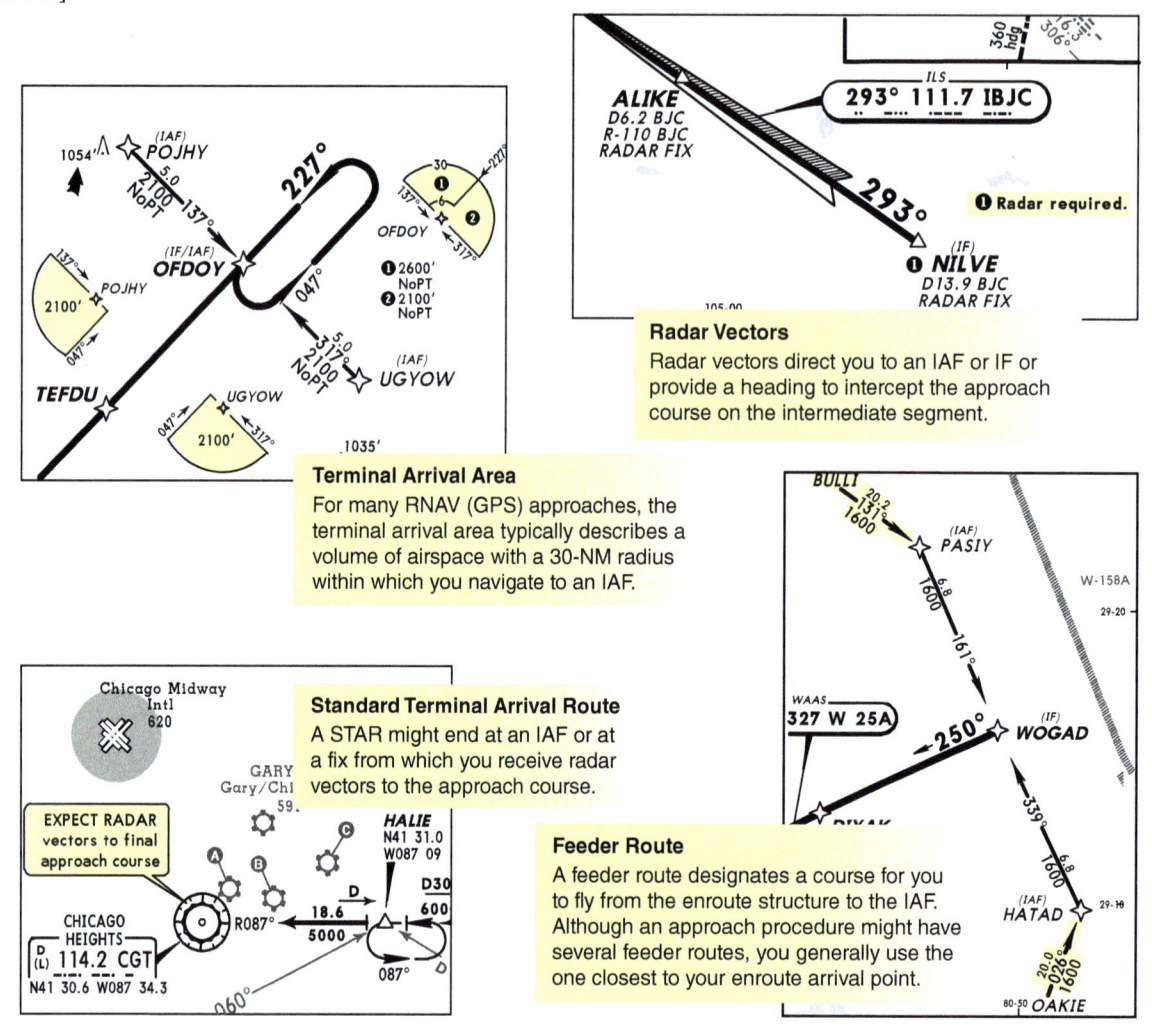

Figure 5-2. These approach excerpts depict transitions to the approach structure.

INITIAL APPROACH SEGMENT

The initial approach segment provides a method for aligning the aircraft with the intermediate or final approach segment by using a DME arc, a course reversal, or a terminal route that intersects the final approach course. The initial approach segment begins at an IAF and usually ends where it joins the intermediate approach segment or at an IF. The letters IAF on an approach chart indicate the location of an IAF and more than one might be available. A given procedure may have several initial approach segments. When more than one exists, each joins a common intermediate segment, although not necessarily at the same location. [Figure 5-3]

INTERMEDIATE APPROACH SEGMENT

The intermediate approach segment positions the aircraft for the final descent to the airport. The intermediate segment, normally aligned within 30° of the final approach course, begins at the IF or intermediate point, and ends at the beginning of the final approach segment. In some cases, an IF is not shown on an approach chart. In this situation, the intermediate segment begins at a point where you are proceeding inbound to the FAF, are properly aligned with the final approach course, and are located within the prescribed distance prior to the FAF. [Figure 5-4]

Terminal Route
The initial approach segment can be a terminal route that intersects the final approach course.

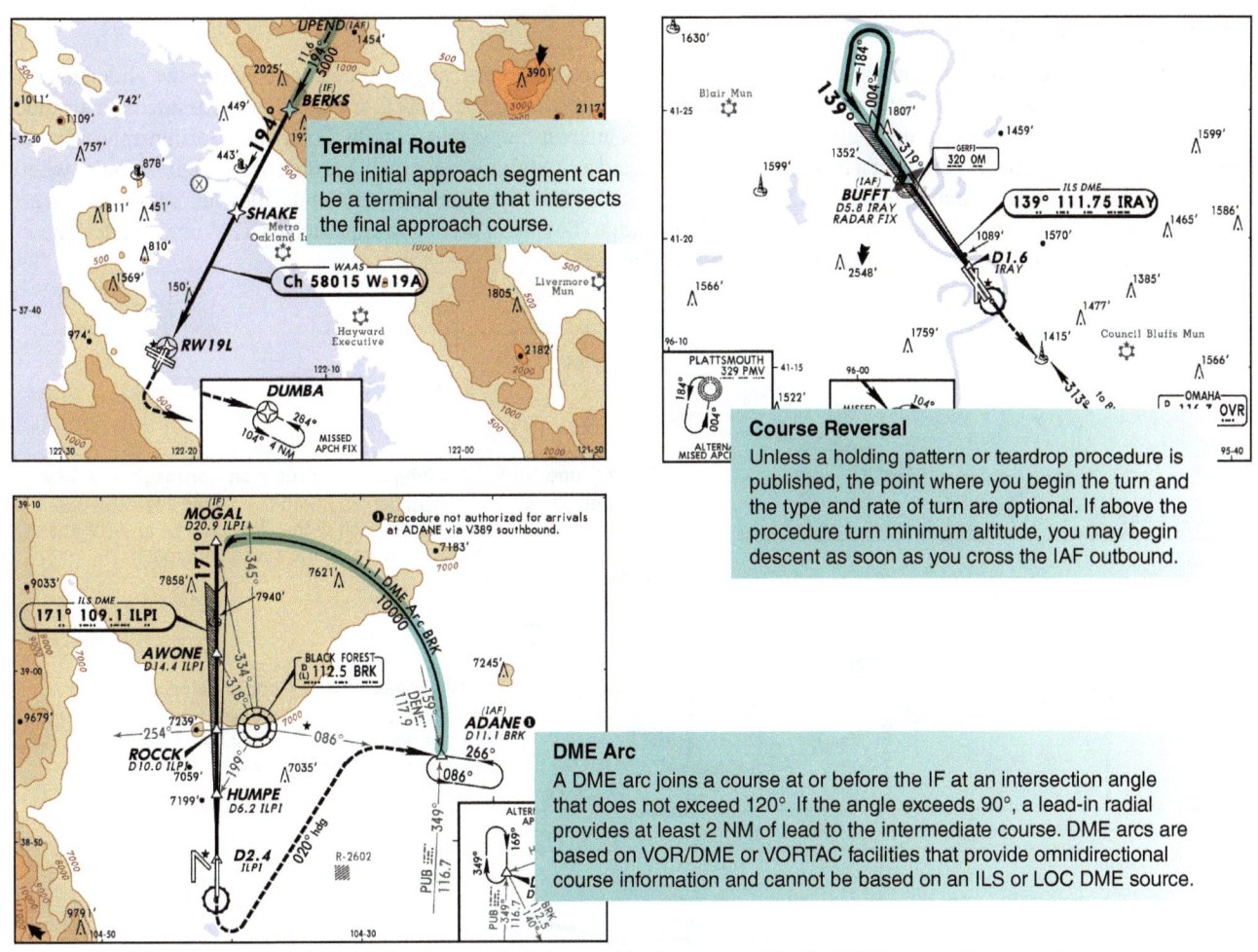

Course Reversal
Unless a holding pattern or teardrop procedure is published, the point where you begin the turn and the type and rate of turn are optional. If above the procedure turn minimum altitude, you may begin descent as soon as you cross the IAF outbound.

DME Arc
A DME arc joins a course at or before the IF at an intersection angle that does not exceed 120°. If the angle exceeds 90°, a lead-in radial provides at least 2 NM of lead to the intermediate course. DME arcs are based on VOR/DME or VORTAC facilities that provide omnidirectional course information and cannot be based on an ILS or LOC DME source.

Figure 5-3. Course, distance, and minimum altitudes are provided for initial approach segments.

No Charted IF
An instrument approach that incorporates a procedure turn is the most common example of an approach that might not have a charted IF. The intermediate segment in this example begins when you intercept the inbound course after completing the procedure turn.

Intermediate Approach Segment
This procedure shows an intermediate approach segment but no charted initial approach segment. You proceed direct to FIRPI IF or are vectored on to the intermediate segment.

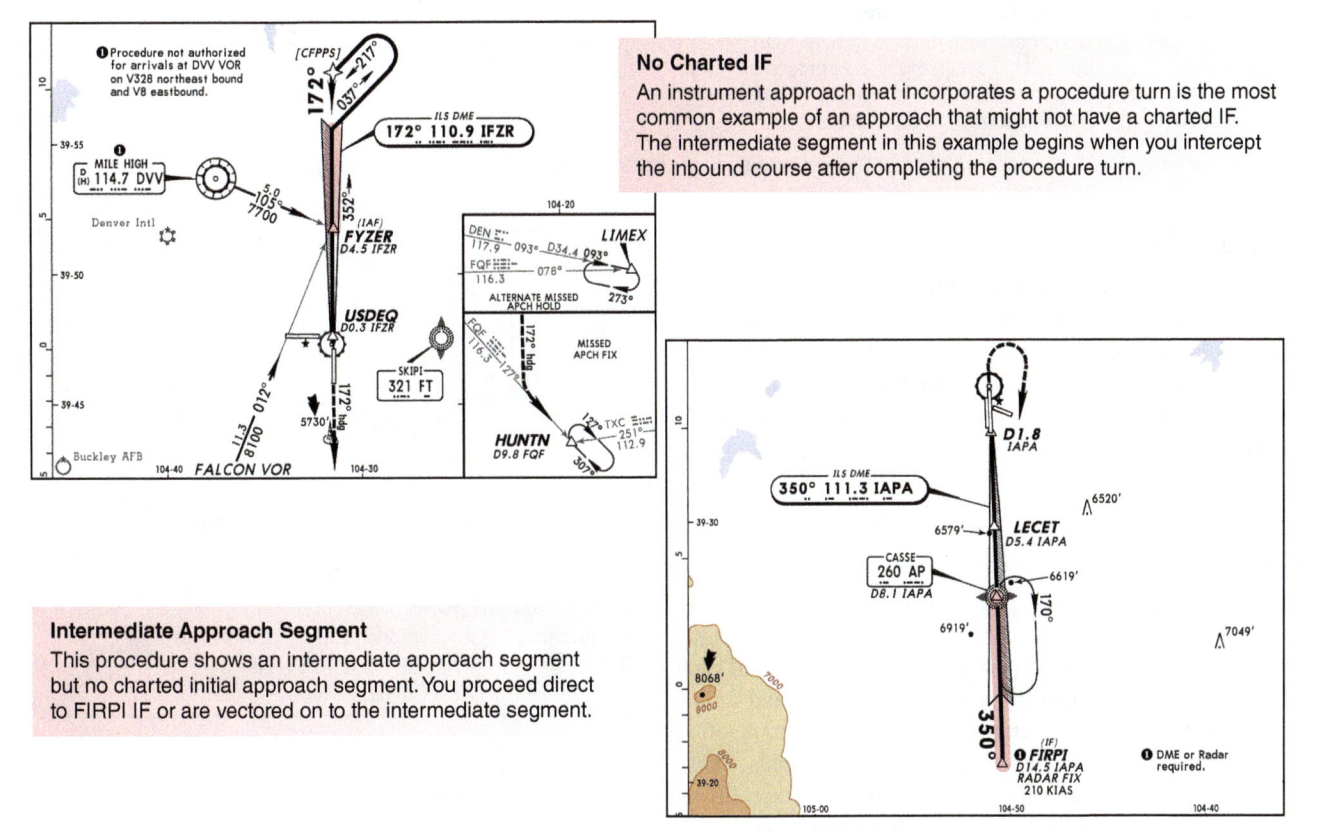

Figure 5-4. You might be vectored on to the intermediate segment to intercept the approach course.

5-3

FINAL APPROACH SEGMENT

The final approach segment for a precision approach or an approach with vertical guidance begins where the glide slope or glide path intercepts the minimum intercept altitude shown on the approach chart. If ATC authorizes a lower intercept altitude, the final approach segment begins upon glide slope or glide path interception at that altitude. For a nonprecision approach, the final approach segment begins either at a designated FAF, depicted as a Maltese cross on the profile view, or at the point where the aircraft is established inbound on the final approach course. The final approach segment ends upon landing or, if you are performing a missed approach, when reaching the decision altitude (DA) for a precision approach or APV, or at the designated missed approach point (MAP) for a nonprecision approach. [Figure 5-5]

Glide Slope/Glide Path Intercept — Precision Approach and APV
The final approach segment begins where the aircraft intercepts the glide slope for a precision approach or the glide path for an APV and ends upon landing or upon beginning the missed approach procedure at the DA.

Final Approach Fix — Nonprecision Approach
The final approach segment begins at the published FAF for a nonprecision approach and ends upon landing or at a fix identified as the MAP.

Final Approach Point — Nonprecision Approach
When the FAF is not published, such as for a VOR or NDB approach that incorporates an on-airport navaid, the final approach segment begins at the final approach point, which is typically where the course reversal intersects the final approach course inbound.

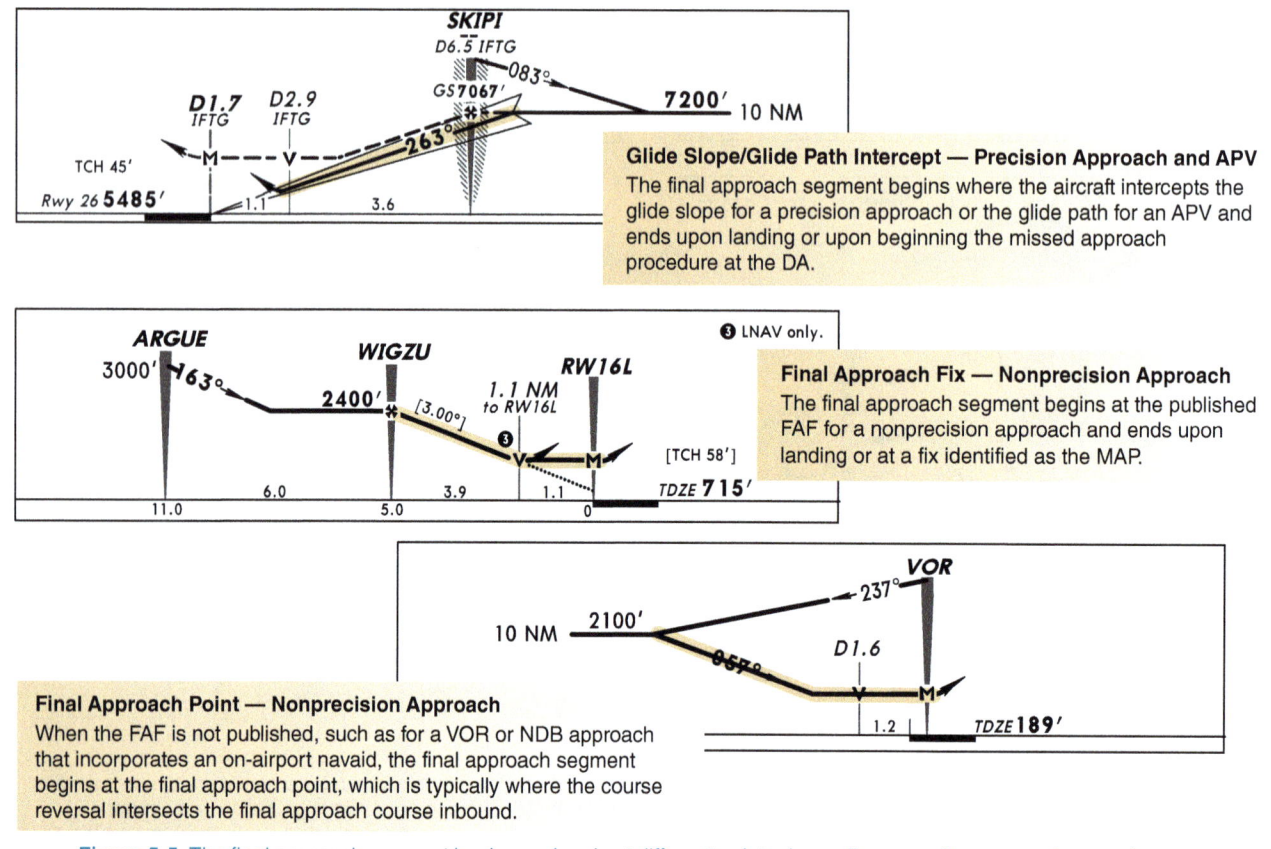

Figure 5-5. The final approach segment begins and ends at different points depending upon the approach procedure type.

MISSED APPROACH SEGMENT

The missed approach segment begins at the DA for precision approaches and for APVs. For nonprecision approaches, this segment begins at the MAP, which is identified as a fix, navaid, or an elapsed time after you cross the FAF. The missed approach segment often includes a holding pattern and ends at a designated point, such as an IAF or enroute fix. [Figure 5-6]

APPROACH PROCEDURE CONSIDERATIONS

You must consider many factors when preparing for and performing approach procedures. To effectively fly an IAP, you must have a thorough knowledge of the elements of each procedure, be able to correctly interpret each chart, and follow SOPs. Most commercial operators dictate SOPs for conducting instrument approaches in their FAA approved manuals. These standards designate company callouts, flight profiles, configurations, and other specific duties for each crewmember.

Missed Approach Hold
To perform a missed approach you typically proceed to WAXEN and hold. However a hold at COTEE is an alternate missed approach procedure.

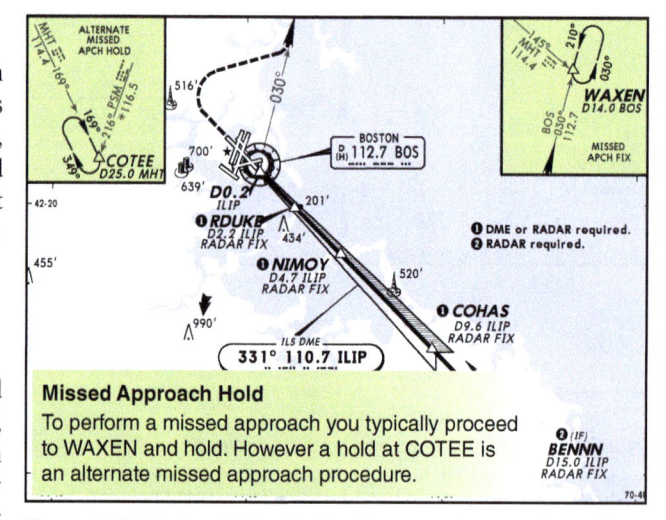

Figure 5-6. Most published missed approach procedures direct you to a holding fix. For the approach procedure shown here, you might receive a clearance to proceed to an alternate holding fix.

STRAIGHT-IN LANDING VS. CIRCLING APPROACH

Straight-in landing minimums normally are specified when the final approach course is positioned within 30° of the runway and a minimum of maneuvering is required to align the airplane with the runway. The heading section at the top of Jeppesen approach charts identifies approach procedures with straight-in landing minimums by using the procedure name and the runway served. The procedure name is based on the navaid or navigation equipment required for the final approach segment. When two or more approaches with straight-in landing minimums with the same type of guidance exist for a runway, a letter suffix is added to the title of the approach so it can be identified easily. These approach charts start with the letter Z and continue in reverse alphabetical order. [Figure 5-7]

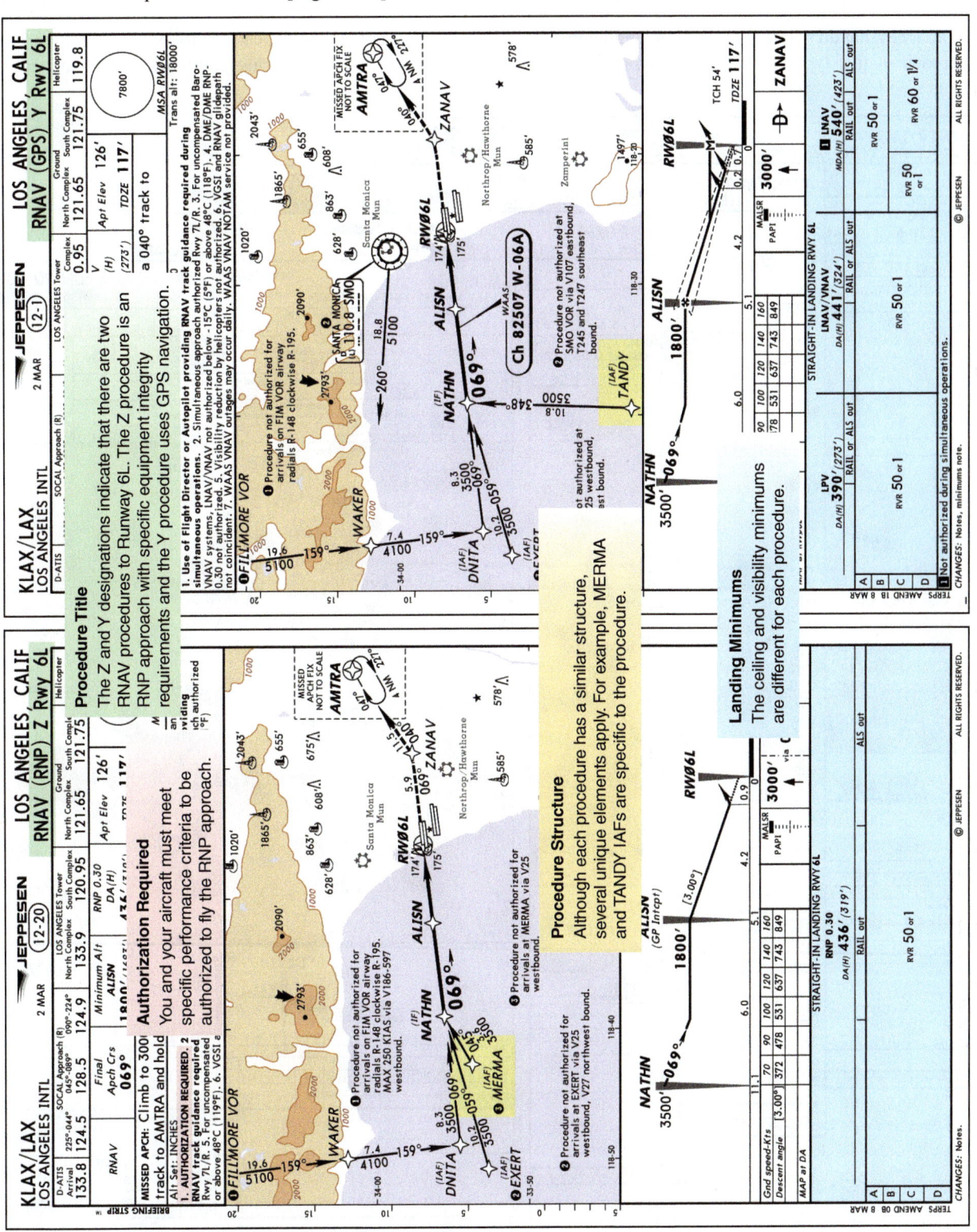

Figure 5-7. The RNAV (RNP) Z Rwy 6L and the RNAV (GPS) Y Rwy 6L approaches at Los Angeles International Airport are to the same runway but have different elements.

5-5

Most approach procedures provide landing minimums for both straight-in and circling minimums, in case you must perform a circling approach to a different runway. However, some approaches only have circling minimums for one of these reasons:

- The final approach course alignment with the runway centerline exceeds 30°.

- The descent gradient is greater than 400 feet per nautical mile from the FAF to the threshold crossing height (TCH). When this maximum gradient is exceeded, the circling-only approach procedure might be designed to meet the gradient criteria limits. This does not preclude a straight-in landing if you can make a normal descent and landing in accordance with the applicable regulations.

Approaches that do not have straight-in landing minimums are identified by the approach type followed by a letter. The first approach of this type created at the airport is labeled with the letter A. The lettering continues in alphabetical order. [Figure 5-8]

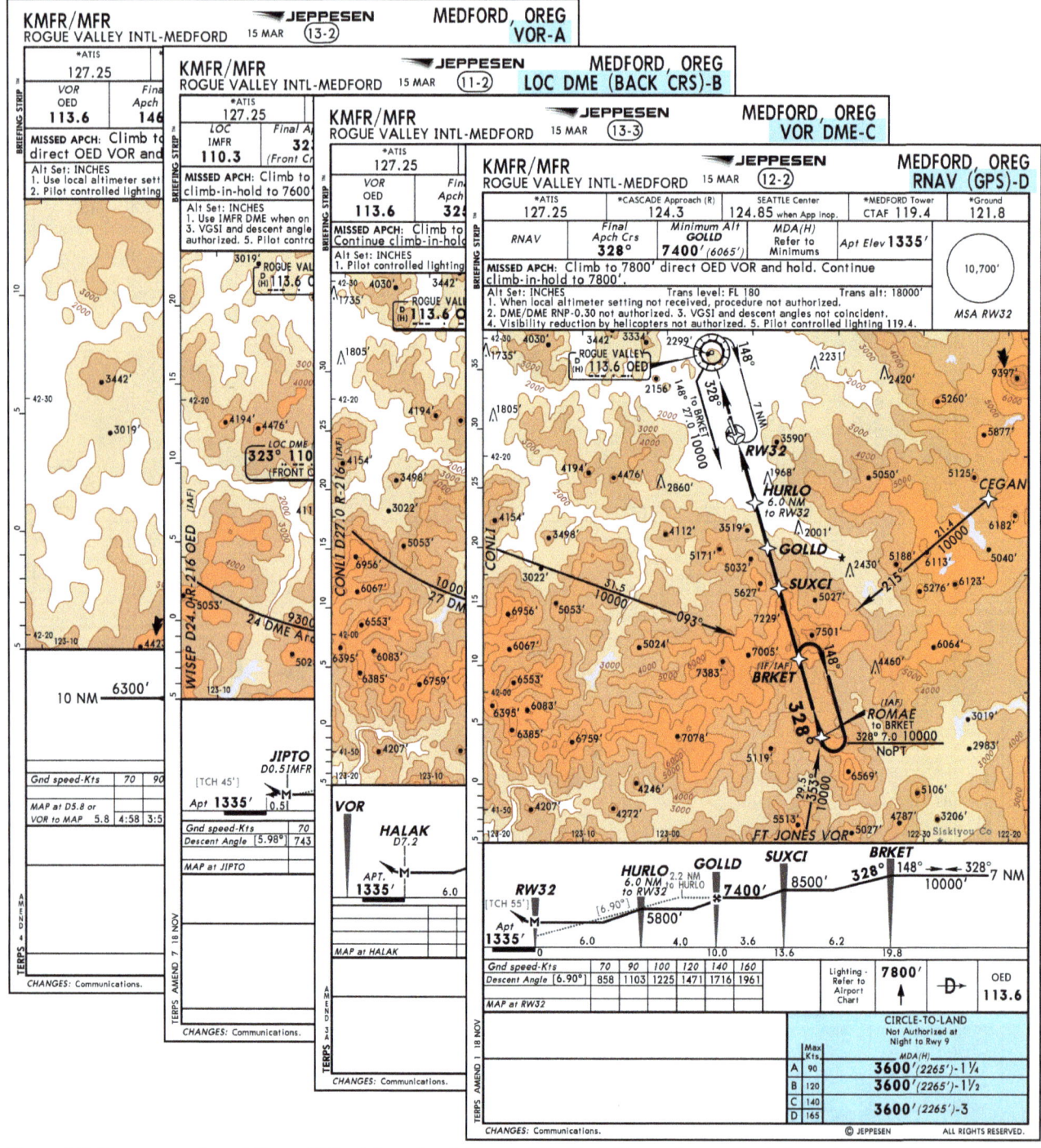

Figure 5-8. Four approaches at Rogue Valley International Airport at Medford, Oregon have only circling minimums. These procedures are identified with the letters A through D in the procedure titles.

STRAIGHT-IN APPROACHES VS. COURSE REVERSALS

In contrast to a straight-in landing, the controller terminology, *"cleared for straight-in approach . . ."* means that you should not perform any published procedure to reverse your course, but does not reference landing minimums. For example, you could be *"cleared for straight-in ILS Runway 25 approach, circle to land Runway 34."* To fly a straight-in approach, you might receive vectors to the final approach course or fly a course from a fix closely aligned with the final approach course. In other situations, you might fly a radius to fix (RF) leg on an RNAV (RNP) approach or you might complete a DME arc.

Some approach procedures do not provide for straight-in approaches unless you are being radar vectored. In these situations, you must complete a course reversal, generally within 10 nautical miles of the primary navaid or fix designated on the approach chart, to establish the airplane inbound on the intermediate or final approach segments. The maximum speed in a course reversal is 200 KIAS. When a procedure turn is depicted on the chart plan view, you may reverse course any way that you want as long as you turn on the same side of the approach course as the symbol. When a course reversal is depicted as a holding pattern or teardrop pattern, you must fly the pattern as charted. [Figure 5-9]

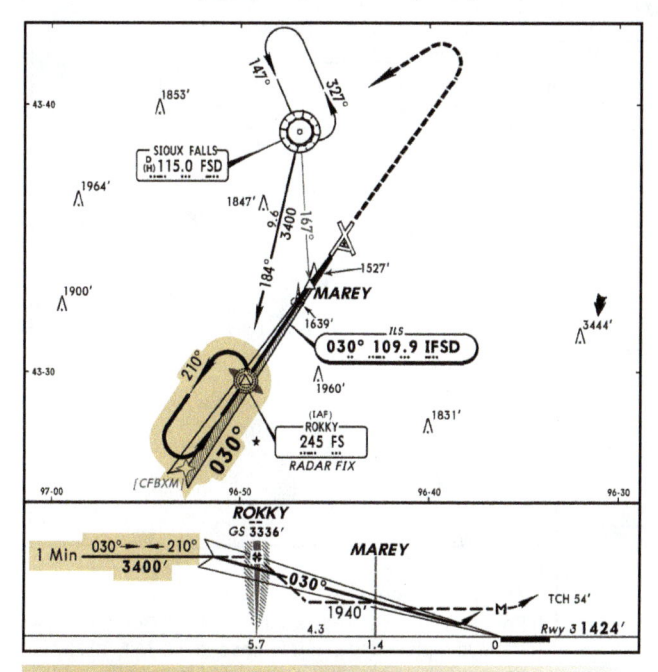

Straight-In Approach
To fly a straight-in approach, you might be cleared to proceed on a course of 240° from Rosewood VORTAC or receive radar vectors to the final approach course.

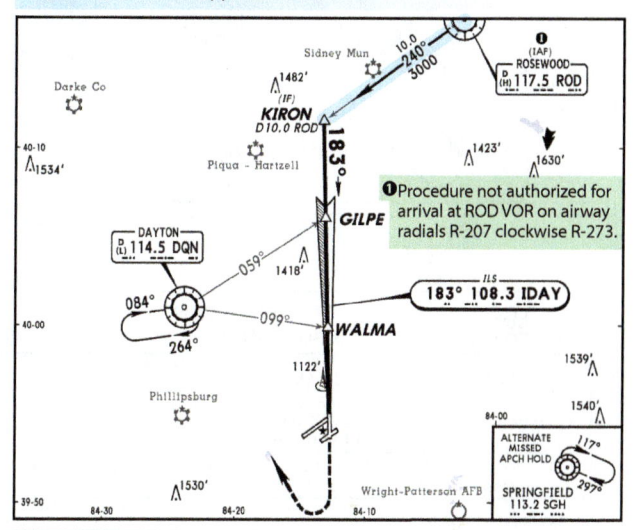

Course Reversal
Unless you receive radar vectors, you must make the proper entry and follow the depicted holding pattern course reversal with one-minute legs to establish the airplane on the inbound course.

Procedure Note
Because of the large amount of course change required, you may not fly from Rosewood VORTAC to KIRON if you are arriving from the southwest on the 207° radial clockwise through the 273° radial.

Figure 5-9. The methods to fly a straight-in approach or a course reversal depend on the specific approach procedure.

ALTITUDES

All altitudes shown in the plan and profile views of Jeppesen approach charts are minimum altitudes above mean sea level unless otherwise indicated. Maximum altitudes are depicted with the altitude value under the word MAXIMUM or MAX. You must maintain altitude at or below the depicted value. You must maintain altitude at the depicted value under the word MANDATORY. Recommended altitudes are depicted with the altitude value under the word RECOMMENDED. You must adhere to altitudes as prescribed because, in certain instances, these altitudes are used as the basis for vertical separation of aircraft by ATC. When a depicted altitude is specified in the ATC clearance, that altitude becomes mandatory.

MINIMUM SAFE/SECTOR ALTITUDE

Minimum safe/sector altitudes (MSAs) are published for emergency use on approach charts. The MSA is normally based on the primary omnidirectional facility on which the IAP is predicated. MSAs are expressed in feet above MSL and normally have a 25 nautical mile radius. This radius may be expanded to 30 nautical miles if necessary to encompass the airport landing surfaces. MSAs provide 1,000 feet clearance over all obstructions but do not necessarily ensure acceptable navigation signal coverage. RNAV (GPS) approaches that use a TAA do not have MSAs because minimum altitudes for areas that extend 30 nautical miles from IAF waypoints are depicted on the chart plan view. [Figure 5-10]

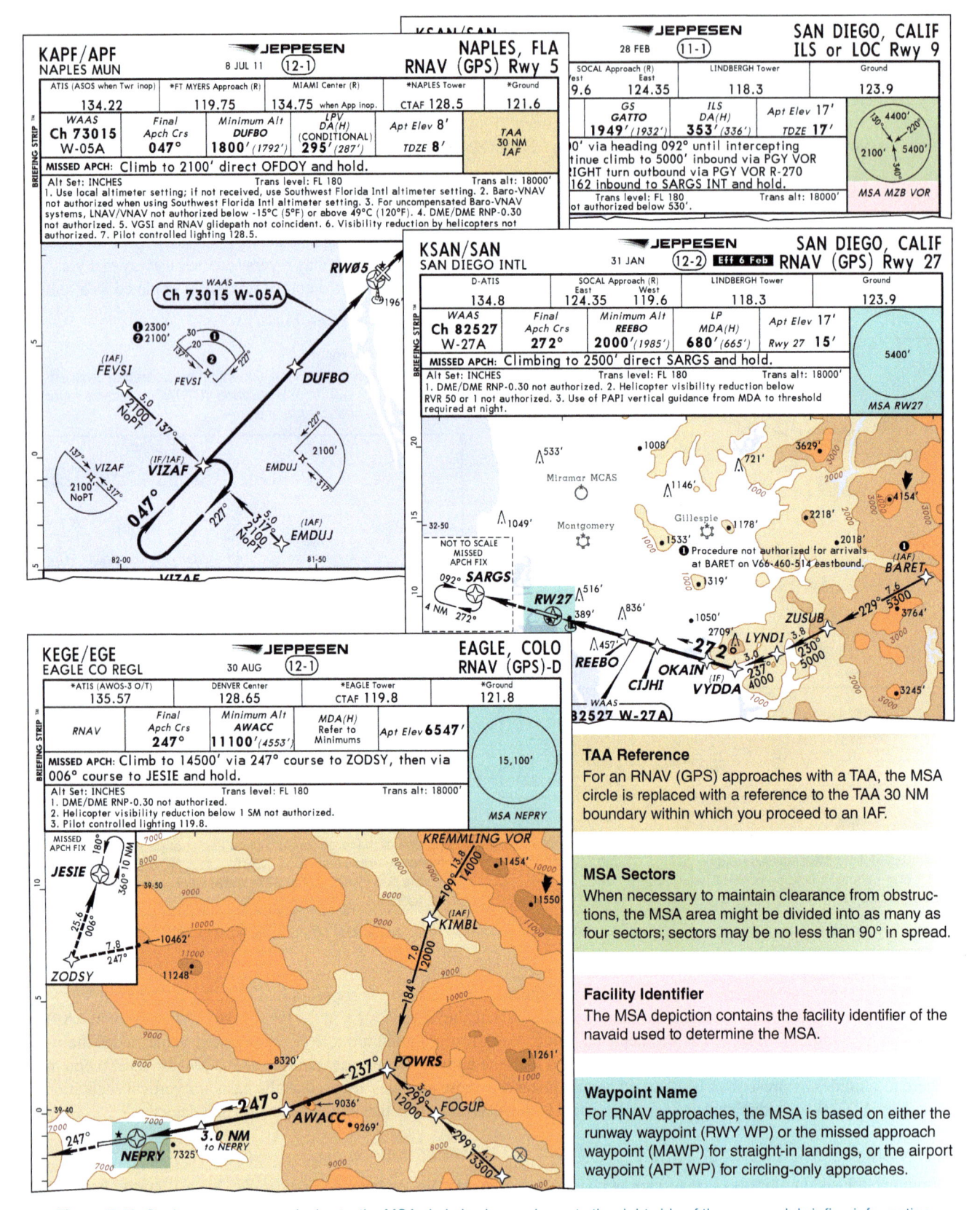

Figure 5-10. On Jeppesen approach charts, the MSA circle is always shown to the right side of the approach briefing information.

FAF OR GLIDE-SLOPE/GLIDE-PATH INTERCEPT ALTITUDE

You must ensure that you know the altitude at the FAF on a nonprecision approach, the charted altitude at which you intercept the glide slope for precision approaches, and the charted altitude for intercepting the glide path for APVs. The altitude at which you actually intercept the glide slope/glide path becomes the FAF for these approaches. Adherence to and cross-check of this altitude has a direct effect on the success of the approach.

Proper airspeed, altitude, and configuration, when crossing the FAF of a nonprecision approach, are essential to flying a stabilized approach and the criteria to accomplish this is outlined in your SOPs. When flying an ILS approach or APV, you must be aware of the glide-slope/glide-path intercept altitude to ensure that you do not follow a false glide slope or other erroneous indication. Many air carriers include a standard callout when the aircraft passes over the FAF of the nonprecision approach underlying the ILS. The pilot monitoring (PM) typically states the name of the fix and the charted glide-slope altitude, thus allowing both pilots to cross-check their respective altimeters and verify the correct indications. [Figure 5-11]

Glide Slope Intercept

In this case, the point at which you intercept the glide slope and the FAF for the localizer approach are at the same position.

Glide Slope Altitude at Fix

For this approach, you intercept the glide slope at 2,000 feet MSL. If you are maintaining the glide slope, you should be at 1,949 feet MSL when you cross GATTO, the FAF for the localizer approach.

Glide Path Intercept

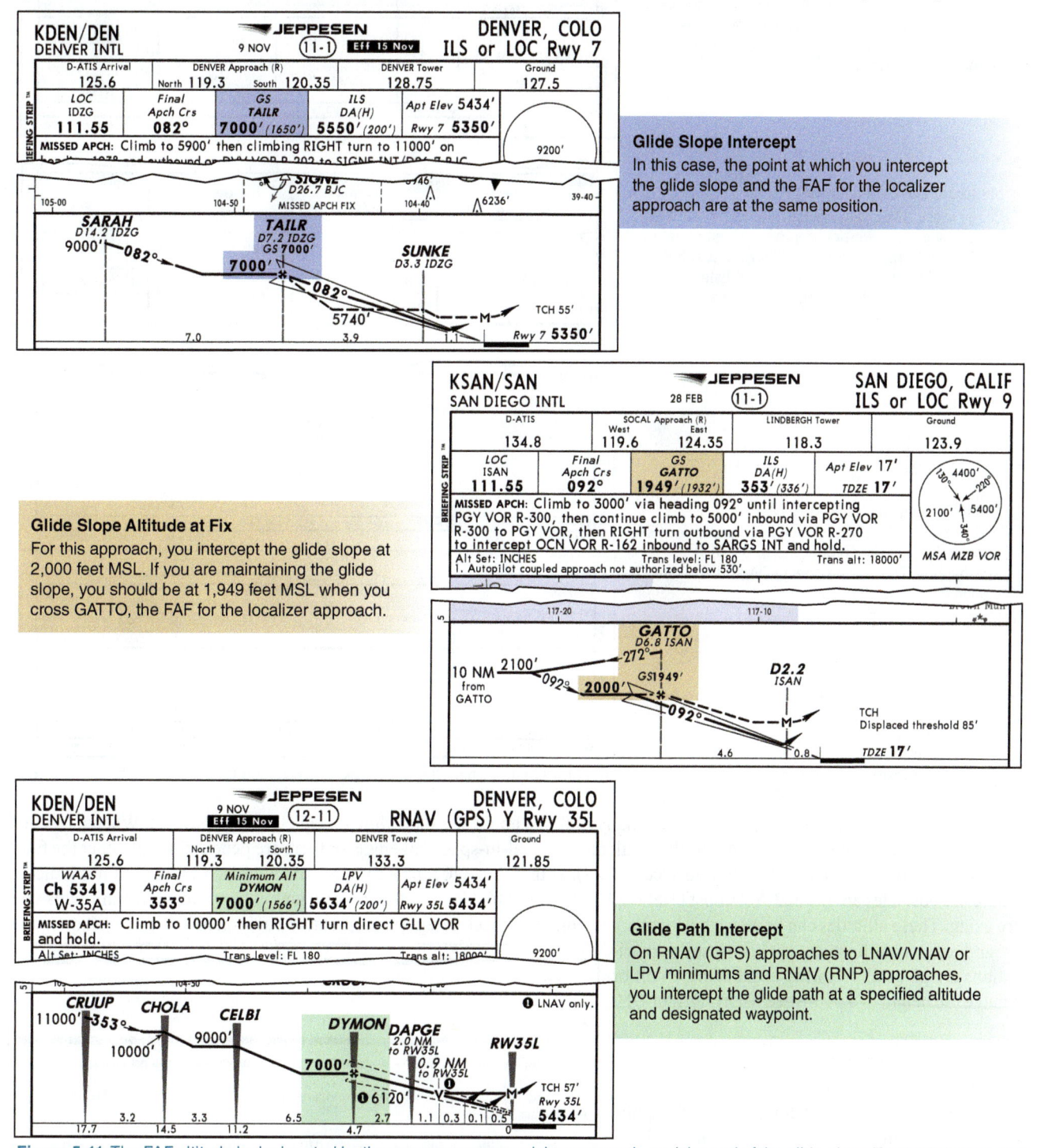

On RNAV (GPS) approaches to LNAV/VNAV or LPV minimums and RNAV (RNP) approaches, you intercept the glide path at a specified altitude and designated waypoint.

Figure 5-11. The FAF altitude is designated by the cross on a nonprecision approach, and the end of the glide-slope "feather" designating the minimum glide-slope intercept altitude on a precision approach.

MINIMUM DESCENT ALTITUDE, DECISION ALTITUDE, AND DECISION HEIGHT

You use a minimum descent altitude (MDA) when you fly nonprecision approaches. You descend to a decision altitude (DA) on category I (CAT I) ILS approaches, and when flying APVs. DAs and MDAs are referenced to MSL and measured with a barometric altimeter. Decision heights (DHs) referenced to AGL and measured by a radio altimeter (RA) apply to special

5-9

authorization (SA) CAT I ILS approaches and CAT II ILS approaches. The height above touchdown (HAT) is shown in parentheses after straight-in landing DAs or MDAs, while the height above the airport (HAA) is indicated after the MDA for circling approaches. [Figure 5-12]

Decision Altitude
DAs in feet MSL with the HAT listed in parentheses apply to CAT I ILS approaches and RNAV approaches with vertical guidance to LPV and LNAV/VNAV minimums.

Minimum Descent Altitude
MDAs in feet MSL with the HAT listed in parentheses apply to nonprecision approaches, such as a localizer-only approach or an RNAV approach to LNAV minimums. MDAs with the HAA listed in parentheses apply to circling approaches.

Decision Height
A DH in feet AGL measured by a radio altimter (RA) applies to SA CAT I approaches and CAT II approaches. The corresponding DA and HAT are shown below the DH.

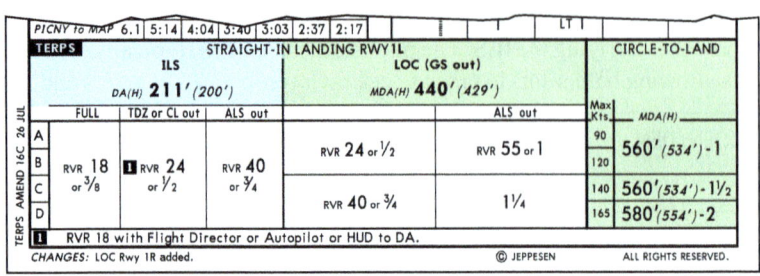

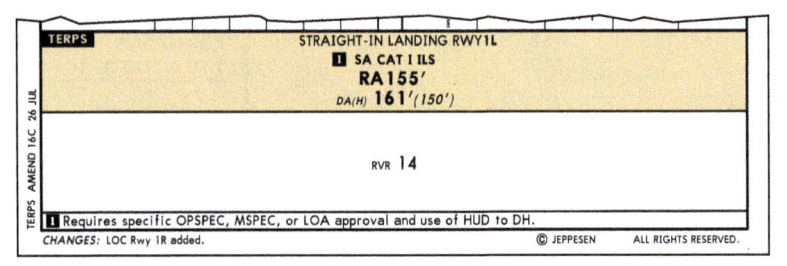

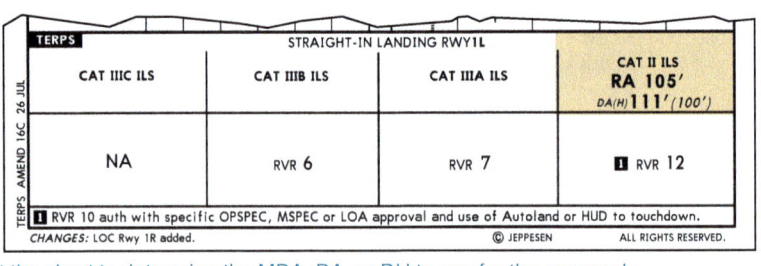

Figure 5-12. You must be able to interpret the chart to determine the MDA, DA, or DH to use for the approach.

The HAT for a CAT I precision approach is normally 200 feet above the touchdown zone elevation (TDZE). When a HAT of 250 feet or higher is published, it might be the result of the signal-in-space coverage, or there are penetrations of either the final or missed approach obstacle clearance surfaces (OCS). If there are OCS penetrations, the approach chart does not indicate where the obstacles are located. You must brief the MDA(H) or DA(H) so that there is no ambiguity as to what minimums you are using. These altitudes can be restricted by many factors. Approach category, inoperative equipment in the aircraft or on the ground, crew qualifications, and company authorizations are all examples of issues that may limit or change the height of a published MDA, DA, or DH.

LANDING MINIMUMS AND OPS SPECS

The primary authorization for the use of specific approach minimums by an individual air carrier is in its FAA approved OpsSpecs: Part C–Airplane Terminal Instrument Procedures, Airport Authorizations and Limitations. This document lists the lowest authorized landing minimums that the company can use while conducting instrument approaches. [Figure 5-13]

5-13. This example of an OpsSpecs document lists landing minimums requirements and limitations for company aircraft and pilots.

For many air carriers, OpsSpecs are the limiting factor for some types of approaches. NDB and circling approaches are two common examples where the OpsSpecs landing minimums might be more restrictive than the charted minimums. Many Part 121 and 135 operators are restricted from conducting circling approaches below a 1,000-foot MDA and 3 statute miles visibility by Part C of their OpsSpecs, and many have specific visibility criteria listed for NDB approaches that exceed visibilities published for the approach (commonly 2 statute miles). In these cases, you must determine which is the more restrictive of the two and comply with those minimums.

In some cases, flight crew qualifications are the limiting factor for the MDA, DA, or DH for an instrument approach. There are many CAT II and III approach procedures authorized at airports throughout the United States, but aircraft and aircrew requirements restrict their use to pilots who have received specific training and aircraft that are equipped and authorized to conduct those approaches. Other rules pertaining to flight crew qualifications also determine the lowest usable MDA, DA, or DH for a specific approach. FARs 121.652 and 135.225 require that you increase the approach minimums and visibility by 100 feet and one-half mile respectively if you have limited experience in the aircraft you are operating. Rules for "high-minimums" pilots are usually derived from a combination of regulations and the company's OpsSpecs. You must consider all of the factors that apply to determine the actual minimums you may use for a specific approach.

VERTICAL DESCENT ANGLE

When flying a nonprecision approach, you must establish a sufficient rate of descent while maintaining an appropriate airspeed to ensure that you reach the MDA prior to the MAP and to provide plenty of time to establish the required visual cues and perform an approach to landing. For nonprecision approaches, Jeppesen charts indicate a vertical descent angle (VDA) and an associated descent rate as a guideline for performing a stabilized descent to arrive at the MDA prior to the missed approach point. Using the VDA helps you maintain a stabilized descent from the FAF to the threshold crossing height (TCH). The vertical descent angle should keep you above the minimum altitudes designated for stepdown fixes; however, it is still your responsibility to monitor your descent and ensure you comply with stepdown fix minimum altitudes. [Figure 5-14]

VNAV DA
Your navigation equipment might enable you to input the VDA to display an advisory glide path. You also might be authorized to follow the advisory glide path and use the MDA as a DA. In this case, you must make a decision upon reaching the MDA to continue the approach to landing or perform a missed approach.

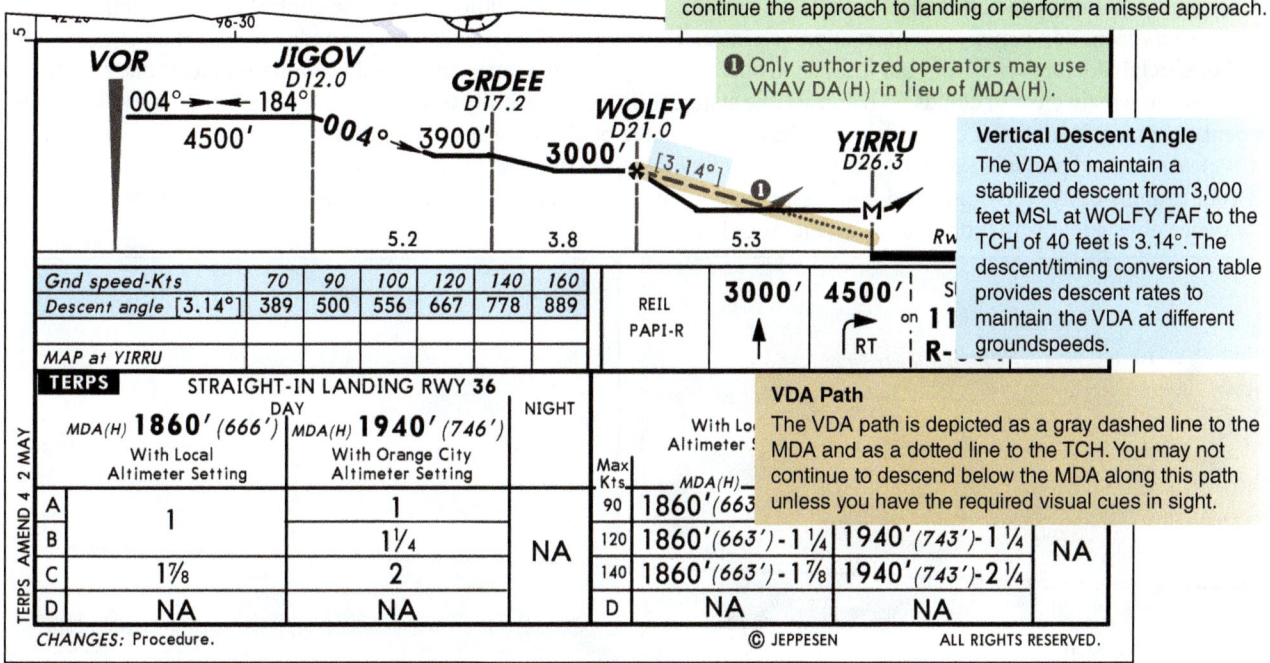

❶ Only authorized operators may use VNAV DA(H) in lieu of MDA(H).

Vertical Descent Angle
The VDA to maintain a stabilized descent from 3,000 feet MSL at WOLFY FAF to the TCH of 40 feet is 3.14°. The descent/timing conversion table provides descent rates to maintain the VDA at different groundspeeds.

VDA Path
The VDA path is depicted as a gray dashed line to the MDA and as a dotted line to the TCH. You may not continue to descend below the MDA along this path unless you have the required visual cues in sight.

Figure 5-14. The VDA enables you to maintain a stabilized descent when flying a nonprecision approach.

TYPES OF APPROACHES

Each approach in the NAS is designed according to the United States Standard for Terminal Instrument Procedures (TERPS) publication. TERPS design criteria bases obstacle clearance for each approach on the surrounding terrain, obstacles, and navaid availability. Final approach obstacle clearance is different for every type of approach but is guaranteed from the start of the final approach segment to the runway (not below the MDA for nonprecision approaches) or MAP, whichever occurs last within the final approach area. Both you and ATC assume obstacle clearance responsibility, but you must maintain an appropriate flight path within the boundaries of the final approach area.

There are numerous types of instrument approaches available in the NAS, including ILS, RNAV (GPS), RNAV (RNP), LOC, VOR, NDB, and radar approaches. Each approach has separate and individual design criteria, equipment requirements, and system capabilities. In addition, if specific conditions are met, you might be cleared for a visual or contact approach while on an IFR flight plan.

VISUAL APPROACH

A visual approach is an ATC authorization for you to proceed visually to the airport of intended landing on an IFR flight plan; it is not an IAP. When it is operationally beneficial, ATC may authorize you to conduct a visual approach to the airport in lieu of the published IAP. You or the controller can initiate a visual approach if the ceiling is reported or expected to be at least 1,000 feet AGL and the visibility is at least 3 statute miles. At airports without weather reporting service there must be reasonable assurance (area weather reports, PIREPs, etc.) that you can descend and perform an approach to landing visually, and AT must inform you that weather information is not available.

Before issuing a visual approach clearance, the controller must verify that you have the airport, or a preceding aircraft that you are to follow, in sight. If you have the airport in sight but do not see the aircraft you are to follow, ATC may issue the visual approach clearance but must maintain responsibility for aircraft and wake turbulence separation. After you report that the airport is in sight, you are responsible for your own separation and wake turbulence avoidance. A visual approach does not have a missed approach segment so if you are unable to complete a visual approach you perform a go-around and ATC provides appropriate separation.

You must remain clear of the clouds at all times while performing a visual approach. At an airport with a control tower, ATC might clear you to fly a visual approach to one runway while other aircraft are flying VFR or IFR approaches to another parallel, intersecting, or converging runway. Radar service is automatically terminated when the controller advises you to change to the tower or advisory frequency.

CONTACT APPROACH

If conditions permit, you can request a contact approach, which is then authorized by the controller. ATC cannot initiate a contact approach. You may fly a contact approach instead of the published procedure to expedite arrival at an airport with an IAP or special IAP (approved for your individual operator) as long as the reported ground visibility is at least one statute mile, and you can remain clear of clouds with at least one statute mile flight visibility throughout the approach. Some advantages of a contact approach are that it usually requires less time than the published instrument procedure, it enables you to retain your IFR clearance, and provides separation from IFR and SVFR traffic. Because obstruction clearance and VFR traffic avoidance is your responsibility, you might find it necessary to descend, climb, or fly a circuitous route to the airport to maintain cloud clearance or terrain/obstruction clearance. [Figure 5-15]

Visual Approach
- You may request or ATC may assign a visual approach.
- You must have the airport in sight, or see a preceding aircraft to follow.
- The ceiling must be at least 1,000 feet AGL with at least 3 SM visibility.

Contact Approach
- You must request a contact approach—ATC cannot initiate the approach.
- ATC may approve a contact approach with 1 SM visibility if you can remain clear of clouds.

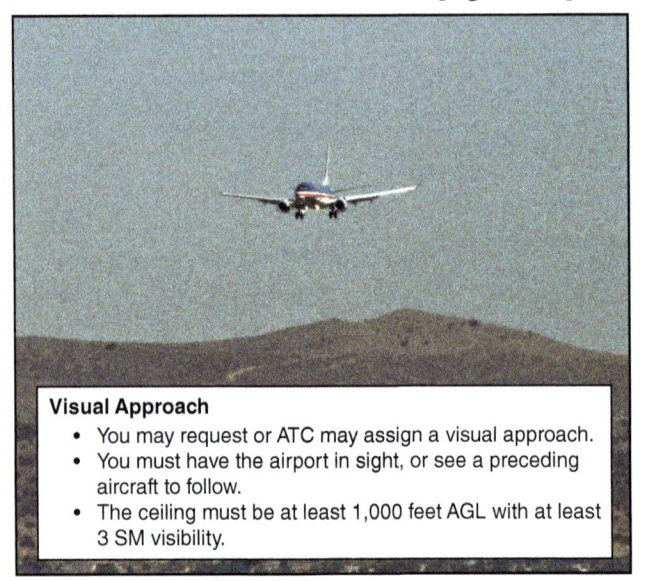

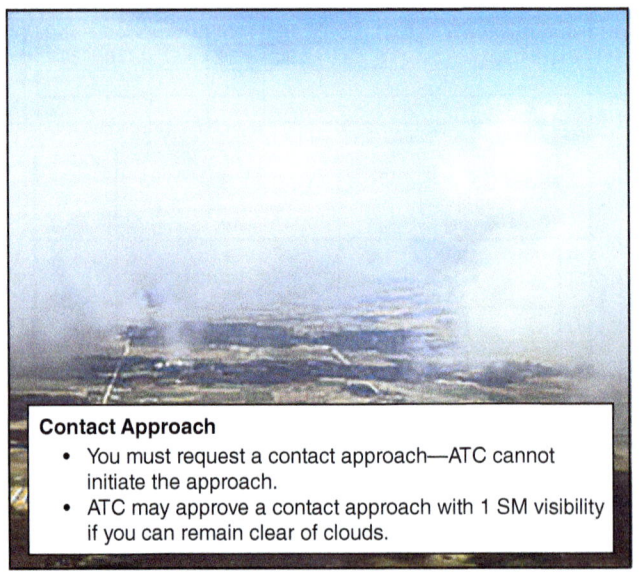

Figure 5-15. The primary differences between a visual approach and a contact approach have to do with requesting the approach and the flight ceiling and visibility.

CHARTED VISUAL FLIGHT PROCEDURE

Charted visual flight procedures (CVFPs) are designed primarily for turbojet aircraft for environmental or noise considerations, as well as when necessary for the safety and efficiency of air traffic operations at some airports with control towers. Before ATC clears you to fly a CVFP, you must have a charted visual landmark or a preceding aircraft in sight, and the ceiling and visibility must be at or above the published minimums. ATC may clear you for a CVFP if the reported ceiling at the airport of intended landing is at least 500 feet above the MVA, and the visibility is at least 3 statute miles, unless higher minimums are published for the particular CVFP. When you accept a clearance to follow a preceding aircraft, you must maintain a safe approach interval and wake turbulence separation. You must advise ATC if you are unable at any point to continue a CVFP or if you lose sight of the preceding aircraft. [Figure 5-16]

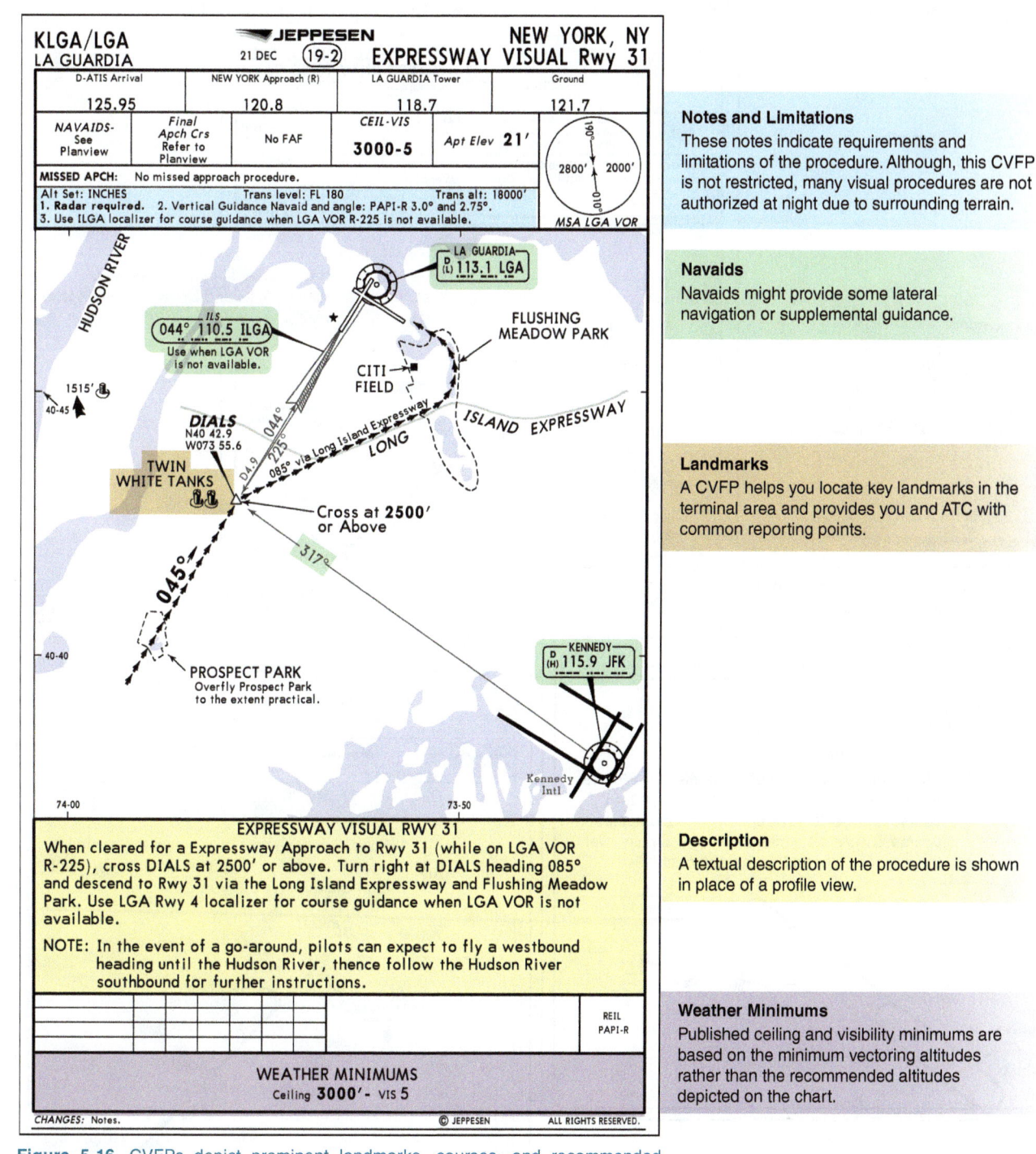

Figure 5-16. CVFPs depict prominent landmarks, courses, and recommended altitudes to specific runways.

RNAV (GPS) APPROACH

RNAV (GPS) approaches and RNAV (RNP) approaches (explained later in this chapter) are the two types of RNAV approaches. RNAV (GPS) approaches are classified as APVs or nonprecision approaches based on whether you use vertical navigation to descend to a DA or lateral guidance only in which case you descend to an MDA.

RNAV (GPS) APPROACH DESIGN

Because RNAV (GPS) procedures are not predicated on ground-based navaids, greater flexibility exists in the approach design. For example, some RNAV (GPS) approach procedures include one or more feeder routes that lead to one or more IAFs for straight-in approaches. Other designs incorporate a holding pattern course reversal. Some designs do not publish an IAF and require radar service to fly to the intermediate approach fix to begin the published approach. [Figure 5-17]

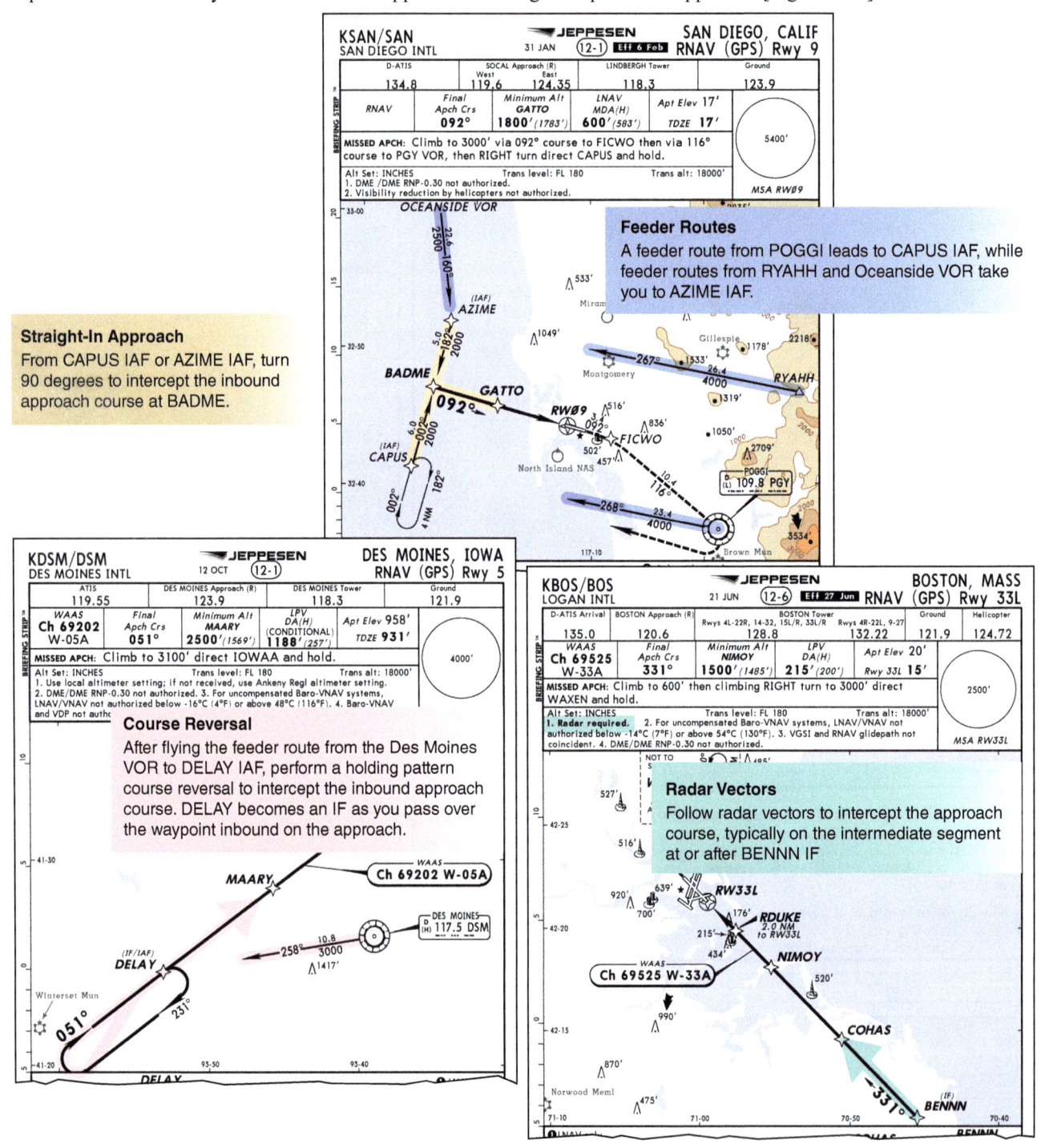

Feeder Routes
A feeder route from POGGI leads to CAPUS IAF, while feeder routes from RYAHH and Oceanside VOR take you to AZIME IAF.

Straight-In Approach
From CAPUS IAF or AZIME IAF, turn 90 degrees to intercept the inbound approach course at BADME.

Course Reversal
After flying the feeder route from the Des Moines VOR to DELAY IAF, perform a holding pattern course reversal to intercept the inbound approach course. DELAY becomes an IF as you pass over the waypoint inbound on the approach.

Radar Vectors
Follow radar vectors to intercept the approach course, typically on the intermediate segment at or after BENNN IF

Figure 5-17. RNAV (GPS) approaches have a variety of designs similar to other approach procedures but are easier to implement because they do not have the limitation of relying on ground-based navaids.

In some cases, RNAV (GPS) approaches are designed with a TAA. This design has some unique features indicated on the approach chart. Icons on the plan view indicate minimum altitudes that you must maintain as you arrive from the enroute structure to a specific IAF, therefore, no MSA is published. In addition, the chart shows a Basic T approach segment configuration that consists of three areas: the straight-in area, the left base area, and the right base area. Modifications to this configuration might be necessary to accommodate operational requirements. [Figure 5-18]

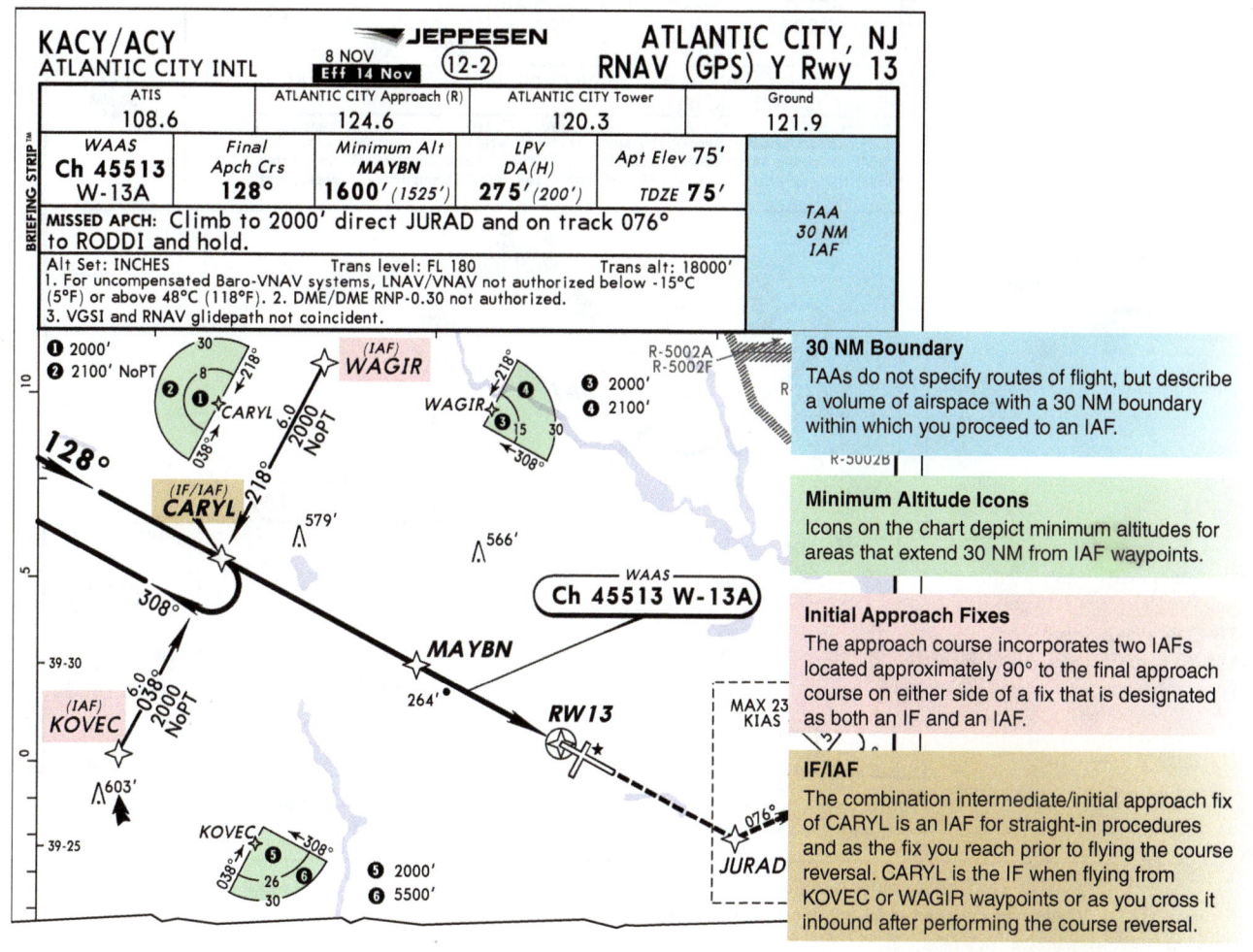

Figure 5-18. The Basic T approach segment configuration is optimum for transition from the enroute to the terminal environment within a TAA.

GPS equipment provides waypoint sequencing for each approach segment. Database coding indicates whether waypoints are fly-over or fly-by, and your GPS equipment provides appropriate guidance for each. For a fly-by waypoint, the GPS equipment anticipates the turn and displays navigation indications to begin the turn so that you do not overshoot the next flight segment. For a fly-over waypoint (depicted by the waypoint symbol enclosed in a circle), navigation indications do not provide guidance for a turn until you pass over the waypoint, followed either by an intercept maneuver to the next flight segment or by direct flight to the next waypoint. [Figure 5-19]

GPS APPROACH EQUIPMENT

To fly RNAV (GPS) approach procedures with lateral navigation, GPS equipment must be certified not just for IFR enroute and terminal navigation but must also be approved for IFR approaches according to the current version of technical standard order (TSO) C129. Additional equipment requirements must be met to fly GPS approaches that incorporate vertical navigation. The primary types of equipment used to perform GPS approaches with vertical navigation are barometric vertical navigation (baro-VNAV) systems or WAAS-certified GPS equipment that is approved according to the most recent version of TSO-C145 or TSO-C146. In addition, AC 20-138 provides guidance for the airworthiness approval of installed GPS and RNAV equipment. You must determine the allowable uses for the specific GPS installation by referring to the airplane flight manual (AFM) or AFM supplement and your OpsSpecs. [Figure 5-20]

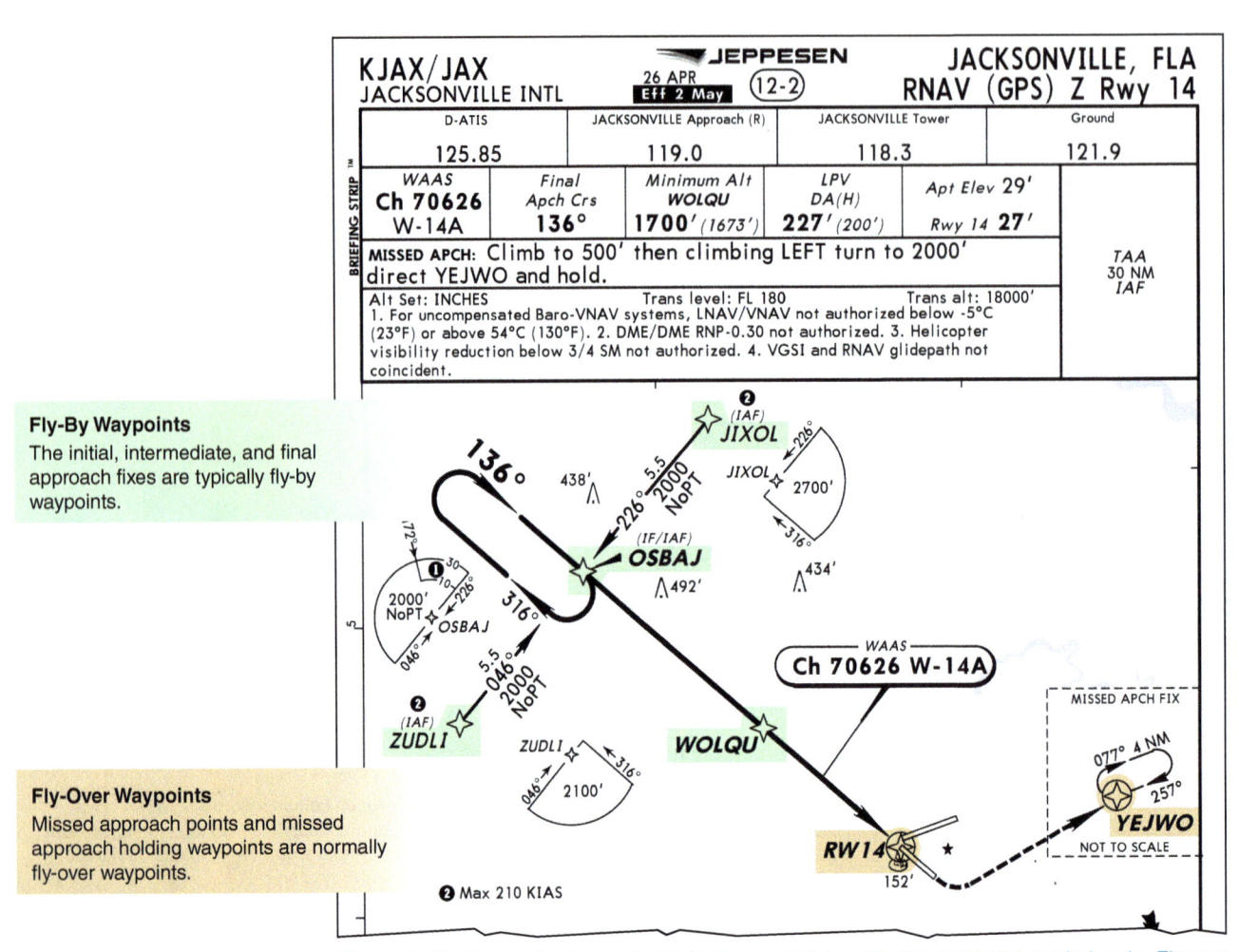

Figure 5-19. Approach charts depict fly-by waypoints with the waypoint symbol only. Fly-over waypoints are shown as the waypoint symbol enclosed in a circle.

Fly-By Waypoints
The initial, intermediate, and final approach fixes are typically fly-by waypoints.

Fly-Over Waypoints
Missed approach points and missed approach holding waypoints are normally fly-over waypoints.

a. The certificate holder is authorized to conduct operations using the types of IAPs listed in Table 1 below, and shall not conduct operations using any other types.

Table 1 – Authorized Instrument Approach Procedures

Nonprecision Approach Procedures Without Vertical Guidance	Approaches With Vertical Guidance (APV)	Precision Approach Procedures
RNAV (GPS)		ILS
VOR		ILS/DME
VOR/DME		ILS/PRM
LOC		
LOCBC		

Figure 5-20. This excerpt from a company's OpsSpecs does not authorize any RNAV (GPS) approaches with vertical guidance.

Baro-VNAV

Baro-VNAV equipment builds a glide path by sensing and then comparing the aircraft's altitude with a calculated altitude for the aircraft's position on the glide path. You must enter the current local altimeter setting on the GPS equipment to ensure an accurate calculated glide path. In addition, there are high and low temperature limitations for the use of baro-VNAV equipment. [Figure 5-21]

WAAS-Certified GPS

WAAS-certified GPS equipment determines a glide path by its vertical and horizontal GPS position and eliminates the errors caused by barometric altimetry. This equipment computes a glide path independent of the altimeter setting, and its operation is not limited by temperature. [Figure 5-22]

KSDM/SDM — JEPPESEN — **SAN DIEGO, CALIF**
BROWN MUN — 13 SEP (62-1) Eff 19 Sep — **RNAV (GPS) Rwy 8L**

*ATIS	SOCAL Approach (R)	*BROWN Tower		
132.35	124.35	CTAF 128.25		
WAAS **Ch 56534** W-08A	Final Apch Crs **082°**	Minimum Alt YAPKI **2400'** (1874')	LPV DA(H) (CONDITIONAL) **726'** (200')	Apt Elev 5 Rwy 8L 5

MISSED APCH: Climb to 940' then climbing LEFT turn to 3000' direct LUGJA and hold.

Alt Set: INCHES   Trans level: FL 180   Trans alt: 18
1. Use local altimeter setting; if not received, use San Diego Intl altimeter setting.
2. Baro-VNAV not authorized when using San Diego Intl altimeter setting. 3. For uncompensated Baro-VNAV systems, LNAV/VNAV not authorized below 2°C (36°F) or above 54°C (130°F). 4. DME/DME RNP-0.30 not authorized. 5. Pilot controlled lighting 128.25.

❶ MISSION BAY VOR(IAF)

❶ Procedure not authorized for arrivals on MZB VOR airway

Local Altimeter Setting
In many cases, using baro-VNAV for vertical navigation on approaches is not authorized without the local altimeter setting. This is because the accuracy of a baro-VNAV glide path depends on using an accurate altimeter setting for the airport.

Temperature Limitations
Some baro-VNAV equipment compensates for extreme temperatures; however, many systems only correct for cold temperature so the high temperature limitation still applies. If you are using baro-VNAV equipment, you must be aware of the equipment's compensation capabilities.

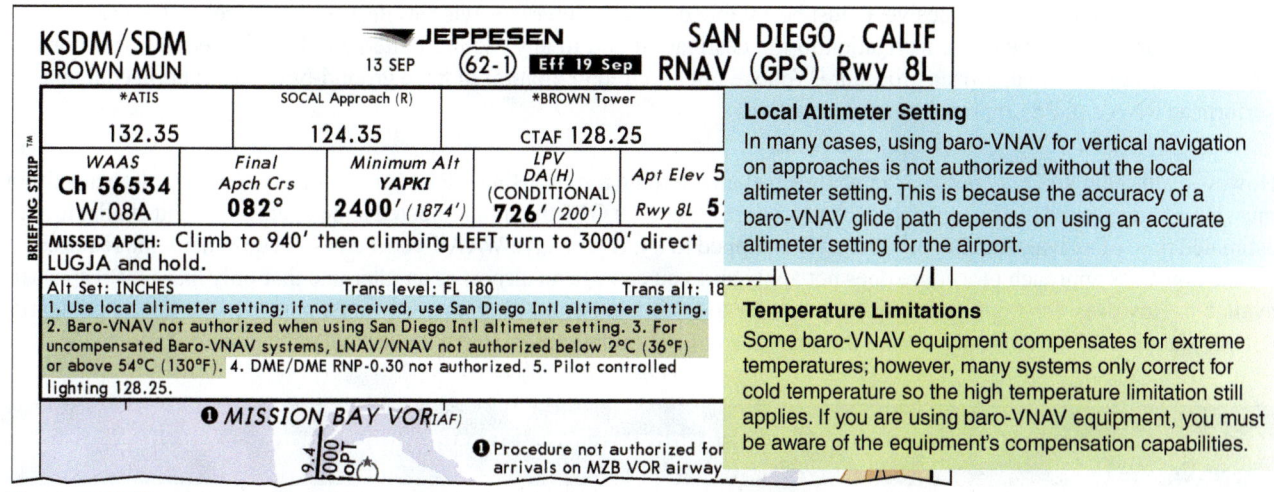

Figure 5-21. The notes section of the approach chart indicates temperature and altimeter setting limitations that apply to using baro-VNAV equipment to fly the approach glide path.

KOKC/OKC — JEPPESEN — **OKLAHOMA CITY, OKLA**
WILL ROGERS WORLD — 11 NOV (12-3) — **RNAV (GPS) Y Rwy 17R**

D-ATIS	OKE CITY Approach (R)	ROGERS Tower	Ground
125.85	124.6	119.35	121.9
WAAS **Ch 50102** W-17A	Final Apch Crs **175°**		

MISSED APCH: Climb to 320
Alt Set: INCHES
1. For uncompensated Baro-VNAV systems, LNAV/VNAV not authorized below -17°C (2°F) or above 35°C (95°F). 2. DME/DME RNP-0.30 not authorized. 3. VGSI and RNAV glidepath not coincident.

WAAS Channel Number
The primary navigation facility box in the briefing section contains the airport's unique WAAS channel number. This number is stored in the GPS equipment database so you are normally not required to enter the WAAS channel number to select an approach.

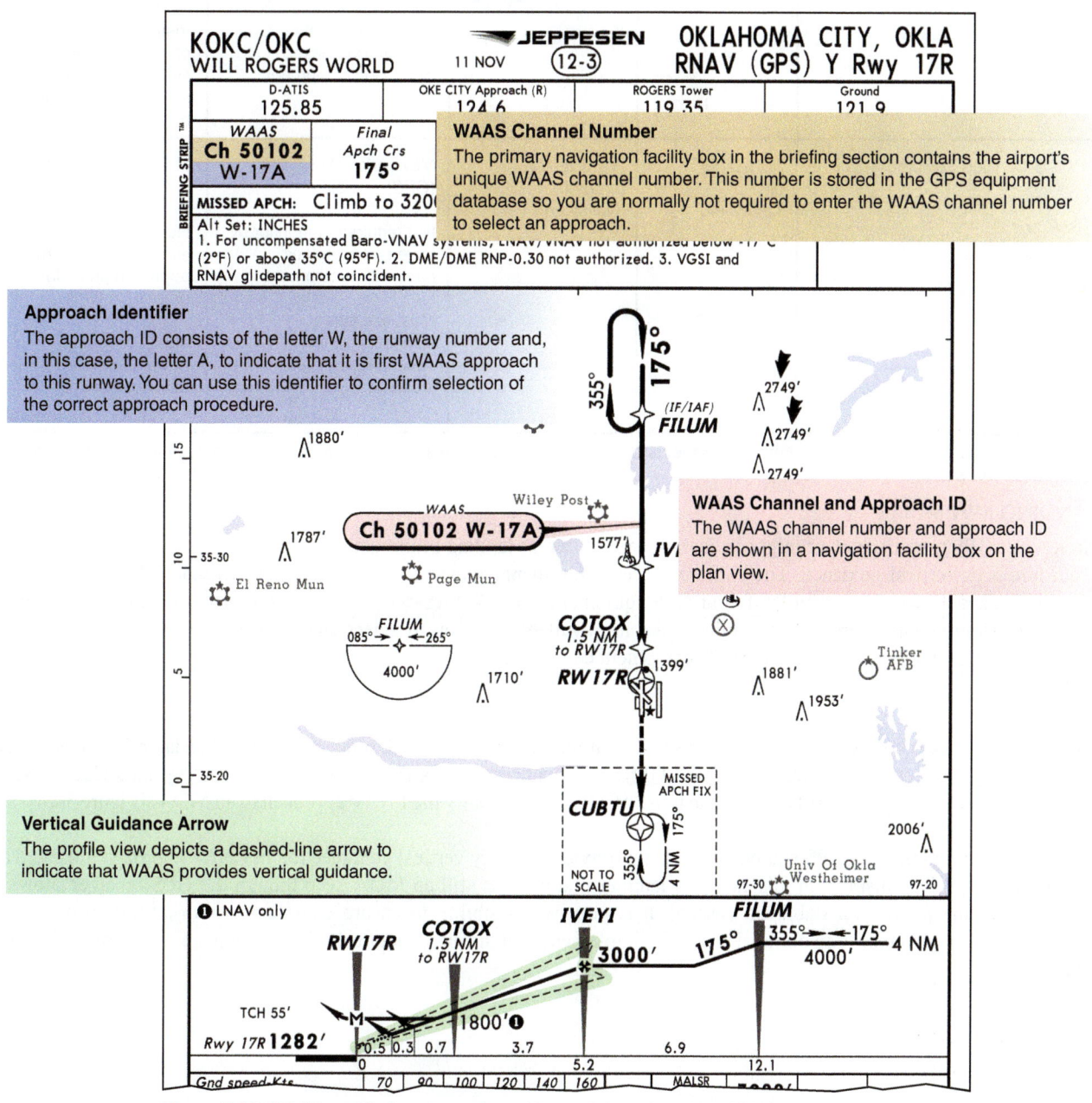

Approach Identifier
The approach ID consists of the letter W, the runway number and, in this case, the letter A, to indicate that it is first WAAS approach to this runway. You can use this identifier to confirm selection of the correct approach procedure.

WAAS Channel and Approach ID
The WAAS channel number and approach ID are shown in a navigation facility box on the plan view.

Vertical Guidance Arrow
The profile view depicts a dashed-line arrow to indicate that WAAS provides vertical guidance.

Figure 5-22. WAAS-certified equipment provides a glide path and WAAS information is displayed on several sections of RNAV (GPS) approach charts.

Aircraft with non-WAAS GPS receivers must be equipped with the alternate avionics necessary to receive the ground-based facilities appropriate for enroute navigation to the destination and to any required alternate, but this requirement does not extend to the destination approach procedure. You are not required to monitor or have ground-based navigation equipment to perform an RNAV (GPS) approach at the destination.

However, although you may perform an approach at an alternate airport using GPS equipment, any required alternate airport must have an approved instrument approach procedure other than GPS that is anticipated to be operational and available at the estimated time of arrival, and that the aircraft is equipped to fly. If you have WAAS-certified GPS equipment, the requirement for the non-GPS approach procedure does not apply and you can use an airport as an alternate that only has a GPS approach available. However, for flight planning purposes for a destination or an alternate, you must consider the lateral navigation (LNAV) landing minimums only, even if the approach has minimums associated with vertical navigation. [Figure 5-23]

GPS Approach Equipment	Certified By	Approved For	Destination Airport	Alternate Airport
Basic IFR Enroute and Approach Certified Equipment	TSO-C129	Lateral Navigation	May perform an RNAV (GPS) approach Not required to monitor or have ground-based navigation equipment	May perform an RNAV (GPS) approach Instrument approach procedure other than GPS and appropriate navigation equipment required
WAAS-Certified Equipment	TSO-C145 or TSO-C146	Vertical and Lateral Navigation	May perform an RNAV (GPS) approach Not required to monitor or have ground-based navigation equipment Must use lateral navigation (LNAV) minimums for flight planning	May perform an RNAV (GPS) approach Not required to have available instrument approach procedure other than GPS Must use lateral navigation (LNAV) minimums for flight planning

Figure 5-23. The aircraft's GPS equipment affects the requirements for performing approach procedures at the destination airport and any required alternate airport.

LANDING MINIMUMS

An RNAV (GPS) approach chart might indicate several different landing minimums for the approach based on whether the procedure uses vertical guidance. The GPS equipment only displays the approach procedures available for the particular equipment capabilities. For example, if your GPS equipment is not WAAS-certified, approach procedures that incorporate landing minimums based on vertical guidance are not available for you to select and activate. You use the appropriate minimums for the approach based on the GPS equipment capabilities.

LNAV

An RNAV (GPS) approach chart that just depicts LNAV minimums means that the procedure is based on lateral guidance only. You can fly approaches to LNAV minimums with GPS equipment certified for IFR approach procedures by TSO-C129. LNAV course guidance has larger integrity limits than those of a localizer. You fly the LNAV approach to an MDA. [Figure 5-24]

If you have WAAS-certified GPS equipment, it might provide advisory vertical guidance for an LNAV approach indicated as LNAV+V on the GPS display. In this case, the landing minimum is still an MDA even though the GPS receiver shows a vertical path that provides a stabilized descent. It is your responsibility to ensure compliance with altitude restrictions. Advisory vertical guidance is an optional capability implemented at the manufacturer's discretion; not a requirement for GPS equipment.

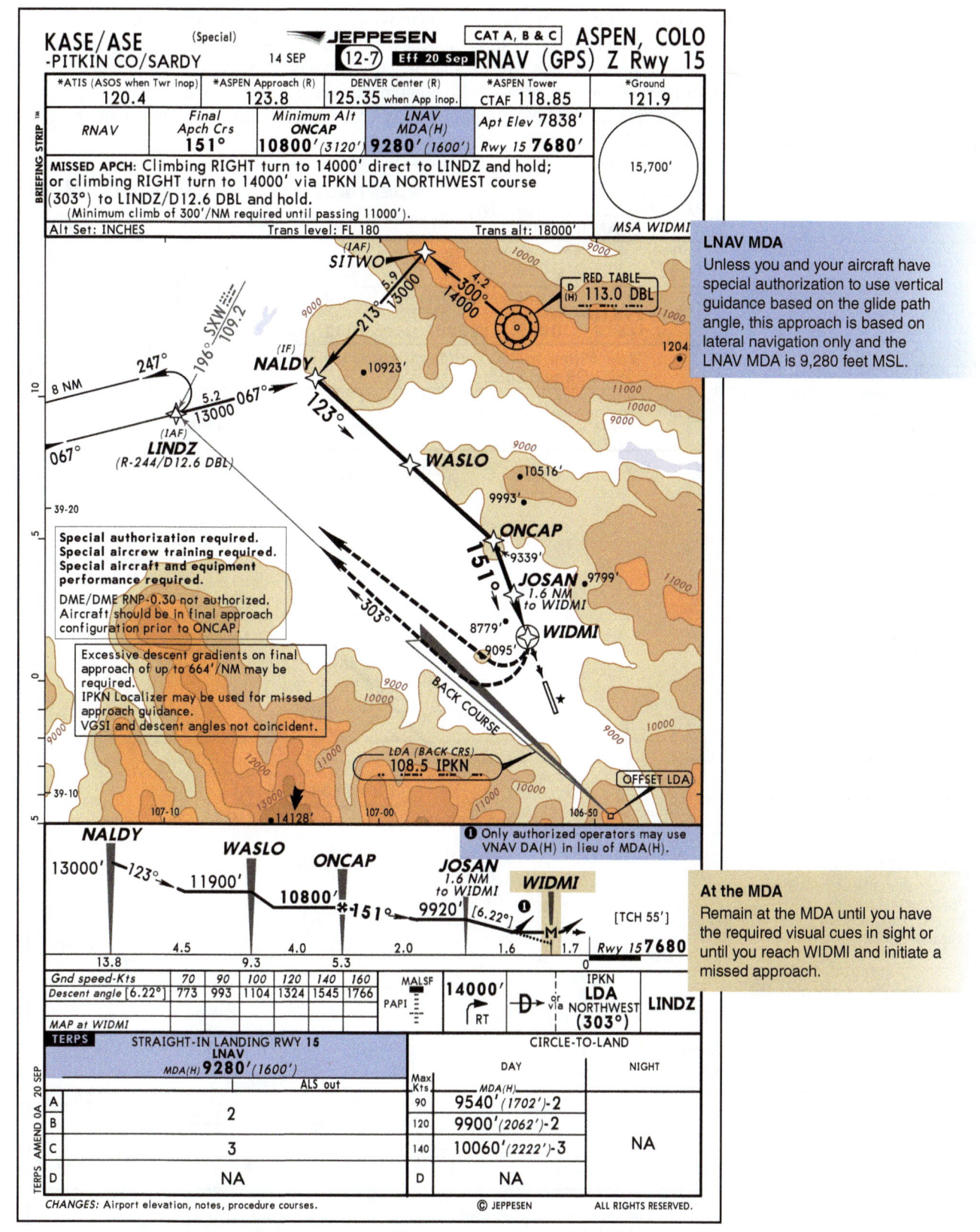

Figure 5-24. An LNAV MDA is based on using lateral navigation indications only.

LNAV/VNAV and LPV

Lateral navigation/vertical navigation (LNAV/VNAV) landing minimums apply to approaches that provide lateral and vertical guidance that is displayed using baro-VNAV or WAAS-certified equipment. The integrity limits for LNAV/VNAV approaches are larger than those of a precision approach. However, the LNAV/VNAV landing minimum is a DA, not an MDA.

5-19

Localizer performance with vertical guidance (LPV) minimums are also provided for RNAV (GPS) approach procedures that have vertical guidance capability. These minimums apply to approaches that provide lateral and vertical guidance with integrity limits that are close to an ILS precision approach. The LPV landing minimum is a DA. Your GPS equipment must be WAAS-certified to fly approaches to LPV minimums; baro-VNAV equipment does not provide the required precision. If WAAS is not available, you must fly the approach to LNAV minimums; WAAS capability does not downgrade from LPV precision to LNAV/VNAV integrity. [Figure 5-25]

LPV DA
You must have WAAS-certified GPS equipment to follow the glide path to the LPV DA of 1,032 feet MSL.

Missed Approach Positions
Jeppesen charts depict three positions along the approach path to begin the missed approach procedure based on each of the approach minimums. The LNAV missed approach point is the RW28 waypoint at the runway threshold. Arrows also indicate the relative positions along the glide path to initiate the missed approach at the LNAV/VNAV and LPV DAs.

LNAV/VNAV DA
If your GPS equipment is not WAAS-certified but you have baro-VNAV capability, you may follow vertical guidance to a DA of 1,146 feet MSL.

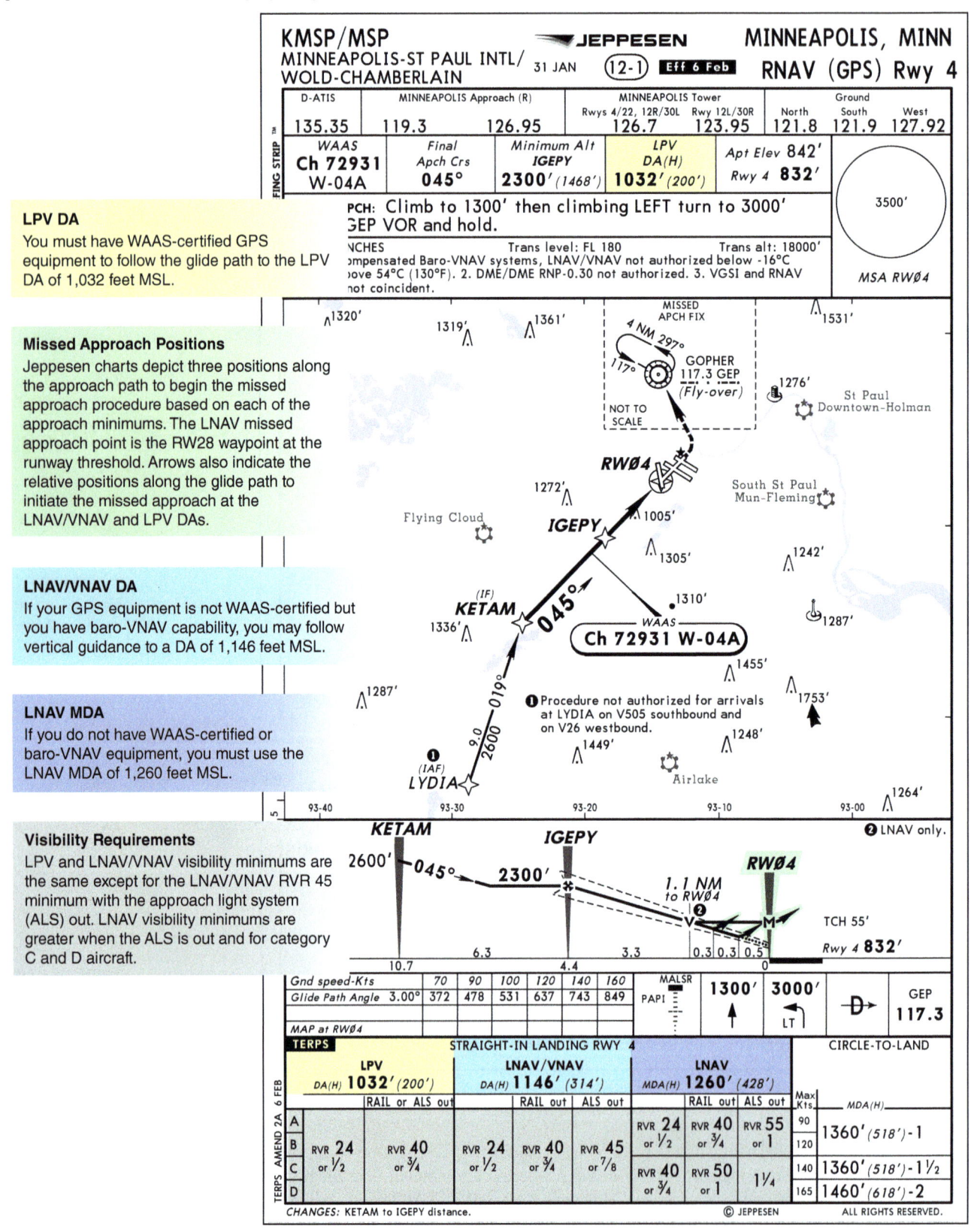

LNAV MDA
If you do not have WAAS-certified or baro-VNAV equipment, you must use the LNAV MDA of 1,260 feet MSL.

Visibility Requirements
LPV and LNAV/VNAV visibility minimums are the same except for the LNAV/VNAV RVR 45 minimum with the approach light system (ALS) out. LNAV visibility minimums are greater when the ALS is out and for category C and D aircraft.

Figure 5-25. You must select the appropriate landing minimums for the approach based on your airplane's equipment capabilities.

LP

Approaches to localizer performance (LP) minimums are commonly referred to as WAAS procedures without vertical guidance. You cannot use baro-VNAV equipment to fly approaches to LP minimums. These approaches have integrity limits close to a localizer and have smaller lateral protected areas than approaches to LNAV minimums. LP and LPV minimums are not published as part of the same approach–each procedure has a different WAAS channel. This means that you cannot perform an LPV approach with vertical guidance and, upon losing WAAS capability, switch to an LP approach. The LP minimum is an MDA and this altitude is often lower than an MDA that is associated with a similar nonprecision approach procedure. Some LP MDAs are as low as 300 feet above touchdown. RNAV (GPS) approaches to LP minimums are typically published in locations where vertical guidance is not feasible due to terrain, obstacles, or other operational limitations. [Figure 5-26]

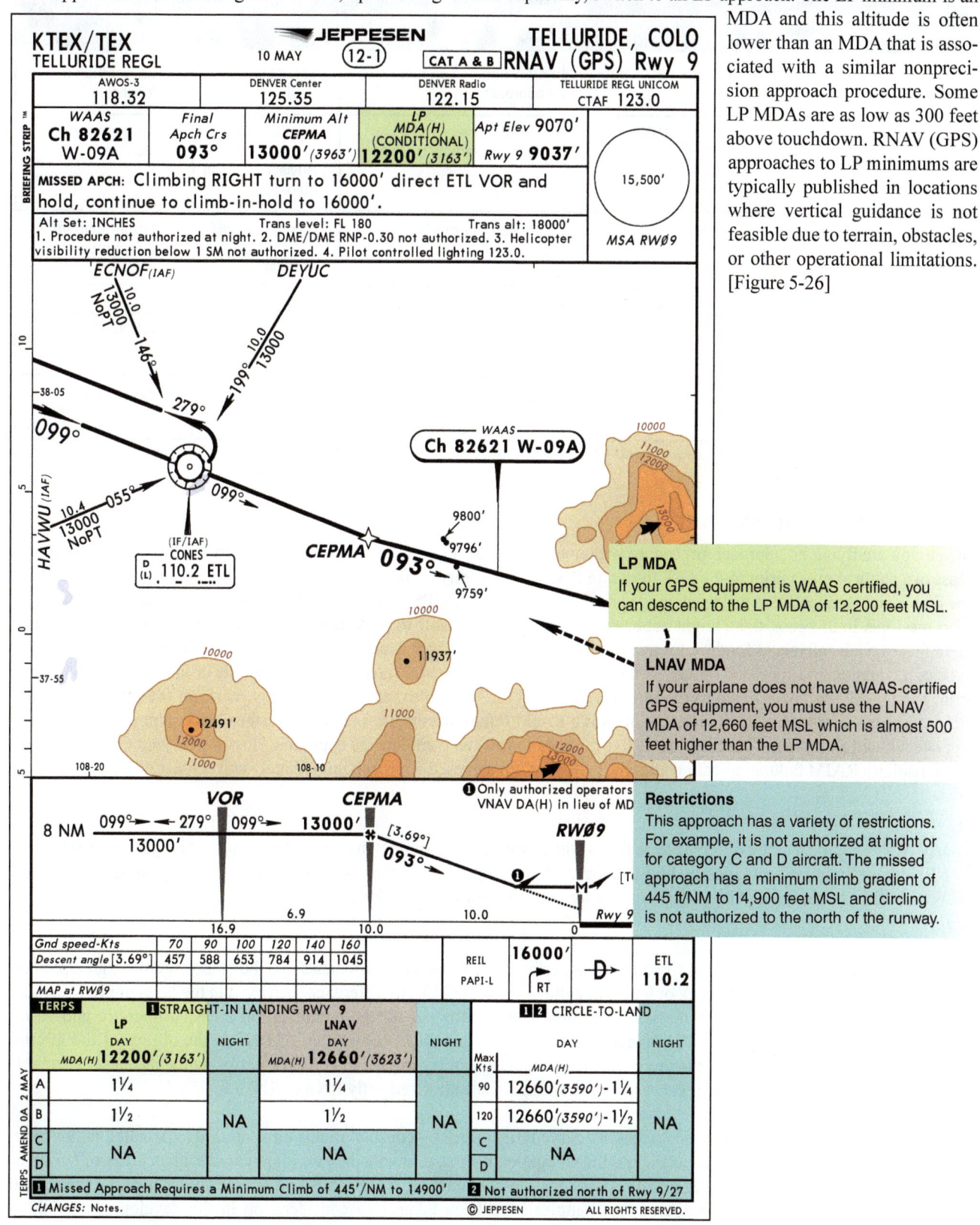

Figure 5-26. Lateral guidance with integrity limits close to a localizer provides more precise navigation to avoid the high terrain surrounding Telluride Regional Airport.

Determining Landing Minimums

To determine the landing minimums to use for an RNAV (GPS) approach procedure, you must have a complete understanding of the procedure and know the capabilities of the airplane's GPS equipment. In addition, you must adhere to the limitations outlined in your company's OpsSpecs. [Figure 5-27]

RNAV (GPS) Approach Minimums	Type of Minimum	Type of Equipment Required	Guidance	Integrity Limits
LNAV	MDA	GPS certified for IFR approaches	Lateral only	Larger than a localizer
LNAV+V	MDA	WAAS or baro-VNAV (for advisory vertical guidance)	Lateral Advisory vertical guidance	Larger than a localizer
LNAV/VNAV	DA	WAAS or baro-VNAV	Lateral Vertical	Larger than an ILS approach
LPV	DA	WAAS	Lateral Vertical	Close to an ILS approach
LP	MDA	WAAS	Lateral only	Close to a localizer

Figure 5-27. This table summarizes the equipment requirements that apply to determining the appropriate landing minimums to use when flying an RNAV (GPS) approach

RAIM FAILURE DURING AN APPROACH

When you are flying an approach procedure with non-WAAS GPS equipment, the receiver performs a RAIM prediction at least two nautical miles prior to the FAF to ensure RAIM availability before it enters approach mode. You should verify that the display has sequenced to approach mode prior to the FAF. If the GPS receiver detects an integrity problem, it displays an alert message. In this case, there might not be enough satellites available to provide RAIM, or RAIM has detected a potential error that exceeds tolerances for the current phase of flight. If RAIM is not available when you set up the approach, use another type of navigation and approach system. If the receiver does not sequence into the approach mode or indicates RAIM failure prior to the FAF, do not descend to the DA or MDA. Proceed to the missed approach point, perform the missed approach procedure, and contact ATC as soon as possible. If a RAIM failure occurs after the FAF fix, the GPS equipment continues to operate without a failure indication for up to five minutes so you can complete the approach. However, if your GPS equipment **does** display a RAIM failure indication after the FAF, perform a missed approach immediately and contact ATC.

RNAV (RNP) APPROACH

RNAV (RNP) approaches are designed to be flown with any type of equipment that meets the required navigation performance (RNP) integrity requirements specified for the approach procedure. To perform RNP approaches, you and your aircraft must meet authorization required (AR) performance criteria that is outlined in AC 90-101, *Approval Guidance for RNP Procedures with AR*.

Operational approval for aircraft and flight crews to perform RNAV (RNP) approaches may be authorized through OpsSpecs, management specifications (MSpecs), or letters of authorization (LOA) and differences can exist in the level of precision that each aircraft system is qualified to meet. A minimum RNP type is part of the authorization for each operator and varies depending on aircraft configuration or operational procedures. A critical component of RNP is the ability of the aircraft navigation system to monitor its achieved performance and to identify to you whether the performance meets set standards during an operation. You must also receive specific training to be authorized to fly RNAV (RNP) approaches.

Key components of RNAV (RNP) approaches are curved flight tracks—constant radius turns around a fix called radius to fix (RF) legs. These turns, which are encoded into the navigation database, enable the aircraft to avoid critical areas of terrain or conflicting airspace while preserving positional accuracy by maintaining precise, positive course guidance along the curved track. Winds, aircraft speeds, and aircraft bank angles have been taken into consideration in the development of these procedures. [Figure 5-28]

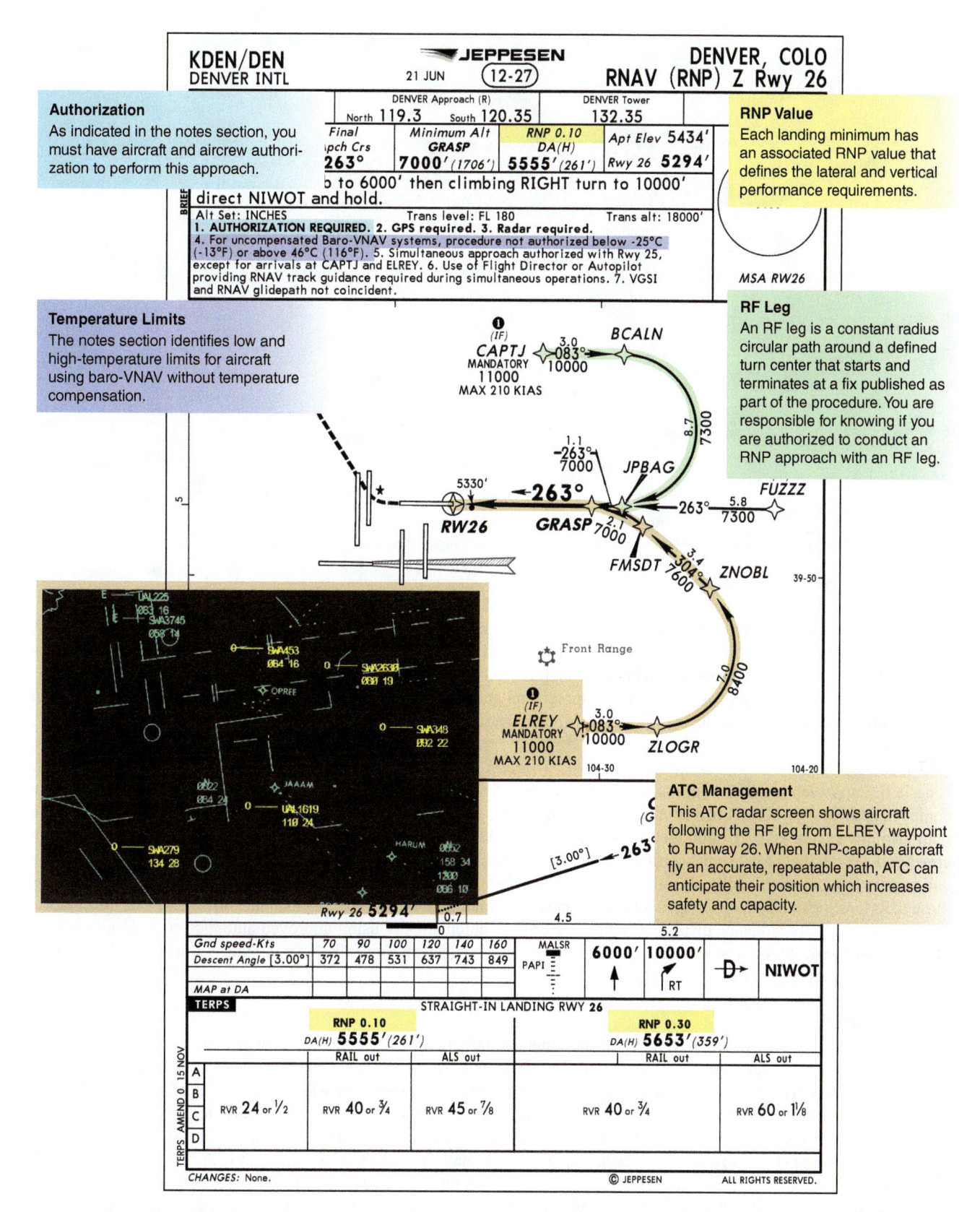

Figure 5-28. RNAV (RNP) approaches have unique features and specific aircraft and flight crew requirements. You and your aircraft must be authorized to fly these approaches.

ILS APPROACH

A single instrument landing system (ILS) can accommodate 29 arrivals per hour on a single runway. Two or three parallel runways operating consecutively can double or triple the capacity of the airport. Capacity is increased through the use of simultaneous parallel, PRM, and converging ILS approaches. ILS approaches of all types are afforded the same obstacle clearance protection and design criteria, no matter how capacity is affected by multiple ILS approaches. [Figure 5-29]

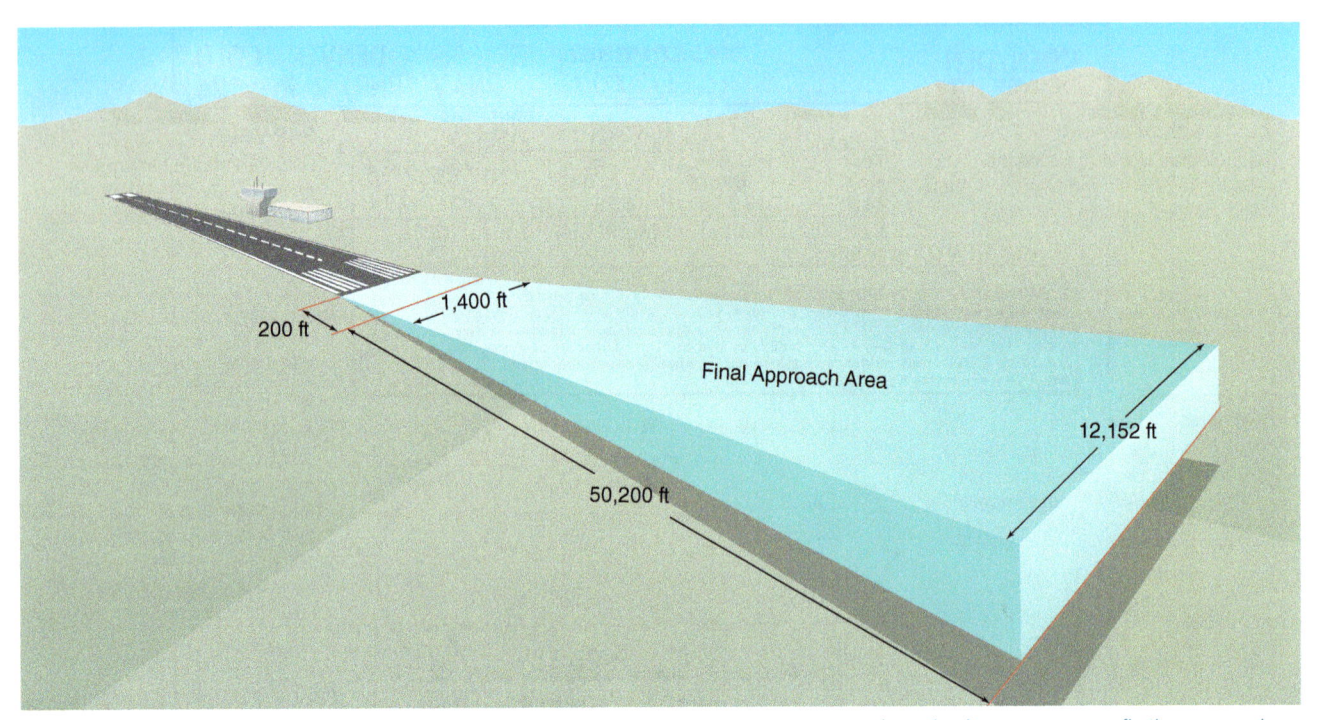

Figure 5-29. The primary protected airspace for the ILS final approach segment ensures obstacle clearance as you fly the approach.

ILS APPROACH CATEGORIES

There are three general classifications of ILS approaches — CAT I, CAT II, and CAT III (autoland). CAT I and CAT II approach categories also include special authorization (SA) approaches and CAT III procedures are further broken down into CAT IIIA, CAT IIIB, and CAT IIIC landing minimums. SA CAT I, CAT II and CAT III approaches require special ground and airborne equipment to be installed and operational and special aircrew training and authorization. The OpsSpecs of individual air carriers detail the requirements of these types of approaches and the approach performance criteria. Lists of locations where each operator is approved to conduct CAT II and III approaches can also be found in the OpsSpecs.

CAT I ILS Approaches

A basic ILS approach is a CAT I approach and requires only that you be instrument rated and current, and that the aircraft be equipped appropriately. CAT I ILS approaches typically allow you to descend to a DA that corresponds to a HAT of 200 feet with visibility as low as RVR 1,800 feet in some cases. SA CAT I approaches are established at some airports to allow flight crews and aircraft that have special certification and approval to descend to DAs that correspond to HATs as low as 150 feet and require a minimum visibility of only RVR 1,400 feet. Your company must have approval to perform these approaches through its OpsSpecs or MSpecs or by an LOA. You may perform Category I approaches manually using raw data information, by reference to flight guidance displays (flight directors), or automatically using approved autopilot or autoland systems. However, air carrier operations, particularly with turbine-powered aircraft, typically have minima restricted by OpsSpecs if a flight director or autopilot is not used. [Figure 5-30]

CAT II ILS Approaches

CAT II ILS approaches typically have lower minimums and require special certification for operators, pilots, aircraft, and airborne/ground equipment. Category II operations may be conducted manually using flight director displays. However, you typically perform CAT II ILS approaches using an autopilot or autoland system, or with combinations of systems using both automatic and flight director elements. A CAT II DH is 100 feet and the visibility minimum is RVR 1,200 feet. CAT II ILS approaches require touchdown zone (TDZ) lighting, runway centerline lighting, and an approach light system with sequenced flashing lights (ALSF-1/2). However, with proper approval you may fly an SA CAT II approach without TDZ lighting, RCL, and ALSF-1/2 if medium intensity approach lighting system with runway alignment indicator lights (MALSR) or simplified short approach lighting with runway alignment indicator lights (SALSR) are substituted for ALSF-1/2. In this case, you must use an automatic landing system (autoland) or a HUD to fly the airplane to touchdown. [Figure 5-31]

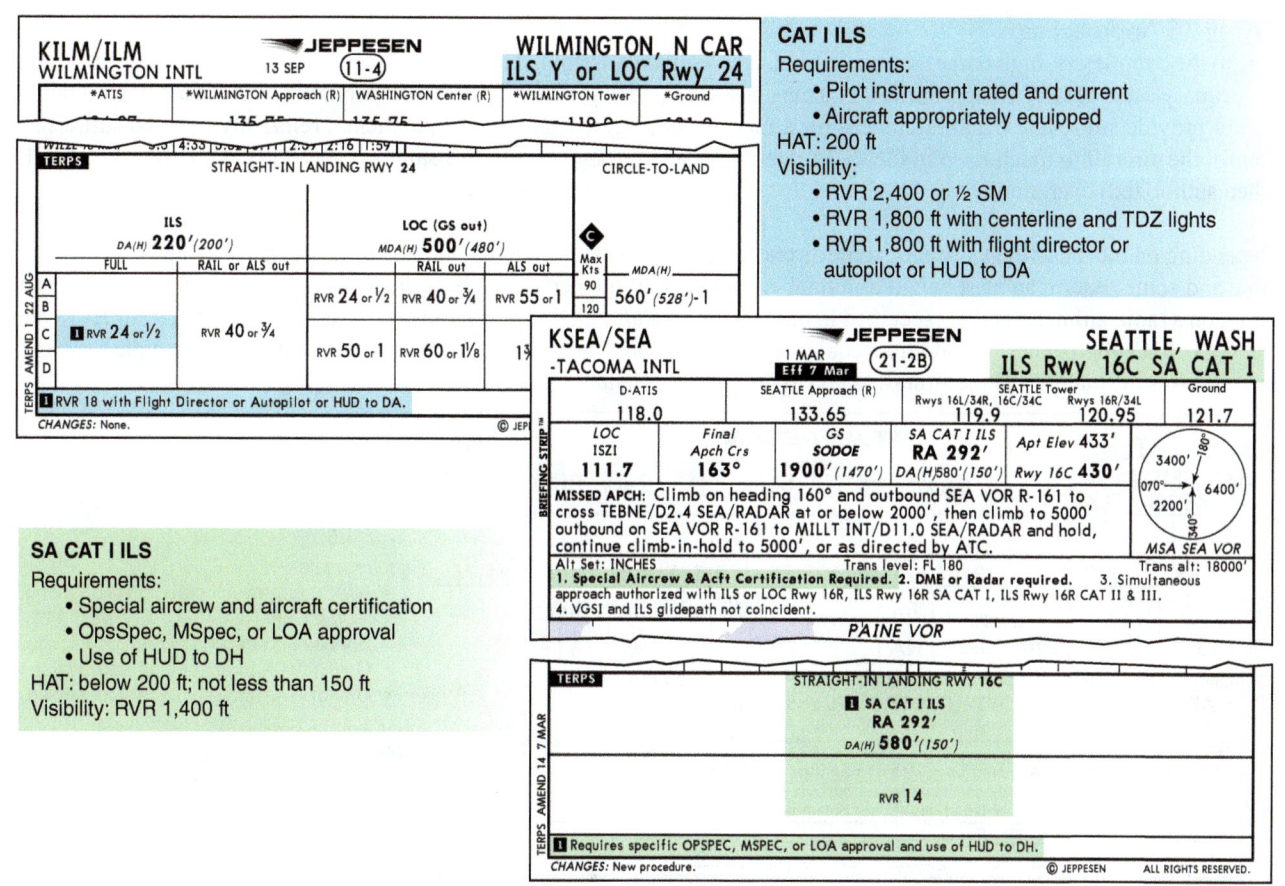

Figure 5-30. You must ensure that you and your aircraft meet the requirements to fly an SA CAT I ILS approach, which specifies lower landing minimums than a basic CAT I ILS.

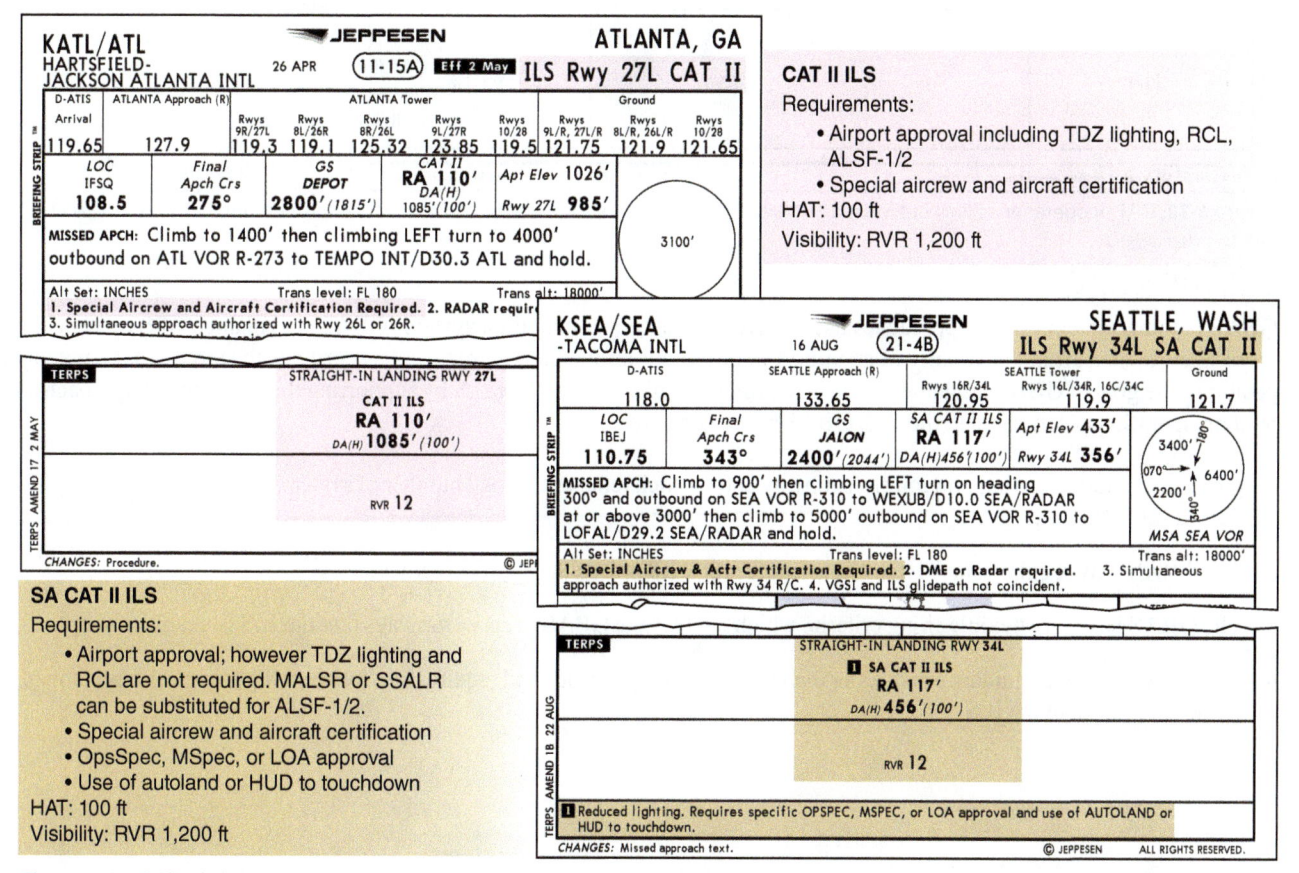

Figure 5-31. CAT II ILS approaches allow low landing minimums if the airport, operator, aircraft, and flight crew meet specific criteria. SA CAT II ILS approaches do not require the same runway lighting as standard CAT II approaches.

5-25

CAT III ILS Approaches

Due to the complexity, high cost of the equipment, and regulatory training requirements, air carrier and military operations are the primary users of CAT III approaches. You must use autoland to perform CAT III operations because the landing minimums do not provide sufficient visual references for a manual landing. The autoland equipment's reliability must be sufficient to control the aircraft to touchdown in CAT IIIA operations and through rollout to a safe taxi speed in CAT IIIB (and CAT IIIC when authorized) operations.

Depending on the auto-flight systems, some aircraft require a DH to ensure that the aircraft is going to land in the touchdown zone and some require an alert height as a final cross-check of the performance of the auto-flight systems. Alert heights are based on a radio altimeter and are specified in the specific aircraft POH/AFM. Because there is no minimum DH or RVR value for CAT IIIC approaches, in addition equipment and training requirements, the primary challenge to implement these operations is the inability of the aircraft to taxi to the gate after landing in this type of weather. [Figure 5-32]

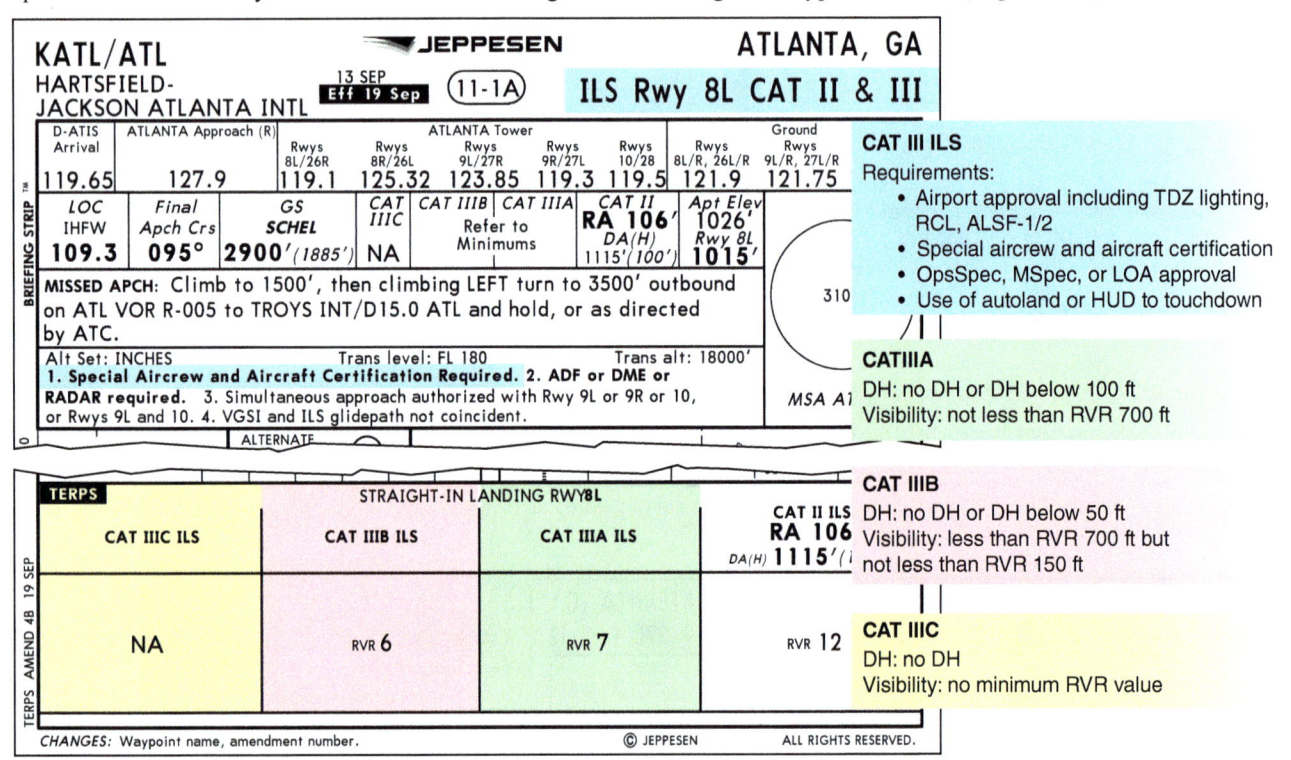

Figure 5-32. CAT III operations allow authorized aircrew and aircraft to perform instrument approaches in weather that would otherwise be prohibitive.

GLS APPROACH

GBAS landing system (GLS) approaches use the ground-based augmentation system (GBAS) to enhance GPS by providing corrections to aircraft in the vicinity of an airport in order to improve the accuracy and integrity of the aircraft's navigational position. The goal of GBAS implementation is to provide an alternative to the ILS by supporting the full range of approach and landing operations. Compared to the ILS, GBAS has several advantages:

- One GBAS station can support multiple runway ends, which reduces the total number of systems at an airport and simplifies airport infrastructure.

- The GBAS only requires one VHF assignment for up to 48 individual approach procedures.

- The GBAS has more flexible siting criteria, which enables the GBAS to serve runways that the ILS is unable to support.

- The GBAS approach guidance is steadier than ILS approach guidance and requires less frequent flight inspections compared to those required of the ILS.

The airport and aircraft equipment must be approved for GLS approach operations. GBAS can provide the required precision and integrity for GLS approaches with CAT I, II, and III minimums and for airport surface operations, such as low-visibility taxiing. [Figure 5-33]

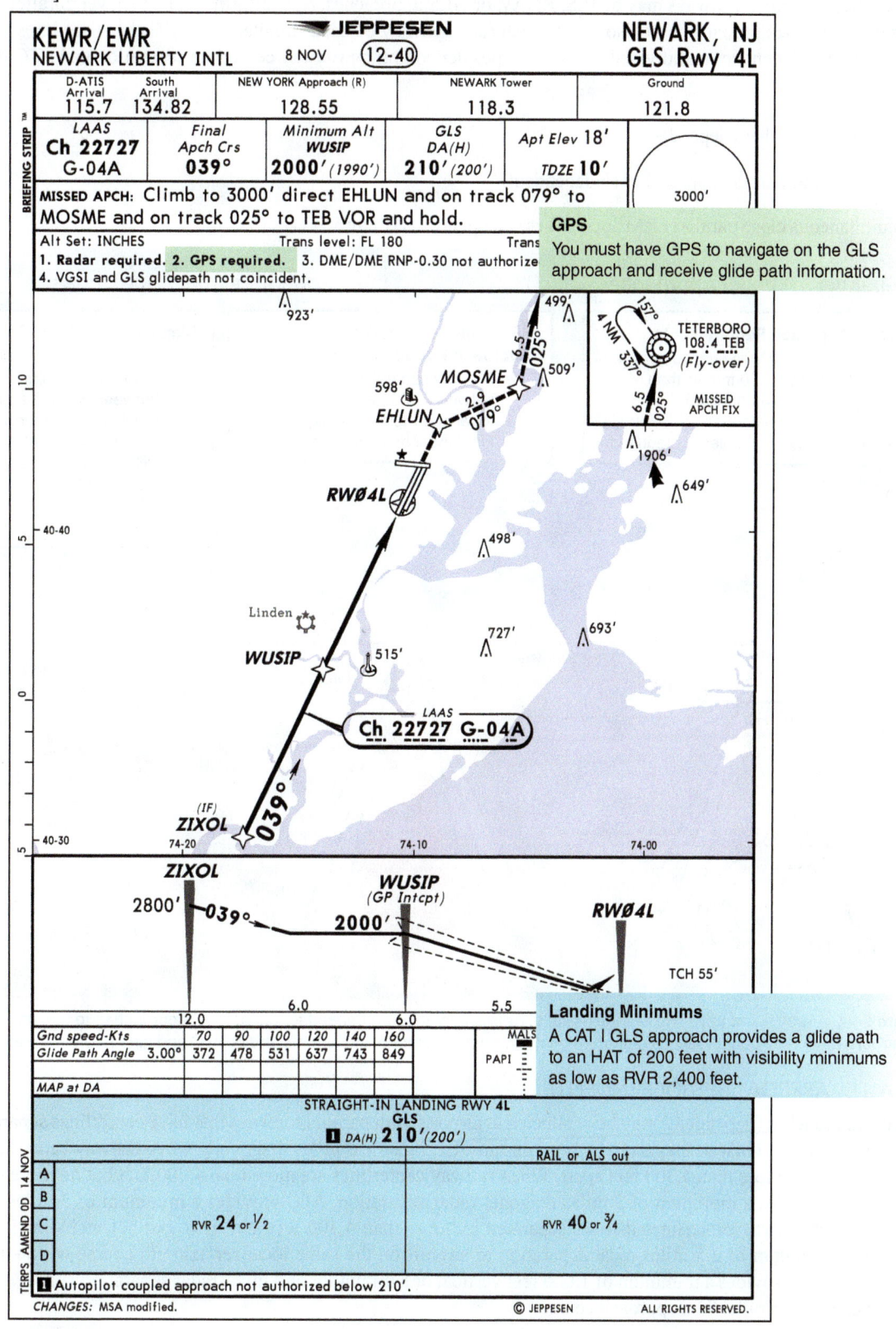

Figure 5-33. The GLS approach provides vertical guidance with navigational accuracy similar to an ILS.

5-27

PARALLEL APPROACHES

At airports that have two or three parallel runway configurations, approach operations may be authorized on each runway. Approaches to parallel runways may be ILS, RNAV, or GLS approaches. ATC informs you whenever parallel approaches are in progress and the approach chart also notes which runways may be used simultaneously. These procedures are classified as dependent or independent and divided into three types depending on runway centerline separation and ATC procedures and aircraft capabilities:

- Parallel approaches (dependent)
- Simultaneous parallel approaches (independent)
- Simultaneous close parallel PRM approaches (independent) [Figure 5-34]

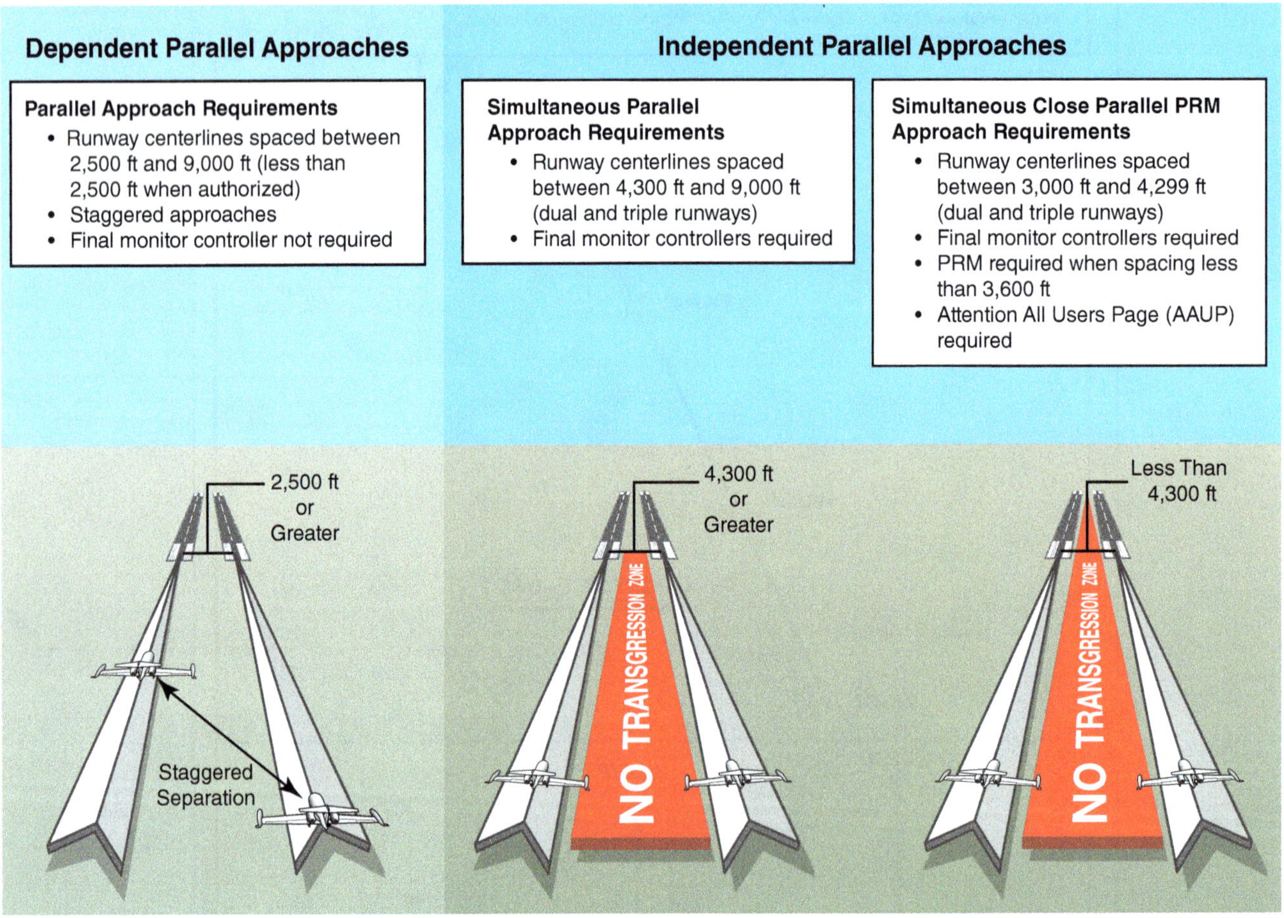

Dependent Parallel Approaches

Parallel Approach Requirements
- Runway centerlines spaced between 2,500 ft and 9,000 ft (less than 2,500 ft when authorized)
- Staggered approaches
- Final monitor controller not required

Independent Parallel Approaches

Simultaneous Parallel Approach Requirements
- Runway centerlines spaced between 4,300 ft and 9,000 ft (dual and triple runways)
- Final monitor controllers required

Simultaneous Close Parallel PRM Approach Requirements
- Runway centerlines spaced between 3,000 ft and 4,299 ft (dual and triple runways)
- Final monitor controllers required
- PRM required when spacing less than 3,600 ft
- Attention All Users Page (AAUP) required

Figure 5-34. Airports that have two or three parallel runways may be authorized to use parallel approaches to maximize the capacity of the airport. Each type of approach is determined by centerline separation minimums and by ATC and aircraft procedures.

PARALLEL APPROACHES (DEPENDENT)

Parallel approaches (dependent) may be conducted at airports with parallel runways that have centerlines separated by at least 2,500 feet. Aircraft must be staggered by a minimum of 1.5 nautical miles diagonally when runway centerlines are at least 2,500 feet but no more than 4,300 feet apart. When runway centerlines are more than 4,300 feet but no more than 9,000 feet apart, ATC provides a minimum of 2 miles diagonal radar separation. ATC provides a minimum of 2 miles diagonal radar separation for runway centerlines that are separated by more than 4,300 feet and up to but not including 9,000 feet. ATC provides a minimum of 2.5 miles radar separation to aircraft on the same localizer/azimuth course within 10 miles of the runway end and provides a minimum of 1,000 feet vertical or a minimum of 3 miles radar separation between aircraft during the turn on to the parallel final approach course.

SIMULTANEOUS PARALLEL APPROACHES (INDEPENDENT)

Simultaneous parallel approaches (independent) are used at authorized airports that have between 4,300 feet and 9,000 feet separation between runway centerlines. A dedicated final monitor controller provides no transgression zone (NTZ) monitoring to ensure separation between aircraft on the adjacent parallel approach course. The NTZ is an area 2,000 feet wide located equidistant between final approach courses. Final monitor controllers track aircraft positions and issue instructions to aircraft observed deviating from the assigned final approach course. NTZ monitoring eliminates the need for staggered approaches. ATC advises you if simultaneous approaches are in progress and the approach chart includes a note identifying the other runways or approaches that may be used simultaneously. You must advise approach control immediately of malfunctioning or inoperative receivers, or if a simultaneous approach is not desired. [Figure 5-35]

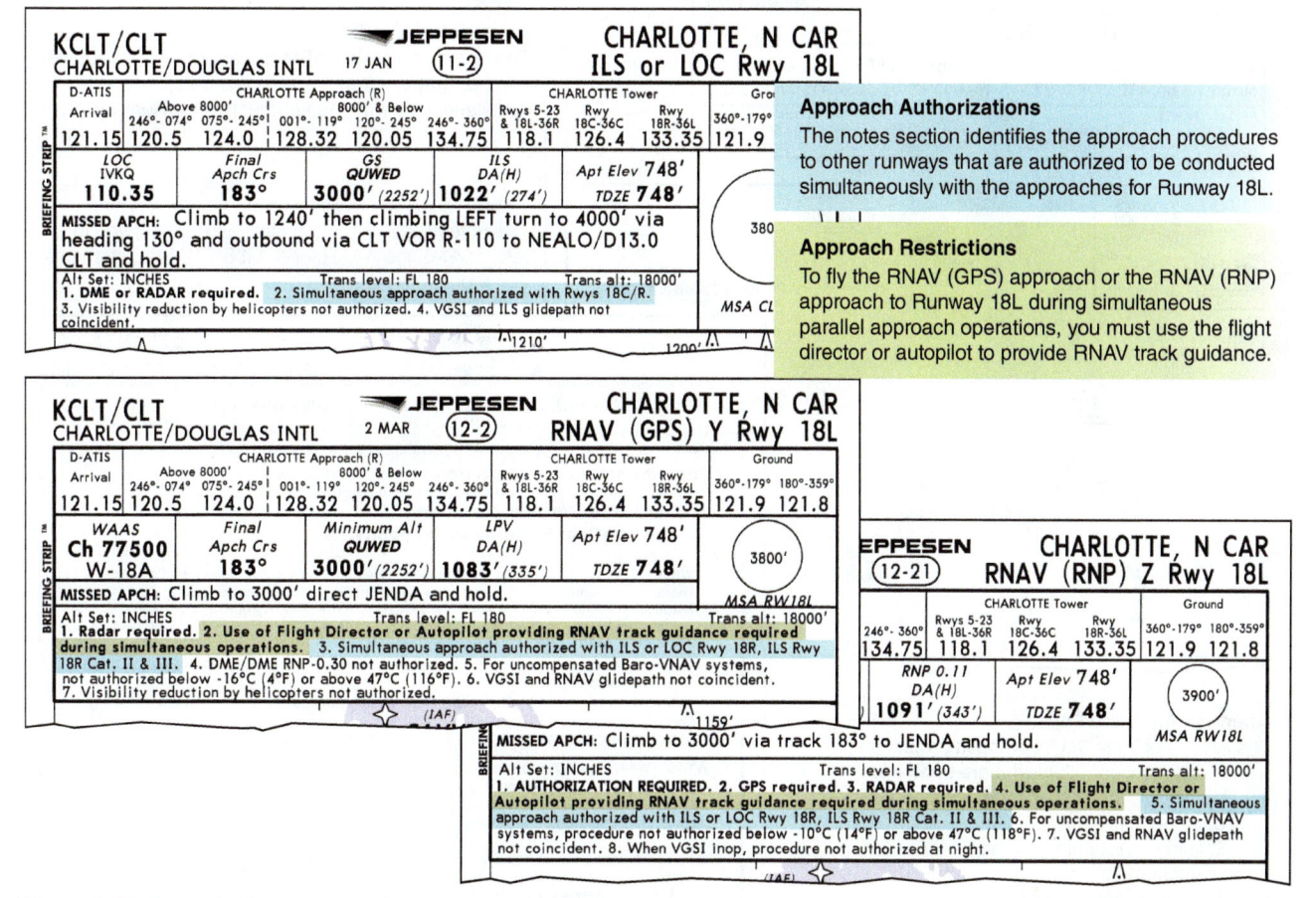

Figure 5-35. Several different types of simultaneous parallel approach procedures are authorized for Runway 18L at Charlotte/Douglas International Airport.

ATC provides 3 miles radar separation or a minimum of 1,000 feet vertical separation during the aircraft's turn on to parallel final approach. You must maintain the assigned altitude until you intercept the glide path, unless cleared otherwise by ATC. You will not be vectored to intercept the final approach course at an angle greater than 30°. If you are observed to overshoot the turn or continue a track that will penetrate the NTZ, the final monitor controller instructs you to return to the final approach course immediately or issues missed approach or breakout instructions. If a deviating aircraft fails to respond to instructions or penetrates the NTZ, ATC issues a breakout instruction to the aircraft on the adjacent final approach course. These are examples of ATC instructions when aircraft deviate during a simultaneous parallel approach procedure:

- Return to Final Instruction – *"Airline Flight 123, you have crossed the final approach course. Turn right immediately and return to the final approach course."* Or *"Airline Flight 123, turn right and return to the final course."*

- Breakout Instruction – *"Traffic alert, Airline Flight 123, turn left immediately heading 230 degrees, climb and maintain 4,000."*

SIMULTANEOUS CLOSE PARALLEL PRM APPROACHES (INDEPENDENT)

Simultaneous close parallel PRM approaches (independent) are conducted to parallel runways with centerlines separated by less than 3,600 feet but by at least 3,400 feet for parallel approach courses, and at least 3,000 feet if one approach course is offset by 2.5° to 3.0°. The precision runway monitor (PRM) system incorporates high-update radar with one second or better update time and a high resolution ATC radar display that contains automated tracking software that can track aircraft in real time. During the approach, the PRM system updates aircraft position and velocity each second and displays a ten second projected position. The system also incorporates visual and aural alerts for the controllers. The PRM approaches require an IAP chart and an Attention All Users Page (AAUP) with a textual description of pilot, aircraft, and procedure requirements necessary to participate in PRM operations. [Figure 5-36]

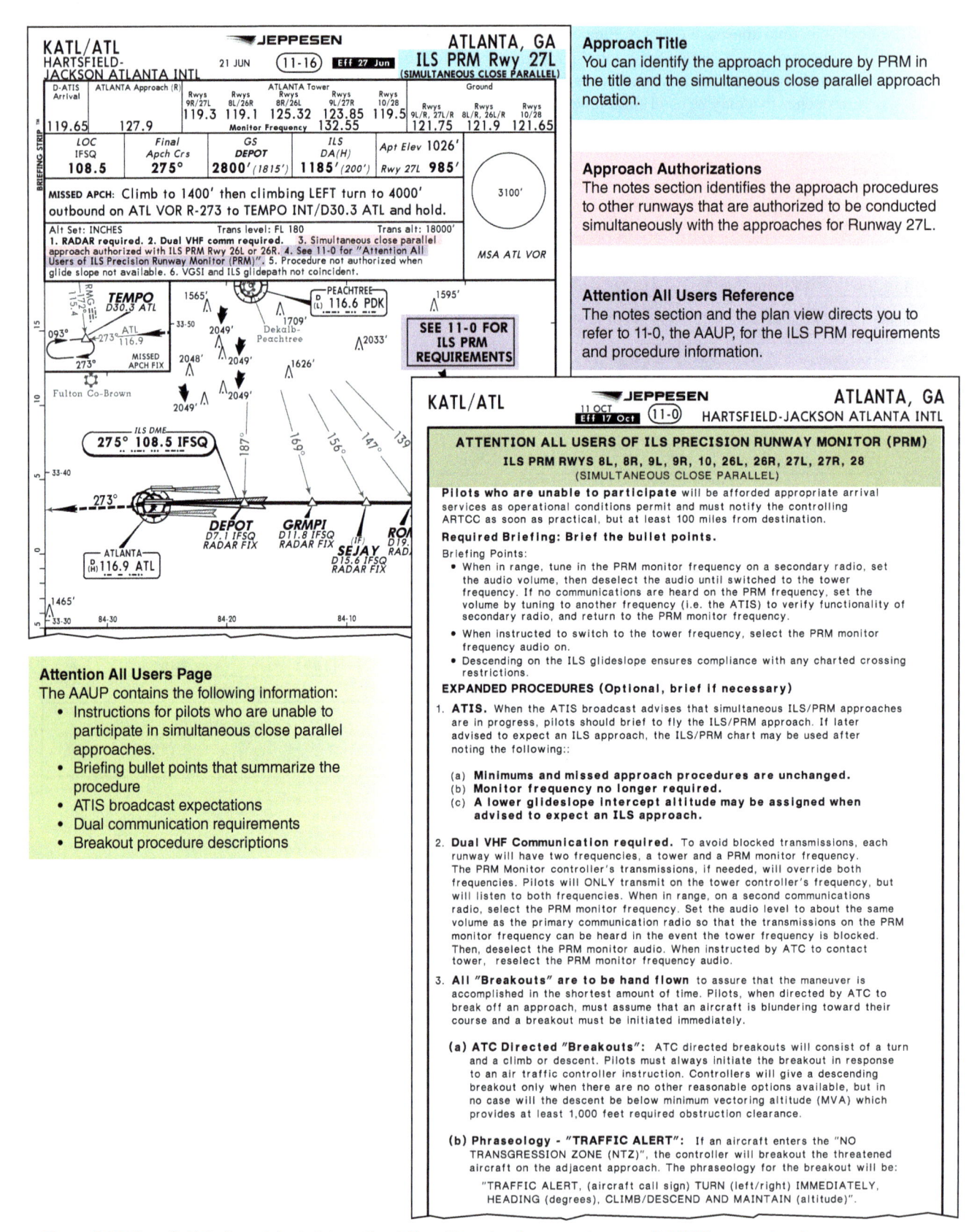

Figure 5-36. Hartsfield-Jackson Atlanta International Airport has simultaneous close parallel PRM approaches to numerous runways.

Simultaneous Offset Instrument Approaches

Simultaneous offset instrument approaches (SOIAs) are classified as simultaneous close parallel PRM approaches. SOIAs allow simultaneous approaches to two parallel runways spaced apart by at least 750 feet but less than 3,000 feet. The SOIA procedure uses an ILS PRM, RNAV PRM or GLS PRM approach to one runway and an offset localizer-type directional aid (LDA) PRM approach with glide slope to the adjacent runway. The procedures and system requirements for SOIA approaches are identical to those used for a typical simultaneous close parallel PRM approach until you near the MAP if you are flying the LDA PRM approach. At the MAP, you must visually acquire the aircraft on the adjacent approach path to then fly a visual segment to landing. The approach charts used in SOIA operations are identical to other PRM approach charts but show a note that provides the separation between the two runways for simultaneous approaches. The LDA PRM approach chart displays the required notations for closely spaced approaches as well as depicting the visual segment of the approach. [Figure 5-37]

Approach Authorizations
The notes section identifies the approach procedures to other runways that are authorized to be conducted simultaneously.

SOIA Reference
A note that provides the separation between the two runways used for simultaneous approaches indicates that this procedure can be conducted as a simultaneous offset instrument approach.

LDA PRM Visual Segment
The LDA PRM approach chart depicts the visual segment of the approach on the plan view and profile view of the approach chart. Procedures for flying the visual segment are also indicated on the AAUP.

LDA PRM Landing Minimums
The LDA PRM landing minimums must be at least a 1,000-foot ceiling and 4 SM visibility. These minimums give you time to see the aircraft on the adjacent approach course and to establish a stabilized descent to the runway on the visual segment of the approach.

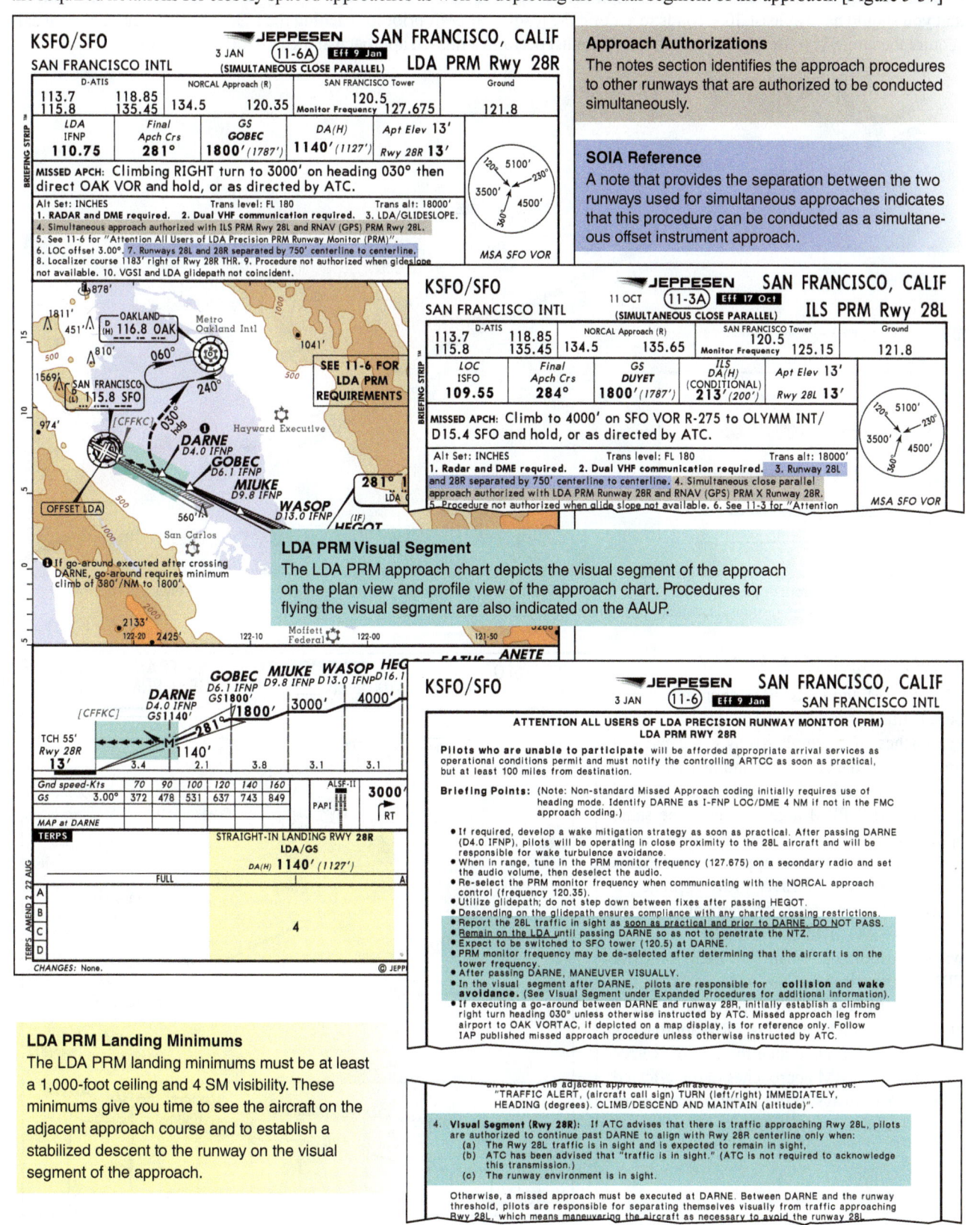

Figure 5-37. The ILS PRM Rwy 28L is paired with the LDA PRM Rwy 28R at San Francisco International Airport as simultaneous offset instrument approaches.

In SOIA operations, aircraft are paired, with the aircraft conducting the LDA PRM approach always positioned slightly behind the aircraft on the adjacent approach path. If you are flying the LDA PRM approach, transition in visual conditions from the LDA MAP to align with the runway so you can stabilize your approach by 500 feet AGL on the extended runway centerline. This point is referred to as the stabilized approach point (SAP)—a design point along the extended centerline of the intended landing runway on the glide slope at 500 feet above the landing threshold. A cloud ceiling for the approach is established so that you should have at least 30 seconds to acquire the leading aircraft prior to reaching the LDA MAP. If you do not visually acquire the aircraft on the adjacent approach, you must perform a missed approach at the MAP. [Figure 5-38]

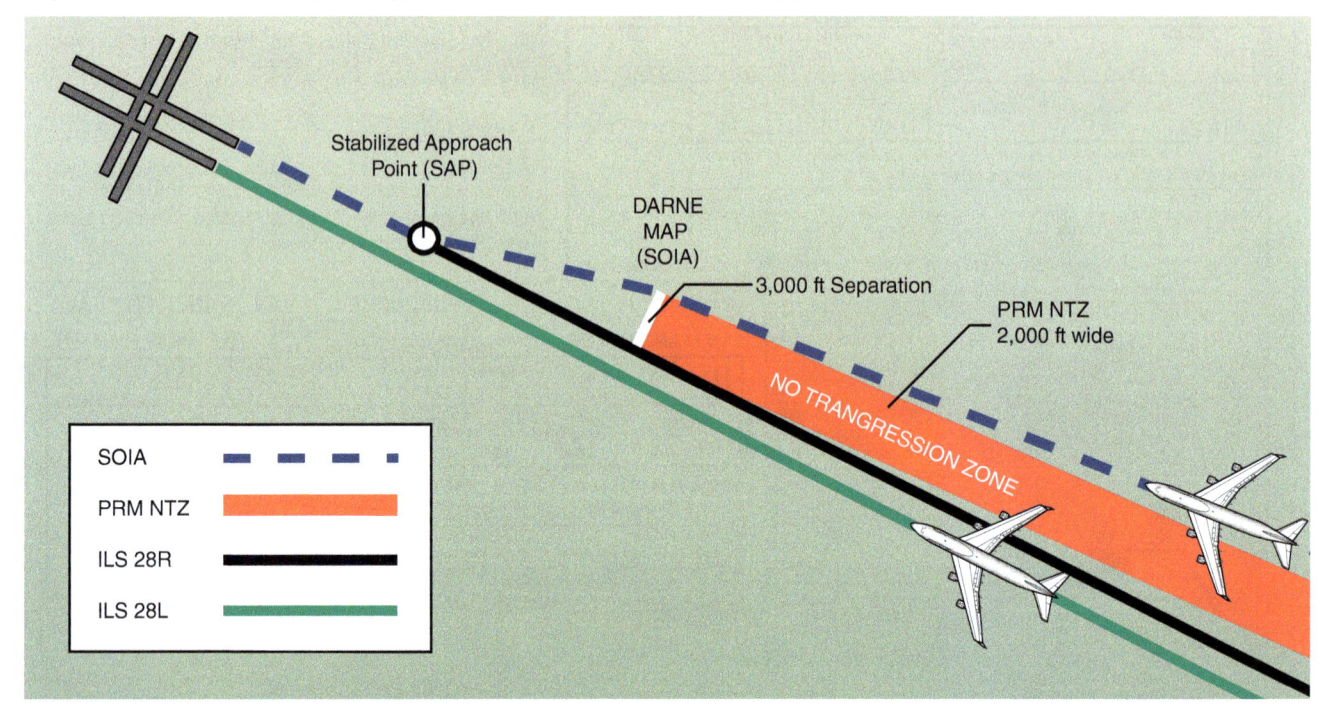

Figure 5-38. This diagram depicts SOIA operations at San Francisco International Airport. Compared to the ILS Rwy 28R course, the LDA Rwy 28R course provides greater aircraft separation during most of the approach.

RNAV PRM and GLS PRM Options

RNAV PRM and GLS PRM approaches may be substituted for: one or both of the ILS PRM approaches in a simultaneous close parallel operation, or the ILS PRM and/or LDA PRM approach in a SOIA operation. An RNAV PRM or GLS PRM approach uses the same applicable notations and the same fixes, crossing altitudes, and missed approach procedures as the ILS PRM or LDA PRM approach it overlays. You must use the vertical guidance for the RNAV PRM or GLS PRM approach when substituting for an ILS PRM or LDA PRM approach. You may request to fly the RNAV PRM or GLS PRM approach in lieu of either the ILS PRM and LDA PRM approaches and ATIS might announce the use of RNAV PRM or GLS PRM approaches to the effected runway or runways in the event of the loss of ground based navaids. [Figure 5-39]

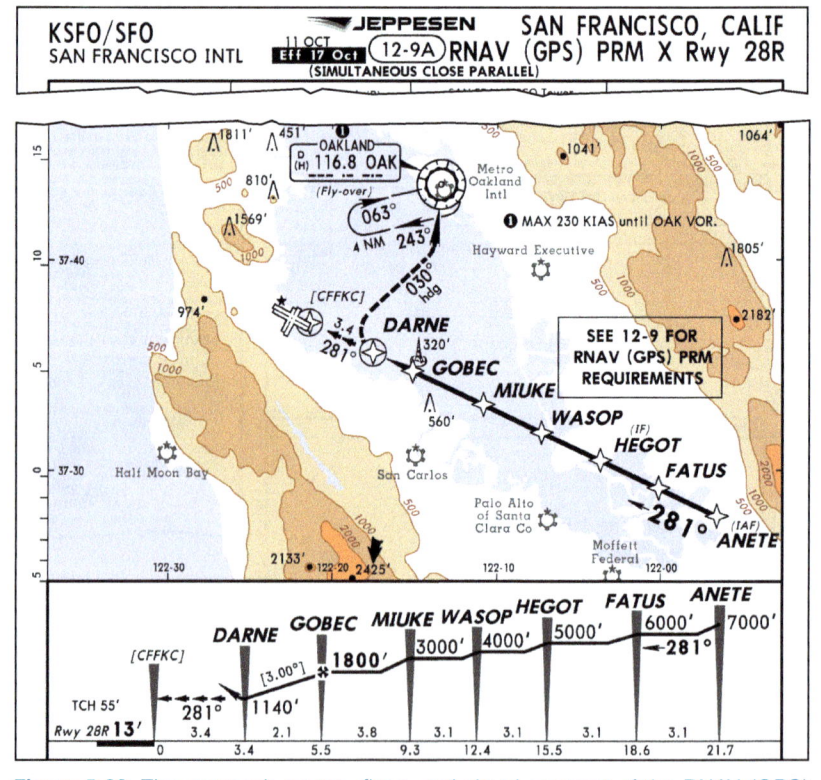

Figure 5-39. The approach course, fixes, and visual segment of the RNAV (GPS) PRM approach to Runway 28R at San Francisco International Airport match those of the LDA PRM approach to this runway.

FMS coding of a SOIA RNAV PRM or GLS PRM approach is different than other RNAV and GLS approach coding. The charted MAP and the FMS-coded MAP, which is the fictitious threshold waypoint (FTP), are not collocated. The FTP is designated in the approach coding as the MAP so that vertical guidance is available to the runway threshold. You may use vertical guidance for situational awareness in the visual segment of the approach. As a result of coding the FTP as the MAP, you must initially fly a heading manually or with the autopilot in heading mode before engaging LNAV when performing a missed approach at or past the charted MAP. Notes on the approach chart and on the AAUP make specific reference to this procedure.

Be aware that the charted MAP is coded as a stepdown fix and some FMSs do not display stepdown fixes inside the FAF. Use the distance from the FTP as shown on the approach chart, or other approved method, to identify the location of the charted MAP. Follow the charted IAP guidance not the map display.

PRM Approach Requirements

Approval for simultaneous close parallel PRM approaches requires that the airport have a PRM system and a final monitor controller who can only communicate with aircraft on the final approach course. Additionally, two tower frequencies are required and the controller broadcasts over both frequencies to reduce the chance of instructions being missed. You must obtain special training before you can accept a clearance for a PRM approach. Part 121 and 135 operators must complete FAA-approved company training that includes the viewing of videos available from the FAA. Advise ATC within 200 nautical miles of the landing airport if you are not qualified or not equipped to fly a PRM approach. Some guidelines that apply to flying PRM approaches are:

- Immediately follow breakout instructions as soon as safety permits.

- Listen to both tower frequencies to avoid missed instructions from stuck mikes or blocked transmissions. The final ATC controller can override the tower frequency if necessary.

- Broadcast only over the main tower frequency.

- Disengage the autopilot for breakouts because hand-flown breakouts are quicker.

- Although the ATC breakout instruction is the primary means of conflict resolution, if you receive a TCAS resolution advisory (RA), immediately follow the TCAS instructions.

SIMULTANEOUS CONVERGING APPROACHES

Simultaneous converging approaches may be established at airports that have runways with an angle between 15° and 100° and each runway must have an ILS. Additionally, separate procedures must be established for each approach and each approach must have a MAP at least 3 nautical miles apart with no overlapping of the protected missed approach airspace. Only straight-in landings are approved for converging ILS procedures. If the runways intersect, the controller must be able to visually separate intersecting runway traffic. Approaches to intersecting runways also have higher minimums; a 700-foot minimum ceiling and no less than 2 statute miles visibility. ATC informs you that converging ILS approaches are being conducted upon initial contact or through ATIS. [Figure 5-40]

LOCALIZER APPROACHES

You might fly the localizer-only portion of an ILS approach if the glide slope is out of service or you cannot, or choose not to, use glide slope guidance. In other cases, you might fly a nonprecision approach specifically designed to use a localizer transmitter without a glide-slope indication. The localizer is able to provide four separate applications from one approach system:

- Localizer approach

- Localizer/DME approach

- Localizer back course approach

- LDA approach

Approach Title
The approach chart title indicates that this is a converging approach.

Approach Authorizations
The notes section indicates that this approach is authorized to be flown simultaneously with the converging ILS Rwy 31R approach and the plan view identifies Runway 31R with the ILS symbol.

Straight-in Landing
Only straight-in landings are approved for converging ILS procedures. No circling minimums are published.

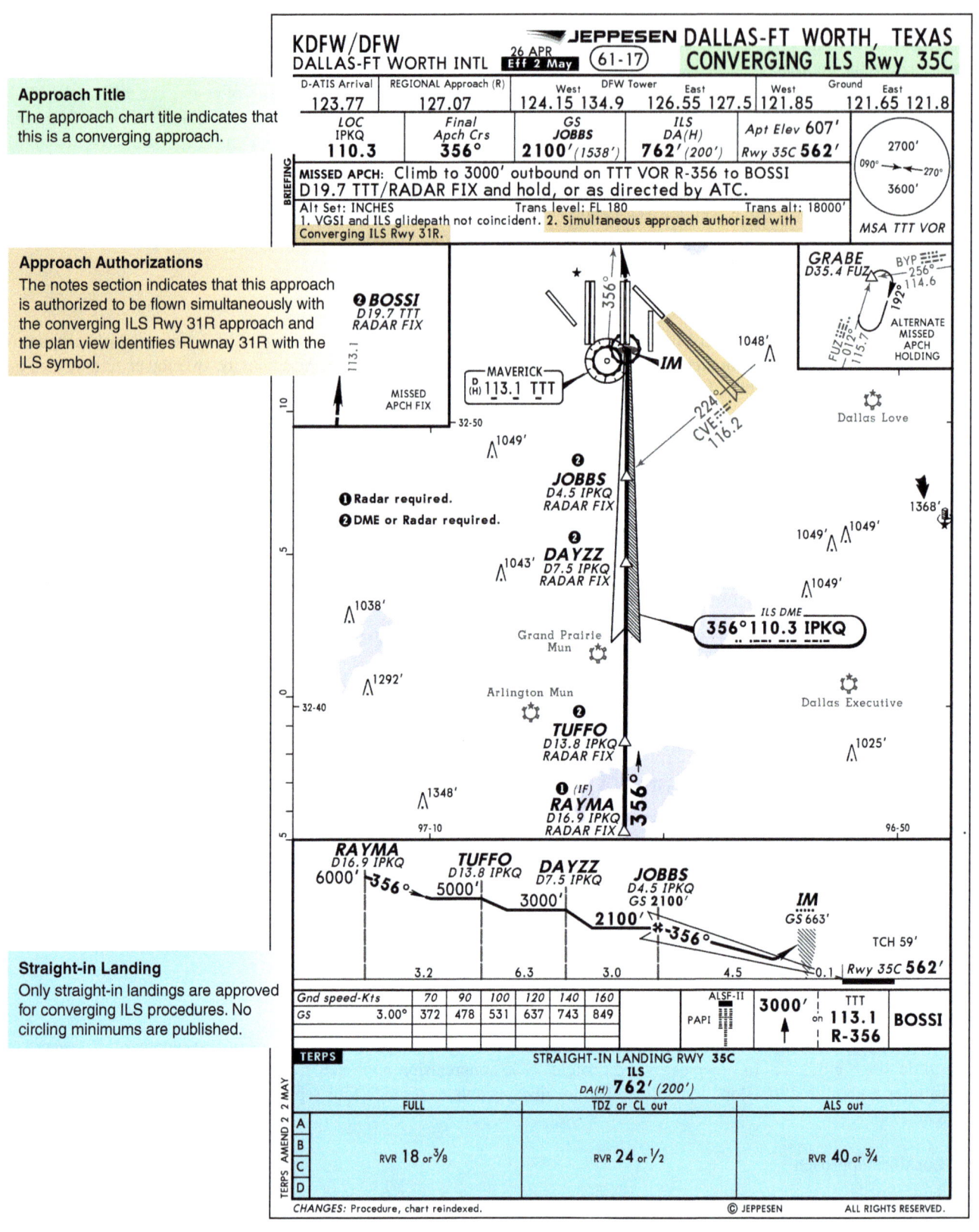

Figure 5-40. Dallas/Fort Worth International Airport makes use of converging ILS approaches because its runway configuration has multiple parallel runways and two offset runways.

LOCALIZER AND LOCALIZER DME

TERPS provides the same alignment criteria for a localizer approach as it does for the ILS because it is essentially the same approach without glide slope vertical guidance. A localizer is always aligned within 3° of the runway, and it is afforded a minimum of 250 feet obstacle clearance in the final approach area. In the case of a LOC DME approach, the localizer installation has a collocated DME installation that provides distance information required for the approach. [Figure 5-41]

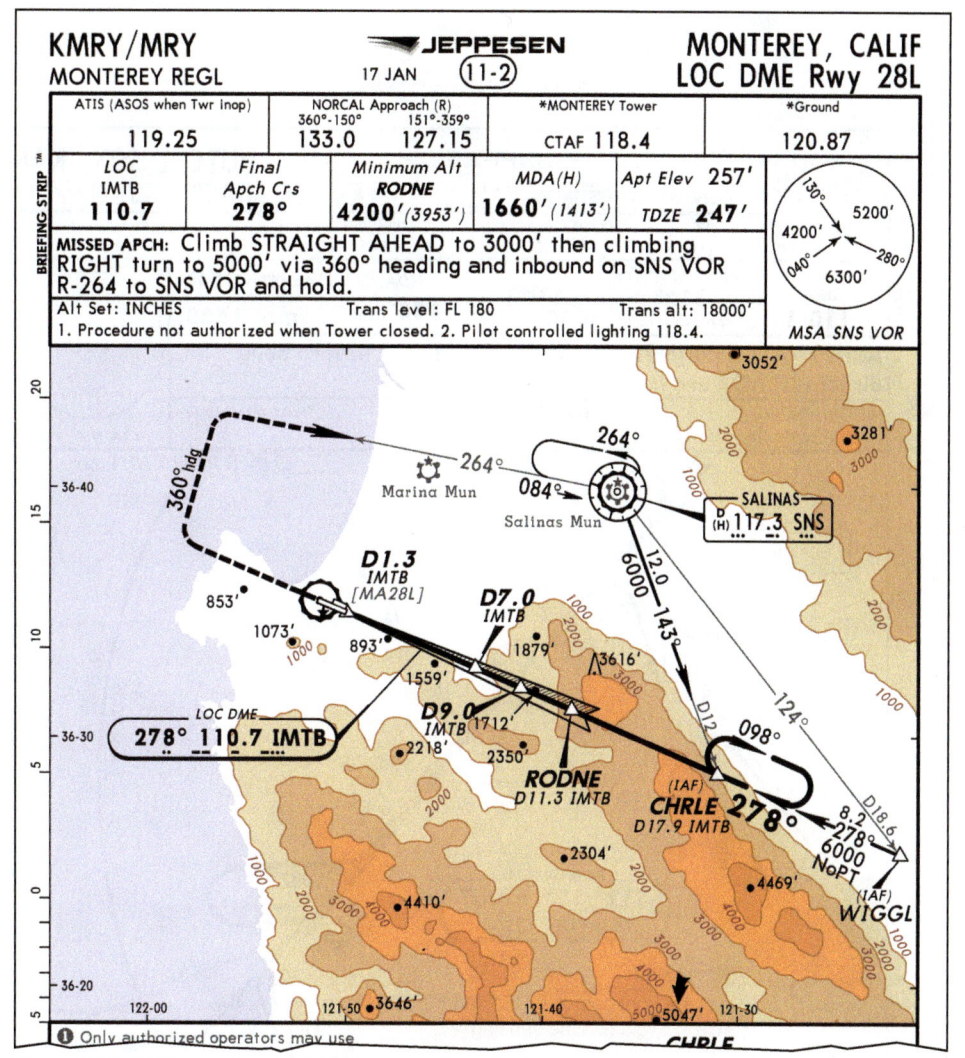

Figure 5-41. High terrain prohibits the use of a ILS glide slope to Runway 28L in Monterey. When flying the localizer approach, you descend to an MDA of 1,660 feet MSL which is 1,413 feet above touchdown.

LOCALIZER BACK COURSE

In locations where an ILS is installed, a back course might be available in conjunction with the localizer. Like the localizer approach, a localizer back course approach does not offer a glide slope, but the back course can project a false glide-slope signal and the glide slope should be ignored. Reverse sensing occurs on the back course using standard VOR equipment. With an HSI (horizontal situation indicator), reverse sensing is eliminated if you set the HSI to the front course. [Figure 5-42]

LOCALIZER-TYPE DIRECTIONAL AID

The localizer-type directional aid (LDA) provides the navigational accuracy of a localizer but the course alignment with the runway exceeds 3°. Although LDA installations do not typically incorporate a glide slope component, LDA PRM approaches (discussed earlier in this chapter) used in conjunction with other approach procedures during SIOAs incorporate a glide slope and a visual component. The availability of a glide slope associated with an LDA is noted on the approach chart.

VOR APPROACH

VOR approaches are nonprecision approaches that use VOR facilities both on and off the airport and can provide MDAs as low as 250 feet above the runway. VOR approaches with on-airport VORs might not have a charted FAF. In this case, the final approach segment begins when you intercept the final approach course inbound after completing the procedure turn. VOR approach procedures often use DME to define approach fixes. When DME is included in the title of the VOR approach, you must have operable DME installed in the aircraft in order to fly the approach from the FAF. [Figure 5-43]

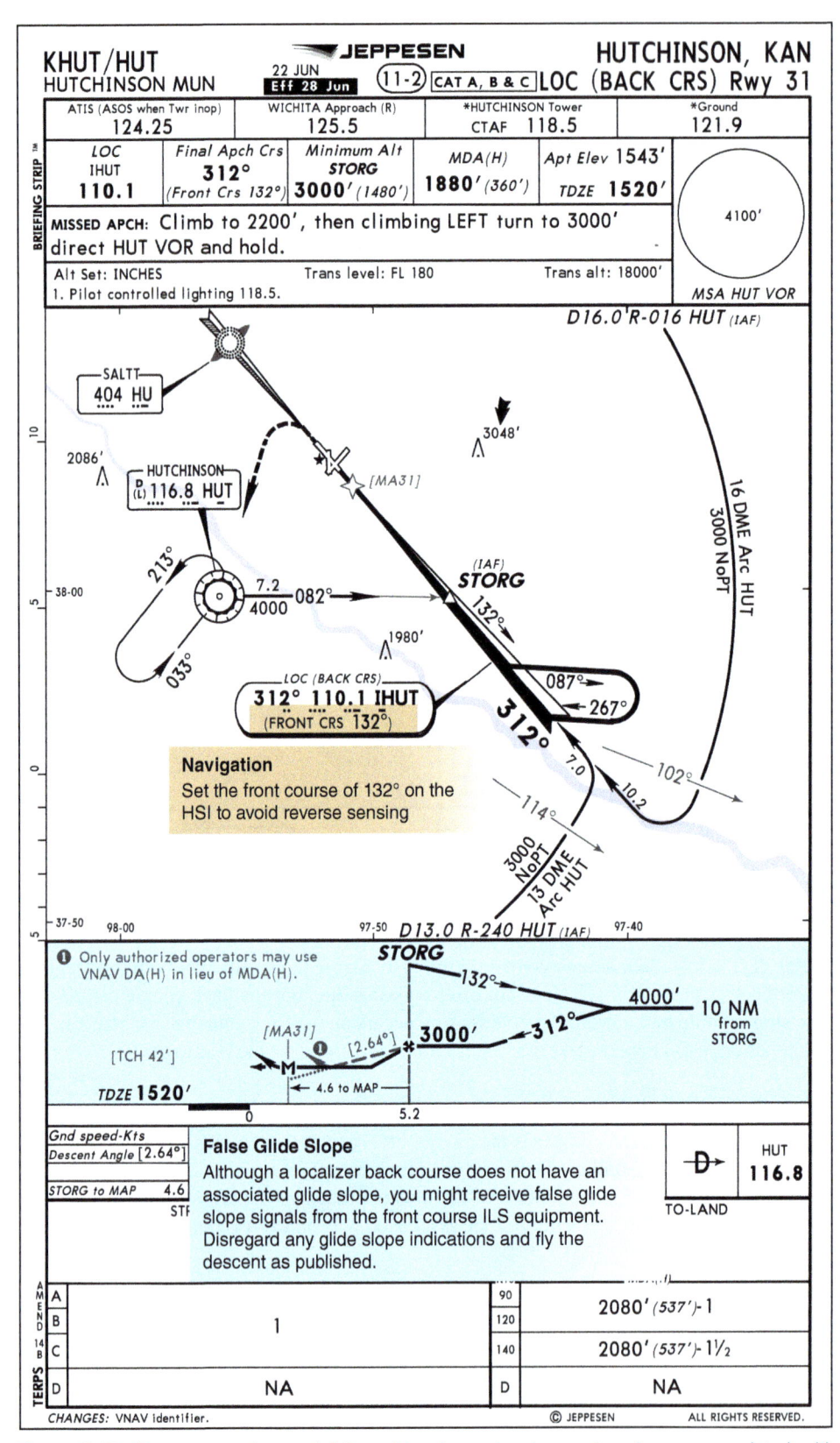

Figure 5-42. Reverse sensing and false glide slope signals are two issues associated with LOC (BACK CRS) approaches.

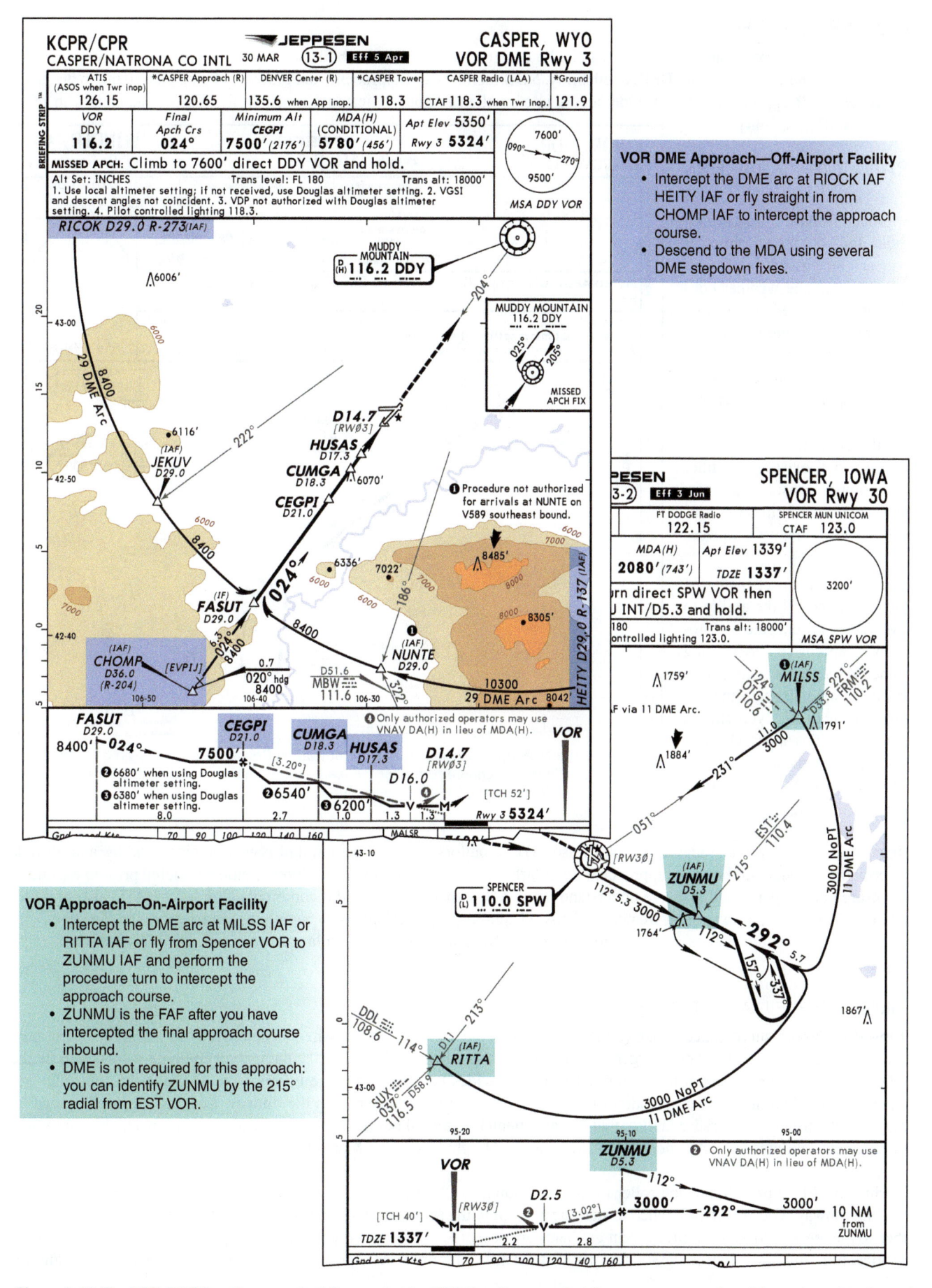

Figure 5-43. The VOR DME Rwy 3 approach at Casper and the VOR Rwy 3 approach at Spencer are examples of the variety of designs of VOR approach procedures based on the location of the VOR and whether DME is required for the procedure.

5-37

NDB APPROACH

Like the VOR approach, an NDB approach can be designed using facilities both on and off the airport, with or without a charted FAF, and with or without DME availability. NDB facilities and approaches are gradually being phased out in the NAS. However, NDB approaches still provide access into smaller, remotely located airports in the United States and in other countries. [Figure 5-44]

RADAR APPROACHES

You may request a radar approach or ATC might offer a radar approach as an option if you are an aircraft in distress regardless of the weather conditions, or as necessary to expedite traffic. Despite the control exercised by ATC in a radar approach environment, it is your responsibility to ensure the landing minimums listed for the approach are appropriate for the existing weather conditions considering personal approach criteria certification and company OpsSpecs.

Perhaps the greatest benefit of a radar approach is the ability to use radar to execute a "no-gyro" approach. Assuming standard rate turns, a controller indicates when to begin and end turns. If available, you should make use of this approach when the heading indicator has failed and you must fly with a partial panel.

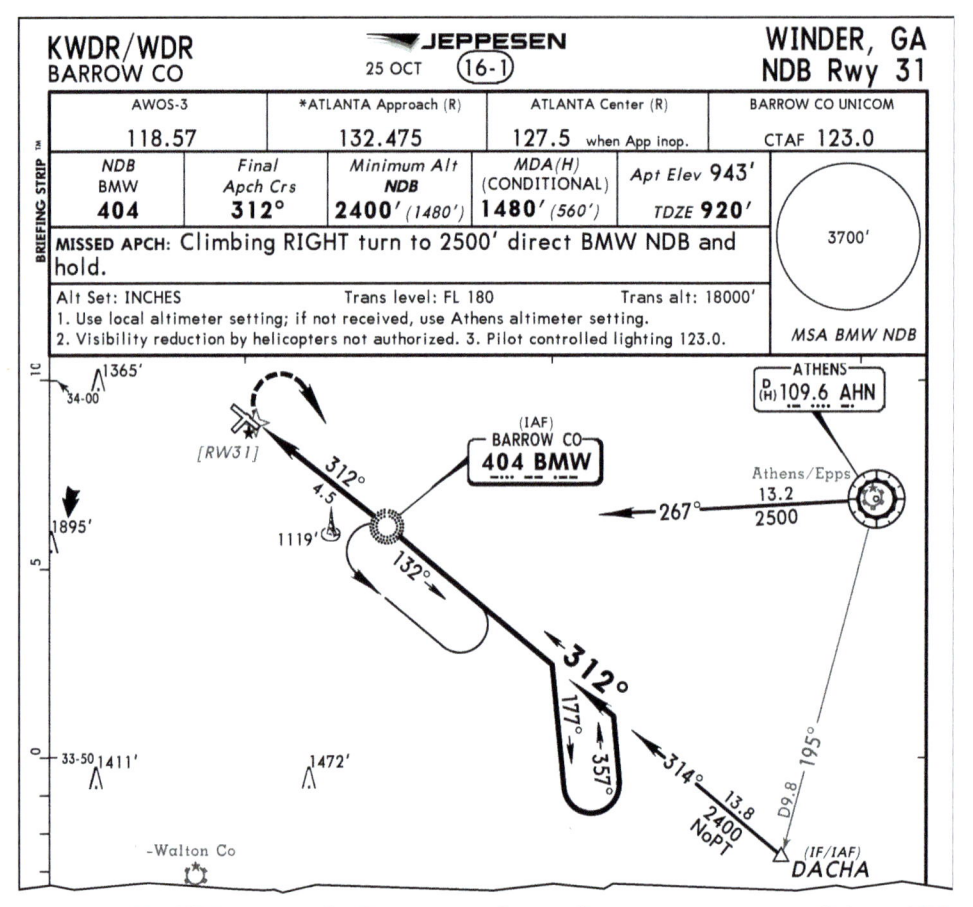

Figure 5-44. The NDB approach for Runway 31 at Barrow County airport uses an off-airport NDB facility. You can fly the procedure turn after intercepting the outbound course from the NDB or fly directly from DACHA to intercept the approach course.

Regardless of the type of radar approach in use, ATC monitors aircraft position and issues specific heading and altitude information throughout the entire approach. Particularly, lost communication procedures should be briefed prior to execution to ensure you have a comprehensive understanding of ATC expectations if radio communication is lost. ATC also provides additional information concerning weather and missed approach instructions when beginning a radar approach. The two types of radar approach procedures available to you in the NAS are airport surveillance radar and precision approach radar approaches.

AIRPORT SURVEILLANCE RADAR

Typically, airport surveillance radar (ASR) approaches are only approved when necessitated for an ATC operational requirement, or in an unusual or emergency situation, such as when you have lost the navigation equipment needed to fly the other instrument approaches at the airport. ASR only provides heading and range information, although the controller can advise you of the altitude where the aircraft should be based on the distance from the runway. An ASR approach procedure may be established at any radar facility that has an antenna within 20 nautical miles of the airport and meets the equipment requirements outlined in FAA Order 8200.1 U.S. Standard Flight Inspection Manual.

During an ASR approach, the controller furnishes headings to fly to align your aircraft with the extended centerline of the landing runway. You are advised when to start the descent to the MDA or, if appropriate, to an intermediate stepdown fix and then to the prescribed MDA. ASR descent gradients are designed to be relatively flat, with an optimal gradient of 150 feet per nautical mile and never exceeding 300 feet per nautical mile. Normally, ATC provides navigation guidance until your aircraft reaches the MAP. At the MAP, ATC terminates guidance and instructs you to execute a missed approach unless you have reported the runway environment in sight. Also, if at any time during the approach the controller considers that safe guidance for the remainder of the approach cannot be provided, guidance is terminated and you are instructed to execute a missed approach. Radar service is automatically terminated at the completion of the approach. [Figure 5-45]

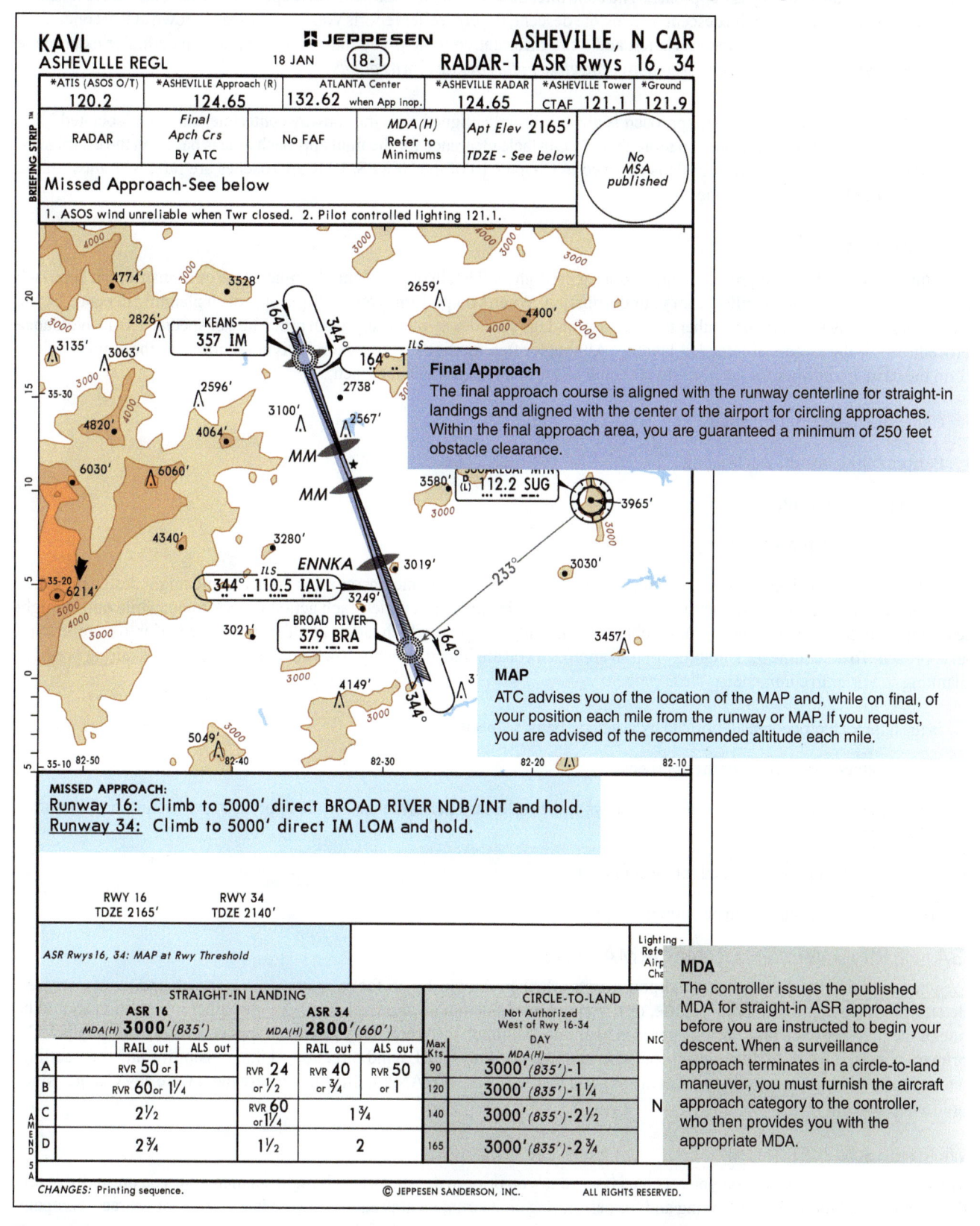

Figure 5-45. The ASR approach is typically available only as a backup procedure. The ASR procedure and landing minimums are published on an approach chart for reference.

PRECISION APPROACH RADAR

Precision approach radar (PAR) provides both vertical and lateral guidance, as well as range, much like an ILS, making it the most precise radar approach available. The controller assigns headings to align your aircraft with the runway centerline and to keep you on the course during the approach. The controller advises you of glide path intercept 10 to 30 seconds before it occurs and you are told when to start the descent. During the descent, the controller reports your range to touchdown at least once each mile and provides you with course deviation and trend information to help you maintain the approach path. For example, a controller might report that you are *"well above the glide path, coming down rapidly."*

The final approach course of a PAR approach is always directly aligned with the runway centerline, and the associated glide slope is typically no less than 2° and no more than 3°. Obstacle clearance for the final approach area is based on the established glide slope angle and the exact formula is outlined in Chapter 10 of the TERPS. PAR approaches are rare, with most of the approaches used in a military setting.

APPROACH PLANNING

Accomplish some of your approach planning during preflight and begin the in-flight planning phase of an instrument approach as far as 100 to 200 nautical miles from your destination. When you perform your in-flight approach planning depends on the aircraft's speed, availability of weather information, and the complexity of the approach procedure or special terrain avoidance procedures for the airport of intended landing. Although often modified to suit each individual operator, these four actions form the basic framework for the in-flight planning phase of an instrument approach:

- Gathering weather information.
- Performing an operational briefing.
- Setting up equipment.
- Performing an approach briefing

The extent of detail a given company includes in their SOPs varies from one operator to another; some might designate which pilot performs each of the above actions, the sequence, and the manner in which each action is performed, while others might leave much of the detail up to individual flight crews and only designate which tasks should be performed prior to commencing an approach. To determine the suitability of a an approach you are intending to fly, ask yourself these questions during preflight planning and prior to commencing the approach:

- Is the approach procedure authorized by your company's OpSpecs?
- Is the weather appropriate for the approach?
- Is the aircraft currently at a weight that allows it the necessary performance for the approach and landing or go around/ missed approach?
- Is the aircraft properly equipped for the approach?
- Am I qualified and current to perform the approach?

GATHERING WEATHER INFORMATION

Weather conditions at the destination airport dictate whether you must plan for an instrument approach and, in many cases, determine which approaches you can use, or if you can even attempt an approach. Gathering weather information should be one of the first steps you take during approach planning. Although there are many possible types of weather information, the primary concerns for in-flight approach decision making are wind speed, wind direction, ceiling, visibility, altimeter setting, temperature, and runway conditions. It is also a good idea to check NOTAMs at this time in case there were any changes since preflight planning.

WEATHER SOURCES

Most of the weather information you receive is issued to you prior to the start of each flight segment, but you normally obtain the weather used for in-flight planning and for performing an instrument approach enroute via government sources, company frequency, or the aircraft communications addressing and reporting system (ACARS).

Air carriers and operators certificated under the provisions of Part 119 (Certification: Air Carriers and Commercial Operators) are required to use the aeronautical weather information systems defined in the OpsSpecs issued to that certificate holder by the FAA. These systems may use basic FAA/National Weather Service (NWS) weather services, contractor or operator-proprietary weather services and/or the enhanced weather information system (EWINS) when approved in the OpsSpecs. As an integral part of EWINS approval, the procedures for collecting, producing, and disseminating aeronautical weather information, as well as the crewmember and dispatcher training to support the use of system weather products, must be accepted or approved. Operators not certificated under the provisions of Part 119 are encouraged to use FAA/NWS products through flight service, direct user access terminal system (DUATS), or the meteorological and aeronautical information (AIS) data link.

The suite of available aviation weather product types is always expanding with the development of new sensor systems, algorithms, and forecast models. The FAA and NWS, supported by the National Center for Atmospheric Research (NCAR) and the Forecast Systems Laboratory, develop and implement new aviation weather product types through a comprehensive process known as the Aviation Weather Technology Transfer (AWTT) process. This process ensures that user needs and technical and operational readiness requirements are met as experimental product types mature to operational application.

WEATHER SOURCE CONSIDERATIONS

Be aware that weather services provided by entities other than the FAA, NWS, or their contractors may not meet FAA/NWS quality control standards. Be aware of the risk of misunderstandings due to nonstandard displays of weather information, incorrect mapping of data, missing data, or an inaccurate time stamp on the product. Therefore, if you are contemplating using such services, consider the following in determining the suitability of the service or product:

- Does the service or product provide all the information that is necessary to make effective aeronautical weather decisions?

- Does the service provide data/products produced by approved aviation weather information sources?

- Is the data or product modified? If so, is the modification process described, and is the final product in a configuration that supports aeronautical weather decision making?

- Are the weather products professionally produced or quality-controlled by a aviation meteorologist?

- Does the provider's quality assurance plan include monitoring generated products and correcting deficiencies as they are discovered?

- Is the product output consistent with original data sources?

- Are education and training materials sufficient to enable you to use the product effectively?

- Are the following key elements of the product intuitive and easy to interpret?

    ○ Type of data/product.

    ○ Currency or age of data/product.

    ○ Method for displaying and decoding the data/product.

    ○ Location/mapping of the data.

Be cautious when using unfamiliar products, or those not supported by technical specifications that satisfy the considerations noted above. When in doubt, use FAA/NWS products with the consultation of a flight service briefer.

IN-FLIGHT WEATHER

The most common method to obtain specific in-flight weather information is to use a source that broadcasts weather for the specific airport. Information about ceilings, visibility, wind, temperature, barometric pressure, and field conditions can be obtained from most types of broadcast weather services transmitted to the aircraft in radio voice format or digital format. [Figure 5-46] These are several services providing in-flight weather information for specific airports:

- Automatic terminal information service (ATIS)—a continuous broadcast of recorded non-control information in selected high activity terminal areas derived from an automated weather observation system or a human weather observer's report.

- AWOS and ASOS—installed at airports and maintained by both government (FAA and NWS) and private entities. FAA-operated AWOS-2 and AWOS-3 systems and NWS-operated ASOSs are approved sources of weather for Part 121 and 135

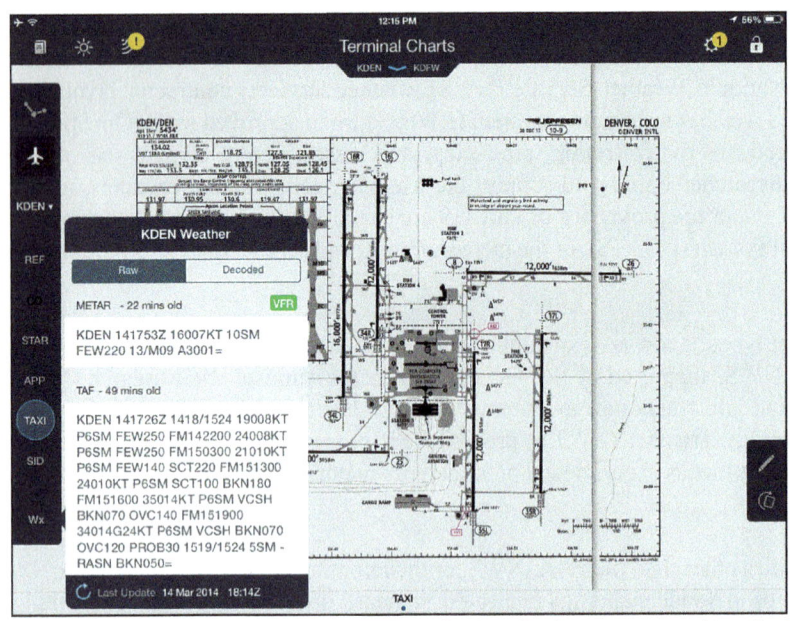

Figure 5-46. Jeppesen FliteDeck Pro EFB application displays enroute and terminal weather, including METARs and TAFs.

IFR operations unless the visibility or altimeter setting is reported missing.

- ARTCC— provides you hourly METAR or non-routine aviation weather report (SPECI) information for airports that have weather observation capability, but lack the appropriate equipment to transmit that information over a radio frequency. You can also obtain this information from Flight Watch.

- Flight information service-broadcast (FIS-B)—provides graphical and textual weather, such as METARs, TAFs, NEXRAD precipitation maps, NOTAMs, TFRs, and PIREPS to aircraft equipped with the 978 UAT link.

- XM WX Satellite Weather—provides continuously broadcast weather information including high-resolution NEXRAD radar, lightning, satellite imagery, METARs, winds aloft, and freezing level.

REGULATORY REQUIREMENTS

There are many practical reasons for reviewing weather information prior to initiating an instrument approach. You must familiarize yourself with the condition of individual airports and runways so that you can make informed decisions regarding fuel management, diversions, and alternate planning. Because this information is critical, the FARs require you to comply with specific weather minimums for planning and performing instrument flights and approaches.

Part 91 Operators

According to FAR 91.103, the pilot in command shall become familiar with all available information concerning a flight prior to departure. Included in this directive is the fundamental basis for you to review NOTAMs and pertinent weather reports and forecasts for the intended route of flight. Include current weather reports and terminal forecasts for all intended points of landing and alternate airports. Although there is no regulatory requirement for Part 91 operators to do so, thoroughly review an airport's current weather conditions prior to initiating an instrument approach so you can form expectations about the outcome of the approach.

Part 135 and Part 121 Operators

Unlike Part 91 operators, Part 135 and Part 121 operators may not depart for a destination unless the forecast weather at that airport will allow an instrument approach and landing. According to FAR 135.219 and FAR 121.613, flight crews and dispatchers may only designate an airport as a destination if the latest weather reports or forecasts, or any combination of them, indicate that the weather conditions will be at or above IFR landing minimums at the estimated time of arrival (ETA). This ensures that you consider weather forecasts when determining the suitability of destinations. You can depart when the forecast weather shows your destination airport will be at or above IFR minimums at the ETA, even if current conditions indicate the airport to be below minimums. Conversely, FAR 135.219 prevents departures when the first airport of intended landing is currently above IFR landing minimums, but the forecast weather is below those minimums at the ETA.

For Part 135, not only is the weather required to be forecast at or above IFR landing minimums for planning a departure, but it also must be above minimums for you to initiate an instrument approach and, once you have initiated the approach, to begin the final approach segment. FAR 135.225 states that pilots may not begin an instrument approach or the final approach segment of an IAP to an airport unless the latest weather report indicates that the weather conditions are at or above the authorized IFR landing minimums for that procedure. This means that Part 135 operators are restricted from passing the IAF and the FAF if the weather is reported below minimums. According to FAR 121.651, Part 121 operators may initiate the approach but may not pass the FAF if the weather is below minimums. Relief from this rule exists for both Part 121 and 135 operators if the aircraft has already passed the FAF when the weather report is received.

The controlling factor for determining whether or not the aircraft can proceed beyond the IAF or FAF is reported visibility. RVR, if available, is the controlling visibility report for determining that the requirements of this section are met. The runway visual value (RVV), reported in statute miles, takes precedent over prevailing visibility. There is no required time frame for receiving current weather prior to initiating the approach. Descent below the MDA, DA, or DH is governed, with one exception, by the same rules that apply to Part 91 operators. The exception is that during Part 121 and 135 operations, the airplane is also required to land within the touchdown zone.

PERFORMING AN OPERATIONAL BRIEFING

Before you can plan for the approach, you must decide which procedure you are most likely to fly from the information that is available to you. Most often, when the flight is being conducted into an airport that has ATIS information, the ATIS specifies the approaches in use. If more than one approach is in use or, you might have to make an educated guess as to which approach ATC will assign you based on the weather, direction of your arrival into the area, any published airport NOTAMs, and previous experience at the specific airport. If you are in contact with the approach control facility, you can query ATC as to which approach you can expect. You may request specific approaches at any time to meet the individual needs of your aircraft equipment or regulatory restrictions and ATC, in most cases, accommodates those requests, providing that workload and traffic permit.

At an airport without a control tower, ATC occasionally gives you the choice of any available instrument approach. In this case, you must choose an appropriate approach based on the expected weather, aircraft performance, direction of arrival, airport NOTAMs, and previous experience at the airport. As you plan your approach, consider several operational elements. For example, you are required to comply with specific airplane performance limitations that govern approach and landing so you must determine your aircraft's performance under specific conditions and in a particular configuration. You must also gather information about the airport and runway to make effective decisions about the approach procedure you intend to fly and your aircraft's capabilities. You should review and brief all this information as you prepare to fly the approach.

AIRPORT AND RUNWAY INFORMATION

As you near your destination, you should perform an approach overview. This includes an initial review of the chart for the expected approach procedure to determine if there are any factors that affect your ability to perform the approach. In addition, you must review the airport chart to determine the runway distance available, the intended turnoff taxiway, and the route of taxi to the parking area. Specific elements to include depend on the type of operation, aircraft characteristics, and OpsSpecs procedures. Landing minimums, terrain and obstacles, unique procedure features, airport information, and taxi considerations are examples of elements to include in an approach overview. [Figure 5-47]

AIRCRAFT PERFORMANCE AND CONFIGURATION

You are required to comply with specific airplane performance limitations that govern approach and landing. The primary goal of these performance considerations is to ensure that the aircraft can remain clear of obstructions throughout the approach, landing, and missed approach/go-around phase of flight and land within the distance required by the FAA. Although you normally complete the majority of in-depth performance planning for a flight under IFR prior to your departure, conduct a review of performance considerations prior to commencing the instrument approach.

Generally speaking, air carriers must have in place an approved method of complying with Subpart I of Parts 121 and 135 (Airplane Performance Operating Limitations), thereby proving the airplane's performance capability for every flight. You must have an approved method of complying with the approach and landing performance criteria in the applicable regulations prior to departing for your intended destination. The primary source of information for performance calculations for all operators, including Part 91, is the approved pilot's operating handbook/airplane flight manual (POH/AFM) for the make and model of aircraft. The AFM is required to contain the manufacturer-determined performance capabilities of the aircraft at each weight, altitude, and ambient temperature that are within the aircraft's listed limitations. Typically, the AFM for a large turbine-powered airplane contains information that enables you to determine that the airplane is capable of performing the following actions, considering the airplane's landing weight and other pertinent environmental factors. You must be able to:

- Land within the distance required by the regulations. Consider how wet or contaminated runway conditions affect the aircraft's performance.

- Climb from the MAP and maintain a specified climb gradient with one engine inoperative.

- Perform a go-around from the final stage of landing and maintaining a specified climb gradient with all engines operating and the airplane in the landing configuration.

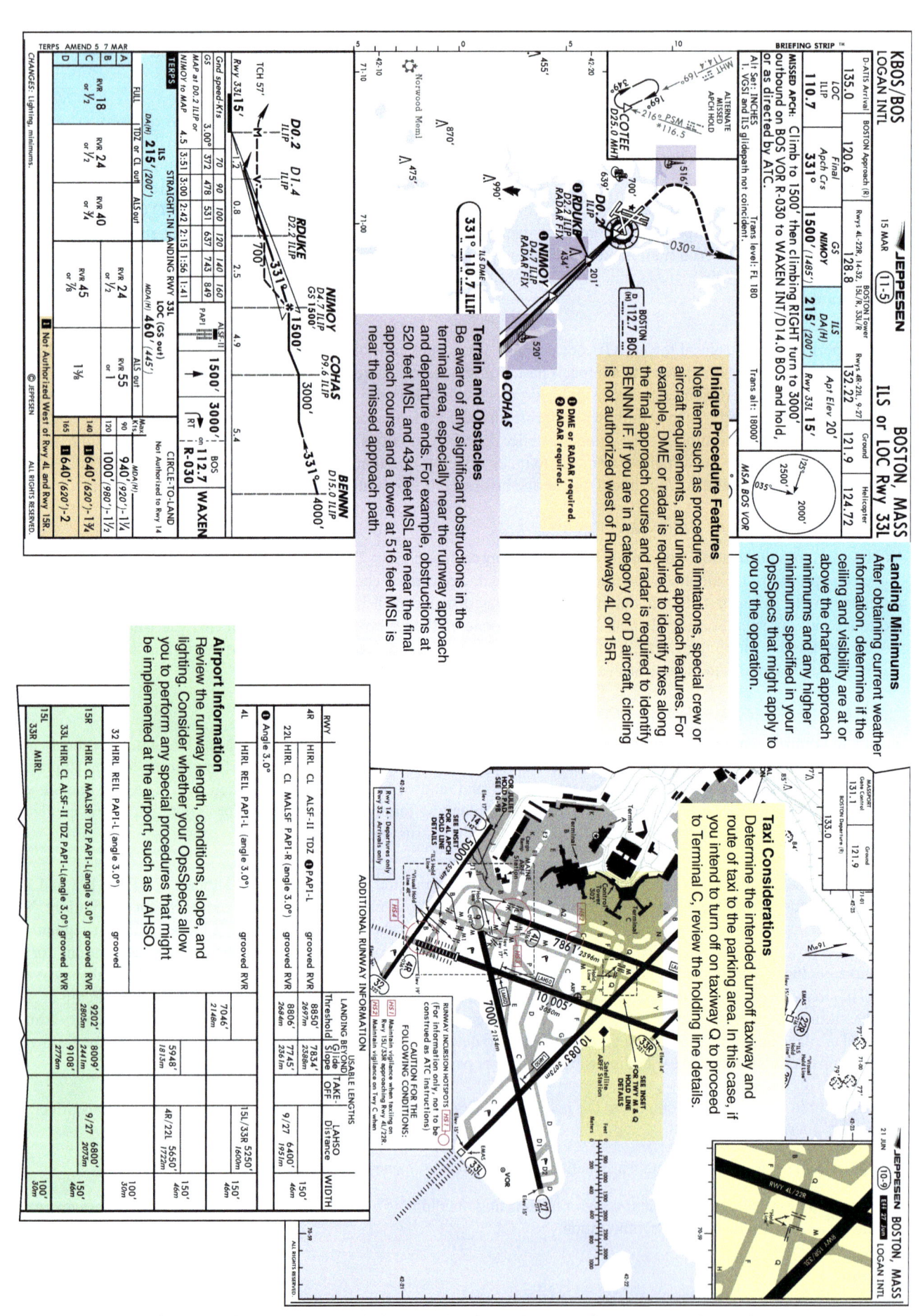

Figure 5-47. Review the approach chart and the airport chart to perform an approach overview.

Many airplanes have more than one allowable flap configuration for a normal landing. Often, a reduced flap setting for landing enables the airplane to operate at a higher landing weight to a runway that has restrictive obstacles in the missed approach climb path or rejected landing climb path. At the full-flap landing speed, the airplane might not have the performance to successfully complete a go-around and avoid any high terrain that might exist on the climb-out path. You must ensure that all-engine and engine-out missed approaches, as well as rejected landings, comply with the regulations regarding the required performance. [Figure 5-48]

Full Landing Flaps Approach
An approach with full landing flaps provides the slowest approach speed, but results in reduced performance in the missed approach climb. The climb performance might not be adequate to clear high terrain.

Reduced Flap Setting Approach
An approach with a reduced flap setting requires a faster approach speed, but results in improved climb performance if a missed approach is necessary.

Figure 5-48. You must consider how the airplane configuration affects performance during a go-around or missed approach.

APPROACH SPEED AND CATEGORY

Two other critical performance factors to consider during the planning phase of an instrument approach are aircraft approach category and planned approach speed. According to FAR 97.3 (b), aircraft approach category means a grouping of aircraft based on reference landing speed (V_{REF}), if specified, or if V_{REF} is not specified, 1.3 V_{S0} (the stalling speed or minimum steady flight speed in the landing configuration) at the maximum certificated landing weight. V_{REF}, V_{S0}, and the maximum certificated landing weight are those values as established for the aircraft by the certification authority of the country of registry. The categories are as follows:

- Category A: Speed less than 91 knots.

- Category B: Speed 91 knots or more but less than 121 knots.

- Category C: Speed 121 knots or more but less than 141 knots.

- Category D: Speed 141 knots or more but less than 166 knots.

- Category E: Speed 166 knots or more.

You are responsible for determining and briefing which category minimums you use for each instrument approach. If you use a higher approach speed on final that places the aircraft in a higher approach category, you must use the minimums for the higher category. Approaches made with inoperative flaps, circling approaches at higher-than-normal straight-in landing speeds, and approaches made in icing conditions for some types of aircraft are all examples of situations that can necessitate the use of a higher approach category. Since an approach category can make a difference in the approach and weather minimums and, in some cases, prohibit you from initiating an approach, you should determine and brief the approach speed and its effects on the approach in the preflight planning phase and prior to initiating an approach.

SETTING UP EQUIPMENT

Company regulations dictate how specific items are set up and others are left to pilot technique. In general, the techniques used by pilots at a specific company are similar. Although this section addresses two-pilot operations, you must set up and verify the same items as a single pilot. Typically, after the anticipated approach and runway have been selected, you use information gathered from ATIS, dispatch (if available), ATC, the specific approach chart for the approach selected, and any other available sources to set up each side of the cockpit. The number of items that you set up ahead of time depends on the level of automation of the aircraft and the avionics available. The pilot monitoring (PM) usually programs the GPS navigation equipment or FMS for the approach and the pilot flying (PF) verifies the information.

Other items to set up include the airspeed bugs based on performance calculations, altimeter bug to DA or MDA, go-around thrust/power setting, the radio altimeter if installed and needed for the approach, and the navigation/communication radios. You also follow checklist procedures to set up aircraft-specific items, such as the autopilot modes, auto-throttles, auto-brakes, pressurization system, fuel system, seat belt signs, anti-icing/de-icing equipment, and igniters.

PERFORMING AN APPROACH BRIEFING

A thorough instrument approach briefing greatly increases the likelihood of a successful instrument approach. Most Part 121 and 135 operators designate specific items to be included in an IAP briefing and the order in which those items are briefed. During an instrument approach briefing, you should identify the airport name and the specific approach procedure to enable other crewmembers the opportunity to cross-reference the chart being used for the brief. This ensures that flight crews intending to conduct an instrument approach have collectively reviewed and verified the information pertinent to the approach. [Figure 5-49]

In addition to the items in the approach briefing section of the chart, you might include items based on the weather conditions, airport environment, your aircraft, the specific approach procedure, and your company's OpsSpecs. For example, you might brief the transition to the approach, traffic situation, or changing weather conditions. Although you have already determined and briefed the airplane performance during the operational briefing, you might restate the runway length and conditions and any aircraft specific items that need emphasis. You might include additional items pertaining to the specific approach, such as CAT II or CAT III considerations and the effect of inoperative equipment. Finally, consider briefing pilot roles during the approach and the transfer of flight controls.

FLYING THE APPROACH

The procedures you use to fly the approach vary based on ATC instructions, the approach procedure details, and your specific aircraft. However, you must consider several basic factors for every approach to adhere to your approach clearance, maintain your course, use the autopilot, fly a stabilized approach, transition to visual conditions, and perform a missed approach.

APPROACH CLEARANCE

According to FAA Order 7110.65, Air Traffic Control, controllers issue clearances authorizing instrument approaches on the basis that, if you make visual contact with the ground before you complete the approach, you continue to follow the entire approach procedure unless you receive approval for a contact approach, ATC clears you for a visual approach, or you cancel the IFR flight plan. Approach clearances are issued based on known traffic. Receiving an approach clearance does not relieve you of your responsibility to comply with the applicable regulations and the notations on approach charts, such as "procedure not authorized at night." The name of the approach, as published, is used to identify the approach in the clearance. Items in parentheses on the approach title are not included in approach clearance phraseology. If a component of the approach aid is inoperative or unreliable, the controller uses the published approach name, but must advise you when the approach clearance is issued that the inoperative or unreliable approach aid component is unusable; for example, *"Cleared ILS Runway 4, glide slope unusable."*

VECTORS TO FINAL APPROACH COURSE

The approach gate is an imaginary point used by ATC as a basis for vectoring aircraft to the final approach course. The gate is established along the final approach course one nautical mile from the FAF on the side away from the airport and is no closer than five nautical miles from the landing threshold. When vectoring your aircraft to the final approach course, the controller is required to ensure the assigned altitude conforms to the following:

- For a precision approach or APV, at an altitude not above the glide slope/glide path or below the minimum glide slope/glide path intercept altitude specified on the approach procedure chart.

- For a nonprecision approach, at an altitude that enables you to descend in accordance with the published procedure.

The controller assigns an altitude to maintain until the aircraft is established on a segment of a published route or IAP. The altitude assigned must guarantee IFR obstruction clearance from the point at which the approach clearance is issued until the aircraft is established on a published route. Part 91.175 (j) prohibits you from making a procedure turn when vectored to a FAF or course, when conducting a timed approach, or when the procedure specifies "NO PT."

Procedure Title, Index Number, and Revision Date
We are planning an ILS to Runway 33 Left at Logan International Airport, Boston, page 11-5, 15 March of 2013

Communication Frequencies
We are talking to Boston Approach on 120.6. Boston Tower set: 128.8. Ground set: 121.9.

Primary Navaid Frequency
Localizer frequency is 110.7.

Final Approach Course
Final approach course is 331°.

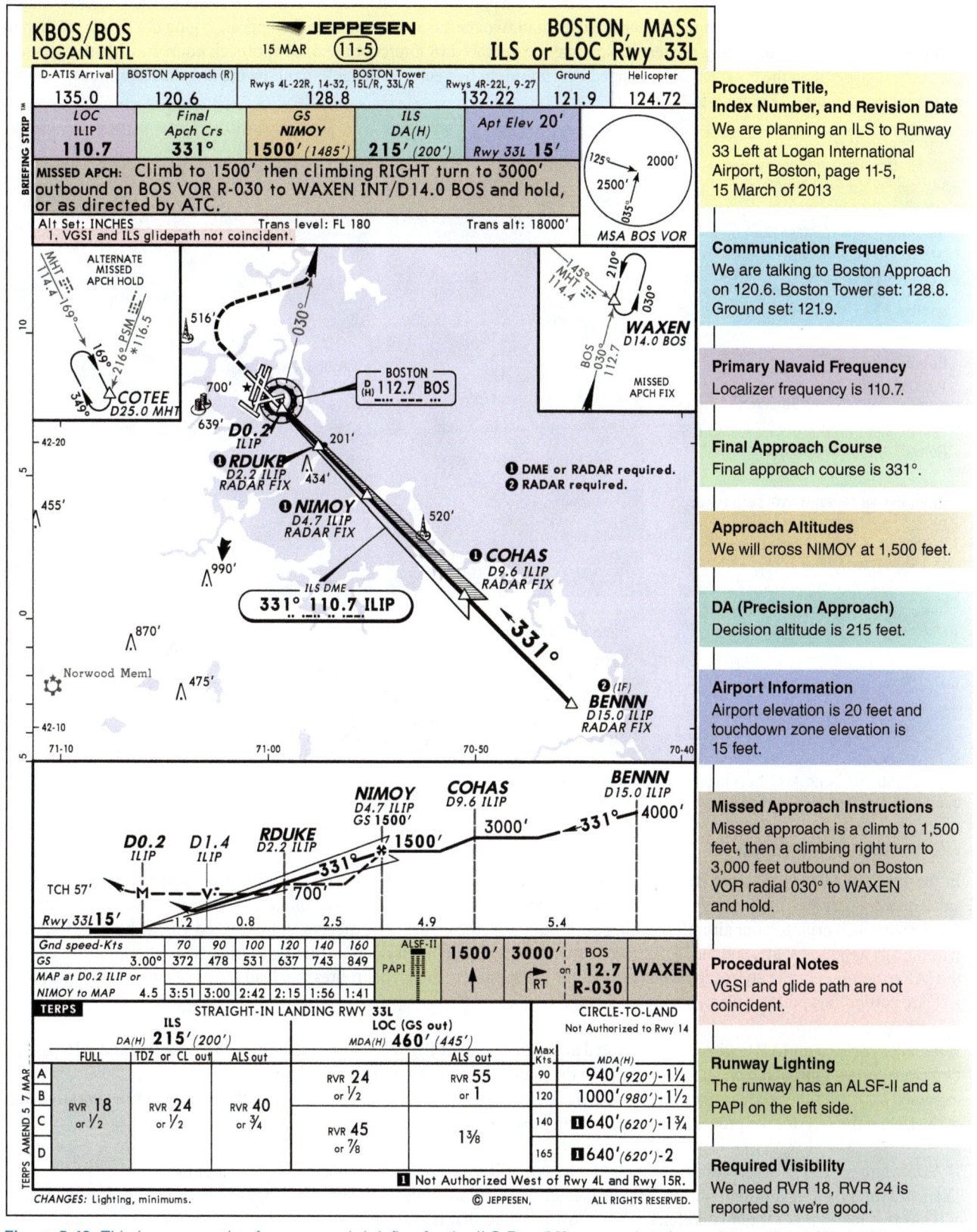

Approach Altitudes
We will cross NIMOY at 1,500 feet.

DA (Precision Approach)
Decision altitude is 215 feet.

Airport Information
Airport elevation is 20 feet and touchdown zone elevation is 15 feet.

Missed Approach Instructions
Missed approach is a climb to 1,500 feet, then a climbing right turn to 3,000 feet outbound on Boston VOR radial 030° to WAXEN and hold.

Procedural Notes
VGSI and glide path are not coincident.

Runway Lighting
The runway has an ALSF-II and a PAPI on the left side.

Required Visibility
We need RVR 18, RVR 24 is reported so we're good.

Figure 5-49. This is an example of an approach briefing for the ILS Rwy 33L approach to Logan International Airport. Your approach briefing might include additional items or state items in a different order based on company procedures and personal technique.

Controllers are required to ensure the intercept to the final approach course is at least two nautical miles outside the approach gate. If the reported ceiling is at least 500 feet above the MVA and the visibility is at least 3 statute miles, aircraft may be vectored to intercept the final approach course closer than two nautical miles outside the approach gate but no closer than the approach gate. If you specifically request it, you may be vectored to intercept the final approach course inside the approach gate but no closer than the FAF. RNAV equipped aircraft might be vectored to the IF to allow the onboard avionics to stabilize on the inbound course. [Figure 5-50]

Intercept Vector
Vectored to intercept a published segment of the final approach course at the MVA of 2,000 feet MSL:

"Four miles from LIMMA. Turn right heading three four zero. Maintain two thousand until established on the localizer. Cleared ILS Runway Three Six approach."

Established
Vectored to the final approach course and now established on a segment of the IAP:

"Seven miles from XRAYE. Cleared ILS Runway Three Six approach."

Established Beyond IAP Segments
Established on the final approach course beyond the IAP segments at 6,000 feet MSL (the MVA is 4,000 feet MSL):

"Eight miles from Alpha. Cross Alpha at or above four thousand. Cleared ILS Runway Three Six approach."

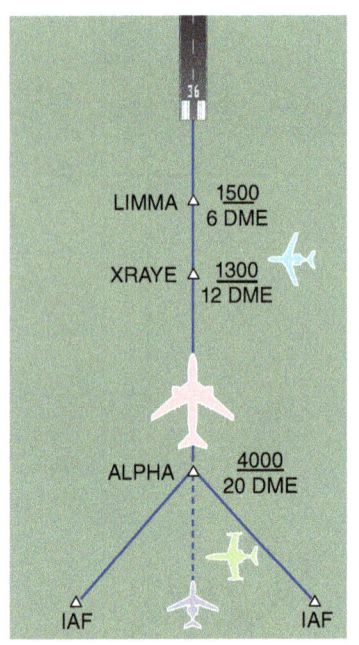

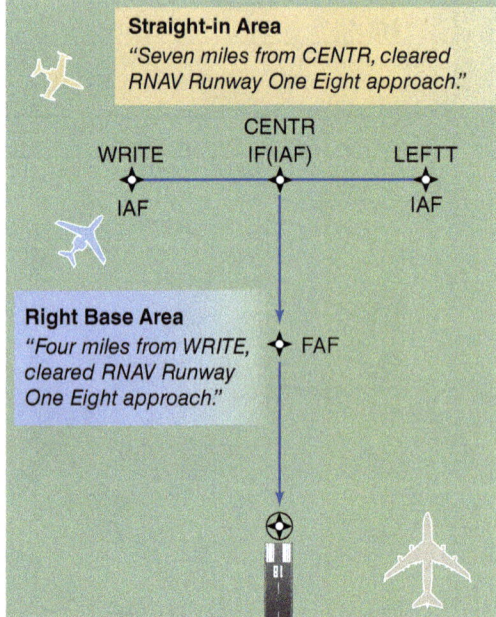

Beyond IAP Segments
Vectored to intercept the final approach course beyond the IAP segments at the MVA of 4,000 feet MSL:

"Five miles from Alpha. Turn right heading three three zero. Cross Alpha at or above 4,000 feet MSL. Cleared ILS runway Three Six approach."

Straight-in Area
"Seven miles from CENTR, cleared RNAV Runway One Eight approach."

Right Base Area
"Four miles from WRITE, cleared RNAV Runway One Eight approach."

Left Base Area
"Fifteen miles from LEFTT, cleared RNAV Runway One Eight approach."

Figure 5-50. Although ATC must follow specific guidelines when providing radar vectors, the controller has several options to position the aircraft on the approach course based on the aircraft position.

NONRADAR ENVIRONMENT

In the absence of radar vectors, an instrument approach begins at an IAF. If you have been cleared to a holding fix and subsequently *"cleared...approach,"* you normally do not receive new routing. Even though ATC might have issued clearance for the approach prior to your aircraft reaching the holding fix, the controller expects you to proceed via the holding fix, which was the last assigned route, and the feeder route associated with that fix, if a feeder route is published on the approach chart, to the IAF to commence the approach. When cleared for the approach, the feeder routes that lead from the enroute structure to the IAF are part of the approach clearance.

If a feeder route to an IAF begins at a fix located along the route of flight prior to reaching the holding fix, and ATC issues a clearance for an approach, you should commence the approach via the published feeder route; for example, the aircraft is not expected to overfly the feeder route and return to it. The controller expects you to commence the approach in a similar manner at the IAF, if the IAF for the procedure is located along the route of flight to the holding fix.

If ATC wants you to fly a direct route to the IAF, the controller states this with phraseology to include the words *"direct...," "proceed direct...,"* or a similar phrase that you can interpret without question. When you are uncertain of the clearance, query ATC as to what route of flight is preferred. You must consider that if approach control services do not exist at the destination airport and the airport is below the coverage area of center radar, off-route transitions to the approach environment might require that you fly the aircraft at a higher altitude than the altitude required for an on-route transition. [Figure 5-51]

Transition to the Approach

Assume you are approaching from the northwest on a direct route to the Durango VORTAC and you are restricted to a minimum IFR altitude of 17,000 MSL due to the unavailability of center radar coverage in the area at lower altitudes. If you arrive on V211 from the northwest to FIMGA IAF, you could obtain clearance to descend to a lower altitude due to the MEA of 11,300 feet MSL. Transitioning to the approach environment at a lower altitude provides a shallower descent and helps you maintain a stabilized arrival and approach.

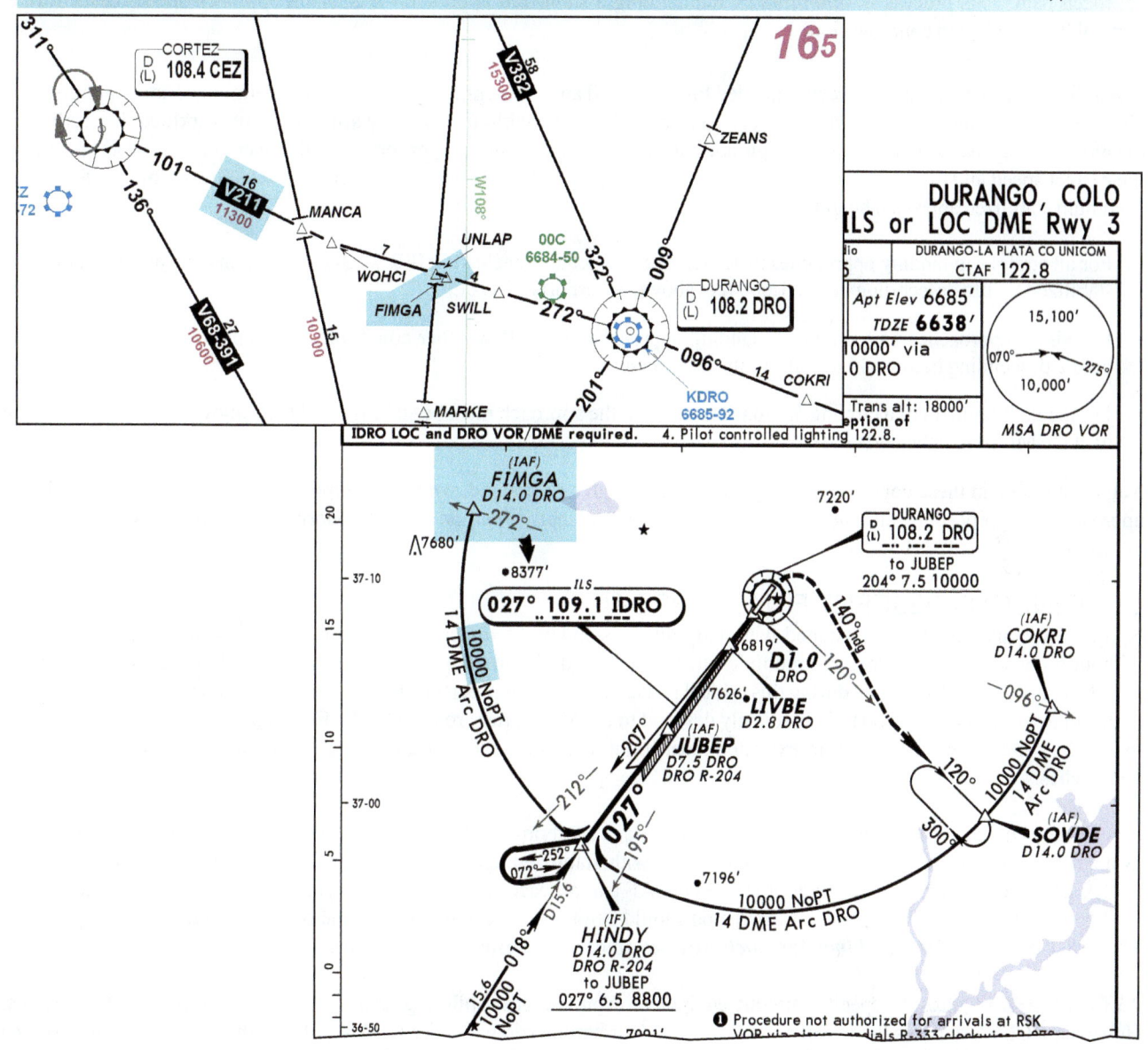

Figure 5-51. In this example, you can set up for a stabilized approach more effectively by flying an on-route transition to the approach on the airway.

USE OF THE AUTOPILOT

You should discuss the use of the autopilot with the other crewmember during the approach briefing, especially regarding the use of the altitude pre-selector and auto-throttles, if your aircraft is so equipped. The POH/AFM for the specific airplane outlines procedures and limitations required for autopilot use during an instrument approach and your OpsSpecs provide guidelines for the tasks the PF and PM perform. Most airplanes with sophisticated auto-flight systems and auto-throttles have the capability to select modes that climb the airplane with maximum climb thrust and descend the airplane with the throttles at idle These airplanes also have the capability to level off at pre-selected altitudes, track localizer, VOR, or RNAV courses, and capture and maintain a glide slope or glide path.

STABILIZED APPROACH

You must continuously evaluate instrument information throughout an approach to properly maneuver the aircraft or to monitor autopilot performance and to decide on the proper course of action when reaching the DA or MAP. Significant speed and configuration changes during an approach can seriously degrade situational awareness and complicate your decision at the

DA or MAP. The swept wing handling characteristics at low airspeeds and slow engine-response of many turbojets further complicate tasks during approach and landing operations. You must begin to form a decision concerning the probable success of an approach before reaching the DA or MAP. While flying the approach, your focus is to determine the displacements from the course and glide slope or glide path centerline and apply control inputs as necessary to achieve and maintain the desired approach path. This process is simplified by maintaining a stabilized approach—a constant approach speed, descent rate, vertical flight path, and configuration.

A stabilized approach is strongly recommended for all aircraft and is essential for safe turbojet operations. Limit configuration changes at low altitudes to those changes that you can easily make without adversely affecting your workload. For turbojets, the airplane must be in an approved configuration for landing or circling, if appropriate, with the engines spooled up, and on the correct speed and flight path with a descent rate of less than 1,000 feet per minute before descending below the following minimum stabilized approach heights:

- For all straight-in landing approaches (this includes contact approaches) in IFR weather conditions, the approach must be stabilized before descending below 1,000 feet above the airport or TDZE.

- For visual approaches and straight-in landing approaches in VFR weather conditions, the approach must be stabilized before descending below 500 feet above the airport elevation.

- For the final segment of a circling approach maneuver, the approach must be stabilized 500 feet above the airport elevation or at the MDA, whichever is lower.

You must maintain these conditions throughout the approach until touchdown for the approach to be considered a stabilized approach. This procedure also helps you recognize a wind shear situation should abnormal indications exist during the approach.

CONTINUOUS DESCENT FINAL APPROACH

Nonprecision approaches are designed with and without stepdown fixes in the final approach segment. Flying stepdowns without a constant descent requires multiple thrust, pitch, and altitude adjustments inside the FAF, which increases your workload and your risk of errors during this critical phase of flight. Nonprecision approaches designed without stepdown fixes in the final segment enable you to immediately descend to the MDA after crossing the FAF. This practice, commonly referred to as "dive and drive," can result in extended level flight as low as 250 feet above the ground and shallow or steep final approaches.

A continuous descent final approach (CDFA) is a technique for flying the final approach segment of a nonprecision approach as a continuous descent. The technique is consistent with stabilized approach procedures and has no level-off altitudes. A CDFA starts from an altitude/height at or above the FAF and proceeds to an altitude/height approximately 50 feet above the landing runway threshold or to a point where you should begin the flare maneuver for the type of aircraft you are flying. AC 120-108, *Continuous Descent Final Approach* provides guidance for effectively flying a CDFA.

To fly a CDFA requires no specific aircraft equipment. You use basic piloting techniques, the FMS and RNAV systems. However, a CDFA requires the use of a published VDA or barometric vertical guidance (GS) on the approach chart. Use the descent/timing conversion table on the approach chart to translate the published VDA or GS into the required rate of descent. AC 120-108 provides further examples of how to determine your descent rate for approaches with and without stepdown fixes after the FAF. [Figure 5-52]

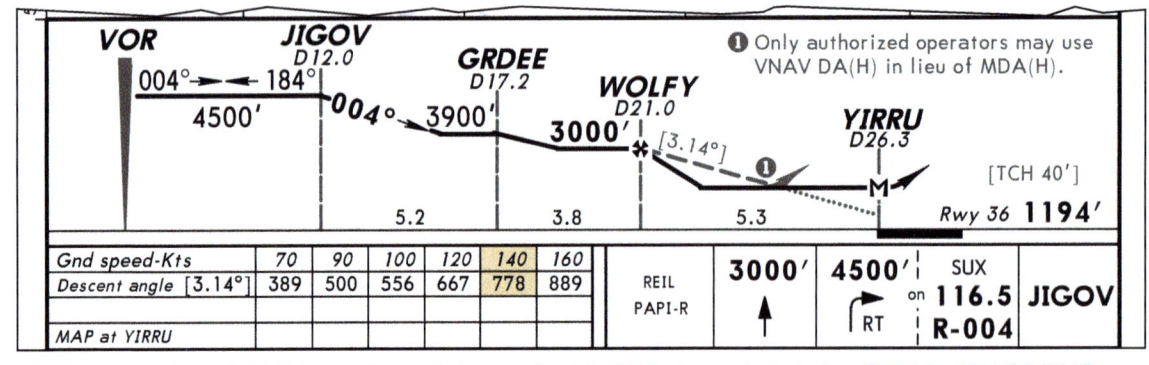

Figure 5-52. At a groundspeed of 140 knots, descend at approximately 778 feet per minute to fly a CDFA for this VOR/DME approach.

TRANSITION TO VISUAL FLIGHT

Stabilized approaches add to the safety of the transition to visual flight because you have already stabilized the approach upon visually acquiring the required references for the runway. One hundred to 200 feet prior to reaching the DA or MDA, most of the PM's attention should be outside of the aircraft in order to visually acquire at least one visual reference for the runway, as required by the regulations. Although you must refer to your specific company procedures, typically the PF stays focused on the instruments until the PM calls out seeing any visual references or states *"runway in sight."* The PF then begins the transition to visual flight. It is common practice for the PM to call out the vertical speed during the transition to confirm to the PF that the instruments are being monitored, thus allowing more of the PF's attention to focus on the visual portion of the approach and landing. The PM also announces any deviations from the stabilized approach criteria. Single-pilot operations can be much more challenging because you must continue to fly by the instruments while attempting to acquire a visual reference for the runway. CAT II and III approaches have specific requirements that may differ from CAT I precision or nonprecision approach requirements regarding transition to visual flight and landing. You can find this information in your OpsSpecs or flight operations manual.

In order to continue to land, the flight visibility must be at least the visibility minimum stated on the instrument approach chart, or as required by regulations The visibility published on an approach chart is dependent on many variables, including the HAT for straight-in landings, or HAA for circling approaches. Other factors include the approach light system coverage, and type of approach procedure.

MISSED APPROACH

Many reasons exist for performing a missed approach. However, the primary reason is that the required flight visibility prescribed in the IAP does not exist or you cannot see the required visual references for the runway upon arrival at the DA or MAP. In addition, according to Part 91, the aircraft must continuously be in a position from which a descent to a landing on the intended runway can be made at a normal rate of descent using normal maneuvers, and for operations conducted under Part 121 or 135, unless that descent rate will allow touchdown to occur within the touchdown zone of the runway of intended landing. CAT II and III approaches call for different requirements as prescribed by the regulations. [Figure 5-53]

Figure 5-53. To descend below the DA or MDA to land, you must establish the runway environment in sight, which includes at least one of these visual references.

You must have flight visibility at or greater than that required for the approach.

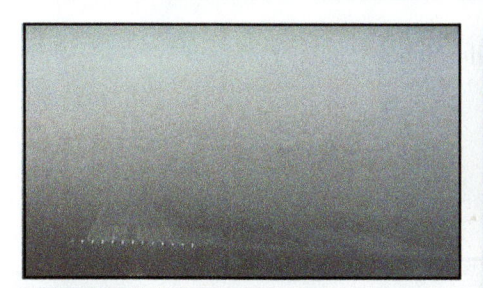

You must be continuously in a position to descend at a normal rate to land on the intended runway by using normal maneuvers and if you are operating under Part 121 or Part 135, your descent rate must allow touchdown to occur within the touchdown zone of the runway.

You must establish the runway environment in sight, which includes at least one of these visual references:
- Approach light system, but you must see the red terminating bars (ALSF-1) or side row bars (ALSF-2) to descend below 100 feet above the touchdown zone elevation
- Runway end identifier lights
- Visual approach slope indicator
- Threshold, threshold markings, or threshold lights
- Touchdown zone, touchdown zone markings, or touchdown zone lights
- Runway, runway markings, or runway lights

After you have begun descent below the DA or MDA, you must perform a missed approach if the required visibility is lost or the runway environment is no longer visible, unless the loss of sight of the runway is a result of normal banking of the aircraft during a circling approach. A missed approach procedure is also required if you perform a rejected landing for any reason, such as personnel and equipment or animals on the runway, or if the approach becomes unstabilized and you cannot perform a normal landing. Performing a missed approach after the DA or MAP below the DA or MDA involves additional risk until established on the published missed approach procedure course and altitude.

At airports with control towers, it is common for ATC to assign alternate missed approach instructions; even so, you should always be prepared to fly the published missed approach. When you perform a missed approach prior to reaching the MAP, you are required to continue along the final approach course, at an altitude above the DA or MDA, until reaching the MAP before making any turns. If you initiate a turn prior to the MAP, obstacle clearance is not guaranteed. It is appropriate after passing the FAF, and recommended, where there are not any climb restrictions, to begin a climb to the missed approach altitude without waiting to arrive at the MAP. The missed approach course begins at the MAP and continues until the aircraft has reached the designated fix and you enter the holding pattern. Prior to reaching the final fix of the missed approach course, ATC might issue further instructions that do not require you to hold.

CFIT PREVENTION

The final approach and landing phase of flight accounts for approximately 40 percent of CFIT accidents. Maintaining situational awareness and flying a stabilized approach is critical to preventing CFIT in IFR conditions. Proper briefings are also key to CFIT prevention. Always perform an approach overview and approach briefing when advised what procedure to expect. If you must fly a nonprecision approach, brief the procedure as a stabilized approach using a constant rate of descent. Brief the missed approach procedure with emphasis on the direction of the initial missed approach turn. The actions you can take to prevent CFIT during approach and landing under IFR can be divided into five categories: altimeters, safe altitudes, ATC procedures, flight crew complacency, and approach procedures:

Altimeters

- Know what altimeter units of measurement are used for the area. Be prepared to convert feet and meters.
- Know the phase of flight to apply the appropriate altimeter setting.
- Use altimeter setting cross-check and readback procedures.
- Cross check radio altimeter and barometric altimeter readings.
- Operate at higher than minimum altitudes during atmospheric anomalies.

Safe Altitudes

- Ensure you have the appropriate charts and brief the altitude information, including terrain and obstructions in the terminal area.
- Know and fly at or above the safe altitudes in the area and know the height of the highest terrain or obstacle.
- Understand terrain clearance limitations for approaches.
- Know TAWS procedures.

ATC Procedures

- Challenge or refuse ATC instructions that you do not understand, that are questionable, or that conflict with your assessment of your aircraft position relative to the terrain.
- Read back clearances and use standard phraseology.
- Do not accept unreasonable clearances.
- Operate the autopilot using the mode that facilitates compliance with ATC instructions.

Flight Crew Complacency

- Know that familiarity can lead to complacency; do not assume that this flight will be like the last flight.
- Follow company SOPs.
- Use effective CRM techniques.
- Be mentally prepared to take the appropriate action at the DA or MAP, which is either performing the missed approach if you do not have the runway environment in sight or transitioning to visual references to land.

Approach Procedures

- Fly the published approach procedure. Do not improvise or invent your own procedures.
- Know what approach and runway aids are available before initiating an approach and use all available aids.
- Identify unique gradient and step-down requirements.
- Review the approach procedures during the approach briefing (preferably before top of descent).
- Fly stabilized approaches and perform a missed approach if your aircraft is not stabilized by 500 feet above the airport elevation in VFR conditions or 1,000 feet above airport elevation in IFR conditions.
- Appropriately use the auto-flight system to fly stabilized approaches and to reduce your workload.

Chapter 6
Helicopter IFR Operations

This chapter provides information on IFR helicopter operations in the NAS. To make this complex subject easier to absorb, the material is organized into four general areas: the helicopter, the pilot, minimums, and approaches.

HELICOPTER IFR CERTIFICATION

Airplanes have been successfully flown by reference to instruments since 1929, but it wasn't until more than 30 years later that the FAA issued the first certification to a helicopter for IFR operations. [Figure 6-1]

The certification requirements for helicopters to operate under IFR are contained in FAR Part 27 for Normal Category rotorcraft, and Part 29 for Transport Category rotorcraft. The requirements for IFR are in addition to the VFR requirements, and many of the IFR requirements for Transport Category helicopters also apply to helicopters in the Normal Category.

These requirements can be organized into the categories of flight and navigation equipment, miscellaneous requirements, stabilization and automatic flight control systems, helicopter flight manual limitations, operations specifications (OpsSpecs), and minimum equipment list (MEL).

FLIGHT AND NAVIGATION EQUIPMENT

FAR 29.1303 lists the basic flight instruments for helicopter IFR operations, with additional requirements listed in Appendix B of Part 29. The requirements include:

- Airspeed Indicator
- Sensitive Altimeter
- Magnetic direction indicator
- Clock
- Free-air temperature indicator
- Gyroscopic pitch and bank (attitude) indicator

Figure 6-1. The Cessna CH-1C Skyhook was the first helicopter certificated by the FAA for IFR operations.

6-1

- Rate-of-climb (vertical speed) indicator
- Magnetic gyroscopic direction indicator
- Standby pitch and bank (attitude) indicator
- Slip/skid indicator
- Speed warning device (if required by Part 29)

MISCELLANEOUS REQUIREMENTS

Appendix B of Part 29 lists some additional equipment requirements, including:

- Overvoltage disconnect
- Indicator of adequate power for each powered flight instrument
- Adequate ice protection of IFR systems
- Alternate static source (single pilot configuration)
- Thunderstorm lights (transport category helicopters)

STABILIZATION AND AUTOMATIC FLIGHT CONTROL SYSTEMS

Helicopter manufacturers normally use a stabilization and/or automatic flight control system (AFCS) in order to meet the stability requirements of Parts 27 and 29. The helicopter you fly might have some or all of these features:

- **Aerodynamic surfaces** are designed to impart some stability or control capability that the basic VFR configuration lacks.

- A **trim system** provides a cyclic centering effect. Trim systems often use a magnetic brake/spring device, controlled by a four-way switch on the cyclic. The trim system supports "hands on" flying of the helicopter.

- A **stability augmentation system (SAS)** provides short-term rate damping control inputs to increase helicopter stability. Like the trim system, the SAS assists "hands on" flying.

- An **attitude retention system (ATT)** returns the helicopter to a selected attitude after a disturbance. You can usually set the desired attitude using a four-way trim switch, or by actuating a "force trim" switch on the cyclic that sets the attitude manually. Depending on the system, attitude retention might be a function of the SAS, or might be the basic "hands off" autopilot function.

- An **autopilot system (AP)** provides for "hands off" flight along specified lateral and vertical paths, such as holding a selected heading, maintaining altitude, holding a particular vertical speed, navigation tracking, and flying an approach. The AP typically has a control panel for mode selection and a system to indicate mode status. The AP might or might not be installed with a flight director system. APs typically control the helicopter about the roll and pitch axes (cyclic control) but some also include yaw axis (pedal control) and collective control servos.

- A **flight director (FD)** provides visual guidance to help you fly selected lateral and vertical modes of operation. The visual guidance is typically provided by a single cue ("vee-bar") presentation superimposed over the attitude indicator. Other FDs use a dual cue display (often called a "cross-pointer"). These two presentations only provide attitude instructions. Some FDs have a three-cue system, which provides information to position the collective as well as attitude cues. When the system detects path errors, or when airspeed errors exceed preset values, the system cues you which collective control inputs to use. The three-cue system pitch command provides the required cues to control airspeed when flying an approach with vertical guidance at speeds slower than the best-rate-of-climb (V_y) speed. When using any flight director, you either move the helicopter's controls manually to satisfy the FD commands or couple the autopilot to the flight director to fly along the desired flight path. Many flight director systems share mode control and indications with the autopilot.

For IFR operations, you might be required to use one or a combination of these systems. During flight operations, you must stay aware of the mode of operation of the augmentation systems, and the control logic and functions employed. For example, a particular FD system has both three-cue and two-cue modes. During an ILS approach using the three-cue mode (lateral, vertical, and collective cues), the flight director collective cue responds to glide-slope deviation, while the horizontal bar of the cross-pointer responds to airspeed deviations. The same system, while flying an ILS in the two-cue mode, the horizontal bar responds to glide-slope deviations. This is especially significant when using two pilots. It is important for you and the other pilot to establish a set of procedures and responsibilities for the control of flight director/autopilot modes for the various phases of flight. Not only does a full understanding of the system modes provide more precise control of the helicopter, it can also help you to identify a fault or failure in the system.

HELICOPTER FLIGHT MANUAL LIMITATIONS

The FAA issues certifications for helicopters to fly IFR with either one or two pilots. For IFR operations with two pilots, the helicopter must have specific equipment installed and functional. Additional equipment is required for single-pilot operations. [Figure 6-2]

The helicopter flight manual (HFM) also contains other specific limitations associated with IFR flight. Here are examples of some typical limitations:

- Minimum equipment required for IFR flight with one pilot or two pilots
- V_{MINI} (minimum speed - IFR)
- V_{NEI} (never exceed speed - IFR)
- Maximum approach angle
- Weight and center of gravity limits
- Aircraft configuration limitations (such as aircraft door positions and external loads)
- Aircraft system limitations (generators, inverters, etc.)
- System testing requirements (many avionics and systems incorporate a self-test feature)
- Pilot action requirements (for example, you must have your hands and feet on the controls during certain procedures)

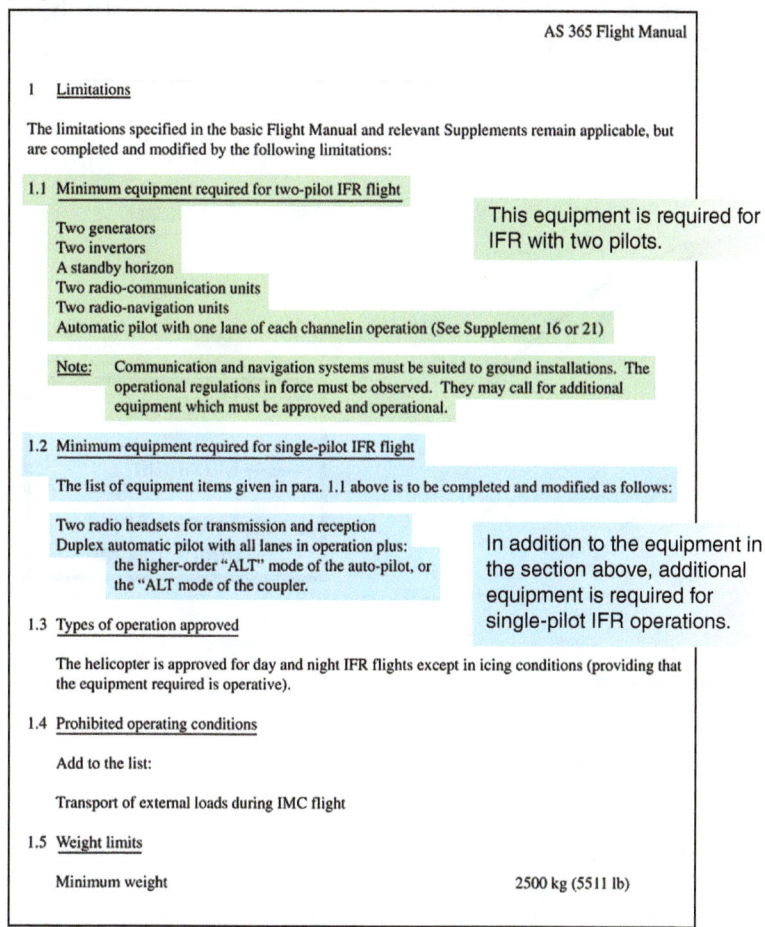

Figure 6-2. The Helicopter Flight Manual (HFM) defines systems and functions that are required to be in operation or engaged for IFR flight in either the single or two pilot configurations.

Final approach angles/descent gradient for public approach procedures can be as high as 7.5 degrees/795 feet per nautical mile. At 70 KIAS (no wind) this gives a descent rate of 925 feet per minute. With a 10-knot tailwind the descent rate increases to 1,056 feet per minute. Certain approach procedures (such as Copter PinS approaches, discussed later) are restricted to helicopters with a maximum V_{MINI} of 70 KIAS and an IFR approach angle that will enable them to meet the final approach angle/descent gradient. If the helicopter you are flying has a V_{MINI} of 70 KIAS, you might not have adequate control margins to fly an approach that is designed with the maximum allowable angle/descent gradient or minimum allowable deceleration distance from the MAP to the heliport. The Copter PinS final approach segment is limited to 70 KIAS because area required for turns and the distance needed to decelerate between the MAP and the heliport might not be adequate at faster speeds. For some helicopters, engaging the autopilot might increase the V_{MINI} to a speed greater than 70 KIAS, or require a speed faster than 70 KIAS in the go-around mode. It might be possible to fly these helicopters manually on the approach, or on the missed approach in a mode other than the go-around mode.

Because slower IFR approach speeds enable the helicopter to fly steeper approaches and reduce the distance from the heliport that is required to decelerate the helicopter, you might want to operate your helicopter at speeds slower than its established V_{MINI}. The provision to apply for a determination of equivalent safety for instrument flight below V_{MINI} and the minimum helicopter requirements are specified in the Advisory Circulars (AC) 27-1, *Certification of Normal Category Rotorcraft* and AC 29-2, *Certification of Transport Category Rotorcraft*. You can obtain guidance for your application from the FAA Rotorcraft Directorate Standards Staff.

Your helicopter flight manual might only provide performance data for the best rate of climb speed. You may use observed performance for similar weight, altitude, temperature, and speed conditions to determine equivalent performance to meet missed approach climb gradients.

When you use an autopilot to fly a missed approach that has a climbing turn, it is important to use the modes that result in the best climb rate, roll rate, and bank angle consistent with safety. For example, autopilots usually provide significantly higher roll rates and bank angles in certain modes, and some systems will accelerate the helicopter in level flight until reaching V_Y before starting a climb unless you select the Airspeed Hold mode when you start the missed approach. Flying a turning missed approach at a higher airspeed or with a reduced turn rate increases the area required for the turn, and might cause you to fly out of the airspace allocated for the missed approach procedure. [Figure 6-3]

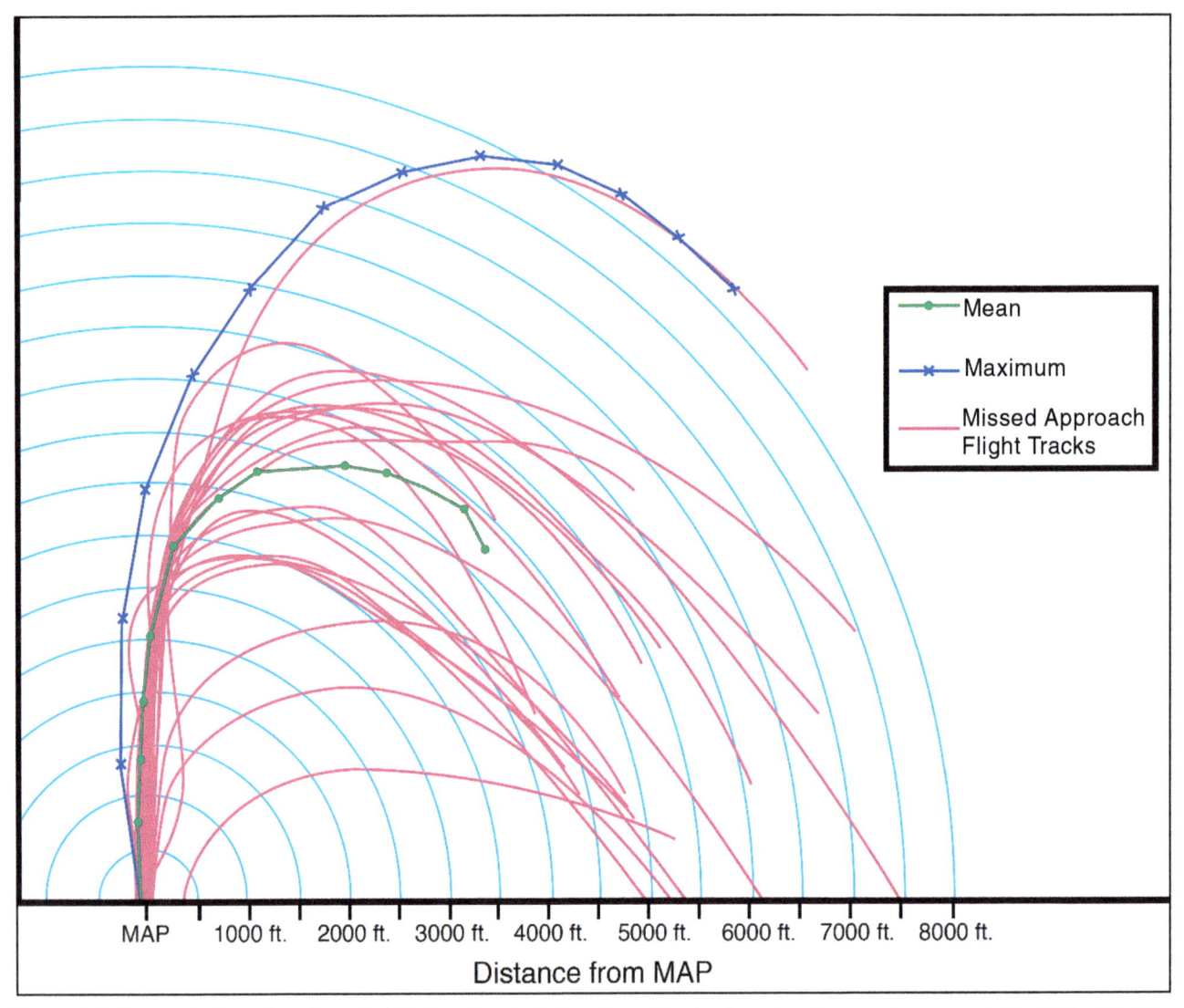

Figure 6-3. The purple lines show the actual flight tracks of a helicopter making turning missed approaches as part of an FAA study. The blue arcs show the distance from the MAP. The larger tracks resulted from higher climb airspeeds and/or lower turn rates.

OPERATIONS SPECIFICATIONS

When you operate a flight under Part 135, the minimums and procedures in your OpsSpecs are more restrictive than those for Part 91 operations. [Figure 6-4]

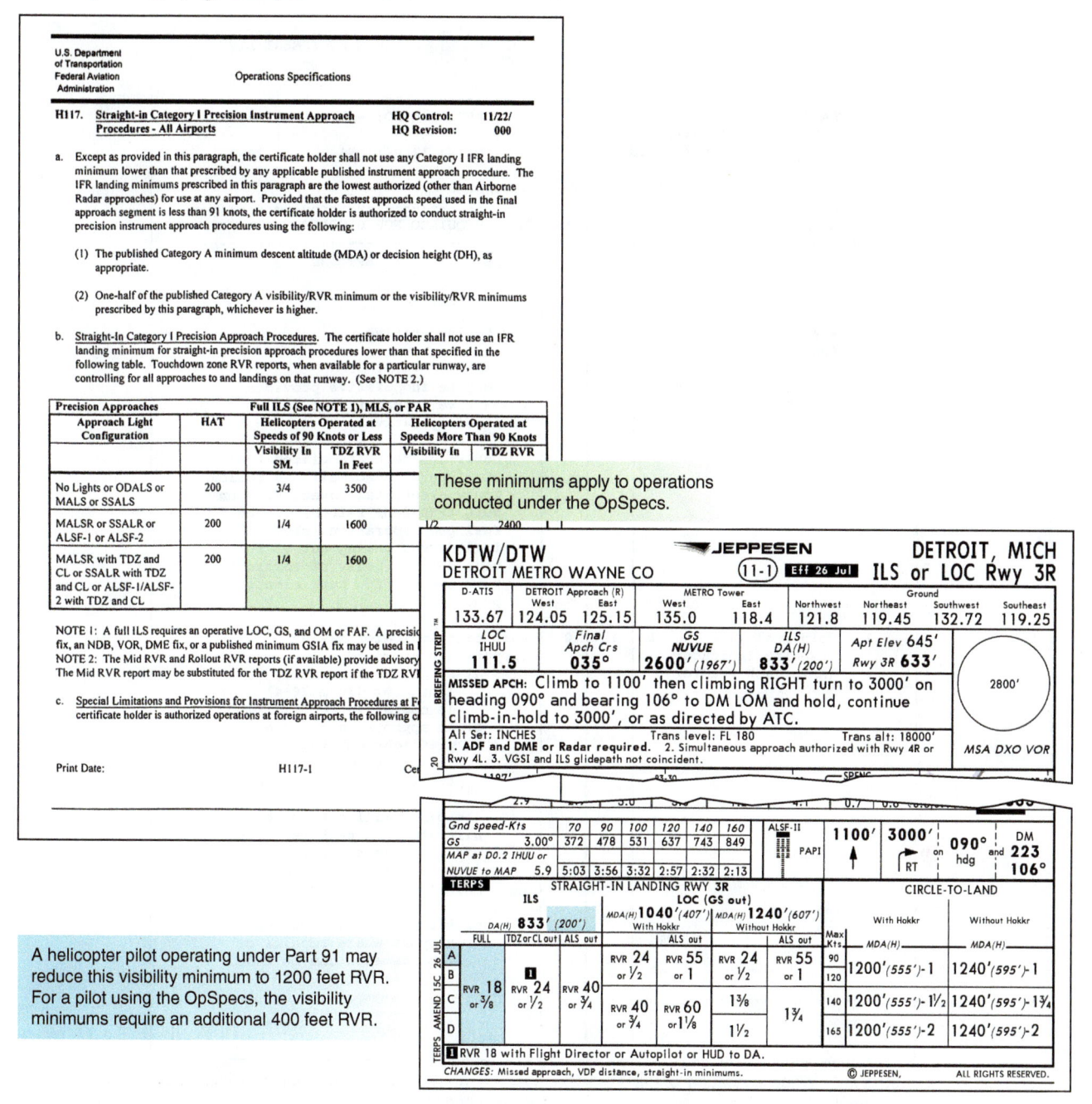

Figure 6-4. This excerpt from a Part 135 OpsSpecs details the minimums for precision approaches. For comparison, the inset shows the minimums for the ILS Rwy 3R approach at Detroit Metro Airport.

Helicopter Emergency Medical Service (HEMS) operators typically have more restrictive OpsSpecs than Part 135 operators. Even when you operate under Part 91, it is a good idea to develop your own personal OpsSpecs based on your personal proficiency, training, and experience.

MINIMUM EQUIPMENT LIST

Under certain circumstances, you are allowed to fly a helicopter under IFR with certain equipment inoperative. The minimum equipment list (MEL) describes the equipment and the conditions you must meet.

In many cases, a helicopter configured for single-pilot IFR may depart IFR with certain equipment inoperative if it has a crew of two pilots. Under Part 91, you may defer certain items without an MEL if those items are not required by the type certificate, regulations, or airworthiness directives (ADs), and the flight can be performed safely without them. Before flight, you must be sure that the inoperative item has been marked inoperative and either disabled or removed, and verify that the event is entered in the aircraft's logbook. [Figure 6-5]

```
                                                    MINIMUM EQUIPMENT LIST

------------------------------------------------------------------------------
 AIRCRAFT:                            | REVISION NO: 4 b    | PAGE:
 MESSERSCHMITT-BOLKOW-BLOHM HELICOPTER |                     |
      MBB-BK 117 SERIES               | DATE: 12/06/1994    | 28-1
------------------------------------------------------------------------------
                          1.  | 2. NUMBER INSTALLED
 SYSTEM &                     ------------------------------------------------
 SEQUENCE            ITEM     |   | 3. NUMBER REQUIRED FOR DISPATCH
 NUMBERS                      |   |--------------------------------------------
 -----------------------------|   |   | 4. REMARKS OR EXCEPTIONS
 28   FUEL                    |   |   |
                              |   |   |
 1.  Fuel Prime Pump      C   | 1 | 0 | May be inoperative.
     Caution Light            |   |   |
                              |   |   |
 2.  Main Tank Transfer   C   | 2 | 1 | One may be inoperative provided
     Pump Caution Lights      |   |   | respective transfer pump is
                              |   |   | verified operative.
                              |   |   |
                              |   |   | (O)Determine that associated fuel
                              |   |   |    pump operates normally as follows:
                              |   |   |    Apply electrical power, turn on
                              |   |   |    FUEL XFER PUMP switch, listen for
                              |   |   |    fuel pump operation, check that
                              |   |   |    fuel is not coming out of fuel
                              |   |   |    vent system (belly of aircraft),
                              |   |   |    turn system off, turn electrical
                              |   |   |    power off.
                              |   |   |
 3.  Main Fuel Tank       B   | 1 | 0 | Main tank indicator may be
     Quantity Indicator       |   |   | inoperative provided:
     (Main Tank Needle)       |   |   |    a) Supply Tank Quantity
                              |   |   |       Indicator (Item 28-4)
                              |   |   |       is operative, and
                              |   |   |    b) An approved alternate
                              |   |   |       preflight gauging method
                              |   |   |       is used to determine
                              |   |   |       total fuel quantity, and
                              |   |   |
                              |   |   | (O) The pilot will ensure that the
                              |   |   |     aircraft fuel tank is topped
                              |   |   |     off and plan the flight to
                              |   |   |     include a 45 minute reserve at
                              |   |   |     normal cruise power.
                              |   |   |
                              |   |   |    c) Aircraft shall not depart
                              |   |   |       airport where repairs or
                              |   |   |       replacements can be made.
```

Figure 6-5. When operating under Part 135, you are not allowed to take off with inoperative equipment unless the operation is authorized in the approved MEL.

PILOT PROFICIENCY

Staying proficient for IFR operations can be a challenge, particularly if you fly different helicopters. Even helicopters of the same make and model might have different avionics installed that change the required equipment or the level of augmentation for a particular operation. The systems and their interactions with each other can be complex, and you need a detailed and thorough understanding to use them safely and efficiently in IFR operations. To stay proficient, you need to maintain a high level of knowledge of system operation, limitations, failure indications and reversionary modes. Trying to accomplish this on your own can be somewhat hit-and-miss, but periodic formal training is both thorough and efficient. Accident statistics and the reports of experienced pilots indicate that investing in professional training is a much better way to stay sharp in the use of these systems than attempting to teach yourself or, worse yet, trying to figure them out on a solo flight in actual IMC.

HELICOPTER VFR MINIMUMS

Helicopters have the same VFR minimums as airplanes with two exceptions. In Class G airspace or under a Special VFR (SVFR) clearance, helicopters have no minimum visibility requirement but must remain clear of clouds and operate at a speed that is slow enough to give the pilot an adequate opportunity to see other aircraft or an obstruction in time to avoid a collision. As a helicopter pilot, you are also authorized to obtain SVFR clearances at airports designated "NO SVFR" in the A/FD or on the sectional chart (Part 91, Appendix D, Section 3). Unlike airplanes, neither helicopter pilots nor the helicopter are required to have instrument certification for SVFR at night. [Figure 6-6]

Helicopter VFR Minimums		
Airspace	**Flight Visibility**	**Distance from Clouds**
Class A	Not applicable	Not Applicable.
Class B	3 SM	Clear of Clouds.
Class C	3 SM	500 feet below. 1,000 feet above. 2,000 feet horizontal.
Class D	3 SM	500 feet below. 1,000 feet above. 2,000 feet horizontal.
Class E: Less than 10,000 feet MSL	3 SM	500 feet below. 1,000 feet above. 2,000 feet horizontal.
At or above 10,000 feet MSL	5 SM	1,000 feet below. 1,000 feet above. 1 statute mile horizontal.
Class G: 1,200 feet or less above the surface (regardless of MSL altitude).		
Day, except as provided in §91.155(b)	None	Clear of clouds.
Night, except as provided in §91.155(b)	None	Clear of clouds.
More than 1,200 feet above the surface but less than 10,000 feet MSL		
Day	1 SM	500 feet below. 1,000 feet above. 2,000 feet horizontal.
Night	3 SM	500 feet below. 1,000 feet above. 2,000 feet horizontal.
More than 1,200 feet above the surface and at or above 10,000 feet MSL	5 SM	1,000 feet below. 1,000 feet above. 1 statute mile horizontal.
B, C, D, E Surface Area Airspace SVFR Minimums		
Day	None	Clear of clouds.
Night	None	Clear of clouds.

Figure 6-6. Except for SVFR and the minimum visibility in Class G at and below 1,200 feet AGL, the VFR minimums for helicopters are the same as for airplanes.

However, the lower minimums for Part 91 operations in Class G airspace and SVFR do not take the place of the VFR minimum requirements of either Part 135 regulations or respective OpsSpecs.

You need to know all of the VFR minimums in order to determine if you can make a point-in-space (PinS) approach, or if you need a SVFR clearance to continue past the MAP. These approaches and procedures are discussed in detail later in this chapter.

HELICOPTER IFR TAKEOFF MINIMUMS

When you fly under Part 91, there are no takeoff minimums other than the requirement to attain V_{MINI} before entering IMC. For most helicopters this requires approximately 1/2 mile and an altitude of 100 feet. If departing with a steeper climb gradient, some helicopters may require additional altitude to accelerate to V_{MINI}. To maximize safety, always consider using the Part 135 standard takeoff visibility minimum of 1/2 SM or the charted departure minimums, whichever is higher. A charted departure to provide protection from obstacles either has a higher visibility, climb gradient, and/or departure path. For Part 135 operations you are required to adhere to the takeoff minimums prescribed by the instrument approach procedures (IAPs) for the airport.

HELICOPTER IFR ALTERNATES

All helicopters operated under IFR must carry enough fuel to fly to the intended destination, fly from that airport to the filed alternate, and continue for 30 minutes at normal cruising speed. You must file for an alternate if weather reports and forecasts at the proposed destination do not meet certain minimums. These minimums differ for Part 91 and Part 135 operators.

PART 91 OPERATORS

When operating under Part 91, you are not required to file an alternate if the ceiling will be at least 1,000 feet above the airport elevation or 400 feet above the lowest applicable approach minimums, whichever is higher, and the visibility is at least 2 SM at the ETA and for one hour after. If an alternate is required, you can use an airport if the ceiling is at least 200 feet above the minimum for the approach to be flown, and visibility at least 1 SM but never less than the minimum for the approach to be flown. If your alternate airport does not have a published instrument approach procedure, the ceiling and visibility minimums must allow you to descend from the MEA, approach, and land under basic VFR.

PART 135 OPERATORS

When you fly under Part 135, you are not required to file an alternate if the ceiling will be at least 1,500 feet above the lowest circling approach MDA for at least one hour before and one hour after your ETA. If a circling instrument approach is not authorized for the airport, the ceiling must be at least 1,500 feet above the lowest published minimum or 2,000 feet above the airport elevation, whichever is higher. For the instrument approach procedure to be used at the destination airport, the forecasted visibility for that airport must be at least 3 SM, or 2 SM more than the lowest applicable visibility minimums, whichever is greater. If you operate under Part 135, alternate landing minimums are described in your OpsSpecs.

HELICOPTER INSTRUMENT APPROACHES

Helicopters can fly a variety of approaches, including standard instrument approaches for airplanes and procedures developed especially for helicopters. Helicopter instrument flight is relatively new compared to airplane instrument flight, so there are not as many approaches designed specifically for helicopters. They vary depending on whether they lead to an airport, a heliport, or a point in space (PinS) from which you can proceed under VFR to a heliport. Some approaches are designated as public, and can be flown by any appropriately-rated pilot in a properly-equipped IFR helicopter. Other procedures are designated as Special, and can only be used by pilots who have undergone specific training for that procedure [Figure 6-7]

Procedure	Helicopter Visibility Minimums	Helicopter MDA/DA	Maximum Speed Limitations
Conventional (non-Copter)	The greater of: one half the Category A visibility minimums, 1/4 statute mile visibility, or 1200 RVR	As published for Category A	The helicopter may initiate the final approach segment at speeds up to the upper limit of the highest Approach Category authorized by the procedure, but must be slowed to no more than 90 KIAS at the MAP in order to apply the visibility reduction.
Copter Procedure	As published	As published	90 KIAS when on a published route/track.
GPS Copter Procedure	As published	As published	90 KIAS when on a published route or track, EXCEPT 70 KIAS when on the final approach or missed approach segment and, if annotated, in holding. Military procedures are limited to 90 KIAS for all segments.

Figure 6-7. Minimums and speed limitations depend on the type of approach procedure.

STANDARD INSTRUMENT APPROACH PROCEDURES TO AN AIRPORT

When flying standard (non-copter) IAPs, you must adhere to the MDA, DA, or DH for Category A, and you may reduce the airplane Category A visibility by 1/2, but not less than 1/4 SM or RVR 1200. Some procedures have the notation "Visibility Reduction by Helicopters NA," which means that the visibility reduction doesn't apply due to obstacles that protrude into the protected area for some portion of the approach.

You can begin the approach at any speed up to the highest approach category authorized, but your speed on final must be reduced to the Category A speed of 90 knots or less before the MAP in order to apply the visibility reduction. For safety, you should fly a constant airspeed on the final approach segment, to comply with the stabilized approach concept. A decelerating approach could make it difficult or impossible to identify wind shear on the approach path.

COPTER ONLY APPROACHES

As the name indicates, Copter approaches are designed specifically for helicopters, so you must use the published minimums with no reductions in visibility requirements. Copter approaches have been designed for both airports and heliports. For Copter approaches other than GPS, you are limited to a maximum airspeed of 90 KIAS on any segment of the approach or missed approach. [Figure 6-8]

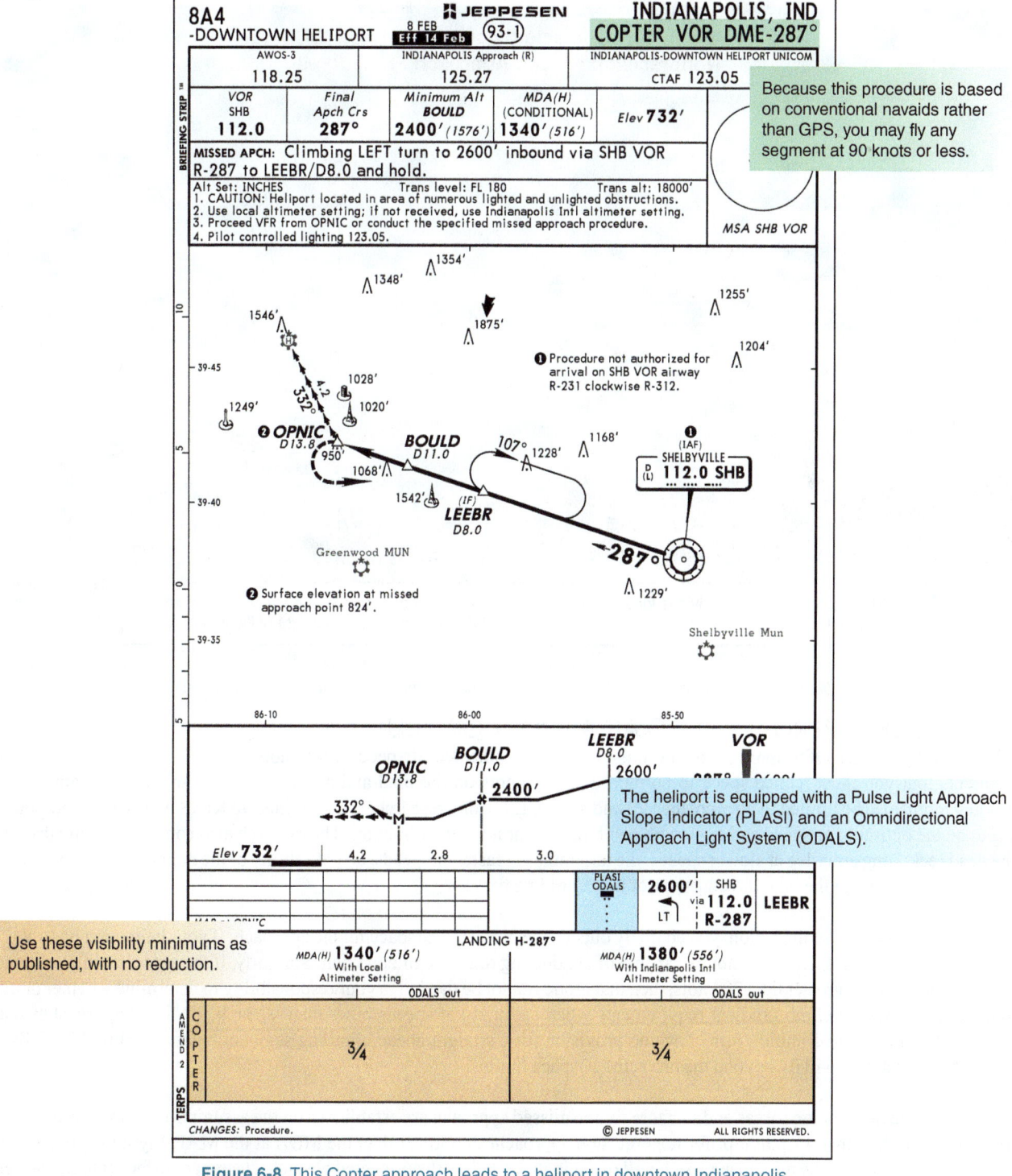

Figure 6-8. This Copter approach leads to a heliport in downtown Indianapolis.

The ability of helicopters to climb steeply and at slow airspeeds is reflected in the design of the missed approach segment of a Copter approach. The OCS for all Copter approaches is a 20:1 inclined plane, which is twice as steep as the OCS used to evaluate the missed approach segment for an airplane. Helicopter climb performance is therefore anticipated to be double the

6-9

airplane's gradient. A minimum climb gradient of at least 400 feet per nautical mile is required unless a higher gradient is published on the approach chart. A helicopter with a groundspeed of 70 KIAS is required to climb at a rate at 467 ft/min (70 KIAS × 400 feet per NM/60 seconds = 467 ft/min.). The advantage of using the steeper missed approach segment is that the missed approach point can be located closer to obstructions, and the MDA might be lower for helicopters than for other aircraft. The minimum required climb gradient of 400 feet per NM for the helicopter in a missed approach will provide 96 feet of required obstacle clearance (ROC) for each NM of flight path. [Figure 6-9]

20:1 Versus 40:1 Obstacle Clearance Surface (OCS) for Nonprecision Missed Approach Procedures

The Copter 20:1 OCS provides for a lower MDA for the helicopter than for the airplane. A climb gradient of 400 ft/NM will allow a required obstacle clearance (ROC) of 96 ft/NM for each NM of flight path.

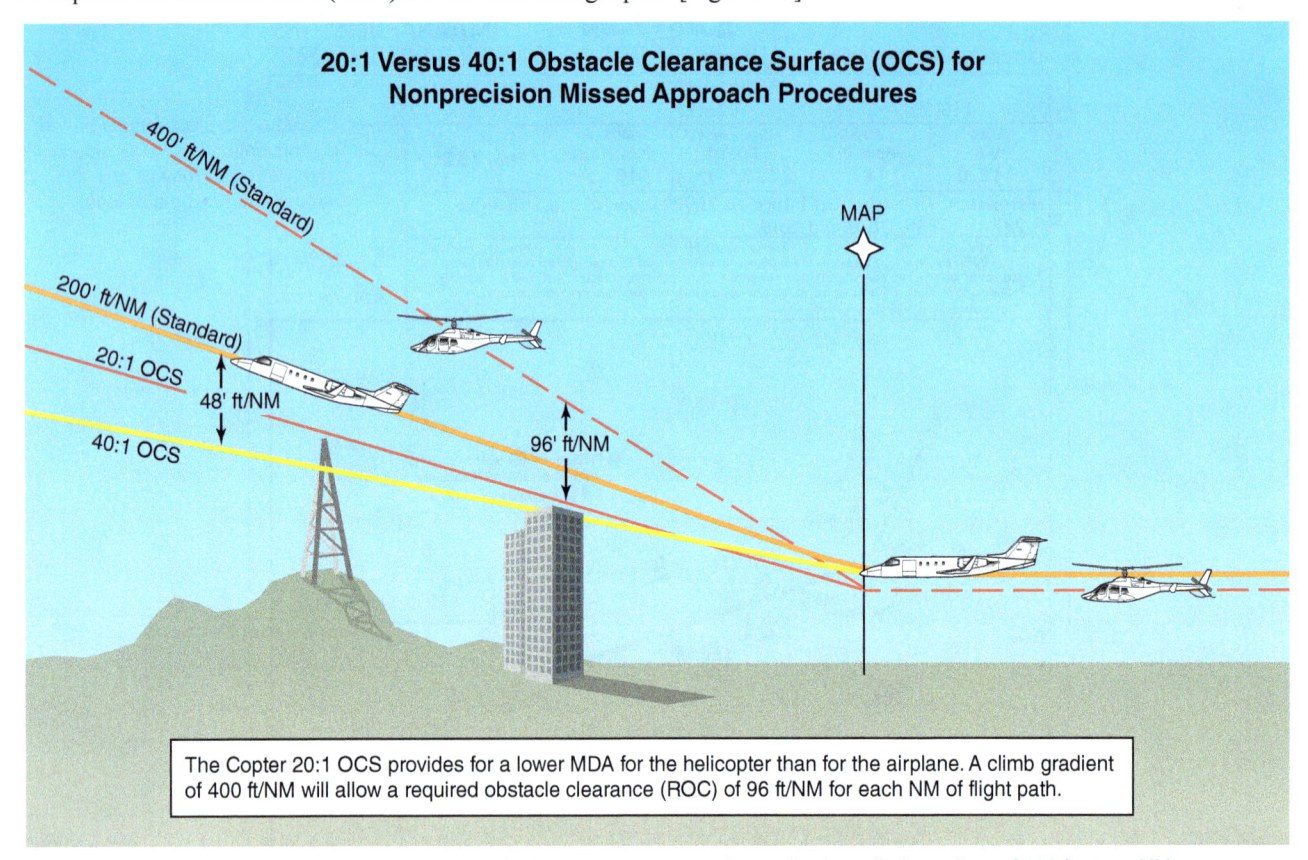

Figure 6-9. During a missed approach, helicopters are expected to maintain a climb gradient of 400 feet per NM.

COPTER GPS APPROACHES TO AN AIRPORT OR HELIPORT

When you fly Copter GPS approaches you must limit your indicated airspeed to 90 knots on the initial and intermediate segments, but you must reduce speed to no more than 70 knots on the final and missed approach segments. If annotated, holding might also be limited to no more than 70 knots. During testing, researchers determined 90 KIAS with a 3 NM outbound leg to be the optimum airspeed and leg length combination for helicopter holding. The research also considered wind drift on the dead reckoning entry leg at slower speeds, the turn radius at faster airspeeds, and the ability of the helicopter in strong wind conditions to intercept the inbound course prior to the holding fix.

If you exceed the 70 knot limitation, you could fly outside the protected airspace for the approach. If your helicopter has a V_{MINI} greater than 70 knots, then it will not be capable of conducting this type of approach. Similarly, if the autopilot in go-around mode climbs at a V_{YI} greater than 70 knots, then that mode cannot be used. It is your responsibility to determine whether or not you can comply with climb gradient requirements when operating at speeds other than V_Y or V_{YI}. Missed approaches that specify an "immediate climbing turn" have no provision for a straight ahead climbing segment before turning. If you fly a straight segment, you will fly beyond the protected airspace limits.

Protected obstacle clearance areas and surfaces for the missed approach are established on the assumption that you initiate the missed approach at the DA point, or for nonprecision approaches no lower than the MDA at the MAP. Flying beyond either point before beginning the missed approach will result in flying below the protected obstacle clearance surface (OCS) and can result in a collision with an obstacle.

APPROACH PROCEDURES TO A VFR HELIPORT

Some helicopter approaches have been developed to provide access to heliports that do not meet the design standards for an IFR heliport. The majority of IFR approaches to VFR heliports are developed in support of HEMS operators. These approaches can be based on conventional ground-based navaids or on an RNAV system such as GPS. Some are public approaches, which require no special training, but many are Special Approaches, which require special pilot training and authorization for use. These instrument procedures are developed as either an approach designed to a specific landing site, or an approach designed to a point-in-space.

APPROACHES TO A SPECIFIC LANDING SITE

The approach is aligned so that when the helicopter reaches the missed approach point, the pilot can make a landing with a course change of 30 degrees or less. The visual segment from the MAP to the landing site is evaluated for obstacle hazards. These procedures carry the notation "Proceed visually from (named MAP) or conduct the specified missed approach." The wording "Proceed visually..." indicates that you must adhere to the **published visibility minimums** for the approach throughout the visual segment from the MAP to the landing site, and you must be able to see specified lights at the heliport before proceeding visually. You must decide before reaching the MAP whether you will have the required visibility, and if not, you must execute the missed approach from the MAP. You are responsible for obstacle or terrain avoidance from the MAP to the landing site. When you reach the MAP (or as soon as practicable afterward), tell ATC whether you are proceeding visually and canceling IFR or executing the missed approach. [Figure 6-10]

POINT-IN-SPACE APPROACHES

Point-in-Space, or PinS, procedures have been developed at locations where the MAP is located more than 2 SM from the landing site, or the path from the MAP to the landing site is populated with obstructions which require avoidance actions, or the flight path requires turns greater than 30 degrees. In some cases, a single PinS procedure can allow you to fly from the MAP to one of several landing areas. These procedures involve a VFR segment between the MAP and the landing area. The procedure specifies a course and distance from the MAP to the available heliports in the area.

The note associated with this procedure is: "Proceed VFR from (named MAP) or conduct the specified missed approach." The wording "Proceed VFR..." has a different meaning than the "Proceed visually..." language in the previous section. In this case, you must determine if the flight visibility meets the **basic VFR minimums**. These procedures require you to determine if you have the visibility available to safely transition from IFR to VFR flight, based on the published minimum visibility, or the weather minimums required by the operating rule, or your OpSpecs (whichever is higher). If you

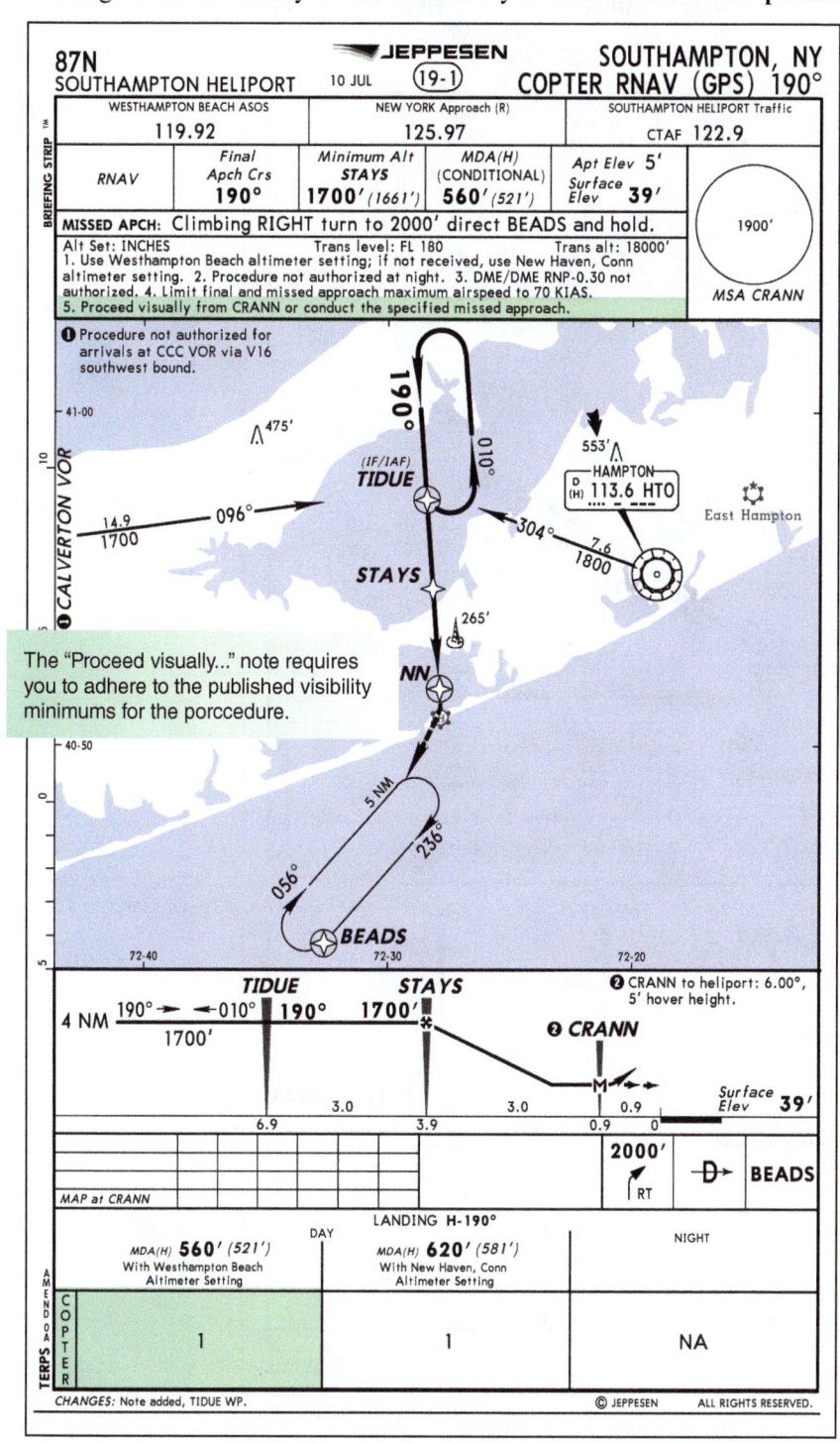

Figure 6-10. The MAP for this Copter GPS approach is less than a mile from the landing site. The visibility minimum is one mile, so if you have the required visibility, you should be able to see the helipad from the MAP.

6-11

don't have the required visibility at or prior to reaching the MAP, you must execute a missed approach. For Part 135 operations, you may not begin the approach unless the latest weather report indicates that the weather conditions are at or above the authorized IFR minimums or the VFR weather minimums (as required by the class of airspace, operating rule, and/or OpSpecs) whichever is higher. You are not required to have visual contact with the landing site, but you must maintain the higher of the VFR weather minimums throughout the visual segment. IFR obstruction clearance areas are not applied to the VFR segment between the MAP and the landing site, so you are responsible for avoiding terrain and obstacles. You must maintain the required visibility until canceling IFR. If SVFR minimums exist and you are in Class B, C, D, or E surface area airspace, you are responsible for obtaining a SVFR clearance. If VFR conditions exist at the MAP, advise ATC of your intent to proceed VFR and cancel IFR. [Figure 6-11]

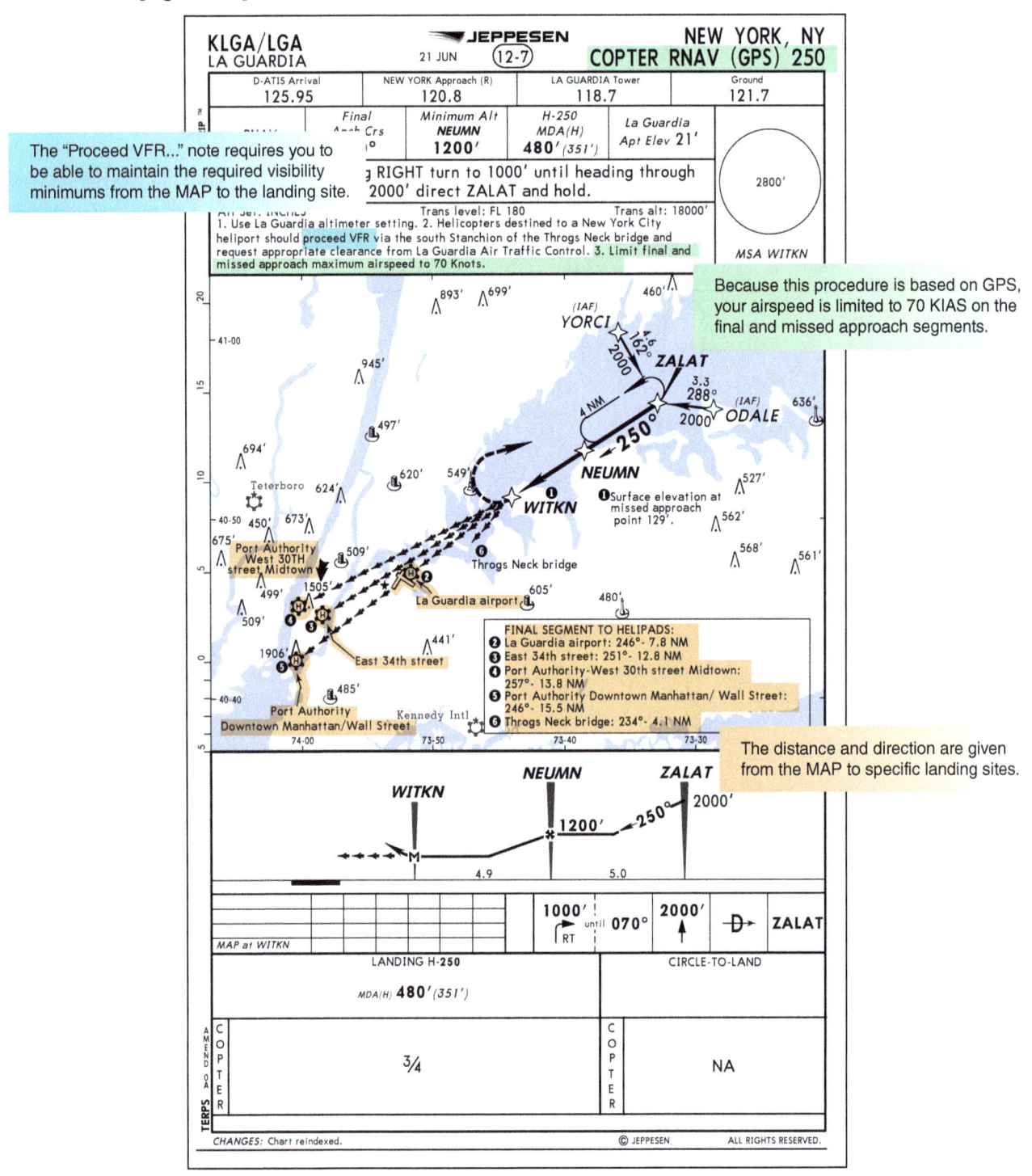

Figure 6-11. This Copter PinS approach allows you to fly VFR from the MAP to La Guardia Airport as well as to heliports in the area.

SPECIAL APPROACHES

Special approach procedures can include approaches to hospitals, oil rigs, or private heliports, as well as airports. Special procedures require Flight Standards approval by a Letter of Authorization for Part 91 operators or by OpsSpecs for Part 135 operators. Due to their unique characteristics, each of these approaches requires specific training. Approach charts include the note: "Special aircrew and aircraft certification required" because the FAA must approve the helicopter and its avionics, and the flight crew must have the required experience, training, and checking. To apply for authorization to use a Special procedure, you must have at least a private pilot helicopter certificate, an instrument helicopter rating, and a type rating if the helicopter requires a type rating. You must also have at least 250 hours as PIC, 100 hours as PIC in helicopters, 50 hours as PIC at night, and 75 hours of actual or simulated instrument flight time, including at least 25 hours of actual or simulated instrument flight time in a helicopter or a helicopter flight simulator, plus the appropriate recent experience, training, and check. To apply for this certification, contact your local Flight Standards District Office.

INADVERTENT FLIGHT INTO IMC

If you fly for a living, chances are you will sometimes need to operate in challenging weather conditions. You might not be able to continue VFR when you encounter conditions that prevent you from seeing the natural horizon, such as fog, snow showers, or night operations over unlit surfaces such as water. Flying in conditions of flat lighting or low visual contrast can cause you to lose depth perception or to misread the size and shape of the topography. Examples include flying over snow or calm, glassy water when the sky is overcast. Low contrast environments can cause you to lose horizontal or surface reference, and obstacles such as wires become invisible to you. To reduce the risk of spatial disorientation, loss of control, or CFIT, slow the helicopter to a speed that will allow you to decelerate within a distance equal to your forward visibility. Look for terrain that provides sufficient contrast to either continue the flight or to make a precautionary landing. If you experience spatial disorientation and a climb into IMC is not feasible (perhaps due to fuel state, icing conditions, or lack of proper equipment) make every effort to land the helicopter with a slight forward descent to prevent any sideward or rearward motion.

It is a good idea to obtain training on avoiding and recovering from inadvertent flight into IMC, with emphasis on avoidance. An unplanned transition from VFR to IFR flight is an emergency that requires a different set of pilot actions. You need to use different navigation and operational procedures, interact differently with ATC, and apply different crewmember resource management (CRM). Consider the terrain under you, airspace, air traffic facilities, weather, and available airport or heliport approaches. Training should emphasize the identification of conditions that lead to inadvertent IMC and a strategy to abandon continued VFR flight in deteriorating conditions. This strategy should include a minimum altitude/airspeed combination that provides for an off-airport/heliport landing, diverting to better conditions, or initiating an emergency transition to IFR. To avoid CFIT, you should be able to readily identify a minimum initial altitude and course that takes you away from higher terrain or provides a safe altitude above it. It is essential to have current IFR en route and approach charts. A GPS receiver with a moving map can help with situational awareness, but be aware that you cannot rely on your GPS for terrain and obstacle avoidance.

Training for an emergency transition to IFR should include full and partial panel instrument flight, unusual attitude recovery, ATC communications, and instrument approaches. In general, an ILS approach should be your first choice, if your helicopter has the equipment. If the helicopter has an IFR approach-capable GPS receiver with a current database, consider making a GPS approach. If neither an ILS nor a GPS procedure is available use another instrument approach.

Upon entering inadvertent IMC, your first priority is to control the helicopter. Keep it simple and take one action at a time.

- **Control.** First use the attitude indicator to level the helicopter. Maintain heading and increase to climb power. Establish climb airspeed at the best angle of climb but no slower than V_{MINI}.

- **Climb.** Climb straight ahead until you have established your crosscheck. Then make turns only to avoid terrain or objects. If ATC has not assigned an altitude to climb to for inadvertent IMC, then you should climb to an altitude that is at least 1,000 feet above the highest known object and contact ATC.

- **Communicate.** Attempt to contact ATC as soon as the helicopter is stabilized in the climb and headed away from danger. If you don't know the appropriate frequency, try to contact ATC on a standard emergency frequency (121.5 VHF or 243.0 UHF). Tell ATC your approximate location, that you have encountered IMC and made an emergency climb, state your altitude, amount of flight time remaining (fuel state), and the number of persons on board. Request a vector to either VFR weather conditions or to the nearest suitable airport/heliport with weather conditions that will support a successful approach. If unable to contact ATC, change the transponder code to 7700 unless ATC has already assigned you a code for inadvertent IMC.

Appendix A
Airborne Navigation Databases

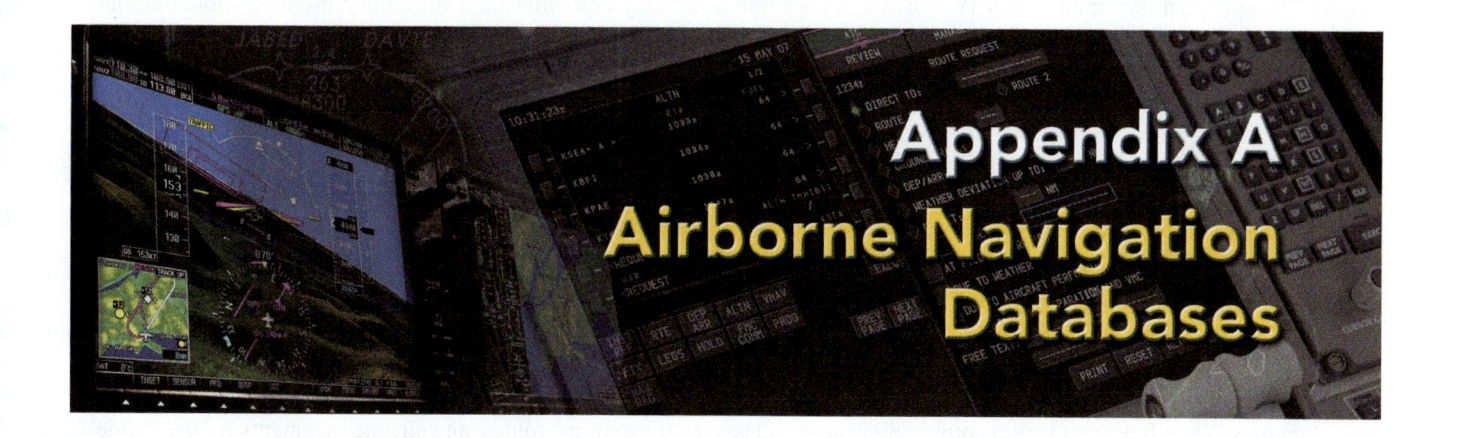

EVOLUTION OF AIRBORNE NAVIGATION DATABASES

There are nearly as many different RNAV platforms operating in the NAS as there are aircraft types. The range of systems and their capabilities is greater now than at any other time in aviation history. From the simplest panel-mounted GPS in a general aviation aircraft to the fully integrated flight management system (FMS) in a commercial airliner, the navigation database is essential. [Figure A-1]

All RNAV systems are capable of determining an aircraft's position over the surface of the earth, but they also must be able to relate that position to the location of other fixes in order to navigate. RNAV systems rely on internal navigation databases to hold detailed information about these fixed points in the airspace or on the earth's surface. In addition to the locations and identifiers of the points required for navigation, the nature of the database makes it possible to provide many other useful pieces of information about a given location.

In 1973, National Airlines installed the Collins RNAV systems in their DC-10 fleet, and a short time later, Delta Air Lines began using an ARMA Corporation RNAV system. Both systems used internal databases, and although the data stored in the two systems was very similar, the designers created the databases to work within the unique electronics of each system. Despite the commonality of the data, there were no standards for format or content, but it was not a problem at the time because so few of the systems were in use. As the use of RNAV systems expanded, designers recognized the need for a world standard for airborne navigation databases.

Figure A-1. Area navigation receivers differ in appearance, operation, and capabilities.

In 1973, Aeronautical Radio, Inc. (ARINC) sponsored the formation of a committee to standardize aeronautical databases. The committee published the first standard (ARINC Specification 424) in 1975, and it has remained the worldwide accepted format for coding airborne navigation databases.

The use of RNAV equipment and their airborne navigation databases has significantly increased the capabilities of aircraft operating in the NAS. Pilots and flight crews are now capable of direct flight over long distances with increasing precision. RNAV equipment is now used by all facets of commercial, corporate, and general aviation. Airborne navigation databases have played a large role in this progress. There are many different types of RNAV systems certified for IFR use in the NAS. The two most prevalent types are GPS and the multi-sensor FMS.

Most GPSs operate as stand-alone RNAV systems. A GPS unit accurately determines the aircraft's present position, but that information is virtually useless without some means of relating it to other locations. The database provides the GPS with position information on the bearings and distances to navigation fixes, enabling the GPS to perform the required geodetic calculations to determine the appropriate tracks, headings, and distances to be flown.

Modern FMS systems are capable of a large number of functions including basic enroute navigation, complex departure and arrival navigation, fuel planning, and precise vertical navigation. Unlike stand-alone navigation systems, most FMSs use several navigation inputs. Typically, they derive the aircraft's current position using a combination of conventional DME signals, inertial navigation sensors, GPS receivers, or other RNAV devices. But like stand-alone navigation avionics, they rely heavily on their internal navigation databases to provide the information needed to perform their numerous functions.

DATABASE CAPABILITIES

The capabilities of airborne navigation databases depend largely on the way they are implemented by the avionics manufacturers. Their functions include providing data on thousands of locations, routes, and airspace segments for use inside the RNAV equipment. In addition, databases can display information to you about airports, ATC frequencies, runways, special use airspace, and much more. These "external" database features add a lot to the value of the RNAV equipment.

Much of the information in an EFB comes from the same source as the database in the aircraft's RNAV avionics, and depending on the database provider, the EFB database can contain much of the same information as the aircraft's FMS or GPS database. Although similar, the information needed for an EFB is significantly different from that needed for onboard navigation avionics, and respective avionics and EFB databases remain independent of each other. For example, the EFB database contains the necessary information to allow replacement of traditional printed instrument charts. EFB charting applications can include terminal charts, enroute moving map (EMM), and airport moving map (AMM). The EFB's terminal charts application uses the same information and layout as the printed chart counterpart. The EMM application uses the same en route data as a GPS or FMS database, but adds additional information specific to charting needs. The EFB AMM database shows the aircraft location relative to elements of the airport environment that are not needed in an airborne navigation database, such as ramps, taxiways, buildings, and hold-short lines.

PRODUCTION AND DISTRIBUTION

In order to understand the capabilities and limitations of airborne navigation databases, you should have a basic understanding of the way databases are compiled and revised by the database provider and processed by the avionics manufacturer.

ROLE OF THE DATABASE PROVIDER

Compiling and maintaining a worldwide airborne navigation database is a large and complex job. Within the United States, the majority of official flight navigation data comes from FAA sources, supplemented by airport managers, state civil aviation authorities, Department of Defense organizations such as the National Geospatial-Intelligence Agency, and branches of the military service. Outside the U.S., the majority of official data is provided by each country's civil aviation authority and compiled in an aeronautical information publication (AIP). Sources provide information to database providers in various formats. It must then be analyzed, edited, and processed before it can be coded into the database. The information changes constantly as new obstructions are built or removed, runways are lengthened or closed, and new procedures are developed, so updating and maintaining navigation database information is a continuous process. Jeppesen supplies the databases used by most avionics manufacturers, both in the U.S. and internationally. To ensure that flight crews have the latest navigation data and the most current changes to the world's airspace system, Jeppesen offers either one-time updates or subscription services.

Changes are incorporated during a 28-day database revision cycle, based on their assigned priority. If the information does not reach the coding phase prior to the cutoff date for the current cycle (the date that new aeronautical information can no longer be included in the next update), it is held out of revision until the next cycle.

Database providers ensure the integrity of the data through a process called a cyclic redundancy check (CRC). A CRC is an error detection algorithm capable of detecting small bit-level changes in a block of data. The CRC algorithm treats a data block as a single (large) binary value. The data block is divided by a fixed binary number (called a "generator polynomial") whose form and magnitude is determined based on the level of integrity desired. The remainder of the division is the CRC value for the data block. This value is stored and transmitted with the corresponding data block. The database provider checks the integrity of the data by reapplying the CRC algorithm prior to distribution. Later, the avionics equipment onboard the aircraft uses the same process to check data integrity.

THE ROLE OF THE AVIONICS MANUFACTURER

When avionics manufacturers develop a piece of equipment that requires an airborne navigation database, they typically form an agreement with a database provider to supply the database for that new avionics platform. The manufacturer determines what information to include in the database for their system. For example, the avionics manufacturer might specify that the database include only runways longer than 4,000 feet. In some cases, the navigation database provider has to significantly reduce the number of records in the database to accommodate the storage capacity of the manufacturer's new product.

Each manufacturer can design its systems to use the data fields in different ways, depending on the needs of the avionics. The manufacturer decides how its equipment handles the records. They make decisions about each field in the record. For instance, a manufacturer might decide not to include the ARINC primary record for an individual runway in the database for a specific model or unit that they manufacture. If the record is included in the tailored database, some of the fields in that record might not be used.

Although standard naming conventions are part of the ARINC 424 specification, each manufacturer chooses how to display the names of fixes and procedures to the pilot. This means that although the approach identifier field for the VOR/DME Runway 34 approach at Eugene Mahlon Sweet Airport (KEUG) in Eugene, Oregon, might be specified in the database as "V34," different avionics platforms can display the identifier in any way the manufacturer deems appropriate. [Figure A-2] An approach identifier in your avionics might not be the same as on navigation charts or on avionics displays from other manufacturers. These differences can also create confusion when you receive approach clearances and other ATC instructions unless you are familiar with your equipment manufacturer's naming conventions.

The manufacturer determines the capabilities and limitations of an RNAV system based on its decisions about that system's processing of the airborne navigation database.

ROLE OF THE USER

Like paper charts, airborne navigation databases require frequent revision to reflect recent changes. Pilots are ultimately responsible for ensuring that they use a current database. This includes checking "NOTAM-type information" concerning errors, which is provided by the avionics manufacturer or the database supplier. You are responsible for learning how the navigation equipment you use handles the navigation database. The manufacturer's documentation is your best source of information regarding the capabilities and limitations of a specific database. [Figure A-3]

Figure A-2. Different avionics manufacturers might display the same information in different formats.

Database Providers	Avionics Manufacturers	Pilots (End Users)
• Collect the Data • Format per ARINC 424 • Revise and Maintain Database	Decide on: • Information to be Included • How Information will be Processed • User Interface	• Ensure Currency • Execute Updates • Responsible for Working Knowledge of Avionics using Database

Figure A-3. For safe IFR operations, database providers, avionics manufacturers, and pilots must all fulfill their responsibilities.

COMPOSITION OF AIRBORNE NAVIGATION DATABASES

Global position is an important concept of RNAV. Short-range navigation deals primarily with azimuth and distance on a relatively small, flat surface, but long-range navigation must have a method of defining positions on the face of a large and imperfect sphere. The latitude-longitude system is currently used to define these positions. Each location in an airborne navigation database must be described by latitude and longitude values in order to be used by avionics systems in navigation calculations.

THE WGS-84 REFERENCE DATUM

Scientists have understood the generally spherical shape of the earth for about 2,500 years. This idea has been refined over time into the current very detailed description of the earth's shape. Unfortunately, the actual topographic shape of the earth's surface is far too complex to be stored as a reference datum in the memories of today's avionics. Likewise, the mathematical calculations necessary to determine distance and direction using such a reference datum would be prohibitively complex. A simplified model of the earth's surface solves both of these problems. This model of the earth is referred to as the Reference Ellipsoid, and when used with other mathematical parameters, it defines the reference for geodetic calculations, which is referred to as the geodetic datum.

The reference datum used in North America for airborne navigation databases is the North American Datum of 1983 (NAD-83), which is essentially equivalent to the World Geodetic System of 1984 (WGS-84). The constellation of GPS satellites is referenced to WGS-84, making it the required datum for flight by reference to a GPS according to FAA Technical Standard Order TSO C129. The International Civil Aviation Organization (ICAO) and the international aviation community recognized the need for a common reference frame and designated WGS-84 as the worldwide geodetic standard.

ARINC 424

First published in 1975, the ARINC 424 document sets forth the air transport industry's recommended standards for the preparation of airborne navigation system reference databases. This document outlines the information to be included in the database for each specific navigation entity (i.e., airports, navaids, airways, waypoints, and approaches), as well as the format in which the data is coded. The ARINC specification determines naming conventions for the database.

ARINC records can be sorted into four general groups: records of fixes, simple routes, complex routes, and miscellaneous records. You don't need in-depth knowledge of all the fields contained in the ARINC 424 records, but familiarity with the types of records contained in the navigation database and their general content can help you to understand how the system operates.

Record — A single line of computer data made up of the fields that define a single entity such as an airport, navaid, route, or waypoint.

Field — A set of columns that defines one aspect of a record, such as an airport's elevation.

Columns — The spaces for data entry that make up the fields on each record. One column can accommodate one character.

RECORDS

The data in an airborne navigation database is organized into records. Each record describes a single navigation entity. Each record is in a standard format with 132 columns or spaces for characters. Not all of the 132 character positions are occupied in every record — some of the positions are left blank to permit like information to appear in the same columns of different records, and others are reserved for possible future record expansion. These records are divided into fields that contain specific pieces of information about the subject of the record. The record type determines what fields are included and how they are organized. For example, the primary record for an airport always contains a field that describes the longest runway at that airport in columns 28 through 30. [Figure A-4] These columns would describe a different characteristic in the record for a VOR or an airway.

Fix Records

Records that describe specific locations on the face of the earth can be considered fix records. Navaids, waypoints, intersections, and airports are all examples of this type of record. These records can be used directly by avionics systems and can be included as parts of more complex records like airways or approaches. Within a fix record, there are several fields that are generally common to all: record type, latitude, longitude, ICAO fix identifier, and ICAO location code. One exception is airports that use FAA identifiers. [Figure A-5]

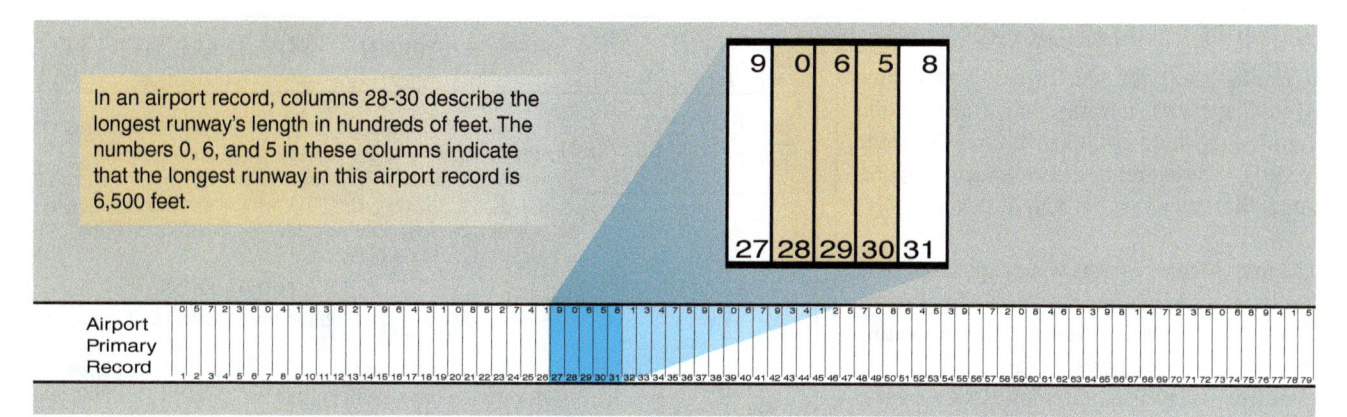

In an airport record, columns 28-30 describe the longest runway's length in hundreds of feet. The numbers 0, 6, and 5 in these columns indicate that the longest runway in this airport record is 6,500 feet.

Figure A-4. This graphic gives you an idea of how an ARINC 424 record is organized. Fields within the record describe specific details about the subject of the record.

Each of these records deals with magnetic variation in a slightly different manner. Magnetic variation must be included in these records so that it can be used to calculate the magnetic courses displayed in the cockpit

Airport	VOR	Waypoint
• Longest Runway • IFR Capability • Magnetic Variation • Airport Elevation • Transition Altitude for Flight Level	• VOR Frequency • Navaid Class • Station Declination • DME Indent	• Waypoint Type • Waypoint Usage • Dynamic Magnetic Variation

For airports, magnetic variation is given as the difference in degrees between the measured values of true north and magnetic north at that location.

For VORs, the field labeled "Station Declination" describes variation in terms of the angular difference between true north and the zero degree radial of the VOR the last time the site was checked.

For a waypoint, the "Dynamic Magnetic Variation" field uses a variation value calculated using a computer model instead of a measured value.

Figure A-5. Fix records of different types contain fields that are specific to the type of fix they describe.

Simple Route Records

Route records describe a flight path instead of a fixed position. Simple route records contain strings of fix records and information on how the fixes should be used by the navigation avionics. A Victor Airway, for example, is described in the database by a series of "enroute airway records" that contain the names of fixes in the airway and information about how those fixes make up the airway. The records include fix identifiers, sequence numbers, route type, required navigation performance (RNP), inbound and outbound magnetic courses (if appropriate), route distance, and minimum and maximum altitudes for the route.

Sequence number fields keep track of the order of fixes within the route. Most routes can be entered from any point and flown in either direction. The sequence number allows the avionics to keep the fixes in order to provide the proper flight path starting from anywhere within the route.

Complex Route Records

Complex route records include those strings of fixes that describe complex flight paths like SIDs, STARs, and instrument approach procedures. Like simple routes, these records contain the names of fixes in the route as well as instructions on how to fly the route. Complex routes also contain several unique fields. For example, some of the fields included in a SID record include the airport identifier, SID identifier, transition identifier, turn direction, recommended navaid, magnetic course, and path/terminator.

Miscellaneous Records

Other types of records coded into airborne navigation databases might include records for restricted airspace, airport minimum safe altitudes, and grid minimum off-route altitudes (MORAs). These records have many unique fields that combine to describe the subject of the record. Some are used by avionics manufacturers, some are not, depending on the individual capabilities of each RNAV unit.

PATH/TERMINATOR CONCEPT

It is important for you to understand how RNAV systems interface with the "Path/Terminator" field included in complex route records. These fields create specific operational limitations within RNAV systems.

The first RNAV systems were capable of only one type of navigation: they could fly directly to a fix. This was sufficient when operating enroute along airways made up of direct routes between fixes. Existing RNAV instrument approaches were no problem for these systems because they consisted mainly of GPS overlay approaches that used direct point-to-point navigation. The need for RNAV equipment to be able to follow more complicated flight paths led to the development of the "Path/Terminator" field that is part of each record for a complex route.

A wide variety of different path/terminators in the ARINC 424 standard enable RNAV systems to follow the flight paths that make up instrument departures, arrivals, and approaches. Within the navigation avionics, they describe the path to follow and the criteria that must be met before each path concludes and the next path begins. Some RNAV (RNP) instrument approach procedures incorporate precision curved flight tracks defined in terms of a radius from a fix with specific initial and end points. Figures A-6 and A-7 illustrate examples of five common path/terminators: track to fix (TF), heading to altitude (VA), direct to fix (DF), heading to radial (VR), and heading to intercept (VI). For a more detailed discussion of coding standards, refer to ARINC Specification 424-15, Navigation System Data Base.

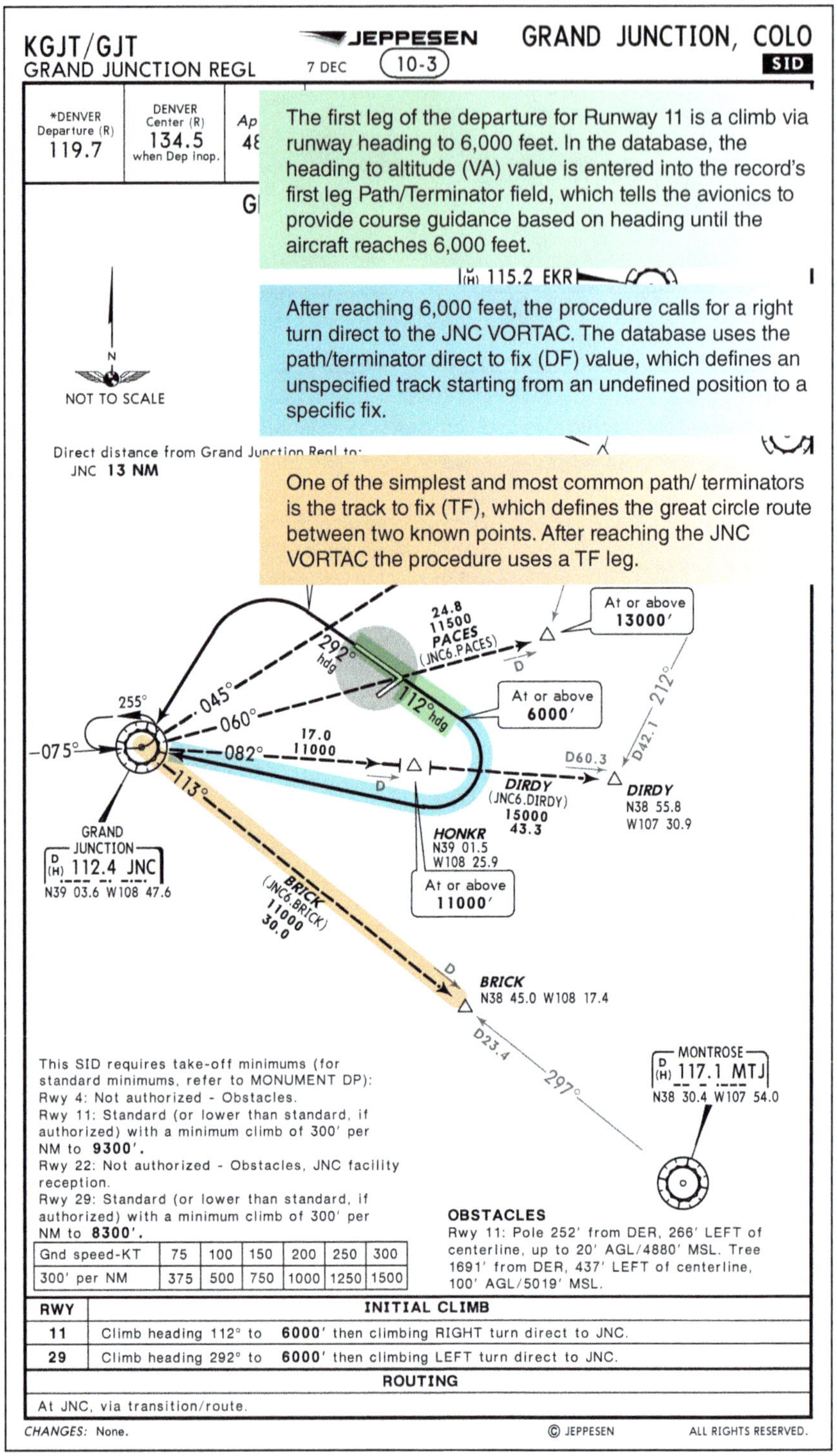

OPERATIONAL LIMITATIONS OF AIRBORNE NAVIGATION DATABASES

One of your biggest concerns in IFR flight is understanding the capabilities and limitations of your aircraft's navigation systems. Considering the large number of RNAV systems and pilot interfaces, it is critical that you study the manufacturer's operating manual for each RNAV system you operate, and that you maintain proficiency in operating those systems in the IFR environment.

Figure A-6. The GRAND JUNCTION SIX DEPARTURE for Walker Field in Grand Junction, Colorado, provides good examples of three types of path/terminators.

RELIANCE ON NAVIGATION AUTOMATION

Cockpit automation has been a factor in a significant fraction of recent aircraft accidents. Misinterpretation, errors in programming or use, and failure to monitor modes and functions can have serious consequences. Given the intimate relationship between automation and the airborne navigation database, it is particularly important to stay proficient and to have a thorough understanding of the limitations of the automation you use. Capabilities, displays, and operating procedures differ widely between systems. Although modern avionics can provide precise guidance throughout all phases of flight, subtle differences in programming or interpretation can lead to unexpected situations.

Most modern RNAV systems are part of an integrated avionics system that receives input from several different navigation and aircraft system sensors. These systems can provide so much information that many well-trained, conscientious, and experienced flight crews have failed to recognize errors in navigation caused by database discrepancies or misuse. The best way to avoid such errors is to be careful when programming, check your work, and be sure the data you enter is accurate and current. Once the transition to RNAV is made during a flight, you must always be capable and ready to revert to conventional navigation if problems arise. While the systems used for IFR are extremely reliable, components can and do fail. Guard against becoming complacent or overly dependent on automated systems. Maintain your hand-flying skills and use other resources, such as charts, to keep track of your position and to verify critical information.

STORAGE LIMITATIONS

As the data in a worldwide database grows more detailed, the space required for data storage increases. The size of GPS and FMS databases has grown exponentially. Some manufacturer's systems have kept up with this growth and some have not. Many of the limitations of older RNAV systems are a direct result of limited data storage capacity. For this reason, avionics manufacturers must make decisions regarding which types of data records are extracted from the master database to be included with their systems, and which data to leave out. For instance, older GPS units rarely include all of the waypoints that are coded into master databases. Typically, even FMS units do not include all of the data that is available from the database providers. The manufacturers often choose not to include certain types of data that they think is unnecessary for the use of the unit. For example, manufacturers of FMS units used in large airplanes might decide not to include airports where the longest runway is shorter than 3,000 feet because large airplanes seldom use those runways.

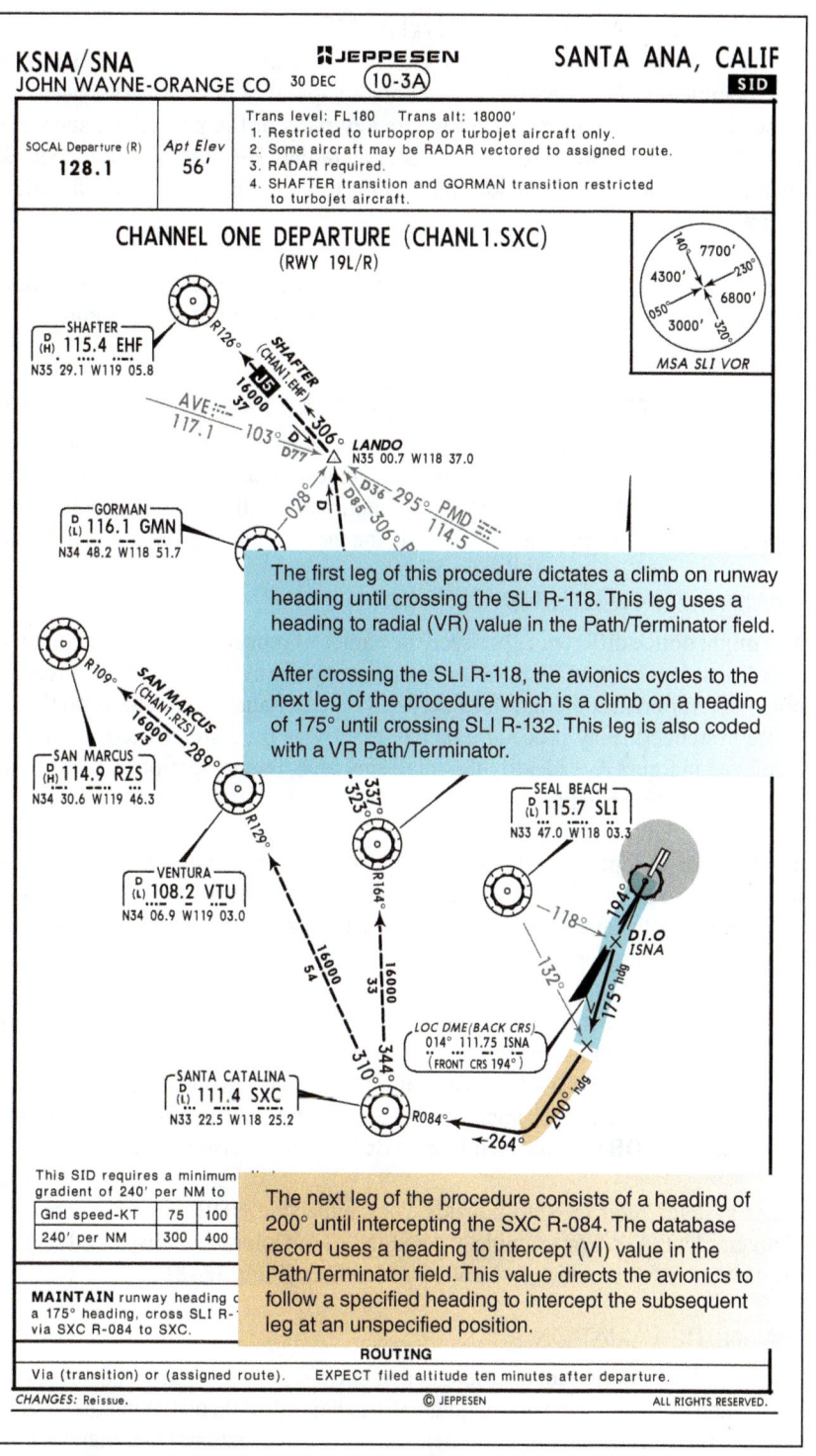

Figure A-7. The CHANNEL ONE DEPARTURE procedure for Santa Ana, California provides examples of two types of path/terminators.

Manufacturers of RNAV equipment can reduce the size of the data storage required in their avionics by limiting the geographic area the database covers. Like paper charts, the amount of data you need to carry in the aircraft is proportional to the size of the coverage area. Depending on the amount of available storage for the data, a database with a large coverage area might include less detailed data. Again, due to the wide range of possible storage capacities, and the number of different manufacturers and product lines, the manufacturer's documentation is your best source of information regarding limitations caused by the storage capacity of your avionics.

A-7

PATH/TERMINATOR LIMITATIONS

You should understand how your RNAV system deals with path/terminators. Some older RNAV systems might ignore this field completely. The lack of path/terminator capability in an RNAV system can cause problems on procedures that include these elements. The system might ignore key parts of the procedure, such as climbs on headings that terminate at specific altitudes or turns after crossing a specific radial. Be sure you understand how your system handles path/terminator characteristics and always review the manufacturer's documentation to familiarize yourself with the capabilities of the RNAV equipment you use.

You should also be aware that some RNAV equipment was designed without the fly-over capability that was discussed in Chapters 2 and 5. This can cause problems if you attempt to use this equipment to fly complex flight paths in the departure, arrival, or approach environments.

INCONSISTENCIES BETWEEN CHARTS AND DATABASES

Many inconsistencies can exist between aeronautical charts and airborne navigation databases. Because so many sources of information go into the production of these materials, and the data is manipulated by several different organizations before it eventually is displayed on RNAV equipment, you are likely to notice differences between your aeronautical charts and the databases. This discussion addresses only the inconsistencies that might be built into the databases.

NAMING CONVENTIONS

You might notice differences between the names of procedures or navaids shown on your charts and those that you see on your RNAV display. Most of them result from the way the avionics manufacturers decide to display the information. The avionics manufacturer creates the interface between the pilot and the database, so the ARINC 424 naming conventions do not apply. Some systems display procedure names exactly as they are charted, but many do not. Although the three different names displayed in figure A-2 identify the same approach, the navigation system manufacturers have used them in different formats in their respective machines.

The fact that multiple navaids can be designated with the same identifier can also create naming discrepancies. A VOR with the identifier "XYZ" might occur several times in a provider's database, so the avionics manufacturer must find a way to differentiate between these fixes within the database. In most cases, navaids with identical identifiers are eliminated when you select a particular geographic region.

Sometimes non-directional beacons (NDBs) and locator outer markers (LOMs) are displayed differently than they are charted. Some of the first airborne navigation databases coded NDBs as waypoints instead of navaids. This necessitated the use of five character identifiers for NDBs. Eventually, the NDBs were coded into the database as navaids, but many older RNAV systems continue to use the five-character identifiers. These systems display the characters "NB" after the charted NDB identifier. Therefore, an NDB with the identifier "ABC" would be displayed as "ABCNB."

Other systems refer to NDB navaids using either the NDB's charted name if it is five or fewer letters, or the one to three character identifier. For example, CASSE NDB in Colorado is displayed on some systems as "CASSE," while other systems might display "AP," which is the NDB's identifier. [Figure A-8]

MAGNETIC VARIATION

The magnetic variation for locations coded into airborne navigation databases can be acquired in several ways. Scientists at the USGS and at other agencies around the world compile data on the magnetic field in five year increments, which is then used to produce a model of the magnetic field called the International Geomagnetic Reference Field (IGRF). Providers of airborne navigation databases typically use the IRGF throughout its five-year lifespan, rather than finding or deriving annual drift values. Sometimes the variation for a given location is calculated internally by the avionics system. These "Dynamic Magnetic Variation" values can be different from those used for locations during aeronautical charting.

Even though ARINC standard records for airways and other procedures contain the appropriate magnetic headings and radials for routes, most RNAV systems do not use this information for enroute flight. The avionics compute the magnetic course internally using the latitudes and longitudes of the waypoints along the route. All of these calculations are based on true north, so the navigation system modifies the result to account for magnetic variation. This can create discrepancies between the charted values and the values derived by the avionics. Some navigation receivers use the magnetic variation, or station declination, contained in the ARINC data records to make calculations, while other systems independently determine the magnetic variation in the general area of the navaid or waypoint.

Even when the avionics system uses variation values from the database, the calculated course might be different from the course depicted on charts. Using the magnetic variation for the region, instead of the actual station declination, can result in differences between charted and calculated courses. Station declination is only updated when a navaid is "site-checked" by the governing authority that controls it. If it has not been site-checked recently, the recorded value is often different from the current magnetic variation for that location. Some avionics systems determine variation internally by consulting an earth model for magnetic variation that has been coded into the avionics memory. Because magnetic variation for a given location changes predictably over time, the avionics might contain a static earth model with fixed variation values that are predicted for the midpoint of the planned lifespan of the unit. In this case, the variation is only correct for one time in the life cycle of the avionics. For example, if the intended life cycle of a GPS unit were 20 years, the variation model might be correct when the GPS unit is 10 years old. Discrepancies would be greatest when the unit is new, and again near the end of its life span.

Another issue that can cause slight differences between charted course values and those in the database occurs when a terminal procedure is coded using "Magnetic Variation of Record." When approaches or other procedures are designed, the designers use specific rules to apply variation to a given procedure. Some controlling government agencies might choose to use the IGRF of an airport to define entire procedures at that airport. This can cause course discrepancies between the charted value and the value calculated using the actual variations from the database.

DIFFERENCES IN REVISION CYCLES

Differences in the lengths of the revision cycles for aeronautical charts and airborne navigation databases can cause discrepancies in the information they contain. Each product has a cutoff date when the revised version of the information is "frozen" and placed into production. New information received after the cutoff date is held for the next revision. Differences between the cutoff dates means that changes that are included in a database can miss the cutoff date for inclusion in a chart, or vice versa.

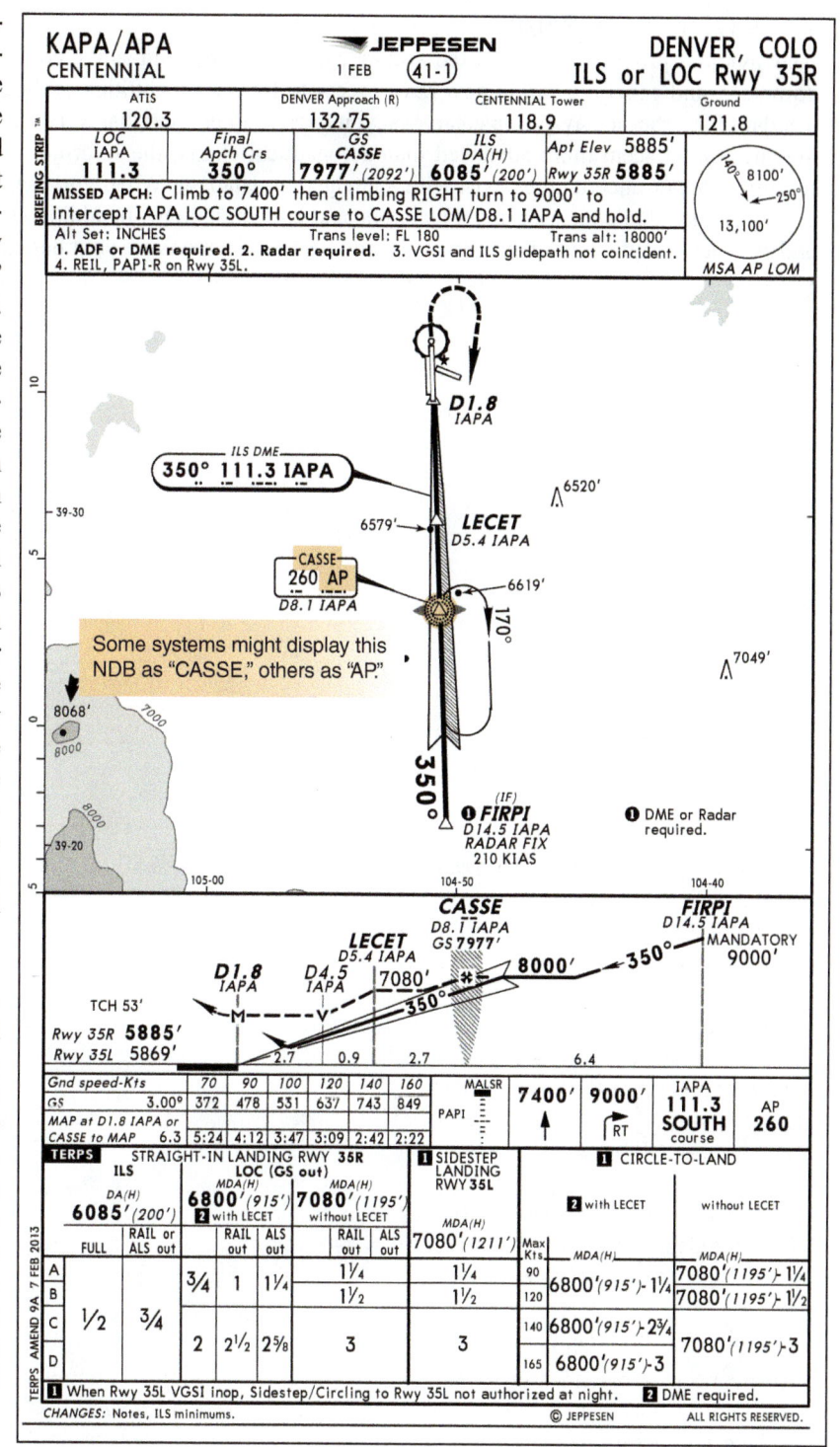

Figure A-8. Naming conventions differ between avionics manufacturers and between avionics displays and aeronautical charts.

EVOLUTION OF RNAV

New avionics provide unprecedented accuracy and precision, and as the costs have come down, all facets of commercial, corporate, and general aviation now have access to RNAV capabilities. Although database providers have implemented a standard for airborne navigation databases, you must keep in mind that RNAV is still an evolving technology. While modern avionics might seem more advanced than aeronautical charts, the information on current charts must be used whenever discrepancies or uncertainties exist with a navigation database. When you use RNAV equipment, you must consider many variables related to databases, manufacturers, and user limitations. In addition to documentation from the database provider and avionics manufacturer, Jeppesen charts and FAA publications are your best sources of information.

Appendix B
Staying Within Protected Airspace

At higher altitudes, protected airspace helps to maintain separation between aircraft. At lower altitudes, protected airspace provides separation from terrain or obstructions as well as from other aircraft flying under IFR. But what does it mean to be established on course? How wide is the protected airspace of a particular route? How can you tell from the cockpit whether your aircraft is at the edge of protected airspace? This appendix is intended to answer these questions and explain the general limits of protected airspace.

WHAT IS PROTECTED AIRSPACE?

Some pilots fly IFR for years without really understanding the size or the limits of the airspace they are allotted. It is difficult to stay within protected airspace unless you have some idea of where the boundaries are and why they are there. At its most basic, the concept of protected airspace is to prevent you from flying into terrain, obstructions, or other aircraft in spite of certain minor errors in your altimeter, your onboard navigation equipment, your autopilot, and the navigation signals transmitted to your aircraft. Most of all, remaining within protected airspace depends on your own flying skills, in terms of precise control of the aircraft, accurate interpretation of your charts, and efficient use of your navigation equipment.

You might assume that flying to the tolerances set out in the FAA Instrument Practical Test Standards (PTS) will keep you within protected airspace, but a note in the PTS makes it clear that the tolerances for IFR flight are established in Part 91. In some cases, flying to the PTS standards does not ensure that you will remain in protected airspace. In certain situations, you could leave protected airspace when flying to PTS standards with a VOR receiver that is legal for IFR flight. [Figure B-1]

You can use a VOR receiver for IFR flight if it indicates within four degrees of the reference when checked at a VOR test facility. With your receiver at the edge of that tolerance, your aircraft could be 11.5 degrees from the centerline, or about 4 NM off the course centerline at 20 NM from the station.

The PTS requires tracking a selected radial within 3/4 of full-scale deflection of the CDI. This equates to 7.5 degrees, which means that you could be 2.6 miles from the course centerline when only 20 NM from the VOR station.

20 NM

11.5 degrees

Primary Protected Airspace

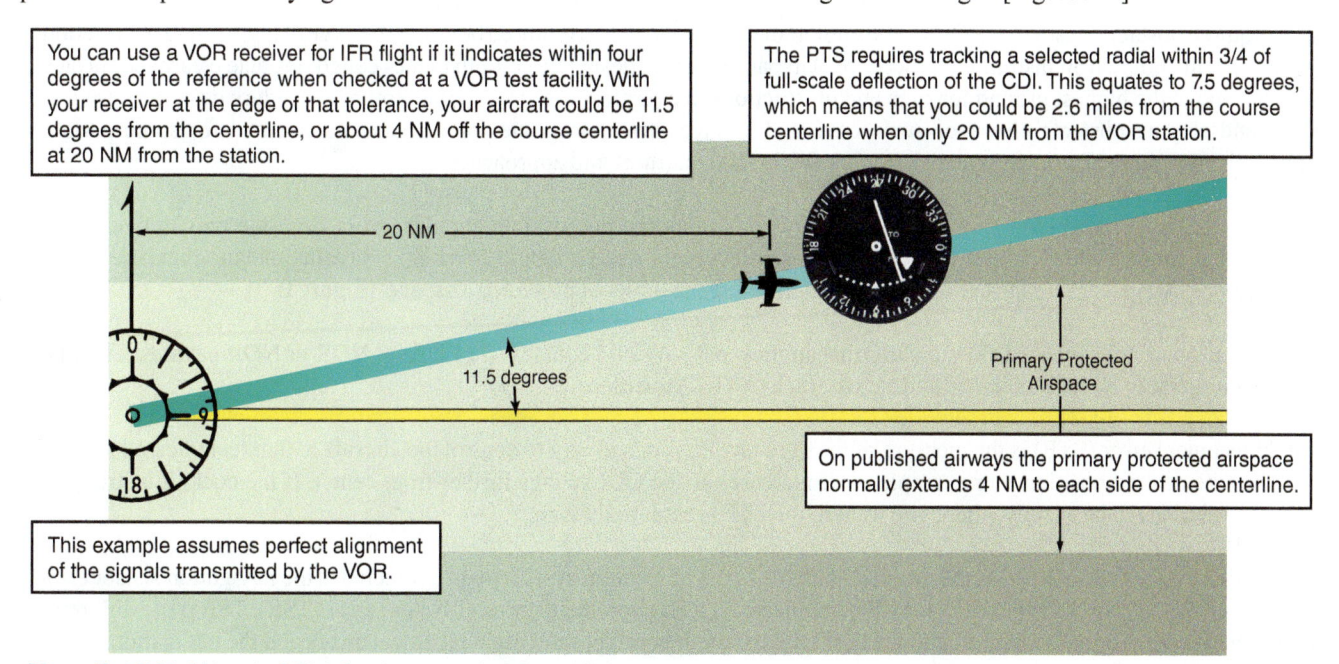

On published airways the primary protected airspace normally extends 4 NM to each side of the centerline.

This example assumes perfect alignment of the signals transmitted by the VOR.

Figure B-1. With 3/4 scale CDI deflection, your aircraft could leave primary protected airspace when only 20 NM from the station, assuming the transmitter is accurate and the receiver has a four degree error.

COURSES AND FIXES

Two concepts are central to staying within protected airspace: courses and fixes. These are already familiar to you, and are fundamental to all navigation. A course is the track over the ground that ATC expects you to follow, and a fix is a specific spot along that track. If you could fly so precisely that you remained on course all the time, the protected airspace for your route might be no wider than the width of your aircraft. The creators of protected airspace understood that it is virtually impossible to keep the aircraft exactly on course all of the time, so protected airspace must be wide enough to accommodate reasonable errors. [Figure B-2]

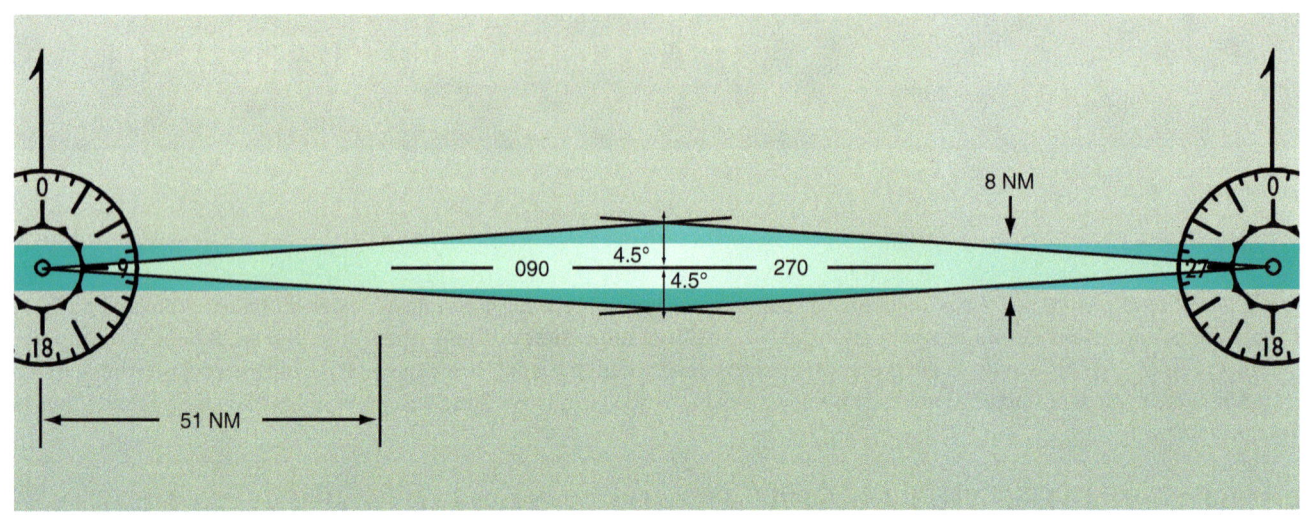

Figure B-2. Airways between VHF navaids are given a width of eight miles to allow tolerances for transmitter alignment errors, receiver accuracy, and piloting abilities.

TERMS

The design of protected airspace is a very detailed and complex process, combining the professional skills of many different experts. They balance a number of different factors, including terrain elevations and contours, runway configurations, traffic considerations, prevailing winds and weather patterns, and the performance capabilities of the aircraft that will use the procedures in order to create airspace that combines functionality with safety. Just to describe the basic guidelines that are used to create an instrument approach requires several hundred pages. Fortunately, you don't need an in-depth knowledge of the details, but you might want to understand some of the terms.

The required obstacle clearance (ROC) is the minimum vertical clearance required between the aircraft and ground obstructions over a specific point in an instrument procedure. Airspace planners designate smooth planes called obstacle clearance surfaces (OCSs) above the highest ground features and obstructions in a particular segment of airspace. Procedure designers use both level and sloping obstacle clearance surfaces. Level surfaces are appropriate for enroute airspace and for some parts of approach procedures. Designers can use sloping OCSs for departures and approaches.

Fix displacement area (FDA) is an area created by combining the permissible angular errors from the two VOR or NDB navaids that define the fix. In theory, a fix is a dimensionless point with no length or width, but reality dictates that it be an area of some size. Airspace planners use the FDA in determining the limits of protected airspace. [Figure B-3]

Fix displacement tolerance (FDT) is an area that applies to RNAV and equates to a FDA for VOR or NDB navaids. The FDT has an along track (ATRK) tolerance and a cross track (XTRK) tolerance.

Flight technical error (FTE) is the measure of the pilot or autopilot's ability to control the aircraft so that its indicated position matches the desired position. For example, FTE increases as the CDI swings further from center. If the cockpit instruments show the airplane to be exactly where you want it, the FTE is essentially zero.

Navigation system error (NSE) is the error attributable to the navigation system in use. It includes the navigation sensor error, receiver error, and path definition error. NSE combines with FTE to produce the total system error (TSE). TSE is the difference between true position of the aircraft and the desired position. It combines the flight technical errors and the navigation system tracking errors.

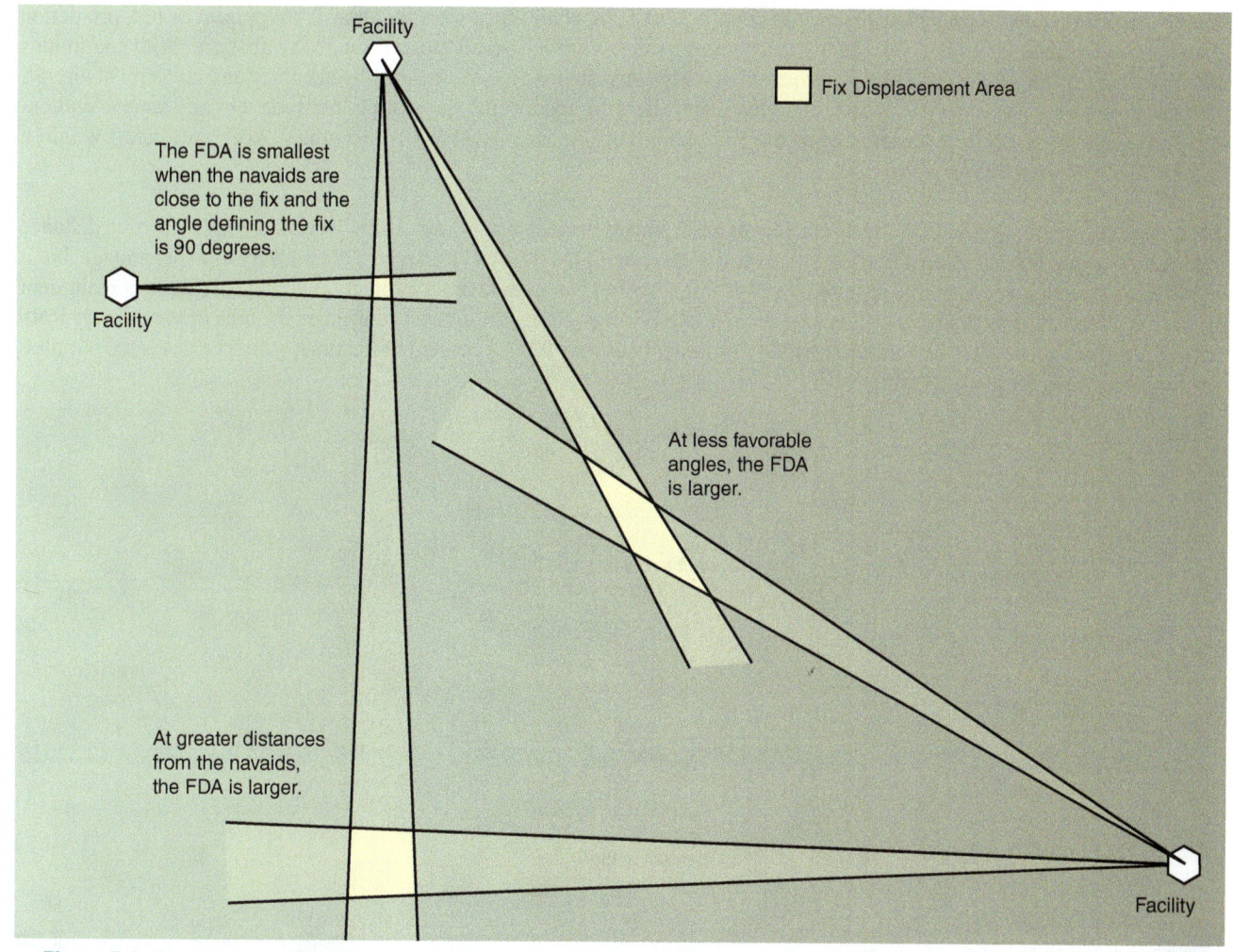

Figure B-3. When using ground-based navaids, the distance and relative angles from the stations define the area required for a fix.

Actual navigation performance (ANP) is an estimate of confidence in the current navigation system's performance. ANP computations consider accuracy, availability, continuity, and integrity of navigation performance at a given moment in time. Required navigation performance (RNP) necessitates the aircraft navigation system monitor the ANP and ensures the ANP does not exceed the RNP value required for the operation. The navigation system must also provide the pilot an alert in the primary field of view when ANP exceeds RNP. [Figure B-4]

Figure B-4. An alerting system in the pilot's primary view must warn if ANP exceeds RNP. This alerting system is comparable to an "OFF" flag for a VOR or ILS.

While you might think of protected airspace as static and existing at all times whether aircraft are present or not, protection from conflicts with other aircraft is dynamic and constantly changing as aircraft move through the airspace. With continuous increases in air traffic, some routes have become extremely congested. At the same time, the accuracy and integrity of aircraft navigation systems has also increased, allowing controllers to reduce the separation between aircraft routes without compromising safety. RNP is a standard for the navigation performance necessary to accurately keep an aircraft within a specific block of airspace.

Containment is a term central to the basic concept of RNP. This is the idea that the aircraft will remain within a certain distance of its intended position (the stated RNP value) at least 95 percent of the time on any flight. This is a very high percentage, but it would not be enough to ensure the required level of safety without another layer of protection outside the basic containment area. This larger area has dimensions that are twice the RNP value, giving the aircraft four times the area of the primary RNP area. Aircraft are expected to be contained within this larger boundary 99.999 percent of the time, which achieves the required level of confidence for safety. [Figure B-5]

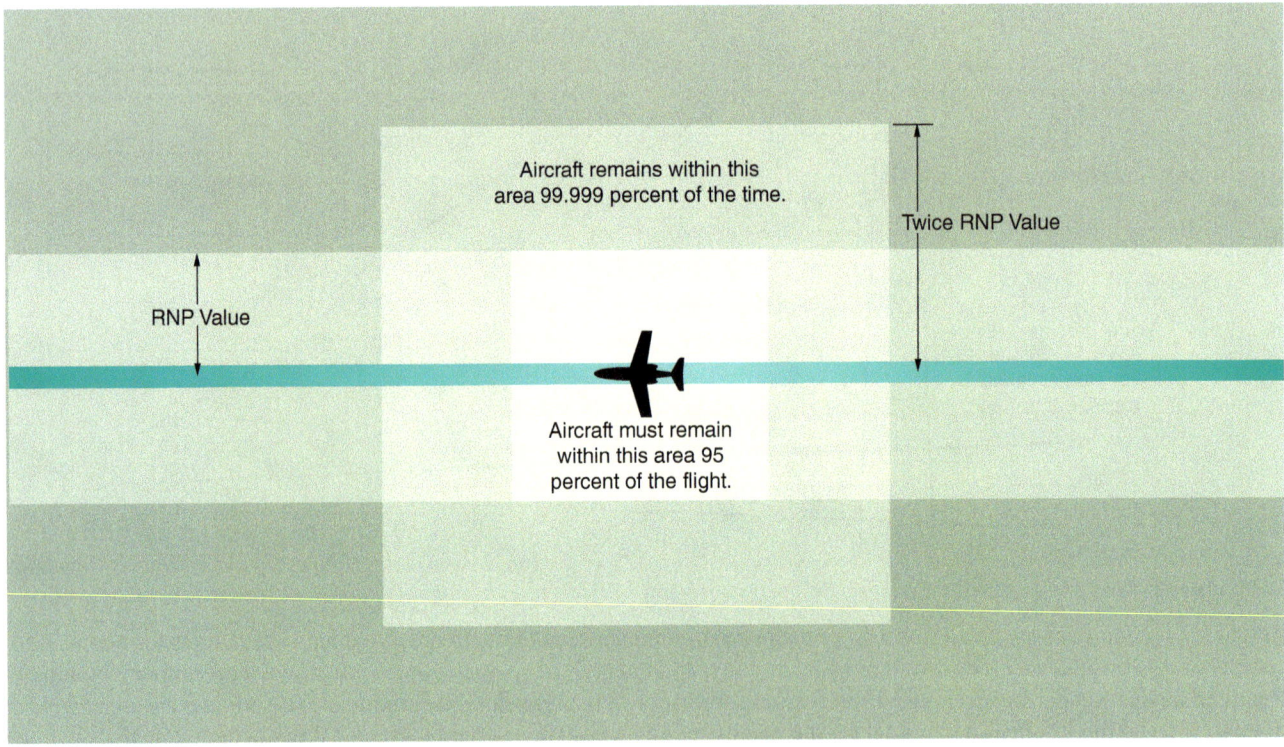

Figure B-5. If maintaining RNP, the aircraft remains in the larger area 99.999 percent of the time, providing an adequate level of safety for reliable separation.

Remaining within protected airspace is largely a matter of staying as close as possible to the centerline of your intended course. There are formal definitions of what it means to be **established on course**, and these are important in practice as well as theory, because controllers often issue clearances contingent on your being established on a course.

You must be established on course before you start a descent on any route or approach segment. The ICAO Procedures for Air Navigation Services – Aircraft Operations (PANS-OPS) Volume I Flight Procedures, specifies, "Descent shall not be started until the aircraft is established on the inbound track." An aircraft is considered established when it is "within half full scale deflection for the ILS and VOR; or within ±5° of the required bearing for the NDB."

In the AIM, "established" is defined as "to be stable or fixed on a route, route segment, altitude, heading, etc." The "on course" concept for IFR is spelled out in Part 91.181, which states that the course to be flown on an airway is the centerline of the airway, and on any other route, along the direct course between the navaids or fixes defining that route.

PROTECTED AIRSPACE FACTORS
Staying within protected airspace depends primarily on five factors:

- Accurate flying

- Accurate navigation equipment in the aircraft

- Accurate navigation signals from ground and space-based transmitters
- Accurate direction by ATC
- Accurate (current) charts and publications

Your primary equipment for vertical navigation is the altimeter.

- Keep in mind that your altimeter is a device that measures pressure changes, not altitude. Never think of your altimeter as an actual altitude indicator. A pressure altimeter is a barometer that measures changes in atmospheric pressure, and by relating these changes to a measured altitude, it converts these changes to a reasonably accurate indicated altitude.

- Certain IFR procedures are annotated "NA" below a given temperature. You can adjust the altimeter to compensate for non-standard atmospheric pressure, but there is no corresponding adjustment for non-standard temperature. This can lead to significant errors when you fly through air that is unusually hot or cold. The errors are more critical when the outside air temperature is cold, because this causes your altimeter to indicate that you are higher than your actual altitude. [Figure B-6]

ICAO Cold Temperature Error Table

Height Above Airport (feet)

Reported Temperature (Degrees Celsius)	200	300	400	500	600	700	800	900	1,000	1,500	2,000	3,000	4,000	5,000
+10	10	10	10	10	20	20	20	20	20	30	40	60	80	90
0	20	20	30	30	40	40	50	50	60	90	120	170	230	280
-10	20	30	40	50	60	70	80	90	100	150	200	290	390	490
-20	30	50	60	70	90	100	120	130	140	210	280	420	570	710
-30	40	60	80	100	120	140	150	170	190	280	380	570	760	950
-40	50	80	100	120	150	170	190	220	240	360	480	720	970	1,210
-50	60	90	120	150	180	210	240	270	300	450	590	890	1,190	1,500

If the temperature is -10 degrees Celsius, and the aircraft altitude is 1,000 feet above the airport elevation, the chart shows that even with the current altimeter setting, you might be 100 feet below the altitude indicated by the altimeter.

Figure B-6. You might not be as high as you think you are. This table gives you an idea of the errors due to low temperatures.

TAKEOFF AND DEPARTURE

Departure procedures are designed using TERPS, a living document that is updated frequently. The OCS is an imaginary plane that extends from the departure end of the runway (DER) along the departure path. The imaginary surface separates airspace with terrain and obstructions from your aircraft. You might think of it as the floor of the departure path. It rises one foot vertically for every 40 feet horizontally, which is 152 feet per NM. Departure design criteria assume you cross the DER at a height of at least 35 feet and maintain an initial climb of at least 200 feet per NM. The difference between the 152 ft/NM OCS and the 200 ft/NM minimum climb gradient provides at least 48 ft/NM of clearance above objects below the OCS. The departure design must also include the acquisition of positive course guidance within 10 NM of the DER for straight departures, or within 5 NM after the turn is completed on departures that require a turn. Positive course guidance means that you have a continuous display of navigational data that enables you to fly along a specific course line, such as a signal from a ground-based navaid, RNAV, or a radar vector. Even if your airplane can climb much more than 200 ft/NM, you must always fly the published departure routing. [Figure B-7]

In a perfect world, the 40 to 1 slope would work for every departure design. But terrain and man-made obstacles often penetrate the 40:1 slope, making it necessary to use alternative requirements. Such cases might require a steeper climb gradient, an increase in the standard takeoff minimums to allow you to "see and avoid" the obstacles, a specific reduction in the runway length, or some combination of these options. If a departure route is specified, it must be flown in conjunction with the other

An obstacle-free departure flight path is based on your aircraft climbing at least 200 feet per nautical mile after it crosses the end of the runway at least 35 feet above the ground.

A slope of 152 feet per nautical mile is assessed for obstacles. If none penetrate this slope, the 200 foot per nautical mile climb gradient provides you with a minimum of 48 feet of obstacle clearance for each mile of flight. If obstacles penetrate this slope, special avoidance procedures such as ceiling and visibility minimums, detailed flight maneuvers, and/or greater climb gradients are specified.

Departure routes are based on positive course guidance acquired within 10 nautical miles from the departure end of the runway on straight departures, and 5 nautical miles after completion of turns on departures requiring turns.

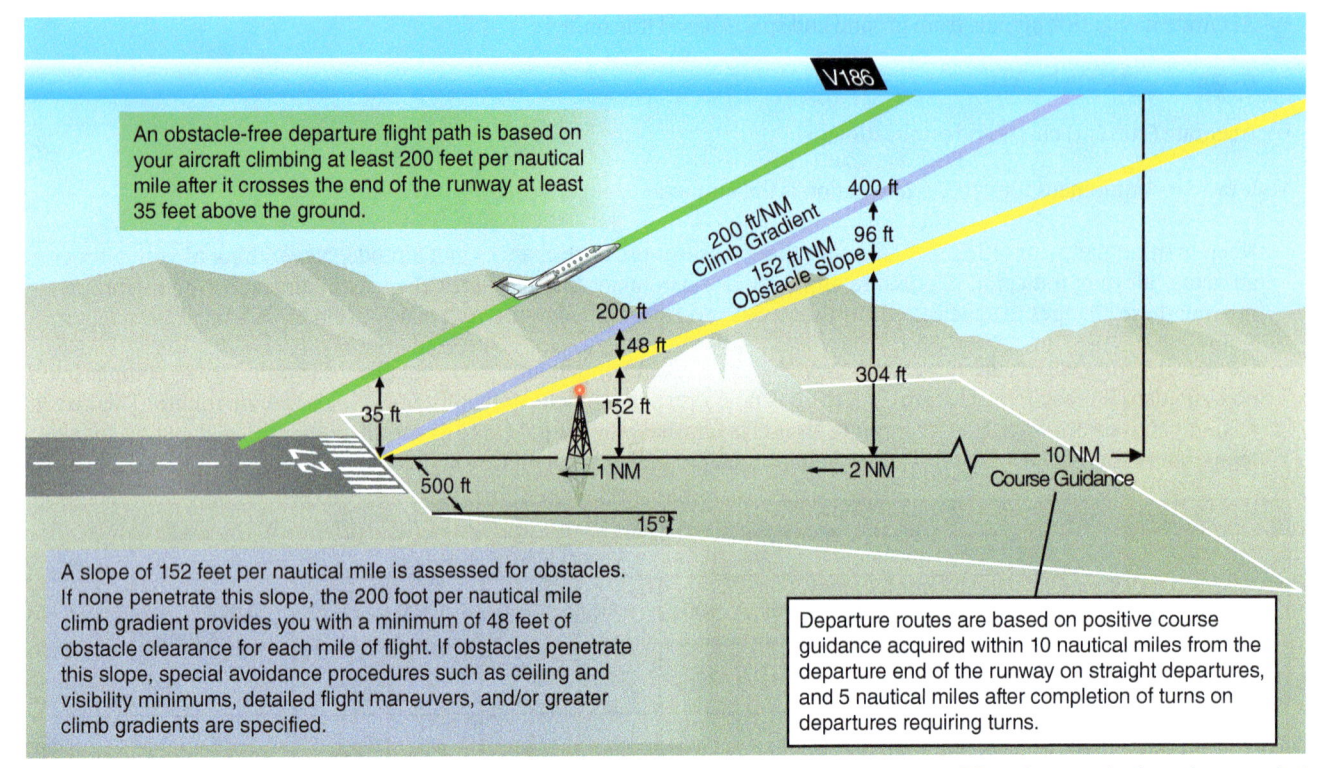

Figure B-7. The Initial Climb Area (ICA) is the segment of the departure procedure that starts at the DER and proceeds along the extended runway centerline to allow an aircraft enough distance to reach an altitude of 400 feet above DER elevation, and to allow the establishment of positive course guidance by all navigation systems. A typical straight departure ICA extends 2-5 nautical miles from the DER along the extended runway centerline. It is 500 feet wide each side of the runway centerline at DER, and diverges at 15°.

options. A published climb gradient in this case is based on the ROC 24 percent rule. To keep the same ROC ratio as standard, when the required climb gradient is greater than 200 feet per NM, the ROC is 24 percent of the total height above the starting elevation gained by an aircraft departing to a minimum altitude to clear an obstacle that penetrates the OCS. The required climb gradient depicted in ODPs is obtained by using the formulas:

Standard Formula

$$CG = \frac{O - E}{0.76\,D}$$

DoD Option*

$$CG = \frac{(48D + 0) - E}{D}$$

where O = obstacle MSL elevation
E = climb gradient starting MSL elevation
D = distance (NM) from DER to the obstacle

Examples:

$$\frac{2049 - 1221}{0.76 \times 3.1} = 351.44$$

Round to 352 ft/NM

$$\frac{(48 \times 3.1 + 2049) - 1221}{3.1} = 315.10$$

Round to 316 ft/NM

*Military only

These formulas are published in TERPS for calculating the required climb gradient to clear obstacles.

The following formula is used for calculating climb gradients for anything other than obstacles (usually ATC requirements):

$$CG = \frac{A - E}{D}$$

where A = "climb to" altitude
E = climb gradient starting MSL elevation
D = distance (NM) from the beginning of the climb

Example:

$$\frac{3000 - 1221}{5} = 355.8 \text{ round to } 356 \text{ ft/NM}$$

NOTE: The climb gradient must be equal to or greater than the gradient required for obstacles along the route of flight.

Obstacles located within 1 NM of the DER that penetrate the 40:1 OCS are referred to as "low, close-in obstacles." Rather than publishing an excessive climb gradient, the height of the obstacle and its location relative to the DER are noted in the Take-off and Obstacle Departure Procedure section of the Jeppesen airport chart or on an obstacle departure chart. (FAA publications place this information in the Take-off Minimums and (OBSTACLE) Departure Procedures section of a given TPP booklet.) The purpose of this note is to identify the obstacle and alert you to the height and location of the obstacle so you can avoid it. [Figure B-8]

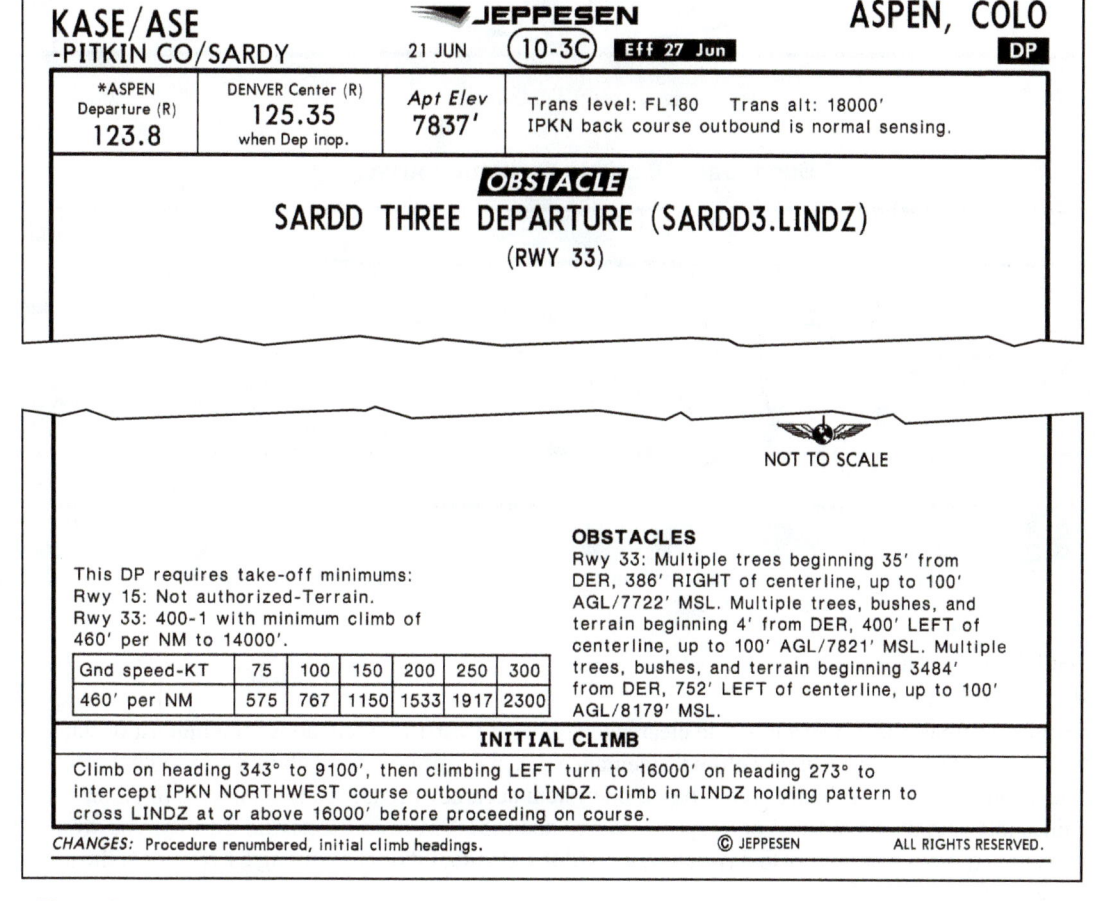

```
KASE/ASE                    JEPPESEN              ASPEN, COLO
-PITKIN CO/SARDY      21 JUN  (10-3C)  Eff 27 Jun               DP

*ASPEN          DENVER Center (R)   Apt Elev   Trans level: FL180   Trans alt: 18000'
Departure (R)       125.35          7837'      IPKN back course outbound is normal sensing.
   123.8         when Dep inop.

                        OBSTACLE
               SARDD THREE DEPARTURE (SARDD3.LINDZ)
                            (RWY 33)
```

                                                    NOT TO SCALE

                                OBSTACLES
                                Rwy 33: Multiple trees beginning 35' from
This DP requires take-off minimums: DER, 386' RIGHT of centerline, up to 100'
Rwy 15: Not authorized-Terrain.   AGL/7722' MSL. Multiple trees, bushes, and
Rwy 33: 400-1 with minimum climb of   terrain beginning 4' from DER, 400' LEFT of
460' per NM to 14000'.   centerline, up to 100' AGL/7821' MSL. Multiple
                                      trees, bushes, and terrain beginning 3484'
| Gnd speed-KT | 75 | 100 | 150 | 200 | 250 | 300 | from DER, 752' LEFT of centerline, up to 100'
| 460' per NM | 575| 767 | 1150| 1533| 1917| 2300| AGL/8179' MSL.

                              INITIAL CLIMB
Climb on heading 343° to 9100', then climbing LEFT turn to 16000' on heading 273° to
intercept IPKN NORTHWEST course outbound to LINDZ. Climb in LINDZ holding pattern to
cross LINDZ at or above 16000' before proceeding on course.
CHANGES: Procedure renumbered, initial climb headings.   © JEPPESEN   ALL RIGHTS RESERVED.

Figure B-8. This departure chart describes both the steeper climb requirements and departure path obstacles.

ENROUTE

All published routes in the NAS are based on specific obstacle clearance criteria. Understanding these obstacle clearance areas helps you to maintain situational awareness and avoid CFIT. Obstacle clearance areas for the enroute phase of flight are identified as primary, secondary, and turning areas. The primary and secondary area obstacle clearance criteria for enroute segments are a function of safety and practicality in flight procedures.

VHF NAVIGATION

By considering factors such as the pilot, the aircraft, and the navigation system being used, airspace planners can compute a total VOR system accuracy factor, along with an associated probability factor. They consider the pilot's ability to track a radial and the flight track resulting from turns at various speeds and altitudes under different wind conditions. In assessing the navigation system, they consider radial alignment displacement, transmitter monitor tolerance, and receiver accuracy. All of these factors are considered during development of enroute criteria. From this analysis, they determined a total system accuracy of ±4.5° 95 percent of the time and ±6.7° 99 percent of the time. The 4.5° figure became the basis for primary area obstacle clearance criteria, airway and route widths, and ATC separation procedures. The 6.7° value provides secondary obstacle clearance area dimensions. [Figure B-9]

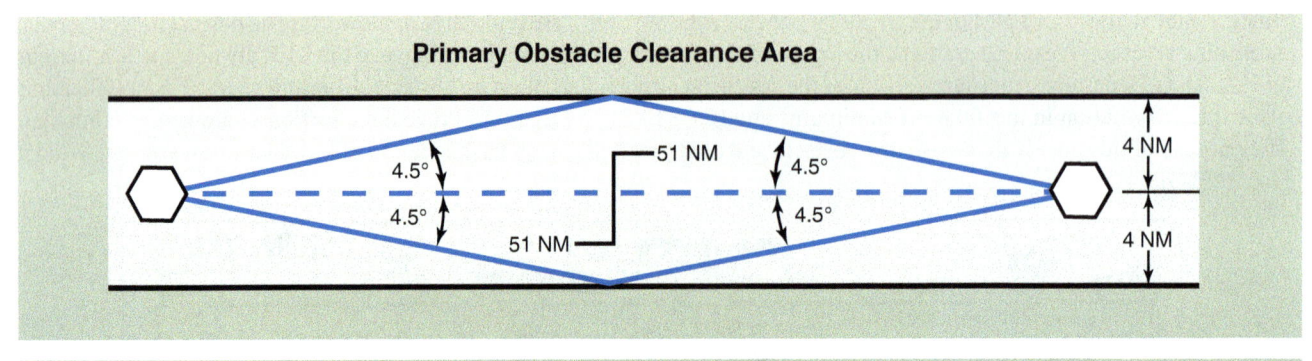

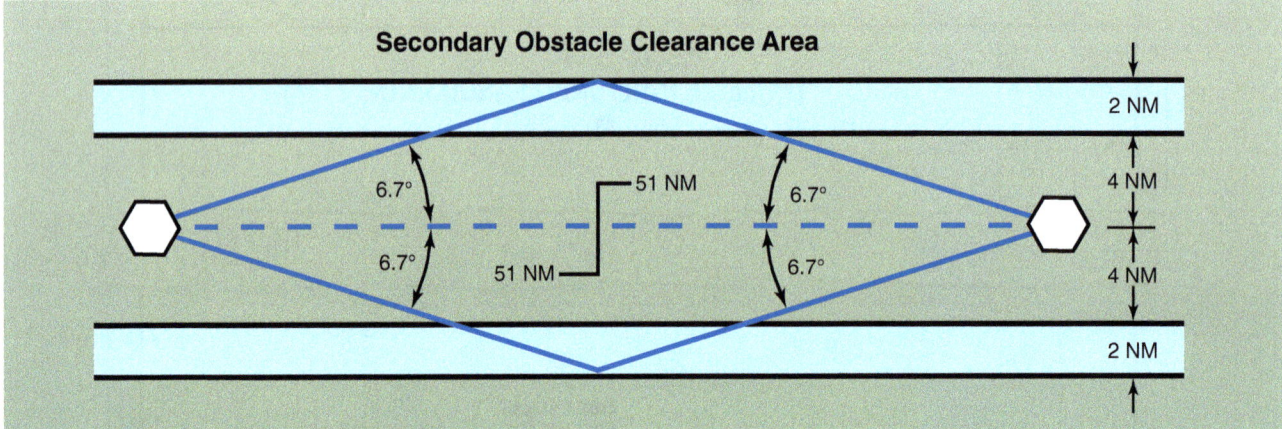

Figure B-9. For VHF navigation, the primary obstacle clearance area is based on 4.5 degree lines from the station, and the secondary obstacle clearance area is based on 6.7 degree lines.

PRIMARY AREA

Non-mountainous Areas

In non-mountainous areas, the primary obstacle clearance area is at least 1,000 feet above the highest obstacle on that route segment. On published routes, the primary obstacle clearance area has a protected width of 8 NM, with 4 NM on each side of the centerline. Protection of the primary area is based on system accuracy of 4.5° from the navaid to either side of the route. These 4.5° lines intersect the boundaries of the primary area about 51 NM from the navaid. Ideally, you would change over from navigating away from that facility to navigating toward the next facility before flying 51 NM from the navaid, but often the navaids are too far apart.

If the distance from the navaid to the changeover point (COP) is more than 51 NM, the outer boundary of the primary area widens beyond the 4 NM width, to include the area between the 4.5° lines. There might be additional differences in the obstacle clearance area if there is an offset COP or a dogleg segment. [Figure B-10]

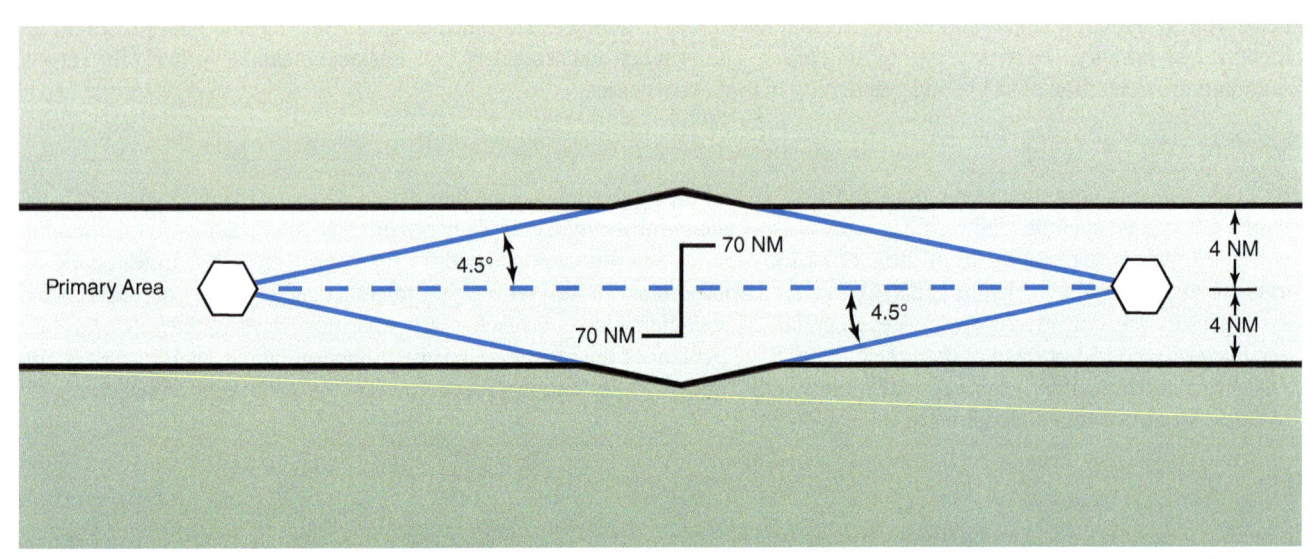

Figure B-10. Beyond 51 NM from the navaid, the primary obstacle clearance area widens along the 4.5° system accuracy lines.

B-8

Mountainous Areas

Mountainous areas for the Eastern and Western U.S. are designated in Part 95. [Figure B-11] In mountainous areas, the lateral boundaries of VHF routes are similar to those in nonmountainous areas, but with some exceptions, the minimum obstacle clearance in mountainous areas is 2,000 feet. The exceptions include some mountainous areas of the Eastern U.S., Puerto Rico, and Hawaii where obstacle clearance is reduced to 1,500 feet, and mountainous areas of the Western U.S. and Alaska where obstacle clearance is reduced to 1,700 feet. The designers consider the following points before they authorize any enroute altitudes that provide less than 2,000 feet of terrain clearance:

- Areas characterized by precipitous terrain
- Weather phenomena peculiar to the area
- Phenomena conducive to marked pressure differentials
- Type of and distance between navigational facilities
- Availability of weather services throughout the area
- Availability and reliability of altimeter resetting points along airways and routes in the area

Altitudes that provide at least 1,000 feet of obstacle clearance over towers or other man-made obstacles may be authorized within designated mountainous areas if the obstacles are **not** located on precipitous terrain where there is high risk of downdrafts and turbulence due to Bernoulli Effect, atmospheric eddies, vortices, waves, and other phenomena that occur when strong winds blow over mountains. Such winds increase the potential hazards.

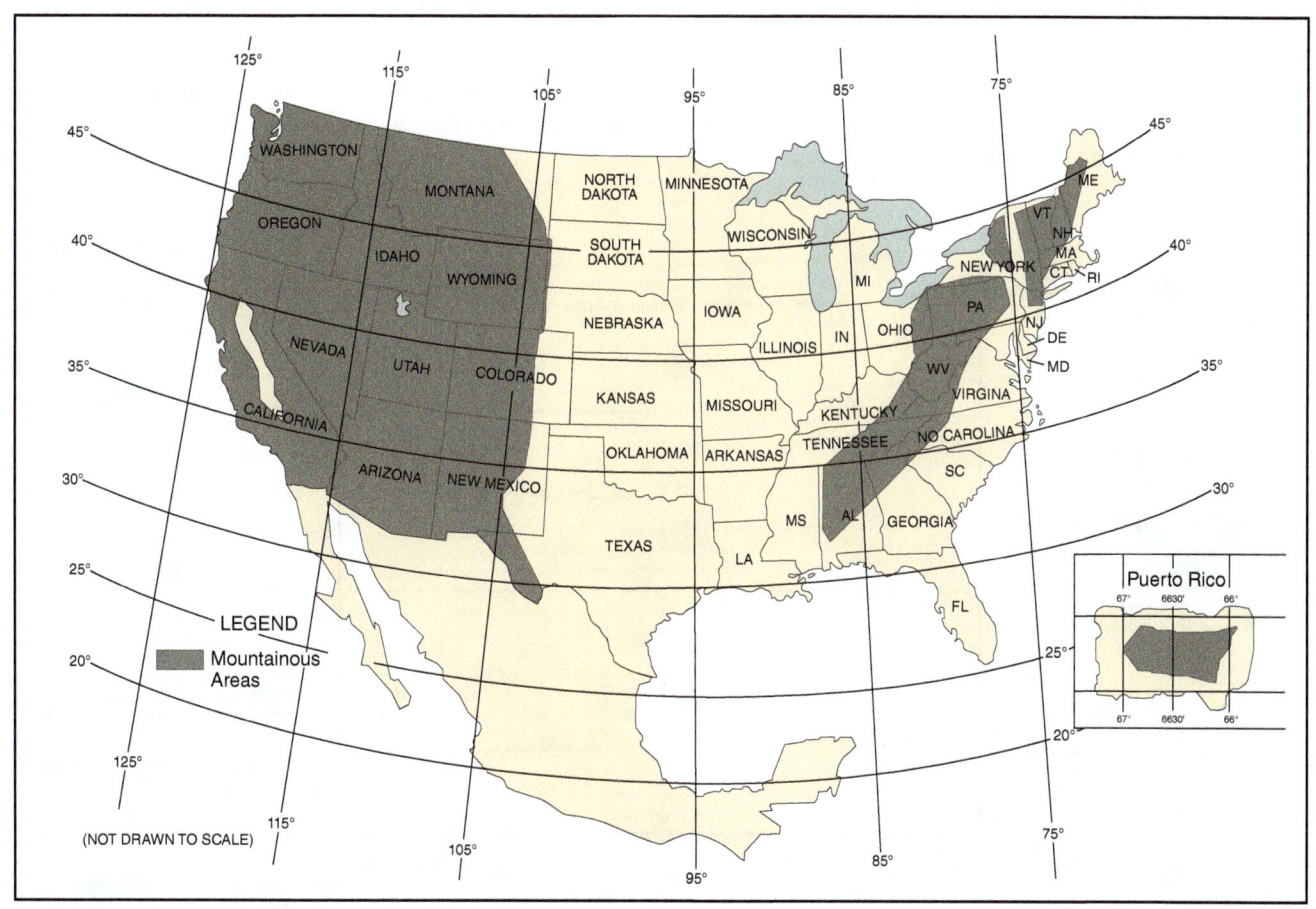

Figure B-11. The darker areas are designated Mountainous Areas. Additional mountainous areas are designated for Alaska, Hawaii, and Puerto Rico.

SECONDARY AREA

The width of the secondary area for VHF routes is also determined by applying a navigation system accuracy factor. For the secondary area, lines diverge at a 6.7° angle from the navaid on each side of the centerline. At a distance of 51 NM from the navaid, these lines are 2 NM from the edges of the primary area. This distance establishes the nominal width for the secondary area, which is 2 NM on each side of the primary area for the entire length of the route within 51 NM of the navaid. If the distance from the navaid to the COP is more than 51 NM, the secondary area widens to follow the 6.7° lines to the COP. [Figure B-12]

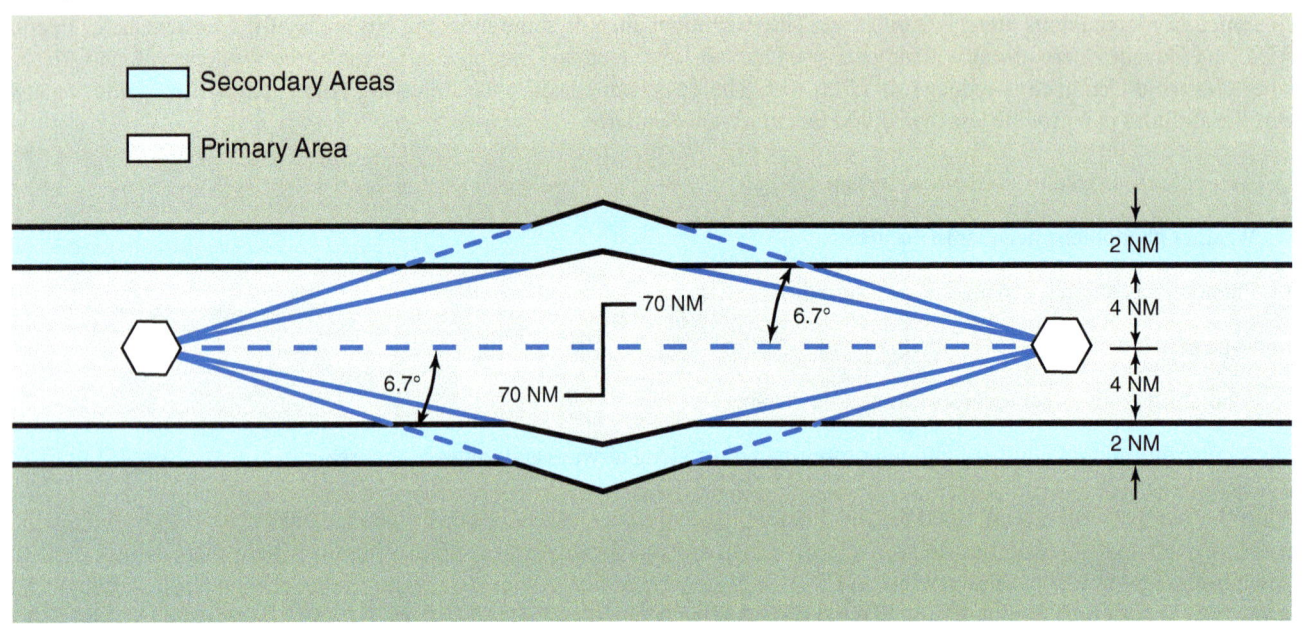

Figure B-12. Both the primary and secondary areas widen along with the system accuracy lines when the COP is more than 51 NM from the navaid.

The bottom surface of the secondary area is not horizontal. This plane begins at a point 500 feet above the obstacle upon which the primary obstacle clearance area is based, and slants upward at an angle that causes it to intersect the outer edge of the secondary area at a point 500 feet higher. [Figure B-13]

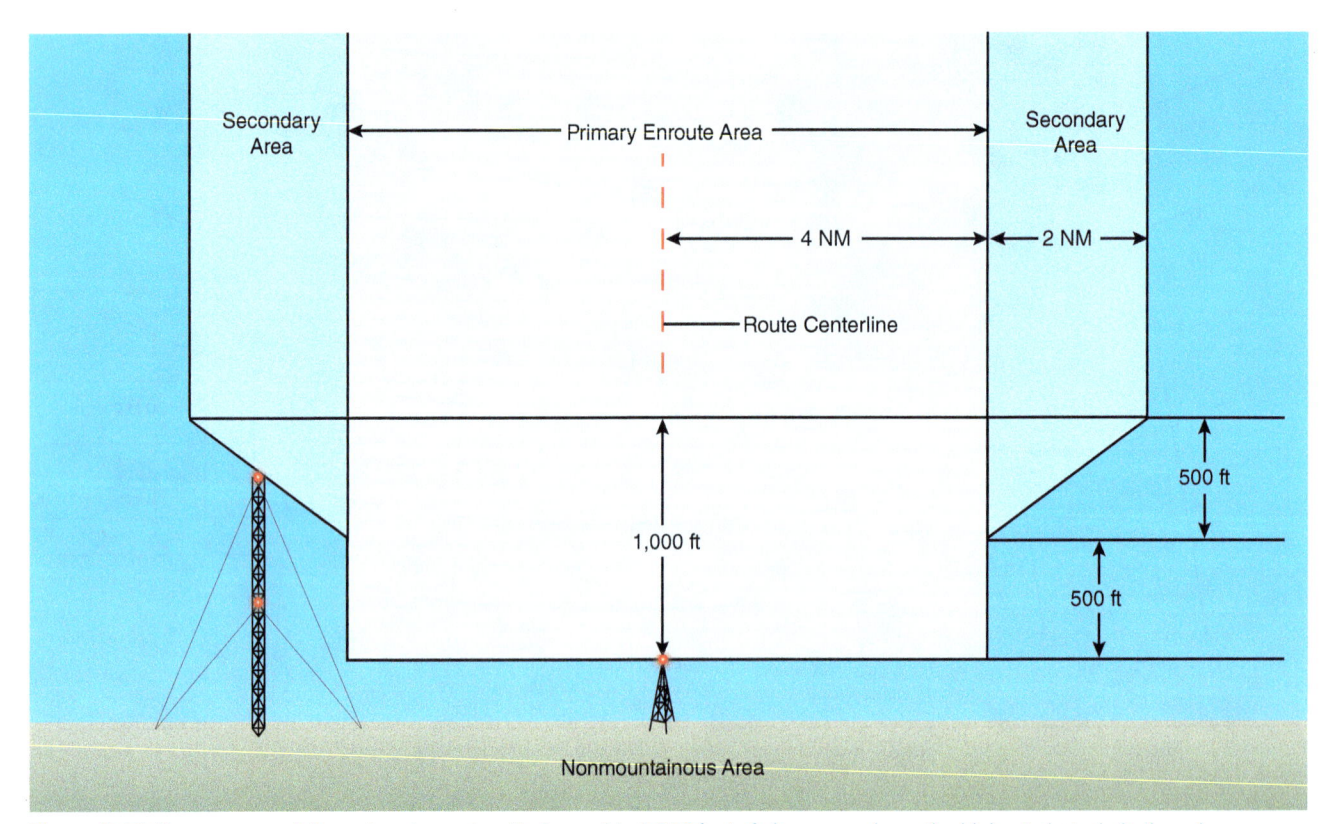

Figure B-13. Over nonmountainous terrain, route criteria provide 1,000 feet of clearance above the highest obstacle in the primary area, but less clearance in the secondary area. At the outer edge of the secondary area, the obstruction clearance tapers to zero.

Because of the additional 1,000 feet of obstacle clearance required in the primary area in mountainous areas, the depth of the secondary area also provides an additional 1,000 feet above obstructions. [Figure B-14]

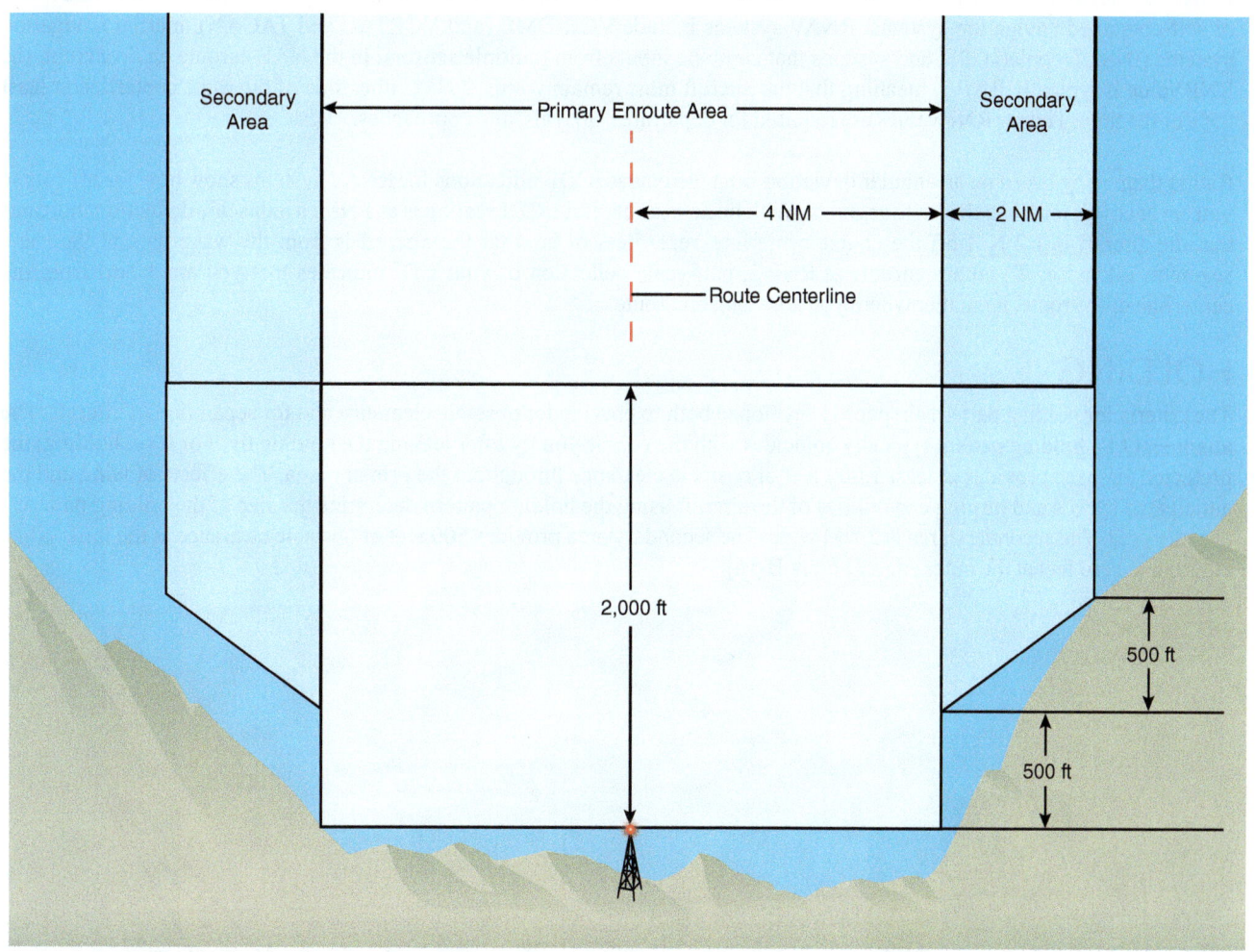

Figure B-14. The interaction of wind and terrain in mountainous areas can create dangerous turbulence, downdrafts, and altimeter errors, so extra clearance is provided above obstacles in both the primary and secondary areas.

TURNING AREA

When you change course on VHF airways and routes, the protected areas are extended to accommodate your aircraft's turn radius. You are expected to lead your turns by starting your turn before you reach the fix. If you turn at the fix or after you pass the fix, you could exceed airway and route boundaries. The turn area provides obstacle clearance for both turn anticipation (turning prior to the fix) and fly-over protection (turning after crossing the fix). Leading your turn is considered part of the requirement for you to fly the centerline of the airway. Many factors enter into the construction and application of the turning area to provide you with adequate obstacle protection, including airspeed limits, the size of the course change, the difference between indicated and true airspeed, and the possibility of a tailwind component. Leading your turn becomes even more important the faster you fly. Failing to lead your turn could cause you to fly outside of protected airspace. [Figure B-15] Due to the high airspeeds used in the flight levels, ATC provides additional IFR separation for course changes.

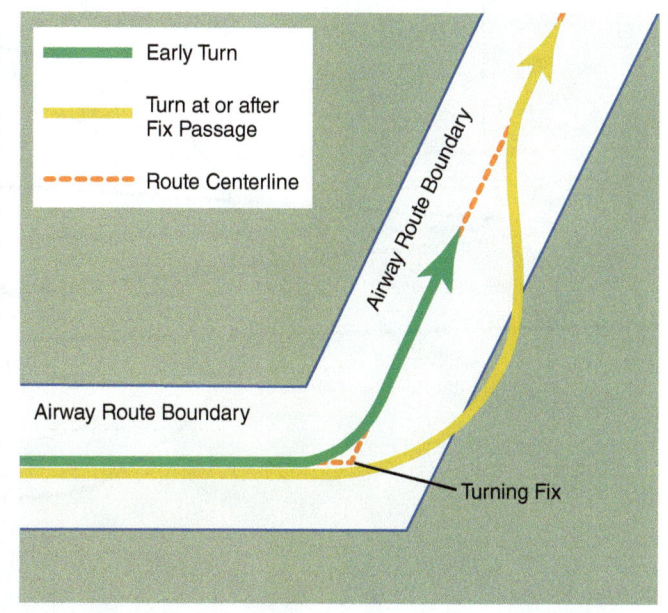

Figure B-15. Failing to lead your turn can cause you to leave the normal route boundaries.

B-11

RNAV

RNAV enables you to fly any desired course within the coverage area of the navigation signals you receive, or within the limits of self-contained navigation systems. RNAV systems include VOR/DME (and VORTAC and TACAN), inertial navigation systems (INS), Doppler, GPS, and systems that combine inputs from multiple sensors. In the NAS enroute environment, the RNP value is typically RNP 2, meaning that the aircraft must remain within 2 NM either side of the route centerline at least 95% of the time. Tighter RNP values are required for departures, arrivals, and approaches.

Rather than being based on an angular deviation from the course, CDI indications for RNAV systems show how far off course you are at any point along the route segment. With linear scaling, if the CDI scaling is at 1 NM, a half scale deflection indicates that the aircraft is 1/2 NM off the course centerline, regardless of how far the aircraft is from the waypoints of the route segment. Likewise, if you are enroute at RNP 2, half-scale deflection of your CDI indicates that you are 1 NM from the centerline of the route, no matter where you are along that route.

HOLDING

The criteria for holding pattern airspace is developed both to provide for obstacle clearance and for separation of aircraft. The alignment of a holding pattern typically coincides with the course you fly after leaving the holding fix. For level holding, the protected airspace provides at least 1,000 feet of obstacle clearance throughout the primary area. The effects of wind and the anticipated speeds and turning capabilities of the aircraft using the holding pattern determine the size of the holding pattern's primary area. The secondary area is 2 NM wide. The secondary area provides 500 feet of obstacle clearance at the inner edge, tapering to zero feet at the outer edge. [Figure B-16]

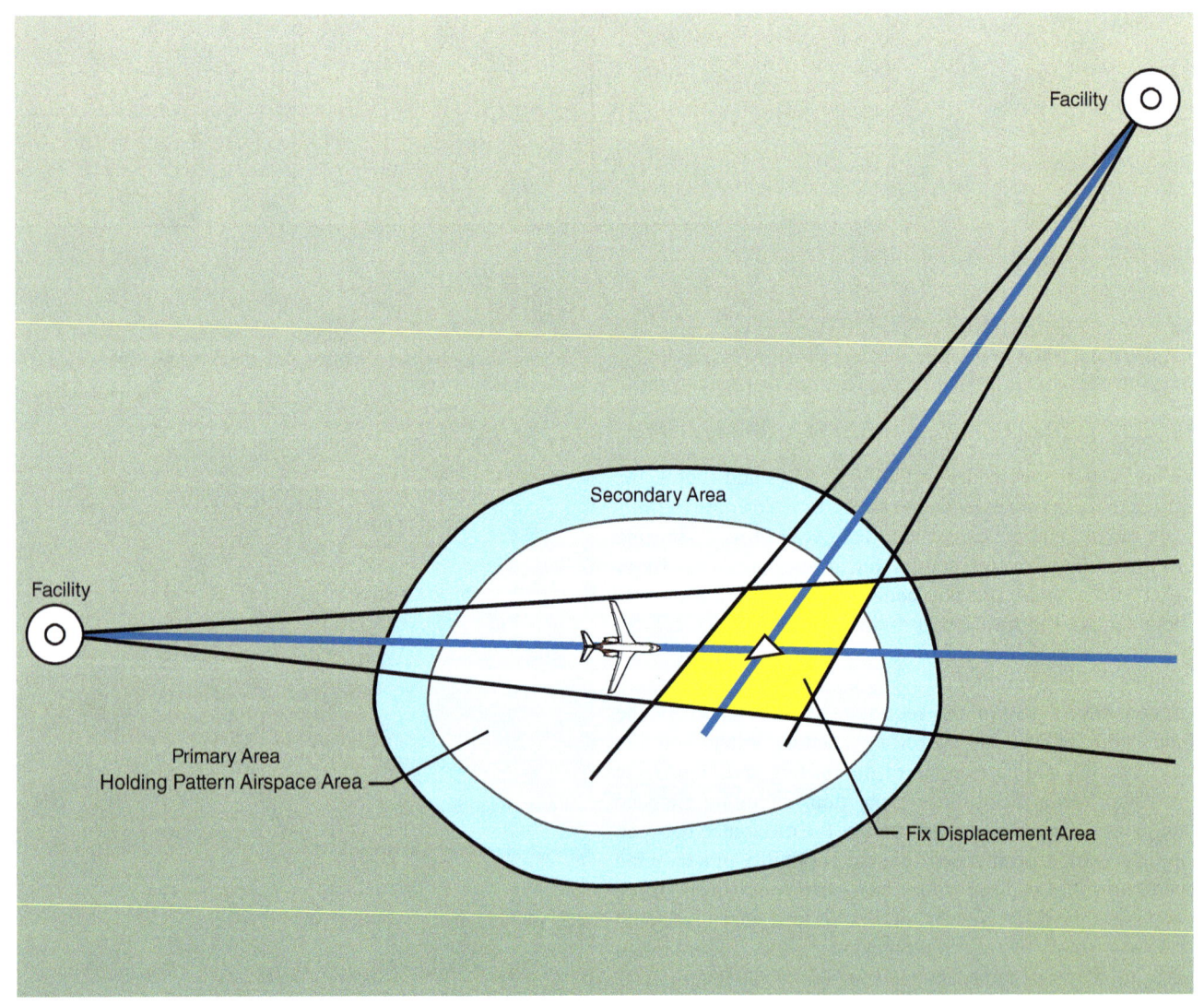

Figure B-16. Protected airspace for a holding pattern takes aircraft turning capabilities and wind effects into consideration.

ARRIVAL AND APPROACH

For approaches, it is not enough to just stay within protected airspace. You must also establish a rate of descent and a track that brings your aircraft to a position from which you can descend to a landing on the intended runway at a normal rate using normal maneuvers. In many ways, coming down through clouds to a precise location is one of the greatest challenges of IFR flight. Likewise, it can be a challenge for airspace designers to create a safe and flyable approach. The ROC must decrease as the aircraft comes closer to the ground, and often there are obstacles near the airport that make it difficult to find a safe path with adequate safety margins. The approach must accommodate aircraft with different approach speeds and turn capabilities, pilots with different levels of skill and proficiency, various combinations of wind and weather, allowances for air traffic flow and other airport operations, radio signal reflections and interference, community noise considerations, contingency plans that anticipate the loss of lighting and electronic components, and the performance of aircraft with different missed approach climb capabilities. Once implemented, the approach provides you with enough protected airspace for safe operations, as long as you fly the procedure correctly and precisely.

TERPS criteria provide obstacle clearance for each segment of an approach procedure. On the initial approach segment, the ROC is approximately 1,000 feet, and it is at least 500 feet on the intermediate approach segment. The final approach segment for a nonprecision approach often has a ROC of 250 feet to the MAP. For a precision approach like an ILS, the ROC decreases between the FAF and the MAP. For the missed approach segment, the ROC increases from zero at the MAP to 1,000 feet where the procedure joins an initial approach segment or the enroute structure. [Figure B-17]

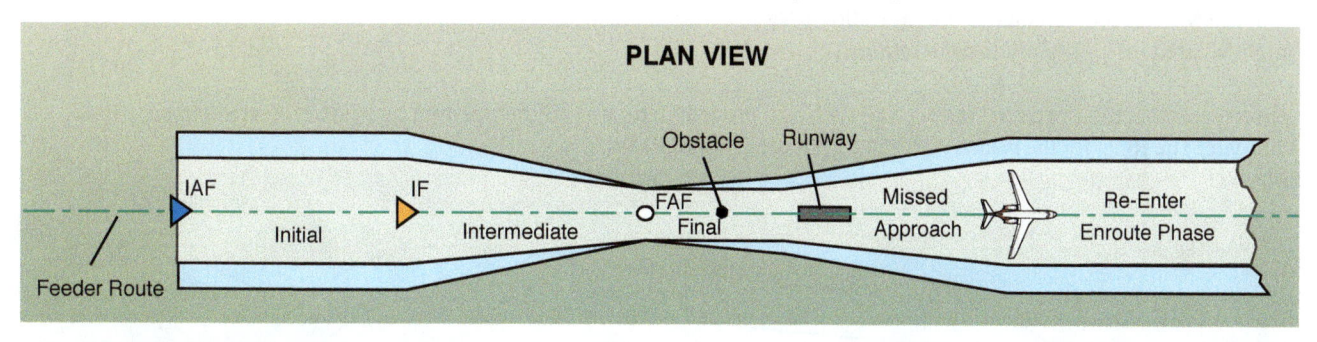

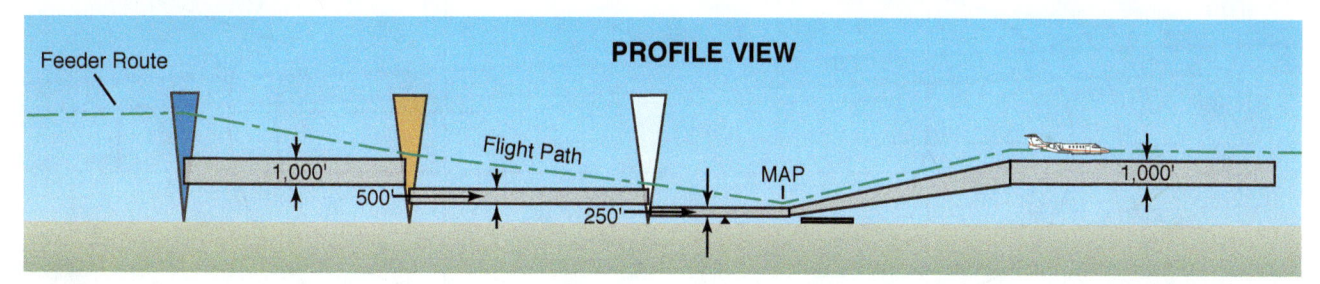

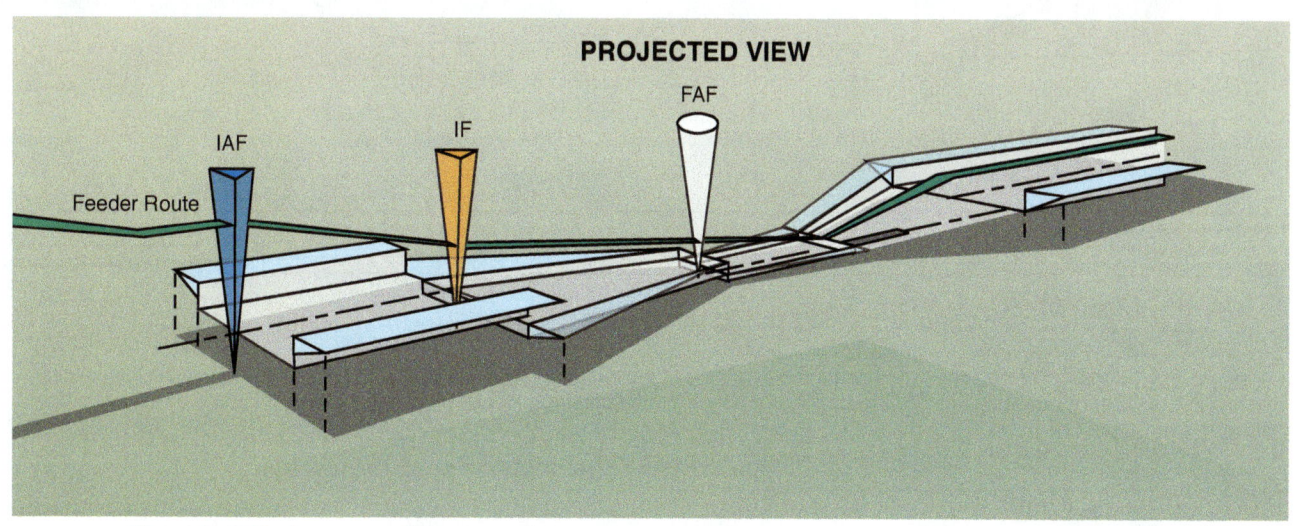

Figure B-17. Each segment of the approach has its own protected airspace criteria. This is a simplified example.

INITIAL APPROACH SEGMENT

The initial approach segment begins at the IAF. When the IF is part of the enroute structure, there might not be an initial approach segment. To accommodate aircraft from various directions, the initial segment might be an arc, radial, course, heading, radar vector, or a combination of these. Procedure turns, holding pattern descents, or high-altitude penetrations are initial approach segments. The ROC for an initial segment is typically 1,000 feet. This segment has lateral dimensions similar to a VHF airway, with a primary area that extends 4 NM to each side of the centerline, and a secondary area 2 NM wide outside the primary area. [Figure B-18]

The optimum descent gradient for this segment is 250 ft/NM, but where necessary, the approach designers can use a descent gradient of as much as 500 ft/NM. Descent gradients up to 1,000 ft/NM might be used for high-altitude penetrations.

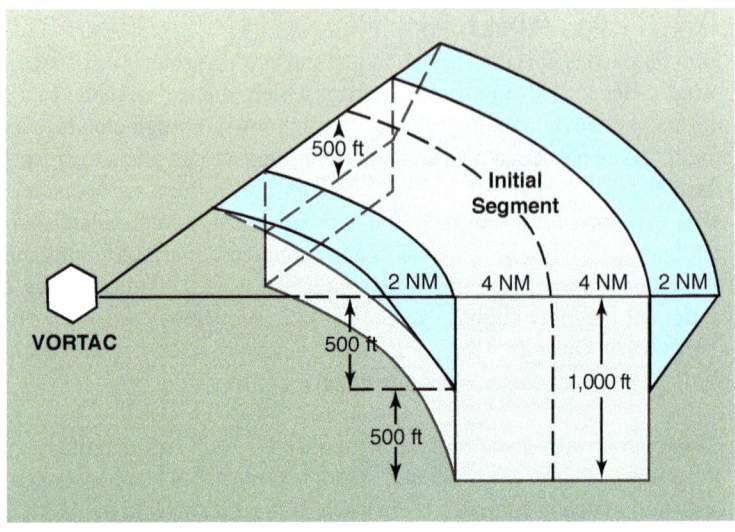

Figure B-18. The dimensions of the protected airspace apply whether the segment is straight or curved.

Approaches that require a course reversal, such as a procedure turn or holding pattern, provide protected airspace based on a template. The ROC for the primary area is 1,000 feet. [Figure B-19]

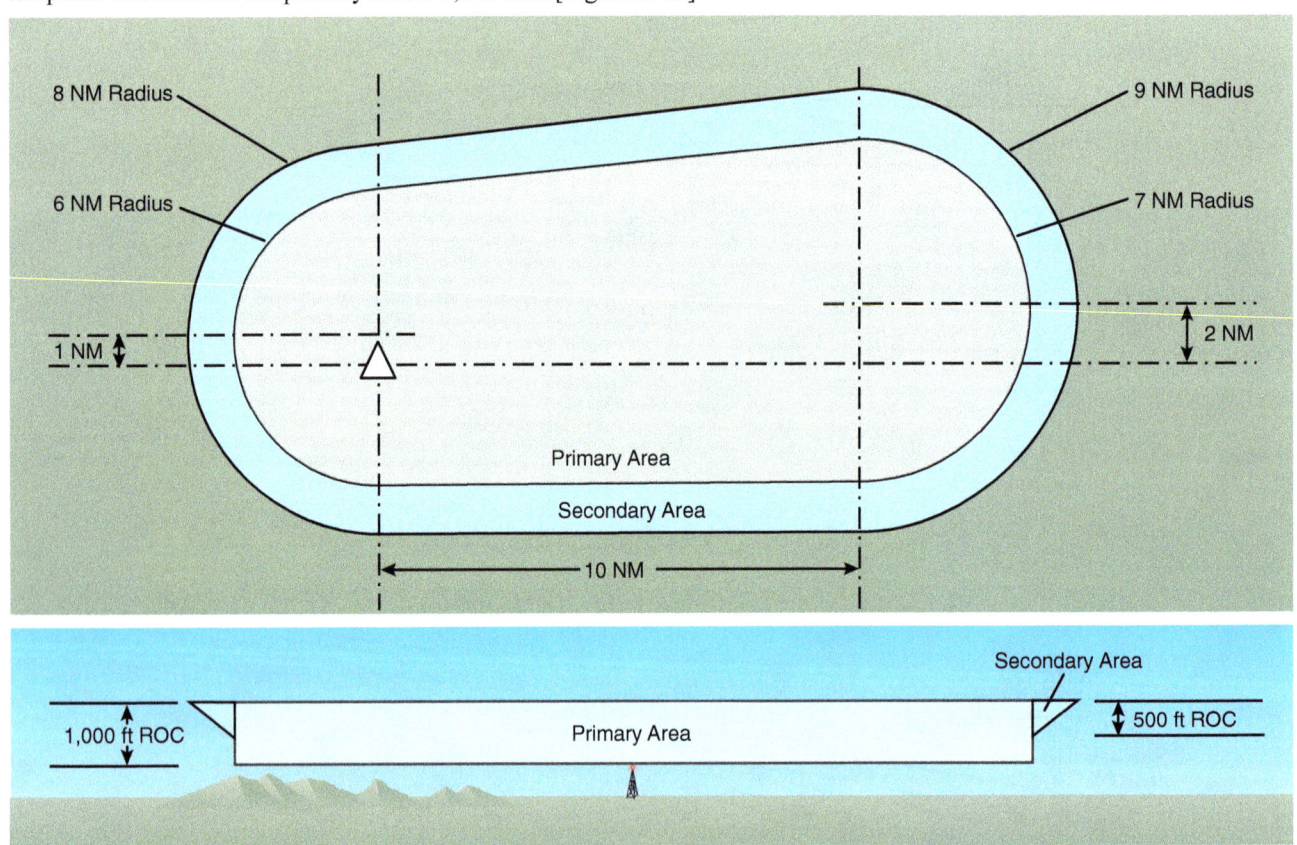

Figure B-19. These dimensions apply to a procedure turn flown at an altitude of 6,000 feet MSL or lower that specifies staying within 10 miles of the fix. Approach designers may reduce the procedure turn distance to as little as five miles for approaches used only by helicopters or Category A aircraft, and the area is somewhat smaller. Likewise, the area is larger for approaches flown above 6,000 feet, and for approaches designed for faster aircraft.

INTERMEDIATE APPROACH SEGMENT

The intermediate approach segment begins at the IF, and is the segment that blends the initial approach into the final approach. This is the segment where you normally reduce your speed and configure the aircraft for landing. For an approach that incorporates a procedure turn, the intermediate approach segment begins when you intercept the inbound course after completing the procedure turn. The intermediate approach segment can be straight or curved. It is at least 5 NM long for Category A and B, and at least 6 NM long for higher categories. The intermediate course might also be longer when the initial course joins the intermediate course at an angle. It is never longer than 15 NM, with 10 NM considered optimum. There are a number of possible configurations depending on the relative locations of the FAF and the procedure turn fix, and whether the fixes are navaids, intersections, or waypoints.

The lateral boundaries of the primary area match those of the segments it joins. The boundaries taper inward as you get closer to the FAF. The primary protected area is 4 NM each side of the centerline at the start of the intermediate approach segment, and tapers to 2 NM from the centerline at the FAF. The primary area provides at least 500 feet of obstacle clearance. The width of the secondary area is also tapered. The lateral boundaries are 2 NM outside the primary area boundaries at the start of this segment, and taper to match the width of the secondary area of the final approach segment at the FAF. The height of the secondary area is 500 feet where it is adjacent to the primary area, and it tapers to zero at the outer edge. [Figure B-20]

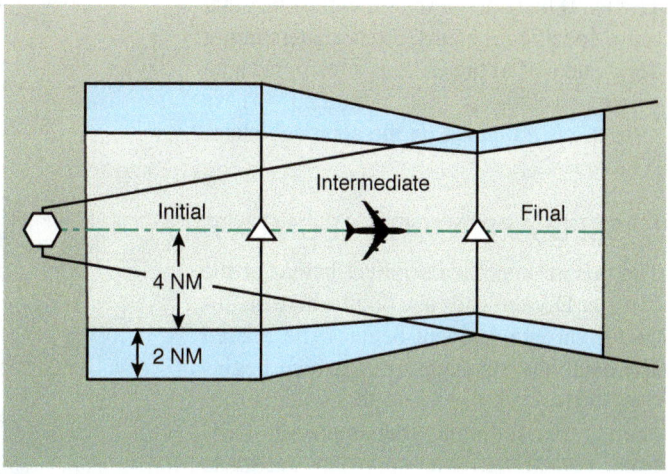

Figure B-20. Both the primary and the he secondary protected areas taper to match their respective areas of the final segment at the FAF.

The descent gradient is relatively flat, with an optimum gradient of 150 feet per mile. On localizer approaches, you might see steeper gradients that coincide with the glide slope of the ILS. When there is a stepdown fix, the maximum descent gradient from the IF point to the stepdown fix is usually 200 feet per NM. The maximum descent gradient from the stepdown fix to the FAF is usually 318 feet per NM.

FINAL APPROACH SEGMENT

The final approach segment can be to a specific runway, or to an airport for a circling approach. On a precision approach, the final approach segment typically begins where the glide slope intersects the minimum glide slope intercept altitude. For a nonprecision approach, the final approach segment begins at the FAF, or when you are established inbound on the final approach course. The final approach segment ends at the MAP or the DA.

The size and shape of the protected airspace for a straight-in final approach depend on the navigation system that guides the approach. In the case of VOR, DME, TACAN, or NDB guidance, the protected airspace also depends on the location of the navaids relative to the final approach. The variations, criteria, and limitations are complex, and well beyond the scope of this book. You can find them in the TERPS in the chapters specific to the facility or system providing navigation guidance.

To create the protected airspace for a circling approach, the designers draw an arc from the threshold of each of the runways included in the approach, and then connect the outermost arcs with tangent lines to define the boundaries of an obstacle evaluation area (OEA). The radius of the arcs is at least 1.3 NM, but the designers adjust the radius upward using a formula that considers true airspeed, bank angle, and the length of the straight segment. This OEA provides 300 feet of ROC. There is no secondary area. [Figure B-21]

Approach designers use a formula to determine the radius for a circling approach.

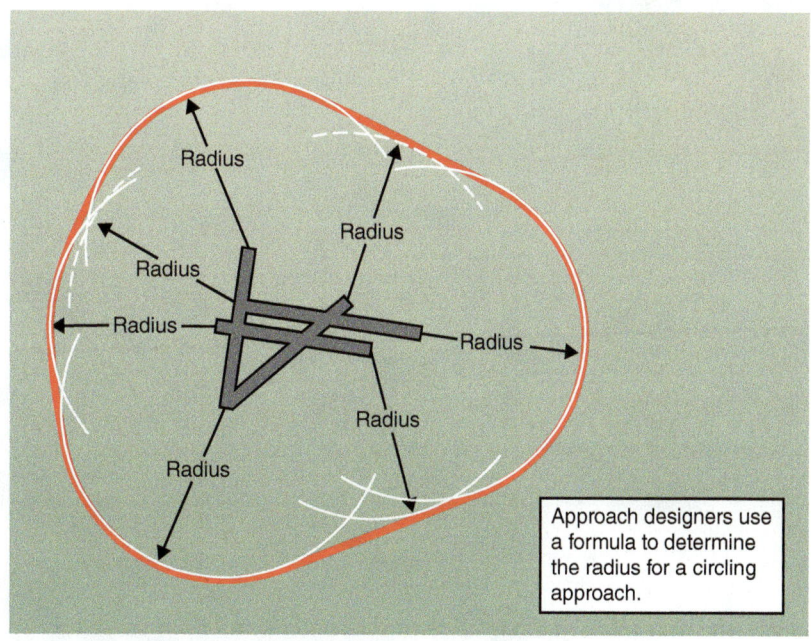

Figure B-21. The OEA for circling approaches provides ROC of 300 feet, with no secondary area.

B-15

To establish the circling MDA, the approach designers using tables and formulas in the TERPs. If there are obstacles in the OEA that cause specific problems, the designers might designate part of the OEA as a restricted area where circling is not permitted. These restrictions are noted on the approach chart. [Figure B-22]

MISSED APPROACH SEGMENT

The missed approach segment begins at the MAP or DA and ends at a point where an initial or enroute segment begins. The missed approach has a sloping OCS, which begins over the MAP at a height determined by subtracting the required final approach ROC from the MDA. The approach designers might have made adjustments to this height based on the glide path angle or other criteria. For a straight missed approach, the slope of the OCS is similar to a departure, increasing one foot vertically for every 40 feet horizontally from the MAP to a height of 1,000 feet. The OCS is level from that point to the fix where the missed approach ends. The missed approach might also specify an interim "climb-to" altitude to identify a turn point. In the secondary area, no obstacle may penetrate a 12:1 slope that extends outward and upward from the 40:1 surface at the inner boundaries of the secondary area. [Figure B-23]

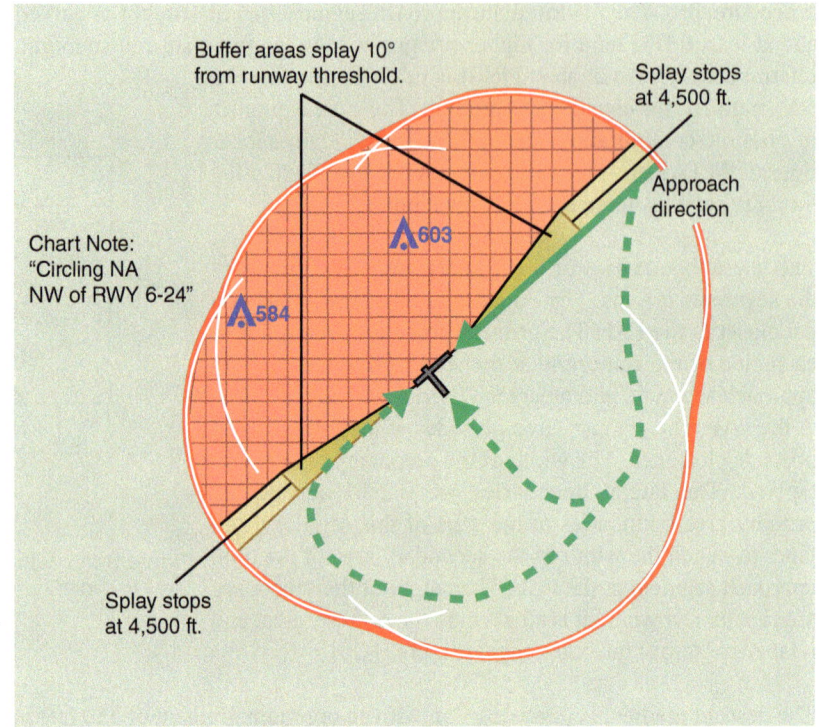

Figure B-22. In most cases runway centerlines define a restricted circling area, but the restricted area excludes a buffer area 10° from the approach path to a distance of 4,500 feet from the threshold.

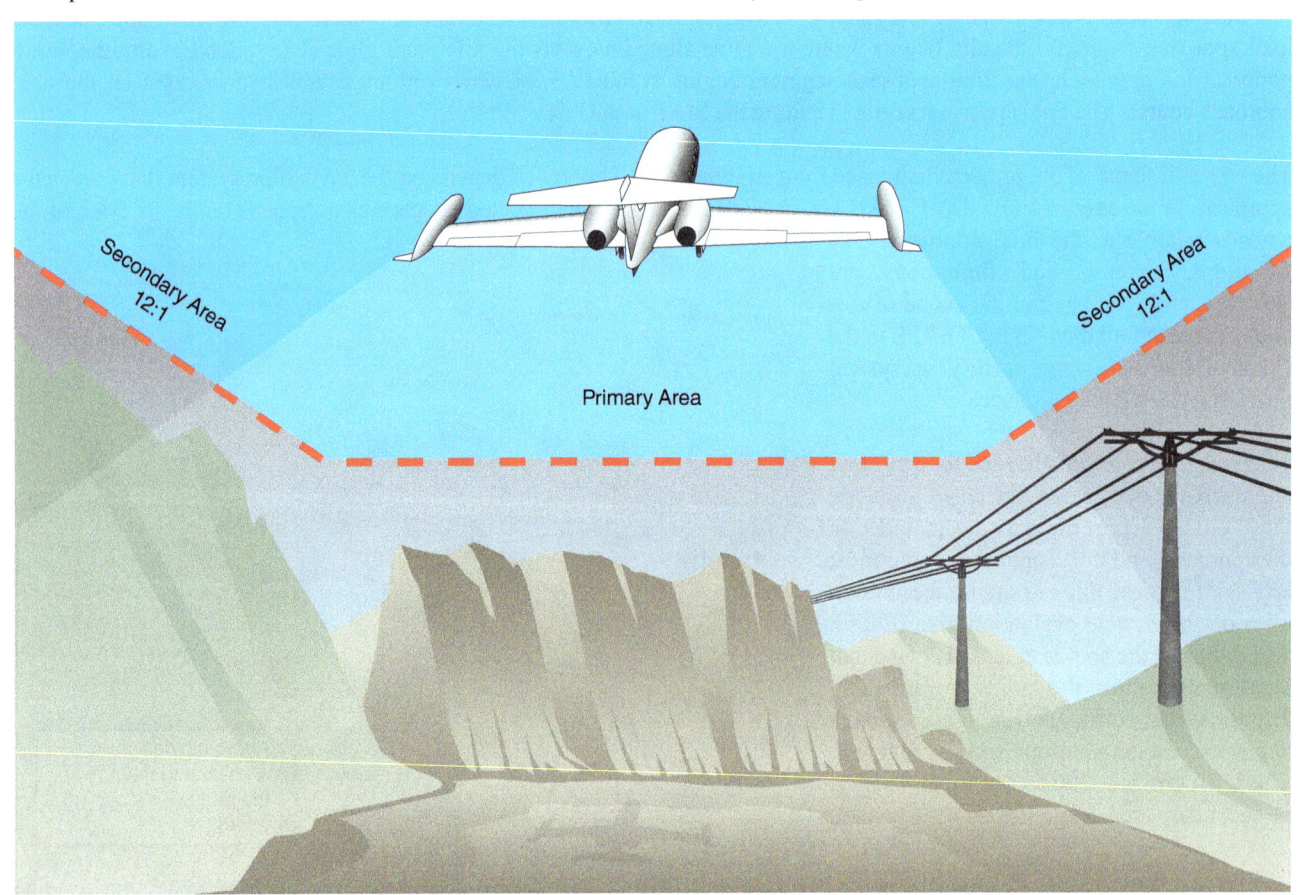

Figure B-23. The missed approach segment has a steeper slope to the secondary OCS than most other segments.

The lateral limits of the protected area widen outward from the width of the protected airspace at the MAP or DA. The angles are such that the primary area is 4 NM each side of the course centerline at a point 15 flying miles from the MAP. When positive course guidance (PCG) is available, a secondary area for the reduction of obstacle clearance is identified within the missed approach area. It has the same width as the final approach secondary area at the MAP, and widens to 2 NM beyond the outer edges of the primary area at 15 miles from the MAP. Where PCG is not available beyond this point, expansion of the area continues until PCG is achieved or the segment terminates. [Figure B-24]

Wherever possible, the designers try to make the missed approach straight or nearly straight. The design of missed approaches with turns is much more complex, and depend on the width of the final approach area at the MAP, the categories of aircraft authorized to use the procedure, and the number of degrees of turn required.

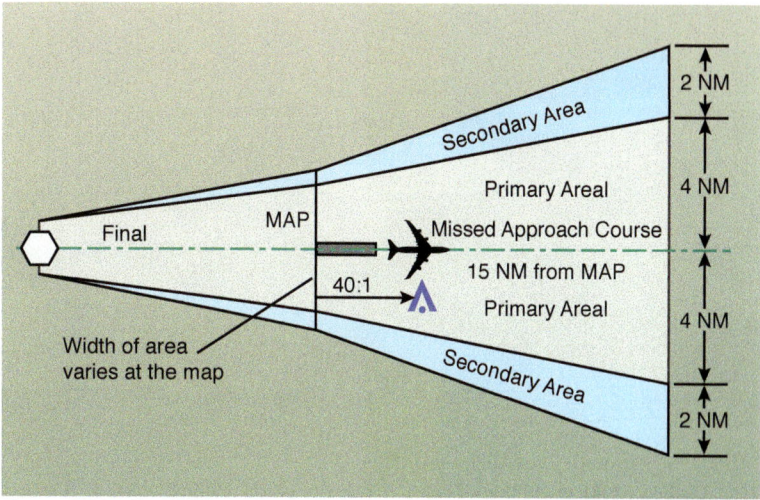

Figure B-24. The lateral boundaries of protected airspace for a straight missed approach widen with distance from the MAP.

The protected airspace descriptions above are typical of standard, uncomplicated approaches. The TERPs document provides additional guidance for other circumstances where the standard approach design is impractical. These include situations where terrain or obstacles are located in the normal approach path, where approach segments are not aligned with each other, where there is a visual component of the procedure, or where the approach must be modified to avoid sensitive areas. This information is not comprehensive and is only provided to give you an idea of how protected airspace is created and the importance of staying well within its boundaries.

Although new navigation systems give you the capability to fly routes and approaches with increased precision, maintaining **situational awareness** is more important than ever. The increasing accuracy and automation of avionics allow approach designers to permit lower minimums and to reduce the size of your protected airspace. There is less margin for error, and pilots have had serious mishaps as a result of misinterpreting cockpit displays, failing to adequately monitor automated systems, or misprogramming their navigation systems. For safety, you should promptly communicate any deviations from assigned altitudes or course centerline. This is especially important when if your flight is close to restricted airspace.

Except in Class A airspace, the protection afforded by staying within protected airspace and adhering to your ATC clearance does not include protection from VFR traffic. Always remember that in VFR conditions you are responsible for avoiding other aircraft. Your IFR clearance does not guarantee separation from VFR aircraft that are climbing, descending, maneuvering, or engaged in any of the myriad other flight activities, from aerobatic practice to fire fighting, from flight instruction to sightseeing. Maintain a sharp visual scan for other traffic whenever you are in VFR conditions.

Appendix C
Acronyms and Glossary

AAUP — Attention All Users Page

AC — advisory circular

ACARS — aircraft communications addressing and reporting system

ACAS — Adverse Conditions Alerting Service

AD — airworthiness directive

ADF — automatic direction finder

ADS — automatic dependent surveillance

ADS-B — automatic dependent surveillance-broadcast

ADS-C — automatic dependent surveillance-contract

ADS-R — automatic dependent surveillance-rebroadcast

AEDT — aviation environmental design tool

AFCS — automatic flight control system

A/FD — Airport/Facility Directory

AFM — airplane flight manual or aircraft flight manual

AFSS — automated flight service station

AGL — above ground level

AIM — Aeronautical Information Manual

AIP — Aeronautical Information Publication

AIRAC — aeronautical information regulation and control cycle

ALAR — approach and landing accident reduction

AMM — airport moving map

ANP — actual navigation performance

ANR — advanced navigation route

AP — autopilot system

APV — approach with vertical guidance

ARINC — Aeronautical Radio, Incorporated

AR — authorization required

ARSR — air route surveillance radar

ARTCC — air route traffic control center

ARTS — automated radar terminal system

ASDE-3 — airport surface detection equipment-3

ASDE-X — airport surface detection equipment-X

ASOS — automated surface observing system

ASR — airport surveillance radar

ATC — air traffic control

ATCSCC — Air Traffic Control System Command Center

ATCT — air traffic control tower

ATIS — automatic terminal information service

ATM — air traffic management

ATOP — advanced technologies and oceanic procedures

ATPA — automated terminal proximity alert

ATRK — along-track

ATS — air traffic service

AWOS — automated weather observing system

AWTT — Aviation Weather Technology Transfer

Baro-VNAV — barometric vertical navigation

B-RNAV — European basic RNAV

CARTS — common automated radar terminal system

CAT — category

CDI — course deviation indicator

CDFA — continuous descent final approach

CDTI — cockpit display of traffic information

CFIT — controlled flight into terrain

CFR — Code of Federal Regulations

CNF — computer navigation fix

COP — changeover point

CRC — cyclic redundancy check

CRM — crew resource management

CSS-Wx — Common Support Services-Weather

CTAF — common traffic advisory frequency

CVFP — charted visual flight procedure

CVS — combined vision system

CWA — center weather advisory

DA — decision altitude

D-ATIS — digital automatic terminal information service

DER — departure end of the runway

DF — direct to fix (path/terminator)

DH — decision height

DME — distance measuring equipment

DOD — Department of Defense

DOT — Department of Transportation

DP — departure procedure

DUATS — direct user access terminal system

DVA — diverse vector area

EFB — electronic flight bag

EFC — expect further clearance

EFVS — enhanced flight vision system

EMM — enroute moving map

EPE — estimated position error

ES — extended squitter

ETA — estimated time of arrival

ETMS — enhanced traffic management system

EVS — enhanced vision system

EWINS — enhanced weather information system

FAA — Federal Aviation Administration

FAF — final approach fix

FANS — future air navigation system

FAP — final approach point

FAST — final approach spacing tool

FD — winds and temperatures aloft forecast

FD — flight director

FDA — fix displacement area

FDC NOTAM — Flight Data Center notice to airmen

FDT — fix displacement tolerance

FIR — Flight Information Region

FIS-B — flight information service-broadcast

FL — flight level

FMS — flight management system

FOC — flight operations center

FOM — flight operations manual

FSDO — flight standards district office

FTP — fictitious threshold waypoint

FSS — flight service station

FTE — flight technical error

GA — general aviation

GAMA — General Aviation Manufacturer's Association

GBAS — ground-based augmentation system

GCO — ground communication outlet

GLS — GBAS Landing System

GPS — global positioning system

GS — glide slope

GS — groundspeed

HAA — height above airport

HAR — High Altitude Redesign

HAT — height above touchdown

HF — high frequency

HFM — helicopter flight manual

HEMS — helicopter emergency medical service

HUD — head-up display

IAF — initial approach fix

IAP — instrument approach procedure

IAS — indicated air speed

ICAO — International Civil Aviation Organization

IF — intermediate fix

IFP — instrument flight procedure

IFR — instrument flight rules

IGRF — International Geomagnetic Reference Field

ILS — instrument landing system

IMC — instrument meteorological conditions

INS — inertial navigation system

IRU — inertial reference unit

KIAS — knots indicated airspeed

LAHSO — land and hold short operations

LDA — localizer-type directional aid

LF — low frequency

LMFS — Lockheed Martin Flight Service

LNAV — lateral navigation

LOA — letter of authorization

LOC — localizer

LOM — locator outer marker

LP — localizer performance

LPV — localizer performance with vertical guidance

LUAW — line up and wait

MAA — maximum authorized altitude

MAHWP — missed approach holding waypoint

MAP — missed approach point

MAWP — missed approach waypoint

MCA — minimum crossing altitude

MDA — minimum descent altitude

MEA — minimum enroute altitude

MEL — minimum equipment list

METAR — aviation routine weather report

MFD — multifunction display

MOA — military operations area

MOCA — minimum obstruction clearance altitude

MORA — minimum off-route altitude

MRA — minimum reception altitude

MSA — minimum safe/sector altitude

MSL — mean sea level

MSpecs — management specifications

MVA — minimum vectoring altitude

NA — not authorized

NAD-83 — North American Datum of 1983

NAS — National Airspace System

NASA — National Aeronautics and Space Administration

NAVAID — navigational aid

NDB — nondirectional beacon

NFDC — National Flight Data Center

NM — nautical mile

NOAA — National Oceanic and Atmospheric Administration

NOTAM — notice to airmen

NOTAM D — distant NOTAM

NPA — nonprecision approach

NPRM — notice of proposed rulemaking

NRR — non-restrictive routing

NRS — navigation reference system

NSE — navigation system error

NTSB — National Transportation Safety Board

NTZ — no transgression zone

NWP — NextGen weather processor

NWS — National Weather Service

OCS — obstacle clearance surface

ODP — obstacle departure procedure

OEA — obstacle evaluation area

OPD — optimized profile descent

OpsSpecs — operations specifications

PA — precision approach

PANS-OPS — Procedures for Air Navigation Services-Aircraft Operations

PAR — precision approach radar

PBN — performance-based navigation

PCG — positive course guidance

PDR — preferential departure route

PF — pilot flying

PFD — primary flight display

PIC — pilot in command

PinS — point-in-space

PIREP — pilot weather report

PM — pilot monitoring

POH — pilot's operating handbook

POI — principle operations inspector

PRM — precision runway monitor

P-RNAV — European precision RNAV

PT — procedure turn

PTP — point-to-point

PTS — FAA Practical Test Standards

QFE — *See glossary.*

QNE — *See glossary.*

QNH — *See glossary.*

RA — radar altimeter

RA — resolution advisory

RAIM — receiver autonomous integrity monitoring

RCAG — remote center air/ground

RCO — remote communications outlet

RF — radius to fix (path/terminator)

RJ — regional jet

RNAV — area navigation

RNP — required navigation performance

ROC — required obstacle clearance

RVR — runway visual range

RVSM — reduced vertical separation minimums

RVV — runway visibility value

RWSL — runway status lights

RWY — runway

SA — special authorization

SAS — stability augmentation system

SID — standard instrument departure

SIGMET — significant meteorological information

SM — statute mile

SMGCS — surface movement guidance and control system

SOIA — simultaneous offset instrument approaches

SOP — standard operating procedure

SPECI — non-routine (special) aviation weather report

SSV — standard service volume

STA — scheduled time of arrival

STAR — standard terminal arrival route

STARS — standard terminal automation replacement system

STC — supplemental type certificate

SVFR — special visual flight rules

SVS — synthetic vision system

TA — traffic advisory

TAA — terminal arrival area

TACAN — tactical air navigation

TAS — true airspeed

TAWS — terrain awareness and warning system

TCAS — traffic alert and collision avoidance system

TCH — threshold crossing height

TDZ — touchdown zone

TDZE — touchdown zone elevation

TEC — tower enroute control

TERPS — U.S. Standard for Terminal Instrument Procedures

TF — track to fix (path/terminator)

TIS — traffic information service

TIS-B — traffic information service-broadcast

TM — traffic management

TMA — traffic management advisor

TMC — traffic management coordinator

TOC — top of climb

TOD — top of descent

TRACON — terminal radar approach control

TSAA — traffic situational awareness with alerts

TSE — total navigation system error

TSO — technical standard order

UAT — universal access transceiver

UHF — ultra high frequency

USAF — United States Air Force

VA — heading to altitude (path/terminator)

VCOA — visual climb over airport

VDA — vertical descent angle

VFR — visual flight rules

VGSI — visual glide slope indicator

VHF — very high frequency

VI — heading to intercept (path/terminator)

VMC — visual meteorological conditions

V_{MINI} — minimum speed—IFR.

VNAV — vertical navigation

V_{NEI} — never exceed speed-IFR.

VOR — very high frequency omnidirectional range

VORTAC — very high frequency omni-directional range/tactical air navigation

VR — heading to radial (path/terminator)

V_{REF} — reference landing speed

V_{SO} — stalling speed or the minimum steady flight speed in the landing configuration

V_X — best angle of climb speed

V_Y — best rate of climb speed

WAAS — wide area augmentation system

WAC — world aeronautical chart

WGS-84 — World Geodetic System of 1984

WP — waypoint

XTRK — cross-track

GLOSSARY

Aircraft Approach Category — A grouping of aircraft based on reference landing speed (V_{REF}), if specified, or if V_{REF} is not specified, 1.3 V_{S0} (the stalling speed or minimum steady flight speed in the landing configuration) at the maximum certificated landing weight. V_{REF}, V_{S0}, and the maximum certificated landing weight are those values as established for the aircraft by the certification authority of the country of registry.

Aircraft Communications Addressing and Reporting System (ACARS) — A digital commercial system that enables you to communicate with company personnel and send email-type messaging to ATC without verbal transmission.

Airport Chart — Charts that provide graphical depictions of airport layouts. Jeppesen IFR terminal chart subscriptions include a separate airport chart for every airport with an instrument approach. Each airport chart depicts information such as runway data, taxiway identifiers, airport latitude and longitude, communication frequencies, and buildings. Takeoff minimums and alternate airport minimums might be depicted on the same chart or on a separate chart along with items such as notices, runway incursion hot spot descriptions, and obstacle departure procedures.

Airport Diagram — See Airport Chart

Airport/Facility Directory (A/FD) — Regional booklets and online products published by the FAA that provide information about all U.S. airports, both VFR and IFR. The A/FD includes runway length and width, runway surface, load bearing capacity, runway slope, airport services, and hazards such as birds.

Airport Surveillance Radar (ASR) — Radar system used by TRACON facilities to direct and coordinate IFR traffic within specific terminal areas. ASR provides relatively short-range coverage in the airport vicinity and serves as an expeditious means of managing terminal area traffic. ATC also uses ASR as an instrument approach aid.

Air Route Surveillance Radar (ARSR) — The long-range radar equipment used in controlled airspace to manage traffic. ARSR facilities relay traffic information to radar controllers at ARTCCs to direct and coordinate IFR traffic.

Air Route Traffic Control Center (ARTCC) — A facility established to provide air traffic control service to aircraft operating on IFR flight plans within controlled airspace and principally during the enroute phase of flight

Air Traffic Control System Command Center (ATCSCC) — A facility that oversees all air traffic control and manages air traffic control at centers where issues cause delays, such as poor weather, traffic overload, or closed runways.

Air Traffic Service (ATS) — An ICAO generic term meaning variously, flight information service, alerting service, air traffic advisory service, air traffic control service (area control service, approach control service, or aerodrome control service).

Approach Gate — An imaginary point used by ATC to vector aircraft to the final approach course. The approach gate is established at one nautical mile from the final approach fix (FAF) on the side of the final approach course away from the airport and is located no closer than five nautical miles from the landing threshold.

Approach with Vertical Guidance (APV) — An instrument approach procedure type that provides lateral guidance and vertical guidance in the form of a glide path display. APVs do not meet precision approach criteria to be classified as precision approaches. RNAV (GPS) and RNAV (RNP) approaches that use vertical guidance are APVs.

Area Navigation (RNAV) — A method of navigation that permits aircraft operations on any desired course within the coverage of station referenced navigation signals or within the limits of self contained system capability.

Automated Surface Observing System (ASOS) — A weather observing system that provides minute-by-minute weather observations such as temperature, dew point, wind, altimeter setting, visibility, sky condition, and precipitation. Some ASOS stations include a precipitation discriminator that differentiates between liquid and frozen precipitation.

Automated Weather Observing System (AWOS) — A suite of sensors that measure, collect, and disseminate weather data. AWOS stations provide a minute-by-minute update of weather parameters such as wind speed and direction, temperature and dew point, visibility, cloud heights and types, precipitation, and barometric pressure. A variety of AWOS system types are available (from AWOS-1 to AWOS-3), each of which includes a different sensor array.

Automatic Dependent Surveillance-Broadcast (ADS-B) — A surveillance system that incorporates GPS satellites, aircraft transmitters, and aircraft and ground receivers to provide pilots and ground control personnel with specific information about the position and speed of aircraft in the area. Two forms of ADS-B equipment apply to aircraft—ADS-B Out and ADS-B In. ADS-B Out signals travel line-of-sight from transmitting aircraft to ATC ground receivers or aircraft receivers. In order to receive the signal and display traffic information in your aircraft you must also have ADS-B In capability. ADS-B continuously and automatically broadcasts aircraft speed, altitude, position, and other data once per second.

Automatic Terminal Information Service (ATIS) — A recorded broadcast available at most airports with an operating control tower that includes crucial information about runways and instrument approaches in use, specific outages, and current weather conditions, including visibility.

Changeover Point (COP) — The point where a frequency change is necessary between navigation aids when other than the midpoint on an airway, to receive course guidance from the facility ahead of the aircraft instead of the one behind. COPs divide an airway or route segment and ensure continuous reception of navigational signals at the prescribed minimum enroute IFR altitude.

Charted Visual Flight Procedure (CVFP) — A procedure established at some towered airports for environmental or noise considerations, as well as when necessary for the safety and efficiency of air traffic operations. Designed primarily for turbojet aircraft, CVFPs depict prominent landmarks, courses, and recommended altitudes to specific runways.

Cockpit Display of Traffic Information (CDTI) — The display and user interface for information about air traffic within approximately 80 miles. It typically combines and shows traffic data from TCAS, TIS-B, and ADS-B. Depending on features, the display may also show terrain, weather, and navigation information.

Combined Vision System (CVS) — A cockpit display that unites synthetic and enhanced systems. A CVS might include database-driven synthetic vision images combined with real-time sensor images superimposed and correlated on the same display.

Contact Approach — An approach where an aircraft on an IFR flight plan, having an ATC authorization, operating clear of clouds with at least one mile flight visibility, and a reasonable expectation of continuing to the destination airport in those conditions, may deviate from the instrument approach procedure and proceed to the destination airport by visual reference to the surface. This approach is only authorized when requested by the pilot and the reported ground visibility at the destination airport is at least one statute mile.

Continuous Descent Final Approach (CDFA) — A technique for flying the final approach segment of a nonprecision approach as a continuous descent. A CDFA starts from an altitude/height at or above the FAF and proceeds to an altitude/height approximately 50 feet above the landing runway threshold or to a point where you should begin the flare maneuver for the type of aircraft you are flying.

Controlled Flight Into Terrain (CFIT) — An accident in which a fully qualified and certificated crew flies a properly functioning airplane into the ground, water, or obstacles with no apparent awareness by the pilots.

Database Field — The collection of characters needed to define one item of information.

Database Record — A single line of computer data made up of the fields necessary to define fully a single useful piece of data.

Decision Altitude (DA) — An altitude referenced to mean sea level, the altitude at which you must decide whether to continue the approach or perform a missed approach. You descend to a DA on CAT I ILS approaches, and when flying approaches with vertical guidance (APV).

Decision Height (DH) — A height referenced to AGL and measured by a radio altimeter (RA), the altitude at which you must decide whether to continue the approach or perform a missed approach. DHs apply to special authorization (SA) CAT I ILS, CAT II ILS, and some CAT III ILS approaches.

Descend Via — A clearance that instructs you to follow the altitudes published on a STAR. You are not authorized to leave your last assigned altitude unless specifically cleared to do so. If ATC amends the altitude or route to one that is different from the published procedure, the rest of the charted descent procedure is canceled. ATC assigns you any further route, altitude, or airspeed clearances, as necessary.

Digital ATIS (D-ATIS) — An alternative method of receiving ATIS reports by aircraft equipped with datalink services capable of receiving information in the cockpit over their ACARS unit.

Diverse Vector Area (DVA) — An area established at an airport when it is necessary to vector aircraft below the minimum vectoring altitude (MVA) to assist in the efficient flow of departing traffic. DVA design requirements are outlined in TERPS and allow for the vectoring of aircraft immediately off the departure end of the runway below the MVA.

Dynamic Magnetic Variation — In a navigation database, a field for magnetic variation in the record for a waypoint that is calculated from a computer model instead of a measured value.

Electronic Flight Bag (EFB) — A device that exists both as a mobile device or as equipment that is installed in the aircraft. EFBs display flight plans, routes, checklists, flight operations manuals, regulations, minimum equipment lists (MELs), moving map and weather displays, approach charts, airport diagrams, logbooks, and operating procedures. You can use the EFB to calculate aircraft performance and accomplish many tasks traditionally handled by a dispatcher. AC 120-76 outlines the capabilities and limitations of each of the three classes of EFBs. Classes are primarily based on whether the EFB is portable and the placement of the equipment in the cockpit.

Enhanced Flight Vision System (EFVS) — A real-time imaging sensor that provides highly accurate vision performance in low visibility conditions and projects an image onto a head-up display (HUD). Required visual references become visible in the image before they are visible naturally out the window. FAR 91.175(l) allows you to continue an approach below the DA or MDA to 100 feet above the runway using an EFVS provided specific conditions outlined in the regulation are met.

Enhanced Vision System (EVS) — A display of the forward external scene topography through the use of imaging sensors, such as forward looking infrared, millimeter wave radiometry or radar, and low-light-level image intensifying. An EVS can be displayed on primary flight displays (PFD), navigation displays, or class 3 EFBs.

Feeder Route — A route depicted on IAP charts to designate courses for aircraft to transition from the enroute structure to the IAF.

Field — See Database Field

Flight Information Region (FIR) — Airspace of defined dimensions within which flight information service and alerting service are provided. Flight information service is a service provided for the purpose of giving advice and information useful for the safe and efficient conduct of flights. Alerting service is a service provided to notify appropriate organizations regarding aircraft in need of search and rescue aid, and assist such organizations as required.

Flight Information Service-Broadcast (FIS-B) — An automatic dependent surveillance-broadcast (ADS-B) service that provides graphical and textual weather, as well as aeronautical information to aircraft equipped with the 978 UAT link. METARs, TAFs, NEXRAD precipitation maps, NOTAMs, TFRs, and PIREPS are just some of the many types of information you receive.

Flight Level (FL) — A level of constant atmospheric pressure related to a reference datum of 29.92 in.Hg. Each flight level is stated in three digits that represents hundreds of feet. For example, FL250 represents an altimeter indication of 25,000 feet.

Flight Management System (FMS) — A flight computer system that uses a large database to allow routes to be pre-programmed and fed into the system by means of a data loader. The FMS is constantly updated with respect to position accuracy by reference to conventional navaids, inertial reference system technology, or GPS.

Floating Waypoints — Waypoints that represent airspace fixes at a point in space not directly associated with a conventional airway. Floating waypoints might be established for such purposes as ATC metering fixes, holding points, RNAV-direct routing, gateway waypoints, STAR origination points, and SID terminating points.

Fly-By Waypoint — A waypoint that requires the use of turn anticipation to avoid overshooting the next flight segment.

Fly-Over Waypoint — A waypoint that precludes any turn until the waypoint is overflown, and is followed by either an intercept maneuver of the next flight segment or direct flight to the next waypoint.

Geodetic Datum — The reference surface from which geodetic calculations are made.

Grid Minimum Off-Route Altitude (Grid MORA) — An altitude derived by Jeppesen or provided by government civil aviation authorities that provides terrain and man-made structure clearance within the section outlined by latitude and longitude lines.

Ground-Based Augmentation System (GBAS) — A system that provides a GPS position correction more precise than WAAS that covers a localized area, generally 20 to 30 miles around an airport. GBAS can pinpoint an aircraft's location to within three feet and can provide the required precision and integrity for extremely precise instrument approaches with Category (CAT) I and CAT II/III minimums and for airport surface operations, such as low-visibility taxiing.

Ground Communication Outlet (GCO) — An unstaffed, remotely controlled ground/ground communications facility that enables you to contact flight service and ATC by VHF radio to a telephone connection to obtain an instrument clearance or close a VFR/IFR flight plan.

Head-up Display (HUD) — A transparent display that presents critical flight data on a display positioned between the pilot and the windscreen. The HUD enables you to look outside the flight deck while simultaneously viewing the primary flight instruments and approach navigation information.

Height Above Touchdown (HAT) — The height of the decision altitude (DA) or minimum descent altitude (MDA) above touchdown zone elevation for straight-in landings.

Instrument Landing System (ILS) — A precision instrument approach system that normally consists of the following electronic components and visual aids; localizer, glide slope, outer marker, middle marker, and approach lights.

International Civil Aviation Organization (ICAO) — A specialized agency of the United Nations whose objective is to develop standard principles and techniques of international air navigation and to promote development of civil aviation.

Intersection — The point at which two VOR radial position lines cross on a route, usually intersecting at a good angle for positive indication of position, resulting in a VOR/VOR fix.

Lateral Navigation (LNAV) — Landing minimums provided for RNAV (GPS) approach procedures that have lateral navigation guidance only. You can fly an approach to LNAV minimums with GPS equipment certified for IFR approach procedures by TSO-C129. LNAV course guidance has larger integrity limits than those of a localizer. The LNAV minimum is an MDA.

Lateral navigation/vertical navigation (LNAV/VNAV) — Landing minimums that apply to RNAV (GPS) approaches that provide lateral and vertical guidance. You can fly an approach to LNAV/VNAV minimums using baro-VNAV or WAAS-certified equipment. The integrity limits for LNAV/VNAV approaches are larger than those of a precision approach. The LNAV/VNAV landing minimum is an MDA.

Localizer Performance (LP) — Landing minimums that apply to RNAV (GPS) approaches that provide lateral guidance with integrity limits close to a localizer and have smaller lateral protected areas than approaches to LNAV minimums. Approaches to LP minimums are published in locations where vertical guidance is not feasible due to terrain, obstacles, or other operational limitations. The LP minimum is an MDA Your GPS equipment must be WAAS-certified to fly approaches to LP minimums.

Localizer Performances with Vertical Guidance (LPV) — Landing minimums provided for RNAV (GPS) approach procedures that have vertical guidance capability. These minimums apply to approaches that provide lateral and vertical guidance with integrity limits that are close to an ILS precision approach. The LPV landing minimum is a DA. Your GPS equipment must be WAAS-certified to fly approaches to LPV minimums.

Magnetic Variation — The difference in degrees between true north and magnetic north at that location.

Maximum Authorized Altitude (MAA) — A published altitude representing the maximum usable altitude or flight level for an airspace structure or route segment. It is the highest altitude on a federal airway, jet route, RNAV low or high route, or other direct route for which an MEA is designated at which adequate reception of navigation signals is assured.

Metering Fix — A fix along an established route over which aircraft are metered prior to entering terminal airspace, at or above 10,000 feet above the airport elevation to facilitate a profile descent, rather than controllers using delaying vectors or a holding pattern at low altitudes.

Mid-RVR — The RVR readout values obtained from sensors located midfield of the runway.

Mileage Break — A point on a route where the leg segment mileage ends, and a new leg segment mileage begins, often at a route turning point.

Minimum Crossing Altitude (MCA) — The lowest altitude at certain fixes at which the aircraft must cross when proceeding in the direction of a higher minimum enroute IFR altitude. MCAs are established in all cases where obstacles intervene to prevent you from maintaining obstacle clearance during a normal climb to a higher MEA after passing a point beyond which the higher MEA applies.

Minimum Descent Altitude (MDA) — The lowest altitude, expressed in feet above mean sea level, to which descent is authorized on final approach or during circle-to-land maneuvering in execution of a nonprecision instrument approach procedure where no glide slope or glide path is provided.

Minimum Enroute Altitude (MEA) — The lowest published altitude between radio fixes that assures acceptable navigational signal coverage and meets obstacle clearance requirements between those fixes. The MEA prescribed for a Federal airway or segment, RNAV low or high route, or other direct route applies to the entire width of the airway, segment, or route between the radio fixes defining the airway, segment, or route.

Minimum Obstruction Clearance Altitude (MOCA) — The lowest published altitude in effect between radio fixes on VOR airways, off-airway routes, or route segments that meets obstacle clearance requirements for the entire route segment. This altitude also assures acceptable navigational signal coverage only within 22 NM of a VOR.

Minimum Reception Altitude (MRA) — An altitude Determined by FAA flight inspection traversing an entire route of flight to establish the minimum altitude the navigation signal can be received for the route and for off-course navaid facilities that determine a fix. When the MRA at the fix is higher than the MEA, an MRA is established for the fix, and is the lowest altitude at which an intersection can be determined.

Minimum Safe/Sector Altitudes (MSA) — An altitude published for emergency use on approach charts. The MSA is normally based on the primary omnidirectional facility on which the IAP is predicated or a specific waypoint for an RNAV approach. MSAs are expressed in feet above MSL and normally have a 25 nautical mile radius. MSAs provide 1,000 feet clearance over all obstructions but do not necessarily ensure acceptable navigation signal coverage.

Minimum Vectoring Altitude (MVA) — An altitude established by the FAA for use by ATC in radar areas where ATC provides radar vectors. The MVA provides 1,000 feet of clearance above the highest obstacle in nonmountainous areas and 2,000 feet above the highest obstacle in designated mountainous areas. While being radar vectored, IFR altitude assignments by ATC are normally at or above the MVA.

National Airspace System (NAS) — The U.S. airspace system that combines a vast collection of facilities, equipment, procedures, and airports operated by thousands of people to provide a safe and efficient flying environment.

Navigation Reference System (NRS) — A grid of waypoints overlying the U.S. that provides flexible flight planning and gives ATC the ability to more efficiently manage tactical route changes for aircraft separation, traffic flow management, and weather avoidance.

Navigational Gap — Referred to as an MEA gap on an enroute chart, describes a distance along an airway or route segment where a gap in navigational signal coverage exists. The navigational gap may not exceed a specific distance that varies directly with altitude.

Nondirectional Radio Beacon (NDB) — An L/MF or UHF radio beacon transmitting nondirectional signals whereby the pilot of an aircraft equipped with direction finding equipment can determine bearing to or from the radio beacon and "home" on or track to or from the station.

Nonprecision Approach (NPA) — An instrument approach procedure type that provides only lateral guidance. Examples of nonprecision approaches include localizer, VOR, and NDB approaches, and RNAV (GPS) approaches without vertical guidance.

Obstacle Clearance Surface (OCS) — Designated by airspace planners, level or inclined planes above the highest and features and obstructions in a particular segment of airspace. Level surfaces are appropriate for enroute airspace and for some parts of approach procedures and sloping OCSs are used for departures and approaches.

Obstacle Departure Procedure (ODP) — A procedure established to ensure obstacle clearance and might be depicted textually or graphically, depending on complexity. ODPs simply provide obstacle clearance—they do not include ATC-related climb requirements. The primary emphasis of ODP design is to use the least onerous route of flight to the enroute structure while attempting to accommodate typical departure routes.

Operations Specifications (OpsSpecs) — A published document required by FAR 119.5 to be issued to commercial operators to define appropriate authorizations, limitations, and procedures based on the type of operation, equipment, and pilot qualifications. The OpsSpecs are an extension of the regulations; therefore, they are legal, binding contracts between a properly certificated air transportation organization and the FAA for compliance with the regulations applicable to their operation.

Performance-Based Navigation (PBN) — A framework for defining navigation that is not constrained by the location of ground-based navigation aids. PBN provides navigation performance requirements that are defined by the accuracy, integrity, continuity, and functionality needed for an operation in a particular airspace environment.

Point-in Space (PinS) Approach — A helicopter approach typically developed at locations where the MAP is located more than 2 SM from the landing site, or the path from the MAP to the landing site is populated with obstructions which require avoidance actions, or the flight path requires turns greater than 30°. In some cases, a single PinS procedure can allow you to fly from the MAP to one of several landing areas. These procedures involve a VFR segment between the MAP and the landing area. The procedure specifies a course and distance from the MAP to the available heliports in the area.

Precision Approach (PA) — An instrument approach procedure type that provides lateral guidance and vertical guidance in the form of a glide slope. This approach provides the most accurate guidance and must meet specific standards of precision and integrity limits. The most common precision approach is the ILS.

Precision Runway Monitor (PRM) — A high-update-rate radar surveillance system used at selected capacity-constrained airports to provide simultaneous close parallel PRM approaches and simultaneous offset instrument approaches (SOIA). The PRM system incorporates high-update radar with one second or better update time and a high resolution ATC radar display that contains automated tracking software that can track aircraft in real time.

Preferential Departure Route (PDR) — A specific departure route from an airport or terminal area to an enroute point where there is no further need for flow control. It may be included in a departure procedure or a preferred IFR route.

Preferred IFR Routes — A system of routes that help you and dispatchers plan a flight to minimize route changes and to aid in the efficient, orderly management of air traffic using airways and jet routes. Low and high altitude preferred IFR routes provide a systematic flow of air traffic in the major terminal and enroute flight environments. Filing preferred routes results in fewer air traffic delays and better efficiency for departure, enroute, and arrival ATC service.

QFE — Mean sea level pressure corrected for temperature, adjusted for a specific site or datum like an airfield

QNE — The standard altimeter setting of 29.92 in. Hg or 1013.2 mb/hPa (used to display pressure altitude)

QNH — The barometric pressure as reported by a particular station—the local altimeter setting (used to display height above sea level)

Receiver Autonomous Integrity Monitoring (RAIM) — A method for GPS equipment to monitor and compare signals from multiple satellites to ensure an accurate signal.

Record — See Database Record.

Reduced Vertical Separation Minimums (RVSM) — Any airspace between and including FL290 and FL410, where aircraft are separated by 1,000 feet vertically. Each aircraft must be in compliance with specific RVSM criteria. A program must be in place to assure continued airworthiness of all RVSM critical systems. Pilots, flight crews, dispatchers, and flight operations must be properly trained and operational procedures, such as checklists, must be established and published in the Ops Manual and AFM, plus operators must participate in a height monitoring program.

Reference Landing Speed (V_{REF}) — The speed of the airplane, in a specified landing configuration, at the point where it descends through the 50-foot height in the determination of the landing distance.

Remote Communications Outlet (RCO) — An unmanned communications facility remotely controlled by air traffic personnel. RCOs serve flight service and are UHF or VHF. RCOs extend the communication range of the air traffic facility. RCOs were established to provide ground-to-ground communications between ATC specialists and pilots located at a satellite airport for delivering enroute clearances, issuing departure authorizations, and acknowledging IFR cancellations or departure/landing times.

Reporting Point — A geographical location in relation to which you report the position of your aircraft. See Compulsory Reporting Points.

Required Navigation Performance (RNP) — Implemented by the FAA and the International Civil Aviation Organization (ICAO), a set of standards that apply to both airspace and navigation equipment. The RNP value designates the lateral performance requirement associated with a procedure. The required performance is obtained through a combination of aircraft capability and the level of service provided by the corresponding navigation infrastructure. RNAV (RNP) approaches are designed to be flown with any type of equipment that meets the RNP integrity requirements specified for the approach procedure.

Rollout RVR — The RVR readout values obtained from sensors located nearest the rollout end of the runway.

Runway Incursion Hot Spots — Locations that have been identified by an airport's controlling authority as having a history of collision risk or runway incursion where pilots and airport vehicle drivers must heighten their attention. Typically these hot spots are locations of intersecting runways, or areas that cannot be seen from the tower. Jeppesen visually depicts hot spot locations on airport charts for those airports with reported hot spots and includes a textual description of the nature of the hazard found at each hot spot.

Runway Incursion — An event formally defined by the FAA as "any occurrence at an aerodrome involving the incorrect presence of an aircraft, vehicle, or person on the protected area of a surface designated for the landing and takeoff of aircraft."

Runway Visual Range (RVR) — Runway visual range (RVR) is an instrumentally derived value, based on standard calibrations, that represents the horizontal distance a pilot can see down the runway. It is based on the sighting of either high intensity runway lights or on the visual contrast of other targets, whichever yields the greater visual range. Unlike prevailing or runway visibility, RVR is based on what a pilot in a moving aircraft should see looking down the runway and is reported in hundreds of feet. You must use the RVR value for takeoff minimums below RVR 1600. However, RVR values of 1,600 feet or greater may be converted to statute miles if RVR is not being reported.

Runway Visibility Value (RVV) — The visibility determined for a particular runway by a transmissometer. A meter provides a continuous indication of the visibility (reported in miles or fractions of miles) for the runway. RVV is used in lieu of prevailing visibility in determining minimums for a particular runway.

Special Instrument Approach Procedure — A procedure approved by the FAA for individual operators, but not published in FAR 97 for public use.

Standard Instrument Departure (SID) — Charted procedures designed at the request of ATC to increase the capacity of terminal airspace, effectively control the flow of traffic with minimal communication, and reduce environmental impact through noise abatement procedures. While obstacle protection is always considered in SID routing, the primary goal is to reduce ATC/pilot workload while providing seamless transitions to the enroute structure. SIDs reduce radio congestion, enable more efficient use of the airspace, and simplify departure clearances to increase airspace capacity and provide benefits to airspace users.

Standard Terminal Arrival Route (STAR) — A procedure that provides a common method for departing the enroute structure and navigating to the destination. A STAR is a preplanned instrument flight rules ATC arrival procedure published for pilot use in graphic and textual form to simplify clearance delivery procedures. STARs provide pilots with a transition from the enroute structure to an outer fix, an instrument approach fix, or arrival waypoint in the terminal area, and they usually terminate with an instrument or visual approach procedure.

Surface Movement Guidance and Control System (SMGCS) — A system that facilitates the safe movement of aircraft and vehicles at airports where scheduled air carriers are conducting authorized operations. The SMGCS low visibility taxi plan includes the improvement of taxiway and runway signs, markings, and lighting, as well as the creation of SMGCS low visibility taxi route charts.

Synthetic Vision System (SVS) — A computer-generated image of the surrounding topography and airport environment created from a database of terrain, obstacles, and cultural features and a navigation source for the aircraft's position, altitude, heading, and track. The image is displayed from the flight crew's perspective or as a plan view moving map on primary flight displays (PFD), navigation displays, or class 3 EFBs.

Terminal Arrival Area (TAA) — An RNAV (GPS) approach design that consists of icons on the plan view indicating minimum altitudes that you must maintain to ensure obstacle clearance as you arrive from the enroute structure to a specific IAF. The TAA Basic T approach segment configuration consists of three areas: the straight-in area, the left base area, and the right base area. Modifications to this configuration might be necessary to accommodate operational requirements.

Terminal Radar Approach Control (TRACON) — An ATC facility that uses radarscopes to monitor an area with a 50-mile radius around an airport up to an altitude of 17,000 feet. TRACON controllers provide IFR separation, vector aircraft, and sequence arrivals for the control tower's airspace.

Threshold Crossing Height (TCH) — The AGL height at which you cross the threshold if you continue the approach to a landing while maintaining the glide slope/path or vertical descent angle.

Top of Climb (TOC) — The point at which cruise altitude is first reached. TOC is calculated based on current aircraft altitude, climb speed, and cruise altitude.

Top of Descent (TOD) — The point at which you initiate a descent from cruise altitude. You calculate the TOD manually or through an FMS, based upon the altitude of the approach gate or IAF.

Touchdown RVR — The RVR visibility readout values obtained from sensors serving the runway touchdown zone.

Touchdown Zone Elevation (TDZE) — The highest elevation in the first 3,000 feet of the landing surface.

Tower Enroute Control (TEC) — The control of IFR enroute traffic within delegated airspace between two or more adjacent approach control facilities. Tower enroute control reallocates airspace both vertically and geographically to allow flight planning between city pairs while remaining within approach control airspace. This service is designed to expedite air traffic and reduces ATC and pilot communication requirements.

Traffic Alert and Collision Avoidance System (TCAS) —. A system that used Mode S and Mode C transponder signals to plot the positions of nearby aircraft so you can maintain awareness of the traffic situation in the vicinity of your aircraft. TCAS II provides airspace surveillance, intruder tracking, threat detection, and avoidance maneuver generations.

Traffic Information Service-Broadcast (TIS-B) — A ground-based, radar-derived service that enables aircraft with ADS-B In and the 978 UAT link to see other transponder-equipped aircraft that are not ADS-B equipped. The cockpit display shows all aircraft in radar contact with controllers—ADS-B equipped or not—within 15 miles, plus or minus 3,500 feet. In addition to in-flight enroute traffic, ADS-B works at low altitudes and on the ground so that it can be used to monitor aircraft surface movement and airport operations.

Traffic Management Advisor (TMA) — Software that helps air traffic controllers to sequence arriving air traffic. The TMA computes the sequences and scheduled times of arrival to the outer meter arc, meter fix, final approach fix, and runway threshold for each aircraft to meet the sequencing and scheduling constraints entered by the traffic management coordinator.

Traffic Management Coordinator (TMC) — Air traffic controllers that create a plan to deliver aircraft, safely separated, to the TRACON at a rate that does not exceed the capacity of the TRACON and the destination airports. The TMC's plan is based on the current and future traffic flow and consists of sequences and scheduled times of arrival (STAs) at meter fixes.

Transition Altitude — Within the U.S., the altitude you are at with the altimeter set at QNH below FL180. QNH is the barometric pressure as reported by a particular station—the local altimeter setting (used to display height above sea level).

Transition Layer — The layer that you pass through as you climb and descend to flight levels. The transition layer is the airspace between the transition altitude and the transition level. The transition level is the lowest flight level available to use above the transition altitude. If you are descending through the transition layer, set the altimeter to local station pressure (QNH). When climbing through the transition layer, use the standard altimeter setting of 29.92 in. Hg or 1013 (QNE).

Transition Level — The lowest flight level available to use above the transition altitude.

Turn Anticipation — The capability of RNAV systems to determine the point along a course, prior to a waypoint where a turn should be initiated, to provide a smooth path to intercept the succeeding course, and to enunciate the information to the pilot.

User-defined Waypoint — Waypoints that you create for use in your own RNAV equipment. User-defined waypoints are unpublished airspace fixes that are designated geographic locations to help provide positive course guidance for navigation and a means of checking progress on a flight. You communicate these waypoints to ATC in terms of bearing and distance, or latitude/longitude.

Vertical Descent Angle (VDA) — An angle indicated on approach charts for nonprecision approaches to use as a guideline for performing a stabilized descent from the FAF to the threshold crossing height (TCH)

Vertical Navigation (VNAV) — A function of many RNAV units that allows flight crews to display an internally generated vertical descent path that allows a constant rate descent to landing minimums during approaches that would otherwise include multiple level-offs.

Visual Approach — A visual approach is an ATC authorization for an aircraft on an IFR flight plan to proceed visually to the airport of intended landing; it is not an IAP. Also, there is no missed approach segment. When it is operationally beneficial, ATC may authorize pilots to conduct a visual approach to the airport in lieu of the published IAP. A visual approach can be initiated by a pilot or the controller.

Waypoint (WP) — A predetermined geographical position used for route or instrument approach definition, progress reports, published VFR routes, visual reporting points or points for transitioning or circumnavigating controlled or special use airspace. They may be defined relative to a VORTAC station or in terms of latitude/longitude coordinates. RNAV waypoints are specified geographical locations that define an RNAV route or the flight path of an aircraft employing area navigation. Waypoints may be any of the following types: predefined, published, floating, user-defined, fly-by, or fly-over.

Wide Area Augmentation System (WAAS) — A series of ground stations that generate a corrective message that is transmitted to the aircraft by a geostationary satellite. This corrective message improves navigational accuracy by accounting for positional drift of the satellites and signal delays caused by the ionosphere and other atmospheric factors. In addition, WAAS-certified GPS equipment provides vertical glide path information for RNAV (GPS) instrument approach procedures.

Index

A

AAUP. *See* Attention All Users Page
AC
   20-138 Airworthiness Approval of Positioning and Navigation Systems 1-14
   90-100 U.S. Terminal and Enroute RNAV Operations 2-19, 4-5
   90-101 RNP Procedures with AR 5-22
   120-76 Electronic Flight Bags 1-18
ACARS 1-21, 2-12, 5-40
ACAS. *See* Adverse Conditions Alerting Service; *See* airborne collision avoidance system
actual navigation performance B-3
adequate visual reference 2-8
ADS-B 1-10
ADS-C 1-11
ADS-R 1-11
advanced technologies and oceanic procedures. *See* ATOP
Adverse Conditions Alerting Service 1-8
advisory vertical guidance 5-18
AEDT. *See* aviation environmental design tool
aeronautical information
   disseminating 1-24
   publication A-2
AeroNav products 1-24
afterburner climb 3-17
airborne collision avoidance system 1-22
air charter 1-6
aircraft communications addressing and reporting system. *See* ACARS
airport
   chart 1-21, 2-2
   moving map 2-1, A-2
   qualification chart 1-31, 4-12
   signs, marking, lighting 2-3
   surface detection equipment-model X 1-20
   surface movement 1-2, 1-20
   surveillance radar 1-9
air route
   surveillance radar 1-9
   traffic control center 1-7, 3-1

airspeed
   maximum holding 3-20
   restrictions 4-3
air traffic control system command center 1-7
air traffic service route designators. *See* ATS route designators
airways
   low frequency 3-8
   VHF 3-2
ALAR. *See* approach and landing accident reduction
alternate minimums
   airplane 2-12
   helicopter 6-7
altimeter setting, IFR enroute 3-14
altitude
   IFR cruising 3-14
   IFR enroute 3-10
   maximum authorized 3-12
   minimum crossing 3-11
   minimum enroute 3-11
   minimum holding 3-19
   minimum obstruction clearance 3-12
   minimum off-route 3-13
   minimum reception 3-12
   minimum safe 2-24
   minimum vectoring 2-22
ANP. *See* actual navigation performance
approach
   angle for helicopters 6-3
   briefing 5-40, 5-46
   category 5-45
   clearance 5-46
   gate , 4-1
   identifier 5-17
   overview 5-43
   procedures, helicopter 6-8
   procedure types 5-1
   speed 5-45
   with vertical guidance. *See* APV
approach and landing accident reduction 1-4
APV 5-1, 5-4

I-1

area charts 1-28
area navigation. *See* RNAV
ARINC Specification 424 A-1, A-4
ARSR. *See* air route surveillance radar
ARTCC. *See* air route traffic control center
ASDE-X. *See* airport surface detection equipment-model X
ASOS 2-11, 5-41
ASR. *See* airport surveillance radar
ASR approach 5-38
ASRS report
   altitude restriction 4-4
   arrival vectors 4-13
ATCSCC. *See* air traffic control system command center
ATOP 1-22
ATPA. *See* automated terminal proximity alert
ATS route designators 3-10
ATT. *See* attitude retention system
Attention All Users Page 5-29
attitude retention system 6-2
autoland 5-24
automated radar terminal system 1-10
automated surface observing system. *See* ASOS
automated terminal proximilty alert 1-24
automated weather observing system. *See* AWOS
automatic dependent surveillance-broadcast. *See* ADS-B
automatic dependent surveillance-contract. *See* ADS-C
automatic dependent surveillance-rebroadcast. *See* ADS-R
automatic flight control system, helicopter 6-2
automatic landing system. *See* autoland
automation, cockpit A-6
autopilot
   helicopter 6-2
   use for approach 5-49
aviation environmental design tool 1-22
aviation, military 1-6
Aviation Weather Technology Transfer 5-41
avionics manufacturer database A-3
AWOS 2-11, 5-41
AWTT. *See* Aviation Weather Technology Transfer

B

back course, localizer 5-35
baro-VNAV 1-14, 5-15, 5-16
beacon-only (radar) sites 1-9
breakout instruction 5-29
briefing
   approach 5-40, 5-46
   operational 5-43
   pilot navigation SID 2-18
   STAR 4-6
   taxi operations 1-3
   vector SID 2-17
B-RNAV. *See* European basic RNAV

C

CARTS. *See* common automated radar terminal system
catch points 3-7

categories
   approach 5-45
   runway incursion 1-2
CAT I, II, and III approach procedures 5-24
CDFA. *See* continuous descent final approach
ceiling and visibility
   alternate requirements 2-12
   visual and contact approach 5-12
certification
   EFB 1-18
   GPS approach equipment 5-15
   helicopters, IFR 6-1
CFIT 1-1, 2-24, 4-13
CF leg. *See* course to fix leg
changeover point 3-3, B-8
charted visual flight procedure 5-13
charter, air 1-6
circling approach 5-6, B-15
clearance
   approach 5-46
   bar lights, SMGCS 1-20, 2-4
   descend via STAR 4-9
   descent 3-18
   holding 3-18
   SID 2-20
   STAR 4-5
climb
   enroute 3-17
   expedited 3-17
   gradient 2-13, 6-9, B-6
close-in obstacles B-7
cockpit automation A-6
coded RNAV leg types 4-8
cold temperature error table B-5
collision avoidance system, airborne 1-22
combined vision system. *See* CVS
command center, ATC system 1-6
common automated radar terminal system 1-10
Common Support Services–Weather 1-17
communication
   outlet, ground 2-22
   radio failure 3-16
complex route records A-5
computerized voice reservation system 1-19
contact approach 5-12
containment limit, RNP 3-21
continuous descent final approach 5-50
controlled flight into terrain. *See* CFIT
control tower 1-8
converging approaches, simultaneous 5-33
COP. *See* changeover point
copter approach 6-9
course reversal 5-3, B-14
course to fix leg 4-8
CRC. *See* cyclic redundancy check
crossing altitude, minimum. *See* MCA
CSS-Wx. *See* Common Support Services–Weather
curved flight tracks 5-22

CVFP. *See* charted visual flight procedure
CVRS. *See* computerized voice reservation system
CVS 1-23
cyclic redundancy check A-2

D

DA 5-9
database
 identifiers 3-5
 navigation 4-8, A-1
 provider A-2
 revision cycle A-2
data comm program 1-22
D-ATIS. *See* digital ATIS
decision altitude. *See* DA
decision height. *See* DH
delays, arrival 4-4
departure
 end of the runway B-5
 nontowered airports 2-21
 obstacle 2-14, B-7
 pilot/controller responsibility 2-20
 procedures 2-13
 queue management systems 1-19
 radar 2-22
 tower-controlled airports 2-21
dependent parallel approaches 5-28
DER. *See* departure end of the runway
descend via clearance, STAR 4-9
descent
 angle, approach 5-11
 clearances 3-18
 enroute 3-17
 gradient, STAR 4-5
 planning 4-1
 restrictions 4-4
 top of 4-1
designators, route 3-10
DF leg. *See* direct to fix leg
DH 5-9
digital ATIS 2-12
direct to fix leg 4-8, A-6
distance to descend 4-2
diverse vector area 2-22
diversion 3-22
DME arc 5-3
DME/DME/IRU 2-19, 4-5
DME in conjunction with localizer
 5-34
DVA. *See* diverse vector area

E

e-CVRS. *See* computerized voice reservation system
EFB 1-18, 1-24, A-2
EFVS 1-24
electronic flight bag. *See* EFB
emergency diversion 3-22

EMM. *See* enroute moving map
engine failure during IFR departure 2-13
enhanced flight vision system. *See* EFVS
enhanced oceanic climb/descent 1-22
enhanced vision system. *See* EVS
enhanced weather information system 5-41
enroute
 altitude, minimum. *See* MEA
 moving map A-2
 transitions to approach 5-2
environmental design tool 1-22
equipment
 requirements for helicopter IFR operations 6-2
 setup for approach 5-45
ES. *See* extended squitter
established on course B-4
e-STMP. *See* special traffic management program
European basic RNAV 1-16
European precision RNAV 1-16
EVS 1-23
EWINS. *See* enhanced weather information system
expedite climb 3-17
extended squitter 1-11
exterior aircraft lights 1-4

F

FAA Order 8400.10 2-11
failure
 of engine during IFR departure 2-13
 radio communication 3-16
FANS 1-22
FAR
 29.1303 6-1
 91.117 4-3
 91.144 3-14
 91.181 B-4
 91.185 3-16
 121.542 2-24
 121.652 5-11
 135.100 2-24
 135.225 5-11
FAST. *See* Final Approach Spacing Tool
FDA. *See* fix displacement area
FDT. *See* fix displacement tolerance
feeder route 5-2
fictitious threshold waypoint 5-33
final approach
 continuous descent 5-50
 course alignment 5-6
 segment 5-1, 5-4
 vectors to 4-10, 5-46
Final Approach Spacing Tool 1-7
final monitor controller 5-28
FIS-B 1-12
fix
 displacement area B-2
 displacement tolerance B-2
 protected airspace B-2

records A-4
to manual termination leg 4-8
Flight Data Center 1-25
flight director, helicopter 6-2
flight information service-broadcast. *See* FIS-B
flight level
    IFR cruising 3-14
    lowest usable 3-14
flight management system. *See* FMS
flight operations center 1-17
Flight Service, Lockheed Martin 1-8
flight technical error B-2
FliteDeck Pro EFB 2-1
floating waypoints 3-5
fly-over protection B-11
FM leg. *See* fix to manual termination leg
FMS 1-24, 4-6
FOC. *See* flight operations center
FTE. *See* flight technical error
FTP. *See* fictitous threshold waypoint
fuel state awareness 3-20
fuel, time, and distance to descend 4-2
future air navigation system. *See* FANS

G

gap, MEA 3-3
gate, approach 4-1
GBAS 1-14, 5-26
GBAS landing system approach. *See* GLS approach
GCO. *See* ground communication outlet
general aviation 1-6
geographic position marking, SMGCS 2-4
glide-slope/path intercept altitude 5-4, 5-8
GLS approach 5-26
gradient
    climb 2-13, B-6
    descent, STAR 4-5
Grid MORA 3-13
ground-based augmentation system. *See* GBAS
ground communication outlet 2-22

H

handoff between ARTCCs 3-2
HAR. *See* High Altitude Redesign
heading
    to altitude A-6
    to intercept A-6
    to radial A-6
head-up display. *See* HUD
heliport, VFR approach procedures 6-10
High Altitude Redesign 3-4
high-performance climb 3-17
holding 4-4
    high-performance airplanes 3-20
    maximum speed 3-20
    procedures 3-18
    protected airspace B-12
hot spot, runway incursion 2-2, 2-6

HUD 1-23, 5-24

I

identifier
    approach 5-17
    database 3-5
IFR
    alternate minimums 2-12
    enroute altitudes 3-10
    release time 1-19
    slots 1-19
IGRF. *See* international geomagnetic reference field
ILS approach 5-23
inadvertent flight into IMC, helicopter 6-13
independent parallel approaches 5-28
in-flight weather, approach planning 5-41
initial approach segment 5-1, 5-2, B-14
instrument landing system approach. *See* ILS approach
intercept altitude, glide slope/path 5-4, 5-8
intermediate approach segment 5-1, 5-2, B-14
international geomagnetic reference field A-8

J

Jeppesen
    Airport Moving Map 2-1
    as database provider A-2
    charts and flight information 1-26
    FliteDeck Pro EFB 2-1
    NavData 1-26
    NOTAM service 1-32

L

landing minimums
    CAT I, II, III approaches 5-24
    OpsSpecs authorization 5-10
    regulatory requirements 5-42
    RNAV (GPS) approach 5-18
    straight-in vs. circling 5-5
lateral containment limit, RNP 3-21
LDA
    approach 5-35
    PRM approach 5-30
leaving altitude 3-17
leg types, coded RNAV 4-8
LF airways and routes 3-8
lighting/lights
    airport 2-3
    CAT II/III 5-24
    exterior aircraft 1-4
    SMGCS 2-4
limitations
    helicopter flight manual 6-3
    navigation database A-6
    temperature for baro-VNAV 5-17
LMFS. *See* Lockheed Martin Flight Service
LNAV minimums 5-18
LNAV/VNAV minimums 5-19

localizer
   approaches 5-33
      performance minimums. *See* LP minimums
      performance with vertical guidance minimums. *See* LPV minimums
localizer-type directional aid approach. *See* LDA approach
Lockheed Martin Flight Service 1-8
low, close-in obstacles B-7
lowest usable flight level 3-14
low frequency airways and routes. *See* LF airways and routes
low-visibility taxi plans, SMGCS 2-4
LP minimums 5-21
LPV minimums 5-19

M

MAA. *See* maximum authorized altitude
magnetic variation
   navigation databases A-8
   of record A-9
markings, airport 2-3
maximum altitude, approach procedure 5-7
maximum authorized altitude 3-12
maximum holding speed 3-20
MCA 3-11
MDA 5-9
MEA 3-11
MEA gap 3-3
MEL, helicopter 6-5
memory limitations, database storage A-7
military aviation 1-6
minimum altitude
   crossing. *See* MCA
   descent. *See* MDA
   enroute. *See* MEA
   obstruction clearance. *See* MOCA
   off-route. *See* MORA
   reception. *See* MRA
   safe/sector. *See* MSA
   vectoring. *See* MVA
minimum equipment list, helicopter. *See* MEL
minimums
   alternate. *See* alternate minimums
   LNAV 5-18
   LP 5-21
   LPV 5-20
   straight-in landing 5-5
   takeoff B-7
   VFR helicopter 6-7
minimum speed, helicopter. *See* V_{MINI}
missed approach
   procedure 5-51
   segment 5-1, 5-4, B-16
MOCA 3-12
MORA 3-13
mountainous areas protected airspace B-9
moving map, airport 2-1
MRA 3-12
MSA 5-7

MVA 2-22, 3-13

N

naming conventions, navigation databases A-8
NAS
   components 1-5
   design 1-9
   safety 1-1
   tools 1-17
NASA ASRS reports. *See* ASRS reports
National Airspace System. *See* NAS
National Flight Data Center 1-25
navaid service volume 3-3
NavData, Jeppesen 1-26
navigation database 4-8, A-1
navigation, enroute 3-2
navigation gap 3-3
navigation performance, required. *See* RNP
navigation reference system 3-5
navigation system error B-2
NextGen 1-1
NFDC. *See* National Flight Data Center
noise abatement 2-22
non-mountainous areas protected airspace B-8
nonprecision approach 5-1
nonradar environment
   approach clearances 5-48
   position reports 3-16
non-restrictive routing 3-7
nontowered airport departures 2-21
NOTAM service, Jeppesen 1-32
no transgression zone 5-28
NPA. *See* nonprecision approach
NRS. *See* navigation reference system
NSE. *See* navigation system error
NTZ. *See* no transgression zone

O

obstacle
   clearance surface B-2
   departure procedure. *See* ODP
   evaluation area B-15
   low close-in B-7
obstruction clearance altitude, minimum. *See* MOCA
Ocean 21 1-22
oceanic climb/descent 1-22
OCS. *See* obstacle clearance surface
ODP 2-14, B-7
OEA. *See* obstacle evaluation area
off-route altitude, minimum. *See* MORA
offset instrument approach, simlutaneous. *See* SOIA
offset phantom waypoint 3-5
offshore airspace speed restrictions 4-4
online slot reservations 1-19
OPD. *See* optimized profile descent
operational briefing 5-43

I-5

OpsSpecs
   diversion procedures 3-22
   helicopter 6-5
   landing minimums 5-10
   takeoff minimums 2-8
optimized profile descent 1-17, 4-6
Order 8400.10 2-11
overview, approach 5-43
ownship symbol, airport chart 2-1

P

PA. *See* precision approach
parallel approaches 5-28
PAR approach 5-40
path/terminator
   concept A-6
   limitations A-8
PBN. *See* performance-based navigation
PBN Dashboard 1-16
performance-based navigation 1-12
phantom waypoint 3-5
pilot navigation SIDs 2-18
Pilot Portal, Lockheed Martin Flight Service 1-8
pilot's discretion
   climb 3-17
   descent 3-18
PinS approach. *See* point-in-space approach
pitch points 3-7
planning
   approach 5-40
   descent 4-1
   RNAV route 3-6
   taxi 1-2
point-in-space approach 6-11
point-to-point routes 3-8
position
   marking, SMGCS 2-4
   reports 3-15
precision approach 5-1
precision approach radar approach. *See* PAR approach
precision runway monitor approach. *See* PRM approach
preferred IFR routes 3-8
pressure, lowest usable flight level 3-14
prevailing visibility 2-10
PRM approach 1-10, 5-29
P-RNAV. *See* European precision RNAV
publication criteria, National Flight Data Center 1-25

Q

QFE 3-15
QNE 3-15
QNH 3-15
Q-routes 3-6
qualification charts, airport 1-31, 4-11

R

radar
   approach 5-38
   departure 2-22
   reporting procedures 3-15
   systems 1-9
   terminal system, automated 1-10
   vectors to final approach , 4-10, 5-14
radio communication failure 3-16
radius to fix leg 4-8, 5-22
RAIM failure 5-22
random RNAV routes 3-6
reaching altitude 3-17
reception altitude, minimum. *See* MRA
records, airborne navigation database A-4
reduced vertical separation minimums. *See* RVSM
REL. *See* runway entrance lights
release time, IFR 1-19
reports
   position 3-16
   radar and nonradar 3-15
required navigation performance. *See* RNP
required obstacle clearance B-2
reservations, IFR slots 1-19
restrictions
   airspeed 4-3
   altitude 4-4
   descent 4-4
return to final instruction 5-29
revision cycle A-2, A-9
RF leg. *See* radius to fix leg
RNAV
   AC 90-100 U.S. Terminal and Enroute RNAV Operations 2-19, 4-5
   enroute protected airspace B-12
   route waypoint 3-4
   SID 2-19
   STAR 4-5
   T-routes 3-8
RNAV (GPS) approach
   copter 6-10
   design 5-14
   equipment 1-14, 5-15
   landing minimums 5-18
RNAV (RNP) approach 5-22
RNP 1-14, 3-20, B-3
RNP approach. *See* RNAV (RNP) approach
ROC. *See* required obstacle clearance
ROC 24 percent rule B-6
route
   designators 3-10
   feeder 5-2
   LF 3-8
   non-restrictive 3-7
   preferred IFR 3-8
   records, airborne navigation database A-5
   RNAV 3-4
   VHF 3-2

rule of thumb for descent planning 4-2
runway
    entrance lights 1-2
    guard lights, SMGCS 2-4
    incursion avoidance 1-2
    incursion hot spot 2-6
    in sight 5-51
    safety 2-7
    status lights 2-7
    visual range. *See* RVR
RVR 2-9
RVSM 1-17, 3-22
RWSL. *See* runway status lights

S

SA CAT I and II approaches 5-24
satellite weather 5-42
segments. *See* approach segments
service volume, navaid 3-3
SID
    noise abatement 2-22
    pilot navigation 2-18
    RNAV 2-19
    vector 2-17
signs, airport 2-3
simple route records, airborne navigation database A-5
simultaneous approaches
    close parallel PRM (independent) 5-29
    converging 5-33
    offset. *See* SOIA
    parallel (independent) 5-28
slots, IFR 1-19
SMGCS 1-2, 1-20, 2-4
SOIA 5-30
Spacing Tool, Final Approach 1-7
special approach procedure, helicopter 6-13
special authorization approaches. *See* SA CAT I and II approaches
special traffic management program 1-19
special VFR, helicopter 6-7
squawk 7600 3-16
squitter, extended 1-11
stabilization system, helicopter 6-2
stabilized approach 5-49
stand-alone RNAV system A-2
Standard for Terminal Instrument Procedures. *See* TERPS
standard instrument departure. *See* SID
standard minimums, takeoff 2-8
standard taxi routes 2-7
standard terminal arrival route. *See* STAR
standard terminal automation replacement system 1-10
STAR 4-5
STARS. *See* standard terminal automation replacement system
sterile cockpit 2-24
STMP. *See* special traffic management program
stop bar lights, SMGCS 2-4
straight-in landing minimums 5-5

surface movement
    guidance and control system. *See* SMGCS
    procedures 1-2, 1-20, 2-1
surveillance systems, radar 1-9
SVFR. *See* special VFR, helicopter
SVS 1-23
synthetic vision system. *See* SVS

T

TAA 5-2, 5-15
tailored arrivals 4-11
Takeoff and Obstacle Departure Procedure chart section 2-14
takeoff hold lights 1-2
takeoff minimums 2-8
Tango routes. *See* T-routes
TAWS 1-1
taxi
    briefing 1-3
    diagram 2-1
    low visibility 2-4
    routes 2-7
taxiway centerline lights, SMGCS 2-4
TCAS 1-22
TEC. *See* tower enroute control
technical standard order. *See* TSO
temperature restrictions
    baro-VNAV 5-17
    IFR procedures B-5
Terminal and Enroute RNAV Operations, AC 90-100 2-19, 4-5
terminal area, arriving in 4-3
terminal arrival area. *See* TAA
terminal automation replacement system 1-10
Terminal Instrument Procedures, Standards for. *See* TERPS
terminal proximity alert 1-24
terminal radar approach control. *See* TRACON
terminal route 5-3
TERPS 2-13, 5-11, B-5
terrain awareness warning system. *See* TAWS
TF leg. *See* track to fix leg
THL. *See* takeoff hold lights
time, fuel, and distance to descend 4-2
TIS-B 1-12
TMC. *See* traffic management coordinator
TOD 4-1
top of descent. *See* TOD
total system error B-2
tower
    enroute control 3-9
    visibility 2-10
tower-controlled airport departures 2-21
tower-to-tower. *See* tower enroute control
track to fix leg 4-8, A-6
TRACON 1-7
traffic alert and collision avoidance system. *See* TCAS
traffic information service-broadcast. *See* TIS-B
traffic management coordinator 1-7

tranceiver, universal access. *See* UAT
transition
   enroute to approach 5-2
   to visual flight 5-51
transponder 7600 squawk 3-16
trim system, helicopter 6-2
T-routes 3-8
TSE. *See* total system error
TSO
   C129 1-14, 5-15
   C145/C146 1-14, 5-15
turning area B-11
two-way radio communication failure 3-16

U

UAT 1-11
United States Standard for Terminal Instrument Proceudures. *See* TERPS
universal access transceiver. *See* UAT
unpublished waypoints 3-5
unsurveyed grid MORA 3-13
usable flight level, lowest 3-14
user-defined waypoints 3-4
U.S. Terminal and Enroute RNAV Operations, AC 90-100 2-19, 4-5

V

VA. *See* heading to altitude
variation, magnetic
   navigation databases A-8
   of record A-9
VCOA 2-14
VDA 5-11
vector
   area, diverse 2-22
   SID 2-17
vectoring, minimum altitude. *See* MVA
vectors to final approach course 5-14, 5-46
vertical descent angle. *See* VDA
vertical guidance
   advisory 5-18
   approach 5-1, 5-4
   arrow in profile view 5-17
VFR
   heliport approach procedures 6-10
   minimums, helicopter 6-7
VHF airways and routes 3-2
VI. *See* heading to intercept
visibility
   prevailing 2-10
   reduction by helicopters 6-8
   tower 2-10
vision systems 1-23
visual aids, airport 2-3
visual approach 5-12
visual climb over airport. *See* VCOA
visual flight, transition to 5-51
visual reference required for takeoff 2-8
V_{MINI} 6-3
VNAV 5-19
V_{NEI} 6-3
volume, navaid service 3-3
VOR
   approach 5-35
   changeover point 3-3, B-8
   system accuracy B-7
VR. *See* heading to radial
V_{REF} 5-45

W

WAAS
   channel number 5-17
   components 1-12
   GPS equipment 5-15
waypoint
   offset phantom 3-5
   RNAV route 3-4
   user-defined 3-4
weather
   AWOS and ASOS 2-11
   destination airport 5-40
   in-flight 5-41
   requirements, instrument approach 5-42
   satellite broadcast 5-42
wide area augmentation system. *See* WAAS

X

XM WX Satellite Weather 5-42

Z

Z and Y RNAV approach 5-5

Numerical Entries

1, 2, 3 Rule for alternate requirements 2-12
3 to 1 formula for descents 4-2
14 CFR
   29.1303 6-1
   91.117 4-3
   91.144 3-14
   91.181 B-4
   91.185 3-16
   121.542 2-24
   121.652 5-11
   135.100 2-24
   135.225 5-11
24 percent ROC rule B-6
28-day database revision cycle A-2
29.92 in. Hg altimeter setting 3-14
100 feet increase to minimums 5-11

424, ARINC specification A-1, A-4
978 MHz UAT 1-11
1013.2 mb/hPa altimeter setting 3-15
1090 ES 1-11
7600 squawk 3-16
8400.10, FAA Order 2-11